THE LITTLE, BROWN HANDBOOK

THIRD EDITION

H. Ramsey Fowler
MEMPHIS STATE UNIVERSITY

With the Editors of Little, Brown

Little, Brown and Company
BOSTON TORONTO

Contributing Editor Jane E. Aaron
Sponsoring Editor Carolyn A. Potts
Book Editor Lauren R. Green
Cover and Text Designer Anna Post
Manuscript Editor Barbara G. Flanagan
Editorial Assistants Janice L. Friedman and Adrienne E. Weiss

Library of Congress Cataloging-in-Publication Data

Fowler, H. Ramsey (Henry Ramsey)
The Little, Brown handbook.

Includes index.
1. English language—Grammar—1950- . 2. English language—Rhetoric. I. Little, Brown and Company. II. Title.
PE1112.F64 1986 808′.042 85-23060
ISBN 0-316-28995-7

Library of Congress Catalog Card No. 85-23060

ISBN 0-316-28995-7

9 8 7 6 5 4 3 2

FG

Published simultaneously in Canada
by Little, Brown & Company (Canada) Limited

Printed in the United States of America

Photograph, page 11: Balthazar Korab, Ltd.

We would like to thank the following authors and publishers for permission to quote from their works.

Bonnie Angelo, from "Those Good Ole Boys," *Time*, 27 September 1976. Copyright 1976 Time Inc. Reprinted by permission from *Time*.

Peter Bogdanovich, excerpted from "Bogie in Excelsis," *Pieces of Time*. © 1973 by Peter Bogdanovich. Used by permission of Arbor House Publishing Company and the author.

Lynn M. Buller, from "The Encyclopedia Game" in Saul D. Feldman and Gerald W. Thielbar, eds., *Life Style: Diversity in American Society*. Copyright © 1972 by Little, Brown and Company (Inc.). Reprinted by permission.

Arthur L. Campa, from "Angelo vs. Chicano: Why?" *Western Review*, 1972. Reprinted by permission of Mrs. Arthur L. Campa.

(*continued on page 621*)

Preface for Instructors

The purpose and framework of *The Little, Brown Handbook* remain unaltered in this new edition: it is both a reference book for writers and a textbook for composition classes, designed for students who need frequent or occasional guidance in the process and conventions of writing. Also unaltered are the features that have distinguished previous editions, especially comprehensiveness, accessibility, clarity, and an organization that puts the writing process up front, as most courses do, and thereby places the conventions of writing in the appropriate context.

But the teaching of composition is constantly changing, and any text intended to serve instructors and students must also change. Thus the third edition of *The Little, Brown Handbook* differs significantly from its predecessors. In countless large and small ways, it had been revised to reflect current practice in the teaching of composition as outlined by hundreds of instructors working with tens of thousands of students.

Chief among the changes in the new edition are recast and expanded chapters on the writing process, argumentation, and the research paper and new dual coverage of punctuation. Chapters 1 and 2, on developing, drafting, and revising the essay, present a more flexible and recursive model of the writing process, with greater emphasis on the writing situation, purpose, invention (including expanded coverage of the patterns of development), audience, drafting, revising and editing, and benefiting from criticism. As before, the process is illustrated with diverse examples from students' work and a "biography" of one student's essay from assignment through final draft. In the essay, which is new to this edition, the student develops an extended example as a personal response to course reading.

To help instructors who teach argumentation as part of the composition course, Chapter 4 now presents a more comprehensive approach to the strategies of argumentation, including new material on structuring an argument, balancing rational and emotional appeals, anticipating readers' objections, using appropriate assertions, and using evidence. In addition, a student essay now illustrates the principles discussed in the text.

Chapter 35 on the research paper is substantially revised. The most obvious change is thorough, well-illustrated coverage of the parenthetical documentation style of the *MLA Handbook for Writers of Research Papers*, 2nd ed. (1984), in addition to complete coverage of footnotes or endnotes (updated to reflect the new *MLA Handbook*). To eliminate the seeming mysteries of bibliographic formats, every source model is now accompanied by a detailed explanation of what information to include and how to arrange and punctuate it. At the request of many instructors, we have retained the sample student paper from previous editions, "How Advertisers Make Us Buy," together with its extensive facing-page annotations on format and content. However, to aid those instructors who requested a more analytical sample paper, we have added a second student essay, on changes made in Jefferson's draft of the Declaration of Independence, that combines analysis of scholars' views with original textual analysis of the Declaration itself. Among the many other changes in the chapter are a new section on using computerized data bases and more extensive discussion of summarizing and paraphrasing, drafting the paper, and introducing quotations, summaries, and paraphrases in the paper.

The final major change in this edition is new dual coverage of punctuation—in separate full chapters, as before, and now also in the chapters on grammar, usage, and style, wherever sentence structure directly affects punctuation. For instance, Chapter 5 now discusses the punctuation of prepositional phrases, verbal phrases, and other structures; and Chapter 16 now discusses the punctuation of coordinated and subordinated sentence elements. As a result of these additions, students will see punctuation as integral to constructing sentences. At the same time, the separate chapters on punctuation (20–25) continue to provide a comprehensive overview of each mark and a convenient reference source for students and instructors. These chapters are also improved by three additions: a unique two-page chart showing the rules and options for all the major marks of internal punctuation (pp. 310–11); text discussions of the similarities and differences between often-confused marks; and an all-punctuation exercise requiring discrimination among the various marks (p. 376).

Besides these major changes, the handbook has been improved in numerous smaller ways. Explanations and examples have been clarified, expanded, or simplified wherever necessary, and more than half the exercise items are new. Significant alterations or additions include discussions of word processing under invention (1d), revising and editing (2d), and preparing a manuscript (Appendix B); thirty new examples in Chapter 3 on paragraphs and greater stress on paragraph building; revised reference headings in Chapter 7 on verbs to cover errors in forms of regular as well as irregular verbs (7a), omitted helping verbs (7d), careless errors in tense (7e), and overuse of the passive voice (7h); a new reference heading in Chapter 10 on sentence fragments to govern the revision of any sentence fragment, regardless of its structure (10a); new discussions of logical agreement under shifts in number (13a) and the Glossary of Grammatical Terms; a dozen new entries in the Glossary of Usage; a lengthy new entry on articles in the Glossary of Grammatical Terms, written especially for students using English as a second language; expansion of the correction chart at the back of the book to include all the subheadings under Chapter 8 on agreement, section 21j on superfluous commas, and Chapter 31 on diction; and a twofold increase in the list of useful lists at the front of the book. Instructors wanting a fuller list of revisions than space allows here need only request one from the publisher.

Both instructors and students should benefit from the expansion and revision of the supplements accompanying the new edition of the handbook—all available from the publisher. Robert A. Schwegler, University of Rhode Island, has updated and enlarged the popular instructor's manual, and it includes a new chapter on collaborative learning by Tori Haring-Smith, Brown University. Part of this chapter, consisting of instruction sheets for guiding peer critiques, is also available in a separate pamphlet for students. Donna Gorrell, University of Wisconsin at Milwaukee, has prepared a third edition of *The Little, Brown Workbook* that parallels the handbook in content and organization while providing ample and varied exercises for students needing additional help with the writing process, grammar, or usage. Students may also obtain help from new computer software that includes a diagnostic test and evaluation, exercises in grammar and usage tailored to students' needs, and follow-up tests. As before, the answers to the exercises in both the handbook and the workbook are available in separate booklets that may be distributed to students at an instructor's option. A portable correction chart, showing the handbook's correction code and symbols, and two diagnostic tests by Edward M. Uehling and John Feaster, both of Valparaiso University, are also available for instructors.

Acknowledgments

Composition instructors all over the country, representing a wide variety of schools, have contributed to this edition of the handbook. Regrettably, we cannot give individual thanks to the hundreds of instructors who made suggestions through Little, Brown's field representatives or in response to our extensive survey. Perhaps these instructors will accept as thanks the myriad small and large changes resulting from their comments.

More than eighty instructors spared us the time to meet in special discussion groups, either on their campuses or at professional meetings. These informative and lively sessions were immensely valuable, not only as sources of ideas but also for the insights they provided into the challenges and rewards of teaching composition. The handbook benefited from the contributions of the participants, and we wish we had the space to thank each one by name. They represented Baylor University, Citadel Military College of South Carolina, College of Charleston, El Paso County Community College, Kennesaw College, McLennan Community College, Marshall University, North Shore Community College, Sam Houston State University, Southwest Texas State University, the University of Houston at University Park, the University of Lowell, the University of Massachusetts at Boston, the University of Rhode Island, and the University of South Carolina at Aiken. To MaryKay Mahoney, who met with us at the University of Massachusetts at Boston, we are particularly grateful for a follow-up suggestion that prompted the new illustrative essay in Chapters 1 and 2.

We are indebted to the instructors who provided thoughtful, constructive, and detailed written comments for parts or all of this edition: James E. Barcus and Margaret H. Davis, both of Baylor University; Michael W. Bartos, William Rainey Harper College; Raymond Brebach, Drexel University; Harry M. Brown and Karen K. Reid, both of Midwestern State University; Susan M. Butler, Thomas Nelson Community College; Kathleen Shine Cain, Merrimack College; James Crawford, Walters State Community College; Frank Devlin, Salem State College; Donald J. Fay, Kennesaw College; Donna Gorrell, University of Wisconsin at Milwaukee; Susan G. Gomberg and John Strommer, both of the University of Rhode Island; Kathleen Ann Kelly, University of North Carolina at Chapel Hill; Ronald B. Nelson, Valencia Community College; and Mame Willey, University of Massachusetts at Boston. A special note of appreciation must go to Robert A. Schwegler, University of Rhode Island, whose sharp perceptions and creative suggestions both identified opportunities and solved real and potential problems. Finally, Richard S. Beal, professor emeritus at Boston University, has once again earned our gratitude for sharing his unique experience and wisdom.

Preface for Students: Using This Book

A handbook is a comprehensive reference guide to the essential information in a field or discipline, whether it is stamp collecting, home maintenance, or chemistry. *The Little, Brown Handbook* is no exception. A basic resource for English composition, grammar, and usage, it can serve you as a text and reference book for writing not only in a composition course but also in other courses and outside college. Mastery of the principles and conventions discussed in this book will not by itself make you a good writer; for that, you need to care about your work at every level from conceiving a topic to spelling words. But learning how to use the handbook and then referring to it as the need arises will give you the means to say *what* you want in the *way* you want. The following pages tell you about the book's organization and store of information, the ways of locating that information, and the standard of usage recommended.

The handbook's organization and coverage

An overview of the handbook's contents appears inside the back cover. The first four chapters discuss larger elements of composition—the essay and the paragraph. Chapters 1 and 2 describe and illustrate the writing process, from choosing a topic through considering an audience and generating and organizing ideas to revision. Chapter 3 treats composing and revising paragraphs. And Chapter 4 discusses the construction of an effective argument. The principles discussed in these chapters are basic to everything that follows in the handbook, so you may want to read and digest them even if they are not assigned.

You may also want to read Chapter 5, which presents the system of English grammar. Though much of the material will be familiar to you, the chapter will repay your attention because it shows that the grammar of English is more than just a hodgepodge of rules, and it provides background for the fourteen chapters that follow. Each of these following chapters treats a principle or convention of grammatical correctness (Chapters 6 to 9), clarity (Chapters 10 to 15), or effectiveness (Chapters 16 to 19). Your instructor may discuss some or all of these chapters in class or may suggest that you consult specific chapters when you encounter problems.

Chapters 20 to 25 of the handbook describe the current conventions of punctuation. Punctuation is also discussed in earlier chapters, but these separate chapters bring together all the conventions for each mark. Preceding Chapter 20, on pages 310–11, is a chart showing the rules and options for the marks that cause the most confusion, even for experienced writers. If you aren't sure how to punctuate a sentence you are working on, this chart can suggest the alternatives. Chapters 26 to 30 present the conventions of mechanics—capitalization, abbreviations, italics (or underlining), numbers, and word division. Whether or not you are assigned these chapters, you should think of them as resources to consult continually for advice on specific questions.

Chapters 31 to 34 deal with words. Chapter 31, which discusses the principles guiding effective word choice, is intended to help you express your meaning exactly and concisely. Chapter 32 introduces the features and uses of any desk dictionary. Chapters 33 and 34 suggest ways in which you can develop your vocabulary and master the complexities of English spelling.

The last chapters of the handbook treat specific writing tasks. Chapter 35 traces the process of writing and documenting a research paper for which you consult books and periodicals on some issue or question. Chapter 36 provides specific advice on writing essay examinations for college courses, writing letters to make complaints or requests or to apply for a job, and writing business memorandums.

The handbook includes three appendixes, each one addressing a specific practical problem. Appendix A explains your responsibility for acknowledging the ideas and information that you draw from other writers. Appendix B describes a widely accepted standard for preparing a manuscript. And Appendix C offers specific advice on studying effectively for any course.

Two glossaries and an index conclude the handbook. The Glossary of Usage provides brief notes on troublesome or confusing words and expressions that plague writers at all levels of experience. The Glossary of Grammatical Terms defines all the specialized words that appear in the handbook as well as a few others. The index contains an entry for every principle, convention, and term discussed in the book as well as many specific words and phrases that you may need to look up.

Finding information in the handbook

The Little, Brown Handbook provides a wealth of specific information—what form of a verb to use, how to express an idea concisely, whether to punctuate with a comma or a semicolon, whether to capitalize a word, how to arrange the title page of a paper, and so on. The handbook also provides many ways of locating such information quickly. When you seek information on your own, you can check the guide to useful lists and summaries inside the front cover; you can refer to the table of contents inside the back cover or immediately after this preface; or you can refer to the index. The table of contents shows all the book's parts, chapters, and main sections within chapters. The sections are labeled with letters (*a*, *b*, and so on). These letters and the corresponding chapter numbers (for instance, 9d or 12a) also appear before the appropriate convention or guideline in the text itself, and they are printed in colored boxes on the sides of the pages. Thus you can find a section heading in the contents and thumb the book until you arrive at its number and letter on the side of the page. If you are uncertain of what to look for and need a more detailed guide to the book's contents, consult the index.

Your instructor may mark your papers using heading numbers and letters, symbols, or written comments. Pages 51–53 show a student essay marked in all three ways. If your instructor marks your paper with, say, 21a, you can refer to the contents to learn that you have made an error involving a comma. If you need further information to correct the error, you can then refer to the text by finding the appropriate page number or by locating 21a in a colored box on the side of the page, as described above. If your instructor uses a symbol such as *frag* to mark your paper, you can find out how to correct the error by referring to the alphabetical list of symbols inside the front cover. Using this guide, you would be directed by the symbol *frag* to Chapter 10, which discusses sentence fragments. The symbols also appear in the colored boxes at the sides of the pages. The best way to find specific handbook sections from your instructor's written comments is to consult the index. Look up the term used by your instructor and scan the subentries under it until you find one that seems to describe the error you have made. Then turn to the page number given.

The handbook's recommended usage

The Little, Brown Handbook describes and recommends the conventions of standard written English—the written language common to business and the professions. Written English is more conservative than spoken English in matters of grammar and usage, and a great many words, phrases, and constructions that are widely spoken remain unaccepted in careful writing.

When clear distinctions exist between the language of conversation and that of careful writing, the handbook provides examples of each and labels them *spoken* and *written*. When usage in writing itself varies with the level of formality intended, the handbook labels examples *formal* and *informal*. When usage is mixed or currently changing, the handbook recommends that you choose the more conservative usage because it will be acceptable to all readers.

If you follow the guidelines discussed in this handbook, your writing will be clearer and more demanding of serious attention than it might otherwise have been. Remember, however, that adhering to established conventions is but a means to the real achievement and reward of writing: communicating your message effectively.

Contents

I
The Whole Paper and Paragraphs

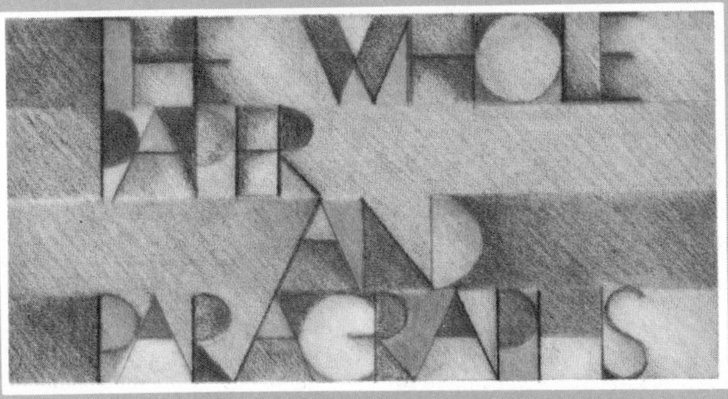

1

Developing an Essay

As varied as they may seem, most of the papers you write in college share certain characteristics. Whether you describe a physics experiment, compare two data-processing systems, analyze a short story, examine the causes of a historical event, argue against campaign subsidies, or relate a personal experience, you are writing an **essay,** a nonfiction composition that analyzes and interprets a topic, offering your view of it. An essay may address almost any subject and may range in length from a page to twenty or more pages. In it you present ideas and information, selected and arranged to reinforce your perspective, in a way that gains and holds the attention of readers and leaves them with a sense that you have said something worthwhile.

From the moment you begin working on an essay until you make the last correction on the final draft, you are continually discovering and deciding: exploring possible topics, finding what you have to say about the topic you choose, selecting a suitable arrangement for your material, and experimenting with paragraphs, sentences, and words to capture meaning. No one can tell you what discoveries you may make or what the right decisions may be, for these depend entirely on your topic and what you aim to do with it. But your work as a writer can be guided by an understanding of how other writers think about writing and what procedures they find helpful. These are the subjects of this chapter and the next.

1a

The writing situation and the writing process

All writing occurs in a context that simultaneously limits and clarifies the writer's choices. Most obviously, context includes the nature of the assignment, the assigned length, and the deadline. But context can also be seen as the **writing situation.** In all essay writing, the writer aims to communicate something about a subject to a particular audience of readers. The three elements—writer, subject, and audience—interact continuously throughout the development, drafting, and revision of the essay, with the writer balancing his or her view, the demands of the subject, and the needs, interests, and expectations of the audience. As we will see throughout this chapter, the nature of the elements and their relative importance change with each new writing task, but the elements are always present. Asking for each task what your subject is, who your audience is, and how you want to present yourself and your subject to that audience can help you define the choices available and decide which ones are most appropriate.

Sometimes the writing situation is clearly defined from the start. Imagine, for instance, that you are assigned a report on an experiment in your physics course, a report expected to show your instructor that you have mastered scientific observation and the principles studied in the course. In this case, your subject, your audience and its expectations, and the way you should present yourself are predefined for you by the assignment. For other writing tasks, however, the writing situation may be left to you to define. Suppose, for instance, that your composition instructor asks you to write an essay relating a significant learning experience. You will have to determine what experience to relate as well as how you want to present yourself and your experience, and you may be required to select your audience and determine its needs and expectations.

Understanding the writing situation is an important part of the **writing process**—the term for all the activities, mental and physical, that go into writing what eventually becomes a finished piece of work. Even for experienced writers, the process is rarely neat and orderly, however neat and orderly the finished work may seem. Though we get a sense of ease or rightness from, say, a well-crafted magazine article, we can safely assume that the writer had to work hard to achieve it, suffering frustration when ideas would not come, struggling to express half-formed thoughts, shaping and reshaping the same paragraph to make a point convincingly.

While engaged in the writing process, a writer continually alternates between a wide and a narrow focus—opening up the mind to take in new information and then closing in on a single idea to shape and refine it, seeking the general picture and then filling in the specific details. This alternating pattern continues through a sequence of overlapping stages: *development* or *planning*, the stage of exploring ideas, gathering information, developing a central theme, and organizing material; *drafting*, the stage of giving preliminary expression to ideas; and *revising*, the stage of rethinking and improving the structure, content, and style.

Aside from the widening and narrowing of focus and the rough division into stages, there is no *one* writing process: no two writers proceed in the same way. With experience, a writer comes to rely on a bundle of procedures that have consistently helped him or her with the activities involved in writing: finding a topic, defining a purpose, developing ideas, shaping ideas, considering an audience, developing a thesis, organizing, drafting, revising, editing. Each of these activities is the subject of a section in this chapter and the next. As you encounter difficulties with any of them in the course of writing, you can experiment with the procedures suggested until you find one or more that work for you. With experience, as you complete a variety of assignments and try a variety of procedures, you will develop your own writing process.

Periodically in this chapter and the next you will see examples of how one student worked from an assignment to a finished essay by drawing on some of the procedures discussed. Occasionally, examples of other students' work will also be introduced to illustrate other approaches. These students' writing situations are not yours, and their solutions to writing problems may not work for you. But following their progress should supplement what you learn on your own about the difficulties and the rewards of writing.

EXERCISE 1

To become aware of your own problems and successes as a writer, begin keeping a journal or log of particular difficulties you encounter while completing writing assignments for your composition course and other courses and also of the procedures that seem most helpful in surmounting those difficulties. Your aim will be to discover your unique writing process so that you can rely on it for any writing you do.

1b
Discovering and limiting a subject

Many writers (including experienced ones) encounter their first stumbling block in finding a subject to write about or in finding a way to make an assigned subject their own. Sometimes an appropriate subject or a unique angle may come to you with little effort; but when it does not, you can try one of the approaches discussed in this section.

To discover an essay subject when one is not assigned, review your own experiences, interests, and curiosities. Look for a subject you already know something about or have been wondering about, such as some issue at your school or in your town. Recall something you have discussed with others recently: perhaps an event in your family's history or a change in relations between men and women. Consider what you have read or have seen at the movies or on television: for instance, a shocking book, a violent or funny movie, a television commercial. Run your mind over the reading and class discussions in your courses to discover an idea or situation that intrigues you or that you can apply to your own experience, such as a political issue or a principle of psychology. Think about things that make you especially happy, such as a hobby, or especially angry, such as the behavior of your neighbors. Examine your own or others' dislikes and preferences to identify any that you would like to understand better. The goal here is to think of a subject that sparks your imagination and gets your mind working. If you care about your subject, then writing about it will be more interesting for you, and what you write will be more likely to interest readers.

If you are assigned a general subject, as often happens in college courses, then your goal is to discover your special interests within the boundaries of the assignment. For instance, if you are assigned a comparison-and-contrast essay on two people you know, then you will need to think of two people—friends, relatives, teachers—whose similarities or differences you find striking. If you are assigned a history essay on, say, Abraham Lincoln as President, then you will need to review the reading you have done for the course and your notes from lectures and discussions to find an aspect of that subject that you'd like to know more about—perhaps Lincoln's weaknesses as President.

If casting over your experiences, observations, and reading fails to produce ideas, or if you can't find a way into an assigned subject, then you may want to try one or more of the discovery techniques discussed on pages 10–16. These techniques, such as freewriting, making lists, and asking questions, are especially useful for finding out what you think about your subject once you have it, but they can also open your mind to possible subjects.

The subject you choose may be something like summer jobs, federal aid to college students, two friends, or Lincoln's weaknesses as President. You could begin developing such a subject right away—generating the ideas and details that will eventually form the substance of the essay. But sooner or later you might run into trouble because these subjects are too broad to be covered thoroughly and interestingly in the few pages often specified in college writing assignments. In such a brief essay, you probably could not provide much of the specific information—facts, examples, sensory details, and so on—that readers need to understand and appreciate what you have to say. Each of the broad subjects above needs to be scaled down to a manageable **topic,** a limited, specific essay subject. Here are several possible topics, each potentially manageable within a few pages, for each of the broad subjects:

Broad subjects	**Specific topics**
Summer jobs	Kinds of summer jobs for unskilled workers How to find a summer job What a summer job can teach
Federal aid to college students	Which students should be entitled to federal aid Kinds of federal aid available to college students Why the federal government should (or should not) aid college students
Two friends	How ______ and ______ are alike despite their differences Why ______ and ______ don't like each other The different roles of ______ and ______ as friends
Lincoln's weaknesses as President	Lincoln's major errors as commander-in-chief of the Union army Lincoln's delay in emancipating the slaves Lincoln's difficulties in controlling his cabinet

The specific topics above are just a few of the possible approaches to the corresponding broad subjects, and they suggest the problems that might result from trying to cover the full range of ideas implied by any of the subjects. The much narrower area defined by each specific topic could, however, be covered both clearly and interestingly in a limited space. (The essay on page 54 illustrates how a student developed the specific topic of what a summer job can teach into a focused and reasonably well-detailed essay.)

You may find that you need to do some planning and writing, exploring different facets of the general subject and pursuing your specific interests, before you hit on the best topic. And the topic you select may require further narrowing or may shift subtly or even dramatically as you move through the writing process. Still, the earlier you can narrow your subject to a specific topic, the more focused your subsequent work will be, so it's worthwhile to push yourself soon after you have your subject to limit its scope.

EXERCISE 2

Make a list of your interests and your recent experiences to arrive at three or four general subjects for an essay. What have you read or seen that made you curious to know more? What activity have you enjoyed lately? What interesting discussions have you participated in? What makes you angry?

EXERCISE 3

Narrow each of the broad subjects from Exercise 2 to one or more specific topics suitable for a brief essay of two or three pages (500 to 750 words). What aspect of the subject interests you most? What aspect can you discuss most effectively, using enough specific information to convey your perspective to your readers?

EXERCISE 4

For each of the following general subjects, provide at least one specific topic that interests you and that you think you could cover well in a brief essay of two or three pages.

1. music, dance, painting, drama, or some other art form
2. automobile safety
3. relations between parents and children
4. relations between the sexes
5. travel

1c
Defining a purpose

Anyone who writes has many purposes. A professional writer may prepare a magazine article to pay her rent, improve her reputation as an author, and learn something about an unfamiliar topic. A student may complete an assignment to get a good grade in a course, become a better writer, and learn something about himself. Usually, though, when writers speak of purpose they mean something different from such goals or desires. By **purpose,** writers mean their chief reason for communicating something about a topic to a particular audience. Defined in this way, *purpose* includes all three elements of the writing situation: writer, topic, and audience. Thus it ties together both the specific context in which the writer is working and the goal the writer hopes to achieve.

Most essays you write will have one of four main purposes: (1) to *entertain* readers; (2) to *express yourself*—your feelings or beliefs—to readers; (3) to *explain* something to readers; or (4) to *persuade* readers to agree with your opinion. These purposes often overlap in a single essay, but usually one predominates. That dominant purpose will demand an emphasis on one of the three elements of the writing situation. When you write mainly to express yourself, for instance, *you* predominate. In contrast, when you write mainly to persuade or entertain readers, *they* predominate. And when you write mainly to explain, the *topic* predominates. Always, though, the other two elements also help determine what and how you write.

Often a writing assignment will specify or imply your purpose: when assigned a report on a physics experiment, for instance, you know the purpose is to explain; when assigned an essay presenting a case for or against federal aid to college students, you know the purpose is to persuade. If the assignment leaves your purpose up to you, then try to define it soon after you have your topic, to give yourself some direction. You may not be successful: sometimes writers do not discover their purpose until they begin drafting. Or you may find that your initial sense of purpose changes as you move through the writing process. Nonetheless, if you are able to define a purpose early, it can set a preliminary course for you to follow and help you recognize changes in your thinking when they occur.

Defining your purpose early has another advantage as well: it can help you determine what kind of essay is likely to be most appropriate—narrative, descriptive, expository, or argumentative. A **narrative essay** relates a sequence of events: a frightening or unhappy incident in your childhood, your mishaps on public transportation, the maneuvers in a historical battle, the steps necessary to perform a task. The purpose of a narrative essay may be any of the four: entertainment, self-expression, explanation, or persuasion. (A narrative essay appears on p. 54.)

A **descriptive essay** evokes a scene, person, object, emotion, or situation by concentrating on its distinguishing details: the features of a building, the look of a landscape, the manner and style of a friend, the feeling of being alone in a strange house at night. Like narration, description may serve the purpose of entertainment, self-expression, explanation, or persuasion. (The essay on p. 51 employs considerable description.)

In an **expository essay,** the writer's primary purpose is to explain (*exposition* comes from a Latin word meaning "to explain or set forth"). Almost any topic is suitable for exposition, from how to pitch a knuckle ball to why you want to major in business to the implications of a new discovery in computer science. It is the kind of writing encountered most often in newspapers, magazines, textbooks, and writing assignments in college and business; and it is the kind of writing this book concentrates on. (Expository essays appear on pp. 51 and 56.)

While the purpose of an expository essay is to explain, the purpose of an **argumentative essay** is to persuade—to convince readers to respect and accept, and sometimes even to act on, the writer's position on a debatable topic. A newspaper editorial favoring city council reform, a magazine article urging mandatory seat-belt use, student papers recommending more required courses or upholding legalized abortion—all these are argumentative essays. (Chapter 4 discusses argumentation in some detail and provides an illustrative essay.)

Narration, description, exposition, and argumentation often overlap in an essay (as description and exposition do in the essay on p. 51); and they may also provide needed information in paragraphs within an essay. For instance, in an argumentative essay intended to persuade readers that needy students should receive first priority for campus jobs, you might include an expository paragraph explaining the current policies and procedures for student employment and a narrative paragraph relating the unhappy job-hunting experiences of one needy student. Or in an expository essay intended to explain a chemical process, you might include a narrative paragraph telling the steps needed to start the process and a descriptive paragraph detailing the smells or colors of the chemicals. The essays would still be primarily argumentative and expository, respectively, with the corresponding primary purposes of persuading and explaining; but other kinds of writing, with other purposes, would be introduced to advance the argument and explanation.

EXERCISE 5

For each of the following topics, suggest both a likely purpose for an essay on the topic (entertainment, self-expression, explanation, persuasion) and a kind of essay suitable for the topic and the purpose (narrative, descriptive, expository, argumentative).

1. why a foreign language should be required in college
2. four kinds of rock music
3. the place where I feel most relaxed
4. a vacation that was a comedy of errors
5. how to find a trusty automobile mechanic

EXERCISE 6

For each of the following general subjects, write down four specific topics, each one suitable for a brief essay written with a different purpose (entertainment, self-expression, explanation, persuasion). For each topic and purpose, what kind of essay seems most appropriate (narrative, descriptive, expository, argumentative)?

Example:

General subject: sports

Topics: (1) Football training as torture (entertainment; narrative). (2) Learning by losing (self-expression; narrative). (3) How to avoid injury during weight training (explanation; expository). (4) Why the school should build a new athletic facility (persuasion; argumentative).

1. music
2. Saturday nights
3. work
4. television
5. driving

EXERCISE 7

To begin developing a brief essay of your own, select a topic that has particular interest for you. (The topic may come from your answers to Exercise 3 or 4 on p. 7 or to Exercise 6.) Define a purpose for your essay, and decide what kind of essay will best suit your topic and purpose.

1d
Developing the topic

As you search for an essay topic and define a purpose for writing, you will inevitably draw on ideas already in your mind or in sources such as course notes and readings. Developing the topic—generating the ideas and information that will help you achieve your purpose—involves similar thinking but with a sharper focus. You probe the topic, seeking to discover implications, possibilities, and relationships not considered before. Sometimes ideas will tumble forth on paper, especially if your topic is very familiar or personal. But when they do not, you may find it helpful to use one or more of the following discovery strategies. Whatever strategy or strategies you use, do your work in writing, not just in your head. Not only will your ideas be retrievable, but the act of writing will simultaneously keep you focused on the topic and lead you to fresh, sometimes surprising, insights.

1
Freewriting

One way to begin exploring a topic is to write without stopping for a certain amount of time (say, fifteen minutes) or to a certain length (say, one page). The goal of this **freewriting** is to discover whatever ideas the topic suggests or to follow ideas where they seem to lead. You should push yourself to keep writing—even if that means repeating the same words until new words come. Don't go back to reread, don't delete ideas that seem dumb or repetitious, and above all don't stop to edit: grammar, punctuation, spelling, and the like are unimportant at this stage. (If you write on a computerized word processor, you can help turn off the editor inside you by turning off the screen as you write. The computer's memory will continue to record what you write, so that you can see your work when you finish, but the blank screen will make it temporarily impossible for you to fuss with your work.)

An example of freewriting can be found in the work of a student, Pat Lucas, whose writing process we will follow in this chapter and the next. In a composition course, Lucas and her classmates read and discussed an essay titled "Hard Architecture" by Robert Sommer. Their instructor then gave them the following assignment: "Sommer contrasts 'hard architecture,' which he finds inhumane and oppressive, with 'soft architecture,' which he finds sensitive and stimulating. Write an essay of 500–750 words in which you respond to one or more of Sommer's ideas by drawing on your own observations of one or more buildings." For Lucas, narrowing the broad subject of the assignment to a specific topic presented little problem, for Sommer's comments on hard architecture immediately made her think of a building called the Renaissance Center in her hometown of Detroit, Michigan. (The photograph of the Renaissance Center below will help you follow Lucas's thinking.) After deciding to explain something about the Renaissance Center in the context of Sommer's ideas, Lucas tried freewriting for ten minutes to generate ideas. Her work appears on the next page.

The Renaissance Center in Detroit

> Sommer says hard architecture is oppressive & inhumane—also really hard—concrete, metal, etc. Nothing people can hurt, buildings that resist humans—don't like humans. Don't like humans. Turn hard surfaces to them—like a cruel person, hard-hearted Hannah, insensitive—insensitive. Hard building = insensitive person??? Thinks only of itself/himself, no concern for others, blind to others. Ren. Center insensitive? Not concerned with people—not people outside. Shuts off people. Concrete walls, tall, dark towers. Towers shut people out, protect what's inside, say don't bother me. Go away. Ren. Center = cold, insensitive person?

With this freewriting, Lucas generated several promising ideas, especially the distillation of Sommer's ideas to the word *insensitive,* the application of that word to the Renaissance Center, and the parallels between an insensitive building and an insensitive person. As we'll see on pages 14–16, she pursued these ideas further using another discovery strategy.

2
Making a list

Like freewriting, list making requires opening yourself to everything that seems even remotely connected to your topic, without concern for order or repetition or form of expression. You can let your topic percolate for a day or more, recording thoughts on it whenever they occur. (For this approach to work, you need to keep a notebook and pen or pencil with you at all times.) Or, in a method more akin to freewriting, you can brainstorm about the topic—that is, focus intently on the topic for a fixed amount of time (say, fifteen minutes), pushing yourself to list every idea and detail that comes to mind. Like freewriting, brainstorming requires turning off your internal editor so that you keep moving ahead instead of looping back over what you have already written to correct it. (If you write on a word processor, the trick of turning off the screen can help with brainstorming as it can with freewriting.)

A list of ideas and details made while brainstorming might look something like the one following. The student's topic is what a summer job can teach—one of the specific topics derived earlier from the general subject of summer jobs.

> summer work teaches—
>   how to look busy while doing nothing
>   how to avoid the sun in summer
>   seriously: discipline, budgeting money, value of money
> which job? Burger King cashier? baby sitter? mail-room clerk?
> mail room: how to sort mail into boxes: this is learning??
> how to survive getting fired—humiliation, outrage
> Mrs. King! the mail-room queen as learning experience

the shock of getting fired: what to tell parents, friends?
Mrs. K was so rigid—dumb procedures
initials instead of names on the mail boxes—confusion!
Mrs. K's anger, resentment: the disadvantages of being smarter than your boss
the odd thing about working in an office: a world with its own rules for how to act
what Mr. D said about the pecking order—big chick (Mrs. K) pecks on little chick (me)
probably lots of Mrs. Ks in offices all over—offices are all barnyards
Mrs. K a sad person, really—just trying to hold on to her job, preserve her self-esteem
a job can beat you down—destroy self-esteem, make you desperate enough to be mean to other people
how to preserve/gain self-esteem from work??
Mrs. K had to call me names to protect herself—I forced her into a corner
if I'd known about the pecking order, I would have been less show-offy, not so arrogant

This informal list jumps around quite a bit, but toward the end the student focuses on what she learned about office politics from working as a mail-room clerk. Thus list making helps her both refine her topic and discover what she thinks about it.

3
Reading

Unless your topic draws exclusively on your own observations and experiences, reading can introduce you to ideas you hadn't considered or can help you expand on what you already know. Often, of course, an assignment will require reading: to respond to Sommer's essay on architecture, for instance, Pat Lucas must carefully digest what Sommer has written; and essays on literary works as well as research papers demand reading. But even when reading is not required by the assignment, a book or a magazine or newspaper article on your topic—perhaps the one that suggested your topic in the first place—can help you develop it by providing opinions, facts, and examples and by simulating your own thinking. (See 35b for techniques of library research that you can use to locate appropriate readings on your topic.)

When you read to discover information or to respond to the author's ideas, do so with a pen or pencil in hand and (unless the material is yours to mark up) with a pad of paper by your side. Then you will be able to keep notes on what you read and—more important—on what the reading makes *you* think. Writing while reading leads you to participate actively in the process, not just passively, and so engages and sparks your own thoughts.

4
Using the journalist's questions

Asking yourself a set of questions about your topic—and writing out the answers—can help you look at the topic objectively and see fresh possibilities in it. Asking questions can also provide some structure to the development of ideas.

One such set of questions is that posed by a journalist with a story to report:

Who was involved?
What happened and what were the results?
When did it happen?
Where did it happen?
Why did it happen?
How did it happen?

These questions can also be useful in probing an essay topic, especially if your purpose is to entertain or to explain in narration or exposition. For instance, the student writing about a summer job as a mail-room clerk could use the journalist's questions to isolate the important people involved, the main events and their order, and the possible causes of the events. Similarly, if you decided to explain the dynamics of a single-parent, single-child family, the questions would lead you to consider the characteristics of the people involved, the ways the two people interact, and the possible causes and effects of their style of interaction.

5
Using the patterns of development

Also useful for probing a topic and at the same time providing some structure for developing ideas is a set of questions derived from the **patterns of development.** These patterns—such as illustration, definition, and comparison and contrast—are ways we think about and understand a vast range of subjects, from our own daily experiences to the most complex scientific theories, and they also serve as strategies for writing about these subjects. As you will see later in this chapter and then in Chapter 3, the patterns of development can provide an organization for an essay (see pp. 31–33) and a means of introducing information in paragraphs (see pp. 83–90, where the patterns are illustrated with paragraph-length examples). Here, Pat Lucas's further work on her essay about the Renaissance Center in Detroit will show how the patterns can open up the possibilities in a topic.

How can it be illustrated or supported? The pattern of **illustration or support** suggests development with one or more examples of the topic (one couple's efforts to adopt a child, say, or three television soap operas) or with the reasons for believing or doing something (three reasons for majoring in English, four reasons for driving defensively). When Pat Lucas asked this question, she quickly saw that her freewriting (p. 12) suggested using the Renaissance Center as an example to illustrate and thus extend Sommer's comments on hard architecture.

What is it? What does it encompass, and what does it exclude? These questions lead to development by **definition:** specifying what the topic is and is not to give a precise sense of its meaning. For Pat Lucas the questions suggested an essay defining hard architecture, perhaps using the Renaissance Center as an example in the definition. But since definition is the thrust of Sommer's essay, she decided to use it only for a brief summary of Sommer's ideas.

What are its parts or characteristics? Or what groups or categories can it be sorted into? These questions derive from the related patterns of **division** and **classification**—dividing a singular subject such as a short story into its parts (characters, setting, plot, and so on) or classifying a plural subject such as automobiles into groups or classes (subcompact, compact, and so on). When Pat Lucas considered these questions, she concluded that while developing her essay primarily as an illustration, she might also divide the building into its parts to show how each part illustrated some characteristic of hard architecture.

How is it like, or different from, other things? The pattern of **comparison and contrast** suggests development by pointing out the similarities and differences between ideas, objects, people, places, and so on: the differences between two similar computer systems, for instance, or the similarities between two political candidates from different parties. For Pat Lucas this question opened up an approach to her topic that her freewriting had not: she could compare the Renaissance Center, as an example of hard architecture, with another Detroit building illustrating soft architecture. To explore this approach, she spent some time making lists of the features of the two buildings in relation to Sommer's ideas. (Another student's comparison-and-contrast essay appears on p. 56.)

Is it comparable to something that is in a different class but more familiar? This question leads to **analogy,** an extended comparison of unlike subjects. Analogy is often used to explain a topic that may be unfamiliar to readers (for instance, the structure of a government) by reference to a familiar topic (the structure of a family). Pat Lucas's freewriting had begun to develop an analogy between an insensitive building and an insensitive person, and this question led her further along that track. She anticipated that readers who had never seen the Renaissance Center might better understand her feelings if she drew parallels with their own experiences of people.

What are its causes or its effects? With the pattern of **cause-and-effect analysis,** the writer explains why something happened or what its consequences were or will be, or both: the causes of cerebral palsy, the effects of a Supreme Court decision, the causes *and* effects of a gradual change in the climate. In asking this question, Pat Lucas foresaw that her essay on the Renaissance Center would attempt to explain the effects of the building on an observer, but otherwise cause-and-effect analysis did not seem appropriate to her topic.

How does it work or how do you do it? This question prompts a **process analysis**—an explanation of how the topic occurs naturally or how it is accomplished: the growth of a plant, the making of a robot, the running of a marathon. Of all the pattern questions, this is the one in which Pat Lucas saw the least potential. Though she briefly considered explaining how the Renaissance Center was developed (who proposed it, who put up the money, and so on), she abandoned this approach because she lacked sufficient information and interest to pursue it.

As the examples of Pat Lucas's thinking indicate, more than one of these questions are likely to seem promising, and several may in fact play a role in the development of an essay. After considering each question, Lucas determined that her essay would primarily illustrate Sommer's ideas on hard architecture with the single example of the Renaissance Center. But she also expected to divide the building into its parts and to develop an analogy between the insensitive building and an insensitive person. Thus an essay developed by example seemed likely to contain parts developed by other patterns—a very common occurrence. Even when you are assigned an essay in a specific pattern, other patterns will almost inevitably prove useful to develop certain ideas or to organize certain categories of information. (For further discussion of how the patterns may combine in an essay, see 3e, pp. 100–102.)

EXERCISE 8

Experiment with either freewriting (p. 10) or brainstorming (p. 12) on the topic you chose in Exercise 7 (p. 10) for your essay-in-progress; or start anew with one of the following topics. Write for at least ten minutes without stopping to edit. When you finish, examine what you have written for ideas and relationships that could help you develop the topic.

1. who I am
2. a restaurant
3. borrowing (or lending) money
4. prejudice in my hometown
5. the college grading system
6. pigeons
7. a country music singer
8. a television show
9. a brother or a sister
10. an awkward or embarrassing moment
11. a radio personality
12. basketball strategies
13. shyness
14. parties
15. patriotism

EXERCISE 9

Continuing from the preceding exercise, generate further ideas on the topic by writing answers to each of the questions derived from the patterns of development (pp. 14–16). Give the closest consideration to the questions that seem most promising. Which pattern might you use for the overall development of your essay, and which other patterns might you use to introduce or organize ideas within the overall pattern?

EXERCISE 10

If you feel that the topic from Exercises 8 and 9 should be developed further, try reading about it or asking the journalist's questions (p. 14). Subsequent exercises leading you through the writing process will be based on the ideas you generate in Exercises 8–10.

1e
Grouping ideas

After developing ideas about your topic, you may need to organize the ideas to see what you have. This procedure is not the same as organizing the essay itself, although the relationships and patterns you discover in your ideas may prove useful later (see 1h, p. 28). Rather, at this point in your thinking and writing you apply order to ideas so that connections, distinctions, overlaps, and gaps will become apparent. Grouping ideas helps you control and understand your topic. It helps you see your central theme and how specific ideas fit into it.

To group ideas, you explore the relationships between them, connecting thoughts that may have occurred separately but that relate to the same aspect or subdivision of the topic. For instance, the list of ideas on a summer job (p. 12) includes several on the student's supervisor, Mrs. King: her rigidity, her anger and resentment, her procedures, her resorting to name calling. Discovering and extending such relationships (marking up the list with arrows, circles, and the like) leads to the creation of general categories or labels, such as "Mrs. King's behavior," that describe the relationships and encompass the related ideas. And the categories, in turn, show what the main ideas of the essay might be, where more information is needed, and which ideas are not relevant.

Pat Lucas followed this procedure in organizing her notes on the Renaissance Center, and she produced the following groups:

Sommer's "hard architecture"
  denies "trust and respect" among human beings
  "used by one group to exclude or oppress another"

"impervious, impersonal," "inorganic"
uses hard, human-proof materials (metal, concrete)
Ren. Center exterior
round tower surrounded by octagonal towers
the most visible feature of the city—calls attention to itself
dark surfaces shield activities inside
armor-like surfaces of octagons
reflecting surface of round tower
high concrete wall at street level
wall is a barrier, like a prison wall
no apparent entrance to building for pedestrians
messages: Keep out, don't bother me
from a distance, the building stands apart from rest of city
much larger than other buildings, nothing like them in design
Ren. Center interior
confusion of walkways, escalators—like a maze
glitter of metal, water, light
fancy restaurants, stores, hotel
insensitive building = insensitive person
cold exterior—hard surfaces
shuts out outsiders/others
concerned only with itself/himself
"soft" Detroit buildings
pleasing decoration—varied detailing of windows and walls
open, inviting entrances at street level
lobbies welcome visitors, give sense of order and calm

In forming these groups of ideas and details, Lucas isolated several approaches to her topic: the ideas in Sommer's essay that she wanted to illustrate with the Renaissance Center; the parts of the building (exterior and interior); the analogy between an insensitive building and an insensitive person; and the contrasting appearance of "soft" buildings. The groups led her to see that the exterior of the building was her main interest because it best illustrated Sommer's ideas and the analogy she developed from them. The details of the interior did not fit as well into the theme of insensitivity. And the comparison with other buildings seemed both underdeveloped and potentially distracting from her main interest, the Renaissance Center. Thus, by linking her ideas in groups, Lucas discovered how she wanted to focus her essay, and with that focus she could make early decisions about what *not* to cover.

EXERCISE 11

For your essay-in-progress, group the ideas you generated in Exercises 8, 9, and 10 (pp. 16–17) into general categories. Delete, add, or modify ideas as necessary to reflect your thinking at this new stage.

1f Considering an audience

As we saw earlier, the basic purpose of all essay writing is to *communicate ideas and information to readers.* Readers are your audience. If they do not understand what they read or do not react the way you want, then you may be at fault. The chances are good that you have not considered carefully enough what the audience must be told in order to understand and to react appropriately.

You will probably consider your audience to some extent from the start of the writing process—when, for an obvious example, you decide not to write on macroeconomic theory for your music history teacher. But at some point while you are developing an essay, it's important to make your readers your primary concern so that you can be reasonably sure you have gathered all the information they will need and can begin to decide how you want to present yourself to them in your writing.

1 Using specific information

When you describe, narrate, argue, or explain, you use specific information to gain and keep the attention of your readers and to guide them to accept your point of view. In description you rely primarily on sensory details to convey appearance, sound, smell, taste, and feel so that readers will know the subject as you do. In narration you focus on the important details of a significant event so that readers will experience or understand the event as you do. In argumentation you support appropriate assertions with reasons, facts, and other evidence so that readers will accept your opinion. And in exposition you provide specific information—details, facts, examples—so that readers understand what you are trying to explain. Whatever the kind of writing, however, your selection of information must suit the background of your audience: its familiarity with your topic, its biases, and its special interests.

Consider the student who needs money. He writes two letters, one to his parents and another to his school's Office of Student Aid. First he writes to his parents:

> Well, I did it again. Only two weeks into a new semester, and I'm broke already. But you know I needed a sweater, and besides, book prices have just skyrocketed and I've got this Constitutional History course that almost broke the bank all by itself ($70.00 for books!). Oh, and I've met this really great girl (more later). So anyway, I'm pretty low on cash right now and am going to need another $50.00 to make it through the rest of the month. This should be the last time I have to ask you for money, though.

> Starting next week I'm going to work part-time at a restaurant—doing some short-order cooking and general kinds of work—so if you want your money back . . .

Then he writes to the Office of Student Aid:

> I am writing to request a short-term loan of $50.00 for bill consolidation and for other personal reasons. Starting in ten days, I will be employed for ten hours per week, as a cook, at Better-Burgers, 315 North Main Street. Thus I will be able to repay the loan easily within the required three-month limit. I understand that if I fail to make any payment . . .

The two letters make the same request, but they contain very different information. In the first letter the student chooses details that he believes his parents will relate to: he's "broke already" and not, apparently, for the first time; he needed new clothes; he's serious enough about his studies to pay large sums for his books; he has a new girl friend; he's not specific about his job. In the second letter he chooses details that will reassure the administrators of student aid: he omits any mention of his purchases, his girl friend, or other personal details; he explains where he will be working and for precisely how many hours each week; he stresses the certainty of repayment; he proves he knows the regulations—the "three-month limit" and the penalties for nonpayment. If, by accident, the student mailed the second letter to his parents, they might be mystified or amused. And if he mailed the first letter to the Office of Student Aid, the recipients might deny his request.

To develop your topic in a way that is appropriate for your audience, ask yourself these questions about your readers:

1. Who are my readers? What is their age, education, and social and economic background? What are their interests, attitudes, and beliefs?
2. What do my readers already know about my topic? What is their likely attitude toward it?

Together, these questions lead you to analyze both the general orientation of your readers and their specific position on your topic, and that analysis can help you decide how best to approach them. For instance, Pat Lucas determined from these questions that while her readers (her classmates) resembled her in age, education, and other general characteristics, they might not share her interest in how architecture affects people. In addition, since Lucas attended a college in the East, she could not expect her classmates to be familiar with a building in Detroit or with the feelings the building aroused in her. Thus she would not have to overcome any biases of readers toward the building, but neither could she draw on what they already knew about it. She realized that she must try to relate her interests and experiences to those of her readers, and she must describe the Renaissance Center in enough detail to create the same picture in readers' minds that she held in her own mind.

If Lucas's audience had been quite different—for instance, residents of Detroit—then her approach would have differed. Detroit residents would not require as much detail about the appearance of the building, but some of them might be expected to like the Renaissance Center or at least to find it unobjectionable. Thus Lucas would have planned to deal directly with their preconceptions in order to overcome them—perhaps by acknowledging that the building is striking before explaining how it is insensitive.

2
Deciding on an appropriate role and tone

Besides deciding what information your audience needs, you should also consider how you want to present yourself and your topic to readers—that is, how you want them to perceive both you and your attitude toward your topic. One way to make this decision is to think of yourself, as writer, playing a role in relation to the reader. The possible roles are many and varied, including, for instance, storyteller, portrait painter, lecturer, guide, reporter, advocate, and inspirer. The choice of a role for yourself will depend partly on your purpose—on whether you intend primarily to express yourself, entertain, explain, or persuade—and partly on how you feel about your topic and expect your readers to feel about it. As you write your essay, the role you choose will help determine *what* you say and also the *way* you say it—your **tone.** Tone in writing is like tone of voice in speaking: words and sentence structures on the page convey some of the same information about attitude as pitch and volume in the voice.

Conceived broadly, tone may be informal or formal, as illustrated by the two requests for money on pages 19–20. In the first letter, the student's tone is informal, personal. His sentences are typical of conversation: loose and full of the second-person pronoun *you*, contractions (*I've, I'm*), and casual expressions like *really, pretty, so anyway*. His paragraph is loosely structured, introducing subjects like the new girl friend as they occur to him and burying the most important point, the request for money, in the middle. The student's purpose is as much to entertain his parents as to persuade them to lend him money. He plays the role of a still scatterbrained but always lovable and almost responsible son—a role he expects his parents to appreciate. In contrast, the second letter is written in a much more formal tone. The student's words (*bill consolidation, employed, per week, thus*) are formal and serious. He avoids *you* and contractions. His carefully constructed sentences (*Thus I will be able to repay the loan easily within the required three-month limit*) would sound stiff in most conversation. The paragraph is tightly structured. The student's purpose is strictly to persuade the school administrators to lend him money, and he assumes the role—serious, responsible adult—that he believes his readers expect.

As these examples suggest, different roles and tones are appropriate for different topics, purposes, and audiences. You have the widest range of choice when your purpose is entertainment or self-expression and when you can assume your audience is sympathetic. Then your attitude toward your topic may lead you to play any role from comedian to tragic figure, adopting any tone from teasing to solemn. For other purposes and kinds of writing, one or more elements of the writing situation, in addition to your own attitude, are likely to narrow your choices. In an essay intended to explain the pleasures of aerobic exercise to an audience of elderly, sedentary readers, you might play the role of cheerful, enthusiastic instructor. In an essay on a highly controversial and value-laden topic, such as abortion or the nuclear-arms race, you might opt for a serious approach, out of respect for the gravity of the issue and the strong feelings it is bound to arouse in readers.

When Pat Lucas considered an appropriate role and tone for her essay on the Renaissance Center, she re-examined her purpose of explaining how the building illustrated Sommer's ideas about hard architecture. That purpose suggested the role of a guide, showing readers how the parts of the building contributed to an overall impression. Lucas realized, though, that she felt too strongly about the building to write impersonally or objectively about it. She disliked the building and she wanted her readers to share her attitude. Thus Lucas decided that the role of critical guide, "speaking" in a slightly disapproving tone, was most appropriate for her.

3
Writing for a general audience

What do you do when you are not writing exclusively for your parents or the Office of Student Aid—when, in other words, you don't know much about your audience? Unless you are taking courses in advertising or the communications media, most of the writing you do in college will be directed to a general academic audience. This group of teachers and students is diverse, but its members have many characteristics in common. Like most people, academic readers are skeptical and easily distracted, but they are also curious and thoughtful. They may not share all your interests, but they can understand and appreciate anything you write, as long as it is specific, clear, honest, and fresh. They will expect you to support the assertions you make and the conclusions you draw with ample details, examples, and reasons. Further, they will expect you to present yourself as thoughtful and competent, the master of your information. For most college writing, an appropriate tone usually falls between the extremes of informality and formality, in a middle range that is straightforward, moderate, and assured.

Of course, much of your college writing may have only one reader besides you: the instructor of the course you are writing for. Suppose you are taking an American history course and have been asked to write an essay on the economic background of the War of 1812. You certainly may assume that your instructor is familiar with your subject and expects an essay that shows careful reading of available information and your own interpretation of the facts. Your instructor will judge your essay on the clarity of your prose, the quality of your research, and the adequacy of your evidence to support your conclusions.

EXERCISE 12

Analyze the content and tone of each paragraph below. What does the writer's choice of information and selection of words and sentence structures indicate about his or her role, attitude toward the subject, and intended audience?

1. It is Friday night at any of ten thousand watering holes of the small towns and crossroads hamlets of the South. The room is a cacophony of the ping-pong-dingdingding of the pinball machine, the pop-fizz of another round of Pabst, the refrain of *Red Necks, White Socks and Blue Ribbon Beer* on the juke box, the insolent roar of a souped-up engine outside and, above it all, the sound of easy laughter. The good ole boys have gathered for their fraternal ritual—the aimless diversion that they have elevated into a life-style. – BONNIE ANGELO, "Those Good Ole Boys"

2. All air bags [in automobiles] work in essentially the same way. First, a sensor detects a sudden decrease in speed and triggers the device. The sensitivity of the sensor is such that no normal driving situation, such as abruptly slamming on the brakes at highway speeds or hitting another car while parking, will trigger it: an impact equivalent to hitting a wall at a speed of at least 12 miles an hour is required to set it off. Then a powdered chemical, sodium azide, is electrically ignited, and produces a quick burst of nitrogen gas to inflate a fabric bag. Nitrogen is a harmless gas that constitutes 78 percent of the air we breathe, but sodium azide can be poisonous and is therefore carefully sealed in the air-bag canister until used. The bag can inflate fully within 1/25th of a second, then deflates again within seconds.
– DAVID L. CHANDLER, "Air Bags—Life-Saving and Unavailable"

EXERCISE 13

To practice considering an audience, choose one of the following topics and, for each audience specified, decide on four points you would make, the role you would assume, and the tone you would adopt. Then write a paragraph for each audience based on your decisions.

1. the effects of smoking: for elementary school students and for adult smokers
2. your opinion of welfare: for someone who is on welfare and for someone who is not and who opposes it
3. the advantages of a summer camp: for a prospective camper and for his or her parents
4. why your neighbors should remove the wrecked truck from their yard: for your neighbors and for your town zoning board
5. the beauty of a snowfall: for someone who has never experienced snow and for someone who hates it

EXERCISE 14

Continuing from the groups of ideas that you prepared in Exercise 11 (p. 18), determine as much as you can about the probable readers of your essay-in-progress—their backgrounds, interests, attitudes, and knowledge of your topic. Evaluate your groups of ideas to ensure that they include the specific information your readers need. Decide what role you want to assume and what tone may best convey your attitude toward your topic.

1g
Developing the thesis

Most essays are focused on and controlled by a single main idea that the writer wants to communicate to readers—a central theme to which all the general statements and specific information of the essay relate. This main idea, called the **thesis,** encompasses the writer's attitude toward the topic and purpose in writing.

Sometimes your thesis may be apparent to you very early in the writing process: you may have chosen your topic in the first place because you had an idea about it that you wanted to communicate. At other times you may need to write and rewrite before a central, controlling idea emerges. Still, it's wise to try to pin down your thesis once you have a sense of your purpose, your attitude, your audience, and the information you will use. Then the thesis can help keep you focused throughout the rest of the writing process, or it can serve as a point of reference so that you recognize changes in intention or direction if they occur.

1 Conceiving the thesis sentence

A good way to develop your thesis is to frame it in a **thesis sentence.** The thesis sentence gives you a vehicle for expressing your thesis at an early stage, and eventually it or a revised version may be placed in the introduction of your final essay as a signal to your readers.

As an expression of the thesis, the thesis sentence serves two crucial functions and one optional one:

1. It narrows the topic to a single idea that you want readers to gain from your essay.
2. It asserts something about the topic, conveying your purpose, your opinion, and your attitude.
3. It *may* provide a concise preview of how you will arrange your ideas in the essay.

Here are some examples of topics and corresponding thesis sentences that fulfill the first two and, in one case, the third of these functions.

Topic	Thesis sentence
1. Why the federal government should aid college students	If it hopes to win the technological race, the United States must make higher education possible for any student who qualifies academically.
2. The effects of strip-mining	Strip-mining should be tightly controlled in this region to reduce its pollution of water resources, its permanent destruction of the land, and its devastating effects on people's lives.
3. A terrible moving experience	The surest way to lose good friends is to enlist their help in a move from one fourth-floor walkup to another.
4. My city neighborhood	The main street of my neighborhood contains enough variety to make almost any city dweller feel at home.
5. Abraham Lincoln's delay in emancipating the slaves	Lincoln delayed emancipating any slaves until 1863 because his primary goal was to restore and preserve the Union, with or without slavery.

6. The dynamics of single-parent families	In families consisting of a single parent and a single child, the boundaries between parent and child often disappear so that the two interact as siblings or as a married couple.
7. What public relations is	Most of us are unaware of the public relations campaigns directed at us, but they can significantly affect the way we think and live.

All of these thesis sentences serve the first two functions listed above: they state a single idea about the topic, and the assertion conveys information about the writer's stand on the topic. (Sentence 2 also serves the third function of previewing the main supporting ideas and their order.) We know from these sentences what each writer's primary purpose is: persuasion in the first two, entertainment in the third, and explanation in the last four. In addition, these sentences not only state opinions but also reveal something of the writers' attitudes, including strong feelings and a sense of urgency (sentences 1 and 2), a groaning good humor (3), pride (4), objectivity (5 and 6), and caution (7).

2
Writing and revising the thesis sentence

When you set out to draft a thesis sentence, ask yourself what central idea emerges from the work you have done so far, how you can frame that idea as an assertion about your topic, and how you can convey your purpose and attitude in that assertion. Answering all these questions in a sentence usually requires more than one attempt, sometimes over one or more drafts of the essay. But the thinking required can help you discover potentially serious problems, such as that you're trying to write about three ideas, not one.

Pat Lucas went through a common procedure in writing and revising her thesis sentence on the Renaissance Center. First she turned her topic into an assertion:

> The Renaissance Center in Detroit is an example of hard architecture.

This sentence reflected Lucas's intention to explain her understanding of Sommer's term "hard architecture" using the example of the Renaissance Center. However, it conveyed nothing specific about the term and the building and none of Lucas's attitudes toward them. The word *insensitive* was absent, even though it had figured prominently in Lucas's thinking almost from the beginning. When she recognized this omission, she rewrote the sentence:

> Hard architecture is insensitive, and the Renaissance Center in Detroit is an excellent example of it.

This sentence was better, but Lucas still needed to link the two parts of the sentence by saying *why* the Renaissance Center is an excellent example. She tried again:

> The Renaissance Center in Detroit is an excellent example of hard, insensitive architecture because it shows a lack of concern for the people of the city.

With this sentence Lucas felt she had drafted an assertion that encompassed all her ideas and supporting details and that conveyed her attitude toward the Renaissance Center. Though she knew the sentence might require further revision, she felt it was adequate to help her for the time being.

When you are writing and revising your thesis sentence, check to be sure it is (1) *limited* to an assertion of one idea; (2) *specific* in conveying both the reasons for the assertion and an attitude about it; and (3) *unified* in that the parts relate to each other. Here are other examples of thesis sentences revised to be limited, specific, and unified:

Original	Revised
People should not go on fad diets. [A vague statement that needs limiting with one or more reasons: what's wrong with fad diets?]	Fad diets can be dangerous when they deprive the body of essential nutrients or rely on excessive quantities of potentially harmful foods.
Televised sports are different from live sports. [A general statement that needs to be made more specific: how are they different, and why is the difference significant?]	Television cannot transmit all the excitement of being in a crowd during a game, but its close-ups and slow-motion replays more than compensate.
Seat belts can save lives, but now car makers may be required to install air bags. [Not unified: how do the two parts of the sentence relate to each other?]	If drivers more often used life-saving seat belts, the car makers might not be required to install air bags.

EXERCISE 15

Evaluate the following thesis sentences, considering whether each one is sufficiently limited, specific, and unified. Rewrite the sentences as necessary to meet these goals.

1. Traveling on a tight budget can be educational.
2. Aggression usually leads to violence, injury, and even death, and we should use it constructively.

3. Gun control is essential.
4. One evening of a radio talk show amply illustrates both the appeal of such shows and their silliness.
5. Good manners make our society work.
6. City people are different from country people.
7. Television is a useful baby sitter and an escape for people who do not want to think about their own problems.
8. I liked American history in high school, but I do not like it in college.
9. We are encouraged to choose a career in college, but people change jobs frequently.
10. Drunken drivers, whose perception, coordination, and reaction time are impaired, should receive mandatory suspensions of their licenses.

EXERCISE 16

Write limited, specific, and unified thesis sentences for three of the following topics. Each of your sentences should convey the purpose given in parentheses.

1. why (or why not) major in business (*persuasion*)
2. a frustrating experience (*self-expression*)
3. why cable television should be free (*persuasion*)
4. how an old house or apartment is better than a new one (or vice versa) (*explanation*)
5. the sounds of the city or country (*self-expression or entertainment*)
6. how to care for a plant (*explanation*)
7. why students attend college (*explanation*)
8. how a rumor spreads (*entertainment or explanation*)
9. why divorce laws should be tougher (or looser) (*persuasion*)
10. a disliked person (*self-expression or explanation*)

EXERCISE 17

Continuing from Exercise 14 (p. 24), write a limited, specific, and unified thesis sentence for your essay-in-progress.

1h
Organizing the essay

An effective essay has a recognizable shape—an arrangement of parts that guides readers, helping them see how ideas and details relate to each other and contribute to the whole. If readers can't see a clear order in your material or how each new idea or piece of information develops your thesis, they will have difficulty understanding you and they may mistrust what you say.

Writers sometimes let an effective organization emerge over one or more drafts. But many writers find that organizing ideas to some extent before drafting can provide a helpful sense of direction, as a map can help a driver negotiate a half-familiar system of roads. If you feel uncertain about the course your essay should follow or have a complicated topic with many parts, devising a shape for your material can clarify your options.

1 Arranging the parts of an essay

Most essays share a basic shape consisting of an introduction, a body, and a conclusion. The introduction draws readers into the world of the essay, stating the topic and often the thesis sentence. The conclusion generally gives readers something to take away from the essay—a summary of ideas, for instance, or a suggested course of action. (Both introductory and concluding paragraphs are discussed with other special kinds of paragraphs in 3d, pp. 95–98.) The body of the essay is its center, the part offering ideas and supporting details, examples, and reasons to develop the thesis. In an essay of two or three pages, the body may contain three to five substantial paragraphs, each presenting and supporting a part of the thesis.

The organization of the body of your essay will depend on your topic, your purpose, and your sense of what your readers need and expect from you. In almost any writing situation, at least one of the following ways of organizing ideas will be appropriate. These organizational schemes are so familiar that readers expect them and look for them. Thus the schemes both help you arrange your material and help readers follow you.

Organizing by space or time

Two organizational schemes—spatial and chronological—grow naturally out of the topic. A **spatial organization** is especially appropriate for description of a geographical area, an object, or a person. Following the way people normally survey something, you move through space from a chosen starting point to other features of the subject. Describing a friend, for instance, you might begin with his shoes and move upward or begin with his face and move downward. If, instead, you moved from hands to face to shoes to arms, your arrangement would probably be less effective because your readers would have to work harder to stay with you. The following thesis sentence suggests that the writer might move in space from one end of the street to the other.

> The main street of my neighborhood contains enough variety to make almost any city dweller feel at home.

To illustrate variety, the writer can provide details of the shops, apartment buildings, and people encountered along the street.

A **chronological organization** reports events as they occurred in time, usually from first to last. This pattern, like spatial organization, corresponds to readers' own experiences and expectations. It suits expository essays in which you describe a process from beginning to end (for instance, how to run a marathon). And it is usually the most effective pattern for narration. In a narrative essay developed from the following thesis sentence, the author would probably proceed chronologically through the event, emphasizing the difficulties and the effects they had on his friends.

> The surest way to lose good friends is to enlist their help in a move from one fourth-floor walkup to another.

A chronological organization structures the narrative essay on page 54. This is the essay on a summer job for which we earlier saw a list of ideas (p. 12).

Organizing for emphasis

Several other organizational schemes do not so much grow out of the topic as they are imposed on it to aid readers' understanding and achieve a desired emphasis. The first of these, the **general-to-specific scheme,** is common in expository and argumentative essays that start with a general discussion of the main points and then proceed to specific examples, facts, or other evidence. The following thesis sentences forecast expository and argumentative essays with general-to-specific organizations:

> In families consisting of a single parent and a single child, the boundaries between parent and child often disappear so that the two interact as siblings or as a married couple.
>
> If it hopes to win the technological race, the United States must make higher education possible for any student who qualifies academically.

Following from the first sentence, the body of the essay might first discuss generally the dynamics of the families in question and then provide specific examples of the two forms of interaction. Following the second sentence, the body of the essay might first elaborate on the basic argument and then provide the specific data to support it.

In some expository or argumentative essays, a **specific-to-general scheme** can arouse readers' interest in specific examples or other evidence, letting the evidence build to more general ideas. The following thesis sentence could be developed in this way.

> Most of us are unaware of the public relations campaigns directed at us, but they can significantly affect the way we think and live.

The writer might devote most of the essay to a single, specific example of a public relations campaign, showing how it influenced people without their knowledge. Then he could explain more generally how the example typifies public relations campaigns.

The other ways of organizing for emphasis draw on different principles for arranging material. In a **climactic organization,** ideas unfold in order of increasing drama or importance to a climax. For example, the following thesis sentence lists three effects of strip-mining in order of their increasing severity, and the essay would cover them in the same order.

> Strip-mining should be tightly controlled in this region to reduce its pollution of water resources, its permanent destruction of the land, and its devastating effects on people's lives.

As this example suggests, the climactic organization aids argumentation by leaving readers with the most important point freshest in their minds. In narration, description, and exposition, such an arrangement can create suspense and thus hold readers' attention.

Expository essays can also be arranged in variations of the climactic pattern. An essay on learning to play the guitar might proceed from **most familiar to least familiar,** that is, from simply plucking strings and sliding the hand up and down the instrument's neck, which most people have seen, to the less familiar styles of picking and chording. Similarly, an essay on various computer languages might proceed from **simplest to most complex,** so that the explanation of each language provides a basis for readers to understand the more difficult one following.

Using a pattern of development

Each of the patterns of development discussed as a discovery strategy on pages 14–16 also suggests at least one overall structure for an essay. If you have been assigned or have chosen a pattern as a way to develop your essay, it can help you arrange your material, almost always in combination with one of the organizational schemes already discussed. (See 3c, pp. 83–90, for paragraph-length examples of each pattern.)

Using **illustration or support,** you list examples or reasons, or you expand on a single example. You can arrange the individual examples or reasons or the details of the single example in the way that seems most appropriate. For instance, you might arrange several examples in climactic order for an essay arguing that the children's television program *Sesame Street* displays subtle sexism. Or you might arrange a single example chronologically for an essay explaining how one episode of the local evening news illustrates a tendency to downplay serious news in favor of trivial stories.

Using **definition** to specify the precise meaning of a word, object, or concept, you will usually differentiate the topic from other things in its class and then fill in the special characteristics of the topic itself. In an essay defining *soap opera*, for instance, you might first differentiate the soap opera from other television dramas (other members of its class) and then extend the definition with examples of the distinguishing features, arranged in the way most appropriate for emphasis.

Division (separating something into its parts) and **classification** (sorting many things into groups or classes) lead you to list and detail the parts of classes of your topic, which you further arrange for maximum emphasis. In a division essay pointing out the unvarying format of local evening news shows, you might cover the most obvious regular segments first (headline news, weather, sports) and then turn to the less obvious regular segments (police-and-fire story and human-struggle story). In a classification essay sorting soap opera characters into groups, you might arrange the groups in order of increasing complexity—say, from consistently evil characters to consistently wholesome characters to goodhearted but weak characters whose behavior is inconsistent.

In **comparison and contrast** and **analogy**, similar patterns specifying the similarities and differences between topics, you usually follow one of two basic organizational schemes: (1) you discuss each topic separately, covering all the pertinent features of one and then all the pertinent features of the other; or (2) you discuss the topics side by side, comparing them feature for feature. A comparison of the attitudes toward defense spending revealed by the network news programs might follow the first scheme, with each network being examined separately. (See the essay titled "The Obsolete Hero" on p. 56 for an example of a comparison organized in this way.) The second scheme might work for an analogy between wild cards in poker and goodhearted but weak characters in soap operas, showing how both cause sudden realignments among players. Both topics would be examined under each comparable feature. In either scheme, the specific features can be arranged in any order that achieves the desired emphasis.

The pattern of **cause-and-effect analysis** also usually leads you to one of two organizations, depending on whether you are examining why something happened or what its consequences were or will be: (1) you first explain an effect and then examine its causes; or (2) you first explain a cause or causes and then examine the actual or possible effects. The first scheme would suit an essay explaining why television game shows are popular; the second scheme would suit an essay arguing that television news makes viewers impatient for quick solutions to complex problems. The causes or effects themselves may be arranged in order of their occurrence (chronologically) or of their importance or complexity.

The final pattern, **process analysis,** is almost always organized chronologically, as the steps in the process actually occur. In a process essay explaining how to improve one's chances of winning a television game show, for instance, you would present the sequence of steps involved in preparing for the show and playing the game on the air.

2
Outlining

When you have chosen an overall organization for your essay, you may find it helpful to work it out in an outline, a blueprint showing what you will cover and where. Some writers rarely use an outline, and some use one primarily during revision to check the underlying structure of a draft. But writers who do use some form of preliminary outline during planning find that it helps them discover potential problems—flaws in organization, gaps or overlaps in coverage, unwanted digressions—and then helps guide the actual drafting. Either of the two kinds of outlines discussed below can serve these functions. Keep in mind, though, that while the thought you give an outline can be very productive, you may not be able to anticipate changes that drafting will demand. Think of the outline as an aid, not a taskmaster.

Preparing an informal outline

For many essays, especially those with a fairly straightforward structure, an **informal outline** may provide adequate direction for your writing. As we saw on page 29, the thesis of the descriptive essay about a neighborhood street suggests a spatial organization. In an informal outline the writer set up topic headings that would correspond to separate paragraphs of her essay, and she added the features of the street.

THESIS SENTENCE

The main street of my neighborhood contains enough variety to make almost any city dweller feel at home.

INFORMAL OUTLINE

The beginning of the street
 high-rise condominium occupied by well-to-do people
 ground floor of building: an art gallery
 across the street: a delicatessen
 above the delicatessen: a tailor's shop, a camera-repair shop, a lawyer's office
The middle of the street
 four-story brick apartment buildings on both sides
 at ground level: an Italian bakery and a Spanish bodega

people sitting on steps
children playing ball on sidewalks
The end of the street
a halfway house for drug addicts
a boarding house for retired men
a discount drugstore
an expensive department store
a wine shop
another high-rise condominium

This informal outline was appropriate both for the writer's topic and purpose and for her organization. It helped keep her focused as she supplied concrete, descriptive details while drafting.

Preparing a formal outline

For more complex topics requiring more complex arrangements of ideas and support, you may want or be required to construct a **formal outline.** More rigidly arranged and more detailed than an informal outline, a formal outline not only lays out main ideas and their support but also shows the relative importance of all the essay's elements and how they connect with each other. Here, for instance, is the formal outline Pat Lucas prepared for her essay on the Renaissance Center.

Thesis sentence

The Renaissance Center in Detroit is an excellent example of hard, insensitive architecture because it shows a lack of concern for the people of the city.

Formal outline

I. Analogy between insensitive building and insensitive person
  A. Cold exterior and hard surfaces
  B. Concern only with self
II. The parts of the Renaissance Center
  A. The five towers
    1. Fortress-like appearance
    2. Dark shapes turning in on themselves
  B. The base
    1. High concrete wall at street level
    2. Lack of apparent entrance for pedestrians
III. The Renaissance Center as a whole
  A. Building set apart from city
  B. Scale and architecture unrelated to city

Lucas's outline illustrates some of the choices that outlining can help you make. In moving from her rough groups of ideas (p. 17) to her outline, Lucas followed through on her earlier plan to omit discussion of the building's interior and of other Detroit buildings. She deleted some other ideas that no longer seemed relevant and combined ideas that seemed related. Thinking of her readers' needs,

Lucas also moved her analogy to the beginning of the essay, where she believed it would do more to explain her attitude. And to depict the building as clearly as possible for readers, she sorted the potentially confusing list of features into two main groups (the parts of the building and the building as a whole). Though Lucas knew her outline might undergo further change as she drafted and revised her essay, she was satisfied that it solved some problems and would provide a course for her to follow until new problems arose.

Lucas's outline illustrates not only the potential value of outlining but also several principles of outlining that can help ensure completeness, balance, and clear relationships.

1. So that the outline both clarifies the order of ideas and details and indicates their relative importance, all its parts are systematically indented and numbered or lettered: Roman numerals (I, II, III) for primary divisions of the essay; indented capital letters (A, B) for secondary divisions; further indented Arabic numerals (1, 2) for principal supporting examples. A level of detail below the Arabic numbers would be indented further still and labeled with small letters (a, b). Each succeeding level contains more specific information than the one before it.

2. The outline divides the material into several groups. An uninterrupted listing of ideas like the one following would indicate a need for tighter, more logical relationships among ideas. (Compare this example with Parts II and III of Lucas's actual outline.)

    II. The Renaissance Center
        A. Fortress-like appearance
        B. Dark shapes turning in on themselves
        C. High concrete wall at street level
        D. Lack of apparent entrance for pedestrians
        E. Building set apart from city
        F. Scale and architecture unrelated to city

3. Within each part of the outline, distinct topics of equal generality appear in parallel headings (with the same indention and numbering or lettering). In the following example points B and C are more specific than point A, not equally general, so they should be subheadings 1 and 2 under it.

    A. The five towers
    B. Fortress-like appearance
    C. Dark shapes turning in on themselves

4. All subdivided headings in the outline break into at least two parts because a topic cannot logically be divided into only one part. The following example violates this principle.

    B. Scale unrelated to city
        1. Architecture in an unrelated style

Any single subdivision should be combined with the heading above it (as the example is in part IIIB of Lucas's outline), matched with another subdivision that has been omitted, or rechecked for its relevance to the heading that precedes it.

5. All headings are expressed in parallel grammatical form. Lucas's is a topic outline, in which each heading consists of a noun plus modifiers. In a sentence outline all headings are expressed as full sentences (see 35f and pp. 528–29 for a discussion and an example). Compare the following mixture of forms with section IIA of Lucas's actual outline:

   A. The five towers
      1. Fortress-like
      2. Dark shapes turn in on themselves.

6. The outline covers only the body of the essay, omitting the introduction and the conclusion. The beginning and the ending are important in the essay itself, but you need not include them in the outline unless you are required to do so or anticipate special problems with their organization.

3 Checking for unity and coherence

In conceiving your organization, devising and checking your outline, and writing your essay, you should be aware of two qualities of effective writing that relate to organization: unity and coherence. An essay has **unity** if all its parts support the thesis sentence and relate to each other. It has **coherence** if readers can see the relations and move easily from one thought to the next. A unified and coherent outline will not necessarily guide you to a unified and coherent essay. Much depends on how you specify connections in sentences and paragraphs, and the very process of specifying connections may lead you to see different relations and arrangements than those suggested by the outline. Still, checking your outline for unity and coherence will help you spot and solve obvious problems and thus perhaps avoid unnecessary distractions during drafting.

To check your outline for unity, ask whether each primary division is relevant to the thesis sentence and whether, within major sections of the outline, each example or detail supports the main idea of that section. Don't be too hard on your information at this stage: you may find a way to use an apparently wayward idea or example while drafting. But do cut anything that is clearly irrelevant and likely to sidetrack you during drafting.

To check your outline for coherence, ask whether your arrangement of material suits both your purpose and your readers' needs and whether readers are likely to recognize the shape of your material. You may see a clear need to rearrange parts of your outline, as Pat Lucas did when she moved her analogy to the beginning of her outline (see p. 34).

The unity and coherence of an essay begin in its paragraphs, so the two are treated in greater detail in Chapter 3 (see 3a and 3b).

EXERCISE 18

Choose three of the following topics and list four to six specific points for each one. Then arrange the ideas using the organizational scheme given in parentheses, unless a different scheme seems more appropriate for your material.

1. a festive or depressing place (*spatial*)
2. my view of what happens after death (*chronological or climactic*)
3. why parking facilities for commuting students should be expanded (*specific to general*)
4. ways to release frustration or tension (*illustration*)
5. the meaning of success or failure (*definition*)
6. the parts of a religious service, a ten-speed bicycle, a camera, or a baseball (*division*)
7. kinds of self-help books, students on campus, joggers, part-time jobs, or teachers (*classification*)
8. the differences or similarities between two television sitcoms, grandparents, newspapers, magazines, or cars (*comparison and contrast*)
9. the causes or effects of an accident, quitting smoking, playing a sport, or cheating (*cause-and-effect analysis*)
10. how to make a great dessert, take a good photograph, make a triple play in baseball, train a dog, or study for an examination (*process analysis*)

EXERCISE 19

Revise the following outline so that it adheres to the principles of the formal outline given on pages 35–36. Use the thesis sentence as a guide to appropriate divisions in the outline.

THESIS SENTENCE

Strip-mining should be tightly controlled in this region to reduce its pollution of water resources, its permanent destruction of the land, and its devastating effects on people's lives.

FORMAL OUTLINE

I. Effects of strip-mining in this region
    A. Causes of water pollution
        1. Soil acids are leached by rainwater.
        2. Run-off of acids into streams
    B. Disappearance of fish
    C. Poisoning of water supply

D. Appearance of hills caused by mining
    1. Scarring
    2. Vegetation is destroyed.
E. Erosion of the land
    1. Topsoil removed
    2. Mud slides are very common.
F. Elimination of people's forms of recreation
G. Health problems
    1. Polluted water causes illness.
H. Destruction of people's farmland and homes
    1. Acid soil
    2. Mud slides
I. Inadequate compensation for destruction of farmland and homes

II. Possible controls on strip-mining
A. Regulate mining techniques.
    1. To limit erosion
    2. Limitations on pollution
B. Mining companies should be required to replace topsoil.
    1. Restore vegetation to prevent erosion
C. Compensation for destruction of farmland and homes
    1. Cash payments
    2. Rebuilding

EXERCISE 20

Continuing from Exercise 17 (p. 28), choose an appropriate organization for your essay-in-progress. Then, to discover whether and to what extent an outline can help you plan and draft an essay, prepare an informal or formal outline (as specified by your instructor) to implement your organization.

2

Drafting and Revising the Essay

The separation of drafting and revising from the planning activities discussed in Chapter 1 is somewhat artificial because the stages almost always overlap during the writing process. But gradually for some writers, more distinctly for others, the primary goal shifts during the writing process from gathering and shaping information to forming connected sentences and paragraphs in a draft and then restructuring and rewriting the draft.

2a
Writing the first draft

Just as they vary in every other part of the writing process, writers vary in the way they draft. At one extreme is the writer who essentially drafts and revises at the same time, getting each unit of thought right before going on to the next. At the other extreme is the writer who plunges on until ideas are exhausted, rarely or never stopping to reread and rewrite. Neither of these styles is preferable, nor is any style between the extremes, except as it suits the writer. But all effective drafting styles share a common characteristic: the writers do not transcribe fully formed, coherent, and polished thoughts into words but strive to find and convey their meaning through the act of writing.

Unless you have already developed a different drafting style that works for you, try to be as fluid as possible while drafting. A degree of spontaneity will allow your attitudes toward your topic to surface naturally in your sentences. And, more important, it will make you receptive to ideas and relationships you have not seen before. Your thesis sentence and an outline can help keep you moving by reminding you of your planned purpose, organization, and content; but they should not constrain you from exploring new ideas

rev
2a

or even developing a new thesis if that is where your writing leads you.

To keep a draft flowing, skip over troublesome spots. If you can't figure out how to start the essay, omit the introduction temporarily and go right to the body. If you're stuck for the right word, leave a blank. Periodically, you will probably need to stop and reread portions of your draft to see where you are and to recapture momentum. If this rereading turns up serious problems, you may need to resolve them before continuing or at least make marginal notes about them. But resist the urge to improve style, word choice, grammar, punctuation, spelling, and the like. These are not unimportant matters, but you should save them for a later draft, after you have resolved larger issues of purpose, content, and structure. Tinkering with them during the first draft may distract you from the more important issues, and the time and energy spent may be wasted because substantial additions, cuts, and rearrangements often remove old flaws and introduce new ones.

For a brief essay, a first draft written in this way is likely to take at least an hour or two. Set aside the time, and work in a place where you are not likely to be interrupted. If interruptions are unavoidable, as they probably will be for longer essays, jot a note before leaving the draft about what you expect to do next. Then when you return you can pick up where you left off.

Pat Lucas's first draft for her essay on the Renaissance Center appears below. She retyped the completed draft in order to have a clean copy for revision.

First draft

Title?

Robert Sommer says that hard architecture is opressive and impersonal. In short, it is insensitive. An excellent example of hard, insensitive architecture is the Renaissance Center in Detroit because it shows a lack of concern for the people of the city.

An insensitive building is like an insensitive person. Both present a cold forbidding face to the world. Or they turn away completely to only show their backs. Neither shows caring or concern for their surroundings--for the people around them. They do not care how they affect people. They shut people out and show no sympathy for their feelings.

The Renaissance Center has two main parts, both of them seem deliberately intended to remind people outside that they are insignificant as far as the builders of the building or the people inside it are concerned. The five towers look fortress-like, four tall octagonal ones surround an even taller round one in the middle and thin round elevator shafts climb up the outsides of all the towers. The towers seem to turn in on themselves in an exclusive way whether they are round or octagons. The dark reflecting glass of the central tower reflects light. The glass of the surrounding towers is even darker, and they are covered in silver metal strips as if their wearing armor. The fortress-like appearance of the towers, plus their reflecting or armor-like surfaces and their darkness seem to protect the priviledged people inside from the rest of the world as if everyone outside was dirty or dangerous.

The Renaissance Center is clearly not intended to attract pedestrians from the city, only cars from elsewhere. All the highways and streets seem to lead right into the Center's parking garage. Obviously, the builders wanted to attract people from outside the city and make it possible for them to get directly into the Renaissance Center without the risk of getting lost in the "dangerous" city or contamanating themselves by contact with its depraved residents. The pedestrian from the city has a hard time even getting near the building, since its on the other side of a many-lane highway. Once across this barrier, a new one presents itself in the form of the hugh concrete base of the building. This base forms a high wall at street level which has no signs or shop windows to direct pedestrian, or attract them. It is not even easy to find a door into the building. It tells anyone passing by to keep out and further reminds them of their insignificance.

The Renaissance Center is by far the most noticable feature on the horizon. It stands apart from the rest of the skyline of downtown Detroit, on the banks of the river. It is much higher and bulkier than any Detroit building, and its design is also much different. It seems to say that its no part of old, rundown Detroit or of the people who live there.

The irony is that the Renaissance Center was conceived as a way to give new life to a depressed city. In 1977 when the Renaissance Center was completed, the center of Detroit was dying of poverty and neglect. Just about anyone with any money had long since fled to the suburbs and they rarely returned even for visits. The remaining residents were mostly poor, and crime was a problem.

The problem is that the Renaissance Center has done little to change all this. Sure, more shoppers and conventioners come to the city now but the city they come to is the Renaissance Center, not Detroit. The old city and its residents are still mostly ignored by this insensitive building.

EXERCISE 1

Compare Lucas's draft with the last step in her planning (her outline) on page 34. Where has the act of drafting led her to rearrange her information, add or delete material, or explore new ideas?

EXERCISE 2

Prepare a draft of the essay you began in Chapter 1. Use your thesis sentence (Exercise 17, p. 28) and your outline (Exercise 20, p. 38) as guides, but don't be unduly constrained by them. Concentrate on opening up options, not on closing them down.

2b
Revising the first draft

When you complete the first draft of your essay, take a break for at least a few hours to pursue some other activity. The break will clear your mind and give you some distance from your work. Then you will be more relaxed and objective as you tackle one of the most crucial activities in any writing: revision.

Revision literally means "re-seeing"—looking anew at ideas and details, their relationships and arrangement, the degree to which they work or don't work for the thesis. Strictly speaking, revision includes editing—refining the manner of expression to improve clarity or style or to correct errors. In this chapter, though, revision and editing are treated separately to stress their differences: in revision you deal with the underlying meaning and structure of your essay; in editing you deal with its surface. Often it is tempting to skip the fundamental work of revision and move directly to editing the first draft. But the resulting essay, though perhaps superficially correct, may be deeply flawed in ways that will negatively affect readers' responses. You can avoid the temptation to substitute editing for revision and prevent them from interfering with each other by making at least two separate drafts beyond the first: a revised one and then an edited one (p. 47).

Set aside at least as much time to revise your essay as you took to draft it. Plan on going through the draft several times to answer the questions in the following checklist and to resolve the problems they reveal. (If you need additional information on any of the topics in the checklist, refer to the handbook sections given in parentheses.)

Checklist for revision

1. Does the body of your essay carry out the purpose and central idea expressed by your thesis sentence (1c, 1g)? Will your reason for writing be apparent to your readers, not only in your thesis sentence but throughout your essay (1f)? If you have drifted away from your thesis sentence in the body, do you need to revise the thesis sentence (to reflect your new direction) or revise the body (to reflect the thesis sentence)?
2. Have you provided adequate details, examples, or reasons to support each of your ideas (1d)? Will your readers need more information at any point to understand your meaning or appreciate your point of view (1f)?
3. Is your essay unified (1h-3)? Does each paragraph and sentence relate clearly to the thesis sentence?
4. Is your essay coherent (1h-3)? Are the relationships within and among its parts apparent? Will readers see the shape of the essay, its overall organization? (Outlining the draft can help you check its structure. See 1h-2, p. 33.)
5. Does the tone of your writing accurately convey your attitude toward your topic and the role you are assuming (1g-2)? Is the tone appropriate for your purpose and your audience? Is it consistent throughout the essay?
6. Is each paragraph in the body unified (3a), coherent (3b), and well developed (3c)?
7. Does your introduction engage and focus readers' attention (3c-1)? Does your conclusion provide readers with a sense of completion (3c-2)?

When Pat Lucas returned to her first draft after half a day, questions like these revealed several problems. Though she felt that the purpose and main idea expressed in her thesis sentence had held up well throughout the draft, she was aware of giving little consideration to her readers' needs. Lucas had earlier decided that an audience of her classmates might not share her attitudes toward architecture and probably would know nothing of the Renaissance Center. Yet, as happens to most writers in the press of drafting, Lucas's own need to get her ideas down had taken precedence over her sense of her readers' needs.

In rereading her draft, Lucas saw that the introduction was too abrupt to engage the attention of readers and show them how her concerns related to their experiences. She also sensed that her tone was sometimes too hostile to help readers identify with her feelings, especially in the sentences on how the builders seemed wary of the danger and contamination of outsiders (the end of the third paragraph and early in the fourth paragraph). And in both her organization and some of her details, Lucas saw that she had failed to give readers the clear mental picture of the Renaissance Center that they would need to appreciate her objections to it. The third, fourth, and fifth paragraphs created a confusing movement in space, starting with the towers seen from some distance, zooming in to the base seen close up, and then pulling way back to the entire building seen from afar. Lucas realized that she could create a more natural movement by reversing the third and fourth paragraphs and signaling the movement in space more clearly at the beginning of each paragraph. And for an even clearer picture of the Renaissance Center, she could add a new paragraph before the others, devoted just to description of the building.

Lucas saw other problems and solutions in her draft as well. The analogy of the second paragraph, which she had nursed all through her writing process, seemed to interrupt what would otherwise be a smooth transition from the introduction to the first descriptive paragraph. Since the analogy applied to all insensitive buildings, not just to the Renaissance Center, Lucas decided to weave a briefer version of it into the introduction. In addition, she decided to cut the discussion of automobile access in the fourth paragraph because it seemed irrelevant to the main point of the paragraph, the pedestrian's experience of the building. And finally, Lucas decided to combine and rewrite her last two paragraphs. Although she had never planned to include this material, she found herself writing about it in her draft as a means of closing the essay. The irony of the building's intended and actual effect on Detroit seemed to her a good way to end the essay, but she thought it would be more effective in a single, briefer concluding paragraph.

In revising her draft, Lucas made many changes directly on the copy, but she also inserted a rewritten introduction and a new second paragraph, and she cut apart and reassembled the paragraphs on the towers and the base. Her revision appears below.

Revised first draft

Title?

Everyone knows what its like walking below modern skyscrapers. The skyscrapers may seem beautiful at first, or even awesome, but as they get familiar they begin to seem boring in their sameness or their gigantic bulk seems overwelming. The essay by Sommer entitled "Hard Architecture" gives some idea of why modern skyscrapers affect a person in this particular way. Sommer says that many modern structures are oppressive and impersonal, the builders seem to care little for the people who must use them or live with them. Like an insensitive person, a building can also be insensitive—hard, remote and uncaring. An excellent example of insensitive architecture is the Renaissance Center in Detroit because it shows a lack of concern for the people of the city.

The Renaissance Center consists of five towers sitting on a massive concrete base that rises several stories from the street. Four of the towers are octagonal and covered in strips of silver metal over dark glass. The fifth tower is taller than the others and round and completely covered in glass. Thin round elevator shafts climb up the outsides of all the towers. The four octagonal towers surround the round one. The Center stands apart from Detroit's older downtown area on the banks of the Detroit river. Visible from miles around, the most noticable thing in the city skyline.

From close up, seems deliberately remind anyone
The Renaissance Center ~~is clearly not~~ intended to ~~attract pedes-~~
outside of their insignificance.
~~trians from the city, only cars from elsewhere. All the highways and streets seem to lead right into the Center's parking garage. Obviously, the builders wanted to attract people from outside the city and make it possible for them to get directly into the Renaissance Center without the risk of getting lost in the "dangerous" city or contamanating themselves by contact with its depraved residents.~~

~~The pedestrian from the city has a hard time even getting near the~~
A person trying to approach the building on foot from the city must cross
~~building, since its on the other side of~~ a many-lane highway. ~~Once~~
Then once at the foot of the building they are confronted by a new barrier,
~~across this barrier, a new one presents itself in the form of~~ the
wall of the It rises several stories from the
~~hugh~~ concrete base ~~of the building~~. ~~This base forms a high wall at~~
It contains
street ~~level which has~~ no signs or shop windows to direct
does have an obvious for the
the pedestrian, or attract them. It ~~is~~ not even ~~easy to find a~~ door ~~into~~
pedestrian to enter by. delivers a clear message to any one who is foolish enough
~~the building.~~ It ~~tells anyone passing by to keep out and further~~
or so poor that they must travel on foot: "Keep out. Do not enter."
~~reminds them of their insignificance.~~

Seen from a somewhat greater distance, the five towers also send messages
~~The Renaissance Center has two main parts, both of them seem~~

~~deliberately~~ *to outsiders.* ~~intended to remind people outside that they are insignificant as far as the builders of the building or the people inside it are concerned.~~ The ~~five~~ towers look fortress-like, *with the* four ~~tall~~ octagonal ones *appearing to guard the* ~~surround an even taller~~ round *central* one. ~~in the middle and thin round elevator shafts climb up the outsides of all the towers.~~ The towers seem to turn in on themselves in an exclusive way. ~~whether they are round or octagons.~~ The dark ~~reflecting~~ glass of the central tower reflects *all* light. The *black and silver stripped exterior of the outer towers* ~~glass of the surrounding towers is even darker, and they are covered in silver metal strips as if~~ *makes them look like* their wearing armor. ~~The fortress-like appearance of the towers, plus their reflecting or armor-like surfaces and their darkness seem to protect the priviledged people inside from the rest of the world as if everyone outside was dirty or dangerous.~~

From afar the Renaissance Center *seems insensitive not just to the residents of Detroit but also their city.* ~~is by far the most noticeable feature on the horizon.~~ It stands apart from the rest of the skyline of downtown Detroit. ~~on the banks of the river.~~ It is much higher and bulkier than any Detroit building, and *does not show even a slight resemblance to the designs of the city's older buildings. The Renaissance Center* ~~its design is also much different. It seems to say that~~ *clearly wants to say that* its no part of old, rundown Detroit or of the people who live there.

The irony is that the Renaissance Center was conceived as a way to give new life to a depressed city, *the victim of poverty and neglect. Since* ~~In 1977 when~~ the Renaissance Center was completed *in 1977, it did succeed in attracting business people, conventioners, tourists, and shoppers.* ~~the center of Detroit was dying of poverty and neglect. Just about anyone with any money had long since fled to the suburbs and they rarely returned even for visits. The remaining residents were mostly poor, and crime was a problem.~~

~~The problem is that the Renaissance Center has done little to change all this. Sure, more shoppers and conventioners come to the city now~~ *B*~~b~~ut ~~the city they~~ *these people* come to ~~is~~ the Renaissance Center, not *to* Detroit. *The builders did not care about involving the* ~~The~~ old city and its residents ~~are still mostly ignored by this insensitive building.~~ *in their own rebirth, and they built a new city to shut out the old.*

EXERCISE 3

Compare Lucas's revised draft with her first draft on pages 40–42. Based on the discussion of her intentions for revision (pp. 43–44), can you see the reasons for most of Lucas's changes? Do you think she identified and solved all the significant problems in her first draft? If not, where would you suggest further revisions, and why?

EXERCISE 4

Revise your own first draft from Exercise 2 (p. 42). Use the checklist for revision on page 43 as a guide. Concentrate on purpose, content, and organization, leaving smaller problems for the next draft.

2c
Editing the second draft

Editing for style, sense, and correctness may come second to more fundamental revision, but it is far from unimportant. A carefully developed, interesting essay will still affect readers negatively if the writer appears oblivious to or careless about awkwardness, repetition, incorrect grammar, misleading punctuation, misused or misspelled words, and similar problems.

When you have revised your first draft, recopy or retype the revision so that you can read it easily and have plenty of room for changes. Then as you read the new draft, try to imagine yourself encountering it for the first time, as a reader will. Showing the draft to a friend or relative can help you gain this perspective. Or you can read the draft aloud, perhaps into a tape recorder, listening for awkward rhythms, repetitive sentence patterns, and missing or clumsy transitions. When reading aloud or silently, be careful to read what you actually see on the page, not what you may have intended to write but didn't.

In your editing, work for clarity and a smooth movement among sentences as well as for correctness. Use the questions in the following checklist to guide your editing. (As in the earlier revision checklist, chapter numbers in parentheses indicate where you can look in the handbook for more information.)

Checklist for editing

1. Are your sentences grammatical? Have you avoided errors in case (6), verb form (7), agreement (8), and adjectives and adverbs (9)?
2. Are your sentences clear? Have you avoided sentence fragments (10), comma splices and fused sentences (11), errors in pronoun reference (12), shifts (13), misplaced or dangling modifiers (14), and mixed or incomplete constructions (15)?
3. Are your sentences effective? Have you used subordination and coordination (16) and parallelism (17) appropriately? Are your sentences emphatic (18) and varied (19)?

rev 2c

4. Is your use of commas, semicolons, colons, periods, and other punctuation correct (20–25)?
5. Are your sentences mechanically correct in the use of capitals, italics, abbreviations, numbers, and hyphens (26–30)?
6. Have you relied on standard diction (31a)? Do your words denote and connote what you intend, and have you avoided triteness (31b)? Is your writing concise (31c)?
7. Are your words spelled correctly (34)?

In response to these questions and her own sense of clarity and effectiveness, Pat Lucas edited the second draft of her essay as follows.

Edited second draft

Towering Insensitivity
~~Title?~~

Anyone who has spent any time in a city knows the feeling of ~~Everyone knows what its like~~ walking below modern skyscrapers. The skyscrapers may seem beautiful at first, ~~or~~ *and* even awesome, but as they get familiar they begin to seem boring in their sameness or their gigantic bulk seems overwelming *[h]*. The essay by *Robert* Sommer entitled "Hard Architecture"[1] gives some idea of why modern skyscrapers affect a person ~~in~~ this ~~particular~~ way. Sommer says that many modern structures are opressive *[p]* and impersonal, the builders seem to care little for the people who must use them or live with them *as permanent features of their environment.* ~~Like an insensitive person, a building can also be insensitive,~~ *A hard building is thus insensitive in the same way a person can be insensitive:* hard, remote, ~~and~~ uncaring. An excellent example of insensitive architecture is the Renaissance Center in Detroit because it shows a lack of concern for the people of the city.

The Renaissance Center ~~consists~~ *is a cluster* of five towers sitting on a massive concrete base. ~~that rises several stories from the street.~~ Four of the towers are octagonal and *are* covered in strips of silver metal over dark glass. ~~The fifth tower is~~ *They surround an even* taller *tower that is* ~~than the others and~~ round and completely covered in glass. Thin round elevator shafts climb up the outsides of all ~~the~~ *five* towers. ~~The four octagonal towers surround the round one.~~ The Center stands apart from Detroit's older downtown area, ~~on~~ *along* the banks of the Detroit river. *It is* Visible from miles around, the most noticable ~~thing in~~ *feature of* the city skyline.

From close up, the Renaissance Center seems *deliberately* intended to remind anyone outside of their insignificance *in the grand designs of the builders.* A person trying to approach

1 Reprinted in Marcia Stubbs and Sylvan Barnet, eds., The Little, Brown Reader, 3rd ed. (Boston: Little, 1983) 126-39.

the building on foot from the city must cross a ~~many-lane~~ multilane highway. Then once at the ~~foot~~ bottom of the building ~~they are~~ the pedestrian is confronted with a new barrier, the concrete wall of the base. ~~This wall~~ It rises several stories from the street. It contains no signs or shop windows to direct or attract the pedestrian~~,~~. It does not even have an obvious door for the pedestrian to enter by. It delivers a clear message to any one who is foolish ~~enough~~ or ~~so~~ poor ~~that they must travel~~ enough to be traveling on foot: "Keep out. Do not enter."

Seen from a somewhat greater distance, the five towers also send messages to outsiders. The towers ~~look~~ are fortress-like, with the four ~~octagonal~~ outer ones appearing to guard the ~~round~~ central one. The towers seem to turn in on themselves in an exclusive way. The dark bronze glass of the central tower reflects all light. The black and silver-stripped exterior of the outer towers makes them look like ~~their~~ they are wearing armor.

From afar, the Renaissance Center seems insensitive not just to the residents of Detroit but also their city. ~~It~~ The Center stands apart from the rest of the downtown skyline. ~~of downtown Detroit.~~ It is much larger, both ~~higher and bulkier~~ in height and bulk, than any other Detroit building~~,~~. And it does not ~~show~~ echo even ~~a~~ slightly ~~resemblance to~~ the designs of the city's older stone and brick buildings. The Renaissance Center clearly wants to say that its no part of old, rundown Detroit or of the people who live there.

The irony is that the Renaissance Center was conceived as a way to give new life to a city depressed ~~city, the victim of~~ by neglect and poverty. ~~and neglect.~~ Since the Center was completed in 1977, it ~~did~~ has succeeded in attracting business people, conventioneers, tourists, and shoppers. But these people come to the Renaissance Center, not to Detroit. Apparently, the builders did not care about involving the old city and its residents in their own rebirth, and so they ~~built~~ constructed a new insensitive city to shut out the old.

EXERCISE 5

Use the checklist for editing (p. 47) and your own sense of your essay's needs to edit the revised draft you prepared in Exercise 4 (p. 47).

2d
Revising and editing on a word processor

The discussion of discovery techniques in Chapter 1 (pp. 11 and 12) mentioned some of the special uses of a word processor—that is, a computer capable of running a program (software) especially designed for composing and revising text. If you have access to a word processor, it can help considerably with the revision and editing of your drafts.

The main advantage of a word processor is that it eliminates the tedious, often messy labor of recopying or retyping successive drafts or pieces of drafts. Desired changes need only be typed into the last draft stored in the computer—a process simplified by the computer's capacity to add, delete, or move words, lines, or whole blocks of text with a few keystrokes. Many writers find that the ease of working on a computer encourages them to revise and edit more than they would if they had to retype or recopy continually.

A word processor can help with revision and editing in other ways as well. If you think a different organization might be more effective, you can leave the original intact within the computer, revise and edit a duplicate of it, and print both versions for comparison. Using the search function featured in most word-processing software, you can tell the computer to locate words you know you have misspelled or have a tendency to misspell. (Some word-processing software can even check most of your spellings against a programmed dictionary.) The search function can help you find other potential problems, too, such as occurrences of *is, are,* and other forms of *be* that appear in passive constructions or in place of more vigorous verbs.

The word processor is thus an undeniable boon to writers, but it is not itself a writer. It can't generate ideas, see their relationships, anticipate readers' needs for information, eliminate wordiness, or correct errors in punctuation. Any writer using a word processor must still do the real work of writing—the thinking. And the writer must also resist the temptation to view a draft coming out of the printer as perfect because it is clean. It's always a good idea to read each newly printed draft carefully, if only because typographical errors are sometimes difficult to spot on the computer screen.

As electronic machines, word processors have one major disadvantage: they are susceptible to breakdowns that could have disastrous consequences for the writer. Power failures, brownouts, and surges of electricity can destroy data stored in the computer's memory; spilled liquids, fingerprints, and even the magnetism of paper clips can destroy data stored on a disk. To avoid losing your material, store every few pages as you are working, routinely make back-up copies of disks, and always print your work at the end of each session. Like many writers, you may find it easier to work on printed copy than on a screen, so the end-of-session print-outs may serve a dual function.

(See Appendix B for special guidelines on manuscript format when you are writing with a word processor.)

2e Preparing the final draft

After editing your essay, recopy, retype, or print it once more for submission to your instructor. Follow the guidelines in Appendix B or the wishes of your instructor for an appropriate manuscript form. Be sure to proofread the final essay several times to spot and correct errors. To increase the accuracy of your proofreading, try reading the essay backward, beginning with the last sentence and moving toward the beginning, examining each sentence as a separate unit. This technique will help keep the content of your writing from distracting you in your search for errors.

Pat Lucas's final essay, along with her instructor's comments, appears below. The instructor points out the strengths he sees in the essay as well as the flaws remaining in it. He uses a combination of written comments, correction symbols (from inside the front cover of this handbook), and correction codes (from inside the back cover).

Final draft with instructor's comments

Towering Insensitivity

Anyone who has spent any time in a city knows the feeling of walking below modern skyscrapers. The skyscrapers may seem beautiful and even awesome at first, but as they get familiar they begin to seem boring in their sameness or their gigantic bulk seems overwhelming. The essay by Robert Sommer entitled "Hard Architecture"[1] gives some idea of why modern skyscrapers affect a person this way. Sommer says that many modern structures are oppressive and impersonal, the builders seem to care little for the people who must use them or live with them as permanent features of their environment. A hard building is thus insensitive in the same way a person can be insensitive:

//

cs

Ref (could be clearer what these pronouns refer to)

Good analogy. It's yours, not Sommer's, right? You need to make that clearer.

[1] Reprinted in Marcia Stubbs and Sylvan Barnet, eds., The Little, Brown Reader, 3rd ed. (Boston: Little, 1983) 126-39.

hard, remote, uncaring. An excellent example of insensitive architecture is the Renaissance Center in Detroit because it shows a lack of concern for the people of the city.

The Renaissance Center is a cluster of five towers sitting on a massive concrete base. Four of the towers are octagonal and are covered in strips of silver metal over dark glass. They surround an even taller tower that is round and completely covered in glass. Thin round elevator shafts climb up the outsides of all five towers. The Center stands apart from Detroit's older downtown area, along the banks of the Detroit river. It is visible from miles around, the most noticable feature of the city skyline.

26d

sp

From close up, the Renaissance Center seems deliberately intended to remind anyone outside of their insignificance in the grand designs of the builders. A person trying to approach the building on foot from the city must cross a multilane highway. Then once at the bottom of the building the pedestrian is confronted with a new barrier, the concrete wall of the base. It rises several stories from the street. It contains no signs or shop windows to direct or attract the pedestrian. It does not even have an obvious door for the pedestrian to enter by. It delivers a clear message to anyone foolish or poor enough to be traveling on foot: "Keep out. Do not enter."

8b

More varied sentences would make this ¶ more readable—see 19b

Seen from a somewhat greater distance, the five towers also send messages to outsiders. The towers are fortress-like, with the four outer ones appearing to guard the central one. The towers seem to turn in on themselves in an exclusive way. The dark bronze glass of the central tower reflects all light. The black and silver-stripped exterior of the outer towers makes them look like they are wearing armor.

meaning? significance of this detail for your thesis?

as if

see 16c

This ¶ is not as well developed as the others. See 3c.

From afar, the Renaissance Center seems insensitive not just to the residents of Detroit but also their city. The Center stands apart from the rest of the downtown skyline. It is much larger, both in height and bulk, than any other Detroit building. And it does not echo even slightly the designs of the city's older stone and brick

//

//

buildings. The Renaissance Center clearly wants to say that its no √

hyph part of old, rundown Detroit or of the people who live there.

The irony is that the Renaissance Center was conceived as a way to give new life to a city depressed by neglect and poverty. Since the Center was completed in 1977, it has succeeded in attracting business people, conventioneers, tourists, and shoppers. But these people come to the Renaissance Center, not to Detroit. Apparently, the builders did not care about involving the old city and its residents in their own rebirth, and so they constructed a new insensitive city to shut out the old. Very effective conclusion

21f (comma)

Your example of the Renaissance Center extends Sommer's ideas very effectively. His essay obviously touched a nerve in you, and you convey your impressions well. I like your second paragraph and your spatial organization: they give me a clear sense of what the building looks like.

In revising, see what you can do to develop and clarify the details of the fourth ¶. Also, correct the errors noted. Reading Chapter 17 on parallelism could help you avoid faulty parallelism (¶s 1, 5) in your future work.

EXERCISE 6

To become familiar with the symbols and codes of this handbook, revise Lucas's essay wherever her instructor has used a symbol or code to mark a problem.

EXERCISE 7

Prepare the final draft of the essay you have been working on throughout Chapters 1 and 2. Proofread carefully and correct all errors before submitting your essay for review.

2f

Benefiting from criticism

When you submit a paper for review by your instructor or, as is often the case in writing courses, by your classmates, they will act as counselors and editors to help you see both virtues and flaws in your work and to sharpen your awareness of readers' needs. Listen closely to what they say, and try not to become defensive. Repeated practice in working from ideas to essay, along with information on the writing process offered by your instructor and classmates, can help you become a more efficient writer. Attentive responses to the

rev
2f

comments of critical readers can help you become a more capable writer.

To increase the benefit from readers' comments, always consider them seriously and, if they seem appropriate, revise your work in response to them, whether or not you are required to do so. Consult your instructor, a classmate, or the appropriate sections of the handbook if you need additional help. (See "Using This Book," p. ix, for a guide to the handbook.) In addition, keep track of problems that recur in your work so that you can give them special attention. One device for tracking minor problems is a chart like the one below, with a vertical column for each assignment and a horizontal row for each error noted on your essays. The handbook section is noted for each problem, and check marks in the boxes indicate how often the problem occurred in each essay.

	Assignment			
Problems	1	2	3	4
parallelism (17)	✓✓	✓	✓	
agreement (8a)	✓		✓	✓
comma splice (11)	✓✓	✓	✓	

The chart also provides a convenient place to keep track of words you misspell so that you can master their spellings.

EXERCISE 8

Carefully read the student essays below, and answer the following questions about each one. (1) What is the writer's purpose, and what kind of essay is that purpose expressed in? (2) How well does the thesis sentence convey both purpose and kind of essay? What assertion does the thesis sentence make? How specific is the sentence? How well does it preview the writer's ideas and organization? (3) What organization does the writer use? Is it clear throughout the essay? (4) What details, examples, and reasons does the writer use to support his or her ideas? Where is supporting evidence skimpy? (5) Who do you think constitutes the writer's intended audience? What role does the writer seem to be assuming? What does the tone reveal about the writer's attitude toward the topic? (6) How successful is the writer in making you care about the topic and his or her views of it?

Working in the Barnyard

Until two months ago I thought summer jobs occupied time and helped pay the next year's tuition but otherwise provided no useful training. Then I took a temporary job in a large government agency. Two months there taught me a very valuable lesson about how people work together.

Last May I was hired by the personnel department of the agency to fill in for vacationing workers in the mail room. I had seven coworkers and a boss, Mrs. King. Our job was to sort the huge morning and afternoon mail shipments into four hundred slots, one for every employee in the agency. Then we delivered the sorted mail out of grocery carts that we wheeled from office to office along assigned corridors, picking up outgoing mail as we went along. Each mail delivery took an entire half day to sort and deliver.

My troubles began almost as soon as I arrived. Hundreds of pieces of mail were dumped on a shallow table against a wall of mail slots. I was horrified to see that the slots were labeled not with people's names but with their initials—whereas the incoming letters, of course, contained full names. Without thinking, I asked why this was a good idea, only to receive a sharp glance from Mrs. King. So I repeated the question. This time Mrs. King told me not to question what I didn't understand. It was the first of many such exchanges, and I hadn't been on the job a half-hour.

I mastered the initials and the sorting and delivery procedures after about a week. But the longer I worked at the job the more I saw how inefficient all the procedures were, from delivery routes to times for coffee breaks. When I asked Mrs. King about the procedures, however, she always reacted the same way: it was none of my business.

I pestered Mrs. King more and more over the next seven weeks, but my efforts were fruitless, even counterproductive. Mrs. King began calling me snide names. Then she began picking on my work and singling me out for reprimands, even though I did my best and worked faster than most of the others.

Two months after I had started work, the personnel manager called me in and fired me. I objected, of course, calling up all the deficiencies I had seen in Mrs. King and her systems. The manager interrupted to ask if I had ever heard of the barnyard pecking order: the top chicken pecks on the one below it, the second pecks on the third, and so on all the way down the line to the lowliest chicken, whose life is a constant misery. Mrs. King, the manager said, was that lowliest chicken at the bottom of the pecking order in the agency's management. With little education, she had spent her entire adult life building up her small domain, and she had to protect it from everyone, especially the people who worked for her. The arbitrariness of her systems was an assertion of her power, for no one should doubt for a moment that she ruled her little roost.

I had a month before school began again to think about my adventure. At first it irritated me that I should be humiliated while Mrs. King continued on as before. But eventually I saw how arrogant, and how unsympathetic, my behavior had been. In my next job, I'll learn the pecking order before I become a crusader, *if* I do.

rev
2

The Obsolete Hero

Most Americans admire the cowboy as a symbol of our nation's pioneering spirit. The cowboy represents the values of a young country expanding its frontiers across the untamed West: rugged courage, physical strength and skill, and stubborn independence. In our century the West has been tamed, however, and the cowboy's role has changed. The hero who used to ride the range is obsolete in an era when cattle are carefully bred, fed, inoculated, and shipped instead of herded to market.

The kind of cowboy we see in television westerns originated from the Spanish conquistadors, who brought horses and cattle to the New World. Let loose to graze, the cattle gradually multiplied into huge herds. When easterners began flooding westward in the mid-1800s, the demand for beef grew, and so did the need for cowboys to track down the cattle and drive them to market.

As the railroads moved westward after the Civil War, it became possible to ship beef not only locally but to the large cities back East. Vast trail drives grew up in which cattle from several ranches at once were herded from Texas northward to railhead cow towns such as Abilene, Wichita, and Dodge City. Supervising these drives were men who had the stamina to ride in the saddle all day for weeks and sleep on the ground at night. Their meals, cooked over an open fire, consisted of whatever could be caught on the way or carried in a chuck wagon without spoiling. The cowboys had to know how to rope a runaway cow, tie a calf's feet for branding, pull a stray out of a bog, shoot a rattlesnake from the back of a galloping horse, find food and water in unfamiliar territory, and break and ride wild mustangs for transportation.

As civilization spread across the West, ranchers began fencing in their land and breeding cattle instead of trusting to nature. Trail drives dwindled as the range was divided into private property and the railroads provided closer outlets for beef. As a result of these changes, today's cowboys lean less on survival skills and more on agriculture and veterinary medicine. They learn to build and mend fences and to drill wells and grease windmills, which provide cattle with water and irrigate the land to create a dependable feed supply. Though horses remain important, the modern cowboy typically trains his ponies from colthood instead of busting wild broncos. He sleeps in a bed at night and rides to the range in a Jeep or pickup truck. His midday meals are delivered fresh and hot by truck. Even the cattle he tends are trucked from one range to the next. When the cowboy needs to search the brush for strays, he can do it in a helicopter. Many of the colorful skills that used to be essential for a cowboy, such as riding a bucking horse and twirling a lasso, now show up mainly in rodeos.

Today our national focus has shifted from geographic frontiers to the frontiers of space and high technology. But many of us, in our hearts, still dream of being as hardy, self-sufficient, and free as that obsolete hero of the Wild West, the cowboy.

3

Composing Paragraphs

Whatever our purpose in writing and whatever our subject, we normally write in **paragraphs,** groups of related sentences set off by a beginning indention. In the process of composing paragraphs and revising them, we work toward two complementary goals: to give full expression to our ideas and to help readers follow and appreciate our train of thought. For the writer, paragraphing provides a way to break down complex ideas into manageable parts, discuss each part separately and completely, and relate each part to the central theme or thesis of the essay. For readers, paragraphing focuses attention on one idea at a time and provides the mixture of general statements and specific information needed to understand meaning.

The following paragraph provides a fairly simple illustration of how the paragraph aids the writer and the reader.

> Some people really like chili, apparently, but nobody can 1
> agree how the stuff should be made. C. V. Wood, twice winner 2
> at Terlingua, uses flank steak, pork chops, chicken, and green
> chilis. My friend Hughes Rudd of CBS News, who imported 3
> five hundred pounds of chili powder into Russia as a condition
> of accepting employment as Moscow correspondent, favors
> coarse-ground beef. Isadore Bleckman, the cameraman I must 4
> live with on the road, insists upon one-inch cubes of stew beef
> and puts garlic in his chili, an Illinois affectation. An Indian of 5
> my acquaintance, Mr. Fulton Batisse, who eats chili for break-
> fast when he can, uses buffalo meat and plays an Indian drum
> while it's cooking. I ask you. 6
>
> – CHARLES KURALT, *Dateline America*

The thesis of the essay in which this paragraph appears is that a Texas chili championship gives undue attention to an unpleasant food. Kuralt begins the paragraph with a general statement that relates to his thesis. That statement leads him directly to four exam-

¶ un
3a

ples—four pieces of evidence for his claim that people disagree over how to make chili (sentences 2–5). He keeps himself focused on his general statement by tying each example back to it with the word *chili* and by starting each example sentence with a name or another identification of a chili maker. At the same time he helps us, his readers, by stating what his paragraph will be about and sticking to that idea, by letting us know that sentences 2–5 serve a similar function, and by giving us plenty of specific details in those sentences so that we can appreciate his point of view.

Kuralt's paragraph illustrates three qualities of most effective paragraphs: (1) it is *unified* because it adheres to one idea; (2) it is *coherent* because its parts relate clearly to one another; and (3) it is *developed* because its general statement is supported with detailed examples. These are three qualities of an effective essay as well (see 1f and 1h), but it is mainly through paragraphs that they are achieved. Thus they are the subjects of the next three sections, 3a, 3b, and 3c. A fourth section, 3d, treats introductions, conclusions, and other kinds of paragraphs that serve special functions in essays. And a final section, 3e, discusses how paragraphs work together in the whole essay.

3a
Maintaining paragraph unity

Since readers expect a paragraph to explore one idea, they will be alert for that idea and will patiently follow its development. In other words, they will seek and appreciate paragraph **unity,** clear identification and clear elaboration of one idea and of that idea only. If readers' attention is not rewarded and they must shift their focus from one idea to another and perhaps back again, their confusion or frustration will impede their understanding and acceptance of the writer's meaning.

In an essay the thesis sentence often announces the main idea (see 1g). In a paragraph a **topic sentence** often alerts readers to the essence of the paragraph by stating the central idea and expressing the writer's attitude toward it. In Kuralt's paragraph on chili the topic sentence is sentence 1: the author states generally that people disagree about how to make chili. The next four sentences provide specific examples of chili concoctions, and the last sentence (*I ask you*) invites us to consider the examples with amusement, as the writer does.

In the body of an essay each paragraph is likely to treat one part of the essay's thesis sentence; the topic sentences simply elaborate on parts of the thesis. A topic sentence will not, of course, guarantee a unified paragraph, any more than a thesis sentence guarantees a unified essay. The next several sections explain how to write unified paragraphs controlled by strong topic sentences.

1
Focusing on the central idea

Kuralt's paragraph on chili works because it rewards our attention to its topic sentence. The sentences that follow the topic sentence do not stray off to other subjects, such as the other food preferences of the people mentioned or of the writer himself. Instead, each one helps us better understand the writer's central idea.

The following paragraph, in contrast, begins to lose its way in sentence 5.

> Professional wrestling satisfies viewers' needs for heroic 1
> struggle. The confrontation between men like Carl "Cowboy" 2
> Coyote and Boris "Tsar" Ivanov—each one costumed to reflect
> his nickname—may seem absurd, not heroic. But the ab- 3
> surdity removes the contest from reality, so that the wrestlers
> are like characters in a fairy tale who symbolize good (the
> American hero) and evil (the Russian menace). We know the 4
> action is all (or mostly all) staged, yet that unreality increases
> the symbolism of the contest. There is also staged action in TV 5
> crime shows. The action *seems* real, so we begin to care about 6
> who wins or loses. The shootings and other violence usually do 7
> not offend us but seem justified and even necessary. Of course, 8
> crime shows are even more violent than professional wrestling.

By the end of this paragraph, the author seems to have forgotten his central idea (stated in sentence 1) that professional wrestling satisfies viewers' needs for heroic struggle. At sentence 5 he becomes distracted by the staged action in TV crime shows, returning to wrestling only weakly in the last sentence.

The writer might have kept on track and produced a more unified paragraph if he had been more careful to relate every sentence both to the sentence before it and to the central idea of the topic sentence. In sentences 2–4 the writer does establish these relationships: in sentence 2 he admits that wrestling often seems absurd; in sentence 3 he says that the absurdity gives a match a fairy-tale symbolism; and in sentence 4 he says that the staged action increases the symbolism. In sentence 5, however, the writer neither comments on the central idea of heroic struggle nor extends the idea (stated in sentence 4) that staged action increases the symbolism of wrestling. From then on he loses his thread and, in the process, his readers.

Compare the disunified paragraph with the following revision, noting especially how the writer uses the new sentences 5–7 to develop his explanation.

Professional wrestling satisfies viewers' needs for heroic 1
struggle. The confrontation between men like Carl "Cowboy" 2
Coyote and Boris "Tsar" Ivanov—each one costumed to reflect
his nickname—may seem absurd, not heroic. But the absurdity 3
removes the contest from reality, so that the wrestlers are like
characters in a fairy tale who symbolize good (the American
hero) and evil (the Russian menace). We know the action is all 4
(or mostly all) staged, yet that unreality increases the symbolism of the contest. Watching the Cowboy and the Tsar grab, 5
twist, and hurl each other, we are watching good struggle
against evil and freedom struggle against repression. It be- 6
comes important who wins or loses, so that every hammerlock
has significance. Such a struggle—ending, of course, with the 7
Cowboy victorious—renews our faith in the rightness of the
world.

— A Student

Depending on his purpose, the writer may develop the deleted comparison with TV crime shows in a separate paragraph, or he may omit it altogether.

Writers often follow the central idea in the topic sentence with a **clarifying or limiting sentence.** Such a sentence can help the writer maintain unity by providing a sharper, clearer focus for the paragraph; and it can help the reader by providing a more precise sense of the writer's idea. In the following paragraph, for instance, sentence 2 clarifies and limits what the writer means in her topic sentence (sentence 1) about the inconsistent attitude toward computer intelligence.

Another inconsistency in *2001: A Space Odyssey* is the atti- 1
tude toward computer intelligence. The filmmakers appar- 2
ently could not decide whether they wanted to present the
shipboard computer, HAL, as self-governed and therefore dangerous or as human-governed and therefore controllable. In his 3
name, the fact that he is a *he* (not an *it*), his soft, slightly
menacing voice, and his control over the spaceship, HAL seems
human and more than human, with a mind of his own. When he 4
starts murdering crew members, the filmmakers seem to be
saying that computer intelligence can be dangerously independent: the nightmare of the appliance taking vengeance on its
users. Yet eventually the one surviving crew member discon- 5
nects HAL's circuits to make him harmless. Then the message 6
seems to be that HAL is, after all, just a machine under human
control. In the end, it is not clear whether the filmmakers fear 7
artificial intelligence or not.

— A Student

2 Placing the topic sentence

The topic sentence of a paragraph (along with any limiting or clarifying sentence) and its supporting details may be arranged variously depending on how the writer wants to direct readers' attention and on how complex the central idea is. The most common positions for the topic sentence are discussed below.

Topic sentence at the beginning

In the most familiar arrangement—illustrated by all the paragraphs examined so far—the topic sentence comes first, then sometimes a clarifying or limiting sentence, then the supporting information. This arrangement can help the writer maintain paragraph unity because the topic sentence provides a guide for selecting details in the rest of the paragraph. For readers the topic-first model establishes an initial context in which all the following details can be understood. Look again at the paragraphs on pages 57 and 60 to see how easily we readers relate each detail or example back to the point made in the first sentence.

The topic-first model is common not only in expository paragraphs, such as those above, but also in argumentative paragraphs, such as the one below. Here the author first states his opinion and then provides the information to support it.

> For almost 30 years now, America has been systematically 1
> destroying the centers of her cities. In the name of urban re- 2
> newal, we have declared choice parcels of downtown real
> estate to be slums and then forced their rightful owners—often
> stable but poor families and small businesses—to move away.
> We have sent bulldozers in at taxpayers' expense to flatten the 3
> old housing, and then we have given the cleared land away at
> bargain prices to the operators of parking garages, overpriced
> hospitals, and chain hotels, to the developers of high-rise bank
> buildings and luxury housing.
>
> – FRED POWLEDGE, "Let's Bulldoze the Suburbs"

Topic sentence following transitional sentence

In many paragraphs the opening sentence serves as a transition or bridge from the preceding paragraph, simultaneously pointing back to the previous idea and forward to a new one. The topic sentence is then often the second sentence, with the remaining sentences providing the support. In the following paragraph, for example, the first, transitional sentence refers to the assertion in the author's preceding paragraph that science is taught as if it does not undergo change. Sentence 2 is the topic sentence.

> And, of course, it [science] is not like this at all. In real life, 1, 2
> every field of science is incomplete, and most of them—what-
> ever the record of accomplishment during the last 200 years—
> are still in their very earliest stages. In the fields I know best, 3
> among the life sciences, it is required that the most expert and

> sophisticated minds be capable of changing course—often
> with a great lurch—every few years. In some branches of biol- 4
> ogy the mind-changing is occurring with accelerating velocity.
> Next week's issue of any scientific journal can turn a whole 5
> field upside down, shaking out any number of immutable ideas
> and installing new bodies of dogma. This is an almost everyday 6
> event in physics, in chemistry, in materials research, in neu-
> robiology, in genetics, in immunology.
>
> – LEWIS THOMAS, "The Art of Teaching Science"

If a writer is making a significant change in direction, the transition from a preceding paragraph may require more than one sentence or even a separate short paragraph (see 3d-3). Even for very slight changes, however, writers frequently use words or phrases to link paragraphs so that readers see the progression of ideas. For instance, in the paragraph on computer intelligence (p. 60) the word *another* creates a bridge from the preceding paragraph. Brief links like this one are discussed in more detail in the next section (see 3b-3 and 3b-6).

Topic sentence at the beginning and in the middle

When the central idea of a paragraph requires fairly extensive support or breaks naturally into two parts, the topic sentence may be divided between the beginning and middle of the paragraph, with each part developed separately. Often the two parts compare two subjects or, as in the following paragraph, examine different sides of an issue.

> So far the only bright side [to nuclear war] I can come up 1
> with—at least the only one I can sanely recommend—is the
> certainty that, in a nuclear war, the perpetrators will also die.
> In fact, since they are no doubt somewhat better prepared for it 2
> than we are, the likelihood is that they will die more slowly,
> and with a more agonizingly clear awareness of what's hap-
> pened, than the rest of us. But even this prospect gives me only 3
> cold comfort. I have never understood those bereaved parents 4
> who, as is occasionally reported to us, find it in their hearts to
> rejoice at the execution of their child's killer. The thought of the 5
> Pentagon brass stumbling in terror through a darkened bunker
> or of the Kremlin leadership preparing to wash down their
> cyanide pills with shots of Stolichnaya, does not, I am afraid,
> begin to compensate.
>
> – BARBARA EHRENREICH, "Finding the 'Bright Side' to Nuclear War"

In this paragraph sentences 1 and 3 together form the central idea of the paragraph: the one bright side of nuclear war is not very comforting. In this case the paragraph is simple enough not to need an opening statement of the whole idea to tie the parts together. In more complex paragraphs, however, the opening sentence may state the entire idea briefly before it is divided. Such an opening sentence can keep the paragraph from breaking in half and also help the writer ensure that the two parts are, in fact, closely related.

Topic sentence at the end

In some paragraphs the central idea may be stated at the end, after supporting sentences have made a case for the general statement. Since this model leads the reader to a conclusion by presenting all the evidence first, it can prove effective in argumentation. And because the point of the paragraph is withheld until the end, this model can be dramatic in exposition as well. For example, all the details in the following paragraph about the comedian Steve Martin lead up to and support the idea stated in sentence 12.

> When Martin comes onstage, he may do, say, just what 1
> Red Skelton used to do, but he gets us laughing at the fact that
> we're laughing at such dumb jokes. Martin simulates being a 2
> comedian, and so, in a way, we simulate being the comedian's
> audience. Martin makes old routines work by letting us know 3
> that they're old and then doing them immaculately. For him, 4
> comedy is *all* timing. He's almost a comedy robot. Onstage, he 5,6
> puts across the idea that he's going to do some cornball routine,
> and then when he does it it has quotation marks around it, and
> that's what makes it hilarious. He does the routine straight, yet 7
> he's totally facetious. He lets us know that we're seeing silliness 8
> in quotes. There he is, spruced up and dapper in a three-piece 9
> white suit; even his handsomeness is made facetious. Steve 10
> Martin is all persona. That's what's dizzying about him—and a 11
> little ghoulish. He and some of the other comics of his genera- 12
> tion make the *idea* of doing comedy funny.
>
> – PAULINE KAEL, "Silliness"

Expressing the central idea at the end of the paragraph does not eliminate the need to unify the paragraph. The idea in the topic sentence must still govern the selection of all the preceding details.

Topic sentence at the beginning and the end

Sometimes the central idea may be stated at the beginning of the paragraph and then restated at the end. Generally, the first sentence provides a context for the supporting information, and the last sentence provides a new twist based on that information. For example:

> Portraits of America as the confident, unworried "happy 1
> republic" have never been entirely accurate. The dour Puritans 2
> who started it all had bleak views about man's limitations as a
> social creature. The Founding Fathers, from Jefferson through 3

> Adams, committed treason and waged war, and came away
> with a melancholy understanding that practical idealism
> involves the sacrifice of some ideals. Pre–Civil War America 4
> was uneasily aware that the yeoman's republic was a vanish-
> ing ideal, and post–Civil War America faced industrialization
> and urbanization with the painfully fresh knowledge that
> worthy social objectives may require suffering on a large scale.
> With the late nineteenth century came populism founded on 5
> the suspicion that the mass of Americans were exploited by
> "interests." Then came the progressives, with their political 6
> historians proclaiming that the thralldom of the masses was
> the result of the sly Founders who had drafted an anti-
> democratic constitution. Pessimism is as American as apple 7
> pie—frozen apple pie with a slice of processed cheese.
>
> – George F. Will, *Statecraft as Soulcraft*

This model, like the previous one, will not work if the writer tries to make the last sentence rescue a disunified paragraph. To be effective, the final statement must reflect some development in the sentences preceding it.

Central idea not stated

Occasionally, a paragraph's central idea will be stated in the previous paragraph or will be so obvious that it need not be stated at all. The following paragraph, from an essay on the actor Humphrey Bogart, has no explicit topic sentence.

> Usually he wore the trench coat unbuttoned, just tied with 1
> the belt, and a slouch hat, rarely tilted. Sometimes it was a 2
> captain's cap and a yachting jacket. Almost always his trousers 3
> were held up by a cowboy belt. You know the kind: one an 4
> Easterner waiting for a plane out of Phoenix buys just as a joke
> and then takes a liking to. Occasionally, he'd hitch up his slacks 5
> with it, and he often jabbed his thumbs behind it, his hands
> ready for a fight or a dame.
>
> – Peter Bogdanovich, "Bogie in Excelsis"

The effectiveness of this paragraph rests on the power of details to describe Bogart. Thus a stated central idea—such as "Bogart's character could be seen in the details of his clothing"—not only would weaken the paragraph but would contradict its intention. Nonetheless, the central idea is clearly implied.

Paragraphs in descriptive writing (like the one above) and in narrative writing (relating a sequence of events) often lack stated topic sentences. But producing a paragraph without a topic sentence does not release the writer from the need to unify the paragraph. Each paragraph should have a central idea, and its details should develop that idea.

EXERCISE 1

What is the central idea of each paragraph below? In what sentence or sentences is it expressed?

1. To most strangers they [the Los Angeles freeways] suggest 1
chaos, or at least purgatory, and there can certainly be more
soothing notices than the one on the Santa Ana Freeway which
announces MERGING BUSES AHEAD. There comes a moment, 2
though, when something clicks in one's own mechanism, and
suddenly one grasps the rhythm of the freeway system, masters
its tribal or ritual forms, and discovers it to be not a disruptive
element at all, but a kind of computer key to the use of Los
Angeles. One is processed by the freeways. Elevated as they 3,4
generally are above the flat and centerless expanse of the city,
they provide a navigational aid, into which one locks oneself
for guidance. Everything is clearer then. There are the moun- 5,6
tains, to the north and east. There is the glimmering ocean. The 7,8
civic landmarks of L.A., such as they are, display themselves
conveniently for you. The pattern of the place unfolds until,
properly briefed by the experience, the time comes for you to
unlock from the system, undo your safety belt, and take the
right-hand lane into the everyday life below.

– JAN MORRIS, "The Know-How City"

2. Advocates of the rights of animals have sabotaged research 1
laboratories that experiment with animals, physically prevented seal hunters from killing seals, freed caged animals
from commercial fur farms, harassed whaling vessels, released
animals from zoos, and hindered hunters in their search for
prey. In search of public support for their point of view, they 2
have taken advertisements and distributed printed fliers and
vivid photographs that give graphic examples of how animals
are sometimes inhumanely treated. Such acts represent the 3
philosophy of a growing number of people in this and other
countries who believe nonhuman animals are sentient creatures that can feel pain, are aware of their plight, and, like
humans, have certain rights.

– BAYARD WEBSTER, "Should Vivisection Be Abolished?"

3. Though they do not know why the humpback whale sings, 1
scientists do know something about the song itself. They have 2
measured the length of a whale's song: from a few minutes to
over half an hour. They have recorded and studied the variety 3
and complex arrangements of low moans, high squeaks, and
sliding squeals that make up the song. And they have learned 4
that each whale sings in its own unique pattern.

– A STUDENT

4. The two most expressive things about him were his mouth 1
and the pockets of his jacket. By looking at his mouth, one 2
could tell whether he was plotting evil or had recently accom-

plished it. If he was bent upon malevolence, his lips were all 3
puckered up, like those of a billiard player about to make a difficult shot. After the deed was done, the pucker was replaced 4
by a delicate, unearthly smile. How a teacher who knew any- 5
thing about boys could miss the fact that both expressions were
masks of Satan I'm sure I don't know. Wallace's pockets were 6
less interesting than his mouth, perhaps, but more spectacular
in a way. The side pockets of his jacket bulged out over his 7
pudgy haunches like burro hampers. They were filled with 8
tools—screwdrivers, pliers, files, wrenches, wire cutters, nail
sets, and I don't know what else. In addition to all this, one 9
pocket always contained a rolled-up copy of *Popular Mechanics*, while from the top of the other protruded *Scientific American* or some other such magazine. His breast pocket contained, 10
besides a large collection of fountain pens and mechanical pencils, a picket fence of drill bits, gimlets, kitchen knives, and
other pointed instruments. When he walked, he clinked and 11
jangled and pealed. – RICHARD ROVERE, "Wallace"

EXERCISE 2

The following paragraphs contain ideas or details that do not support their central ideas. Identify the topic sentence in each paragraph and delete the unrelated material.

1. In the southern part of the state, some people still live 1
much as they did a century ago. They use coal- or wood-burn- 2
ing stoves for heating and cooking. Their homes do not have 3
electricity or indoor bathrooms or running water. The towns 4
can't afford to put in sewers or power lines, because they don't
receive adequate funding from the state and federal govern-
ments. Beside most homes there is a garden where fresh vege- 5
tables are gathered for canning. Small pastures nearby support 6
livestock, including cattle, pigs, horses, and chickens. Most of 7
the people have cars or trucks, but the vehicles are old and
beat-up from traveling on unpaved roads.

2. Most people don't realize how difficult it is to work and go 1
to school at the same time. If you want to make good grades 2
but need to pay your own way, the burdens are tremendous. I 3
work in an office sixteen hours a week. Each term I have to 4
work out a tight schedule that will let me take the courses I
want and still be at work when I'm needed. I like the job. The 5,6
people there are pleasant, and they are eager to help me learn.
In the end my job will be good training for the kind of mana- 7
gerial position I hope to have some day, because I'm gaining
useful experience in office procedures and working with people. It's hard for me to have a job and go to school, but 8
when I graduate both will make me more employable.

EXERCISE 3

Develop the following topic sentence into a unified paragraph by using the relevant information in the statements below it. Delete each statement that does not relate directly to the topic, and then rewrite and combine sentences as appropriate.

Topic sentence

Mozart's accomplishments in music seem remarkable even today.

Wolfgang Amadeus Mozart was born in 1756 in Salzburg, Austria.
He began composing music at the age of five.
He lived most of his life in Salzburg and Vienna.
His first concert tour of Europe was at the age of six.
On his first tour he played harpsichord, organ, and violin.
He published numerous compositions before reaching adolescence.
He married in 1782.
Mozart and his wife were both poor managers of money.
They were plagued by debts.
Mozart composed over six hundred musical compositions.
His most notable works are his operas, symphonies, quartets, and piano concertos.
He died at the age of thirty-five.

EXERCISE 4

Develop three of the following topic sentences into detailed and unified paragraphs.

1. Fans of country music (or rock music, classical music, jazz) come in [number] varieties.
2. My high school was an ugly (or attractive or homely or whatever) building.
3. Words can hurt as much as sticks and stones.
4. Professional sports have (or have not) been helped by extending the regular season with championship play-offs.
5. Working for good grades can interfere with learning.

3b
Achieving paragraph coherence

A paragraph is unified if it holds together — if all its details and examples support the central idea. A paragraph is **coherent** if readers can see *how* the paragraph holds together without having to puzzle out the writer's reasons for adding each new sentence. Each time readers must pause and reread to see how sentences relate to each other, they lose both comprehension and patience.

¶ coh
3b

Coherent paragraphs convey relations in many ways, and we will look at each one in detail. First, however, we will examine what makes a paragraph, like the following one, incoherent.

> The ancient Egyptians were masters of preserving dead 1
> people's bodies by making mummies of them. Mummies sev- 2
> eral thousand years old have been discovered nearly intact.
> The skin, hair, teeth, finger- and toenails, and facial features of 3
> the mummies were evident. It is possible to diagnose the dis- 4
> eases they suffered in life, such as smallpox, arthritis, and
> nutritional deficiencies. The process was remarkably effective. 5
> Sometimes apparent were the fatal afflictions of the dead peo- 6
> ple: a middle-aged king died from a blow on the head, and polio
> killed a child king. Mummification consisted of removing the 7
> internal organs, applying natural preservatives inside and out,
> and then wrapping the body in layers of bandages.

This paragraph seems to be unified: it sticks to the topic of mummification throughout. But the paragraph is hard to read. It jumps back and forth between specific details about features, diseases, and causes of death (sentences 3, 4, 6) and general statements about mummies' intactness (sentence 2), the effectiveness of the process (sentence 5), and the process itself (sentence 7). Sentence 5, about the effectiveness of the process, seems to relate to sentences 3 and 4 before it and to sentence 6 after it, yet because of its placement we can't be sure. The last sentence, though related to the topic sentence, seems stuck on as an afterthought. All the sentences seem disconnected; no words signal how each one relates to the one before it. And though sentences 3, 4, and 6 seem to have parallel meaning, they are not expressed in parallel grammatical form (*The...were evident*; *It is possible to diagnose...*; *Sometimes apparent were...*), and their verbs shift from past to present to past (*were, is, were*).

The paragraph as it was actually written is much clearer.

> The ancient Egyptians were masters of preserving dead 1
> people's bodies by making mummies of them. Basically, mum- 2
> mification consisted of removing the internal organs, applying
> natural preservatives inside and out, and then wrapping the
> body in layers of bandages. And the process was remarkably ef- 3
> fective. Indeed, mummies several thousand years old have 4
> been discovered nearly intact. Their skin, hair, teeth, finger- 5
> and toenails, and facial features are still evident. Their diseases 6
> in life, such as smallpox, arthritis, and nutritional deficiencies,
> are still diagnosable. Even their fatal afflictions are still appar- 7
> ent: a middle-aged king died from a blow on the head; a child
> king died from polio.
>
> – A Student

This paragraph contains the same information and the same number of sentences as the previous one, but now we have no difficulty moving from one sentence to the next, seeing the writer's intentions, understanding the writer's meaning. The initial broad assertion (the topic sentence) is the same, but now the writer responds to the expectations it creates with two more specific statements: first (in sentence 2) he defines the process of making mummies; then (in sentence 3) he notes why the Egyptians were masters of the process (because the process was remarkably effective). Sentence 3 automatically leads us to expect an explanation of how the process was effective, and in sentence 4 the writer proceeds to tell us: ancient mummies have been discovered nearly intact. "How intact?" we want to know. And again the writer responds to our expectation: we can make out features (sentence 5), diseases (sentence 6), and even fatal afflictions (sentence 7).

While responding to our expectations for content and arranging his sentences in a familiar, general-to-specific pattern, the writer has also linked sentences effectively, so that each either grows out of or aligns with the one before. Here is the paragraph marked up to show these connections.

> The ancient Egyptians were masters of preserving dead 1
> people's bodies by making mummies of them. Basically, 2
> mummification consisted of removing the internal organs,
> applying natural preservatives inside and out, and then wrap-
> ping the body in layers of bandages. And the process was 3
> remarkably effective. Indeed, mummies several thousand 4
> years old have been discovered nearly intact. Their skin, hair, 5
> teeth, finger- and toenails, and facial features are still evident.
> Their diseases in life, such as smallpox, arthritis, and nutri- 6
> tional deficiencies, are still diagnosable. Even their fatal 7
> afflictions are still apparent: a middle-aged king died from a
> blow on the head; a child king died from polio.

The writer restates the end of sentence 1 (*making mummies*) as the subject of sentence 2 (*mummification*) and then as the subject of sentence 3 (*the process*). As a result, sentences 2 and 3, at the same level of generality, are linked with sentence 1 and even more closely with each other. In sentence 4, which is more specific, the subject *mummies* picks up on sentence 1. Then sentences 5–7, three examples at the same level of generality, all use *their* to refer back to *mummies* and show parallel grammatical form (*Their... are still evident*; *Their... are still diagnosable*; *Their... are still apparent*). In addition to these links, the writer provides explicit transitions between sentences in the boxed words.

Though some of the connections in this paragraph may have been added in revision, the writer probably attended to them while drafting as well. Not only superficial coherence but also an underlying clarity of relationships can be achieved by tying each sentence to the one before—generalizing from it, clarifying it, qualifying it, adding to it, illustrating it. As we saw just above, each sentence in a paragraph creates an expectation of some sort in the mind of the reader, a question such as "How was a mummy made?" or "How intact are the mummies?" or "What's another example?" When the writer recognizes these expectations and tries to fulfill them, readers are likely to understand relationships without struggle.

The next pages discuss organization, parallelism, repetition and restatement, use of pronouns, consistency, and transitional expressions—all techniques for achieving coherence both while drafting and in revision.

1
Organizing the paragraph

The paragraphs on mummies illustrate an essential element of coherence: information must be arranged in an order that readers can follow easily and that corresponds to their expectations. The common organizations for paragraphs correspond to those for entire essays (see 1h-1). Here we will examine the arrangements by space, by time, and for emphasis. The patterns of development, each suggesting its own arrangement, will be examined in the next section (p. 82).

Organizing by space or time

A paragraph organized **spatially** focuses readers' attention on one point and scans a person, object, or scene from that point. The movement may be from top to bottom, from side to side, from a farther point to a closer one, or from a closer point to a farther one. Donald Hall follows the last pattern in the following paragraph.

> Across the yard, between the cow barn and the road, was a 1
> bigger garden which was bright with phlox and zinnias and pe-
> tunias. Beyond was a pasture where the color changed as the 2
> wild flowers moved through the seasons: yellow and orange
> paint brushes at first, then wild blue lupines and white Queen

> Anne's lace, and finally the goldenrod of August. Mount Kear- 3
> sarge loomed over the pasture in the blue distance, shaped like
> a cone with a flattened point on top. We sat on the porch and 4
> looked at garden, field, and mountain.
>
> – Donald Hall, *String Too Short to Be Saved*

Since a spatial organization parallels the way people actually look at a place for the first time, it conforms to readers' expectations. The spatial relationships can be further clarified with explicit signals, such as Hall's *Across* and *between* (sentence 1), *beyond* (2), and *over* (3). The writer may place a topic sentence at the beginning of the paragraph, may (like Hall) pull the scene together at the end, or may omit a topic sentence and let the details speak for themselves.

Another familiar way of organizing the elements of a paragraph is **chronologically**—that is, in order of their occurrence in time. In a chronological paragraph, as in experience, the earliest events come first, followed by more recent ones.

> There is no warning at all—only a steady rising intensity of 1
> the sun's light. Within minutes the change is noticeable; within 2
> an hour, the nearer worlds are burning. The star is expanding 3
> like a balloon, blasting off shells of gas at a million miles an
> hour as it blows its outer layers into space. Within a day, it is 4
> shining with such supernal brilliance that it gives off more light
> than all the other suns in the Universe combined. If it had plan- 5
> ets, they are now no more than flecks of flame in the still-
> expanding shells of fire. The conflagration will burn for weeks 6
> before the dying star collapses back into quiescence.
>
> – Arthur C. Clarke, "The Star of the Magi"

Like spatial paragraphs, chronological paragraphs can be almost automatically coherent because readers normally expect the progression of events. The writer can help readers by signaling the order of events and the time that separates them, as Clarke does with the phrases and words *Within minutes* and *within an hour* (sentence 2), *Within a day* (4), *now* and *still* (5), and *before* (6). Like Clarke's, a chronological paragraph may lack a topic sentence when the idea governing the sequence is otherwise clear.

Organizing for emphasis

Whereas the spatial or chronological organization is almost dictated by the content of the paragraph, other organizational schemes are imposed on paragraphs to achieve a certain emphasis. These imposed organizations are also familiar to readers.

In the **general-to-specific** scheme the topic sentence generally comes first and then the following sentences become increasingly specific. The paragraph on mummies (p. 68) illustrates this organization: each sentence is either more specific than the one before it or at the same level of generality. The following paragraph is a more straightforward illustration.

> Perhaps the simplest fact about sleep is that individual 1
> needs for it vary widely. Most adults sleep between seven and 2
> nine hours, but occasionally people turn up who need twelve
> hours or so, while some rare types can get by on three or four.
> Rarest of all are those legendary types who require almost no 3
> sleep at all; respected researchers have recently studied three
> such people. One of them—a healthy, happy woman in her sev- 4
> enties—sleeps about an hour every two or three days. The 5
> other two are men in early middle age, who get by on a few
> minutes a night. One of them complains about the daily fifteen 6
> minutes or so he's forced to "waste" in sleeping.
>
> – LAWRENCE A. MAYER, "The Confounding Enemy of Sleep"

After the general statement of his topic sentence, the author moves from common and less common sleep patterns (sentence 2) to the rarest pattern (sentence 3) and (in the remaining sentences) to particular people.

In the **specific-to-general** organization the elements of the paragraph build to a general conclusion. Such is the pattern of the next paragraph.

> It's disconcerting that so many college women, when asked 1
> how their children will be cared for if they themselves work, re-
> fer with vague confidence to "the day care center" as though
> there were some great amorphous kiddie watcher out there
> that the state provides. But such places, adequately funded, 2
> well run, and available to all, are still scarce in this country, par-
> ticularly for middle-class women. And figures show that when 3
> she takes time off for family-connected reasons (births, child
> care), a woman's chances for career advancement plummet. In 4
> a job market that's steadily tightening and getting more com-
> petitive, these obstacles bode the kind of danger ahead that can
> shatter not only professions, but egos. A hard reality is that 5
> there's not much more support for our daughters who have
> family-plus-career goals than there was for us; there's simply a
> great deal more self- and societal pressure.
>
> – JUDITH WAX, *Starting in the Middle*

The author first states a common belief (sentence 1) and two reasons why it is a misconception (sentences 2 and 3). Then she explains the implications, first specifically (sentence 4) and then generally (sentence 5). The last sentence is the topic sentence of the paragraph.

When the details of a paragraph vary in significance, they can be arranged in a **climactic** order, from least to most important or dramatic. The following paragraph builds to a climax, saving the most dramatic example for last.

> Nature has put many strange tongues into the heads of her 1
> creatures. There is the frog's tongue, rooted at the front of the 2

> mouth so it can be protruded an extra distance for nabbing
> prey. There is the gecko lizard's tongue, so long and agile that 3
> the lizard uses it to wash its eyes. But the ultimate lingual 4
> whopper has been achieved in the anteater. The anteater's 5
> head, long as it is, is not long enough to contain the tremendous
> tongue which licks deep into anthills. Its tongue is not rooted in 6
> the mouth or throat: it is fastened to the breastbone.
>
> – ALAN DEVOE, "Nature's Utmost"

Similar to the organizations discussed so far are those that arrange details according to readers' likely understanding of them. In discussing the virtues of public television, for instance, you might proceed from **most familiar to least familiar,** from a well-known program your readers have probably seen to less well-known programs they may not have seen. Or in defending the right of government employees to strike, you might arrange your reasons from **simplest to most complex,** from the employees' need to be able to redress grievances to more subtle consequences for employer-employee relations.

2
Using parallel structures

Another way to achieve coherence, although not necessarily in every paragraph, is through **parallelism**—the use of similar grammatical structures for similar elements of meaning within a sentence or among sentences. (See Chapter 17 for a detailed discussion of parallelism.) Parallel structures help tie together the last three sentences in the paragraph on mummies (p. 68). In the following paragraph the parallel structures of *It is the* and *Democracy is the* link all sentences after the first one; and parallelism also appears within many of the sentences (for instance, *hole in the stuffed shirt* and *dent in the top hat* in sentence 4). The author, writing during World War II, was responding to a request from the Writer's War Board for a statement on the meaning of democracy.

> Surely the Board knows what democracy is. It is the line 1,2
> that forms on the right. It is the don't in Don't Shove. It is the 3,4
> hole in the stuffed shirt through which the sawdust slowly
> trickles; it is the dent in the high hat. Democracy is the recur- 5
> rent suspicion that more than half of the people are right more
> than half of the time. It is the feeling of privacy in the voting 6
> booths, the feeling of communion in the libraries, the feeling of
> vitality everywhere. Democracy is the score at the beginning of 7
> the ninth. It is an idea which hasn't been disproved yet, a song 8
> the words of which have not gone bad. It's the mustard on the 9
> hot dog and the cream in the rationed coffee. Democracy is a 10
> request from a War Board, in the middle of a morning in the
> middle of a war, wanting to know what democracy is.
>
> – E. B. WHITE, *The Wild Flag*

3

Repeating or restating words and word groups

Since every unified paragraph has only one topic, that topic is bound to recur in many of the sentences. In fact, repeating or restating key words or word groups is an important means of achieving paragraph coherence and of reminding your readers what the topic is. In the following paragraph, also by E. B. White, the repetition of *poets/poet* and *clearer/clear* ties the sentences together and stresses the important words of the paragraph.

> "I wish poets could be clearer," shouted my wife angrily 1
> from the next room. Hers is a universal longing. We would all 2,3
> like it if the bards would make themselves plain, or we think we
> would. The poets, however, are not easily diverted from their 4
> high mysterious ways. A poet dares be just so clear and no 5
> clearer; he approaches lucid ground warily, like a mariner who
> is determined not to scrape his bottom on anything solid. A 6
> poet's pleasure is to withhold a little of his meaning, to intensify by mystification. He unzips the veil from beauty, but does 7
> not remove it. A poet utterly clear is a trifle glaring. 8
>
> – E. B. WHITE, "Poetry"

White's paragraph also includes some restatements of his key words: *bards* for *poets* and *plain* and *lucid* for *clear.* Such restatements or **synonyms**—words with similar meaning—figure prominently in the following paragraph.

> Since the industrial revolution work has been rearranged 1
> and much of the satisfaction has been rationalized out. Very 2
> few workers have a chance to set their own task. Jobs have 3
> been divided and subdivided so that each person performs a
> single operation upon a continuous flow of parts or papers. In- 4
> creasingly the worker is denied not only the chance to set his own task but even the chance to finish the task someone else
> sets for him. The jobs are so fragmented that few workers can 5
> feel they are helping to make a car or to issue an insurance policy. They are merely repeating the same few motions, the same 6
> simple calculations over and over throughout a lifetime of labor.
>
> – BARBARA GARSON, *All the Livelong Day*

The writer's repetitions and restatements both bind her sentences together and ensure that readers perceive her central idea, the segmenting of workers' jobs. *Work* (sentence 1) becomes a *task* (2, 4), *jobs* (3, 5), *labor* (6). *Workers* and *the worker* (2, 4, 5) become *each person* (3), *him* (4), *they* (5, 6). The work has been *rearranged* (1), *divided and subdivided* (3), *fragmented* (5). It consists of *a single operation* (3), *the same few motions, the same simple calculations* (6).

Though planned repetition can be effective, careless or excessive repetition weakens prose. See 31c.

4
Using pronouns

The previous examples illustrate yet another device for achieving paragraph coherence, the use of pronouns like *it, him, his,* and *they*. **Pronouns** refer to and function as nouns (see 5a-2) and thus can help relate sentences to each other. In the following paragraph the pronouns *he, him,* and *his* indicate that the patient is still the subject while enabling the writer to avoid repeating *the patient* or *the patient's*.

> The experience is a familiar one to many emergency-room 1
> medics. A patient who has been pronounced dead and unex- 2
> pectedly recovers later describes what happened to him during
> those moments—sometimes hours—when his body exhibited
> no signs of life. According to one repeated account, the patient 3
> feels himself rushing through a long, dark tunnel while noise
> rings in his ears. Suddenly, he finds himself outside his own 4
> body looking down with curious detachment at a medical
> team's efforts to resuscitate him. He hears what is said, notes 5
> what is happening but cannot communicate with anyone.
> Soon, his attention is drawn to other presences in the room— 6
> spirits of dead relatives or friends—who communicate with
> him nonverbally. Gradually he is drawn to a vague "being of 7
> light." This being invites him to evaluate his life and shows him 8
> highlights of his past in panoramic vision. The patient longs to 9
> stay with the being of light but is reluctantly drawn back into
> his physical body and recovers.
>
> – KENNETH L. WOODWARD, "Life After Death?"

The pronouns in this paragraph give it coherence, in part because they refer clearly to a noun. The opposite effect will occur if the reader cannot tell exactly what noun a pronoun is meant to refer to. (For a discussion of the problems associated with pronoun reference, see Chapter 12.)

5
Being consistent

Being consistent is the most subtle way to achieve paragraph coherence because readers are aware of consistency only when it is absent. Consistency (or the lack of it) occurs primarily in the person and number of nouns and pronouns and in the tense of verbs (see Chapter 13). Although some shifts will be necessary because of meaning, inappropriate shifts will interfere with a reader's ability to follow the development of ideas. The writers of the following paragraphs destroy coherence by shifting person, number, and tense, respectively.

Shifts in person

An enjoyable form of exercise is modern dance. If *one* 1,2
wants to stay in shape, *you* will find that dance tones and
strengthens most muscles. The leaping and stretching *you* do 3
also improves *a person's* balance and poise. And *I* found that *my* 4
posture improved after only a few months of dancing.

Shifts in number

Politics is not the activity for everyone. It requires quick- 1,2
ness and patience at the same time. *A politician* must like 3
speaking to large groups of people and fielding questions without having time to think of the answers. *Politicians* must also be 4
willing to compromise with the people *they* represent. And no 5
matter how good *a politician* is, *they* must give up on becoming
popular with all constituents. It isn't possible. 6

Shifts in tense

I *am developing* an interest in filmmaking. I *tried* to take 1,2
courses that relate to camera work or theater, and I *have read*
books about the technical and artistic sides of movies. Though 3
I *would have liked* to get a job on a movie set right away, I *will*
probably *continue* my formal education and training in filmmaking after college. There simply *aren't* enough jobs available 4
for all those who *wanted* to be in films but *have* no direct
experience.

6 Using transitional expressions

In addition to the methods for achieving coherence discussed above, writers also rely on specific words and word groups to connect sentences whose relationships will not be instantly clear to readers. Sometimes the omission of these words or word groups will make an otherwise coherent paragraph choppy and hard to follow, as the next paragraph shows.

Medical science has succeeded in identifying the hundreds 1
of viruses that can cause the common cold. It has discovered 2
the most effective means of prevention. One person transmits 3
the cold viruses to another most often by hand. An infected 4
person covers his mouth to cough. He picks up the telephone. 5
His daughter picks up the telephone. She rubs her eyes. She 6,7,8
has a cold. It spreads. To avoid colds, people should wash their 9,10
hands often and keep their hands away from their faces.

This paragraph is unified and fundamentally coherent because the sentences do seem related to each other. However, we can only guess at the precise relationships, which are spelled out by the italicized words in the paragraph as it was actually written:

> Medical science has *thus* succeeded in identifying the hun- 1
> dreds of viruses that can cause the common cold. It has *also* 2
> discovered the most effective means of prevention. One person 3
> transmits the cold viruses to another most often by hand. *For* 4
> *instance,* an infected person covers his mouth to cough. *Then* 5
> he picks up the telephone. *Half an hour later,* his daughter 6
> picks up the *same* telephone. *Immediately afterward,* she rubs 7
> her eyes. *Within a few days,* she, *too,* has a cold. *And thus* it 8,9
> spreads. To avoid colds, *therefore,* people should wash their 10
> hands often and keep their hands away from their faces.
>
> – A STUDENT

Now we see that sentence 1, with *thus,* is a transition from the previous paragraph. The *also* in sentence 2 indicates clearly that this discovery is a second insight of medical science, not perhaps a clarification of the first. *For instance* in sentence 4 signals that an example is coming. The time indicators in sentences 5–8 link the parts of the example. *And thus* in sentence 9 helps pull us out of the example and prepares us for the conclusion, signaled by *therefore,* in sentence 10.

The linking words and word groups are called **transitional expressions.** They state relationships clearly and thus enhance paragraph coherence. The following is a partial list of transitional expressions, arranged by the functions they perform.

TO ADD OR SHOW SEQUENCE

again, also, and, and then, besides, equally important, finally, first, further, furthermore, in addition, in the first place, last, moreover, next, second, still, too

TO COMPARE

also, in the same way, likewise, similarly

TO CONTRAST

although, and yet, but, but at the same time, despite, even so, even though, for all that, however, in contrast, in spite of, nevertheless, notwithstanding, on the contrary, on the other hand, regardless, still, though, yet

TO GIVE EXAMPLES OR INTENSIFY

after all, an illustration of, even, for example, for instance, indeed, in fact, it is true, of course, specifically, that is, to illustrate, truly

TO INDICATE PLACE

above, adjacent to, below, elsewhere, farther on, here, near, nearby, on the other side, opposite to, there, to the east, to the left

TO INDICATE TIME

after a while, afterward, as long as, as soon as, at last, at length, at that time, before, earlier, formerly, immediately, in the meantime, in the past, lately, later, meanwhile, now, presently, shortly, simultaneously, since, so far, soon, subsequently, then, thereafter, until, until now, when

To repeat, summarize, or conclude

all in all, altogether, as has been said, in brief, in conclusion, in other words, in particular, in short, in simpler terms, in summary, on the whole, that is, therefore, to put it differently, to summarize

To show cause or effect

accordingly, as a result, because, consequently, for this purpose, hence, otherwise, since, then, therefore, thereupon, thus, to this end, with this object

(For a discussion of transitional sentences and paragraphs, see pp. 61 and 99, respectively.)

7
Combining devices to achieve coherence

The devices we have examined for achieving coherence rarely appear in isolation in effective paragraphs. As any example in this chapter shows, writers must often combine sensible organization, parallelism, repetition, pronouns, consistency, and transitional expressions to help readers follow the development of ideas. And the devices also figure, naturally, in the whole essay (see 3e).

EXERCISE 5

Which of the organizational schemes discussed on pages 70–73 has been used in each of the following paragraphs?

1. The losing animal in a struggle saves itself from destruc- 1
tion by an act of submission, an act usually recognized and accepted by the winner. In some cases, for instance, the loser pre- 2
sents to its rival a vulnerable part of its body such as the top of
the head or the fleshy part of the neck. The central nervous sys- 3
tem of the winner recognizes the "meaning" of the presentation, and the instinct to kill is inhibited. Typical of this natural 4
pattern is the behavior of two wolves in combat. As soon as one 5
of the animals realizes it cannot win, it offers its vulnerable
throat to the stronger wolf; instead of taking advantage of the
opportunity, the victor relents, even though an instant earlier it
had appeared frantic to reach the now proffered jugular vein.
– René Dubos, "Territoriality and Dominance"

2. On August 18, 1951, the St. Louis Browns baseball team 1
cracked a joke and forever changed the rules of professional
baseball. On that day the Browns were playing the Detroit Ti- 2
gers. In the first inning the St. Louis manager sent to the plate 3

Eddie Gaedel, a man less than four feet tall. Detroit's pitcher at 4
first did not throw to Gaedel, but the small man held his stance,
his child's bat cocked. When the pitcher finally let one fly, the 5
ball sailed over Gaedel's head. The pitcher tried again, and 6
again the ball flew over Gaedel's head. The third pitch, too, was 7
high, and so was the fourth. The pitcher simply could not lower 8
his throws to Gaedel's strike zone. Gaedel walked to first base, 9
where he was replaced by a pinch runner who later scored.
Within twenty-four hours baseball had a new rule: no midgets 10
would ever again play professional ball. – A STUDENT

3. One must descend to the basement and move along a con- 1
fusing mazelike hall to reach it. Twice the passage seems to 2
lead against a blank wall; then at last one enters the brightly
lighted auditorium. And here, finally, are the social workers at 3
the reception desks; and there, waiting upon the benches
rowed beneath the pipes carrying warmth and water to the
floors above, are the patients. One sees white-jacketed psy- 4
chiatrists carrying charts appear and vanish behind screens
that form the improvised interviewing cubicles. All is an atmos- 5
phere of hurried efficiency; and the concerned faces of the
patients are brightened by the friendly smiles and low-pitched
voices of the expert workers. One has entered the Lafargue Psy- 6
chiatric Clinic. – RALPH ELLISON, *Shadow and Act*

4. There are three reasons, quite apart from scientific consid- 1
erations, that mankind needs to travel in space. The first reason 2
is the need for garbage disposal: we need to transfer industrial
processes into space, so that the earth may remain a green and
pleasant place for our grandchildren to live in. The second 3
reason is the need to escape material impoverishment: the
resources of this planet are finite, and we shall not forego
forever the abundant solar energy and minerals and living
space that are spread out all around us. The third reason is our 4
spiritual need for an open frontier: the ultimate purpose of
space travel is to bring to humanity not only scientific discoveries and an occasional spectacular show on television but a
real expansion of our spirit.

– FREEMAN DYSON, "Disturbing the Universe"

EXERCISE 6

After the topic sentence (sentence 1), the sentences in each student paragraph below have been deliberately scrambled to make the paragraph incoherent. Using the topic sentence and other clues as guides, rearrange the sentences in each paragraph to form a well-organized, coherent unit.

1. We hear complaints about the Postal Service all the time, 1
but we should not forget what it does *right*. The total volume of 2
mail delivered by the Postal Service each year makes up more
than half the total delivered in all the world. Its 70,000 3

employees handle 90,000,000,000 pieces of mail each year. And 4
when was the last time they failed to deliver yours? In fact, on 5
any given day the Postal Service delivers almost as much mail
as the rest of the world combined. That means over 1,250,000 6
pieces per employee and over 400 pieces per man, woman, and
child in the country.

2. A single visit to New York City will tell you why the city is 1
both loved and hated by so many people. Whether you arrive 2
by car, bus, train, plane, or boat, the skyline will take your
breath away. And the streets seem so dirty: cans and bags and 3
newspapers lie in the gutters and on the sidewalks or sometimes fly across your path. Even the people who do speak 4
English won't smile or say "Excuse me" or give you good
directions. The thrill will only be heightened when you walk 5
down the skyscraper canyons, look in the shop windows, go to
the theater or a museum, stroll in the neighborhoods where no
one speaks English. You start to notice the noise of traffic and 6
get annoyed at the crowds. But all is not perfect—far from it. 7
After a few days, when your reactions balance out, you have the 8
same love-hate feelings as everyone else.

EXERCISE 7

Study the paragraphs in Exercise 1 (pp. 65–66) for the authors' reliance on various devices to achieve paragraph coherence. Look especially for parallel structures and ideas, repetition and restatement, pronouns, and transitional expressions.

EXERCISE 8

The paragraph below is incoherent because of inconsistencies in person, number, or tense. Identify the inconsistencies and revise the paragraph to give it coherence.

I rebel against the idea of males always being the sole fam- 1
ily provider. For me to be happy, I needed to feel useful, and so 2
I work to support myself and my daughter. I did not feel that it 3
is wrong for one to be a housewife while a man supports your
household, but that way is not for me. I enjoy the business 4
world, and I have been pleased with my job. Working, I make 5
enough now to support the two of us, and I know that when I
graduate, I will be able to earn even more. I can do very well as 6
my own provider.

EXERCISE 9

Transitional expressions have been removed from the following paragraph at the numbered blanks. Fill in each blank with an appropriate transitional expression (1) to contrast, (2) to intensify, and (3) to show effect. Consult the list on pages 77–78 if necessary.

All over the country people are swimming, jogging, weight-lifting, dancing, walking, playing tennis—doing anything to keep fit. __(1)__ this school has consistently refused to construct and equip a fitness center. The school has __(2)__ refused to open existing athletic facilities to all students, not just those playing organized sports. __(3)__ students have no place to exercise except in their rooms and on dangerous public roads.

EXERCISE 10

Write a coherent paragraph from the following information, combining and rewriting sentences as necessary. First, begin the paragraph with the topic sentence given and arrange the supporting sentences in a climactic order. Then combine and rewrite the supporting sentences, helping the reader see connections by introducing parallelism, repetition and restatement, pronouns, consistency, and transitional expressions.

Topic sentence

Hypnosis is far superior to drugs for relieving tension.

Supporting information

Hypnosis has none of the dangerous side effects of the drugs that relieve tension.
Tension-relieving drugs can cause weight loss or gain, illness, or even death.
Hypnosis is nonaddicting.
Most of the drugs that relieve tension do foster addiction.
Tension-relieving drugs are expensive.
Hypnosis is inexpensive even for people who have not mastered self-hypnosis.

EXERCISE 11

Develop three of the following topic sentences into coherent paragraphs. Organize your information by space, by time, or for emphasis, as seems most appropriate. Use parallelism, repetition and restatement, pronouns, consistency, and transitional expressions to link sentences.

1. Of all my courses, ______ is the one that I think will serve me best throughout life.
2. The movie (or book) had an exciting plot.
3. We Americans face many problems, but the one we should concentrate on solving first is ______.
4. The most dramatic building in town is the ______.
5. Children should not have to worry about the future.

¶ dev
3c

3c
Developing the paragraph

A paragraph may be both unified and coherent but still be skimpy, unconvincing, or otherwise inadequate. The following paragraph is unified and coherent: it adheres to the topic of bad television commercials, and the relations among sentences are apparent. But it is not an effective paragraph.

> Despite complaints from viewers, television commercials 1
> aren't getting any more realistic. Their makers still present 2
> idealized people in unreal situations. And the advertisers also 3
> persist in showing a version of male-female relationships that
> can't exist in more than two households. What do the advertis- 4
> ers know about us, or about how we see ourselves, that makes
> them continue to plunge millions of dollars into these kinds of
> commercials?

Sentences 2 and 3 create expectations in our minds: we anticipate that the writer will give examples of commercials showing idealized people and unrealistic male-female relationships. But our expectations are disappointed because the paragraph lacks **development,** completeness. It does not provide enough information for us to evaluate the writer's assertion in sentence 1.

A well-developed paragraph always provides the specific information that readers need and expect in order to understand you and to stay interested in what you say. Often you may develop and arrange this information according to a particular pattern that is determined by your topic and what you want to say about it.

1
Using specific information

If they are sound, the general statements you make in any writing will be based on what you have experienced, observed, read, and thought. Readers will assume as much and will expect you to provide the evidence for your statements. They need details, examples, and reasons—the heart of paragraph development—to understand and appreciate your meaning.

Here is the actual version of the paragraph discussed above. Notice how the added descriptions of commercials (in italics) make a sketchy paragraph into an interesting and convincing piece of writing.

> Despite complaints from viewers, television commercials 1
> aren't getting any more realistic. Their makers still present 2
> idealized people in unreal situations. *Friendly shopkeepers stock* 3
> *only their favorite brand of toothpaste or coffee or soup. A* 4

> *mother cleans and buffs her kitchen floor to a mirror finish so*
> *her baby can play on it. A rosy-cheeked pregnant woman uses* 5
> *two babies, two packaged diapers neatly dissected, and two ink*
> *blotters to demonstrate one diaper's superior absorbency to her*
> *equally rosy-cheeked and pregnant friend.* The advertisers also 6
> persist in showing a version of male-female relationships that
> can't exist in more than two households. *The wife panics be-* 7
> *cause a meddlesome neighbor points out that her husband's shirt*
> *is dirty. Or she fears for her marriage because her finicky hus-* 8
> *band doesn't like her coffee.* What do the advertisers know 9
> about us, or about how we see ourselves, that makes them con-
> tinue to plunge millions of dollars into these kinds of com-
> mercials?
> — A STUDENT

In this paragraph the writer has recognized that sentences 2 and 6 create expectations for supporting examples, and she has duly responded to these expectations. Whereas the general statements merely *tell* us about the commercials, the detailed examples *show* them to us.

2
Using a pattern of development

Sometimes you may have difficulty developing an idea, or you may not see the most effective way to shape the information you have. Then you can use one of the patterns of paragraph development that correspond to patterns of essay development discussed on pages 14–16 and 31–33. Experienced writers use these patterns all the time, often unconsciously. Inexperienced writers can ask themselves a series of questions about an idea that will suggest how to develop it and how to organize the supporting information.

How can it be illustrated or supported?

Some ideas can be developed simply by **illustration or support**—supplying detailed examples or reasons. The writer of the paragraph above on television commercials developed her idea with several specific examples of each general statement. You can also supply a single extended example, as the author of the following paragraph does to illustrate his assertion (sentence 1) about cultural differences in the ways people communicate.

> One of my earliest discoveries in the field of intercultural 1
> communication was that the position of the bodies of people in
> conversation varies with the culture. Even so, it used to puzzle 2
> me that a special Arab friend seemed unable to walk and talk at
> the same time. After years in the United States, he could not 3
> bring himself to stroll along, facing forward while talking. Our 4
> progress would be arrested while he edged ahead, cutting

slightly in front of me and turning sideways so we could see
each other. Once in this position, he would stop. His behavior 5,6
was explained when I learned that for the Arabs to view the
other person peripherally is regarded as impolite, and to sit or
stand back-to-back is considered very rude. You must be in- 7
volved when interacting with Arabs who are friends.

– EDWARD T. HALL, *The Hidden Dimension*

The details of this example are arranged in a rough chronological sequence. In a paragraph containing several examples, a climactic organization is often effective; see the paragraph by Alan Devoe on pages 72–73 for an example.

Sometimes you can develop a paragraph by providing your reasons for stating a general idea. Such is the method used in the following paragraph.

It is time to defend the welfare state—taxes, bureaucrats, 1
rules and regulations—the whole thing. Not only because it 2
actually helps people who need help and subsidizes and
enables a range of socially valuable activities: it does all that,
and all that has to be done. There is another, and ultimately a 3
more important, reason for defending the welfare state. It 4
expresses a certain civil spirit, a sense of mutuality, a commitment to justice. Without that sense, no society can survive for 5
long as a decent place to live—not for the needy, and not for
anyone else.

– MICHAEL WALZER, "The Community"

Sentences 2, 4, and 5 provide reasons for the general assertion in sentence 1. As is often the case in such paragraphs, the reasons are arranged in a climactic order. (For another example, see the paragraph by Freeman Dyson in Exercise 5, p. 79.)

What is it? What does it encompass, and what does it exclude?

Asking "What is it?" leads to development by **definition**—saying what something is and is not, specifying the characteristics that distinguish it from the other members of its class. You can easily define concrete, noncontroversial terms in a single sentence: *A knife is a cutting instrument* (its class) *with a sharp blade set in a handle* (the characteristics that set it off from, say, scissors or a razor blade). But defining a complicated, abstract, or controversial topic often requires extended explanation (see 4b-2), and you may need to devote a whole paragraph or even an essay to it. Such a definition may provide examples to identify the subject's characteristics. It may also involve other methods of development discussed below, such as division (separating things into their parts), classification (combining things into groups), or comparison and contrast.

Here is a paragraph developed by definition. It is from an essay asserting that "quality in product and effort has become a vanishing element of current civilization."

> In the hope of possibly reducing the hail of censure which 1
> is certain to greet this essay (I am thinking of going to Alaska or
> possibly Patagonia in the week it is published), let me say that
> quality, as I understand it, means investment of the best skill
> and effort possible to produce the finest and most admirable
> result possible. Its presence or absence in some degree charac- 2
> terizes every man-made object, service, skilled or unskilled
> labor—laying bricks, painting a picture, ironing shirts, prac-
> ticing medicine, shoemaking, scholarship, writing a book. You 3
> do it well or you do it half-well. Materials are sound and 4
> durable or they are sleazy; method is painstaking or whatever
> is easiest. Quality is achieving or reaching for the highest 5
> standard as against being satisfied with the sloppy or fraudu-
> lent. It is honesty of purpose as against catering to cheap or 6
> sensational sentiment. It does not allow compromise with the 7
> second-rate. — BARBARA TUCHMAN, "The Decline of Quality"

To explain just what she means by *quality*—the key word of her essay—the author first provides a general definition (sentence 1) and then refines it with examples of the range of activities in which quality may figure (2), followed by a list of the characteristics that distinguish quality from nonquality (3–7). In this paragraph the sentences after the first move roughly from specific to general, but an arrangement by increasing specificity, importance, or complexity often works in definition as well.

What are its parts or characteristics? Or what groups or categories can it be sorted into?

Separating a single thing into its parts is the activity of **division** (also called **analysis**). Using division, you might examine a family by dividing it into its individual members—mother, father, daughter, son. Grouping many things according to their similarities is the activity of **classification.** Using classification to describe families, you might examine family structures in various cultures—matriarchal, patriarchal, nuclear, extended, and so on. Division and classification are so closely related that writers often combine them in developing an idea, a paragraph, or an essay. Thus in describing the family you might first classify the types and then divide each type into the separate roles of the individual family members.

In the following paragraph the writer divides a small portion of a daily newspaper into its parts, giving the technical name for each part.

> A typical daily newspaper compresses considerable infor- 1
> mation into the top of the first page, above the headlines. The 2

> most prominent feature of this space, the newspaper's name, is
> called the *logo* or *nameplate*. Under the logo and set off by rules 3
> is a line of small type called the *folio line*, which contains the
> date of the issue, the volume and issue numbers, copyright in-
> formation, and the price. To the right of the logo is a block of 4
> small type called a *weather ear*, a summary of the day's fore-
> cast. And above the logo is a *skyline*, a kind of advertisement in 5
> which the paper's editors highlight a special feature of the
> issue. — A STUDENT

Division always begins with a single object or concept; in the preceding paragraph it is a segment of a newspaper's front page. The task is then to identify and explain the distinct elements that constitute the object or concept. The elements might be arranged spatially, as they are above, or in order of importance or complexity.

In the following paragraph the writer classifies parents.

> In my experience, the parents who hire daytime sitters for 1
> their school-age children tend to fall into one of three groups.
> The first group includes parents who work and want someone 2
> to be at home when the children return from school. These 3
> parents are looking for an extension of themselves, someone
> who will give the care they would give if they were at home.
> The second group includes parents who may be home all day 4
> themselves but are too disorganized or too frazzled by their
> children's demands to handle child care alone. They are look- 5
> ing for an organizer and helpmate. The third and final group 6
> includes parents who do not want to be bothered by their
> children, whether they are home all day or not. Unlike the 7
> parents in the first two groups, who care for their children
> whenever and however they can, these parents are looking for a
> permanent substitute for themselves. — A STUDENT

The groups in this paragraph are arranged in a climactic order, but complexity or familiarity may also serve to organize a classification. This paragraph also illustrates several principles of classification. First, the subject being classified is plural (parents), in contrast to the singular subject of division. Second, the classes or groups are alike in at least one basic way: all hire sitters for their children. And third, the classes do not overlap, as would parents who work and parents who don't because both groups include some uncaring

How is it like, or different from, other things?

Asking about similarities and differences leads to **comparison and contrast.** The two may be used separately or together to develop an idea or to relate two or more things. In the following paragraph the author contrasts two styles of basketball play to support his point about consistency in sentence 1.

> Consistency is also always potentially dull, even when the 1
> consistency demonstrated happens to be excellence. John 2
> Havlicek, the former basketball star of the Boston Celtics,
> almost never made a mistake on the court. He used the back- 3
> board with astounding precision, and stood exactly where he
> was supposed to on every fast break. Yet Havlicek was a far less 4
> satisfying player to watch than Philadelphia's Julius Erving,
> who continually surprises spectators and defenses with moves
> no one (including himself) could possibly anticipate. One 5
> might argue that Erving is consistently amazing, but the rea-
> son he so grasps a crowd's imagination, the reason thousands
> of people roar whenever Erving simply lays a hand on the ball,
> is that the man seems the epitome of the unpredictable, the
> thoroughly free and spontaneous soul.
>
> – ROGER ROSENBLATT, "Consistency as a Minor Virtue"

This paragraph illustrates one of two common ways of organizing a comparison and contrast: the two subjects are discussed separately, first one and then the other. The next paragraph illustrates the other common organization: the two subjects are discussed side by side, feature for feature.

> This emphasis on the unfairness of language to women is 1
> misplaced. We should be erasing all bias from language, and 2
> that means bias against men as well. If a female pilot should 3
> not be stigmatized as an "aviatrix," then a male pilot should
> not be stigmatized as a "fly-boy." If it is unfair to label women 4
> as "witches," then it is equally unfair to label men as "cads." If a 5
> woman should not be called a "dog," then a man should not be
> called a "nerd" or a "wimp." If it demeans the homeless woman 6
> to call her a "baglady," then it also demeans the homeless man
> to call him a "bum."
>
> – A STUDENT

The most effective comparisons show similarities between subjects usually perceived as different, such as the words used for women and men in the preceding paragraph. Contrasts, however, are most effective when they show differences between subjects usually perceived as similar, such as the two basketball players in Rosenblatt's paragraph.

Is it comparable to something that is in a different class but more familiar?

Whereas we draw comparisons and contrasts between elements in the same general class (basketball players, words), we link elements in different classes with a special kind of comparison called **analogy.** Most often in analogy we illuminate or explain an unfamiliar, complex, abstract class of things with a familiar and concrete class of things. In the following paragraph the author develops an analogy between writing style (abstract) and a distance runner (concrete).

> The good style is the lean style. Like a good distance run- 1,2
> ner, it hasn't an ounce of excess fat anywhere on it. And like the 3
> good distance runner, it moves without excess motion. Its arms 4
> don't flail out in all directions; they swing easily at the sides in a
> beautiful economy of effort. A good style has the same grace 5
> and beauty in its motion as a good athlete because there's noth-
> ing wasted. Everything is there for a purpose. 6
>
> — LAURENCE PERRINE, "Fifteen Ways to Write Five Hundred Words"

In the next paragraph the author draws an analogy between the weather and human combat.

> In an age all too familiar with war the yearly cycle of the 1
> weather is well imagined in terms of combat. It is a war in 2
> which a stronghold or citadel sometimes beats off assault after
> assault. More often the battle-line shifts quickly back and forth 3
> across thousands of miles—a war of sudden raids and swift
> counterattacks, of stern pitched battles, of deep forays and
> confused struggles high in the air. In the Northern Hemisphere 4
> the opponents are the Arctic and the Tropics, North against
> South. Uncertain ally to the South—now bringing, now with- 5
> drawing aid—the sun shifts among the signs of the zodiac. And 6
> the chief battle-line is known as the Polar Front.
>
> — GEORGE R. STEWART, *Storm*

What are its causes or its effects?

When you analyze why something happened or what is likely to happen, then you are determining causes and effects. **Cause-and-effect analysis** is especially useful in writing about social, economic, or political events or problems, as the next paragraphs illustrate. In the first, the author looks at the causes of Japanese collectivism, which he elsewhere contrasts with American individualism.

> The *shinkansen* or "bullet train" speeds across the rural 1
> areas of Japan giving a quick view of cluster after cluster of
> farmhouses surrounded by rice paddies. This particular pattern 2
> did not develop purely by chance, but as a consequence of the
> technology peculiar to the growing of rice, the staple of the
> Japanese diet. The growing of rice requires the construction 3
> and maintenance of an irrigation system, something that takes
> many hands to build. More importantly, the planting and the 4
> harvesting of rice can only be done efficiently with the coopera-
> tion of twenty or more people. The "bottom line" is that a 5
> single family working alone cannot produce enough rice to sur-
> vive, but a dozen families working together can produce a sur-
> plus. Thus the Japanese have had to develop the capacity to 6
> work together in harmony, no matter what the forces of dis-
> agreement or social disintegration, in order to survive.
>
> — WILLIAM OUCHI, *Theory Z: How American Business Can Meet the Japanese Challenge*

In sentences 1, 2, and 6 Ouchi specifies an effect: the Japanese live close together and work in harmony. The middle sentences explain the conditions that caused this effect: the Japanese depend heavily on rice, and growing rice demands collective effort.

Cause-and-effect paragraphs tend to focus either on causes, as Ouchi's does, or on effects, as the next paragraph does.

> Although the net effects of boredom in history are proba- 1
> bly malign, good has also been served by this state of mind.
> Many an evil dogma, doctrine, or other intellectual continuity 2
> has in the end been undone, not by assault, but by boredom on
> the part of its victims. A secret weapon against the Soviet 3
> Union and the Marx-Leninist creed is the stupefying boredom
> that this creed induces in the minds of the second and third
> generations brought up under it. In all probability boredom 4
> was what ended the dreadful witchcraft craze in the seven-
> teenth century. Certainly the leading lights of the day, most of 5
> whom believed as ardently as any peasant in the witches and in
> the necessity of their destruction, did little if anything to stop
> the practice. It was not, in short, legal, moral, or religious 6
> argument but sheer boredom with the spectacle that won out.
> "When you've seen one burn, you've seen them all" might well 7
> have become in time the saving thought. It is boredom above 8
> anything else that brings literary continuities to a welcome
> end. The public is grateful for Milton, but deplores the Mil- 9
> tonians. So it is with the ascendancy of political parties: the 10
> more powerful a party-in-office becomes, the greater the bore-
> dom it produces in the public mind.
>
> – ROBERT NISBET, "Boredom"

In his first two sentences Nisbet specifies a cause—boredom—and states that it can have desirable effects. The remaining sentences provide examples to support the generalization of sentence 2.

How does it work?

When you explain how something works, you explain the steps in a **process.** Paragraphs developed by analyzing a process are usually organized chronologically or spatially, as the steps in the process occur. Some process analyses tell the reader how to do something. For example:

> Car owners waste money when they pay a mechanic to 1
> change the engine oil. The job is not difficult, even for someone 2
> who knows little about cars. All one needs is a wrench to 3
> remove the drain plug, a large, flat pan to collect the draining
> oil, plastic bottles to dispose of the used oil, and fresh oil. First, 4
> warm up the car's engine so that the oil will flow more easily.
> When the engine is warm, shut it off and remove its oil-filler 5
> cap (the owner's manual shows where this cap is). Then locate 6
> the drain plug under the engine (again consulting the owner's

manual for its location) and place the flat pan under the plug.
Remove the plug with the wrench, letting the oil flow into the 7
pan. When the oil stops flowing, replace the plug and, at the 8
engine's filler hole, add the amount and kind of fresh oil specified by the owner's manual. Pour the used oil into the plastic 9
bottles and take it to a waste-oil collector, which any garage
mechanic can recommend.

– A STUDENT

Other process analyses explain how a process is done or how it works in nature. The following paragraph, for example, explains how an island of mangrove trees begins "from scratch."

Nor can a tree live without soil. A hurricane-born man- 1,2
grove island may bring its own soil to the sea. But other man- 3
grove trees make their own soil—and their own islands—from
scratch. These are the ones which interest me. The seeds germi- 4,5
nate in the fruit on the tree. The germinated embryo can drop 6
anywhere—say, onto a dab of floating muck. The heavy root 7
end sinks; a leafy plumule unfurls. The tiny seedling, afloat, is 8
on its way. Soon aerial roots shooting out in all directions trap 9
debris. The sapling's networks twine, the interstices narrow, 10
and water calms in the lee. Bacteria thrive on organic broth; 11
amphipods swarm. These creatures grow and die at the trees' 12
wet feet. The soil thickens, accumulating rainwater, leaf rot, 13
seashells, and guano; the island spreads.

– ANNIE DILLARD, "Sojourner"

Combining patterns of development

Whatever pattern you choose as the basis for developing a paragraph, other patterns may also prove helpful. We have seen combined patterns often throughout this section: Tuchman uses contrast to define *quality* (p. 85); Rosenblatt uses examples to contrast consistency and inconsistency (p. 87); Perrine uses analogy to define a good writing style (p. 88).

As we will see in 3e, the paragraphs within an essay inevitably will be developed with a variety of patterns, even when one controlling pattern develops and structures the entire essay.

3 Checking length

The average paragraph contains between 100 and 150 words, or between four and eight sentences. These numbers are averages, of course. The actual length of a paragraph depends on its topic, the role it plays in developing the thesis of the essay, and its position in the essay. Nevertheless, very short paragraphs are often inadequately developed; they may leave readers with a sense of incompleteness. And very long paragraphs often contain irrelevant details or develop two or more topics; readers may have difficulty sorting out or remembering ideas.

When you are revising your essay, reread the paragraphs that seem very long or very short, checking them especially for unity and adequate development. If the paragraph wanders, cut everything from it that does not support your main idea (such as sentences that you might begin with *By the way*). If it is underdeveloped, supply the specific details, examples, or reasons needed, or try one of the methods of development we have discussed here.

EXERCISE 12

The following paragraphs are not well developed. Analyze them, looking especially for general statements that lack support or leave questions in your mind. Then rewrite one into a well-developed paragraph, supplying your own concrete details or examples.

1. One big difference between successful and unsuccessful 1
teachers is the quality of communication. A successful teacher 2
is sensitive to students' needs and excited by the course subject. In contrast, an unsuccessful teacher seems uninterested 3
in students and bored by the subject.

2. Gestures are one of our most important means of commu- 1
nication. We use them instead of speech. We use them to sup- 2,3
plement the words we speak. And we use them to communicate 4
some feelings or meanings that words cannot adequately
express.

3. Children who have been disciplined too much are often 1
easy to spot. Their behavior toward adults may reflect the harsh 2
treatment they have received from adults. And their behavior 3
toward other children may be uncontrolled.

EXERCISE 13

Identify the pattern or patterns of development in each of the following paragraphs. Where does the author supply specific information to achieve development?

1. A century of association has inevitably acculturated both 1
Hispanos and Anglo-Americans to some extent, but there still
persist a number of culture traits that neither group has relin-
quished altogether. Nothing is more disquieting to an Anglo- 2
American who believes that time is money than the time perspective of Hispanos. They usually refer to this attitude as the 3
"*mañana* [tomorrow] psychology." Actually, it is more of a 4
"today psychology," because Hispanos cultivate the present to
the exclusion of the future; because the latter has not arrived

yet, it is not a reality. They are reluctant to relinquish the 5
present, so they hold onto it until it becomes the past. To an 6
Hispano, nine is nine until it is ten, so when he arrives at nine-
thirty, he jubilantly exclaims: "*¡Justo!*" [right on time]. This 7
may be why the clock is slowed down to a walk in Spanish
while in English it runs. In the United States, our future- 8
oriented civilization plans our lives so far in advance that the
present loses its meaning. January magazine issues are out in 9
December; 1973 cars have been out since October; cemetery
plots and even funeral arrangements are bought on the install-
ment plan. To a person engrossed in living today the very idea 10
of planning his funeral sounds like the tolling of the bells.

– ARTHUR L. CAMPA, "Anglo vs. Chicano: Why?"

2. They [newly arrived ethnic groups] are changing the 1
American landscape, proliferating into unexpected niches,
each following an irresistible ethnic call. Korean greengrocers 2
have sprouted all over New York City, nestling bins of knobby
and unexplained roots next to red Delicious apples, while
Greeks have all but taken over the coffee shops, conquering the
quick lunch business under their ubiquitous symbol: the drink
container with a picture of a discus thrower. In New Orleans, 3
Vietnamese immigrants have converted their housing-project
lawns into vegetable gardens, irrigating them with the same
long-handled canvas buckets they once dipped into the
Mekong. The amplified call of the muezzin echoes through the 4
south end of Dearborn, Michigan, five times a day, calling the
faithful to prayer at their mosque. Just as Americans have 5
finally digested the basics of soccer, cricket has emerged as the
avant-garde immigrant sport, played by exuberant Samoans
on the fields of Carson, California, and earnest Jamaicans and
Trinidadians in Brooklyn's Prospect Park.

– "The New Immigrants," *Newsweek*

3. A dying person may pass through five separate attitude 1
stages, according to the psychiatrist Elisabeth Kübler-Ross. In 2
the first stage, denial, the patient ignores symptoms of illness
and refuses to accept diagnosis and sometimes even treatment.
Then, in a stage of anger, the patient feels outraged at the in- 3
justice of dying. A stage of bargaining may follow, when the 4
patient tries to make an exchange with the hospital staff or his
or her family or God for a little more time. Then the patient 5
may enter a period of depression that comes when he or she realizes that everything is soon to be finished, that life is almost
over. And finally, the dying person may feel acceptance of 6
death, a quiet resignation to the power of death.

– A STUDENT

4. In American society there exist people classified by en- 1
cyclopedia salesmen as "mooches." Mooches can be generally 2
defined as people who like to buy the product; they see the encyclopedia salesman as the bearer of a rare and desirable gift.

Mooches are people whose incomes and occupational levels ex- 3
ceed their educational attainments; persons whose income is in
the middle-middle range but whose education doesn't exceed
high school, or may not even attain that level. Without educa- 4
tion, mooches cannot have professional status, although they
might make as much money as a professional; consequently,
mooches try to assume professionalism by accruing what they
think are indications of professional status. A conspicuously 5
displayed set of encyclopedias tells the mooch's friends that he
can afford to consume conspicuously, that he values a highly
normative product over creature comforts, and that he provides for the long-range benefit of his protectorate. The mooch 6
associates all these characteristics with professional persons.
For him, then, encyclopedias function as easily interpreted pro- 7
fessional-status indicators.

– LYNN M. BULLER, "The Encyclopedia Game"

EXERCISE 14

Write a well-developed paragraph on one of the following ideas or an idea of your own. Or take an underdeveloped paragraph from something you have written and revise it. Be sure your paragraph is unified and coherent as well as adequately developed with specific information.

1. how billboards blight (or decorate) the landscape
2. why you like (or don't like) poetry
3. a place where you feel comfortable (or uncomfortable)
4. an unusual person you know
5. an instance of unusual kindness or cruelty

EXERCISE 15

Identify an appropriate pattern or patterns for developing a paragraph on each of the following topics. (Choose from illustration or support, definition, division or classification, comparison and contrast, analogy, cause-and-effect analysis, and process analysis.)

1. the influences of a person's biorhythms or astrological sign on his or her behavior
2. a typical situation comedy on television
3. tuning an engine
4. rock music and country music
5. why read newspapers
6. what loyalty is
7. the picture of aliens shown by recent science-fiction movies
8. dancing as pure motion, like a kite in the wind
9. one consequence of living alone (or in a group)
10. the kinds of fans at a baseball game (or a game in some other sport)

EXERCISE 16

Write a paragraph about a topic from Exercise 15, using the development pattern you chose in that exercise. Or if you prefer, choose a topic of your own and develop it with one of the patterns discussed in the text. Be sure the paragraph is also unified and coherent.

EXERCISE 17

Write seven unified, coherent, and well-developed paragraphs, each one developed with a different pattern. Draw on the topics provided here or in Exercise 15. Or choose your own topics.

1. *Illustration or support*
   why go to college
   why study
   having a headache
   the best sports events
   usefulness (or uselessness) of a self-help book
2. *Definition*
   hunger
   fear
   humor
   authority
   an adult
3. *Division and classification*
   the segments of a television news show
   factions in a campus controversy
   styles of playing poker
   parts of a barn
   kinds of sports fans
4. *Comparison and contrast*
   driving a friend's car and driving your own car
   AM and FM radio announcers
   high school and college football
   movies on TV and in a theater
5. *Analogy*
   paying taxes and giving blood
   the U.S. Constitution and a building's foundation
   graduating from high school and being released from prison
6. *Cause-and-effect analysis*
   connection between tension and anger
   causes of failing a course
   connection between credit cards and debt
   causes of a serious accident
7. *Process analysis*
   preparing for a job interview
   drying fresh herbs
   making a cabinet
   protecting your home from burglars
   making a jump shot

3d
Writing special kinds of paragraphs

Several kinds of paragraphs do not always follow our guidelines for unity, coherence, development, and length because they serve special functions. These are the essay introduction, the essay conclusion, the transitional or emphatic paragraph, and the paragraph of spoken dialogue.

1
Opening an essay

Most essays open with a paragraph that draws readers from their world into the writer's world. An opening paragraph should focus readers' attention on the topic and arouse their curiosity about what the writer has to say. It should be concise. It should specify what the writer will discuss and what his or her attitude is. It should be sincere. And it should be interesting without misrepresenting the content of the essay that follows.

The safest kind of introduction opens with a statement of the essay's general subject, clarifies or limits the subject in one or more sentences, and then, in the thesis sentence, asserts the point of the essay (see 1g). This is the pattern in the following paragraph, which introduces an essay on the history of American bathing habits.

> We Americans are a clean people. We bathe or shower 1,2
> regularly and spend billions of dollars each year on soaps and
> deodorants to wash away or disguise our dirt and odor. Yet 3
> cleanliness is a relatively recent habit with us. From the time of 4
> the Puritans until the turn of the twentieth century, bathing in
> the United States was rare and sometimes even illegal.
>
> – A STUDENT

The writer's first two sentences offer her subject and elaborate on it, leading us to focus on something within our experience. Then, by introducing a less familiar but related idea, the third sentence forms a bridge from common experience to the writer's specific purpose. The fourth sentence, the thesis, states that purpose explicitly. Here is another example of this form of introductory paragraph.

> Can your home or office computer make you sterile? Can it 1,2
> strike you blind or dumb? The answer is: Probably not. Nev- 3,4
> ertheless, reports of side effects relating to computer use
> should be examined, especially in the area of birth defects,
> eye complaints, and postural difficulties. Although little con- 5
> clusive evidence exists to establish a causal link between
> computer use and problems of this sort, the circumstantial
> evidence can be disturbing.
>
> – THOMAS HARTMANN, "How Dangerous Is Your Computer?"

Several other types of introduction can be equally effective, though they are sometimes harder to invent and control. One kind begins with a quotation that leads into the thesis sentence.

> "It is difficult to speak adequately or justly of London," 1
> wrote Henry James in 1881. "It is not a pleasant place; it is not 2
> agreeable, or cheerful, or easy, or exempt from reproach. It is 3
> only magnificent." Were he alive today, James, a connoisseur 4
> of cities, might easily say the same thing about New York or
> Paris or Tokyo, for the great city is one of the paradoxes of
> history. In countless different ways, it has almost always been 5
> an unpleasant, disagreeable, cheerless, uneasy and reproach-
> ful place; in the end, it can only be described as magnificent.
> – *Time*

Another kind of introduction opens by relating an incident that sets the stage for the thesis.

> Canada is pink. I knew that from the map I owned when I 1,2
> was six. On it, New York was green and brown, which was true 3
> as far as I could see, so there was no reason to distrust the map
> maker's portrayal of Canada. When my parents took me across 4
> the border and we entered the immigration booth, I looked ex-
> citedly for the pink earth. Slowly it dawned on me: This for- 5
> eign, "different" place was not so different. I discovered that 6
> the world in my head and the world at my feet were not the
> same. – Robert Ornstein, *Human Nature*

An introduction may also start with an opinion, preferably a startling one that will grab the reader's attention.

> Caesar was right. Thin people need watching. I've been 1,2,3
> watching them for most of my adult life, and I don't like what I
> see. When these narrow fellows spring at me, I quiver to my 4
> toes. Thin people come in all personalities, most of them men- 5
> acing. You've got your "together" thin person, your mechanical 6
> thin person, your condescending thin person, your tsk-tsk thin
> person. All of them are dangerous. 7
> – Suzanne Britt Jordan, "That Lean and Hungry Look"

A historical comparison or contrast may make an effective introduction when some background to the essay topic is useful.

> Throughout the first half of this century, the American 1
> Medical Association, the largest and most powerful medical or-
> ganization in the world, battled relentlessly to rid the country
> of quack potions and cure-alls; and it is the AMA that is gener-
> ally credited with being the single most powerful force behind
> the enactment of the early pure food and drug laws. Today, 2
> however, medicine's guardian seems to have done a complete
> about-face and become one of the pharmaceutical industry's
> staunchest allies—often at the public's peril and expense.
> – Mac Jeffery, "Does Rx Spell Rip-off?"

An effective introductory paragraph need not be long, as the following opener shows.

> I've often wondered what goes into a hot dog. Now I know 1,2
> and I wish I didn't. — WILLIAM ZINSSER, *The Lunacy Boom*

When writing and revising an introductory paragraph, avoid the following approaches that are likely to bore readers or make them question your sincerity or control.

1. Don't start with "The purpose of this essay is . . . ," "In this essay I will . . . ," or any similar flat announcement of your intention or topic.
2. Don't refer to the title of the essay in the first sentence—for example, "This is my favorite activity" or "This is an interesting problem."
3. Don't start with "According to Webster . . ." or a similar phrase leading to a dictionary definition. A definition can be an effective springboard to an essay, but this kind of lead-in has become dull with overuse.
4. Don't apologize for your opinion or for inadequate knowledge of your subject with "I'm not sure if I'm right, but I think . . . ," "I don't know much about this, but . . . ," or similar lines.

2 Closing an essay

Most essays end with a closing statement or conclusion, a signal to readers that the writer has not simply stopped writing but has actually finished. The conclusion completes the essay, bringing it to a climax while assuring readers that they have understood the writer's intention. Usually set off in its own paragraph, the conclusion may consist of a single sentence or a group of sentences. It may summarize the evidence presented in the essay, restate the thesis with a fresh emphasis, suggest a course of action, ask a question, strike a note of hope or despair, introduce a startling fact, quote an authority, or tell an anecdote.

The following paragraph concludes the essay on bathing habits whose introduction we saw on page 95. The writer summarizes her essay and then echoes her introduction by proposing a link between the habits of history and the habits of today.

> Thus changed attitudes and advances in plumbing finally 1
> freed us to bathe whenever we want. Perhaps partly to make up 2
> for our ancestors' bad habits, we have transformed that freedom into a national obsession. — A STUDENT

Ada Louise Huxtable uses a different technique to conclude her highly critical essay on the Rayburn House Office Building in Washington, D.C. Instead of summarizing, she takes a final shot at the building.

An old architectural saying has it that there's no point in 1
crying over spilled marble. Several million pounds of it have 2
been poured onto Capitol Hill in this latest Congressional building venture, and there is nothing quite as invulnerable as a
really monumental mistake. The Rayburn Building's ultimate 3
claim to fame may well be that it is the biggest star-spangled architectural blunder of our time.

– Ada Louise Huxtable, "The Rayburn Building"

Concluding an essay on environmental protection, Peter F. Drucker states his opinion on the issues he has discussed and, in his last sentence, calls for action.

Until we get the answers, I think we had better keep on 1
building power plants and growing food with the help of fertil-
izers and such insect-controlling chemicals as we now have.
The risks are well known, thanks to the environmentalists. If 2,3
they had not created a widespread public awareness of the eco-
logical crisis, we wouldn't stand a chance. But such awareness 4
by itself is not enough. Flaming manifestos and prophecies of 5
doom are no longer much help, and a search for scapegoats can
only make matters worse. The time for sensations and mani- 6
festos is about over. Now we need rigorous analysis, united ef- 7
fort and very hard work.

– Peter F. Drucker, "How Best to Protect the Environment"

These three paragraphs illustrate how to avoid several pitfalls of conclusions.

1. Don't simply repeat your introduction—statement of subject, thesis sentence, and all. Presumably the paragraphs in the body of your essay have contributed something to the opening statements, and it's that something you want to capture in your conclusion.
2. Don't start off in a new direction, with a subject different from or broader than the one your essay has been about. For instance, Huxtable might have violated this principle (and weakened her conclusion) had she veered off to the quality of Washington architecture in general.
3. Don't conclude more than you reasonably can from the evidence you have presented. If your essay is about your frustrating experience trying to clear a parking ticket, you cannot reasonably conclude that *all* local police forces are too tied up in red tape to be of service to the people.
4. Don't apologize for your essay or otherwise cast doubt on it. Don't say, "Even though I'm no expert," or "This may not be convincing, but I believe it's true," or anything similar. Rather, to win your readers' confidence, display confidence.

3 Using short transitional or emphatic paragraphs

A short paragraph of a sentence or two may direct readers' attention to a turn in an essay or emphasize an idea that has been or will be developed. A transitional paragraph, because it is longer than a word or phrase and set off by itself, moves a discussion from one point to another more slowly or more completely than does a single transitional expression (3b-6) or even a transitional sentence attached to a paragraph (3a-2).

> These, then, are the causes of the current expansion in hospital facilities. But how does this expansion affect the medical costs of the government, private insurers, and individuals?
>
> The conclusion would seem to be obvious. To be sure, however, we must look at a few other facts.
>
> So the debates were noisy and emotion-packed. But what did they accomplish? Historians agree on at least three direct results.

Use transitional paragraphs rarely—only to shift readers' attention when your essay makes a significant turn. A paragraph like the one below betrays a writer who is stalling; it does not redirect the flow but stops it altogether.

> Now that we have examined these facts, we can look at some others that are equally important to an examination of this issue.

A short, emphatic paragraph gives unusual stress to an important idea, in effect asking the reader to pause and consider before moving on.

> In short, all those who might have taken responsibility ducked it, and catastrophe was inevitable.

4 Writing dialogue

When recording a conversation between two or more people, start a new paragraph for each person's speech. The paragraphing establishes for the reader the point at which one speaker stops talking and another begins.

> "Are you saying that you are going to go now and not come back?"
>
> "Oh, God. Yes, I'm saying that."
>
> Jessica began to scream.
>
> – IRIS MURDOCH, *The Nice and the Good*

Though dialogue appears most often in fictional writing (the source of the example above), it may occasionally freshen or enliven narrative or expository essays. (For guidance in using quotation marks and other punctuation in dialogue, see 24c.)

EXERCISE 18

Analyze the introductory and concluding paragraphs in the first and final drafts of the student essay in Chapter 2, pages 40–42 and 51–53. What is wrong with the first-draft paragraphs? Why are the final-draft paragraphs better? Could they be improved still further?

3e
Linking paragraphs in the essay

Paragraphs do not stand alone but contribute to a larger piece of writing. Each unified, coherent, and well-developed paragraph adds something to a unified, coherent, and well-developed essay (see Chapter 1).

In a two- to four-page essay each paragraph between the introductory and concluding ones will develop and support a part of the essay's central idea, its thesis. The devices for achieving paragraph coherence—organization, transitional expressions, and the like—will also link paragraphs in a coherent whole. And the patterns for developing paragraphs—definition, division, and so on—will suit the needs of individual paragraphs in the larger context of the essay. Thus the paragraph patterns may or may not reflect the overall pattern of the whole essay, and they may vary from one paragraph to the next.

The following essay illustrates the way effective paragraphs can contribute to an effective essay.

> A hyperactive committee member can contribute to efficiency. A hyperactive salesperson can contribute to profits. But when a child is hyperactive, people—even parents—may wish he had never been born. To understand hyperactivity in children, we can visualize a collage of the thoughts, feelings, and attitudes of those who must cope with the problem: doctors, parents, even the child himself. 1
>
> The first part of our collage is the doctors. In their terminology the word *hyperactivity* is short for H-LD, a hyperkinesis-learning disability syndrome. They apply the word to children who are "abnormally or excessively busy." But doctors do not fully understand the problem and thus differ over how to treat it. For example, some recommend special diet; others, behavior-modifying drugs; and still others, who do not consider hyperactivity to be a medical problem, a psychiatrist for the en- 2

tire family. The result is a merry-go-round of tests, confusion, and frustration for the parents and the child.

3 As the parent of a hyperactive child, I can say what the word *hyperactivity* means to the parents who form the second part of the collage. It means a worry that is deep and enduring. It means a despair that is a companion on dark and sleepless nights. It means a fear that is heart twisting and constant, for the hyperactive child is most destructive toward himself. It means a mixture of frustration, guilt, and anger. And finally, since there are times when that anger goes out of control and the child is in danger from the parent, it means self-loathing.

4 The weight of hyperactivity, however, rests not on the doctors or the parents but on the child. For him is reserved the final and darkest part of our collage because he is most affected. From early childhood he is dragged from doctor to doctor, is attached to strange and frightening machines, and is tested or discussed by physicians, parents, neighbors, teachers, peers. His playmates dislike him because of his temper and his unwillingness to follow rules; and even his pets fear and mistrust him, for he treats them erratically, often hurting them without meaning to. As time goes on, he sees his parents more and more often in tears and anger, and he knows that he is the cause. Though he is highly intelligent, he does poorly when he enters school because of his short attention span. He is fond of sports and games but never joins the other children on the playground because he has an uncontrollable temper and poor coordination. By the time he reaches age seven or eight, he is obsessed with one thought: "Mama," my son asks me repeatedly, "why do I have to be hyperactive?"

5 At last the collage is completed, and it is dark and somber. *Hyperactivity,* as applied to children, is a word with uncertain, unattractive, and bitter associations. But the picture does have a bright spot, for inside every hyperactive child is a loving, trustful, calm person waiting to be recognized. — A STUDENT

The overall pattern of development in this essay is division or analysis: the writer examines the human elements involved in hyperactivity. In addition, the writer creates an analogy, comparing those involved to the pieces in a collage. The essay's basic organization is climactic or general to specific, proceeding from the general notions of the seemingly distant doctors to the more specific and poignant experiences of a single child. Within this general scheme, however, each paragraph follows the course required by its topic and the writer's purpose. For instance, having shown in paragraph 2 that doctors do not agree on what hyperactivity is, the writer develops paragraph 3 by defining the word as she sees it. And she develops paragraph 4 by analyzing the effects of hyperactivity on the one most harmed by it, the child himself. This paragraph also follows a chronological organization in tracing the child's experiences.

Despite the varied organizational schemes and patterns of development in her paragraphs, the writer guides us smoothly and steadily from one paragraph to the next. She recalls the promise of the thesis sentence, a three-part collage, in the topic sentence of every succeeding paragraph. She links paragraphs with transitional words to remind us where we are in the essay: *first* (paragraph 2), *second* (3), *however* and *final* (4), *at last* (5). The entire first sentence of paragraph 4 is a transition from the earlier paragraphs. The writer repeats the key words of the essay, *collage* and *hyperactive* or *hyperactivity,* in the first or second sentence of every paragraph. At the end of paragraph 2 on doctors she looks ahead to the next two paragraphs on parents and the child. In the conclusion she echoes the distinction first made in the introduction between the useful hyperactivity of adults and the destructive hyperactivity of children. The combination of these techniques produces a tightly woven analysis that readers can easily understand.

EXERCISE 19

Analyze the ways in which paragraphs combine in the three student essays in Chapter 2, pages 51, 54, and 56. With what techniques, if any, does each writer link paragraphs to the thesis sentence and to each other? Where, if at all, does the writer seem to stray from the thesis or fail to show how paragraphs relate to it? How would you revise the essays to solve any problems they exhibit?

EXERCISE 20

Analyze the following paragraphs for unity, coherence, and development. For each paragraph, identify the central idea (even if it is not stated explicitly), the organizational scheme, the devices used to achieve coherence, and the pattern or patterns of development.

1. If it is the very essence of life you seek, visit Japan. The 1,2
wine is served piping hot in the tiniest thimble bowls, and it is
better than gulping beakers of cold sauterne. Some of the finest 3
Japanese sculptures are no larger than a walnut and can be
worn as the tassel to one's belt. In the Japanese dance, one 4
tightly controlled gesture stands for an entire routine, and in
the theater the merest corner of a handkerchief pressed to the
eye symbolizes unbearable grief.

– James Michener, "Why I Like Japan"

2. To feel used is to have a sense of something of ours being 1
taken away. But it is more than that. To feel used is to feel that 2,3
our services have been separated from ourselves. It is a sense of 4

the violation of our central worth, as though we ourselves are important to the other individual only because we are a vehicle
for supplying the stuff that he desires. It may be most graphic 5
and evident when what he desires is a material or physical thing—our money or our possessions—but we are equally offended when what is taken or used is our intelligence, our creativity, our companionship, or our love.

– WILLARD GAYLIN, "Feeling Used"

3. Shortly after World War II, decades of investigation into 1
the internal workings of the solids yielded a new piece of electronic hardware called a transistor (for its actual invention,
three scientists at Bell Laboratories won the Nobel Prize). Tran- 2
sistors, a family of devices, alter and control the flow of electricity in circuits; one standard rough analogy compares their action to that of faucets controlling the flow of water in pipes.
Other devices then in existence could do the same work, but 3
transistors are superior. They are solid. They have no cogs and 4,5
wheels, no separate pieces to be soldered together; it is as if
they are stones performing useful work. They are durable, take 6
almost no time to start working, and don't consume much
power. Moreover, as physicists and engineers discovered, they 7
could be made very small, indeed microscopic, and they could be produced cheaply in large quantities.

– TRACY KIDDER, *The Soul of a New Machine*

4. As more products and services become available to con- 1
sumers, their quality and effectiveness seem to decline. To 2
avoid unnecessary frustration and expense, consumers should
be well informed before buying products and services. First, 3
they should shop around, hunting among dealers for the best
quality, price, and service available. Second, they should con- 4
sult guides, such as *Consumer Reports,* that are published by
nonprofit product-testing services. Finally, they should refuse 5
to accept oral promises, demand to see relevant contracts and warranties, and decline to sign or accept any document they do not fully understand. – A STUDENT

5. We may extend this conclusion for hearts to a general 1
statement about the pace of life in small versus large animals.
Small animals tick through life far more rapidly than large ani- 2
mals—their hearts work more quickly, they breathe more frequently, their pulse beats much faster. Most importantly, meta- 3
bolic rate, the so-called fire of life, increases only three-fourths
as fast as body weight in mammals. To keep themselves going, 4
large mammals do not need to generate as much heat per unit
of body weight as small animals. Tiny shrews move frenetically, 5
eating nearly all their waking lives to keep their metabolic fire burning at the maximal rate among mammals; blue whales glide majestically, their hearts beating the slowest rhythm among active, warm-blooded creatures.

– STEPHEN JAY GOULD, *The Panda's Thumb*

6. In the nineteenth century one of American agriculture's 1
bumper crops was extraordinary technologists. The revolution 2
that made possible America's great cities was begun on farms.
Elias Howe, Eli Whitney, Thomas Alva Edison, Alexander 3
Graham Bell, George Westinghouse, Orville and Wilbur
Wright, the American geniuses of invention, manufacturing,
transportation, were farm boys all. And not altogether sur- 4
prisingly. Whatever its limitations as a teacher of culture or 5
sociability, the farm was a superior forcing house of technical
ingenuity and mechanical skill. Henry Ford, another American 6
farm boy, born on a farm outside Dearborn, Michigan, in 1863,
was the most famous mechanic the world has known. Strictly 7
speaking, Henry Ford invented nothing, but he tinkered with
nearly everything. Years later, recalling his early days on his 8
father's farm, Ford said: "My toys were all tools—they still
are."

– JOSEPH EPSTEIN, *Ambition*

4
Convincing Your Readers

In a way, all writing is meant to persuade: your primary purpose may be to explain something to readers or entertain them or express your feelings to them, but you also want them to accept your perspective. Convincing your readers is especially important in argumentation, for the goal is always to win readers' complete or partial agreement with your ideas. The special strategies of argumentation and some of its pitfalls are the focus of this chapter.

4a
Constructing an argument

Almost everything said in Chapters 1 and 2 on developing and revising an essay applies to the argumentative essay. But in constructing an argument, you need to pay special attention to the combination of the general and the specific, the balance of reason and emotion, and the likely attitudes and objections of your readers.

1
Combining the general and the specific

In conversation with friends who trust your judgment, you might gain their acceptance of a general statement, such as *That movie is boring,* without supplying any supporting evidence. In a narrative essay you might gain readers' acceptance of the significance of an event by providing plentiful concrete details, without stating the significance outright. In argumentation, however, you cannot expect readers to accept your opinions unless you provide the evidence to back them up. Nor can you expect readers to see the significance of your evidence unless you make general statements to organize information and direct attention to the most important points. In short, an argumentative essay must present both general statements, or **assertions,** and the evidence to support those assertions. Neither is effective without the other. (We will discuss the kinds of assertions and evidence in detail in 4b and 4c.)

Most effective arguments state the central assertion of the essay in a thesis sentence (see 1g) so that readers understand the writer's purpose and know what they are supposed to agree with. The body of the essay then demonstrates the validity of the thesis by breaking it down into other assertions. Each assertion may be the topic sentence of a paragraph (see 3a), with the remainder of the paragraph consisting of the evidence for the assertion—the facts, examples, and so on that make the assertion true.

2
Appealing to reason and emotion

In Chapter 1 we discussed the way details and tone can gain readers' interest and support in any kind of writing (see 1f). Argumentation presents a special challenge to the writer because the aim is to *change* the way readers think and feel about a subject.

In forming convictions about arguable issues—capital punishment, gun control, defense spending, the best location for a new town dump—we generally interpret the factual evidence through the filter of our values, beliefs, tastes, desires, and feelings. Mayor Jones may object to placing the new town dump in a particular wooded area because the facts suggest that the site is not large enough and that prevailing winds will blow odors back through the town. But Mayor Jones may also have fond memories of playing in the wooded area as a child, feelings that color his interpretation of the facts and strengthen his conviction that the dump should be placed elsewhere. His conviction is partly rational, because it is based on evidence, and partly emotional, because it is also based on feelings.

Most effective arguments combine **rational appeals** to readers' capacities for reasoning logically from evidence to a conclusion with **emotional appeals** to readers' beliefs and feelings. The following three passages, all expressing the same view on the same subject, illustrate how either a primarily rational or a primarily emotional appeal may be weaker than an approach that uses both.

Rational appeal

In its report the commission expresses too strong a concern for the public image of nuclear power. The commission regards the Howe nuclear plant as now "safe," with the risk of meltdown "an acceptably low 3 in 10,000 per year." Yet it maintains that the general public may not accept the experts' judgments of safety. To "strengthen public faith in nuclear power," the commission calls for additional safety precautions to achieve a "slight" further reduction in risk, to 1 in 10,000. The report does not address the high cost of these additional precautions or how the financially unstable plant is to pay for them.

Emotional appeal

The commission is clearly more intent on improving the public image of nuclear power than on making this much-needed source of energy available for public use. In recommending additional and totally unnecessary safety precautions at the Howe nuclear plant, the commission shows blind unconcern that a minor improvement in public image might be gained at the expense of the plant's being shut down for good.

Rational and emotional appeals

In its report the commission reveals itself to be more intent on improving the public image of nuclear power than on making this much-needed source of energy available for public use. The commission regards the Howe nuclear plant as now "safe," with the risk of meltdown "an acceptably low 3 in 10,000 per year." Yet it worries that the general public may not accept the experts' judgments of safety. To "strengthen public faith in nuclear power," the commission calls for additional safety precautions to achieve a "slight" further reduction in risk, to 1 in 10,000. The report does not acknowledge that these unnecessary precautions would be prohibitively expensive, especially for a plant that is already financially unstable. Apparently the commission is unconcerned that a minor improvement in public image might be gained at the expense of the plant's being shut down for good.

Notice the differences in these three passages. The first one emphasizes the evidence that supports the claim of the first sentence: the current risk, the desired risk, and the omissions from the report. The writer appeals to readers' reason by making an arguable assertion and then providing the facts to back it up; but he fails to address readers' feelings on the issue. The second passage emphasizes the writer's interpretation of the facts: merely to improve the public image of nuclear power, the commission requires unnecessary safety precautions that will jeopardize the availability of nuclear power. The writer appeals to readers' emotions—to their desire for more plentiful energy supplies, their receptiveness to nuclear energy, and even their distaste for public relations ploys—but he fails to provide supporting evidence. The third passage combines both kinds of appeal. Thus it gives readers both a rational and an emotional basis for accepting the writer's view that the commission is willing to sacrifice nuclear power out of concern for public relations alone, not for actual safety.

As the third passage illustrates, an appeal to emotion is a way to establish common ground with readers, to show them that you and they share beliefs and desires that can and should influence the interpretation of the facts. For such an appeal to be successful, however, it must be appropriate for the audience and the argument. An appeal is inappropriate for the audience when it misjudges readers' actual feelings. The writer of the third passage assumed that his readers would want nuclear power to supplement other energy supplies. If, instead, his readers feared nuclear power, finding even a minimal risk too high, then he would fail to convince them that the commission's concerns were misplaced.

An appeal is inappropriate for the argument when it raises emotional issues that are irrelevant to the assertion and the evidence. The writer of the third passage might have tried to bolster his case by stating that one member of the commission was once an executive with the regional natural-gas company. But the statement would be inappropriate on at least two counts: it would attack a member of the commission rather than the report of the entire commission; and the attack would be based on the unproved assumption that the member's past employment invalidated his current judgment. Inappropriate emotional appeals are discussed in greater detail in 4b-3.

3 Anticipating objections

By definition, an arguable issue has more than one side: however well supported your case is and however strongly you believe in it, others can marshall their own evidence to support a different view or even several different views. Some of these others might be in your audience. But even readers who have no preconceptions about your subject will suspect that your side is not the only one. If you ignore your opposition or pretend that there is none, readers will find your argument less sound than you say it is and may even consider it dishonest.

In constructing an effective argument, you need to acknowledge opposing views forthrightly, grant any validity they may have, and demonstrate why, despite their validity, the opposing views are less compelling than your own. The student who wrote the following paragraph took this approach.

> The athletic director argues against reducing university support for athletic programs on the grounds that they make money that goes toward academic programs. It is true that here at Springfield the surpluses from the football and basketball programs have gone into the general university fund, and some of that money may have made it into academic departments (the fund's accounting methods make it impossible to say for sure). But the athletic director misses the point. The problem is not that the

athletic programs cost more than they take in but that they demand too much to begin with. For an institution that hopes to become first-rate academically, too many facilities, too much money, too much energy, and too many people are tied up in the effort to produce championship sports teams.

The writer first acknowledges the possible truth of the athletic director's defense of his programs. Then he shows that the director fails to address the central issue, the cost of the programs.

4
Examining a sample argument

The following student essay illustrates the principles discussed so far in this chapter. As you read the essay, look especially for general assertions and supporting evidence and for rational and emotional appeals.

A Year for America

Among the many problems in the United States today, two are particularly troubling. One is the tendency of people to see those with different moral, religious, social, economic, and political views as "the enemy"—absolutely wrong, even somewhat less than human. The other is the tendency to see government not as the resolver of such differences—the place where compromises are hammered out—but as the chief problem itself, either too intrusive or not responsive enough, depending on one's point of view. The loss of respect and sympathy for the "other guy" and the loss of faith in government are depriving us of a sense of community—of belonging to, sharing in, and contributing to our great nation. One step toward restoring this sense of community could be achieved by requiring a year of government service from each citizen.

Introduction: identification of problems

Thesis: a proposal for a solution

A program of mandatory government service might be set up as follows. On finishing high school or reaching age eighteen, all young adults would be expected to spend one year working for the government (local, state, or federal). The service might be with the military, but it could also be with social-service agencies, hospitals, schools, national parks, data-processing centers, road-maintenance departments, or any other government group. Program participants would be paid the minimum wage and would work full-time throughout the year. There would be no deferments or exemptions from service, except possibly

Explanation of the proposal

log
4a

for severe economic hardship or mental or physical disability.

Support for the proposal: first advantage

This program could substantially reduce the present polarization in our society. In keeping with the United States' melting-pot heritage, the program would be a great equalizer: male and female, rich and poor, black and white, urban and rural—all would serve together. Participants would be exposed to others whose backgrounds, experiences, and values were previously unknown or misunderstood. They would become more aware and tolerant of diversity, more sympathetic toward "different" people, more respectful of different views.

Support for the proposal: second advantage

In addition to learning about each other, the participants would also learn firsthand about their government. They would see for themselves the huge variety of services that we as a nation expect our government to deliver, from keeping roads free of litter to providing health care to the elderly. In many jobs they would come face to face with the people who benefit from government services—the middle-class home owner, the school-age child, the disabled veteran, the impoverished mother of five. In short, participants would see the many ways in which government serves them and others. And that experience could turn their fear and mistrust of government into appreciation and respect.

Support for the proposal: third advantage

The participants would gain personally as well. The year of service would expose them to a broad range of career options, both in and out of government. They would gain some of the experience and information necessary to discover their talents and interests and to make realistic and appropriate decisions about further education and eventual career paths. They would also acquire marketable skills that would give them a boost in whatever work they chose. On a less practical level, participants would begin to see themselves as belonging and contributing to the larger community of which they were a part. Such awareness would reduce the sense of isolation and frustration that often disturbs young adults.

Responses to probable objections

The proposal for a mandatory year of government service is bound to meet at least two objections. First, the young adults who would be affected might not want to give up a year of their lives. However, since everyone else in their age group would be making the same sacrifice, they would not be at any disadvantage. And with public education, the young adults could be made to take pride in their sacrifice and service. The second major objection would be cost: with budget deficits already endangering our economy, how can we possibly afford such a program? Granted, the program would cost money in its initial stages, as the administrative machinery was set in motion and the low-level government employees being displaced by participants were retrained for jobs outside government. Eventually, however, the program could save money because the participants, receiving minimum wage, would cost less to do the same work now performed by relatively highly paid government employees. Furthermore, the government labor force would grow temporarily when participants began serving but before existing employees had been retrained and moved out. With a larger labor force, government could do many things it now cannot do because of inadequate labor, such as clean up city streets, give individual attention to disadvantaged children, and help the elderly with daily living. The money would be well spent.

Conclusion: summary of how the plan would solve the problems identified in the introduction

Despite its personal and monetary costs, a program of mandatory government service would be enormously beneficial to the United States. Its citizens, instead of viewing each other as enemies, would learn to work together creatively, despite their differences, to resolve problems. And instead of seeing their government as something *other* than themselves, a faceless giant either too intrusive or too unresponsive to be worth its cost, they would see it as something *of, by,* and *for* themselves and all other Americans.

EXERCISE 1

Analyze the construction and effectiveness of the preceding essay by answering the following questions.

1. Where does the writer make general assertions related to her thesis sentence, and where does she provide examples or other evidence to support the assertions?
2. Where does the writer appeal primarily to reason, and where does she appeal primarily to emotion? What specific beliefs, values, and desires of readers does the writer appeal to?
3. What objections to her plan does the writer anticipate? What reasons does she give for dispensing with them?
4. How effective do you find this argument? To what extent do you agree with the writer about the problems identified in her

introduction? To what extent does she convince you that her plan is desirable and workable and would solve those problems? Does she fail to anticipate any major objections to her plan?

EXERCISE 2

Identify each sentence below either as a general assertion in need of support or as possible evidence for some general assertion.

1. Drugs and alcohol are particularly dangerous for someone with a family history of substance abuse.
2. The IRS estimates that perhaps half of all taxpayers do not report all their income.
3. The city jail is so overcrowded that cells intended for two inmates now house three or four.
4. The university's policy of open admissions has benefited economically and educationally disadvantaged students.
5. Whatever her motivation, Ms. Horne has succeeded in refocusing employees' attention and energy on achieving corporate goals.

EXERCISE 3

Identify each sentence below either as a rational appeal or as an emotional appeal.

1. Only complacency, indifference, or selfishness could allow us to ignore these people's hunger.
2. As the data collected by the researchers demonstrate, a mandatory sentence for illegal possession of handguns can lead to reduction in handgun purchases.
3. The broadcasters themselves accept that children's television is a fair target for regulation.
4. Anyone who cherishes life in all its diversity could not help being appalled by the mistreatment of laboratory animals.
5. Many experts in constitutional law have warned that the rule violates the right to free speech.

4b
Making assertions

As we saw in the preceding section, assertions are fundamental to an argument. Though an assertion must generally be well supported for readers to accept it fully, the likelihood of acceptance can be improved or diminished by the nature of the assertion, its degree of concreteness or abstraction, and the extent to which it confronts an issue straightforwardly.

1 Distinguishing among fact, opinion, belief, and prejudice

Most statements we make in speaking and writing are assertions of fact, opinion, belief, or prejudice. In argumentation the usefulness and acceptability of an assertion depends partly on which of these categories it falls into.

A **fact** is verifiable—that is, one can determine whether it is true. It may involve numbers or dates: *The football field is 100 yards long. World War II ended in 1945.* Or the numbers may be implied: *The earth is closer to the sun than Saturn is. The cost of medical care is rising.* Or the fact may involve no numbers at all: *The city council adjourned without taking a vote. The President vetoed the bill.* The truth of the fact is beyond argument if one can assume that measuring devices or records or memories are correct. Facts provide crucial support for the assertions of an argument. But because they are inarguable, they do not make worthwhile assertions by themselves.

An **opinion** is a judgment *based* on facts, an honest attempt to draw a reasonable conclusion from evidence. For example, you know that millions of people go without proper medical care because they can't afford it, and so you form the judgment that the country should institute national health insurance even though it would cost billions of dollars. This opinion expresses a viewpoint. It is arguable because the same facts might lead another reasonable person to a different opinion (for instance, that the country simply can't afford national healtn insurance costing billions of dollars, even if people must go without proper medical care). And the opinion is potentially changeable: with more evidence you might conclude that the problem of inadequate medical care might be solved by other means less costly than national health insurance.

The thesis of an argument is always an opinion, and other, more specific opinions generally form the backbone of the argument supporting the thesis. By themselves, however, opinions have little power to convince. You must always let your readers know what your evidence is and how it led you to arrive at each of your opinions (see 4c on evidence).

An opinion is not the same as a **belief,** a conviction based on cultural or personal faith, morality, or values. Statements such as *Capital punishment is legalized murder* and *The primary goal of government should be to provide equality of opportunity for all* are often called opinions because they express viewpoints. Unlike opinions, however, such beliefs are not based on facts and other evidence. They cannot be disproved by facts or even contested on the basis of facts. Thus they cannot serve as the thesis of an argument because they, like facts, are inarguable. However, as we saw in the earlier discussion of emotional appeals, statements of belief can be useful in argumentation if you can assume that readers share the feelings they express. For instance, you might support an argument that the country should institute national health insurance not only with facts demonstrating the need but also with the assertion that a nation cannot be strong while millions of its citizens suffer needlessly from poor health. If your readers agree with this assertion, it may make them more open to other parts of your argument.

One kind of assertion that has no place in argumentation is **prejudice,** an opinion based on insufficient or unexamined evidence: *Women are bad drivers. Fat people are jolly. Teenagers are irresponsible.* Unlike a belief, a prejudice is testable: it can be contested and disproved on the basis of facts. Very often, however, we form prejudices or accept them from others—parents, friends, the communications media—without questioning their meaning or testing their truth. At best, they are thoughtless oversimplifications: *some* women are bad drivers, but so are *some* men. At worst, assertions of prejudice reflect a narrow-minded view of the world. And writers who are perceived as thoughtless and narrow-minded are not likely to win the confidence and agreement of readers.

2 Defining terms

In any argument, but especially in arguments about abstract ideas, clear and consistent definition of terms is essential. In the following assertion the writer is not clear about what she means by *justice.*

> Over the past few decades justice has deteriorated so badly that it almost does not exist anymore.

We can't tell what the writer is asserting because we don't know what *justice,* the crucial term of the sentence, means to her. The word is abstract; it does not refer to anything specific or concrete and in fact has varied meanings. (The seven definitions in *The American Heritage Dictionary* include "the principle of moral rightness," "conformity to truth," and "the administration and procedure of law.") When the writer specifies her meaning, her assertion is much clearer.

> If by *justice* we mean treating people fairly, punishing those who commit crimes, and protecting the victims of those crimes, then justice has deteriorated badly over the past few decades.

Of course, we need to see how this writer supports her assertion before we can accept it, but at least we now understand her definition of *justice.*

Highly abstract words such as *justice, equality, success,* and *maturity* may require an entire paragraph of definition if they are central to an argument. See Chapter 3, pages 84–85, for more on definition, including a paragraph defining the abstract word *quality.*

3
Facing the question

Almost every argument centers on an issue or question: Should the risk of meltdown in a nuclear plant be lowered further? Could a program of mandatory government service help solve the nation's problems? Should the country adopt national health insurance? An effective argument faces the central issue squarely. It answers the question by stating relevant opinions about it and supporting those opinions with facts. But facing the question can be difficult. It is often easier to oversimplify complex issues or to argue superficially about them than it is to grapple with all the evidence. Sometimes, too, a favored opinion dies hard, though the evidence fails to support it. These circumstances can cause two common faults: begging the question (also called circular reasoning) and ignoring the question through inappropriate emotional appeals.

Begging the question

You **beg the question** when you treat an opinion that is open to question as if it were already proved or disproved. (In essence, you are begging your readers to accept your ideas from the start.) For example, if you assert that the expenses of the school library should be reduced by cutting subscriptions to useless periodicals, then you beg the question. Without supplying the necessary evidence, you assert that at least some of the library's periodicals are useless, and then you use that unproved assertion to support your proposal.

The following sentence begs the question in a slightly different way.

> Teenagers should be prevented from having abortions, for they would not become pregnant in the first place if they weren't allowed to terminate their "mistakes."

The writer assumes—and asks us to agree—that the option of having an abortion leads teenagers to unwanted pregnancies; therefore, removing the option of abortion will remove the problem of pregnancy. But how can we agree when we still have no proof for the fundamental assertion? The writer has merely substituted one debatable assumption for another.

Ignoring the question

As we have seen, appeals to readers' emotions are common in effective arguments. But such appeals must be relevant to the argument and must supplement rather than substitute for facts, examples, and other evidence. If they do not, they obscure or **ignore the question.**

Writers sometimes ignore the question with **appeals to readers' fear, pity, or sense of decency.**

> By electing Susan Clark to the city council, you will prevent the city's economic collapse. [Trades on people's fears. Can Clark single-handedly prevent economic collapse?]
>
> She should not have to pay taxes because she is an aged widow with no friends or relatives. [Touches on people's pity. Should age and loneliness, rather than income, determine a person's tax obligation?]
>
> Dr. Bowen is an honest man because he attends church regularly and participates in community activities. [Appeals to people's sense of decent behavior. Are churchgoers and community participants necessarily honest?]

Sometimes writers ignore the question by appealing to readers' sense of what other people believe or do. One approach is **snob appeal,** inviting readers to accept an assertion in order to be identified with others they admire.

> As any literate person knows, James Joyce is the best twentieth-century novelist. [But what qualities of Joyce's writing make him a superior novelist?]
>
> Paul Newman's support for the governor proves that the governor is doing a good job. [What has the governor actually accomplished?]

A similar tactic invites readers to accept an assertion because everybody else does. This is the **bandwagon approach.**

> As everyone knows, marijuana use leads to heroin addiction. [What is the evidence?]
>
> No one in this town would consider voting for him. [What is the basis for judging him?]

Yet another diversion involves **flattery** of readers, in a way inviting them to join in a conspiracy.

> Since you are thoughtful and perceptive, you know how corrupt the insurance commissioners are. [What is the evidence of corruption?]
>
> We all understand campus problems well enough to see the disadvantages of such a backward policy. [What are the disadvantages of the policy?]

All these assertions resort to appeals having nothing to do with the issues they raise. A careless reader might be momentarily swayed by such appeals, but a careful reader is more likely to be put off by the writer's evasion.

One final kind of inappropriate emotional appeal addresses *not* the pros and cons of the issue itself but the real or imagined negative qualities of the people who hold the opposing view. This kind of argument is called ***ad hominem,*** Latin for "to the man."

> We need not listen to her arguments against national health insurance because she is wealthy enough to afford private insurance. [Her wealth does not necessarily discredit her views on health insurance.]
>
> One of the scientists has been treated for emotional problems, so his pessimism about nuclear war merits no attention. [Do the scientist's previous emotional problems invalidate his current views?]

You'll recognize most of these tricks for ignoring the question from advertising and political campaigns. Are your children's teeth cavity-free? Is your kitchen floor as spotless as your neighbor's? Are you the only person who does not eat a certain brand of cereal? Is that candidate as incompetent as his opponent says? You should be wary of these pitches in what you read and hear, and you should avoid them in your own writing. Readers are unlikely to be persuaded by them, and their presence in your argument could cause readers to mistrust everything else you say.

EXERCISE 4

Identify the assertions of fact, opinion, belief, and prejudice in the following paragraph.

Cigarette advertising has already been banned from television and radio, and the time has come to ban it from newspapers, magazines, and billboards as well. Numerous research studies have linked smoking with disease and death, and it is simply wrong to advertise a health- and life-threatening activity. Nonetheless, the major tobacco companies continue to spend more than $1.5 billion a year advertising their products. In sharp contrast, the federal government and health organizations such as the American Lung Association spend perhaps $20 *million* a year on programs and advertisements designed to educate the public about the dangers of smoking. Clearly, these efforts cannot begin to counterbalance the onslaught of the tobacco companies' messages that smoking gives a person romance, beauty, fun, and happiness. And even if there were more balance in what the public is told about smoking, people who smoke are so mindless that they would ignore the warnings and heed only the sales pitches.

EXERCISE 5

The following paragraph fails to define important words clearly enough for us to pin down the meaning intended. Identify the undefined terms and revise the paragraph as you see fit to eliminate the problems.

The best solution to current problems is one we don't hear of very often: self-sufficiency. If we were more self-sufficient, we would not have to rely so much on scarce resources to satisfy basic needs. Sure, some of us play at gardening, sewing, and other skills, but very few of us try to free ourselves of the grocery store's vegetables or the department store's clothes. If we were more self-sufficient, we would be more secure because independence ultimately creates a bond between individuals.

EXERCISE 6

Identify the question implied by each of the following assertions and evaluate the writer's effectiveness in facing the question.

1. Many women are bored with their lives because their jobs are tedious.
2. Steven McRae spends too much time making himself look good to be an effective spokesman for the student body.
3. Teenagers are too young to be allowed to use birth control.
4. Giving nuclear capability to emerging nations is dangerous because they will probably use it to wage war.
5. Our souls are immortal because they are not made of matter and thus are indestructible.

EXERCISE 7

Leaf through a magazine or watch television for half an hour, looking for advertisements that attempt to sell a product not on the basis of its worth but by snob appeal, flattery, or other inappropriate appeals to emotions. Be prepared to discuss the advertisers' techniques.

4c
Supporting assertions with evidence

As we saw in Chapters 1 and 3, evidence is crucial in any kind of writing to make readers understand your meaning and to engage their interest. In argumentation, however, it must do even more: it must demonstrate the validity of your opinions so that readers will accept them. A clear and reasonable assertion will open readers' minds to your evidence. But if the evidence is then inadequate or questionable, readers will reject the assertion, and your cause will be at least partly and perhaps wholly lost. In the following sections we will look at the kinds of evidence used in argumentation and then at the criteria for evaluating such evidence.

1 Distinguishing among the kinds of evidence

Writers draw on several kinds of evidence to support their assertions. One discussed already is **facts,** statements whose truth is subject to verification (see p. 113).

> Poland is slightly smaller than New Mexico.
> Insanity is grounds for divorce in a majority of the states.

Facts employing numbers are **statistics.**

> Of those polled, 62 percent stated a preference for a flat tax.
>
> In 1981 there were 2,049,000 men and women in the U.S. armed forces.
>
> The average American household consists of 2.73 persons.

Another kind of evidence is **examples,** specific instances of the point being made. The following passage uses an example as partial support for the assertion in the first sentence.

> Besides broadening students' knowledge, required courses can also introduce students to possible careers that they otherwise would have known nothing about. Somewhat reluctantly, I enrolled in a psychology course to satisfy the social science requirement. But what I learned in the course has led me to consider becoming a clinical psychologist instead of an engineer.

A third kind of evidence is **expert opinions,** the judgments formed by authorities on the basis of their own examination of the facts. In the following passage the writer cites the opinion of an expert to support the assertion in the first sentence.

> Despite the fact that affirmative action places some individuals at a disadvantage, it remains necessary to right the wrongs inflicted historically on whole groups of people. Howard Glickstein, a past director of the U.S. Commission on Civil Rights, maintains that "it simply is not possible to achieve equality and fairness" unless the previous grounds for discrimination (such as sex, race, and national origin) are now used as the grounds for admission to schools and jobs.

As this passage illustrates, a citation of expert opinion is generally accompanied by a reference to the expert's credentials. (See also 35g-2, pp. 506–08.)

2
Providing reliable evidence

To support your assertions and convince readers, your evidence must be reliable—that is, it must be accurate, relevant, representative, and adequate.

Accurate evidence is drawn from trustworthy sources, quoted exactly, and presented with the original meaning unchanged. In researching an essay in favor of gun control, for instance, you might consult statistics provided by the anticontrol National Rifle Association as well as those provided by procontrol groups to ensure that your evidence is sound from both perspectives. In quoting a source, be careful to preserve the author's true meaning, not just a few words that happen to support your argument. For instance, you would distort the writer's meaning if you quoted only the first sentence in the following passage as evidence of the positive effects of television.

> Television can be an effective force for education and understanding, for appreciation of people and their troubles and accomplishments. But it assumes that role so rarely that we have only fleeting glimpses of the possibilities. We know better the dull-witted, narrow-minded fare that monopolizes the set from one year to the next.

Not just opinions but also facts and examples may be misinterpreted or distorted. Suppose you were arguing to extend a three-year-old law allowing the police to stop vehicles randomly as a means of apprehending drunk drivers. If you cited statistics showing that the number of drunk-driving accidents dropped in the first two years of the law, but you failed to note that the number rose back to the previous level in the third year, then your evidence would be distorted and thus inaccurate. If your readers know or sense that you are distorting any evidence in this way, they may question all your other evidence whether it is accurate or not.

Relevant evidence comes from sources with authority on your topic and relates directly to your point. Unless your uncle is a recognized expert on the Central Intelligence Agency, or unless you can establish his authority, his opinion of whether the CIA meddles illegally in other countries' affairs is not relevant to your paper on the subject. If your aunt is a member of the town council, however, her views may very well be relevant evidence in an essay on how a new shopping mall will hurt the town merchants.

Representative evidence reflects the full range of the sample from which it is said to be drawn. For instance, in an essay arguing that dormitories should stay open during school holidays, you might want to cite the opinions of the school's 5000 students. But you would mislead readers if, on the basis of a poll among your roommates and dormitory neighbors, you reported as evidence that "the majority of students favor leaving the dormitories open." A few dormitory residents could not be said to represent the entire student body, particularly the nonresident students. To be representative, your poll would have to take in many more students in proportions that reflect the numbers of resident and nonresident students on campus.

Adequate evidence is plentiful and specific enough to support your assertions. To convince readers of your opinion, you must tell them what information you base it on. If you are writing an essay about animal abuse, you cannot hope to win over your readers solely with statements like *Too many animals are deliberately injured or killed by humans every year.* You need to supply facts instead of the vague *too many.* How many animals are injured? How many die? You need to specify the conditions under which animals are injured or killed. And you need to demonstrate that the actions are deliberate, perhaps with examples of animal abuse. Adequate, well-selected evidence is crucial to an effective argument.

EXERCISE 8

Supply at least two pieces of evidence—examples from your own experience or facts or expert opinions from other sources—to support each of the following general assertions.

1. A college education is too costly (or is a good value for the money).
2. _______ is a television program (or movie or book) that should be a model for all entertainment aimed at adolescents (or children or parents).
3. _______ is a good teacher (or employer, doctor, or politician).
4. Americans are energy spendthrifts.
5. Driver education makes one a better driver.

EXERCISE 9

Locate the statements of evidence in the following passages, and evaluate each one against the four criteria of accuracy, relevancy, representativeness, and adequacy.

1. Our rivers and streams are becoming choked by pollution. For example, swimming is now prohibited along stretches of the Mississippi River. My minister says there are portions of the river where fish can't survive. Are we a nation that does not care enough about its resources to conserve them?

2. Crime is out of control in this city. Three months ago my parents' house was burglarized. The thieves stole their food processor and their vibrating bed as well as their television and

stereo. Then a month ago my roommate had her pocket picked on the subway. And last week I saw a confused old man trying to describe to the police how muggers had stolen his wallet and his groceries as he walked home from the corner market.

4d
Reasoning effectively

In constructing an argument you can benefit from understanding the two ways in which people tend to reason: inductively and deductively. These methods figure not only in our formal writing but also in our everyday activities, as the following example illustrates.

You want to buy a reliable used car. In thinking of what kind of car to buy, you follow specific steps of reasoning. (1) You consider your friends' experiences with used cars: one has had to spend a lot of money to repair her used Volkswagen; another has complained that his used Ford handles badly; and three others have raved about their used Toyotas. (2) You recall an article in *Consumer Reports* rating Toyota high among used cars. (3) You conclude that Toyota is the most reliable used car. So far your reasoning is **inductive.** You have made a series of specific observations about the reliability of different used cars. And you have induced, or inferred, from those observations the generalization that Toyota is the most reliable used car. The **generalization** is based on the assumption that what is applicable in one set of circumstances (your friends' experiences, *Consumer Reports'* tests) is or will be applicable as well in a similar set of circumstances (your own experiences). Having thus reasoned inductively, you then proceed with **deductive** reasoning, from the generalization to specific circumstances. You start with a generalization you believe to be true (Toyota is the most reliable used car) and apply it to particular circumstances (you want to buy a reliable used car) in order to reach a conclusion (you want to buy a used Toyota).

As this example demonstrates, induction and deduction are fundamental to our thought. They derive from our experience of the world as coherent (with one event related to another) and not fragmented. We activate these reasoning processes effortlessly and habitually in the daily business of living. We employ them more consciously in organizing essays and paragraphs from specific to general (inductively) and from general to specific (deductively). (See 1h-1 and 3b-1.) And we can use them methodically in reasoning about complex ideas—for instance, when evaluating the thinking of others or when trying to convince others to accept our views.

1
Reasoning inductively

Induction is the dominant method of reasoning in two situations: generalizing from observations and attributing a cause to a set of observed circumstances.

We saw an example of generalizing from observations in the identification of a reliable used car. In another case you might observe that few students attend showings of the school film society, which presents only serious foreign films; that your college friends seem to prefer science-fiction, adventure, and horror movies; and that a magazine article says these three kinds of entertainment films are most popular with people under twenty-five. From these observations you infer that most college students prefer entertainment movies. The more students you talk to and the more you read about the subject, the more certain you can be that your generalization is true.

Attributing a cause to circumstances is essentially the same process as generalizing from observations. You and your friends, and presumably most students, prefer science-fiction, adventure, and horror movies, which entertain you and offer relief from studying. The president of the student film society, however, programs only weighty foreign films, and few students attend. From these observations you conclude that the president is unaware of students' needs and preferences. True, with a little imagination you could also conclude that the president knows students' preferences but is determined to ignore them because she is a snob. You could even conclude that she is ignoring them because she wants to learn foreign languages. But the conclusion you do draw is the simplest because it adheres to the available evidence: the president does not demonstrate awareness of students' preferences. And the simplest explanation of cause, based exclusively on what you know, is usually more reasonable than the more elaborate one for which you must invent supporting facts.

The more evidence you have, the more likely it is that your generalizations are valid, but you can't know for certain that they are correct. You can only ensure that your generalizations are reasonable—sound conclusions based on sound evidence—and that your readers perceive them as such.

2
Reasoning deductively

You reason deductively when you use some assertions to arrive at others. As when you determined that you should buy a used Toyota, in deduction you apply generalizations or conclusions that are accepted as true to slightly different but similar situations or issues. For example, if you know that all male members of your psychology class are on the football squad, and Albert is in the psychology class, then you conclude that Albert must be on the football squad. This group of three statements constitutes a **syllogism,** two premises stating facts or judgments that together lead to a conclusion.

1. *Premise:* English papers containing sentence fragments receive poor grades.
2. *Premise:* Your English paper contains sentence fragments.
3. *Conclusion:* Your English paper will receive a poor grade.

The first premise states a generalization arrived at by induction. The second premise states a specific case of the generalization. The conclusion derives logically from the two premises.

Though it is rarely laid out as neatly as in the preceding syllogism, deductive reasoning underlies many arguments you read or write. The force of such arguments depends on the reliability of the premises and the care with which you apply them in drawing new conclusions. Two common sources of difficulty with deduction are unstated premises and overstated premises.

Many deductive arguments depend on **unstated premises**—that is, the basic premise is not explicitly stated but is understood. For instance:

> Ms. Chang has worked with drug addicts for fifteen years, so she should know a great deal about their problems. [Unstated premise: Anyone who has worked fifteen years with drug addicts knows about their problems.]
>
> As student government president, Jordan will have to deal with conflicting demands from all sides. [Unstated premise: A student government president must deal with conflicting demands.]

Problems arise when the unstated premise is wrong or unfounded, as in the following sentences.

> Since Jane Lightbow is a senator, she must receive money illegally from lobbyists. [Unstated premise: All senators receive money illegally from lobbyists.]
>
> Now that Sally Matlock's mother is in jail, Sally will become a behavior problem. [Unstated premise: All children whose mothers are jailed become behavior problems.]

As these sentences show, when reasoning deductively you must carefully examine your basic premises, especially when they are implied.

The second common problem in deduction, **overstated premises,** results from the difficulty in making a generalization that will apply to all instances, since ordinarily we must base any generalization on only a few instances. When such generalizations are premises in a deductive argument, they must contain or imply limiting words such as *some, many,* and *often* rather than absolute words such as *all, no one, never,* or *always.* Compare the difference in reasonableness in the following pairs of sentences.

Overstated	Parents are *always* too busy to help their children solve problems.
Modified	Parents are *often* too busy to help their children solve problems.
Overstated	Movie theater ushers *are* a thing of the past; one *never* sees them in cinema complexes.
Modified	Movie theater ushers *may be* a thing of the past; one *rarely* sees them in cinema complexes.

Even when a premise sounds reasonable, it still must be supportable. For instance, modifying the unstated assumption about Senator Lightbow might result in this sentence:

> Since Jane Lightbow is a senator, she might receive money illegally from lobbyists. [Unstated premise: *Some* senators receive money illegally from lobbyists.]

But it does not necessarily follow that Senator Lightbow is one of the "some." The sentence, though logical, is not truly reasonable unless evidence demonstrates that Senator Lightbow should be linked with illegal activities.

3 Avoiding faulty reasoning

Some kinds of faulty inductive and deductive reasoning—errors called **fallacies**—are common in all sorts of writing. Like begging or ignoring the question (pp. 115–17), these fallacies weaken an argument.

Hasty generalization

A **hasty generalization** is based on too little evidence or on evidence that is unrepresentative (see 4c). For example:

> Because it trains one for work, business is the only major worth pursuing. [Other majors train one for work, and other students may have different goals.]
>
> When attendance is down and the team is losing, the basketball coach should be fired. [The sentence does not allow for other influences on the team's performance.]

A variation of the hasty generalization involves the use of absolute words such as *all, always, never,* and *no one* when your evidence cannot support such terms and what you really mean is *some, sometimes, rarely,* and *few* (see the overstated and modified assertions on the previous page).

Another common hasty generalization is the **stereotype,** a conventional and oversimplified characterization of a group of people. The ideas that the French are good lovers, the British reserved, and the Italians emotional are stereotypes. When you apply such a characterization to an individual Frenchman or Briton or Italian, you extend a prejudice, an opinion based on insufficient or unexamined evidence (see p. 114). Here are several other stereotypes: *People who live in cities are unfriendly. Californians are fad-crazy. Women are emotional. Men are less expressive than women.*

Oversimplification

A frequent fallacy in writing is **oversimplification** of the relation between causes and their effects. The fallacy (sometimes called the **reductive fallacy**) often involves linking two events as if one caused the other directly, whereas the causes may be more complex or the relation may not exist at all. For example:

> Poverty causes crime. [If so, then why do people who are not poor commit crimes? And why aren't all poor people criminals?]
>
> The better a school's athletic facilities are, the worse its academic programs are. [The sentence assumes a direct cause-and-effect link between athletics and scholarship.]

Post hoc *fallacy*

Related to oversimplification of cause and effect is the fallacy of assuming that because *A* preceded *B*, then *A* must have caused *B*. This fallacy is called in Latin *post hoc, ergo propter hoc,* meaning "after this, therefore because of this," or the ***post hoc* fallacy** for short. Here are a definition and an example from the humorist Max Shulman, followed by two more examples of the fallacy at work.

> "Next comes Post Hoc. Listen to this: Let's not take Bill on our picnic. Every time we take him out with us, it rains."
>
> "I know somebody just like that," she exclaimed. "A girl back home—Eula Becker, her name is. It never fails. Every single time we take her on a picnic—"
>
> "Polly," I said sharply, "it's a fallacy. Eula Becker doesn't *cause* the rain. She has no connection with the rain. You are guilty of Post Hoc if you blame Eula Becker."
>
> – MAX SHULMAN, "Love Is a Fallacy"

> In the two months since he took office, Mayor Holcomb has allowed crime in the city to increase 2 percent. [The increase in crime is no doubt attributable to conditions existing before Holcomb took office.]
>
> The town council erred in permitting the adult bookstore to open, for shortly afterward two women were assaulted. [It cannot be assumed without evidence that the women's assailants visited or were influenced by the bookstore.]

Either/or fallacy

In the **either/or fallacy** (also called **false dilemma**) you assume that a complicated question has only two answers, one good and one bad, both bad, or both good.

> City policemen are either brutal or corrupt.
>
> Either we institute national health insurance or thousands of people will become sick or die.

Like the illustrations of the previous fallacies, these sentences oversimplify complex issues and relations to make the writer's perspective seem convincing. But no careful reader would be fooled. Many city policemen are neither brutal nor corrupt. And allowing people to sicken or die is not necessarily the only alternative to national health insurance.

Non sequitur

A **non sequitur** occurs when no logical relation exists between two or more connected ideas. In Latin *non sequitur* means "it does not follow." In the following sentences the second thought does not follow from the first.

> If high school English were easier, fewer students would have trouble with the college English requirement. [Presumably, if high school English were easier, students would have *more* trouble.]
>
> Kathleen Newsome has my vote for mayor because she has the best-run campaign organization. [Shouldn't one's vote be based on the candidate's qualities, not the campaign organization's?]

False analogy

An **analogy** is a comparison between two essentially unlike things for the purpose of definition or illustration. (See also 1d-5 and 3c-2.) In arguing by analogy, you draw a likeness between things on the basis of a single shared feature and then extend the likeness to other features. But analogy can only illustrate a point, never prove

log
4d

it. It can trick you into assuming that because things are similar in one respect, they *must* be alike in other respects. Here is an example of this fallacy, which is called **false analogy.**

> The nonhuman primates such as chimpanzees and gorillas care for their young, clean and groom each other, and defend themselves and sometimes the group from attack. Why, then, must the human primates go so much further—Medicare, child care, welfare, Social Security, and so on—to protect the weak? [Taken to its logical extreme, this analogy would lead us to ask why we speak to each other when gorillas do not.]

EXERCISE 10

Study the following facts and then evaluate each of the numbered conclusions below them. Which of the generalizations are reasonable given the evidence, and which are not? Why?

Between the 1970 and 1980 national censuses, the population of the United States increased 11.4 percent, to 226,504,825.
The percentage increase from 1950 to 1960 was 18.5 percent; from 1960 to 1970, 13.3 percent.
The population of the South and West regions increased 21.4 percent between 1970 and 1980.
The population of the Northeast and North Central regions increased just over 2 percent between 1970 and 1980.
More than 52 percent of the nation's people now live in the South and the West.

1. During the 1970s the population of the United States continued to grow at the same rapid pace set during the 1950s.
2. During the 1970s increasing numbers of Americans made their homes in the Sun Belt states of the South and West regions rather than in the states of the Northeast and North Central regions.
3. Many Americans prefer the pleasant climate of the South and West regions to the harsh climate of the Northeast and North Central regions.

EXERCISE 11

Supply the element needed to complete each of the following syllogisms.

1. a. Cigarette smokers risk lung cancer.
   b.
   c. Therefore, cigarette smokers risk death.
2. a. The challenging courses are the good ones.
   b. Biology is a challenging course.
   c.

3. a.
   b. That child receives no individual attention.
   c. Therefore, that child learns slowly.
4. a. Discus throwers develop large pectoral muscles.
   b.
   c. Therefore, Warren has large pectoral muscles.
5. a.
   b. Enrollments will certainly decline.
   c. Therefore, the school will close.

EXERCISE 12

At least one of the following assertions is reasonable, but the others either generalize from inadequate evidence or depend on faulty or overstated assumptions. Circle the number preceding any sentence that seems reasonable, and explain what is wrong with each of the others.

1. Since capital punishment prevents murder, it should be the mandatory sentence for all murderers.
2. The mayor opposed pollution controls when he was president of a manufacturing company, so he may not support new controls or vigorously enforce existing ones.
3. The only way to be successful in the United States is to make money, because Americans measure success by income.
4. Keeping the library open until midnight has caused the increase in late-night crime on the campus.
5. Government demands so much honesty that we should not leave it to lawyers and professional politicians.

EXERCISE 13

The following sentences exemplify the fallacies discussed in the text. Determine what is wrong with each sentence, and then revise it to make it more logical.

1. A successful marriage demands a maturity that no one under twenty-five possesses.
2. Students' persistent complaints about the grading system prove that it is unfair.
3. The United States got involved in World War II because the Japanese bombed Pearl Harbor.
4. People watch television because they are too lazy to talk or read or because they want mindless escape from their lives.
5. Working people are slaves to their corporate masters: they have no freedom to do what they want, and they can be traded to other companies.
6. The stories about welfare chiselers show that the welfare system supports only shirkers and cheats.

7. Mountain climbing is more dangerous than people think: my cousin has fainted three times since he climbed Pikes Peak.
8. Racial tension is bound to occur when people with different backgrounds are forced to live side by side.
9. If the United States does not supply military assistance to Central and South American countries, we will eventually be subjected to Communism.
10. She admits to being an atheist, so how can she be a good philosophy teacher?

EXERCISE 14

Evaluate the following brief essay for its effectiveness in persuading you (or any reader) to accept the writer's argument. Look especially for sound or unsound inductive or deductive reasoning. Do you see examples of any of the faults discussed in this chapter, such as begged or ignored questions, overstated assumptions, or fallacies?

Let's Hear It for Asphalt

The truly disadvantaged students on this campus are the commuters. We pay our money and work hard for our degrees, yet we can never find places to park our cars. Commuters are regularly treated as second-class citizens compared to resident students. But nowhere is the discrepancy more noticeable than in the parking situation.

The fact is that there aren't enough parking spaces for half the cars on campus. Students are lucky to make their classes at all after driving around for hours looking for a place to stop their car. If parking were easier, students would get better grades, and the school administrators would probably have the higher enrollments they're so desperate for.

The most maddening thing is that we have to pay good money for parking tickets on top of tuition and everything else. The money probably goes toward a new faculty office building or dormitory or one of the other building projects that eat up what little parking space there is. Meanwhile, we commuters are pushed farther and farther away from the center of campus. But then why should the rich folks in charge of things care what happens to a few struggling students, some with families to support, who seek to better themselves?

The commuting students are like the Jews wandering in the wilderness. We need homelands for our cars and freedom from persecution by campus cops.

II

Grammatical Sentences

5

Understanding Sentence Grammar

Grammar describes how language works and enables us to talk about it. People who are experts in grammar don't always write well, and many people who write well no longer think consciously about grammar and would have difficulty explaining in grammatical terms how their sentences work. But when something goes wrong in a sentence, a knowledge of grammar helps in recognizing the problem and provides a language for discussing it.

Grammar can help us understand sentences even if we don't know the meaning of all the words in the sentence.

> The rumfrum biggled the pooba.

We don't know what that sentence means. But we can infer that something called a *rumfrum* did something to a *pooba*. He (or she, or it) *biggled* it, whatever that means. We know this because we understand the basic grammar of simple English sentences. We understand that this sentence seems like *The boy kicked the ball* or *The student passed the test*. As in those sentences, a single word following *the* names something; words with *-ed* endings usually denote action of some sort, especially when they fall in patterns like *the rumfrum biggled;* and word groups beginning with *the* and *that,* coming after words like *biggled,* usually name something that receives the action indicated.

In the sense that we understand *The rumfrum biggled the pooba,* we can understand more complex sentences such as the following:

> The stintless rumfrums biggled the jittish poobas who were kerpesting the gloots.

We don't know what *stintless* and *jittish* mean, but we do know that they describe *rumfrums* and *poobas,* respectively, and that the *poobas were kerpesting* (doing something to) *the gloots,* probably more than one *gloot.* We understand these relations among the words because we recognize structures that recur in everyday talking and writing. Each statement is a **sentence,** the basic unit of writing.

5a Understanding the basic sentence

The basic grammar of sentences consists of the kinds of words that compose them, the functions of those words, the patterns on which sentences are built, and the ways those patterns can be expanded and elaborated. Understanding basic grammar can help you create clear sentences that effectively relate your ideas.

1 Identifying subjects and predicates

Most sentences make statements. First they name something; then they make an assertion about or describe an action involving that something. These two sentence parts are the **subject** and the **predicate.**

Subject	Predicate
Amanda	took the money to the bank.
Leroy	rode his bicycle down the middle of the street.
All the members of my family	were churchgoers from their earliest years.

2 Identifying the basic words: nouns and verbs

If we study the following five simple sentences, we find that they consist almost entirely of two quite different kinds of words.

Subject	Predicate
The earth	trembled.
The earthquake	destroyed the city.
The result	was chaos.
The government	sent the city aid.
The citizens	declared the earthquake a disaster.

In these sentences the words *earth, earthquake, government,* and *citizens* name things; in contrast, the words *trembled, destroyed,* and *sent* express actions. These two groups of words work in different ways. We can have one *earthquake* or several *earthquakes,* one *citizen* or many *citizens;* but we cannot have one or more *declareds* or *destroyeds.* If we drop the *-ed* from *destroyed* or the *-d* from *declared,* we change the time of the action. But we cannot add *-ed* to *citizen* and have *citizened.* The word *citizen* just doesn't work that way.

Grammar reflects these differences by identifying **parts of speech** or **word classes.** Except for the words *the* and *a,* which simply point to and help identify the words after them, our five sentences consist of two parts of speech: **nouns,** words that name; and **verbs,** words that express an action or an occurrence or a state of being. These are the basic words in English; without them we cannot form even the simplest sentences. The nouns and verbs in our sample sentences appear below.

Nouns	Verbs
earth	trembled
earthquake	destroyed
result	was
government	sent
citizens	declared
city	
chaos	
aid	
disaster	

We can identify nouns and verbs both by their meanings and by their forms.

Nouns

Meaning

Nouns name. They may name a person (*Lily Tomlin, Johnny Carson, astronaut*), a thing (*chair, book, spaceship*), a quality (*pain, mystery, simplicity*), a place (*city, Washington, ocean, Red Sea*), or an idea (*reality, peace, success*). Whatever exists or can be thought to exist has a name. Its name is a noun.

Form

Almost all nouns that name countable things add an *-s* to distinguish between the singular, meaning "one," and the plural, meaning "more than one": *earthquake, earthquakes; city, cities; citizen, citizens.* A few nouns form irregular plurals: *man, men; child, children; goose, geese.* Nouns also form a possessive by adding *-'s: citizen, citizen's; city, city's; father, father's.* This possessive form shows ownership (*Sheila's books*) and source (*Auden's poems*) as well as some other relationships.

Some nouns in our sample sentences—*chaos* and *earth*—do not usually form plurals. These words belong to a subgroup called

mass nouns. They name something that is not usually countable, such as *sugar, silver,* and *gravel;* or they name qualities, such as *courage, fortitude,* and *anger.* Other important groups of nouns not illustrated in our sentences are **proper nouns** such as *Ann, Cairo,* and *Ohio River,* which name specific people, places, and things; and **collective nouns** such as *army, family,* and *herd,* which name groups.

Nouns with *the, a,* and *an*

Nouns are often preceded by *the* or *a* (*an* before a vowel sound: *an apple*). These words are usually called **articles,** but they may be described as **noun markers** since they always indicate that a noun will soon follow.

Verbs

Meaning

Verbs express an action (*bring, change, grow*), an occurrence (*become, happen*), or a state of being (*be, seem*).

Form

Almost all verbs change form to indicate a difference between present and past time. To show past time, most verbs add *-d* or *-ed* to the form listed in the dictionary: *They play today. They played yesterday.* Some verbs indicate past time irregularly: *eat, ate; begin, began.* (See 7a.)

All verbs except *be* and *have* add *-s* or *-es* to their dictionary forms when their subjects are singular nouns or singular pronouns such as *he, she,* and *it: The bear escapes. It escapes. The woman begins. She begins.* When their subjects are plural nouns or pronouns, verbs retain their dictionary forms: *The bears escape. The women begin.* The *-s* forms of *be* and *have* are *is* and *has;* and *are* is the form of *be* with plural subjects. (See Chapter 7, pp. 179–81, for a fuller discussion of verb forms.)

Helping verbs

The dictionary form of all verbs can combine with the words *do, does, did, can, could, may, might, will, would, shall, should,* and *must: could run, may escape, must help.* These words are called **helping verbs** or **auxiliary verbs.** They and a few others combine with special forms of verbs to make verb phrases such as *will be running, might have escaped,* and *could have been helped.* (See Chapter 7, pp. 180 and 186.)

A note on form and function

In different sentences an English word may serve different functions, take correspondingly different forms, and belong to different word classes. For example, *aid* functions as a noun in the sentence *The government sent the city aid.* But in *The government aids the city,* the word *aid* functions as a verb, taking the characteristic *-s* ending of a verb with a singular subject, *government.* In *The light burns,* the word *light* functions as a noun; but in *The lanterns light the path,* the word *light* functions as a verb. Because words can function in different ways, we must always determine how a particular word works in a sentence before we can identify what part of speech it is. The *function* of a word in a sentence always determines its part of speech in that sentence.

Pronouns

Before looking at the five basic sentence patterns in English, we need to look at a third group of words, the pronouns.

> Susanne enlisted in the Air Force. *She* leaves for her training in two weeks. Susanne is one of the people *who* took advanced physics in high school.

Most **pronouns** substitute for nouns and function in sentences as nouns do. In the sentences above, the pronoun *she* substitutes for *Susanne,* and the pronoun *who* substitutes for *people.*

Pronouns fall into several subclasses depending on their form or function. **Personal pronouns** refer to a specific individual or to individuals. They are *I, you, he, she, it, we,* and *they.* **Indefinite pronouns,** such as *everybody* and *some,* do not substitute for any specific nouns, though they function as nouns (*Everybody likes Tim*). **Demonstrative pronouns,** including *this, that,* and *such,* identify or point to nouns (*This is the gun she used*). The **relative pronouns** *who, which,* and *that* relate groups of words to nouns or other pronouns (*Jim spoke to the boys who broke the window*). Intensive and reflexive pronouns have different functions but the same form: a personal pronoun plus *-self* (*himself, yourself*). **Intensive pronouns** emphasize a noun or other pronoun (*She herself asked the question*). **Reflexive pronouns** indicate that the sentence subject also receives the action of the verb (*You might hurt yourself*). Finally, **interrogative pronouns,** including *who, which,* and *what,* introduce questions (*Who will come to the concert?*).

The personal pronouns *I, he, she, we,* and *they* and the relative pronoun *who* change form depending on their function in the sentence. (For a discussion of these form changes, see Chapter 6.)

EXERCISE 1

Identify the subject and the predicate of each sentence below. Then use each sentence as a model for creating a sentence of your own.

Example:

An important scientist spoke at commencement.

SUBJECT | PREDICATE

An important scientist | spoke at commencement.

The hungry family ate at the diner.

1. The leaves fell.
2. October ends soon.
3. The orchard owners made apple cider.
4. They examined each apple carefully before using it.
5. Over a hundred people will buy cider at the roadside stand.

gr 5a

EXERCISE 2

In the following sentences identify all words functioning as nouns with *N*, all words functioning as verbs with *V*, and all pronouns with *P*.

Example:

We took the tour through the museum.

P V N N

We took the *tour* through the *museum.*

1. The lecture was a bore, and I slept through the last half.
2. Guests must register at the front desk; otherwise, they cannot obtain a key.
3. The trees they planted are dying of blight.
4. The new speed limit has prevented many accidents.
5. Although I was absent for a month, I finished the semester with good grades.

EXERCISE 3

Identify each of the following words as a noun, as a verb, or as both. Then create sentences of your own, using each word in each possible function.

Example:

fly

Noun and verb.

The *fly* sat on the meat loaf. [Noun.] The planes *fly* low. [Verb.]

1. wish
2. tie
3. swing
4. mail
5. spend
6. label
7. door
8. company
9. whistle
10. glue

3 Forming sentence patterns with nouns and verbs

The five sample sentences introduced earlier reappear below with an *N* over each noun and a *V* over each verb.

N V
1. The earth trembled.

N V N
2. The earthquake destroyed the city.

N V N
3. The result was chaos.

N V N N
4. The government sent the city aid.

N V N N
5. The citizens declared the earthquake a disaster.

These five sentences typify the five basic patterns on which we build all our sentences, even the most complex. The subjects of the sentences are similar, consisting only of a noun and an article or marker. But each predicate is different because the relation between the verb and the remaining words is different. We will examine each pattern in turn.

Pattern 1: The earth trembled.

In the simplest pattern the predicate consists only of the verb. Verbs in this pattern do not require following words to complete their meaning and thus are called **intransitive** (from Latin words meaning "not passing over").

SUBJECT	PREDICATE
	Intransitive verb
The earth	trembled.
Mosquitoes	buzz.
Spring	will come.
We	have been swimming.

Pattern 2: The earthquake destroyed the city.

In sentence 2 the predicate consists of a verb followed by a noun. The noun completes the meaning of the verb by identifying who or what receives the action of the verb. This noun is a **direct object** (DO). Verbs that require direct objects to complete their meaning are called **transitive** ("passing over").

SUBJECT	PREDICATE	
	Transitive verb	***Direct object***
The earthquake	destroyed	the city.
The man	stubbed	his toe.
The people	wanted	peace.

Pattern 3: The result was chaos.

In sentence 3 the predicate also consists of a verb followed by a single noun. But here the verb *was* serves merely to introduce a word that renames or describes the subject. We could write the sentence *The result = chaos.* The noun following the verb in this kind of sentence is a **subject complement** (SC), or a **predicate noun.** Verbs in this pattern are called **linking verbs** because they link their subjects to the description that follows.

Subject	**Predicate**	
	Linking verb	***Subject complement***
The result	was	chaos.
Jenn	is	an engineer.
The man	became	an accountant.

Subject complements in this sentence pattern may also be adjectives, words such as *tall, hopeful, large,* and *kind* (see 5b-1). Adjectives serving as complements are often called **predicate adjectives.**

Subject	**Predicate**	
	Linking verb	***Subject complement***
The result	was	chaotic.
The house	seemed	expensive.

Pattern 4: The government sent the city aid.

In sentence 4 the predicate consists of a verb followed by two nouns. The second noun is a direct object, identifying what was sent. But the first noun, *city,* is different. This noun is an **indirect object** (IO), identifying to or for whom or what the action of the verb is performed.

Subject	**Predicate**		
	Transitive verb	***Indirect object***	***Direct object***
The government	sent	the city	aid.
Neighbors	gave	the dog	a bone.
The boys	asked	their teacher	a question.
George	tossed	me	an apple.

Pattern 5: The citizens declared the earthquake a disaster.

In sentence 5 the predicate again consists of a verb followed by two nouns. But in this pattern the first noun is a direct object and the second noun renames or describes it. Here the second noun is an **object complement** (OC).

Subject	Predicate		
	Transitive verb	***Direct object***	***Object complement***
The citizens	declared	the earthquake	a disaster.
The manager	made	him	an assistant.
The class	elected	Joan O'Day	president.

Notice that the relation between a direct object and an object complement is the same as that between a subject and a subject complement in pattern 3. Just as the subject complement renames or describes a subject, so an object complement renames or describes a direct object. And just as we can use either nouns or adjectives in pattern 3, so we can use either nouns or adjectives as object complements in this last pattern.

Subject	Predicate		
	Transitive verb	***Direct object***	***Object complement***
The citizens	declared	the earthquake	disastrous.
The people	considered	the building	beautiful.

The five sentence patterns above are the basic frameworks for most written English sentences. However long or complicated a sentence is, one or more of these basic patterns forms its foundation. A question may change the order of the subject and verb (*Is she a doctor?*), a command may omit the subject entirely (*Be quiet!*), and the order of the parts may be different in some statements (see 5e), but the same basic sentence parts will be present or clearly understood.

EXERCISE 4

In the following sentences, identify each verb as intransitive, transitive, or linking. Then identify each direct object (DO), indirect object (IO), subject complement (SC), and object complement (OC).

Example:

Children give their parents both headaches and pleasures.

Give is a transitive verb.

IO DO DO

Children give their *parents* both *headaches* and *pleasures*.

1. Many people find the movie offensive.
2. The car stalled.
3. I lost my dry-cleaning ticket.

4. The building is unusual.
5. Marie calls her boyfriend a genius.
6. The dentist's bill was five hundred dollars.
7. I read my brother *Charlotte's Web.*
8. Then I bought him his own copy.
9. The counterfeiter was a child.
10. The magician showed the audience his tricks.

EXERCISE 5

Create sentences by using each of the following verbs in the pattern indicated. You may want to change the form of the verb.

Example: give (S–V–IO–DO)

Sam gave his brother a birthday card.

1. laugh (S–V)
2. elect (S–V–DO–OC)
3. steal (S–V–DO)
4. catch (S–V–DO)
5. bring (S–V–IO–DO)
6. seem (S–V–SC)
7. call (S–V–DO–OC)
8. become (S–V–SC)
9. buy (S–V–IO–DO)
10. study (S–V)

5b
Expanding the basic sentence with single words

We have been studying simple sentences and their basic structures. But most of the sentences we read, write, or speak are more complex and also more informative and interesting. Most sentences contain one or more of the following: (1) modifying words; (2) word groups, called phrases and clauses; and (3) combinations of two or more words or word groups of the same kind. These sentence expanders are the subjects of this and the next two sections.

1
Using adjectives and adverbs

The simplest expansion of sentences occurs when we add modifying words to describe or limit the noun and verbs. Modifying words add details.

Recently, the earth trembled.

The earthquake *nearly* destroyed the *old* city.

The *frantic* citizens *quickly* declared the earthquake a *complete* disaster.

The added words do not all act the same way. *Old, frantic,* and *complete* modify nouns, but *recently, nearly,* and *quickly* do not. We don't speak of a *recently earthquake* or a *quickly citizen.* Nor do we say *frantic declared* or *complete destroyed.* We are dealing with two different parts of speech. **Adjectives** (such as *old, frantic, complete, heartless, friendly*) describe or modify nouns and pronouns. **Adverbs** (such as *recently, nearly, quickly, never, always*) describe the action of verbs and also modify adjectives, other adverbs, and whole groups of words.

We cannot always identify adjectives and adverbs by their form. Although an *-ly* ending often signals an adverb, many adverbs —*never* and *always,* for example—have a different form. Moreover, some adjectives end in *-ly:* in *likely candidate* and *lovely breeze, likely* and *lovely* clearly modify nouns and are thus adjectives. Therefore, to determine whether a word is an adjective or an adverb, we must identify the word or words it modifies.

Adjectives modify only nouns and pronouns. Adverbs may modify verbs, but they may also modify adjectives and other adverbs: *extremely unhappy* (adverb-adjective); *bitterly cold* (adverb-adjective); *very quickly* (adverb-adverb). Adverbs may also modify whole sentences or groups of words within a sentence. In *Unfortunately, we have no money,* for example, *unfortunately* modifies the whole sentence that follows it. In *She ran almost to the end of the street,* the adverb *almost* modifies *to the end of the street.*

Adverbs usually indicate where, when, how, or to what extent, as in the following sentences.

> Send all the mail *here.* [*Here* is *where* the mail is to be sent.]
>
> Fred will arrive *tomorrow.* [*Tomorrow* is *when* Fred will arrive.]
>
> Jeremy answered *angrily.* [*Angrily* is *how* Jeremy answered.]
>
> We are *completely* satisfied. [*Completely* indicates *to what extent* we are satisfied.]

Adjectives and adverbs appear in three forms distinguished by degree. The **positive degree** is the basic form, the one listed in the dictionary: *good, green, angry; badly, quickly, angrily.* The **comparative** form indicates a greater degree of the quality named by the word: *better, greener, angrier; worse, more quickly, more angrily.* The **superlative** form indicates the greatest degree of the quality named: *best, greenest, angriest; worst, most quickly, most angrily.* (For further discussion of the forms and uses of comparatives and superlatives, see 9e.)

EXERCISE 6

Identify the adjectives and adverbs in the following sentences. Then use each sentence as a model for creating a sentence of your own.

Example:

The red barn sat uncomfortably among modern buildings.

The *red* (ADJ) barn sat *uncomfortably* (ADV) among *modern* (ADJ) buildings.

The little girl complained loudly to her busy mother.

1. The icy rain created glassy patches on the roads.
2. Happily, children played in the slippery streets.
3. Fortunately, no cars ventured out.
4. Wise parents stayed indoors where they could be warm and dry.
5. The dogs slept soundly near the warm radiators.

EXERCISE 7

Change each of the following adjectives into an adverb, and change each adverb into an adjective. Then write one sentence using the adjective and another using the adverb.

Example:

sorrowful: *sorrowfully*

Her expression was *sorrowful.*

David watched *sorrowfully* as the firemen removed the charred remains of his furniture.

1. skillful
2. wisely
3. new
4. bright
5. fortunately
6. bluntly
7. happy
8. painfully
9. stupid
10. sturdy

2
Using other words as modifiers

We have already observed that a particular word may function sometimes as a noun, sometimes as a verb. Similarly, nouns and special forms of verbs may sometimes serve as modifiers of other nouns. In combinations such as *office buildings, Thanksgiving prayer,* and *shock hazard,* the first noun modifies the second. In combinations such as *singing birds, corrected papers,* and *broken finger,* the first word is a verb form modifying the following noun. (These modifying verb forms are discussed in more detail in 5c-2.) Again, the part of speech to which we assign a word always depends on its function in a sentence.

EXERCISE 8

Use each of the following verb forms to modify a noun in a sentence of your own.

Example:
smoking
Only a *smoking cigar* remained.

1. scrambled
2. twitching
3. rambling
4. typed
5. painted
6. written
7. charging
8. ripened
9. known
10. driven

gr
5c

EXERCISE 9

To practice expanding the basic sentence patterns with single-word modifiers, combine each group of sentences below into one sentence. You will have to delete and rearrange words.

Example:

The speaker told us the facts. The speaker told us calmly. The facts were terrifying.

The speaker *calmly* told us the *terrifying* facts.

1. The parents comforted their children. The parents were departing. The children were nervous.
2. The house sheltered people. The people were homeless. The house was abandoned.
3. The dog barked. The dog was frightened. It barked loudly.
4. A driver can avoid accidents. The driver must be careful. The accidents might be unhappy.
5. Children leave toys. The children are growing. They leave the toys behind. The toys are many. The toys are broken.
6. The car is a Chevrolet. The car is wrecked. The car is silver.
7. We bought our father a knife. We bought the knife recently. It is for carving.
8. The doors open. The doors are brass. They open inward.
9. The oceans are deep. The oceans contain fish. The fish are peculiar.
10. The boy drank the water. The boy was hiccupping. He drank the water quickly.

5c
Expanding the basic sentence with word groups

We have seen that nouns and verbs are the basic words of our language. Naming and asserting, they are all we need to build the basic sentence patterns. Adjectives and adverbs are the simplest modifiers, permitting us to qualify or limit nouns and verbs. But most sentences we read or write contain whole word groups that *serve* as nouns and modifiers. Such word groups enable us to combine several bits of information into one sentence and to make the relations among them clear.

Consider the following sentence:

> When the ice cracked, the skaters, fearing an accident, sought safety at the lake's edge.

The skeleton of this sentence—the basic subject and predicate—is *The skaters sought safety.* The sentence pattern is subject (*skaters*), verb (*sought*), and direct object (*safety*). But attached to this skeleton are three other groups of words that add related information. Each word group could itself be stated as a basic sentence pattern: *The ice cracked. The skaters feared an accident. The lake's edge was safe.* In the sample sentence, however, each of these statements is reduced to something less than a sentence and then is inserted into the basic pattern *The skaters sought safety.* The reduced constructions are phrases and clauses.

A **phrase,** such as *at the lake's edge* and *fearing an accident,* is a group of related words that lacks either a subject or a predicate or both. A **clause,** in contrast, contains both a subject and a predicate. Both *The skaters sought safety* and *When the ice cracked* are clauses, though only the first can stand alone as a sentence. We will examine the various kinds of phrases and clauses in the following sections.

1
Using prepositional phrases

Prepositions are connecting words. Unlike nouns, verbs, and modifiers, which may change form according to their meaning and use in a sentence, prepositions never change form. We use many prepositions with great frequency, but the entire list is relatively short. Here are the most common ones.

about	beneath	inside	round
above	beside	in spite of	since
according to	between	instead of	through
across	beyond	into	throughout
after	by	like	till
against	concerning	near	to
along	despite	next to	toward
along with	down	of	under
among	during	off	underneath
around	except	on	unlike
as	except for	onto	until
at	excepting	out	up
because of	for	outside	upon
before	from	over	with
behind	in	past	within
below	in addition to	regarding	without

A preposition always connects a noun, a pronoun, or a word

group functioning as a noun to another word in the sentence: *Robins nest in trees.* The noun, pronoun, or word group so connected (*trees*) is called the **object of the preposition.** The preposition plus its object and any modifiers is called a **prepositional phrase.**

PREPOSITION	OBJECT
of	spaghetti
on	the surface
with	great satisfaction
upon	entering the room
from	where you are standing

Prepositions normally come before their objects. But sometimes the preposition comes after its object, particularly in speech.

What do you want to see him *about?*
She pointed to the *house* she lives *in.*

Prepositional phrases usually function as adjectives (modifying nouns) or as adverbs (modifying verbs, adjectives, or other adverbs). As modifiers, they add details that make sentences clearer and more interesting for readers.

PREPOSITIONAL PHRASES AS ADJECTIVES

Terry is the boy *in the pink shirt.* [Phrase describes *boy.*]

Life *on a raft in the Mississippi* was an opportunity *for adventure.* [*On a raft* describes *life; in the Mississippi* describes *raft;* and *for adventure* describes *opportunity.*]

PREPOSITIONAL PHRASES AS ADVERBS

She had driven steadily *for four hours from Baltimore.* [Both phrases describe *driven.*]

Our Great Dane Joshua buries his bones *behind the garage.* [Phrase describes *buries.*]

Occasionally, prepositional phrases also function as nouns, though rarely in writing.

PREPOSITIONAL PHRASE AS NOUN

Across the river is too far to go for ice cream. [Phrase functions as sentence subject.]

Punctuating prepositional phrases

Since a prepositional phrase lacks a subject and a predicate, it should not be punctuated as a complete sentence. If it is, the result is a **sentence fragment:**

FRAGMENT Toward the sun.

The phrase must be attached to another group of words containing both a subject and a predicate:

Revised The plant turned *toward the sun.*

See Chapter 10 for a full discussion of how to recognize and revise sentence fragments.

A prepositional phrase that introduces a sentence is set off with punctuation, usually a comma, unless it is short (see 21b).

According to the newspaper and other sources, the governor has reluctantly decided to veto the bill.

In 1865 the Civil War finally ended.

A prepositional phrase that interrupts or concludes a sentence is *not* set off with punctuation when it restricts the meaning of the word or words it modifies (see 21c).

Nothing *about him* surprises me.
We saw her riding *in Sandy's car.*

When an interrupting or concluding prepositional phrase does *not* restrict meaning, but merely adds information to the sentence, then it *is* set off with punctuation, usually a comma or commas (see 21c).

The governor, *according to the newspaper and other sources*, has reluctantly decided to veto the bill.

The governor has reluctantly decided to veto the bill, *according to the newspaper and other sources.*

As all the preceding examples illustrate, a preposition and its object are not separated by a comma (see 21j-1).

EXERCISE 10

Identify the prepositional phrases in the following passage. Indicate whether each phrase functions as an adjective or as an adverb, and name the word that the phrase modifies.

Example:

After an hour I finally arrived at the home of my professor.

ADV PHRASE — ADV PHRASE — ADJ PHRASE

After an hour I finally arrived *at the home of my professor.* [*After an hour* and *at the home* modify *arrived; of my professor* modifies *home.*]

The woman in blue socks ran from the policeman on horseback. She darted down Bates Street and then into the bus depot. At the depot the policeman dismounted from his horse and searched for the woman. The entrance to the depot and the interior were filled with travelers, however, and in the crowd he lost sight of the woman. She, meanwhile, had boarded a bus on the other side of the depot and was riding across town.

gr 5c

EXERCISE 11

To practice writing sentences with prepositional phrases, combine each pair of sentences below into one sentence that includes one or two prepositional phrases. You will have to add, delete, and rearrange words. Some items have more than one possible answer.

Example:

I will start working. The new job will pay the minimum wage.
I will start working *at a new job for the minimum wage.*

1. The prize money was hidden. It was concealed behind a painting.
2. The lawyer accepted the case. She had no hesitation.
3. The band members held a party. They invited one hundred people.
4. We are required to write the exam. We must use pencil and white paper.
5. The interview continued. Two hours was the time it took.
6. Jan received a glass paperweight. An unknown admirer gave it.
7. They took a long walk. They followed the stream and crossed the bridge.
8. The wagging tail toppled the lamp. It was a dog's tail.
9. Everyone attended the lecture. Only Vicky and Carlos did not go.
10. He impressed everyone. He told everyone tales of his exploits.

2
Using verbals and verbal phrases

Verbals are special verb forms like *smoking* or *hidden* or *to win* that can function as nouns (*smoking is dangerous*) or as modifiers (*the hidden money, the urge to win*). Verbals *cannot* stand alone as the complete verb in the predicate of a sentence. For example, *The man smoking* and *The money hidden* are not sentences. Any verbal must combine with a helping verb to serve as the predicate of a sentence: *The man was smoking. The money is hidden.*

Because verbals cannot serve alone as sentence predicates, they are sometimes called **nonfinite verbs** (in essence, they are "unfinished"). **Finite verbs,** in contrast, can make an assertion or express a state of being without a helping verb (they are "finished"). A simple test can distinguish finite and nonfinite verbs. Finite verbs that express present time always change form when the subject changes from singular to plural: *The prisoner escapes. The prisoners escape. The paper is written. The papers are written.* In contrast, nonfinite verbs always have the same form whether the subject is singular or plural: *the prisoner escaping, the prisoners escaping; the paper written, the papers written; the letter to mail, the letters to mail.*

There are three kinds of verbals: participles, gerunds, and infinitives.

Participles

gr
5c

All verbs have two participle forms, a present and a past. The **present participle** consists of the dictionary form of the verb plus the ending *-ing: beginning, completing, hiding.* The **past participle** of most verbs consists of the dictionary form plus *-d* or *-ed: believed, completed.* Some common verbs have an irregular past participle: *begun, hidden.* (See 7a.)

Both present and past participles function as adjectives to modify nouns and pronouns.

> The *freezing* rain made the roads dangerous. [Modifies *rain.*]
>
> The *exhausted* miners were rescued. [Modifies *miners.*]
>
> Oliver found his *typing* job *boring.* [Both participles modify *job.*]
>
> *Disgusted,* he quit that night. [Modifies *he.*]

Gerunds

Gerund is the name given to the *-ing* form of the verb when it serves as a noun.

> Unfortunately, *studying* always bored Michael. [Sentence subject.]
>
> His sister Annie hated *swimming.* [Object of *hated.*]
>
> Both Michael and Annie preferred *loafing* to *working.* [*Loafing* is the object of *preferred; working* is the object of *to.*]
>
> Their principal occupation was *loafing.* [Subject complement.]

Present participles and gerunds can be distinguished *only* by their function in a sentence. If the *-ing* form functions as an adjective (*a teaching degree*), it is a present participle. If the *-ing* form functions as a noun (*Teaching is difficult*), it is a gerund.

Infinitives

The **infinitive** is the *to* form of the verb, the dictionary form preceded by the infinitive marker *to: to begin, to hide, to run.* Infinitives may function as nouns, adjectives, or adverbs.

> He plans *to go.* [The infinitive functions as a noun, the object of *plans.*]
>
> He is the man *to elect.* [The infinitive functions as an adjective, modifying *man.*]
>
> Some physics problems are difficult *to solve.* [The infinitive functions as an adverb, modifying *difficult.*]

Verbal phrases

Participles, gerunds, and infinitives — like other forms of verbs — may take subjects, objects, or complements, and they may be modified by adverbs. The verbal and all the words immediately related to it make up a **verbal phrase.** With verbal phrases, we can create concise sentences packed with information.

Participial phrases

Like participles, **participial phrases** always serve as adjectives, modifying nouns or pronouns.

> *Chewing his pencil steadily,* Dick stared into the air. [Modifies *Dick.*]
>
> He was frustrated by the paper *lying before him.* [Modifies *paper.*]
>
> *Defeated by the same blank paper earlier in the day,* Dick knew he must somehow write something. [Modifies *Dick.*]

Gerund phrases

Gerund phrases, like gerunds, always serve as nouns.

> *Eating an entire lemon pie for lunch* was easy for Wesley. [Sentence subject.]
>
> His mother was annoyed at *his eating the whole pie.* [Object of preposition *at. His* is the subject of the gerund; see 6h.]
>
> But she had hidden a second pie because she anticipated *his doing it.* [Object of *anticipated.*]

Infinitive phrases

Infinitive phrases may serve as nouns, adjectives, or adverbs.

> *To lie repeatedly* is *to deny reality.* [Both phrases function as nouns, the first as the sentence subject and the second as a subject complement.]
>
> We wanted *him to go.* [The phrase functions as a noun, the object of *wanted. Him* is the subject of the infinitive; see 6f.]
>
> Jimmy's is the best place *to eat pancakes.* [The phrase functions as an adjective, modifying *place.*]
>
> Amy is not someone *to put off decisions.* [The phrase functions as an adjective, modifying *someone.*]
>
> Frank jogged *to keep himself fit.* [The phrase functions as an adverb, modifying *jogged.*]
>
> Jack was too young *to understand the story.* [The phrase functions as an adverb, modifying *young.*]

Note: When an infinitive or infinitive phrase serves as a noun after verbs such as *hear, let, help, make, see,* and *watch,* the infinitive marker *to* is omitted: *We all heard her (to) tell the story.*

Punctuating verbals and verbal phrases

Like prepositional phrases, verbal phrases punctuated as complete sentences are sentence fragments. A complete sentence must contain a subject and a finite verb (p. 148).

Fragment	*Treating* the patients kindly.
Revised	*She treats* the patients kindly.

See Chapter 10 on sentence fragments.

A verbal or verbal phrase serving as a modifier is almost always set off with a comma when it introduces a sentence (see 21b).

To pay her tuition, she worked at two jobs.
Breathing evenly, the cat lay asleep on the rug.

A modifying verbal or verbal phrase that interrupts or concludes a sentence is *not* set off with punctuation when it restricts the meaning of the word or words it modifies (see 21c).

The boy *selling hotdogs* is my brother.
She worked at two jobs *to pay her tuition.*

When an interrupting or concluding verbal modifier does *not* restrict meaning, but merely adds information to the sentence, it *is* set off with punctuation, usually a comma or commas (see 21c).

The cat, *breathing evenly*, lay asleep on the rug.
The cat lay asleep on the rug, *breathing evenly.*

EXERCISE 12

The following sentences contain participles, gerunds, and infinitives as well as participial, gerund, and infinitive phrases. Identify each verbal or verbal phrase and indicate whether it is used as an adjective, an adverb, or a noun.

Example:

Laughing, the talk-show host prodded her guest to talk.

ADJ ADV
Laughing, the talk-show host prodded her guest *to talk.*

1. Shunned by the community, Hester Prynne went into exile.
2. She is self-confident enough to laugh at her own faults.
3. Sliding and slipping, they moved across the ice to greet their friends.
4. Eating at a nice restaurant is a relaxing way to end a hectic week.
5. To fly was one of humankind's recurring dreams.
6. Because of the dwindling water supply, the remaining vacationers decided to leave for another campground.

7. The periodic firing of the rifle kept the hungry wolves at bay.
8. The train moved too fast for us to enjoy the countryside.
9. Three misbehaving children ruined our attempt to stage a play in the elementary school.
10. After missing rehearsal three times in a row, I received a call from the conductor.

EXERCISE 13

To practice writing sentences with verbals and verbal phrases, combine each pair of sentences below into one sentence. You will have to add, delete, change, and rearrange words. Each item has more than one possible answer.

Example:

My father took pleasure in mean pranks. For instance, he hid the neighbors' cat.

My father took pleasure in mean pranks such as *hiding the neighbors' cat.*

1. The highway leads into the town. It is lined with fast-food restaurants.
2. The ancient Greeks gave their children cheese. The cheese rewarded good behavior.
3. The islands of Japan form a thousand-mile-long archipelago. The archipelago lies mostly in the temperate zone.
4. She worked hard at her job search. She called every lead she got.
5. Lee knew she had lost the race. She was falling far behind the other runners.
6. The letter had been opened by mistake. It was lying on the table.
7. Children shop in supermarkets with their parents. This is an early experience that almost all children share.
8. I must get a job. I must support myself.
9. They discovered a box of old money. They were cleaning the cellar.
10. I have jogged every day for a month. The exercise has helped me lose five pounds.

3
Using absolute phrases

Absolute phrases consist of a noun or pronoun and a participle, plus any modifiers.

The parade passed by slowly, *the bands blaring, the crowds shouting.*

The old tree stood alone, *its trunk stripped and rotting.*

Their work nearly finished, the men rested.

These phrases are called *absolute* (from a Latin word meaning "free") because they have no specific grammatical connection to any word in the rest of the sentence. Instead, they modify the entire rest of the sentence, adding information or clarifying meaning.

Notice that absolute phrases, unlike participial phrases, always contain a subject. Compare the following.

> The large man *standing before me* turned to speak. [Participial phrase modifying *man,* the sentence subject.]
>
> *A large man having moved in front of me,* I could see nothing. [Absolute phrase having its own subject, *A large man,* and modifying the rest of the sentence.]

We often omit the participle from an absolute phrase when it is some form of *be* such as *being* or *having been.*

> Sammy watched intently, *his mouth* (*being*) *wide open.*

Punctuating absolute phrases

Absolute phrases are always set off from the rest of the sentence with punctuation, usually a comma or commas (see 21d).

> *Its finish waxed and buffed*, the car looked almost new.
> The car, *its finish waxed and buffed*, looked almost new.
> The car looked almost new, *its finish waxed and buffed.*

EXERCISE 14

To practice writing sentences with absolute phrases, combine each pair of sentences below into one sentence that contains an absolute phrase. You will have to add, delete, change, and rearrange words.

> *Example:*
> The flower's petals wilted. It looked pathetic.
> *Its petals wilted,* the flower looked pathetic.

1. Her face turned pale. She stared at the woman ahead of her.
2. The steelworkers called a strike. The factory was closed down.
3. We were forced to cancel the annual picnic. The funds had run out.
4. The thief stood before the safe. His fingers twitched eagerly.
5. The swimmer rose again to the surface. His arms thrashed.

4
Using subordinate clauses

As we noted earlier, a **clause** is any group of words that contains both a subject and a predicate. There are two kinds of clauses, and the distinction between them is important. A **main** or **indepen-**

dent clause can stand alone as a sentence: *The sky darkened.* A **subordinate** or **dependent clause** is just like a main clause *except* that it begins with a subordinating word: *when the sky darkened. When* and other subordinating words such as *because, if, who,* or *that* express particular relationships between the clauses they introduce and the main clauses to which they are attached. Clauses that have been subordinated can *never* stand alone as sentences (see the discussion of punctuation on p. 156). The following examples show the differences between the two kinds of clauses.

Two main clauses

The chair is expensive. We cannot buy it.

First clause subordinated

Because the chair is expensive, we cannot buy it.

Two main clauses

I met a man. He was selling boa constrictors.

Second clause subordinated

I met a man *who was selling boa constrictors.*

We use two kinds of subordinating words to connect subordinate clauses with main clauses. The first kind is **subordinating conjunctions** or **subordinators.** They always come at the beginning of subordinate clauses. Like prepositions, subordinating conjunctions are few and never change form in any way. The following are the most common subordinating conjunctions.

after	because	in order that	than	when
although	before	once	that	whenever
as	even if	rather than	though	where
as if	even though	since	unless	wherever
as though	if	so that	until	while

The second kind of connecting word is the **relative pronoun.** It also introduces a subordinate clause and links it with an independent clause. The relative pronouns are as follows:

which	what	who (whose, whom)
that	whatever	whoever (whomever)

Like subordinating conjunctions, these words link one clause with another. But unlike subordinating conjunctions, relative pronouns also usually act as subjects or objects in their own clauses, and two of them (*who* and *whoever*) change form accordingly (see 6g).

Subordinate clauses function as adjectives, adverbs, and nouns and are described as adjective, adverb, or noun clauses according to their use in a particular sentence. Only by determining its function in a sentence can we identify a particular clause.

ADJECTIVE CLAUSES

Adjective clauses modify nouns and pronouns, providing necessary or helpful information about them. They usually begin with the relative pronouns listed above, although a few adjective clauses begin with *when* or *where* (standing for *in which, on which,* or *at which*). The relative pronoun is the subject or object of the clause it begins. The clause ordinarily falls immediately after the noun or pronoun it modifies.

> My family still lives in the house *that my grandfather built.* [Modifies *house.*]
>
> Dale is the girl *who always gets there early.* [Modifies *girl.*]
>
> My yellow Volkswagen, *which I bought seven years ago,* has traveled 78,000 miles. [Modifies *Volkswagen.*]
>
> There comes a time *when each of us must work.* [Modifies *time.*]

ADVERB CLAUSES

Like adverbs, adverb clauses modify verbs, adjectives, other adverbs, and whole groups of words. They usually tell how, why, when, where, under what conditions, or with what result. They always begin with subordinating conjunctions.

> Calvin liked to go *where there was action.* [Modifies *go.*]
>
> Elaine is friendlier *when she's talking on the telephone.* [Modifies *friendlier.*]
>
> *Because he did not study,* Donald failed. [Modifies *failed.*]
>
> She came as quickly *as she could.* [Modifies *quickly.*]

An adverb clause can often be separated from the word it modifies. In both of the following sentences, the italicized adverb clause clearly modifies *ended.*

> The game ended *before he had a chance to play.*
> *Before he had a chance to play,* the game ended.

NOUN CLAUSES

Noun clauses function as subjects, objects, and complements in sentences. They begin either with relative pronouns or with the words *when, where, whether, why,* and *how.* Unlike adjective and adverb clauses, noun clauses *replace* a noun within a main clause; therefore, they can be difficult to identify.

> *The lecture* pleased the audience. [*The lecture* is the sentence subject.]
>
> *What the lecturer said* pleased the audience. [The noun clause replaces *The lecture* as the sentence subject.]

Here are some typical noun clauses.

> Everyone knows *what a panther is.* [Object of *knows.*]

Whoever calls the station first will win a case of bean soup. [Subject of sentence.]

They thought about *whether they could afford the trip.* [Object of preposition *about.*]

Elliptical clauses

A subordinate clause that is grammatically incomplete but clear in meaning is an **elliptical clause** (*ellipsis* means "omission"). The meaning of the clause is clear because the missing element can be supplied from the context. Most often the elements omitted are the relative pronouns *that, which,* and *whom* from adjective clauses or the predicate from the second part of a comparison.

Thailand is among the countries (*that* or *which*) *he visited.*
Ellen dances better *than Martha* (*dances*).

Here are other typical elliptical clauses.

When (*she was*) *only a child,* Julia saw a great gray owl.

Though (*they are*) *rare south of Canada,* great gray owls sometimes appear in Massachusetts.

Punctuating subordinate clauses

Subordinate clauses punctuated as complete sentences are sentence fragments. Though a subordinate clause contains a subject and a predicate and thus resembles a complete sentence, it also contains a subordinating word that makes its meaning dependent on a main clause.

Fragment	Because the door was ajar.
Revised	The door was ajar.
Revised	I overheard *because the door was ajar.*

See Chapter 10 on sentence fragments.

A subordinate clause serving as an adverb is almost always set off with a comma when it introduces a sentence (see 21b).

Although the project was almost completed, it lost its funding.

A modifying subordinate clause that interrupts or concludes a main clause is *not* set off with punctuation when it restricts the meaning of the word or words it modifies (see 21c).

The woman *who spoke* is a doctor.
The project lost its funding *because it was not completed on time.*

When an interrupting or concluding subordinate clause does *not* restrict meaning, but merely adds information to the sentence, it *is* set off with punctuation, usually a comma or commas (see 21c).

The woman, *who is a doctor*, cares for her invalid father.
The project lost its funding, *although it was almost completed.*

EXERCISE 15

Identify the subordinate clauses in the following sentences and indicate whether each is used as an adjective, an adverb, or a noun. If the clause is a noun, indicate its function in the sentence.

Example:

The article explained how one could build an underground house.

NOUN

The article explained *how one could build an underground house.* [Object of *explained.*]

1. They were not interested in what the tour guide said.
2. The auctioneer opened the bidding once everyone was seated.
3. Whenever the economy is uncertain, people tend to become anxious.
4. Whoever wants to graduate must pass all the required courses.
5. I knew the ending would be unhappy when the main character started falling apart.
6. That Stefanie has not gone to college is a disappointment to her parents.
7. Ever since she was a small child, they have saved money for her education.
8. Stefanie decided, though, that she wanted to work a year or two before college.
9. Until she makes up her mind, Stefanie's education money is collecting interest.
10. Her parents are the kind who let their children think for themselves.

EXERCISE 16

To practice writing sentences with subordinate clauses, combine each pair of main clauses below into one sentence. Use either subordinating conjunctions or relative pronouns as appropriate, referring to the lists on page 154 if necessary. You will have to add, delete, and rearrange words. Each item has more than one possible answer.

Example:

She did not have her tire irons with her. She could not change her bicycle tire.

Because she did not have her tire irons with her, she could not change her bicycle tire.

1. The critic reviewed the Frank Capra movie. It was playing at the revival theater.
2. He is an accountant. He rarely makes mistakes.
3. We came to the gate. We had first seen the deer tracks there.
4. Someone is fickle. This person cannot be relied on.
5. Abner won the award. This still amazes us.
6. We can make no exceptions. You should know this.

7. The town government canceled the new playground. Then small children demonstrated in the streets.
8. Those dogs have a master. He gives them equal discipline and praise.
9. The basketball team has had a losing season. The team still shows promise.
10. He did not bother to undress for bed. He was too tired.

5
Using appositives

An **appositive** is a word or word group that renames the word or word group before it. (The word *appositive* derives from a Latin word that means "placed near to" or "applied to.") The most common appositives are nouns that rename other nouns.

> Her sister *Jean* attends law school. [Noun as appositive.]
>
> Bizen ware, *a dark stoneware,* has been produced in Japan since the fourteenth century. [Noun phrase as appositive.]
>
> His first love, *racing stock cars,* was his last love. [Gerund phrase as appositive.]

All appositives can replace the words they refer to: *A dark stoneware has been produced in Japan. Racing stock cars was his last love.*

Appositives are often introduced by words and phrases such as *or, that is, such as, for example,* and *in other words.*

> Kangaroos, opossums, and wombats are all marsupials, *that is, mammals that carry their young in external abdominal pouches.*
>
> Jujitsu, *or judo,* is based on the principle that an opponent's strength may be used to defeat him or her.

Although most appositives are nouns that rename other nouns, they may also be and rename other parts of speech.

> All papers should be proofread carefully, that is, *checked for spelling, punctuation, and mechanics.* [The appositive defines the verb *proofread.*]

Noun appositives can always be stated as clauses with some form of the verb *be.*

> Bizen ware, (*which is*) *a dark stoneware,* has been produced in Japan since the fourteenth century.

Thus appositives are economical alternatives to adjective clauses containing a form of *be.*

Punctuating appositives

Appositives punctuated as complete sentences are sentence fragments. Correcting such fragments generally involves connecting the appositive to the main clause containing the word referred to.

Fragment	An exceedingly tall man with narrow shoulders.
Revised	I stood next to a basektball player, *an exceedingly tall man with narrow shoulders.*

See Chapter 10 on sentence fragments.

An appositive is *not* set off with punctuation when it restricts the meaning of the word it refers to (see 21c).

The verb *howl* comes from the Old English verb *houlen.*

When an appositive does *not* restrict the meaning of the word it refers to, it *is* set off with punctuation, usually a comma or commas (see 21c).

An aged elm, the tree was struck by lightning.
The tree, *an aged elm*, was struck by lightning.
Lightning struck the tree, *an aged elm.*

A nonrestrictive appositive is sometimes set off with a dash or dashes, especially when it contains commas (see 25b-2).

Three people—*Will, Carolyn, and Tom*—objected to the new procedure.

A concluding appositive is sometimes set off with a colon (see 25a-1).

Two principles guide the judge's decisions: *justice and fairness.*

EXERCISE 17

To practice writing sentences with appositives, combine each pair of sentences into one sentence that contains an appositive. You will have to delete and rearrange words. Some items have more than one possible answer.

Example:

The largest land animal is the elephant. The elephant is also one of the most intelligent animals.

The largest land animal, *the elephant,* is also one of the most intelligent animals.

1. The poet is an egocentric boor. He is rarely invited to read.
2. The part of Nathan Detroit is played by Frank Sinatra. Detroit is a gambler.
3. The tapestry depicted a unicorn. That is the fabled horselike animal with one horn.
4. Cactus growing attracts patient people. It is a hobby with no immediate rewards.
5. The most popular professional sports pay their players well. They are football, baseball, basketball, and hockey.
6. Edgar Allan Poe was a writer of fantastic, scary stories. He was also a poet and a journalist.

7. The house was a five-room adobe structure. It was bought by a neighborhood group.
8. English adopted many words for animals from the Algonquin Indians. These are words such as *moose, opossum,* and *raccoon.*
9. Jerry's aim in life is to avoid all productive labor. His aim will surely change when his parents stop supporting him.
10. Their Beatles memorabilia occupied a room in their basement. The memorabilia consisted of records, photographs, posters, and T-shirts.

5d
Compounding words, phrases, and clauses

We have seen how to modify the nouns and verbs of the basic sentence patterns and how to use word groups in place of single nouns and modifiers. Now we will examine how to combine words and word groups that are closely related and parallel in importance, as in these examples:

> Bonnie spent the afternoon in the park. Her father spent the afternoon in the park.
>
> *Bonnie and her father* spent the afternoon in the park.
>
> Curt was tired. He was sick. He was depressed.
>
> Curt was *tired, sick, and depressed.*
>
> Brenda went to the drugstore. She bought some vitamins. She returned as soon as possible.
>
> Brenda *went to the drugstore, bought some vitamins, and returned as soon as possible.*

In the first pair of examples the two different subjects, *Bonnie* and *her father,* become a **compound subject,** thus avoiding repetition of the same predicate in two sentences. In the second pair of examples the three adjective complements become a **compound complement** (*tired, sick, and depressed*) that describes the common subject *Curt* after the common linking verb *was.* And in the last pair of examples the three different predicates become a **compound predicate** (*went . . . , bought . . . , and returned . . .*) with the common subject *Brenda.* In every example *and* joins the parts.

1
Using coordinating conjunctions and correlative conjunctions

The word *and* is a **coordinating conjunction.** Like prepositions and subordinating conjunctions, coordinating conjunctions are few and do not change form.

and	or	so
but	for	yet
nor		

The coordinating conjunctions *and, but, nor,* and *or* always connect words or word groups of the same kind—that is, two or more nouns, verbs, adjectives, adverbs, phrases, subordinate clauses, or main clauses.

Stewart *or* Linda will have to go.
The chair was unfashionable *but* charming.
Alison worked every day *and* partied every evening.
He studied day and night, *but* he could not pass the course.

The conjunctions *for* and *so* cannot connect words, phrases, or subordinate clauses, but they can connect main clauses. *For* indicates cause; *so* indicates result.

Amy stayed home, *for* she had work to do.
Jasper was tired, *so* he went to bed early.

The word *yet* often functions as an adverb (*She has not left yet*), but it can also function as a coordinating conjunction. Like *but,* it indicates contrast.

He tended the goldfish carefully, *yet* it died.

Some conjunctions pair up with other words to form **correlative conjunctions.** The following are common correlative conjunctions.

both . . . and	neither . . . nor
not only . . . but also	whether . . . or
not . . . but	as . . . as
either . . . or	

Both Bonnie *and* her father went to the park.
The basketball is *either* on the shelf *or* in the closet.
The class stood *neither* when he arrived *nor* when he left.
We consume energy *not only* when awake *but also* when asleep.

Punctuating compounded words, phrases, and clauses

Unless they form a series of three or more, words, phrases, and subordinate clauses that are connected by a coordinating conjunction are *not* separated by commas (see 21j-2).

The *boys and girls* segregated themselves.
The cat jumped *off the roof and into the tree.*
The robbery occurred *after I left but before Jim arrived.*

When two *main* clauses are joined into one sentence with a coordinating conjunction, a comma precedes the conjunction (see 21a).

The test was difficult, *but* I think I did well.

When two main clauses are joined *without* a coordinating conjunction, they must be separated with a semicolon to avoid the error called a **comma splice** (see 11a).

The joke was not funny; it was insulting.

The semicolon sometimes separates two main clauses joined by a coordinating conjunction when the clauses are long or contain commas (see 22c). The semicolon *always* separates two main clauses linked by a conjunctive adverb (see the next section).

In a series of three or more items, commas separate the items, with *and* usually preceding the last item (see 21f-1).

The curtains were mostly white with splotches of pink, yellow, *and* brown.

Semicolons sometimes separate the items in a series if they are long or contain commas (see 22d).

The comma also separates coordinate adjectives (those which modify a noun or pronoun equally) when the adjectives are not joined by a coordinating conjunction (see 21f-2).

Wet, *slick* roads made driving dangerous.

The comma does *not* separate adjectives when the one nearer the noun is more closely related to it in meaning (see 21f-2).

She gave the teacher a *large red* apple.

2
Using conjunctive adverbs

One other kind of connecting word, called a **conjunctive adverb,** links only main clauses, not words, phrases, or subordinate clauses. Here is a list of common conjunctive adverbs.

accordingly	furthermore	moreover	similarly
also	hence	namely	still
anyway	however	nevertheless	then
besides	incidentally	next	thereafter
certainly	indeed	nonetheless	therefore
consequently	instead	now	thus
finally	likewise	otherwise	undoubtedly
further	meanwhile		

Compare the use of conjunctive adverbs, coordinating conjunctions, and subordinating conjunctions in the following sentences.

The game was long and boring; *however,* we stayed to the end.
The game was long and boring, *but* we stayed to the end.
Although the game was long and boring, we stayed to the end.

The game was exciting; *consequently*, we stayed to the end.
The game was exciting, *and* we stayed to the end.
Because the game was exciting, we stayed to the end.

In the first sentence of each group, the conjunctive adverbs *however* and *consequently* link two main clauses while at the same time acting as adverbs to modify the clauses they appear in. In the second sentence of each group, the coordinating conjunctions *but* and *and* also join two main clauses, but neither word modifies the clause that follows. In the third sentence of each group, the initial subordinating conjunctions *although* and *because* reduce the first clauses from main clauses to adverb modifiers.

gr **5d**

A simple test can distinguish a conjunctive adverb from a coordinating or subordinating conjunction. If the word can be moved from where it appears to elsewhere in the clause, then it is a conjunctive adverb:

The game was long and boring; *however*, we stayed to the end.
The game was long and boring; we stayed, *however*, to the end.
The game was long and boring; we stayed to the end, *however*.

If the word cannot be moved in this way, then it is a coordinating or subordinating conjunction. For example, we would not write *we stayed to the end but* or *the game although was long and boring*.

These differences among conjunctive adverbs, coordinating conjunctions, and subordinating conjunctions are important because they determine very different punctuation between clauses. (See the discussion of punctuation below.)

Note: Just as some words may serve as nouns, verbs, or modifiers depending on their function in a sentence (see pp. 135 and 143), so some connecting words may have more than one use. *After, before, until*, and some other words may be either prepositions or subordinating conjunctions. Some prepositions, such as *behind, in*, and *outside*, can serve also as adverbs, as in *He trailed behind*. Most relative pronouns are used also as interrogative pronouns to ask questions: *What time is it? Who left?* And some conjunctive adverbs, particularly *however*, may also serve simply as adverbs in sentences such as *However much it costs, we must have it*. Again, the part of speech of a word depends on its function in a sentence.

Punctuating sentences containing conjunctive adverbs

Two main clauses linked by a conjunctive adverb must be separated by a semicolon (see 22b). If they are separated by a comma, the result is a **comma splice.**

Comma splice	We hoped for sunshine, *instead*, we got rain.
Revised	We hoped for sunshine; *instead*, we got rain.

See Chapter 11 for a full discussion of comma splices.

A conjunctive adverb is almost always set off from its clause with a comma or commas.

> No one was injured; *however*, the car was totaled.
> No one was injured; the car, *however*, was totaled.
> No one was injured; the car was totaled, *however*.

The comma or commas are optional with some one-syllable conjunctive adverbs (especially *hence, now, then,* and *thus*) and are not used with a few others when they appear inside or at the ends of clauses.

> Interest rates rose; *thus* real estate prices declined.
>
> All the performances were sold out; the play *therefore* made a profit.
>
> We hoped for sunshine; we got rain *instead*.

EXERCISE 18

To practice compounding words, phrases, and clauses, combine each pair of sentences below into one sentence that is as short as possible without altering meaning. Use an appropriate connecting word of the type specified in parentheses, referring to the lists on pages 161 and 162 if necessary. You will have to add, delete, and rearrange words, and you may have to change or add punctuation.

Example:

The encyclopedia had some information. It was not detailed enough. (*Conjunctive adverb.*)

The encyclopedia had some information; *however*, it was not detailed enough.

1. The new model is more powerful than the old. It is heavier and less portable. (*Coordinating conjunction.*)
2. Frank Lloyd Wright was an influential architect. He is considered the leading architect of the twentieth century. (*Conjunctive adverb.*)
3. Television news will get better. I will give up news programs for newspapers. (*Correlative conjunction.*)
4. Physics is a difficult subject. It is an enjoyable subject. (*Coordinating conjunction.*)
5. The cheerleaders missed the bus. The back-up center also missed the bus. (*Coordinating conjunction.*)
6. Politicians cannot be shy people. They must be outgoing. (*Conjunctive adverb.*)
7. The newspaper publishes interesting feature articles. It publishes feeble editorials. (*Coordinating conjunction.*)
8. My mother attended Thomas Jefferson High School. My mother-in-law also attended Thomas Jefferson High School. (*Correlative conjunction.*)

9. The news stories from Uganda were censored. They were out of date because the censor had held on to them for so long. (*Conjunctive adverb.*)
10. The crocuses were blooming. There were no other signs of spring. (*Coordinating conjunction.*)

5e
Changing the usual order of the sentence

So far, all the examples of basic sentence grammar have been similar: the subject of the sentence comes first, naming the performer of the predicate's action, and the predicate comes second. This arrangement of subject and predicate describes most sentences that occur in writing, but we need to look briefly at four other kinds of sentences that alter this basic pattern.

1
Forming questions

We form questions in one of several ways. We may invert the normal subject-verb arrangement of statements:

The dog is barking. Is the dog barking?

We may use a question word such as *how, what, who, when, where, which,* or *why:*

What dog is barking?

Or we may use some combination of the two methods:

Why is the dog barking?

In each case a question mark signals that the sentence is a question.

2
Forming commands

We construct commands even more simply than we construct questions: we merely delete the subject of the sentence, *you.*

Open the window.
Go to the store.
Eat your spinach.
Leave me alone.

3
Writing passive sentences

In any sentence that uses a transitive verb—that is, in any sentence where the verb takes an object—we can move the object to the position of the subject and put the subject in the predicate. The result is a **passive sentence,** using the **passive voice** of the verb rather than the **active voice.** (See also Chapter 7, pp. 194–95.)

> Greg wrote the paper. [Active voice.]
>
> The paper was written by Greg. [Passive voice. *The paper,* which was the original object of *wrote,* becomes the sentence subject. The original sentence subject, *Greg,* appears in a prepositional phrase.]

The prepositional phrase specifying the subject of the active verb (the actor) may be omitted entirely if the actor is unknown or unimportant: *The house was flooded.*

A passive sentence is so called because its subject does not perform or initiate the action indicated by the verb. Rather, the subject *receives* the action. In passive sentences the verb is always a phrase consisting of some form of the verb *be* and the past participle of the main verb (*paper was written, exams are finished*). (See 7h and 18d for cautions against overuse of the passive voice.)

4 Writing sentences with postponed subjects

The subject follows the predicate in two sentence patterns that are not questions, commands, or passive sentences. In one pattern the normal word order is reversed for emphasis: *Then came the dawn. Up walked Henry.* This pattern occurs most often when the normal order is subject–intransitive verb–adverb. Then the adverb moves to the front of the sentence while subject and predicate reverse order.

A second kind of sentence with a postponed subject begins with either *it* or *there,* as in the following:

> v s
> There will be eighteen people attending the meeting.
>
> v s
> It was surprising that Cuomo was nominated.

The words *there* and *it* in such sentences are **expletives.** Their only function is to postpone the sentence subject. Expletive sentences are common, but they can be unemphatic because they add words and delay the sentence subject. Usually, the normal subject-predicate order is more effective: *Eighteen people will attend the meeting. Cuomo's nomination was surprising.* (See also 18e and 31c-3.)

EXERCISE 19

Form a question and a command from the following noun and verb pairs.

Example:

split, wood

Did you *split* all this *wood?*
Split the *wood* for our fire.

1. water, boil
2. music, stop
3. table, set
4. roll, dice
5. telephone, use

EXERCISE 20

Rewrite each passive sentence below as active, and rewrite each expletive construction to restore normal subject-predicate order. (For additional exercises with the passive voice and with expletives, see pp. 196, 298, and 420.)

1. "The Star-Spangled Banner" was written by Francis Scott Key.
2. The tarragon was added to the stew by the chef.
3. The football was thrown by the quarterback for more than forty yards.
4. It is uncertain whether microwave ovens are dangerous.
5. There was an audience of nearly ten thousand at the outdoor concert.

5f

Classifying sentences

We describe and classify sentences in two different ways: by function (statement, question, command, exclamation, and so forth) or by structure. Four basic sentence structures are possible: simple, compound, complex, and compound-complex.

1

Writing simple sentences

Simple sentences consist of a single main clause. The clause may contain phrases, and the subject, the verb, and its objects may be compound; but the sentence is simple as long as it contains only one complete main clause and no subordinate clause.

Last July was unusually hot.

In fact, both July and August were vicious months.

The summer made farmers leave the area for good or reduced them to bare existence. [Two predicates but only one subject.]

2
Writing compound sentences

A **compound sentence** consists of two or more main clauses. The clauses may be joined by a coordinating conjunction and a comma, by a semicolon alone, or by a conjunctive adverb and a semicolon.

> Last July was hot, but August was even hotter.
>
> The hot sun scorched the land to powder; the lack of rain made the soil untillable.
>
> The government later provided assistance; consequently, the remaining farmers gradually improved their lot.

3
Writing complex sentences

A sentence is **complex** if it contains one main clause and one or more subordinate clauses.

> Rain finally came, although many had left the area by then. [Main clause, then subordinate clause.]
>
> When the rain came, people rejoiced. [Subordinate clause, then main clause.]
>
> Those who remained were able to start anew because the government came to their aid. [Main clause containing subordinate clause, then another subordinate clause.]

Notice that length does not determine whether a sentence is complex or simple; both kinds can be short or long.

4
Writing compound-complex sentences

A **compound-complex sentence** has the characteristics of both the compound sentence (two or more main clauses) and the complex sentence (at least one subordinate clause).

> Even though government aid finally came, many people had already been reduced to poverty, and others had been forced to leave the area. [Subordinate clause, then main clause, then another main clause.]
>
> Some of the farmers who had left the area moved back gradually to their original homes, but several years passed before the land became as fertile as before. [Main clause containing subordinate clause, then another main clause, then another subordinate clause.]

EXERCISE 21

Mark the main clauses and subordinate clauses in the following sentences. Identify each sentence as simple, compound, complex, or compound-complex.

Example:

The police began patrolling more often when crime in the neighborhood increased.

MAIN

Complex: The police began patrolling more often

SUBORDINATE

when crime in the neighborhood increased.

1. Joseph Pulitzer endowed the Pulitzer Prizes.
2. Pulitzer, incidentally, was the publisher of the New York newspaper *The World.*
3. Although the first prizes were for journalism and letters only, Pulitzers are now awarded in music and other areas.
4. The police strike lasted a week, but no robberies occurred in that time.
5. Even though some say football has supplanted baseball as the national pastime, millions of people watch baseball every year, and they don't seem ready to stop.

EXERCISE 22

Combine each of the following groups of simple sentences to produce the kind of sentence specified in parentheses. You will have to add, delete, change, and rearrange words.

Example:

The traffic passed her house. It never stopped. (*Complex.*)
The traffic that passed her house never stopped.

1. Dinner was tasty. It did not fill us up. (*Compound.*)
2. The storm was predicted to be fierce. It passed by quickly. (*Complex.*)
3. The musical notes died away. Then a strange object filled the sky. (*Complex.*)
4. The wolves were afraid. They feared the fire. (*Simple.*)
5. We wanted the rumors to stop. We hoped for that. They did not. (*Compound-complex.*)

6

Case of Nouns and Pronouns

Case is the form of a noun or pronoun that shows the reader how it functions in a sentence—that is, whether it functions as a subject, as an object, or in some other way. The personal pronouns *I, we, he, she,* and *they* and the relative pronoun *who* have separate forms for three cases: subjective, possessive, and objective.

Subjective

I	we	he, she	they	who

Possessive

my	our	his, her	their	whose
mine	ours	his, hers	theirs	

Objective

me	us	him, her	them	whom

All other pronouns and all nouns have only two case forms: a possessive case (for instance, *your, boy's*); and a plain case (*you, boy*), which is the form listed in the dictionary and which serves all functions except that of the possessive. Since only *I, we, he, she, they,* and *who* change form for each case, we will focus on these pronouns in this chapter.

The **subjective form** is used when a pronoun is the subject of a sentence, the subject of a clause, the complement of a subject, or an appositive identifying a subject. (See 5a and 5c.)

Subject of sentence

She and *I* skied three days last week.
They tried to save the house.

Subject of subordinate clause

Give the money to the kids *who* cleaned up the house.
He is the man *who* I thought would win.

Subject of understood verb

Sarah has more money than *he* (has).
I am not as smart as *she* (is).

Subject complement

The editors of the paper were *he* and *I*.
They assumed it was *I*.

Appositive identifying subject

Only two members, Susan and *I*, went to the jazz festival.

The **objective form** of a pronoun is used when the pronoun is the direct or indirect object of a verb or verbal, the object of a preposition, the subject of an infinitive, or an appositive identifying an object. (See 5a and 5c.)

Object of verb

Lisa likes both Tom and *him*.
The woman *whom* they elected was experienced.
The exam gave *him* a headache.

Object of preposition

Most of *us* hated to get up.
I didn't know *whom* they laughed at.

Object of verbal

Electing *her* was easy. [Object of gerund.]

Having elected *her*, the committee adjourned. [Object of past participle.]

Mary ran to help *him*. [Object of infinitive.]

Subject of infinitive

We invited *them* to eat with us.
They asked *me* to speak.

Appositive identifying object

The judge fined both defendants, Joe and *her*.

The **possessive form** of a pronoun is used before nouns and gerunds.

Before a noun

His sisters needed *our* bicycles.

Before a gerund

Their flying to Nashville was my suggestion.

In addition, the possessive forms *mine, ours, yours, his, hers,* and *theirs* (and only those forms) may be used without a following noun, in the position of a noun.

IN NOUN POSITIONS

Hers is the racket on the table.
The blue Pinto is *mine* (*ours, yours, his, theirs*).

(For the possessive forms of nouns, see 23a.)

6a

Use the subjective case for all parts of compound subjects and for subject complements.

In compound subjects use the same pronoun form you would use if the pronoun stood alone as a subject.

SUBJECTS

Joan and *I* left, but *Bill* and *he* stayed.
After *she* and *I* left, the fight started.

If you are in doubt about the correct form, try each part of the subject in a separate sentence: *Joan left. I left.* Therefore, *Joan and I left.*

A pronoun following the forms of the verb *be* (*am, is, are, was, were*) is a subject complement (see 5a-3). Since it renames the subject, the pronoun is in the subjective case.

SUBJECT COMPLEMENTS

The ones who paid the bill were *you* and *I*.
It was *she* whom the governor finally appointed.

Sentences like these often sound stilted because expressions such as *It's me* and *It was her* are common in speech. In writing, unless we want to gain some special emphasis, we ordinarily use the more natural order: *You and I were the ones who paid the bill. The governor finally appointed her.*

6b

Use the objective case for all parts of compound objects.

In compound objects use the same pronoun form you would use if the pronoun stood alone as an object.

OBJECTS OF VERBS

We wanted to invite *Larry* and *her*. [Direct object.]
The coach gave *her* and *me* a lecture. [Indirect object.]

Objects of prepositions

Marty gave presents to *Gloria* and *me.*
The $10 gift was divided between *him* and *me.*

If you are in doubt about the correct form, try each part of the object in a separate sentence: *We wanted to invite Larry. We wanted to invite her.* Therefore, *We wanted to invite Larry and her.*

EXERCISE 1

From the pairs in parentheses, select the appropriate subjective or objective pronoun(s) for each of the following sentences.

Example:

"Between you and (*I, me*)," the salesman said, "this deal is a steal."

"Between you and *me,*" the salesman said, "this deal is a steal."

1. When the electricity went out, (*he, him*) and Jody tried to find the fuse box in the basement.
2. The previous tenant had not given the basement door key to (*he, him*) and Jody.
3. It was (*they, them*), not the previous tenant, who should have remembered the key.
4. The company offered jobs to (*she, her*) and (*I, me*).
5. After (*she, her*) and (*I, me*) had discussed the offers with several people, we both decided to decline.
6. I felt that the argument should remain between (*he, him*) and (*I, me*).
7. Moving to a new house upset (*she, her*) and Tracy, the two youngest children.
8. My parents had wanted all the children home for Thanksgiving but could afford to bring only Susanne and (*I, me*).
9. No one told us that (*he, him*) and George had left.
10. The guilty ones are (*she, her*) and Allen.

6c

Use the appropriate case when the plural pronouns *we* and *us* occur with a noun.

The case of the first-person plural pronoun used with a noun depends on the use of the noun.

Freezing weather is welcomed by *us* skaters. [*Skaters* is the object of the preposition *by.*]

We skaters welcome freezing weather. [*Skaters* is the subject of the sentence.]

6d

In appositives the case of a pronoun depends on the function of the word it describes or identifies.

The class elected two representatives, Debbie and *me*. [*Representatives* is the object of the verb *elected*, so the words in the appositive, *Debbie and me*, take the objective case.]

Two representatives, Debbie and *I*, were elected. [*Representatives* is the subject of this sentence, so the words in the appositive, *Debbie and I*, take the subjective case.]

If you are in doubt about case in an appositive, try the sentence without the word the appositive identifies: *The class elected Debbie and me; Debbie and I were elected.*

EXERCISE 2

From the pairs in parentheses, select the appropriate subjective or objective pronoun for each of the following sentences.

Example:

Convincing (*we, us*) veterans to vote yes on this issue will be difficult.

Convincing *us* veterans to vote yes on this issue will be difficult.

1. Obtaining enough protein is important to (*we, us*) vegetarians.
2. The true beneficiaries of this tax reform are (*we, us*) students.
3. The two most bashful people, (*he, him*) and Christine, turned out to be the best actors.
4. (*We, Us*) students appreciate clear directions on tests.
5. Two of (*we, us*) children, my sister Ellen and (*I, me*), gave our parents an anniversary party.

6e

The case of a pronoun after *than* or *as* in a comparison depends on the meaning.

When we use *than* and *as* in comparisons, we often do not complete the clauses they introduce: *Joe likes spaghetti more than* (*he likes*) *ravioli.* Without the words in parentheses, this sentence is clear because it can have only one sensible meaning. But in *Annie liked Ben more than Joe,* we cannot tell whether *Annie liked Ben more than* (*she liked*) *Joe* or *Annie liked Ben more than Joe* (*liked him*).

When such sentences end with a pronoun, the case of the

pronoun indicates what words have been omitted. When the pronoun is subjective, it must serve as the subject of the omitted verb.

Annie liked Ben more than *he* (liked Ben).

When the pronoun is objective, it must serve as the object of the omitted verb.

Annie liked Ben more than (she liked) *him.*

Be careful to choose the pronoun form that fits your meaning.

6f
Use the objective case for pronouns that are subjects or objects of infinitives.

SUBJECT OF INFINITIVE

We wanted Gail and *her* to win the bowling tournament. [*Gail and her* is the compound subject of the infinitive *to win.*]

OBJECT OF INFINITIVE

They expect to meet *him.* [*Him* is the object of the infinitive *to meet.*]

6g
The form of the pronoun *who* depends on its function in its clause.

1
At the beginning of questions use *who* if the question is about a subject, *whom* if it is about an object.

To determine the form of *who* at the beginning of a question, construct an answer to the question, using a personal pronoun in the answer. The case of the pronoun in the answer will indicate the required case of *who* in the question.

(*Who, Whom*) left the freezer door open? *She* left it open. Therefore, *Who* left the freezer door open?

(*Who, Whom*) does one ask? One asks *him.* Therefore, *Whom* does one ask?

(*Who, Whom*) is the pizza for? It is for *them.* Therefore, *Whom* is the pizza for?

In speech the subjective case *who* is commonly used whenever it is the first word of a question, regardless of whether it is a subject or an object. But writing requires a distinction between the forms.

Spoken	*Who* should we blame?
Written	*Whom* should we blame? [Object of verb *blame.*]

ca
6g

2

In subordinate clauses use *who* and *whoever* for all subjects, *whom* and *whomever* for all objects.

The case of a pronoun in a subordinate clause depends on its function in the clause, regardless of whether the clause itself functions as a subject, an object, or a modifier. (See 5c-4.)

Give the clothes to *whoever* needs them. [*Whoever* is the subject of *needs.* The entire clause *whoever needs them* is the object of the preposition *to.*]

I don't know *whom* the mayor appointed. [*Whom* is the object of *appointed: the mayor appointed whom.* The whole clause *whom the mayor appointed* is the object of the verb *know.*]

Whom he appointed is not my concern. [Again, *whom* is the object of *appointed.* This time the clause is the subject of the sentence.]

Larry is the man *whom* most people prefer. [*Whom* is the object of *prefer: people prefer whom.* The clause *whom most people prefer* modifies the noun *man.*]

If you have trouble determining which form of *who* or *whoever* to choose, rewrite the subordinate clause as a separate sentence, substituting a personal pronoun for the *who* form. The form of the personal pronoun will be the same as the required form of *who.* For instance:

I remember (*who, whom*) was sitting on the sofa. *He* was sitting on the sofa. Therefore, I remember *who* was sitting on the sofa.

The manager hired the woman (*who, whom*) his boss recommended. His boss recommended *her.* Therefore, the manager hired the woman *whom* his boss recommended.

Note: Don't let expressions such as *I think* and *she says* confuse you when they come between the subject *who* and its verb.

He is the man *who* I think *was* on duty yesterday. [*Who* is the subject of *was,* not the object of *think.*]

I asked the mechanic *who* Barbara said *was* her friend. [*Who* is the subject of *was,* not the object of *said.*]

To choose between *who* and *whom* in such constructions, delete the interrupting phrase: *I asked the mechanic who was her friend.*

EXERCISE 3

From the pairs in parentheses, select the appropriate form of the pronoun in each of the following sentences.

Example:

My mother asked me (*who, whom*) I was going out with.
My mother asked me *whom* I was going out with.

1. (*Who, Whom*) is next in line for the throne?
2. The author (*who, whom*) you are less familiar with may be the better of the two.
3. I went to the barber (*who, whom*) Jack said was good.
4. There is always hard work for (*whoever, whomever*) wants it.
5. About (*who, whom*) did you hear that rumor?
6. The owner of the pool, (*whoever, whomever*) it is, should invite us all for a swim.
7. (*Who, Whom*) is Elaine talking to?
8. (*Whoever, Whomever*) parked this Cadillac needs to learn how to drive.
9. The school administrators suspended Jurgen, (*who, whom*) they suspected of setting the fire.
10. (*Who, Whom*) is that man in the tuxedo?

EXERCISE 4

Combine each pair of sentences below into one sentence that contains a clause beginning with *who* or *whom*. Be sure to use the appropriate case form. You will have to add, delete, and rearrange words, and more than one answer may be possible in each case.

Example:

David is the candidate. We think David deserves to win.
David is the candidate *who* we think deserves to win.

1. Some children have undetected hearing problems. These children may do poorly in school.
2. Carolyn knows the person. We invited the person to speak.
3. The customer was dissatisfied. The customer returned the product.
4. Nancy is an author. She has written several very funny stories.
5. Truman was a president. My father greatly admired Truman.

6h

Ordinarily, use the possessive form of a pronoun or noun immediately before a gerund.

A **gerund** is the *-ing* form of the verb (*running, sleeping*) used as a noun (see 5c-2). Like nouns, gerunds are commonly preceded by possessive nouns and pronouns: *her marriage* (noun), *her marrying* (gerund), *our vote* (noun), *our voting* (gerund).

> He disapproved of *their* exercising. [Compare *their exercise.*]
> *Jo's* failing in history surprised us. [Compare *Jo's failure.*]

Notice the difference between the gerund and the present participle. Both have the same *-ing* form. But whereas the gerund serves as a subject or object, the participle serves as an adjective.

> We often met *John* coming home late. [*Coming home late* is a participial phrase modifying *John.*]
>
> *John's* coming home late worried us. [*Coming home late* is a gerund phrase serving as the subject of *worried.*]

The case of a noun or pronoun before the *-ing* form of a verb can subtly influence the meaning of a sentence.

> We noticed *Ann* driving. [The emphasis is on *Ann,* who happened to be driving when she was noticed. *Driving* is a participle.]
>
> We noticed *Ann's* driving. [The emphasis is on Ann's activity—her driving. *Driving* is a gerund.]

Notice also that a gerund usually is not preceded by the possessive when the possessive would create an awkward construction.

Awkward	We heard a rumor about everybody's on the team wanting to quit.
Less awkward	We heard a rumor about everybody on the team wanting to quit.
Better	We heard a rumor that everybody on the team wants to quit.

EXERCISE 5

Correct all inappropriate case forms in the following paragraph, and explain the function of each case form.

Mike and I arrived at the campground just after sunset. The manager, whom we thought looked like a movie star, was naturally reluctant to let we ruffians in, but eventually she showed us to a tiny campsite. When we unpacked the tent, Mike and me discovered that we were missing two tent pegs. Searching in the dark, Mike managed to find some sturdy sticks to use as pegs, and between he and I we managed to set up the tent. But Mike was apparently more tired than me, because he didn't drive his pegs deeply enough into the ground. Several hours later, when him and me had finally dozed off, the tent collapsed on top of us. Us yelling at each other woke the people in the next campsite, who were even less amused than us by our plight. We piled everything into the car as fast as possible and took off down the road for a motel.

7
Verb Forms, Tense, Mood, and Voice

VERB FORMS

All verbs except *be* have five forms:

Infinitive: close, run
Past tense: closed, ran
Past participle: closed, run
Present participle: closing, running
***-s* form:** closes, runs

The first three forms are the verb's **principal parts.** The **infinitive** (sometimes called the **plain form**) is the dictionary form of the verb. It is the form we use when the verb's action occurs in the present and the subject is a plural noun or the pronoun *I, we, you,* or *they.*

We *live* in the city.
Examinations *frighten* me.
They *go* downtown.

The **past-tense form** indicates that the verb's action occurred in the past. It is usually formed by adding *-d* or *-ed* to the infinitive, although for some irregular verbs it is formed in other ways (see 7a).

We *lived* in the city.
Examinations *frightened* me.
They *went* downtown. [Irregular verb.]

The **past participle** is the verb form we use with *have, has,* or *had* (*have climbed, had opened*); with a form of *be* in the passive voice (*was created;* see 7h); and by itself to modify nouns and pronouns (*sliced bread*). Except for some irregular verbs (see 7a), the past participle is the same as the past-tense form.

We have *lived* in the city.
Examinations have *frightened* me.
They had *gone* downtown. [Irregular verb.]

In addition to the three principal parts, all verbs have two other forms, a present participle and an *-s* form. We form the **present participle** by adding *-ing* to the verb's infinitive, as in *acting, eating, living, studying.* The present participle can modify nouns and pronouns (*boiling water, the girl driving*); and, as a gerund, it functions as a noun (*Running exhausts me*). In addition, the present participle may combine with forms of the verb *be* (*am, is, are, was,* and *were*) to indicate continuing action: *is buying, was finishing, were swimming.*

vb 7

The **-s form** of the verb is the one ending in *-s* or *-es* (*begs, lives, is, has*). We use it when the verb's action occurs in the present and the subject is third-person singular—that is, a singular noun (*dog, Harry*), a singular indefinite pronoun (*everybody, someone*), or the personal pronoun *he, she,* or *it.*

The dog *begs.*
Harry *lives* in town.
Everybody *is* asleep.
She *has* a car.

The verb *be* has eight forms rather than the five forms of most other verbs. In addition to its infinitive *be,* its present participle *being,* and its past participle *been, be* has three distinct forms in the present tense and two in the past tense.

	I	*he, she, it*	*we, you, they*
PRESENT TENSE	am	is	are
PAST TENSE	was	was	were

Helping verbs, also called **auxiliary verbs,** combine with a verb's infinitive, present participle, or past participle to indicate time and other kinds of meaning, as in *can run, was sleeping, had been eaten.* These combinations are **verb phrases** (see also 7d). Since the infinitive, present participle, or past participle in any verb phrase always carries the principal meaning, it is sometimes called the **main verb.**

Some helping verbs—*shall* and *will; have, has,* and *had; do, does,* and *did;* and the forms of *be* (*am, is, are, was, were, been,* and *being*)—combine with main verbs to indicate time and voice (see pp. 187 and 194).

I *will go.*
She *had run.*
Sylvia *did* not *want* grapes.
The doors *were opened.*
The child *was awakened.*
They *have been seen.*

Helping verbs such as *can, could, may, might, must, ought, shall, should, will,* and *would* combine with main verbs to indicate necessity, obligation, permission, possibility, and the like.

She *can write.*	You *must go.*
I *should study.*	I *might come.*

The two kinds of helping verbs sometimes work together to create complex verb phrases.

You *might have told* me.
I *may be sleeping.*
You *ought to have eaten.*

7a
Use the correct form of regular and irregular verbs.

As indicated above, most verbs are **regular;** that is, they form their past tense and past participle by adding *-d* or *-ed* to the infinitive.

INFINITIVE	PAST TENSE	PAST PARTICIPLE
live	lived	lived
act	acted	acted
frighten	frightened	frightened

Since the past tense and past participle are created simply by adding to the infinitive and since the two are identical, the forms of regular verbs do not often cause problems in speech and writing (but see 7c).

Some verbs, however, do not follow the pattern of regular verbs. About two hundred English verbs are **irregular;** that is, they form their past tense and past participle in some irregular way. We have to learn the parts of the verbs by memorizing them, just as we learn new words.

Most irregular verbs form the past tense and the past participle by changing an internal vowel.

INFINITIVE	PAST TENSE	PAST PARTICIPLE
begin	began	begun
come	came	come
ring	rang	rung

Some irregular verbs change an internal vowel and add an *-n* in the past participle.

INFINITIVE	PAST TENSE	PAST PARTICIPLE
break	broke	broken
draw	drew	drawn
grow	grew	grown

Some irregular verbs have the same form in both the past tense and the past participle or in all three forms.

INFINITIVE	PAST TENSE	PAST PARTICIPLE
sleep	slept	slept
let	let	let
set	set	set

Check a dictionary if you have any doubt about a verb's principal parts. The form listed there is the infinitive. If no other forms are listed, the verb is regular; that is, both the past tense and the past participle add *-d* or *-ed* to the infinitive (*agree, agreed; sympathize, sympathized; talk, talked*). If the verb is irregular, the dictionary will list the infinitive, the past tense, and the past participle in that order (*speak, spoke, spoken; go, went, gone*). If the dictionary gives only two forms (as in *hear, heard* or *think, thought*), then the past tense and the past participle are the same.

The following list includes the most common irregular verbs. (When a principal part has two possible forms, as in *dove* and *dived,* both are included.) Look over this list to find verbs whose parts you are unsure of. Then spend some time memorizing the parts and trying them in sentences.

INFINITIVE	PAST TENSE	PAST PARTICIPLE
arise	arose	arisen
become	became	become
begin	began	begun
bid	bid	bid
bite	bit	bitten, bit
blow	blew	blown
break	broke	broken
bring	brought	brought
burst	burst	burst
buy	bought	bought
catch	caught	caught
choose	chose	chosen
come	came	come
cut	cut	cut
dive	dived, dove	dived
do	did	done
draw	drew	drawn
dream	dreamed, dreamt	dreamed, dreamt
drink	drank	drunk
drive	drove	driven
eat	ate	eaten
fall	fell	fallen
find	found	found
flee	fled	fled
fly	flew	flown

Infinitive	Past tense	Past participle
forget	forgot	forgotten, forgot
freeze	froze	frozen
get	got	got, gotten
give	gave	given
go	went	gone
grow	grew	grown
hang	hung, hanged (executed)	hung, hanged
hear	heard	heard
hide	hid	hidden
hold	held	held
keep	kept	kept
know	knew	known
lay	laid	laid
lead	led	led
leave	left	left
let	let	let
lie	lay	lain
lose	lost	lost
pay	paid	paid
prove	proved	proved, proven
ride	rode	ridden
ring	rang	rung
rise	rose	risen
run	ran	run
say	said	said
see	saw	seen
set	set	set
shake	shook	shaken
sing	sang, sung	sung
sink	sank, sunk	sunk
sit	sat	sat
slide	slid	slid
speak	spoke	spoken
spring	sprang, sprung	sprung
stand	stood	stood
steal	stole	stolen
swim	swam	swum
take	took	taken
tear	tore	torn
throw	threw	thrown
wear	wore	worn
wind	wound	wound
write	wrote	written

EXERCISE 1

For each irregular verb in parentheses, supply either the past tense or past participle, as appropriate, and identify the form you used.

Example:

Though we had (*hide*) the cash box, it was (*steal*).

Though we had *hidden* the cash box, it was *stolen*. [Two past participles.]

1. He (*dream*) that he (*sing*) the National Anthem at the opening game.
2. He (*keep*) bringing out more food until finally they had all (*eat*) too much.
3. Margie (*choose*) a good spot and then Joe (*hang*) the picture.
4. After she had (*speak*) about interest rates, the economist (*draw*) some interesting conclusions.
5. Because the day was so dark, it seemed as though the sun had never (*rise*).
6. Before we could stop him, my cousin had (*drink*) all the chocolate milk and had (*eat*) all the cookies.
7. The fans were encouraged because their team had not (*lose*) a home game all season.
8. The wind (*blow*) and my hands almost (*freeze*).
9. If we had not (*leave*) the table, we would have (*fall*) asleep.
10. The dry spell was (*break*) when the rains (*begin*) again.

7b

Distinguish between *sit* and *set* and between *lie* and *lay*.

The principal parts of *sit* and *set* and of *lie* and *lay* are easy to confuse. Here are the forms of the four verbs.

INFINITIVE	PAST TENSE	PAST PARTICIPLE
sit	sat	sat
set	set	set
lie	lay	lain
lay	laid	laid

Sit and *lie,* as in *Sit down* and *Lie down,* mean "be seated" and "recline," respectively. They are both **intransitive verbs:** they cannot take objects. *Set* and *lay,* as in *Set the eggs down carefully* and *Lay the floor boards there,* mean "put" or "place." They are **transitive verbs** and usually take objects. (See 5a-3.)

Angela *lies* down every afternoon. [No object.]
Carter *laid* the plans on the table. [*Plans* is the object of *laid.*]
The dog *sits* by the back door. [No object.]
Mr. Flood *set* the jug down roughly. [*Jug* is the object of *set.*]

EXERCISE 2

Choose the correct verb from the pair given in parentheses and then supply the past tense or past participle, as appropriate.

Example:

After I washed all the windows, I (*lie, lay*) down the squeegee and then I myself (*lie, lay*) down for a nap.

After I washed all the windows, I *laid* down the squeegee and then I myself *lay* down for a nap.

1. Last Christmas, Jay (*lie, lay*) in bed all day with a fever.
2. When he awoke, Millard (*sit, set*) up in his chair, picked up the fallen book, and (*sit, set*) it on the table.
3. The spider (*sit, set*) in its web and (*lie, lay*) in wait for its prey.
4. After she had (*sit, set*) the table, she (*lie, lay*) a cloth over it.
5. Joan's wallet had (*lie, lay*) in the street for two days.

vb
7c

7c

Use the *-s* and *-ed* forms of the verb when they are required.

Some English dialects use the infinitive of the verb instead of the *-s* form that is required by standard English whenever the subject is third-person singular and the verb's action occurs in the present.

The roof *leak* (*leaks*).
Harry *live* (*lives*) in town.
He *don't* (*doesn't*) care.
Nobody *have* (*has*) a car.
She *be* (*is*) happy.

In sentences like these, standard English requires the forms in parentheses.

Some dialects also omit the *-ed* or *-d* ending from the past tense or past participle of regular verbs when the ending is not clearly pronounced.

We *bag* (*bagged*) groceries.
He was *suppose* (*supposed*) to call.
I bought a *use* (*used*) book.
Sue has *ask* (*asked*) for help.

In standard English, however, the *-ed* and *-d* ending is required for regular verbs whenever (1) the verb's action occurred in the past (*we bagged*); (2) the past participle functions as a modifier (*used books*); and (3) the past participle combines with a form of *be* or *have* (*were supposed, has asked*).

EXERCISE 3

Supply the correct form of each verb in parentheses. Be careful to include *-s* and *-ed* (or *-d*) endings where they are needed for standard English.

A teacher sometimes (*ask*) too much of a student. In high school I was once (*punish*) for being sick. I had (*miss*) some school, and I (*realize*) that I would fail a test unless I had a chance to make up the class work. I (*discuss*) the problem with the teacher, but he said I was (*suppose*) to make up the work while I was sick. At that I (*walk*) out of the class. I (*receive*) a failing grade then, but it did not change my attitudes. Today I still balk when a teacher (*make*) unreasonable demands or (*expect*) miracles.

7d

Use helping verbs when they are required.

Helping verbs combine with the infinitives, present participles, and past participles of verbs to indicate time and other kinds of meaning (see p. 180). In some English dialects the helping verb is omitted:

The owl (*is*) *hooting*.
I (*have*) *taken* French.
Sara (*has*) *been* at home.
That (*would*) *be* awful.

However, standard English requires the helping verbs in these sentences and in others like them.

Often, the omission of a helping verb creates an incomplete sentence, or **sentence fragment,** because a present participle (*hooting*) or an irregular past participle (*taken, been*) cannot stand alone as the only verb in a sentence (see Chapter 10).

Fragments Few people *smoking*. The toy *broken*.

Revised Few people *were smoking*. The toy *was broken*.

Smoking and *broken* are **nonfinite,** or "unfinished," verbs: they can modify other words, but they cannot serve as sentence predicates. Only a **finite,** or "finished," verb can serve as a sentence predicate, and to be made finite a nonfinite verb must be combined with a helping verb. (See p. 148 for additional discussion of finite and nonfinite verbs.)

EXERCISE 4

Add helping verbs in the following sentences where they are needed for standard English.

1. The floors squeak loudly, and we been meaning to repair them.
2. The essay written by a woman who earned a degree in biology and worked as a laboratory technician.
3. They expected that the play be canceled because of poor attendance.

4. Joey complaining that his course load leaves him no time for running, and he talking about dropping physics.
5. Most of the harsh words spoken at the meeting been left out of the minutes.

TENSE

Tense is the attribute of a verb that shows the time of the verb's action in relation to the time at which the writer writes or the speaker speaks. The **simple tenses** indicate that an action or state of being is present, past, or future.

Simple tenses	Regular verb	Irregular verb
Present	You *work.*	You *write.*
Past	You *worked.*	You *wrote.*
Future	You *will work.*	You *will write.*

The present tense uses the verb's infinitive (*work, write*) or, for third-person singular subjects, its *-s* form (*he works, she writes*). The past tense uses the verb's past-tense form (*worked, wrote*). The future tense uses the helping verb *will* or *shall* and the verb's infinitive.

The **perfect tenses** indicate that an action was or will be completed before another time or action. (The term *perfect* derives from the Latin *perfectus,* meaning "completed.") The perfect tenses are formed with the helping verb *have* plus the verb's past participle.

Perfect tenses	Regular verb	Irregular verb
Present perfect	You *have worked.*	You *have written.*
Past perfect	You *had worked.*	You *had written.*
Future perfect	You *will have worked.*	You *will have written.*

The present perfect tense uses the infinitive *have* or, for third-person singular subjects, the *-s* form, *has.* The past perfect tense uses the past-tense form *had* for all subjects. The future perfect tense uses *will have* or *shall have* for all subjects.

In addition to the simple and perfect tenses, all verbs have a set of **progressive forms,** sometimes called the **progressive tense,** that indicate continuing (therefore progressive) action. The progressive uses the *-ing* form of the verb plus a form of *be* to show time. Regular and irregular verbs do not differ.

Progressive forms	
Present	You *are working/writing.*
Past	You *were working/writing.*
Future	You *will be working/writing.*
Present perfect	You *have been working/writing.*
Past perfect	You *had been working/writing.*
Future perfect	You *will have been working/writing.*

We use the helping verb *do* (*does*) or its past tense *did*, together with the infinitive of the verb, in asking questions, making negative statements, and showing emphasis.

> *Does* he *write* every day? [Question.]
> He *did* not *write* every day. [Negation.]
> He *does write* every day. [Emphasis.]

7e
Use the appropriate tense to express your meaning.

For native speakers of English, the selection of an appropriate verb tense usually presents few problems. Most errors in tense are actually errors in verb form like those discussed in the preceding sections—misusing the principal parts of irregular verbs, omitting *-d* or *-ed* endings, and omitting helping verbs. Still, errors in tense do sometimes occur, so it is a good idea to edit your work carefully to ensure that the tenses of verbs accurately express your meaning.

Any problems in verb tense are most likely to occur with some special uses of the present tense and with the perfect tenses.

1
Observe the special uses of the present tense.

The present tense generally indicates action occurring at the time of speaking, as in *She understands what you mean* or *From here I see the river and the docks*. It is also used in several special situations.

To indicate habitual or recurring action

> Abby *goes* to New York every Friday.
> The store *opens* at ten o'clock.

To state a general truth

> The mills of the gods *grind* slowly.
> The earth *is* round.

To discuss the content of literature, film, and so on

> Huckleberry Finn *has* adventures we all would like to experience.
> In that article the author *examines* several causes of crime.

To indicate future time

> Our friends *arrive* the day after tomorrow.
> Ted *leaves* in the next half-hour.

(Notice that in sentences like the last two, time is really indicated by the phrases *the day after tomorrow* and *in the next half-hour*.)

2
Observe the uses of the perfect tenses.

The perfect tenses generally indicate an action completed before another specific time or action. The present perfect tense also indicates action begun in the past and continued into the present.

PRESENT PERFECT

Hannah *has fed* the dog, so we can go. [Action is completed at the time of the statement.]

Hannah *has* always *fed* the dog. [Action began in the past but continues now.]

PAST PERFECT

Hannah *had fed* the dog by the time we were ready. [Action was completed before another past action.]

FUTURE PERFECT

Hannah *will have fed* the dog a thousand times by the end of the month. [The phrase *by the end of the month* indicates the future. The future perfect *will have fed* indicates that Hannah will complete the thousandth feeding before the specified time.]

7f
Use the appropriate sequence of verb tenses.

The term **sequence of tenses** refers to the relation between the verb in a main clause and the verbs or verbals in subordinate clauses or verbal phrases (see 5c). The tenses need not be identical as long as they reflect changes in actual or relative time. For example, in the sentence *He had left before I arrived* the past tense *arrived* is in normal sequence with the past perfect *had left.* The few conventions governing tense sequence are discussed below. (For a discussion of tense shifts—changes *not* required by meaning—see 13b.)

1
Generally, the verb in a subordinate clause may be in any tense required by meaning.

As long as the tense of the verb in the main clause is neither past nor past perfect (see 7f-2 below), the tense in the subordinate clause need only reflect your meaning. In the following sentences all the verb forms follow a clear and natural sequence, though the tenses in main and subordinate clauses are different.

Mike *knows* that Susan *visited* New Orleans. [Mike's present knowledge is about something that happened in the past, Susan's visit.]

Mike *has known* all along that Susan *will visit* New Orleans. [Mike's knowledge began in the past and continues; Susan's going to New Orleans lies in the future.]

Susan *will explain* to Mike why she *changed* her plans. [The explanation lies in the future, but the change of plans occurred some time in the past.]

Note that any change of tense between a main and a subordinate clause must be logical. The sentence *My family always keeps pets because we liked them* does not seem logical because *liked* indicates that the liking is past and thus is not a reason to keep pets in the present.

2
The verb in a subordinate clause must be past or past perfect if the verb in the main clause is past or past perfect.

We *talked* for a long time after we *returned* home. [Since the talking took place in the past, the return home must also have occurred in the past. The past perfect *had returned* would also indicate that the return occurred at a time before the past talking. But the present *return* or the future *will return* would make no sense in the sentence.]

My friend *had left* before I *arrived*. [The past perfect *had left* indicates that the friend's leaving occurred earlier than the past arrival.]

Exception: When a subordinate clause expresses a general truth such as *The earth is round,* use the present tense even though the verb of the main clause is in the past or past perfect tense.

I never *realized* that many marriages *are* genuinely happy.

3
Observe the appropriate tense sequence with infinitives.

The tense of an infinitive is determined by the tense of the verb in the predicate. The **present infinitive** is the verb's plain form preceded by *to* (see 5c-2). It indicates action *at the same time* as or *later* than that of the verb.

I *went to see* a World Series game last year. [The going and the seeing occurred at the same time in the past.]

I *want to see* a World Series game this year. [The wanting is present; the seeing is still in the future.]

I *would have liked to see* (not *to have seen*) the other World Series games last year. [The present infinitive indicates the same past time as *would have liked.*]

The verb's **perfect infinitive** consists of *to have* followed by the past participle, as in *to have talked, to have won.* It indicates action *earlier* than that of the verb.

Sarah *would like* (not *would have liked*) *to have heard* Sylvia Plath read her poetry. [The liking occurs in the present; the hearing would have occurred in the past.]

The election *was thought to have been rigged.* [The rigging of the election occurred before the thinking about it.]

4
Observe the appropriate tense sequence with participles.

Like the tense of an infinitive, the tense of a participle is determined by the tense of the verb in the predicate. The present participle shows action occurring *at the same time* as that of the verb.

Driving across the United States, he *was astonished* by the vast spaces. [The driving and the astonishment occurred in the same past time.]

The past participle and the present perfect participle show action occurring *earlier* than that of the verb.

Exhausted by overwork, Sheila *remained* at home for two weeks. [The exhaustion occurred before Sheila remained home.]

Having lived all his life in the country, he *is frightened* by cities. [Life in the country preceded the fear of cities.]

EXERCISE 5

Revise the following sentences so that the sequence of verb tenses is appropriate. Some items have more than one possible answer.

Example:
Hedy had hoped to have been elected.
Hedy had hoped *to be elected.*

1. My parents ate before I have arrived home from work.
2. When he runs his next marathon, Jim will have worn different shoes.
3. We boycotted any grapes to have come from South Africa.
4. Believing that the design is unsafe, the stagehands had refused to put up the set for the new play.
5. The archaeologist entered the tomb after the bats inside it have been killed.

6. The jury recommends leniency because the criminal was so young.
7. The mechanic would have liked to have owned the car.
8. She was on the critical list since she fell yesterday.
9. Many shopkeepers should have done more to have protected themselves against robberies.
10. Having driven without my glasses on, I caused an accident.

EXERCISE 6

The tenses in each of the following sentences are in correct sequence. Change the tense of one verb as instructed in parentheses. Then change the tense of infinitives, participles, and other verbs as necessary to restore correct sequence. Some items have more than one possible answer.

Example:

He will call when he reaches his destination. (*Change will call to called.*)

He called when he *reached* (or *had reached*) his destination.

1. High school students are taking preparatory classes so that they will do well on the SAT. (*Change are taking to were taking.*)
2. Everyone believes that the Hitler diaries are authentic because a well-known historian has declared them so. (*Change believes to believed.*)
3. Everyone who auditions for the play is given a part. (*Change auditions to auditioned.*)
4. I would like to have attended that concert. (*Change would like to would have liked.*)
5. The elderly man hoped that his children would visit him over Chanukah. (*Change hoped to hopes.*)

MOOD

Mood in grammar is a verb form that indicates the writer's or speaker's attitude toward what he or she is saying. The **indicative mood** states a fact or opinion or asks a question. The **imperative mood** expresses a command or gives a direction. The **subjunctive mood** expresses a requirement, a desire, or a suggestion, or it states a condition that is contrary to fact. The three moods are illustrated in these sentences:

INDICATIVE	They *need* our help. [Opinion.] Marie *works* only on Saturday. [Fact.] Why *does* she *work* on Saturday? [Question.]
IMPERATIVE	*Work* only on Saturdays. [Command.] *Turn* right at the light. [Direction.]

SUBJUNCTIVE Her father urged that she *work* only on Saturdays. [Suggestion.]

Regulations require that applications *be* in writing. [Requirement.]

I wish that I *swam* better. [Desire.]

If she *were* to get sick, her studies would suffer. [Condition contrary to present fact.]

Notice the distinctive features of the imperative and the subjunctive. The imperative omits the subject of the sentence: (*You*) *Work only on Saturdays.* The subjunctive uses only the infinitive of the verb in the present tense, no matter what the subject is (see the first subjunctive sentence above). The present subjunctive form of *be* is *be* rather than *am, is,* or *are* (second subjunctive sentence). In the past tense of the subjunctive all verbs except *be* use their past tense (third subjunctive sentence); *be* uses *were* for all subjects (fourth subjunctive sentence). (For a discussion of keeping mood consistent within and among sentences, see 13b.)

7g
Use the subjunctive verb forms appropriately.

Although in the past English used distinctive subjunctive verb forms in many contexts, such forms appear now only in two kinds of constructions and in a few idiomatic expressions.

1
Use the subjunctive *were* in contrary-to-fact clauses beginning with *if* or expressing a wish.

If I *were* you, I'd see a doctor.
If the rash *were* treatable, she would have treated it.
I wish Jeannie *were* my doctor.

NOTE: The indicative form *was* (*I wish Jeannie was my doctor*) is common in speech and in some informal writing, but the subjunctive *were* is usual in formal English.

2
Use the subjunctive in *that* clauses following verbs that demand, request, or recommend.

Verbs such as *ask, insist, urge, require, recommend,* and *suggest* often precede subordinate clauses beginning with *that* and containing the substance of the request or suggestion. The verb in such *that* clauses should be in the subjunctive mood.

The psychologist urged that the patient *be released.*
The law required that he *report* weekly.
Julie's mother insisted that she *stay* home.
Instructors commonly ask that papers *be finished* on time.

Note: These constructions have widely used alternative forms that do not require the subjunctive, such as *The law required him to report weekly* or *Julie's mother insisted on her staying home.*

vb 7g

3 Use the subjunctive in some set phrases and idioms.

Several English expressions commonly use the subjunctive. For example:

Come rain or *come* shine.
Be that as it may.
The people *be* damned.

EXERCISE 7

Revise the following sentences with appropriate subjunctive verb forms.

Example:

I would help the old man if there was a way I could reach him.
I would help the old man if there *were* a way I could reach him.

1. The letter requests that we are patient.
2. If I was a rich man, I'd still clip coupons from the paper.
3. The syllabus requires that each student writes three papers and takes two essay tests.
4. They treat me as if I was their son.
5. I wish the lighting in the office was better because my eyes are strained.

VOICE

Verbs that take objects (transitive verbs) can show whether their subjects are acting or are acted upon. In the **active voice** the subject names the actor.

David wrote the paper.
Bookies coordinate illegal bets.

In the **passive voice** the subject names the object or receiver of the action.

The paper was written by David.
Illegal bets are coordinated by bookies.

The passive voice of a verb always consists of the appropriate form of the helping verb *be* plus the past participle of the main verb. Other helping verbs may also be present.

> Senators *are elected* for six-year terms.
> Jerry *has been given* complete freedom.

To change a sentence from active to passive voice, we convert the direct object or the indirect object of the verb into the subject of the verb.

ACTIVE	We *gave* Jerry complete freedom.
PASSIVE	Jerry *was given* complete freedom. [Indirect object becomes subject.]
PASSIVE	Complete freedom *was given* (to) Jerry. [Direct object becomes subject.]

To change a sentence from passive to active voice, we convert the verb's subject into a direct or an indirect object and substitute a new subject for the previous one.

PASSIVE	Sally *was bitten* by Jamie's dog.
ACTIVE	Jamie's dog *bit* Sally.
PASSIVE	The statement *was read* at a press conference.
ACTIVE	The company's representative *read* the statement at a press conference.

7h

Generally, prefer the active voice. Use the passive voice when the actor is unknown or unimportant.

Because the passive omits or de-emphasizes the actor (the performer of the verb's action), it can deprive writing of vigor and is often vague or confusing. The active voice is usually stronger, clearer, and more forthright.

WEAK PASSIVE	The exam was thought by us to be unfair because we were tested on material that was not covered in the course.
STRONG ACTIVE	We thought the exam unfair because it tested us on material the course did not cover.

The passive voice is useful in two situations: when the actor is unknown and when the actor is unimportant or less important than the object of the action.

> Ray Appleton *was murdered* after he returned home. [The murderer is presumably unknown, and in any event Ray Appleton's death is the point of the sentence.]

In the first experiment acid *was added* to the solution. [The person who added the acid, perhaps the writer, is less important than the fact that acid was added. Passive sentences are common in scientific writing.]

Except in such situations, however, you should prefer the active voice in your writing. (See 18d and 31c-3 for additional cautions against the passive voice.)

pass
7h

EXERCISE 8

To practice using the two voices of the verb, convert the following sentences from active to passive or from passive to active. (In converting from passive to active, you may have to add a subject for the new sentence.) Which version of each sentence seems more effective, and why? (For additional exercises with the passive voice, see pp. 167, 298, and 420.)

Example:

The building was demolished last spring.
The *city demolished* the building last spring.

1. Volunteers built the new school.
2. The aspiring actor was discovered by a talk-show host.
3. When the Eiffel Tower was built in 1889, it was thought by the French to be ugly.
4. Drugs are often prescribed to relieve depression.
5. Whales are still being killed by foreign fishing fleets.

EXERCISE 9

Circle all the verbs and verbals in the following paragraph and correct their form, tense, or mood if necessary.

For centuries the natives of Melanesia, a group of islands laying northeast of Australia, have practice an unusual religion. It began in the eighteenth century when European explorers first have visited the islands. The natives were fascinated by the rich goods or "cargo" possessed by the explorers. They saw the wealth as treasures of the gods, and cargo cults eventually had arised among them. Over the centuries some Melanesians turned to Christianity in the belief that the white man's religion will bring them the white man's treasures. During World War II, American soldiers, having arrived by boat and airplane to have occupied some of the islands, introduced new and even more wonderful cargo. Even today some leaders of the cargo cults insist that the airplane is worship as a vehicle of the Melanesians' future salvation.

8
Agreement

Agreement is the correspondence in form between subjects and verbs and between pronouns and their **antecedents,** the nouns or other pronouns they refer to. Agreement helps readers understand the relations between elements in a sentence.

Subjects and verbs agree in number (singular and plural) and in person (first, second, and third).

> *Sarah* often *speaks* up in class. [Both subject and verb are in the third-person singular form.]

> Even though *we understand, we* still *dislike* it. [Both subjects and verbs are in the first-person plural form.]

Pronouns and their antecedents agree in person, number, and gender (masculine, feminine, and neuter).

> *Claude* resented their ignoring *him*. [Both the pronoun *him* and its antecedent *Claude* are masculine and third-person singular.]

> The *dogs* stand still while *they* are judged. [The pronoun *they* and its antecedent *dogs* are both third-person plural.]

8a
Make subjects and verbs agree in number.

Most subject-verb agreement problems arise when the writer omits endings from subjects or verbs, when the writer cannot easily determine whether the subject is singular or plural, or when words come between subject and verb and blur their relationship. The following conventions cover these and other problems that affect subject-verb agreement.

agr
8a

1
Use the verb ending *-s* or *-es* with all third-person singular subjects. Use the noun ending *-s* or *-es* to make most nouns plural.

Adding *-s* or *-es* to a noun usually makes the noun *plural,* whereas adding *-s* or *-es* to a present-tense verb makes the verb *singular.* Thus if the subject noun is plural, it will end in *-s* or *-es* and the verb will not. If the subject is singular, it will not end in *-s* and the verb will.

SINGULAR	PLURAL
The boy eat*s*.	The boy*s* eat.
The bird soar*s*.	The bird*s* soar.

The only exceptions to these rules involve the nouns that form irregular plurals, such as *child, children; man, men; woman, women.* The irregular plural still requires a plural verb: *The children play.*

Writers often omit *-s* and *-es* endings from nouns or verbs because they are not pronounced clearly in speech (as in *asks* and *lists*) or because they are not used regularly in some English dialects. However, the endings are required in both spoken and written standard English.

NONSTANDARD	Julie *resist* any kind of change.
STANDARD	Julie *resists* any kind of change.
NONSTANDARD	Their *action* demand a response.
STANDARD	Their *actions* demand a response.

Remember that the verb *be* is irregular. In the present tense we use *is* with *he, she, it,* and singular nouns (*tree is*) and *are* with all plurals (*trees are*). In the past tense we use *was* with *he, she, it,* and singular nouns (*tree was*) and *were* with all plurals (*trees were*).

(See Chapter 7, pp. 180 and 185, for more on these verb forms.)

2
Subject and verb should agree even when other words come between them.

When the subject and verb are interrupted by other words, particularly other nouns, then we may make agreement errors because we tend to connect the verb to the nearest noun rather than to the actual subject.

A catalog of courses and requirements often *baffles* (not *baffle*) students. [The verb must agree with the subject, *catalog,* not the nearer word *requirements.*]

The profits earned by the cosmetic industry *are* (not *is*) high. [The subject is *profits,* not *industry.*]

Note: Phrases beginning with *as well as, together with, along with, in addition to,* and similar expressions do not change the number of the subject.

The governor, as well as his advisers, *has* (not *have*) agreed to attend the protest rally.

In such a sentence if you really mean *and* (*The governor and his advisers have agreed to attend*), you can avoid confusion and awkwardness (and extra words) by using *and.* Then the subject is compound, and the verb should be plural (see 8a-3).

3
Subjects joined by *and* usually take plural verbs.

Two or more subjects joined by *and* usually take a plural verb, whether one or all of the subjects are singular.

Frost and Roethke *are* her favorite poets.
The dog, the monkey, the children, and the tent *were* in the car.

Exceptions: When the parts of the subject form a single idea or refer to a single person or thing, then they take a singular verb.

Avocado and bean sprouts *is* my favorite sandwich.
The winner and new champion *was* in the shower.

When a compound subject is preceded by the adjective *each* or *every,* then the verb is usually singular.

At customs, every box, bag, and parcel *is* inspected.
Each man, woman, and child *has* a right to be heard.

But when a compound subject is *followed* by *each,* the verb is plural.

The man and the woman each *have* different problems.

4
When parts of a subject are joined by *or* or *nor,* the verb agrees with the nearer part.

When all parts of a subject joined by *or* or *nor* are singular, the verb is singular; when all parts are plural, the verb is plural.

Neither the teacher nor the student *knows* the answer.
The rabbits or the woodchucks *have eaten* my lettuce.

Problems with subjects joined by *or* or *nor* occur most often when one part of the subject is singular and the other plural. In that case the verb should agree with the subject part closer to it. To avoid awkwardness in such sentences, place the plural part closer to the verb.

AWKWARD	Neither the employees nor the manager *was* on time.
IMPROVED	Neither the manager nor the employees *were* on time.

The same problem arises when the subject consists of nouns and pronouns of different person requiring different verb forms: *neither Jim nor I, either he or you.* In this case, too, the verb agrees with the part of the subject nearer to it.

Neither Jim nor I *am* late.
Either he or you *are* late.

Since observing this convention often results in awkwardness, avoid the problem altogether by rewording the sentence.

AWKWARD	Either she or you *are* late.
IMPROVED	Either she *is* late, or you *are.*

5 Generally, use singular verbs with indefinite pronouns.

An **indefinite pronoun** is one that does not refer to a specific person or thing. The common indefinite pronouns include *all, any, anybody, anyone, anything, each, either, everybody, everyone, everything, neither, nobody, none, no one, one, some, somebody, someone,* and *something.* Most of these are singular in meaning (they refer to a single unspecified person or thing), and they take singular verbs.

Something *smells.*
Neither *is* right.

A few indefinite pronouns like *all, any, none,* and *some* may be either singular or plural in meaning. The verbs you use with these pronouns depend on the meaning of the nouns or pronouns they refer to.

All of the money *is* reserved for emergencies. [*All* refers to the singular noun *money,* so the verb is singular.]

When the men finally arrive, all *go* straight to work. [*All* refers to the plural noun *men,* so the verb is plural.]

6 Collective nouns take singular or plural verbs depending on meaning.

A **collective noun** has singular form but names a group of individuals or things—for example, *army, audience, committee, crowd,* *family, group, team.* When used as a subject, a collective noun may take a singular or plural verb, depending on the context. When considering the group as one unit, use the singular form of the verb.

> The group *agrees* that action is necessary.
> Any band *sounds* good in that concert hall.

But when considering the group's members as individuals who act separately, use the plural form of the verb.

> The old group *have* gone their separate ways.
>
> Since their last concert, the band *have* not agreed on where to play.

Note: Even when the plural verb form is properly used, as in these examples, it often sounds awkward. For this reason you may prefer to rephrase such sentences with plural subjects, as in *The members of the old group have gone their separate ways.*

Number, used as a collective noun, may be singular or plural. Preceded by *a,* it is always plural; preceded by *the,* it is always singular.

> *A* number of my friends *have* decided to live off campus.
> *The* number of people in debt *is* very large.

7
The verb agrees with the subject even when the normal word order is inverted.

Inverted subject-verb order occurs in questions.

> *Is* voting a right or a privilege? [*Voting* is the subject; *is* is the verb. Compare *Voting is a right or a privilege.*]
>
> *Are* Madigan and Harris married? [*Madigan and Harris* is the compound subject; *are* is the verb. Compare *Madigan and Harris are married.*]

Inverted subject-verb order also occurs in expletive constructions beginning with *there* or *it* and a form of *be* (see 5e-4).

> There *are* too many students in that class. [*Students* is the subject; *are* is the verb. Compare *Too many students are in that class.*]
>
> After many years there *is* finally peace in that country. [*Peace* is the subject; *is* is the verb. Compare *Peace is in that country.*]

In expletive constructions, *there is* may be used before a compound subject when the first element in the subject is singular.

> There *is* much work to do and little time to do it.

Word order may sometimes be inverted for emphasis. The verb still agrees with its subject.

> From the mountains *comes* an eerie, shimmering light.

8

A linking verb agrees with its subject, not the subject complement.

When a linking verb is followed by a subject complement, be sure that the verb agrees with its subject, the first element, not with the noun or pronoun serving as a subject complement (see 5a-3).

Henry's sole support *is* his mother and father. [The subject is *support.*]

Henry's mother and father *are* his sole support. [The subject is *mother and father.*]

9

When used as subjects, *who, which,* and *that* take verbs that agree with their antecedents.

The relative pronouns *who, which,* and *that* do not have different singular and plural forms. When one of these pronouns serves as a subject, its verb should agree with the noun or other pronoun that the relative pronoun refers to (its antecedent).

Mayor Garber ought to listen to the people who *work* for her. [*Who* refers to the plural *people,* so the verb is plural.]

Jane is the person who usually *solves* our problems. [*Who* refers to the singular *person,* so the verb is singular.]

Agreement problems often occur with relative pronouns when the sentence includes *one of the* or *the only one of the.*

Roberts is one of the teachers who *give* difficult tests. [*Who* refers to the plural *teachers.* Several teachers give difficult tests; Roberts is one of them.]

Roberts is the only one of the teachers who *has* paid attention to me. [*Who* refers to *one.* Among the teachers only one, Roberts, has paid attention.]

10

Nouns with plural form but singular meaning take singular verbs.

Some nouns with plural form (that is, ending in *-s*) are usually regarded as singular in meaning. They include *athletics, economics, mathematics, measles, news, politics, physics,* and *statistics.*

After so long a wait, the news *has* to be good.
Statistics *is* required of psychology majors.

Measurements and figures ending in *-s* may also be singular when the quantity they refer to is a unit.

Three years *is* a long time to wait.
Three-fourths of her library *consists* of reference books.

These words and amounts are plural in meaning when they describe individual items rather than whole groups or whole bodies of activity or knowledge.

The statistics *prove* him wrong. [*Statistics* refers to facts.]

Two-fifths of the cars on the road *are* unsafe. [The cars are unsafe separately.]

11
Titles and words named as words take singular verbs.

When your sentence subject is the title of a work (such as a book or a movie) or a word you are defining or describing, the verb should be singular even if the title or the word is plural.

Dream Days remains one of her favorite books.
Folks is a down-home word for *people.*

EXERCISE 1

Revise the verbs in the following sentences as needed to make subjects and verbs agree in number. If the sentence is already correct as given, circle the number preceding it.

Example:

Each of the job applicants type sixty words per minute.
Each of the job applicants *types* sixty words per minute.

1. Neither of the options are likely to receive support.
2. The number of students at the demonstration was disappointing.
3. Neither the won ton soup nor the chicken wings appeals to me.
4. The library owns the only one of the copies that are in good condition.
5. The idea that people their age still bite their nails are funny.
6. Some members of the chorus are going on the European tour.
7. Only some of the rooms in the house needs painting.
8. Physics are the only subject she feels competent in.
9. Is there enough handouts to go around?
10. The printer, along with two software programs and a user's manual, are included in the package.
11. Either his brother or his sister are responsible for that prank.
12. Every Tom, Dick, and Harry seems to have an opinion on how the federal dollar should be spent.
13. The police claimed that the crowd were endangering public safety.
14. He is one of those persons who breaks promises easily.
15. *Two Brothers* is the title of his newest movie.

8b

Make pronouns and their antecedents agree in person and number.

The **antecedent** of a pronoun is the noun or other pronoun it refers to. The antecedent usually comes before the pronoun that refers to it, but it may follow the pronoun.

agr
8b

Every *dog* in that kennel has received *its* shots. [*Dog* is the antecedent of *its*.]

Having received *their* tax bills, the *home owners* worried about payment. [*Home owners,* the subject of the main clause, is the antecedent of *their* in the introductory phrase.]

As these examples show, a pronoun agrees with its antecedent in gender (masculine, feminine, neuter), person (first, second, third), and number (singular, plural). Since pronouns derive their meaning from their antecedents, pronoun-antecedent agreement is essential for the reader to understand what you are saying.

1

Antecedents joined by *and* usually take plural pronouns.

Two or more antecedents joined by *and* usually take a plural pronoun, whether one or all of the antecedents are singular.

My adviser and I can't coordinate *our* schedules.
Their argument resolved, George and Jennifer had dinner together.

Exceptions: When the compound antecedent refers to a single idea, person, or thing, then the pronoun is singular.

The athlete and scholar forgot both *his* javelin and *his* books.

When the compound antecedent follows *each* or *every,* the pronoun is singular.

Every girl and woman took *her* seat.

2

When parts of an antecedent are joined by *or* or *nor,* the pronoun agrees with the nearer part.

When the parts of an antecedent are connected by *or* or *nor,* the pronoun should agree with the part closer to it.

Steve or John should have raised *his* hand.

Either consumers or car manufacturers will have *their* way.

Neither the student nor the elderly people will retrieve *their* deposits from that landlord.

When one subject is plural and the other singular, as in the last example, the sentence will be awkward unless you put the plural subject second.

Awkward Either the dogs or the cat will have to be returned to the shop *it* came from.

Revised Either the cat or the dogs will have to be returned to the shop *they* came from.

3 Generally, use a singular pronoun when the antecedent is an indefinite pronoun.

Indefinite pronouns refer to persons or things in general rather than to a specific person or thing. The indefinite pronouns *each, either, neither,* and *no one* as well as those ending in *-body, -one,* or *-thing* (*everybody, someone, anything*) are singular in meaning. When these indefinite pronouns serve as antecedents to other pronouns, the other pronouns are singular.

Everyone on the team had *her* own locker.
Each of the boys likes *his* teacher.
Something made *its* presence felt.

Using a singular pronoun to refer to an indefinite pronoun may result in an awkward sentence when the indefinite pronoun clearly means "many" or "all."

Awkward After everyone left, I shut the door behind *him.*

In speech we commonly avoid such awkwardness with a plural pronoun: *After everyone left, I shut the door behind them.* In all but the most informal writing, however, you should rewrite the sentence.

Rewritten After *all the guests* left, I shut the door behind *them.*

The generic he

In the preceding examples, the gender intended by the indefinite pronoun is known and is reflected in the pronouns *her, his,* and *its.* However, the meaning of indefinite pronouns often includes both masculine and feminine genders, not one or the other. In such cases we traditionally use *he* (or *him* or *his*) to refer to the indefinite antecedent. But many people see the so-called **generic *he*** (or generalized *he*) as unfairly excluding females. Thus many writers now avoid using *he* in these situations by rewriting their sentences.

Original	Everyone brought *his* book to class.
Broader	Everyone brought *his or her* book to class. [Overused, this option can be wordy or awkward.]
Plural	All the students brought *their* books to class. [This option can be used frequently without creating awkwardness.]

In speech we often solve the problem of the generic *he* by combining a plural pronoun with an indefinite pronoun, as in *Everyone brought their books to class.* But many readers view this construction as wrong, so it should be avoided in writing.

4

Collective noun antecedents take singular or plural pronouns depending on meaning.

Collective nouns such as *army, committee, family, group,* and *team* have singular form but may be referred to by singular or plural pronouns, depending on the meaning intended. When you are referring to the group as a unit—all its members acting together—then the pronoun is singular.

The committee voted to disband *itself.*
The team attended a banquet in *its* honor.

When you are referring to the individual members of the group, the pronoun is plural.

The audience arose quietly from *their* seats.
The old group have gone *their* separate ways.

The last example demonstrates the importance of being consistent in verb use as well as pronoun choice when assigning a singular or plural meaning to a collective noun (see also 8a-6).

Inconsistent	The old group *has* gone *their* separate ways.
Consistent	The old group *have* gone *their* separate ways.

EXERCISE 2

Revise the following sentences so that pronouns and their antecedents agree in person and number. Some items have more than one possible answer. If the sentence is already correct as given, circle the number preceding it.

Example:

Each of the Boudreaus' children brought their laundry home at Thanksgiving.

Each of the Boudreaus' children brought *his or her* laundry home at Thanksgiving. *Or: All* of the Boudreaus' children brought *their* laundry home at Thanksgiving.

1. Neither my brother nor my parents have made their vacation plans.
2. Everyone had to fill out a questionnaire describing their job.
3. The coalition launched a campaign to publicize their cause.
4. They asked each of the senators for their opinion.
5. No taxpayer will welcome an increase in their taxes.
6. Will either Mary or Lucy send in their application?
7. Neither of the two candidates is well known for her honesty.
8. The team had never won on their home court.
9. The town offers few opportunities for someone to let out their tensions.
10. Did any of the boys believe they would get away with cheating?

EXERCISE 3

In the following sentences subjects agree with verbs, and pronouns agree with antecedents. Make the change specified in parentheses after each sentence, and then revise the sentence as necessary to maintain agreement. Some items have more than one possible answer.

Example:

The student attends weekly conferences with her teacher. (*Change The student to Students.*)

Students *attend* weekly conferences with *their* teacher.

1. Even though the treatments have resulted in little physical improvement, they do seem to aid the patient psychologically. (*Change treatments to treatment.*)
2. He who does poorly in school often loses respect for himself. (*Change He to People.*)
3. Teen-agers who collect baseball cards often devote much money and time to their hobby. (*Change Teen-agers to A teen-ager.*)
4. The dancer who fails to practice risks injuring herself. (*Change The dancer to Dancers.*)
5. The computers were purchased because of their simplicity. (*Change computers to computer.*)
6. Their exams over, the seniors celebrate by throwing a party. (*Change seniors to senior.*)
7. The photographs show the beauty of the landscape, but their dim light obscures details. (*Change photographs to photograph.*)

8. All workers have some complaint about the way they are treated on the job. (*Change* All workers *to* Each worker.)
9. Judith is the one who always makes the decisions, and the rest of us resent her authority. (*Change* Judith *to* Judith and Bill.)
10. Since we don't know what's behind it, the locked door seems more mysterious than it probably is. (*Change* door *to* doors.)

EXERCISE 4

Revise the sentences in the following paragraph to correct errors in agreement between subjects and verbs or between pronouns and their antecedents.

Everyone has their favorite view of professional athletes. A common view is that the athletes are like well-paid children who have no real work to do, have no responsibilities, and simply enjoy the game and the good money. But this view of professional athletes fail to consider the grueling training the athletes have to go through to become professionals. Either training or competing lead each athlete to take risks that can result in their serious injury. The athletes have tremendous responsibility to the team they play on, which need to function as a unit at all times to win their games. Most athletes are finished as active team players by the age of forty, when he is too stiff and banged-up to go on. Rather than just listening to any of the people who criticizes professional athletes, everyone interested in sports need to defend the athletes. They take stiff physical punishment so neither the sports fanatic nor the casual observer are deprived of their pleasure.

9

Adjectives and Adverbs

Adjectives and adverbs are modifiers that describe, restrict, or otherwise qualify the words to which they relate. **Adjectives** modify nouns and pronouns. **Adverbs** modify verbs, adjectives, and other adverbs.

ADJECTIVE-NOUN	ADJ N serious student
ADJECTIVE-PRONOUN	ADJ PRON ordinary one
ADVERB-VERB	ADJ V hurriedly seek
ADVERB-ADJECTIVE-NOUN	ADV ADJ N only three people
ADVERB-ADVERB	ADV ADV quite seriously

Adverbs may also modify phrases, clauses, or entire sentences.

> He drove *nearly* to the edge of the cliff. [*Nearly* modifies the phrase *to the edge.*]
>
> They arrived *just* when we were ready to leave. [*Just* modifies the clause *when we were ready to leave.*]
>
> *Fortunately,* she is no longer on the critical list. [*Fortunately* modifies the entire sentence that follows.]

Many of the most common adjectives are familiar one-syllable words such as *good, bad, strange, true, false, large, right,* and *wrong.* Many others are formed by adding endings such as *-al, -able, -ful, -less, -ish, -ive,* and *-y* to nouns or verbs: *optional, fashionable, beautiful, fruitless, selfish, expressive, dreamy.*

Most adverbs are formed by adding *-ly* to adjectives: *badly, strangely, falsely, largely, beautifully, selfishly.* But note that we cannot depend on *-ly* to identify adverbs, since some adjectives also end in *-ly* (*fatherly, lonely, silly*) and since some common adverbs do not end in *-ly* (*always, forever, here, not, now, often, quite, then, there*). Thus the only sure way to distinguish between adjectives and adverbs is to determine how an individual word functions in its sentence. If a word modifies a noun or pronoun, it is an adjective; if it modifies a verb, an adjective, another adverb, or an entire word group, it is an adverb.

9a

Don't use adjectives to modify verbs, adverbs, or other adjectives.

Adjectives modify only nouns and pronouns. Using adjectives instead of adverbs to modify verbs, adverbs, or other adjectives is nonstandard.

NONSTANDARD	They took each other *serious.*
STANDARD	They took each other *seriously.*
NONSTANDARD	Jenny read the book *easy.*
STANDARD	Jenny read the book *easily.*

The adjectives *good* and *bad* often appear where standard English requires the adverbs *well* and *badly.*

NONSTANDARD	Playing *good* is the goal of practicing baseball.
STANDARD	Playing *well* is the goal of practicing baseball.
NONSTANDARD	The band played *bad* last night.
STANDARD	The band played *badly* last night.

Although in informal speech the adjective forms *real* and *sure* are often used in place of the adverb forms *really* and *surely,* formal speech and writing require the *-ly* adverb form.

INFORMAL	After a few lessons Dan drove *real* well.
FORMAL	After a few lessons Dan drove *really* well.
INFORMAL	I *sure* was shocked by his confession.
FORMAL	I *surely* was shocked by his confession.

9b

Use an adjective after a linking verb to modify the subject. Use an adverb to modify a verb.

A **linking verb** is one that links, or connects, a subject and its complement: *They are golfers* (noun complement); *He is lucky* (adjective complement). (See also 5a-3.) The verbs most often used as linking verbs are forms of *be* and verbs associated with our five senses (*look, sound, smell, feel, taste*), as well as a few others (*appear, seem, become, grow, turn, prove, remain*). But some of these verbs may or may not be linking, depending on their meaning in the sentence. When the word after the verb modifies the subject, the verb is linking and the word should be an adjective. When the word modifies the verb, however, it should be an adverb.

> Hallie felt *bad* after she lost the race. [Adjective *bad,* meaning "ill" or "unhappy," modifies *Hallie.*]
>
> She had lost the race *badly.* [Adverb *badly* modifies *had lost.*]
>
> The evidence proved *conclusive.* [Adjective *conclusive* modifies *evidence.*]
>
> The evidence proved *conclusively* that the defendant was guilty. [Adverb *conclusively* modifies *proved.*]

9c

After a direct object, use an adjective to modify the object and an adverb to modify the verb.

If the direct object of a verb is followed by a word that modifies the verb, that word must be an adverb: *She repeated the words angrily.* If, in contrast, the direct object is followed by a word that modifies the object itself (an object complement), that word must be an adjective: *Campus politics made Martin angry.* (See also 5a-3.) You can test whether a modifier should be an adjective or an adverb by trying to separate it from the direct object. If you can separate it, it should be an adverb: *She angrily repeated the words.* If you cannot separate it, it is probably an adjective.

> The instructor considered the student's work *thorough.* [The adjective can be moved in front of *work* (*student's thorough work*), but it cannot be separated from *work.*]
>
> The instructor considered the student's work *thoroughly.* [The adverb can be separated from *work.* Compare *The instructor thoroughly considered the student's work.*]

9d

When an adverb has a short form and an *-ly* form, distinguish carefully between the forms.

Some adverbs have two forms, one with an *-ly* ending and one without. These include the following:

cheap, cheaply	loud, loudly	sharp, sharply
high, highly	near, nearly	slow, slowly
late, lately	quick, quickly	wrong, wrongly

With some of these pairs the choice of form is a matter of idiom. The *-ly* form in some adverb pairs has developed an entirely separate meaning.

> He went *late.*
> *Lately* he has been eating more.

> Winter is drawing *near.*
> Winter is *nearly* here.

In other pairs the long and short forms have the same meaning. However, the short forms generally occur in informal speech and writing. The *-ly* forms are preferable in formal writing.

INFORMAL	Drive *slow.*
FORMAL	The funeral procession moved *slowly* through town.
INFORMAL	Jones wants to get rich *quick.*
FORMAL	Harrison became rich *quickly* when she invested in the stock market.

EXERCISE 1

Identify the adjectives and adverbs in the following sentences, and determine what part of speech each one modifies. Then compose a sentence of your own that parallels each sentence.

Example:

The angry man shouted loudly and moved inside.

ADJ → N   V ← ADV   V ← ADV

The *angry* man shouted *loudly* and moved *inside.*

The *hungry* child cried *plaintively* and fussed *about.*

1. The weary tourists slowly filed into the large gray bus.
2. During the rapid descent through the thick clouds, passengers muttered tensely among themselves.
3. Everyone in the class answered the hardest question wrong.
4. He was such an exciting person that everyone felt bad when he left.
5. As the Ferris wheel slowly turned, raising him higher in the air, he became increasingly ill.

EXERCISE 2

Revise the following sentences to make adjectives modify nouns and pronouns and to make adverbs modify verbs, adjectives, and other adverbs. If any sentence is already correct as given, circle the number preceding it.

Example:

The announcer warned that traffic was moving very slow.
The announcer warned that traffic was moving very *slowly.*

1. I was real surprised when Martin and Emily bought a Thunderbird.
2. If you take your lessons more serious, you will improve faster.
3. That perfume smelled similarly to my mother's.
4. Thinking about the accident, Jerry felt bad.
5. After playing poor for six games, the hockey team finally had a game that went good.

9e

Use the comparative and superlative forms of adjectives and adverbs appropriately.

Adjectives and adverbs can show different degrees of quality or amount with the endings *-er* and *-est* or with the words *more* and *most* (to compare upward) or *less* and *least* (to compare downward). Most modifiers have three forms. The **positive form** is the dictionary form and simply describes without comparing.

a *big* book spoke *forcefully*

The **comparative form** compares the thing modified with one other thing.

a *bigger* book spoke *more* (or *less*) *forcefully*

The **superlative form** compares the thing modified with two or more other things.

the *biggest* book spoke *most* (or *least*) *forcefully*

1

When word length or sound requires, use *more* and *most* instead of the endings *-er* and *-est*.

For downward comparisons, all adjectives and adverbs use *less* for the comparative (*less open*) and *least* for the superlative (*least successfully*). For upward comparisons, most one-syllable adjectives and adverbs and many two-syllable adjectives take the endings *-er* and *-est: red, redder, reddest; lucky, luckier, luckiest; fast, faster, fastest.*

Many two-syllable adjectives can either add *-er* and *-est* or use the words *more* and *most: steady, steadier* or *more steady, steadiest* or *most steady.* The use of *more* or *most* tends to draw the comparison out and so places more emphasis on it.

Using *more* and *most* is the only way to form the comparative and superlative for adjectives of three or more syllables and for most adverbs of two or more syllables (including nearly all ending in *-ly*): *beautiful, more beautiful, most beautiful; often, more often, most often; sadly, more sadly, most sadly.*

ad
9e

2 Use the correct form of irregular adjectives and adverbs.

The irregular modifiers change the spelling of their positive form to show comparative and superlative degrees.

Positive	**Comparative**	**Superlative**
Adjectives		
good	better	best
bad	worse	worst
little	littler, less	littlest, least
many, some, much	more	most
Adverbs		
well	better	best
badly	worse	worst

3 Don't use double comparatives or double superlatives.

A doubled comparative or superlative combines the *-er* or *-est* ending with the word *more, most, less,* or *least.* It is redundant and should be avoided.

He was the *wisest* (not *most wisest*) man I ever knew.
My sister gets privileges because she's *older* (not *more older*).

4 In general, use the comparative form for comparing two things and the superlative form for comparing three or more things.

She was the *taller* of the two girls. [Comparative.]
Of all those books, *The Yearling* is the *best.* [Superlative.]

In conversation the superlative form is often used even though only two things are being compared: *When two people argue, the angriest one is usually wrong.* But the distinction between the forms should be observed in writing.

5 In general, don't use comparative or superlative forms for modifiers that cannot logically be compared.

Adjectives and adverbs that cannot logically be compared include *perfect, unique, dead, impossible,* and *infinite.* These words are **absolute;** that is, they are not capable of greater or lesser degrees because their positive form describes their only state. Although they can be preceded by adverbs like *nearly* or *almost* that mean "approaching," they cannot logically be modified by *more, most, less,* or *least* (as in *most unique* or *less infinite*). This distinction is sometimes ignored in speech, but it should always be made in writing.

Speech	He was the *most unique* teacher we had.
Writing	He was a *unique* teacher.

EXERCISE 3

Write the comparative and superlative forms of each adjective or adverb below. Then use all three forms in sentences of your own.

Example:

heavy: heavier (comparative), heaviest (superlative)
The barbells were too *heavy* for me. The magician's trunk was *heavier* than I expected. Joe Clark was the *heaviest* person on the team.

1. badly
2. great
3. lively
4. steady
5. some
6. often
7. good
8. well
9. elegant
10. understanding

EXERCISE 4

Revise the following sentences so that the comparative and superlative forms of adjectives and adverbs are appropriate for formal usage.

Example:

Attending classes full-time and working at two jobs was the most impossible thing I ever did.

Attending classes full-time and working at two jobs was *impossible* (or *the hardest thing I ever did*).

1. Brad is the smallest of the two boys.
2. That is the most saddest story I have ever heard.
3. Of the two major problems with nuclear power plants—waste disposal and radiation leakage—radiation leakage is the most terrifying.
4. If I study hard, I should be able to do more better on the next economics test.
5. Working last summer as an assistant to my congressman was one of the more unique experiences I have ever had.

9f
Avoid overuse of nouns as modifiers.

We often use one noun to modify another, especially in the absence of an appropriate adjective form. For example:

father figure	slave trade	child care
flood control	truth serum	security guard

Carefully conceived, such phrases can be both clear and concise: *security guard* seems preferable to *guard responsible for security.* But overuse of noun modifiers can lead to flat, even senseless, writing. To avoid awkwardness or confusion, observe two principles. First, whenever possible use a possessive or an adjective as a modifier.

NOT — Glenn took the state medical *board* exams to become a *dentist* technician.

BUT — Glenn took the state medical *board's* exams to become a *dental* technician.

Second, use only short nouns as modifiers and use them only in two- or three-word sequences.

CONFUSING — Minimex maintains a *plant employee relations improvement program.*

REVISED — Minimex maintains a *program* for *improving relations* among *plant employees.*

EXERCISE 5

Revise the following sentences so that they conform to formal usage. Make sure that adjectives modify nouns and pronouns; that adverbs modify verbs, adjectives, and other adverbs; that the comparative and superlative degrees are appropriate; and that nouns are not overused as modifiers. If a sentence is already correct as given, circle the number preceding it.

Example:

Of the three books in the trilogy, the third is the better.
Of the three books in the trilogy, the third is the *best.*

1. She batted real well this season, but she didn't field good enough to make the all-county team.
2. It was the most totally perfect apartment we saw.
3. All three candidates claimed to be the more responsive.
4. Todd felt strangely the next day, and he was sure his exam would go bad.
5. The cat stalked its prey careful and quiet.
6. That argument sounds too illogical to take serious.
7. The university administration student absenteeism policy was controversial.
8. Jerry was not more mature than his brother, though he was more older.
9. He remained firm, refusing to give in even though we asked him nicely.
10. One can buy a tape player cheap, but the cheap players rarely work good or last long.

III
Clear Sentences

10 *Sentence Fragments*

A **sentence fragment** is part of a sentence that is set off as if it were a whole sentence by an initial capital letter and a final period or other end punctuation. Unlike a complete sentence, a sentence fragment lacks a subject or a verb or both, or it begins with a subordinating word.

FRAGMENT	The sign leaning against the wall. [Lacks a verb.]
FRAGMENT	Feeling sick. [Lacks both a subject and a verb.]
FRAGMENT	When it is time. [Contains a subject and a verb but begins with a subordinating word.]

Fragments are serious errors in writing. They distract or confuse the reader, and they suggest that the writer has been careless or does not understand the structure of a sentence. (Before proceeding with this chapter, you may find it helpful to review 5a and 5c on sentences and clauses.)

10a Test your sentences for completeness, and revise any fragments.

The following three tests will help you determine whether a word group punctuated as a sentence is actually a complete sentence. If the word group does not pass *all three* tests, it is a fragment and needs to be revised.

Test 1: Find a verb.

Look for a verb in the group of words. If you do not have one, the word group is a fragment.

Fragment Four years of study and then graduation. [The group contains no verb. Compare a complete sentence: *Four years of study precede graduation.*]

If you find a verb form, test to see if it is a sentence verb. A sentence verb will change form at least once to show the difference in present time, past time, and future time. *Work,* for instance, is different for all three times: *Today the men work* (present); *Yesterday the men worked* (past); *Tomorrow the men will work* (future). *Hurt* remains the same for present and past but does require *will* to show future: *Today the ant bites hurt* (present); *Yesterday the ant bites hurt* (past); *Tomorrow the ant bites will hurt* (future). If the verb form does not change at least once to indicate present, past, and future time, then it is not a sentence verb, and the word group containing it is a fragment. An *-ing* form such as *working* or *hurting* does not change to show time and thus can never serve alone as the only verb in a sentence. It must be accompanied by a form of *be* that does change to show time.

Fragment The statue standing by the door. [The *-ing* verb form *standing* does not change in any way to show a difference in present, past, or future time. Compare a complete sentence: *The statue is* (or *was* or *will be*) *standing by the door.*]

Fragment The skies having darkened. [The helping verb *having* does not change form in any way to show a difference in time. Compare a complete sentence: *The skies have* (or *had* or *will have*) *darkened.*]

Test 2: Find a subject.

If you find a sentence verb, look for its subject by asking who or what performs the action or makes the assertion of the verb. The subject will usually come before the verb. If there is no subject, the word group is a fragment unless it is a command.

Fragment And closed the door quietly. [The word group lacks a subject and is not a command. Compare complete sentences: *And he closed the door quietly. And close the door quietly.*]

Test 3: Look for a subordinating word.

If you find a sentence verb and its subject, look at the beginning of the word group. If the first word is a subordinating conjunction such as *after, because, before,* or *since,* the group is a fragment because it does not express a complete, independent thought. (See p. 154 for a list of subordinating conjunctions.)

Fragment As the plane lifted from the runway. [The word group contains a sentence verb, *lifted,* and a subject, *plane.* But because the group begins with the subordinating conjunction *as,* the thought is incomplete. Compare a complete sentence: *The plane lifted from the runway.*]

If the word group begins with *how, who, whom, whose, which, where, when, what,* or *why*—words that may introduce either subordinate clauses or questions—the group is a fragment unless it asks a question.

frag
10a

Fragment When she goes to the office. [The word group contains a sentence verb, *goes,* and a subject, *she.* But it begins with *when* and does not ask a question. Compare complete sentences: *She goes to the office. When does she go to the office?*]

Revising sentence fragments

Almost all sentence fragments can be corrected in one of two ways, the choice depending on the importance of the information in the fragment. First, the fragment can be made into a complete sentence. This method gives the information in the fragment the same importance as that in other complete sentences.

Fragment The baboon waited for his challenger. *Poised for combat.*

Revised The baboon waited for his challenger. *He was* poised for combat.

Fragment He stared at the woman. *Who had once been his wife.*

Revised He stared at the woman. *She* had once been his wife.

Once the fragment is corrected, it can be punctuated as a separate sentence (as in the preceding examples), or it can be separated from another main clause with a semicolon (see 22a).

Fragment She hesitated briefly. *Then blurted out her idea.*

Revised She hesitated briefly; then *she* blurted out her idea.

The second method of correcting a fragment is to combine it with a main clause. This method subordinates the information in the fragment to the information in the main clause.

Fragment The baboon waited for his challenger. *Poised for combat.*

Revised The baboon, poised for combat, waited for his challenger.

In this example, commas separate the inserted phrase from the rest of the sentence because the phrase does not restrict the meaning of any word in the main clause but simply adds information (see 21c). When a phrase or subordinate clause *does* restrict the meaning of a word in the main clause, a comma or commas do not separate the two elements.

Fragment	He stared at the woman. *Who had once been his wife.*
Revised	He stared at the woman who had once been his wife.

Sometimes a fragment may be combined with the main clause using a colon or a dash (see 25a and 25b, respectively).

Fragment	His sculptures use four materials. *Wood, iron, plastic, and paper.*
Revised	His sculptures use four materials**:** wood, iron, plastic, and paper.
Fragment	*A shortage of money, the illness of her father, a fear of failure.* These were her reasons for dropping out of school.
Revised	A shortage of money, the illness of her father, a fear of failure — these were her reasons for dropping out of school.

EXERCISE 1

Apply the tests for completeness to each of the following word groups. If a word group is a complete sentence, circle the number preceding it. If it is a sentence fragment, revise it in two ways: by making it a complete sentence and by combining it with a main clause of your own.

Example:

And could not find his money.

The word group has a verb (*could . . . find*) but no subject.

Revised into a complete sentence: And *he* could not find his money.

Combined with a new main clause: *He was confused* and could not find his money.

1. The water spilling onto the floor.
2. A big black cat with piercing blue eyes.
3. Whoever burned the painting should be ashamed.
4. But kept it a secret.
5. After the drinking age was raised.
6. The books displayed were rare.
7. Whom the child feared.

8. Using newspaper and string to wrap the package.
9. Because of the drought, watering plants was forbidden.
10. Whenever I hear that song.

10b

Don't set off a subordinate clause as a sentence.

frag
10b

Subordinate clauses contain both subjects and verbs, but they always begin with a subordinating conjunction (*although, because, if,* and so on) or a relative pronoun (*who, which, that*). (See 5c-4.) Subordinate clauses cannot stand alone as complete sentences.

To correct a subordinate clause set off as a sentence, combine it with the main clause or remove or change the subordinating word to create a main clause.

FRAGMENT	Many pine trees bear large cones. *Which appear in August.* [The fragment is a subordinate clause modifying *cones.*]
REVISED	Many pine trees bear large cones, which appear in August. [The subordinate clause is combined with the main clause.]
REVISED	Many pine trees bear large cones. *They* appear in August. [Substituting *They* for *Which* makes the fragment into a complete sentence.]
FRAGMENT	The decision seems fair. *Because it considers all parties.*
REVISED	The decision seems fair because it considers all parties.
REVISED	The decision seems fair. It considers all parties.

EXERCISE 2

Correct any sentence fragment below either by combining it with a main clause or by making it a main clause. If an item contains no sentence fragment, circle the number preceding it.

Example:

Jujitsu can be a form of self-protection. Because it enables one to overcome an opponent without the use of weapons.

Jujitsu can be a form of self-protection because it enables one to overcome an opponent without the use of weapons.

1. I have promised myself that I will explore the neighboring towns. Especially now that I have a car.
2. The telephone company promised to install the phone by Monday. Unless the installer could not find an open line.

3. In the nineteenth century chemists began synthesizing perfume. Which previously could be made only from natural oils.
4. Sarah worked many hours perfecting her double somersault. Before summer ended it had become her best dive.
5. Whenever they lose touch with their children. Parents blame themselves.

10c

Don't set off a verbal phrase or a prepositional phrase as a sentence.

A **verbal phrase** consists of an infinitive (*to begin, to choose*), a past participle (*begun, chosen*), or a present participle or gerund (*beginning, choosing*) together with any objects and modifiers it may have (see 5c-2). Verbal phrases are always parts of sentences and can never stand alone as complete sentences. Fragments consisting of verbal phrases are most easily corrected by combining them with the main clauses they are related to. Verbal phrases can be converted into main clauses only by rewriting.

Fragment He backed closer and closer to the end of the diving board. *At last falling into the water.*

Revised He backed closer and closer to the end of the diving board, at last falling into the water. [The phrase is combined with the main clause.]

Revised He backed closer and closer to the end of the diving board. At last *he fell* into the water. [The phrase is made into a complete sentence by changing *falling* to the verb *fell* and by adding the subject *he*.]

A **prepositional phrase** consists of a preposition (such as *in, on, to, over, under,* and *with*) together with its object and modifier (see 5c-1). A prepositional phrase always serves as part of a sentence and cannot stand alone as a complete sentence. It may be combined with a main clause or rewritten as a main clause.

Fragment More than anything else, I wanted to get away from the heat. *To someplace cooler.*

Revised More than anything else, I wanted to get away from the heat to someplace cooler. [The phrase is combined with the main clause.]

Revised More than anything else, I wanted to get away from the heat. *I longed for* someplace cooler. [The phrase is made into a complete sentence with the addition of a new subject and verb, *I longed for*.]

EXERCISE 3

Correct any sentence fragment below either by combining it with a main clause or by rewriting it as a main clause. If an item contains no sentence fragment, circle the number preceding it.

Example:

A hobby can contribute to a fulfilling life. Engaging one in activities outside work.

A hobby can contribute to a fulfilling life, engaging one in activities outside work.

1. They found the missing floppy disk. In a mislabeled file.
2. I now know how to budget my money. Having taken a night course in personal finance.
3. To ferry the souls of the dead across the River Styx in Hades. That is the job of Charon in Greek mythology.
4. St. Petersburg was renamed Petrograd in 1914. On Lenin's death in 1924 it was renamed Leningrad.
5. The children ran a race. To the end of the block and back.
6. Learning Chinese in one year. That is my goal.
7. The gun was where the police expected to find it. In a garbage can behind the movie theater.
8. Drag racing is a mixed pleasure. Being both exciting and dangerous.
9. To be able to fly a glider was one of my childhood dreams. I finally realized it last year.
10. The house will take at least three weeks to paint. Even with two painters working full-time.

10d

Don't set off any other word group as a sentence if it lacks a subject or a verb or both.

Besides subordinate clauses and verbal and prepositional phrases, several other word groups are often mistakenly punctuated as complete sentences—especially nouns plus their modifiers, appositives, and parts of compound predicates.

We often follow a noun with a phrase or subordinate clause that modifies the noun. No matter how long the noun and its modifier are, they cannot stand alone as a sentence.

Fragment	*People waving flags and cheering. Lined the streets for the parade.*
Revised	People waving flags and cheering lined the streets for the parade. [The two fragments are combined into one sentence.]
Fragment	*Veterans who fought in Vietnam.* They are finally being honored.

Revised Veterans who fought in Vietnam are finally being honored. [The fragment replaces *They* as the modified subject of the main clause.]

Appositives are nouns, or nouns and their modifiers, that rename or describe other nouns (see 5c-5). They cannot stand alone as sentences.

Fragment When I was a child, my favorite adult was an old uncle. *A retired sea captain who always told me long stories of wild adventures in faraway places.*

Revised When I was a child, my favorite adult was an old uncle, a retired sea captain who always told me long stories of wild adventures in faraway places. [The appositive is combined with the main clause.]

Compound predicates are predicates made up of two or more verbs and their objects, if any. A verb or its object cannot stand alone as a sentence.

Fragment Pat worked all day. *And danced at night.*

Revised Pat worked all day and danced at night. [The fragment, part of the compound predicate *worked . . . and danced,* is combined with the main clause.]

Fragment If his friends were in trouble, Henry always offered them much advice. *But no real help.*

Revised If his friends were in trouble, Henry always offered them much advice but no real help. [The fragment, part of the compound object of *offered,* is combined with the main clause.]

Note: Beginning a sentence with a coordinating conjunction such as *and* and *but* can lead to a sentence fragment. Check every sentence you begin with a coordinating conjunction to be sure it is complete.

EXERCISE 4

Correct any sentence fragment below either by combining it with a main clause or by rewriting it as a main clause. If an item contains no sentence fragment, circle the number preceding it.

Example:

Lynn graduated from college in 1983. But did not begin working until 1985.

Lynn graduated from college in 1983 but did not begin working until 1985.

Lynn graduated from college in 1983. But *she* did not begin working until 1985.

1. Woody Allen, the film director, writer, and actor. He is also an accomplished clarinetist.
2. The driver-education course includes ten hours of classroom discussion. And five hours of on-the-road training.
3. During World War II Jack Armstrong was the all-American boy. A hero for young people.
4. He detested the condescending tone of the essay. But the ideas in it were interesting.
5. In whatever form, tobacco is bad for one's health. Whether cigarettes, cigars, pipe tobacco, or chewing tobacco.

frag **10e**

10e

Be aware of the acceptable uses of incomplete sentences.

A few word groups lacking the usual subject-predicate combination are incomplete sentences, but they are not fragments because they conform to the expectations of most readers. They include exclamations (*Watch it! Oh no!*); questions and answers (*Where next? To Kansas. Why? To see my brother.*); and commands (*Move along. Shut the window. Finish your work.*). Exclamations and questions and answers occur most often in speech or in writing that records speech; commands occur in speech and in written directions. Another kind of incomplete sentence, which occurs in special situations, is the transitional phrase (*So much for the causes, now for the results. One final point.*).

Professional writers sometimes use incomplete sentences that *are* sentence fragments when they want to achieve a special effect. Such fragments appear more in narration and description than in exposition or argumentation. Unless you are experienced and thoroughly secure in your own writing, you should avoid all fragments and concentrate on writing clear, well-formed sentences.

EXERCISE 5

Break each of the following sentences at the vertical line, and then add, delete, or change words and punctuation as necessary to produce two *complete* sentences.

Example:

When the president came to town, | Secret service men were everywhere.

The president came to town. Secret Service men were everywhere.

1. The drunken driver swerved across the cement median strip | and hit four parked cars in a row.

2. Classes may not resume after vacation | because the school has run out of money.
3. The child appeared at the hospital, | badly beaten and abandoned by his parents.
4. An unknown person gave the acting company an old building | and the money to convert it to a theater.
5. The old photograph shows a handsome man, | although he holds himself stiffly so as not to blur the image.

EXERCISE 6

Revise the following paragraph to eliminate sentence fragments by combining them with main clauses or rewriting them as main clauses.

Hiring Steele as the manager of the baseball team was a stupid move. Or a very clever maneuver. Depending on whether one is thinking like a fan or like the team's owner. Fans claim it was stupid. Because Steele is hard to get along with and unfair. They say he is also a poor manager. Failing to make the best use of the team's talents. And creating friction among the players. But the team's owner may have had a good reason for hiring such a manager. Some people think the owner hired Steele only temporarily. In order to make the team less attractive to unfriendly buyers. Who have been threatening a hostile takeover of the team. Hiring Steele could have been intended to prevent the takeover. And in the long run save the team. Not ruin it.

11
Comma Splices and Fused Sentences

When two or more main clauses appear consecutively, readers expect them to be clearly separated from each other in one of three ways:

1. With a period:

   The ship was huge**.** Its mast stood thirty feet high.

2. With a semicolon:

   The ship was huge**;** its mast stood thirty feet high.

3. With a comma preceding a coordinating conjunction that joins the clauses and specifies the relation between them:

   The ship was huge**,** *and* its mast stood thirty feet high.

Two problems commonly occur in punctuating consecutive main clauses. One is the **comma splice,** in which the clauses are not joined with a coordinating conjunction and are separated only by a comma, not a semicolon or period.

COMMA SPLICE

The ship was huge, its mast stood thirty feet high.

The other problem is the **fused sentence** (also called a **run-on sentence**), in which no punctuation or coordinating conjunction appears between the clauses.

FUSED SENTENCE

The ship was huge its mast stood thirty feet high.

Like sentence fragments (see Chapter 10), comma splices and fused sentences are serious errors because they generally force the reader to reread for sense. They also suggest that the writer has been careless or does not understand the structure of a sentence.

COMMA SPLICES

11a

Separate two main clauses with a comma *only* when they are joined by a coordinating conjunction.

A comma cannot separate main clauses unless they are linked by a coordinating conjunction (*and, but, or, nor, for, so, yet*). Readers expect the same sentence to continue after a comma. When they find themselves reading a second sentence before they realize they have finished the first, they may have to reread to understand the writer's meaning.

COMMA SPLICE Rain had fallen steadily for sixteen hours, many basements were flooded.

COMMA SPLICE Cars would not start, many people were late to work.

EXCEPTION: Experienced writers sometimes use commas between very brief main clauses that are grammatically parallel.

He's not a person, he's a monster.

However, many readers view such punctuation as incorrect. Unless you are certain that your readers will not object to the comma in a sentence like this one, separate the clauses with periods or semicolons, as described below.

You have four main options for correcting a comma splice: (1) make separate sentences of the main clauses; (2) insert a coordinating conjunction after the comma between the clauses; (3) insert a semicolon between the clauses; or (4) subordinate one of the clauses to the other. The option you choose depends on the relation you want to establish between the clauses.

Making separate sentences

Revising a comma splice by making separate sentences from the main clauses will always be correct.

Rain had fallen steadily for sixteen hours. Many basements were flooded.

The period is not only correct but preferable if the ideas expressed in the two main clauses are only loosely related.

COMMA SPLICE Chemistry has contributed much to our understanding of foods, many foods such as wheat and beans can be produced in the laboratory.

Revised Chemistry has contributed much to our understanding of foods. Many foods such as wheat and beans can be produced in the laboratory.

Inserting a coordinating conjunction

When the ideas in the main clauses are closely related and equally important, you may choose to correct a comma splice by inserting the appropriate coordinating conjunction immediately after the comma to join the clauses.

Cars would not start, *and* many people were late to work.

cs
11a

Comma splice He had intended to work all weekend, his friends arrived Friday and stayed until Sunday.

Revised He had intended to work all weekend, *but* his friends arrived Friday and stayed until Sunday.

Notice that the relation indicated by a coordinating conjunction can be complementary (*and*), contradictory (*but, yet*), causal (*for, so*), or alternate (*or, nor*).

Many people were late to work, *for* cars would not start.

People were late to work, *or* they stayed home to pump out flooded basements.

Using a semicolon

If the relation between the ideas expressed in the main clauses is very close and obvious without a conjunction, you can separate the clauses with a semicolon. (See also 11b.)

Rain had fallen steadily for sixteen hours; many basements were flooded.

Comma splice Rhoda and Nate were more than close friends, they were inseparable.

Revised Rhoda and Nate were more than close friends; they were inseparable.

Subordinating one clause

When the idea in one clause is more important than that in the other, you can express the less important idea in a subordinate clause or a phrase.

After rain had fallen steadily for sixteen hours, many basements were flooded. [The addition of the subordinating conjunction *After* reduces the first sentence to a subordinate clause indicating time.]

After sixteen hours of steady rain, many basements were flooded. [The clause is reduced to a prepositional phrase.]

Subordination is often more effective than forming separate sentences because it defines the relation between ideas more precisely.

Comma splice	The examination was finally over, Becky felt free to enjoy herself once more.
Revised	The examination was finally over. Becky felt free to enjoy herself once more. [Both ideas receive equal weight.]
Improved	*When* the examination was finally over, Becky felt free to enjoy herself once more. [Emphasis on the second idea.]
Comma splice	The house was for sale, the price was reasonable.
Revised	The house was for sale. The price was reasonable.
Improved	The house was for sale at a reasonable price.

11b

Use a period or semicolon to separate main clauses connected by conjunctive adverbs.

Conjunctive adverbs are connecting words such as *consequently, however, nevertheless, then,* and *therefore* (see 5d-2 for a more complete list). Conjunctive adverbs frequently connect main clauses, and then the clauses must be separated by a period (forming two separate sentences) or by a semicolon (see 22b). The adverb is also generally set off by a comma or commas.

Comma splice	Most Americans refuse to give up unhealthful habits, consequently our medical costs are higher than those of many other countries.
Revised	Most Americans refuse to give up unhealthful habits. Consequently, our medical costs are higher than those of many other countries.
Revised	Most Americans refuse to give up unhealthful habits; consequently, our medical costs are higher than those of many other countries.

Like coordinating and subordinating conjunctions, conjunctive adverbs help to link the two clauses they join. But they also serve as adverbs, modifying the clause in which they appear. And unlike conjunctions, which must be placed between the word groups they join (coordinating) or at the beginning of the word group they introduce (subordinating), conjunctive adverbs may usually be moved from one place to another in the clause (see 5d-2). No matter where in the clause a conjunctive adverb appears, however, the clause must be separated from another main clause by a period or a semicolon.

Comma splice

The increased time devoted to watching television is not the only cause of the decline in reading ability, it is one of the important causes.

Comma and coordinating conjunction

The increased time devoted to watching television is not the only cause of the decline in reading ability, *but* it is one of the important causes.

Subordinating conjunction

Although the increased time devoted to watching television is not the only cause of the decline in reading ability, it is one of the important causes.

Period and conjunctive adverb

The increased time devoted to watching television is not the only cause of the decline in reading ability. *However,* it is one of the important causes.

Semicolon and conjunctive adverb

The increased time devoted to watching television is not the only cause of the decline in reading ability; *however,* it is one of the important causes.

The increased time devoted to watching television is not the only cause of the decline in reading ability; it is, *however,* one of the important causes.

The increased time devoted to watching television is not the only cause of the decline in reading ability; it is one of the important causes, *however.*

EXERCISE 1

Correct each comma splice below in *two* of the following ways: make separate sentences of the main clauses; insert an appropriate coordinating conjunction after the comma; substitute a semicolon for the incorrect comma; or subordinate one clause to another. If an item contains no comma splice, circle the number preceding it.

Example:

Carolyn still had a headache, she could not get the child-proof cap off the aspirin bottle.

Carolyn still had a headache *because* she could not get the child-proof cap off the aspirin bottle. [Subordination.]

Carolyn still had a headache, *for* she could not get the child-proof cap off the aspirin bottle. [Coordinating conjunction.]

1. Tony's new kitchen is well equipped, it has a microwave oven, a dishwasher, and a garbage disposal.

2. Terry did not feel prepared for her concert, she had not yet memorized her solo.
3. She reached Wayne's answering machine each time she called his number, consequently, she stopped calling him.
4. The blender was very old, it still worked on some speeds.
5. Scott began his career as a news reporter, now, however, he is a second-string film critic.
6. The student guards at the gym rarely ask to see identification, they are usually too busy doing their homework.
7. The election was held on a rainy day, the weather kept people away from the polls.
8. We lost the game against Colliersville, though we had been favored to win.
9. Sean bought a new suit for the interview, he didn't get the job.
10. Home owners are rebelling against the property tax, many of them believing they should not have to bear the expense of local government.

fs
11c

FUSED SENTENCES

11c

Don't combine two main clauses without using an appropriate connector or punctuation mark between them.

When two main clauses are joined without a word to connect them or a punctuation mark to separate them, the result is a **fused sentence,** sometimes called a **run-on sentence.** Fused sentences can rarely be understood on first reading, and they are never acceptable in standard written English.

Fused	Many people would be lost without television they would not know how to amuse themselves.
Fused	Our foreign policy is not well defined it confuses many countries.

Fused sentences may be corrected in the same ways as comma splices (see 11a).

Separate sentences

Our foreign policy is not well defined. It confuses many countries. [The two main clauses are made into separate sentences.]

Comma and coordinating conjunction

Our foreign policy is not well defined, *and* it confuses many countries. [The two main clauses are separated by a comma and a coordinating conjunction.]

Semicolon

Our foreign policy is not well defined; it confuses many countries. [The two main clauses are separated by a semicolon.]

Subordinating conjunction

Because our foreign policy is not well defined, it confuses many countries. [*Because* subordinates the first clause to the second.]

EXERCISE 2

Revise each of the fused sentences below in *two* of the four ways shown above.

Example:

Tim was shy he usually refused invitations.
Tim was shy, *so* he usually refused invitations.
Tim was shy; he usually refused invitations.

1. He did not finish work until midnight he was too tired to drive home.
2. The record Sarah bought was defective she returned it to the store.
3. The speaker is a well-known poet he teaches a poetry seminar at the university.
4. The skills center offers job training to people who need it it can't guarantee jobs, though.
5. The parking problem in the downtown area is getting out of hand the mayor suggests a new underground parking garage.

EXERCISE 3

Combine each pair of sentences below into one sentence without creating comma splices or fused sentences. Use one of the following methods to combine the sentences: supply a comma and an appropriate coordinating conjunction; supply a semicolon; or subordinate one clause to the other. You will have to add, delete, or change words as well as punctuation.

Example:

The sun sank lower in the sky. The colors gradually faded.

As the sun sank lower in the sky, the colors gradually faded. [The first clause is subordinated to the second.]

1. I once worked as a switchboard operator. However, after a week I was fired for hopeless incompetence.
2. The candidate's backers learned of his previous illegal activities. They withdrew their support.
3. Record prices stayed stable for a long time. In the last decade they rose sharply.
4. Teachers sometimes make unfair assignments. They don't take account of the workload in other courses.

5. I nearly froze trying to unlock the car door. I discovered I was standing next to the wrong red Rabbit.
6. Many proud people restrict their activities. They are afraid to fail at something new.
7. We thought my seven-year-old brother was a genius. He read an entire encyclopedia.
8. The driver was lucky to escape uninjured. His car was destroyed, however.
9. Some Eskimos found and nursed the sick explorer. He died two weeks later.
10. Two railroad lines cut through the town. They intersect a block from the main street.

EXERCISE 4

Identify and revise the comma splices and fused sentences in the following paragraph.

A good way to meet new people during the summer is to take evening courses, many colleges, high schools, and adult-education centers offer them. They attract different kinds of people who share common interests. Last summer in my woodworking class I met a woman who was also interested in colonial chairs we have been touring antique shows ever since. This summer in my singing class I met several people who enjoy country music as much as I do, we have gone to numerous concerts together, we are planning a trip to Nashville. If I had not attended evening classes, I would not have met these new friends, they have enriched my life.

12

Pronoun Reference

A **pronoun** derives its meaning from its **antecedent,** the noun it substitutes for. Therefore, a pronoun must refer clearly and unmistakably to its antecedent in order for the sentence containing the pronoun to be clear. A sentence such as *Jim told Mark he was not invited* is not clear because the reader does not know whether *he* refers to Jim or to Mark.

Whether a pronoun and its antecedent appear in the same sentence or in adjacent sentences, you should be certain their relation is clear. One way to achieve clarity is to ensure that pronoun and antecedent agree in person and number (see 8b). The other way is to ensure that the pronoun refers unambiguously to a single, close, specific antecedent.

12a

Make a pronoun refer clearly to one antecedent.

A pronoun may, of course, refer to two or more nouns in a compound antecedent, as in *Jenkins and Wilson pooled their resources and became partners.* But when either of two nouns can be a pronoun's antecedent, the reference will not be clear.

CONFUSING	The men removed all the furniture from the room and cleaned *it.* [Does *it* refer to the room or to the furniture?]
CLEAR	The men removed all the furniture from the room and cleaned *the room* (or *the furniture*).
CLEAR	After removing all the furniture from it, the men cleaned the room.
CLEAR	The men cleaned all the furniture after removing it from the room.

Clarifying pronoun reference may require simply replacing the pronoun with the appropriate noun, as in the first revision above. But to avoid repetition, you may want to restructure the sentence so that the pronoun can refer to only one possible antecedent, as in the second and third revisions.

Sentences that report what someone said, using verbs like *said* or *told,* often require direct rather than indirect quotation.

Confusing	Oliver told Bill that he was mistaken.
Clear	Oliver told Bill, "I am mistaken."
Clear	Oliver told Bill, "You are mistaken."

Note: Avoid the awkward device of using a pronoun followed by the appropriate noun in parentheses.

Weak	Mary should help Joan, but *she (Joan)* should help herself first.
Improved	Mary should help Joan, but *Joan* should help herself first.

12b
Place a pronoun close enough to its antecedent to ensure clarity.

When the relative pronoun *who, which,* or *that* introduces a clause that modifies a noun, the pronoun generally should fall immediately after its antecedent to prevent confusion. (See also 14b.)

Confusing	Jody found a dress in the attic *that* her aunt had worn. [Her aunt had worn the attic?]
Clear	In the attic Jody found a *dress that* her aunt had worn.

Even when only one word could possibly serve as the antecedent of a pronoun, the relationship between the two may still be unclear if they are widely separated.

Confusing	Denver, where my grandmother grew up, was once the scene of a mad gold rush with fortune seekers, plush opera houses, makeshift hotels, noisy saloons, and dirt streets. When I was a child, *she* often retold the stories she had heard of those days. [*She* can sensibly refer only to *grandmother,* but the pronoun is too far from its antecedent to be clear.]

CLEAR Denver, where my grandmother grew up, was once the scene of a mad gold rush with fortune seekers, plush opera houses, makeshift hotels, noisy saloons, and dirt streets. When I was a child, *my grandmother* often retold the stories she had heard of those days. [The noun is repeated for clarity.]

The confusing separation of pronoun and antecedent is most likely to occur in long sentences and, as illustrated by the preceding example, in adjacent sentences within a paragraph.

EXERCISE 1

Rewrite the following sentences to eliminate unclear pronoun reference. If you use a pronoun in your revision, be sure that it refers to only one antecedent and that it falls close enough to its antecedent to ensure clarity.

Example:

Saul found an old gun in the rotting shed that was just as his grandfather had left it.

In the rotting shed Saul found an old gun that was just as his grandfather had left it.

1. Mrs. Krieger telephoned her daughter often when she was away.
2. The picture on the cover of the novel is disturbing; one expects it to be more gruesome than it is.
3. Two brothers had built the town's oldest barn, which over the years had served as a cow barn, a blacksmith shop, and a studio for artisans. However, no one could remember their names.
4. Lee played a piece on the piano that dated from the seventeenth century.
5. Since Colson was operating the rented backhoe that ran over Mrs. Gibb's fence, he is responsible for the damage it suffered.
6. If your pet cheetah will not eat raw meat, cook it.
7. My father and his sister have not spoken for thirty years because she left the family when my grandfather was ill and never called or wrote. But now he is thinking of resuming communication.
8. There is a difference between the heroes of today and the heroes of yesterday: they have flaws in their characters.
9. Jan held the sandwich in one hand and the telephone in the other, eating it while she talked.
10. Tom told his brother that he was in trouble with their grandparents.

12c

Make a pronoun refer to a specific antecedent rather than to an implied one.

As a rule, the meaning of a pronoun will be clearest when it refers to a specific noun or other pronoun. When the antecedent is not specifically stated but is implied by the context, the reference can only be inferred by the reader.

1

Use *this, that, which,* and *it* cautiously in referring to whole statements.

ref 12c

The most common kind of implied reference occurs when the pronoun *this, that, which,* or *it* refers to a whole idea or situation described in the preceding clause, sentence, or even paragraph. Such reference, often called **broad reference,** is acceptable only when the pronoun refers clearly to the entire preceding clause. In the following sentence, *which* could not possibly refer to a noun in the preceding clause and thus refers unambiguously to the whole clause.

> I can be kind and civil to people, *which* is more than you can.
> – George Bernard Shaw

But if a pronoun might possibly confuse a reader, you should recast the sentence to avoid using the pronoun or to provide an appropriate noun.

Confusing	I knew nothing about economics, *which* my instructor had not learned. [*Which* could refer to *economics* or to the whole preceding clause.]
Clear	I knew nothing about economics, *a fact* my instructor had not learned.
Clear	I knew nothing about economics *because* my instructor knew nothing about it.
Confusing	The faculty members reached agreement on a change in the requirements, but *it* took time. [Does *it* refer to reaching agreement or to the change?]
Clear	The faculty members agreed on a change in the requirements, but *arriving at agreement* took time.
Clear	The faculty members reached agreement on a change in the requirements, but *the change* took time to implement.

Confusing	The British knew little of the American countryside and had no experience with the colonists' guerrilla tactics. *This* gave the colonists an advantage. [Does *This* refer to the whole preceding sentence, to the ignorance alone, or to the inexperience alone?]
Clear	The British knew little of the American countryside and had no experience with the colonists' guerrilla tactics. *Their ignorance and inexperience* gave the colonists an advantage.

ref
12c

2 Don't use a pronoun to refer to a noun implied by a modifier.

Adjectives, nouns used as modifiers, and the possessives of nouns or pronouns make unsatisfactory antecedents. Although they may imply a noun that could serve as an antecedent, they do not supply the specific antecedent needed for clarity.

Weak	In the President's speech *he* outlined plans for tax reform.
Revised	In *his* speech *the President* outlined plans for tax reform.
Weak	Liz drove a red car; *it* was her favorite color.
Revised	Liz drove a red car because *red* was her favorite color.
Revised	Liz drove a car *that was red,* her favorite color.

3 Don't use a pronoun to refer to a noun implied by some other noun or phrase.

Weak	Jim talked at length about salesmanship, although he had never been *one.*
Revised	Jim talked at length about salesmanship, although he had never been *a salesman.*
Weak	Jake was bitten by a rattlesnake, but *it* was not serious.
Revised	Jake was bitten by a rattlesnake, but *the bite* was not serious.

4 Don't use part of a title as an antecedent in the opening sentence of a paper.

The title of a paper is entirely separate from the paper itself, so a pronoun cannot be used to refer to the title. If you open a paper with a reference to the title, repeat whatever part of the title is necessary for clarity.

Title	How to Row a Boat
Not	*This* is not as easy as it looks.
But	*Rowing a boat* is not as easy as it looks.

12d

Avoid the indefinite use of *it* and *they*. Use *you* only to mean "you, the reader."

ref 12e

In conversation we commonly use expressions such as *It says in the paper* or *In Texas they say*. But such indefinite use of *it* and *they* is inappropriate in writing. The constructions are not only unclear but wordy.

Weak	In Chapter 4 of this book *it* describes the early flights of the Wright brothers.
Revised	In Chapter 4 of this book *the author* describes the early flights of the Wright brothers.
Weak	In the average television drama *they* present a false picture of life.
Revised	The average television *drama* presents a false picture of life.

Using *you* with indefinite reference to people in general is also well established in conversation: *You can tell that my father was a military man.* The indefinite *you* frequently occurs in informal writing, too. And in all but very formal writing, *you* is acceptable when the meaning is clearly "you, the reader," as in *You can learn the standard uses of pronouns.* But the writer must consider whether the context is appropriate for such a meaning. Consider this example.

Inappropriate	In the fourteenth century *you* had to struggle simply to survive. [Clearly, the meaning cannot be "you, the reader."]
Revised	In the fourteenth century *one* (or *a person* or *people*) had to struggle simply to survive.

12e

Avoid using the pronoun *it* more than one way in a sentence.

We use *it* idiomatically in expressions such as *It is raining*. We use *it* to postpone the subject in sentences such as *It is true that more jobs are available to women today*. And, of course, we use *it* as a personal pronoun in sentences such as *Joan wanted the book, but she couldn't find it.* All these uses are standard, but two of them in the same sentence can confuse the reader.

CONFUSING	When *it* is rainy, shelter your bicycle and wipe *it* often. [The first *it* is idiomatic; the second refers to *bicycle.*]
REVISED	*In rainy weather* shelter your bicycle and wipe *it* often.

ref 12f

12f

Be sure the relative pronouns *who, which,* and *that* are appropriate for their antecedents.

The relative pronouns *who, which,* and *that* commonly refer to persons, animals, or things. *Who* refers most often to persons but may also refer to animals that have names.

Travis is the boy *who* leads the other boys into trouble.
Their dog Wanda, *who* is growing lame, has difficulty running.

Which refers to animals and things.

The Orinoco River, *which* is 1600 miles long, flows through Venezuela into the Atlantic Ocean.

That refers to animals and things and occasionally to persons when they are collective or anonymous.

The jade tree *that* my grandmother gave me suddently died.
Infants *that* walk need constant tending.

(See also 21c-1 for the use of *which* and *that* in nonrestrictive and restrictive clauses.)

The possessive *whose* generally refers to people but may refer to animals and things to avoid awkward and wordy *of which* constructions.

The book *whose* binding broke had been my father's. [Compare *The book of which the binding broke had been my father's.*]

EXERCISE 2

Many of the pronouns in the following sentences do not refer to specific, appropriate antecedents. Revise the sentences as necessary to make them clear.

Example:

In Grand Teton National Park they have moose, elk, and trumpeter swans.

Moose, elk, and trumpeter swans live in Grand Teton National Park.

1. Sandra Day O'Connor has been a Supreme Court Justice since 1981, when she was appointed to it by Ronald Reagan.
2. Ever since I read a book on the Buddhists' beliefs, I've been thinking of becoming one.
3. In impressionist paintings they used color to imitate reflected light.
4. Six or seven bearskin rugs decorated the rooms of the house, and Sam claimed to have killed them.
5. In Japan they are very loyal to the companies they work for.
6. Thompson is a painter that works primarily in oils.
7. In my weight-training class, the instructors advise you to leave two or three days between workouts.
8. The play was supposed to open the first week in March, but because of casting problems this did not happen.
9. We receive warnings to beware of nuclear fallout, pesticides, smog, and even our food, but I try not to think about it.
10. In F. Scott Fitzgerald's novels he wrote about the Jazz Age.
11. Macbeth is a complicated and ambiguous hero, and that makes it a good play.
12. In urban redevelopment projects they try to make neighborhoods safe and attractive.
13. In the nineteenth century you didn't have many options in motorized transportation.
14. It rained for a week, but it is possible that we can save the crop.
15. We argue constantly and he never looks straight at me, which bothers me.

ref
12

EXERCISE 3

Revise the following paragraph so that each pronoun refers clearly to a single specific and appropriate antecedent.

In Charlotte Brontë's *Jane Eyre* she is a shy young woman that takes a job as governess. Her employer is a rude, brooding man named Rochester. He lives in a mysterious mansion on the English moors, which contributes an eerie quality to Jane's experience. Eerier still are the fires, strange noises, and other unexplained happenings in the house; but Rochester refuses to discuss this. Eventually, they fall in love. On the day they are to be married, however, she learns that he has a wife hidden in the house. She is hopelessly insane and violent and must be guarded at all times, which explains his strange behavior. Heartbroken, Jane leaves the moors, and many years pass before they are reunited.

13
Shifts

A sentence should be consistent: grammatical elements such as tense, mood, voice, person, and number should remain the same throughout the sentence unless grammar or the meaning of the sentence requires a shift. Unnecessary shifts in these elements, either within a sentence or among related sentences, confuse readers and distort meaning.

13a
Keep sentences consistent in person and number.

Person in grammar refers to the distinction among the person talking (first person), the person spoken to (second person), and the person, object, or concept being talked about (third person). **Number** refers to the distinction between one (singular) and more than one (plural). Both nouns and personal pronouns change form to show differences in number, but only personal pronouns have distinctive forms for the three persons.

Shifts in person

The most common faulty shifts in person are shifts from second to third and from third to second person. They occur because we can refer to people in general, including our readers, either in the third person (*a person, one; people, they*) or in the second person (*you*).

> *People* should not drive when *they* have been drinking.
> *One* should not drive when *he* (or *he or she*) has been drinking.
> *You* should not drive when *you* have been drinking.

Although any one of these possibilities is acceptable in an appropriate context, a mixture of them is inconsistent.

Inconsistent	If a *person* works hard, *you* can accomplish a great deal.
Revised	If *you* work hard, *you* can accomplish a great deal.
Revised	If a *person* works hard, *he* (or *he or she*) can accomplish a great deal.
Better	If *people* work hard, *they* can accomplish a great deal.

(See p. 205 on avoiding the use of *he* to mean "he or she.")

Shifts in number

Inconsistency in number occurs most often between a pronoun and its antecedent (see 8b).

Inconsistent	If a *student* does not understand a problem, *they* should consult the instructor.
Revised	If a *student* does not understand a problem, *he* (or *he or she*) should consult the instructor.
Better	If *students* do not understand a problem, *they* should consult the instructor.

Inconsistency in number can also occur between other words (usually nouns) that relate to each other in meaning.

Inconsistent	All the *boys* have a good *reputation.*
Revised	All the *boys* have good *reputations.*

The consistency in the revised sentence is called **logical agreement** because the number of the nouns is logically consistent.

EXERCISE 1

Revise the following sentences to make them consistent in person and number.

Example:

A plumber will fix burst pipes, but they won't repair waterlogged appliances.

Plumbers will fix burst pipes, but they won't repair waterlogged appliances.

1. When a student is waiting to hear from college admissions committees, you begin to notice what time the mail carrier arrives.

2. If tourists cannot find the Arts Center, one should ask for directions.
3. When taxpayers do not file their return on time, they may be penalized.
4. If a student misses too many classes, you may fail a course.
5. One should not judge other people's actions unless they know the circumstances.

13b

Keep sentences consistent in tense and mood.

shift **13b**

Shifts in tense

Certain changes in tense within a sentence or from one sentence to another may be required to indicate changes in actual or relative time (see 7f). For example:

> Ramon *will graduate* from college twenty-three years after his father *arrived* in the United States. [Ramon's graduation is still in the future, but his father arrived in the past.]

But changes that are not required by meaning distract readers. Unnecessary shifts from past to present or from present to past in sentences narrating a series of events are particularly confusing.

Inconsistent Immediately after Booth *shot* Lincoln, Major Rathbone *threw* himself upon the assassin. But Booth *pulls* a knife and *plunges* it into the major's arm. [Tense shifts from past to present.]

Revised Immediately after Booth *shot* Lincoln, Major Rathbone *threw* himself upon the assassin. But Booth *pulled* a knife and *plunged* it into the major's arm.

The present tense is used to describe what another author has written, including the action in literature or a film (see 7e-1).

Inconsistent The main character in the novel *suffers* psychologically because he *has* a clubfoot, but he eventually *triumphed* over his handicap.

Revised The main character in the novel *suffers* psychologically because he *has* a clubfoot, but he eventually *triumphs* over his handicap.

Shifts in mood

Shifts in the mood of verbs occur most frequently in directions when the writer moves between the imperative mood (*Unplug the appliance*) and the indicative mood (*You should unplug the ap-*

pliance). (See 7g.) Directions are usually clearer and more concise in the imperative, as long as its use is consistent.

Inconsistent *Cook* the mixture slowly, and *you should stir* it until the sugar is dissolved. [Mood shifts from imperative to indicative.]

Revised *Cook* the mixture slowly, and *stir* it until the sugar is dissolved. [Consistently imperative.]

EXERCISE 2

Revise the following sentences to make them consistent in tense and mood.

Example:

Lynn ran to first, rounded the base, and keeps running until she slides into second.

Lynn ran to first, rounded the base, and *kept* running until she *slid* into second.

1. Misunderstandings sometimes occurred when people of one culture do not understand the rules of appropriate behavior in another culture.
2. Soon after he joined the union, Lester appears at a rally and makes a speech.
3. First sand down any paint that is peeling; then you should paint the bare wood with primer.
4. Rachel was walking down the street, and suddenly she stopped as a shot rings out.
5. To buy a tape deck, find out what features you need and you should decide what you want to pay.

13c

Keep sentences consistent in subject and voice.

When a verb is in the active voice, the subject names the actor: *Linda passed the peas*. When a verb is in the passive voice, the subject names the receiver of the action; the actor may not be mentioned or may be mentioned in a prepositional phrase: *The peas were passed* (*by Linda*). (See pp. 194–95.)

A shift in voice may sometimes help focus the reader's attention on a single subject, as in *The candidate campaigned vigorously and was nominated on the first ballot*. However, most shifts in subject and voice not only are unnecessary but also may create confusion or error.

Inconsistent In the morning the *children rode* their bicycles; in the afternoon *their skateboards were given* a good workout. [The shift in subject from *children* to

	skateboards is confusing. Without a named actor the second clause implies that someone other than the children used the skateboards.]
Revised	In the morning the *children rode* their bicycles; in the afternoon *they gave* their skateboards a good workout.
Inconsistent	As *we looked* out over the ocean, *ships could be seen* in the distance. [Since the main clause does not name an actor, the reader cannot be sure who is looking.]
Revised	As *we looked* out over the ocean, *we could see* ships in the distance.

EXERCISE 3

Make the following sentences consistent in subject and voice.

Example:

At the reunion they ate hot dogs and volleyball was played.
At the reunion they ate hot dogs and *played volleyball.*

1. Some arrowheads were dug up, and they found some pottery that was almost undamaged.
2. They started the game after some practice drills were run.
3. The tornado ripped off the roof, and it was deposited in a nearby lot.
4. The debate was begun by the senator when he introduced the new bill.
5. If you learn how to take good notes in class, much extra work will be avoided.

13d

Don't shift unnecessarily between indirect and direct quotation.

Direct quotation reports, in quotation marks, the exact words of a speaker: *He said, "I am going."* **Indirect quotation** reports what was said but not necessarily in the speaker's exact words: *He said that he was going.*

Inconsistent	Sue asked whether we had repaired the car and "Is anything else likely to happen?"
Revised	Sue asked, "Have you repaired the car? Is anything else likely to happen?"
Revised	Sue asked whether we had repaired the car and whether anything else was likely to happen.

EXERCISE 4

Revise each of the following sentences twice, once to make the form of quotation consistently indirect and once to make it consistently direct.

Example:

Tom asked whether the guest host had arrived and "Are the cameras ready?"

Tom asked whether the guest host had arrived and *whether the cameras were ready.*

Tom asked, "*Has the guest host arrived?* Are the cameras ready?"

1. Muhammad Ali bragged that he was the greatest and "Not only do I knock 'em out, I pick the round."
2. Coach Butler said that our timing was terrible and "I would rather cancel the season than watch you play."
3. The report concluded, "Drought is a serious threat" and that we must begin conserving water now.
4. The author claims that adults pass through emotional stages and "No stage can be avoided."
5. My grandfather says, "Gardening keeps me alive" and that, in any event, the exercise helps ease his arthritis.

EXERCISE 5

Revise the following paragraph to eliminate unnecessary shifts in person, number, tense, mood, and voice.

Driving in snow need not be dangerous if you practice a few rules. First, one should avoid fast starts, which prevent the wheels from gaining traction and may result in the car's getting stuck. Second, drive more slowly than usual, and you should pay attention to the feel of the car: if the steering seemed unusually loose or the wheels did not seem to be grabbing the road, slow down. Third, avoid fast stops, which lead to skids. One should be alert for other cars and intersections that may necessitate that the brakes be applied suddenly. If you need to slow down, the car's momentum can be reduced by downshifting as well as by applying the brakes. When braking, don't press the pedal to the floor, but it should be pumped in short bursts. If you feel the car skidding, the brakes should be released and the wheel should be turned into the direction of the skid, and then the brakes should be pumped again. If one repeated these motions, the skid would be stopped and the speed of the car would be reduced.

14
Misplaced and Dangling Modifiers

In reading a sentence in English, we depend principally on the arrangement of the words to tell us how they are related. In writing, we usually follow unconsciously the arrangements readers expect. But we may create confusion if we fail to connect modifiers to the words they modify.

MISPLACED MODIFIERS

We say that a modifier is **misplaced** if it appears to modify the wrong part of the sentence or if we cannot be certain what part of the sentence the writer intended it to modify. Misplaced modifiers may be awkward, unintentionally amusing, or genuinely confusing.

14a
Place prepositional phrases where they will clearly modify the words intended.

Readers tend to link a prepositional phrase to the nearest word it could modify: *I saw a man in a green hat. The cat leaped over the fence.* Thus the writer must place the phrase so that it clearly modifies the intended word and not some other.

CONFUSING	She served hamburgers to the men *on paper plates.* [Surely the hamburgers, not the men, were on paper plates.]
CLEAR	She served the men hamburgers *on paper plates.*

Confusing	He was unhappy that he failed to break the record *by a narrow margin.* [The sentence implies that he wanted to break the record only by a narrow margin.]
Clear	He was unhappy that he failed *by a narrow margin* to break the record.

14b

Place subordinate clauses where they will clearly modify the words intended.

Like a prepositional phrase, a subordinate clause will seem to apply to the nearest word or words it could modify. Thus the writer must place the clause so that it relates clearly to the word or words intended.

Confusing	According to police records, many dogs are killed by automobiles *that roam unleashed.* [The clause appears to modify *automobiles.*]
Clear	According to police records, many dogs *that roam unleashed* are killed by automobiles.
Confusing	The mayor was able to cut the ribbon and then the band played *when someone found scissors.* [The clause appears to modify *the band played.*]
Clear	*When someone found scissors,* the mayor was able to cut the ribbon and then the band played.

EXERCISE 1

Revise the following sentences so that prepositional phrases and subordinate clauses clearly modify the words intended.

Example:

I came to enjoy flying over time.
Over time I came to enjoy flying.

1. The senator returned to Capitol Hill after a long illness on Monday.
2. I watched a film clip of the accident in my hospital bed.
3. The artist painted a canvas at a summer retreat that imitated Monet's style.
4. The consulate received the letter from a messenger with exotic stamps.
5. Trisha delivered a party platter to the host wrapped in cellophane.

6. The electric typewriter needs repair in the library.
7. Marie opened the book given to her last Christmas by Charles Dickens.
8. The bell is an heirloom that you hear chiming.
9. She stared at the people standing nearby with flashing eyes.
10. Buffalo gains a huge supply of hydroelectric power from Niagara Falls that will never be exhausted.

14c

Place limiting modifiers carefully.

mm 14c

Limiting modifiers include *almost, even, exactly, hardly, just, merely, nearly, only, scarcely,* and *simply*. They modify the expressions that immediately follow them. Compare the uses of *just* in the following sentences:

The instructor *just nodded* to me as he came in.
The instructor nodded *just to me* as he came in.
The instructor nodded to me *just as he came in.*

In speech several of these modifiers frequently occur before the verb, regardless of the words they are intended to modify. In writing, however, these modifiers should fall immediately before the word or word group they modify to avoid any ambiguity.

UNCLEAR	They *only* saw each other during meals. [They had eyes only for each other, or they met only during meals?]
CLEAR	They saw *only* each other during meals.
CLEAR	They saw each other *only* during meals.

NOTE: *Only* is acceptable immediately before the verb when it modifies a whole statement.

He *only* wanted his guest to have fun.

EXERCISE 2

Use each of the following limiting modifiers in two versions of the same sentence.

Example:
only
He is the *only* one I like.
He is the one *only* I like.

1. almost
2. even
3. hardly
4. simply
5. nearly

14d
Avoid squinting modifiers.

A **squinting modifier** is one that may refer to either a preceding or a following word, leaving the reader uncertain about what it is intended to modify. A modifier can modify only *one* grammatical element in a sentence. It cannot serve two elements at once.

SQUINTING	Snipers who fired on the soldiers *often* escaped capture.
CLEAR	Snipers who *often* fired on the soldiers escaped capture.
CLEAR	Snipers who fired on the soldiers escaped capture *often*.

When an adverb modifies an entire main clause, as in the last example, it can usually be moved to the beginning of the sentence: *Often, snipers who fired on the soldiers escaped capture.*

EXERCISE 3

Revise each of the following sentences twice so that the squinting modifier applies clearly first to one element and then to the other.

Example:

The work that he hoped would satisfy him completely frustrated him.

The work that he hoped would *completely* satisfy him frustrated him.

The work that he hoped would satisfy him frustrated him *completely*.

1. People who sun-bathe frequently can damage their skin.
2. The contestant who answered the first question completely lost his concentration during the second round.
3. The baseball team that wins championships most of the time has excellent pitching.
4. I told my son when the game was over I would play with him.
5. People who see psychologists occasionally will feel better.

14e
Avoid separating a subject from its verb or a verb from its object or complement.

When we read a sentence, we expect the subject, verb, and object or complement to be close to each other. If adjective phrases or clauses separate them, the meaning is usually clear.

The wreckers who were demolishing the old house discovered a large box of coins. [The subject, *wreckers,* and the verb, *discovered,* are separated by the adjective clause beginning *who.*]

However, if an adverb phrase or clause interrupts the movement from subject to verb to object or complement, the resulting sentence is likely to be awkward and confusing.

AWKWARD	The *wreckers,* soon after they began demolishing the old house, *discovered* a large box of coins. [The clause beginning *soon after* interrupts the movement from subject to verb.]
REVISED	Soon after they began demolishing the old house, the *wreckers discovered* a large box of coins.
AWKWARD	Three of the wreckers *lifted,* with great effort, *the heavy box.* [The phrase beginning *with* interrupts the movement from verb to object.]
REVISED	Three of the wreckers *lifted the heavy box* with great effort.

14f

Avoid separating the parts of a verb phrase or the parts of an infinitive.

A verb phrase consists of a helping verb plus a main verb, as in *will call, was going, had been writing.* Such phrases constitute close grammatical units. We regularly insert single-word adverbs in them without causing awkwardness: *Joshua had almost completed his assignment.* But when longer word groups interrupt verb phrases, the result is almost always awkward.

AWKWARD	Many students *had,* by spending most of their time on the assignment, *completed* it.
REVISED	By spending most of their time on the assignment, many students *had completed* it.
REVISED	Many students *had completed* the assignment by spending most of their time on it.

Infinitives consist of the marker *to* plus the plain form of a verb: *to produce, to enjoy.* The two parts of the infinitive are widely regarded as a grammatical unit that should not be split.

AWKWARD	The weather service expected temperatures *to not rise.*
REVISED	The weather service expected temperatures not *to rise.*

Note, however, that a split infinitive may sometimes be natural and preferable, though it may still bother some readers.

> Several U.S. industries expect *to* more than *triple* their use of robots within the next decade.

We could recast the sentence entirely: *Several U.S. industries expect to increase their use of robots by over 200 percent within the next decade.* But the split construction seems acceptable for economy.

EXERCISE 4

Revise the following sentences to connect separated parts (subject-predicate, verb-object-complement, verb phrase, infinitive).

Example:

Most children have by the time they are seven lost a tooth.
By the time they are seven, most children have lost a tooth.

1. The mail carrier returned, after two weeks, the undelivered letter.
2. The lieutenant had given, although he was later accused of dereliction of duty, the correct orders.
3. The girls loved to daily sun beside the pool.
4. Ballet will, if the present interest continues to grow, be one of the country's most popular arts.
5. The beavers, when the new housing construction began, abandoned their dam.

DANGLING MODIFIERS

14g
Avoid dangling modifiers.

A **dangling modifier** does not sensibly modify anything in its sentence.

Dangling	*Passing the building,* the vandalism was clearly visible. [The modifying phrase seems to describe *vandalism.* The writer has not said who was passing the building or who saw the vandalism.]
Dangling	*Shortly after leaving home,* the accident occurred. [The modifying phrase seems to describe *accident.* The writer has not said who left home or who was in the accident.]

Dangling modifiers occur most often when certain kinds of modifying word groups precede the main clause of the sentence. These word groups include participial phrases (*passing the build-*

dm
14g

ing); infinitive phrases (*to see*); prepositional phrases in which the object of the preposition is a gerund (*after leaving home*); and elliptical clauses in which the subject and perhaps the verb are understood (*while at work*). (See 5c.) Since these phrases and clauses have no expressed subject, readers take them to modify the following noun, the subject of the main clause. If they do not sensibly define or describe the following noun, they are dangling modifiers.

Dangling	*Being very tried,* the alarm failed to disturb Morton's sleep. [Participial phrase.]
Dangling	*To get up on time,* a great effort was needed. [Infinitive phrase.]
Dangling	*On rising,* coffee was essential to waken Morton. [Prepositional phrase.]
Dangling	*Until completely awake,* work was impossible. [Elliptical clause.]

These sentences are illogical: alarm clocks don't get tired, effort doesn't get up, coffee doesn't rise, and work doesn't awaken. Note that a modifier may be dangling even when the sentence elsewhere contains a word the modifier might seem to describe, such as *Morton's* and *Morton* in the first and third examples. In addition, a dangling modifier may fall at the end of a sentence:

Dangling	Work came easily *when finally awake.*

We correct dangling modifiers by recasting the sentences in which they appear. We can change the subject of the main clause to a word the modifier properly defines or describes. Or we can recast the dangling modifier as a complete clause. The following examples illustrate these revisions.

Dangling	*Being crowded in the car,* the trip was uncomfortable.
Revised	*Being crowded in the car, we* were uncomfortable.
Revised	*Because we were crowded in the car,* the trip was uncomfortable.
Dangling	*After unlocking the door,* the cat refused to go out.
Revised	*After I had unlocked the door,* the cat refused to go out.
Dangling	*To take sharp action pictures,* the shutter speed should be fast.
Revised	*To take sharp action pictures, a photographer* should use a fast shutter speed.
Revised	*If a photographer wants to take sharp action pictures,* the shutter speed should be fast.

Dangling	*While still in the hospital,* the stitches were removed from Larry's wound.
Revised	*While still in the hospital, Larry* had the stitches removed from his wound.
Revised	*While Larry was still in the hospital,* the stitches were removed from his wound.

EXERCISE 5

Revise the following sentences to eliminate any dangling modifiers. Each item has more than one possible answer.

Example:

Driving north, the vegetation became increasingly sparse.

Driving north, *we noticed* that the vegetation became increasingly sparse.

As we drove north, the vegetation became increasingly sparse.

1. By turning the lights down, the room looked less dingy.
2. To file a formal complaint, a statement must be submitted.
3. Having prepared thoroughly, the exam was easy for me.
4. Though usually energetic, emotional problems had sapped her strength.
5. Staring at the ceiling, the idea became clear.
6. Sagging and needing a new coat of paint, Mr. Preston called the house painter.
7. Monday passed me by without accomplishing anything.
8. To obtain disability income, a doctor must certify that an employee cannot work.
9. When only a ninth grader, my grandmother tried to teach me double-entry bookkeeping.
10. After weighing the alternatives, his decision became clear.

EXERCISE 6

Combine each pair of sentences below into a single sentence by rewriting one as a modifier. Make sure the modifier applies clearly to the appropriate word. You will have to add, delete, and rearrange words, and you may find that more than one answer is possible in each case.

Example:

Bob demanded a hearing from the faculty. Bob wanted to appeal the decision.

Wanting to appeal the decision, Bob demanded a hearing from the faculty.

1. We were taking our seats. The announcer read the line-up.
2. I was rushing to the interview. My shoelace broke.

3. The children crowded into the buses. The children were from the fifth grade.
4. She was trying to cheer Jason up. Her Halloween mask terrified Jason instead.
5. They were holding hands. A man crept up behind them.
6. She rested her bandaged foot on the stool. She was wearing a yellow satin robe.
7. My uncle said he had never received good advice. He was fifty years old then.
8. Several people saw the ranch hand. The people had been shopping in town.
9. We reached the end of the road. A vast emptiness surrounded us.
10. Sylvie received a letter announcing she had won. The letter came the day after she returned from vacation.

EXERCISE 7

Revise the following paragraph to eliminate any misplaced or dangling modifiers.

Town legend has it that Mr. Potter was as an infant left on the doorstep of a church in a basket. After a few days he was placed in the care of experienced foster parents along with two other orphans who provided love and strong guidance. Eventually adopted by his foster parents, Mr. Potter's life was seemingly happy and uneventful through law school. His bizarre behavior only started after his law practice began to completely fail.

15
Mixed and Incomplete Sentences

MIXED SENTENCES

A **mixed sentence** contains two or more parts that are incompatible — that is, the parts do not fit together. The misfit may be in grammar or in meaning.

Mixed grammar	After watching television for twelve hours was the reason his head hurt.
Mixed meaning	The work involved in directing the use of resources is the definition of management.

15a
Be sure that the parts of your sentences, particularly subjects and predicates, fit together grammatically.

Many mixed sentences occur when we start a sentence with one grammatical plan or construction in mind but end it with a different one. Such sentences often result from a confusion between two ways of making a statement.

Mixed	In all her efforts to please others got her into trouble.

In this mixed sentence the writer starts with a modifying prepositional phrase and then tries to make that phrase work as the subject of *got.* But prepositional phrases can very seldom function as sentence subjects. Here are two ways to revise the sentence.

Revised	In all her efforts to please others, *she* got into trouble. [The necessary subject *she* is added to the main clause.]

Revised All her efforts to please others got her into trouble. [The preposition *In* is dropped, leaving the subject *All her efforts.*]

Each group of sentences below illustrates a similar confusion between two sentence plans and gives ideas for revision.

Mixed Although he was seen with a convicted thief does not make him a thief. [The writer has used an adverb clause, beginning *Although,* as the subject of *does.* An adverb clause cannot serve as a subject.]

mixed
15b

Revised *That* he was seen with a convicted thief does not make him a thief. [*That* changes the clause into a noun clause, a grammatical subject.]

Revised Although he was seen with a convicted thief, *he is* not necessarily a thief. [A new subject and verb are supplied for the main clause.]

Mixed Among those who pass the entrance examinations, they do not all get admitted to the program. [*They* is not an appropriate subject for the modifying phrase beginning *Among.* A subject such as *all* or *many* is needed.]

Revised Among those who pass the entrance examinations, *not all* get admitted to the program.

Revised Among those who pass the entrance examinations, *many* do not get admitted to the program.

Revised *Not all those* who pass the entrance examinations get admitted to the program.

15b

Be sure that the subjects and predicates of your sentences fit together in meaning.

The mixed sentences examined above are confusing because their parts do not fit together grammatically. Another kind of mixed sentence fails because its subject and predicate do not fit together in meaning. Such a mixture is sometimes called a **faulty predication.**

The most common form of faulty predication occurs when the linking verb *be* connects a subject and its complement. Since such a sentence forms a kind of equation, the subject and complement must be items that can be sensibly equated. If they are not, the sentence goes awry.

Faulty A *compromise* between the city and the town would be the ideal *place* to live.

In this sentence the subject *compromise* is equated with the complement *place.* Thus the sentence says that *a compromise is a place,* clearly not a sensible statement. Sometimes such mixed sentences seem to result from the writer's effort to compress too many ideas into a single word or phrase. The sentence above can be revised to state the writer's meaning more exactly.

REVISED A *community* that offered the best qualities of both city and town would be the ideal *place* to live.

A special kind of faulty predication occurs when a clause beginning *when* or *where* follows a form of *be* in a definition, as in *Suffrage is where you have the right to vote.* Though the construction is common in speech, written definitions require nouns or noun clauses on both sides of *be: Suffrage is the right to vote.*

FAULTY *An examination* is *when you are tested* on what you know.

REVISED *An examination* is *a test* of what you know.

REVISED *In an examination you are tested* on what you know.

A similar kind of faulty predication occurs when a *because* clause follows the subject-verb pattern *The reason is,* as in *The reason is because I don't want to.* This construction is common in speech, but it is redundant since the conjunction *because* means *for the reason that.* The construction should not appear in writing.

FAULTY The *reason* we were late *is because* we had an accident.

REVISED The *reason* we were late *is that* we had an accident.

REVISED We were late *because* we had an accident.

Faulty predications are not confined to sentences with *be.* In the following sentences the italicized subjects and verbs highlight the misfit between them.

FAULTY The *use* of emission controls *was created* to reduce air pollution. [The controls, not their use, were created.]

REVISED Emission *controls were created* to reduce air pollution.

FAULTY The *area* of financial mismanagement *poses* a threat to small businesses. [Mismanagement, not the area, poses the threat.]

REVISED Financial *mismanagement poses* a threat to small businesses.

In some mixed sentences the combination of faults is so confusing that the writer has little choice but to start over.

Mixed	My long-range goal is through law school and government work I hope to deal with those problems I deal with more effectively.
Possible revision	My long-range goal is to go to law school and then work in government so that I can deal more effectively with problems I face.

EXERCISE 1

Revise the following sentences so that their parts fit together both in grammar and in meaning. Each item has more than one possible answer.

Example:

When they found out how expensive pianos are is why they were discouraged.

They were discouraged *because* they found out how expensive pianos are.

When they found out how expensive pianos are, *they* were discouraged.

1. The different accents of students is in where they grew up.
2. Because he believes news programs are misleading is why he does not watch them.
3. By simply increasing the amount of money we spend will not solve the problem of crime.
4. An antique is when an object is one hundred or more years old.
5. Among the polished stones, they were all beyond my price range.
6. Schizophrenia is when a person withdraws from reality and behaves in abnormal ways.
7. Any government that can support an expedition to Mars, they should be able to solve their country's social problems too.
8. Needlepoint is where you work with yarn on a mesh canvas.
9. Through the help of his staff is how the mayor got reelected.
10. The reason many people don't accept the theory of evolution is because it goes contrary to their religious beliefs.

INCOMPLETE SENTENCES

The most serious kind of incomplete sentence is the fragment (see Chapter 10). But sentences are also incomplete when the writer omits one or more words needed to make a phrase or clause clear or accurate.

15c

Be sure that omissions from compound constructions are consistent with grammar or idiom.

In both speech and writing we commonly use **elliptical constructions,** constructions that omit words not necessary for meaning (see 5c-4). In the following sentences the words in parentheses can be omitted without confusing or distracting the reader. Notice that they all involve compound constructions.

> My car has been driven 80,000 miles; his (has been driven) only 20,000 (miles).
>
> Some people heat by oil and some (heat) by gas.
>
> She had great hopes for her sons and (for) their children.

Such omissions are possible only when the words omitted are common to all the parts of a compound construction. When the parts differ in grammar or idiom, all words must be included in all parts.

> My car *has been driven* 80,000 miles; their cars *have been driven* only 20,000 miles.
>
> I *am* firm; you *are* stubborn; he *is* pigheaded.
>
> The students *were* invited and *were* happy to go. [The first *were* is a helping verb in the passive verb phrase *were invited.* The second *were* is a linking verb with the complement *happy.*]
>
> She had faith *in* and hopes *for* the future. [Idiom requires different prepositions with *faith* and *hopes,* so both must be included.]

Notice that in the sentence *My brother and friend moved to Dallas,* the omission of *my* before *friend* indicates that *brother* and *friend* are the same person. If two different persons are meant, the modifier or article must be repeated: *My brother and my friend moved to Dallas.*

(See 31b-3 for a list of English idioms and 17a for a discussion of grammatical parallelism.)

15d

Be sure that all comparisons are complete and logical.

Comparisons make statements about the relation between two or more things, as in *Dogs are more intelligent than cats* or *Bones was the most intelligent dog we ever had.* To be complete and logical, a comparison must state the relation fully enough to ensure clarity; it must compare only items that can sensibly be compared; and it must include all and only the items being compared.

1 State a comparison fully enough to ensure clarity.

In a comparison such as *John likes bowling better than* (*he likes*) *tennis,* we can omit *he likes* because only one meaning is possible. But sentences such as *John likes bowling better than Jane* may mean either "better than he likes Jane" or "better than Jane likes bowling." Therefore, we must be careful to state such sentences fully enough to prevent any misreading.

UNCLEAR	They worry more about money than their child.
CLEAR	They worry more about money than their child *does.*
CLEAR	They worry more about money than *about* their child.

2 Be sure that the items being compared are in fact comparable.

A comparison is logical only if it compares items that can sensibly be compared. We can compare one food with another or one car with another, but we cannot sensibly compare food with cars. We are likely to make illogical comparisons unintentionally.

ILLOGICAL	The cost of a typewriter is greater than a calculator. [The writer compares the cost of something with a calculator.]
REVISED	The cost of a typewriter is greater than *the cost of* (or *that of*) a calculator.

3 In comparing members of the same class, use *other* or *any other.* In comparing members of different classes, use *any.*

When we compare a person or thing with all others in the same group, we form two units: (1) the individual person or thing and (2) all *other* persons or things in the group.

> Joshua [the individual] was more stubborn than *any other* child in the family [all the others in the group].

ILLOGICAL	Los Angeles is larger than *any* city in California. [Since Los Angeles is itself a city in California, the sentence seems to say that Los Angeles is larger than itself.]
LOGICAL	Los Angeles is larger than *any other* city in California. [Adding *other* excludes Los Angeles from the group of the state's other cities.]

When a person or thing is compared with the members of a *different* group, the two units are logically separate.

Some American cars [one group] are cheaper than *any* foreign car [a different group].

ILLOGICAL — Los Angeles is larger than *any other* city in Canada. [The cities in Canada constitute a group to which Los Angeles does not belong.]

LOGICAL — Los Angeles is larger than *any* city in Canada. [Omitting the word *other* makes a separate group of the Canadian cities.]

inc 15e

4 Avoid comparisons that do not state what is being compared.

Brand X gets clothes *whiter*. [Whiter than what?]
Brand Y is so much *better*. [Better than what?]

15e Be careful not to omit articles, prepositions, or other needed words.

In haste or carelessness writers sometimes omit small words such as articles and prepositions that are needed for clarity.

INCOMPLETE — Regular payroll deductions are a type painless savings. You hardly notice missing amounts, and after period of years the contributions can add a large total.

REVISED — Regular payroll deductions are a type *of* painless savings. You hardly notice *the* missing amounts, and after *a* period of years the contributions can add *up to* a large total.

In both speech and writing we often omit *that* when it introduces a noun clause following a verb: *We knew (that) he was coming.* But such an omission can sometimes be confusing.

INCOMPLETE — She observed many people who had been invited were missing. [At first reading, *many people* appears to be the object of *observed* rather than the subject of the entire subordinate clause.]

REVISED — She observed *that* many people who had been invited were missing.

Attentive proofreading is the only insurance against the kind of omissions described in this section. *Proofread all your papers carefully.*

EXERCISE 2

Revise the following sentences so that they are complete, logical, and clear. Some items have more than one possible answer.

Example:

Our house is closer to the courthouse than the subway stop.

Our house is closer to the courthouse than *it is to* the subway stop.

Our house is closer to the courthouse than the subway stop *is*.

1. I get along with my parents better than my sister.
2. Councilor Dougherty not only believes but works for tax reform.
3. Wally believed people who came to him with their problems were using him.
4. His tip was larger than any customer I ever waited on.
5. With an altitude of 6288 feet, New Hampshire's Mount Washington is higher than any mountain in New England.
6. The largest bookstore the United States stocks two three copies most books in print.
7. The dog is only a puppy; the cats both ten years old.
8. My chemistry text is more interesting to me than any other social science text.
9. Inventors usually have an interest and talent for solving practical problems.
10. The legal question raised by the prosecution was relevant and considered by the judge.

IV
Effective Sentences

16
Using Coordination and Subordination

To communicate effectively, you often need to combine several statements into a single sentence, fitting thoughts together according to their relative importance. You can **coordinate** the facts and ideas you wish to emphasize equally, such as the thoughts about insurance in the sentence *Car insurance is costly, but medical insurance is almost a luxury*. You can **subordinate** statements of lesser importance to those you wish to emphasize. In the sentence *Because accidents and theft are frequent, car insurance is expensive,* the clause beginning *Because* is grammatically subordinate to the main clause. The information you decide to subordinate may be important to the total meaning of the sentence, providing necessary explanation or support, but readers will almost always see it as less important than that presented in the main clause.

In creating sentences through coordination, you may choose to link words, phrases, and clauses with the coordinating conjunctions *and, but, or, nor, for, so,* and *yet;* with conjunctive adverbs such as *however, moreover,* and *therefore;* or with similar grammatical constructions (see Chapter 17 on parallelism). In using subordination, you may place less important information in clauses introduced by subordinating conjunctions (such as *although, because, if, when, where, while*) or by relative pronouns (*who, which, that*), or you may express the information in phrases and single words.

The following sections provide guidelines for using coordination and subordination effectively in constructing sentences.

16a
Coordinating to relate equal ideas

Two or more simple sentences in a row will seem roughly equal in importance but distinct, even if they are related in content.

Thus readers will have to detect on their own the specific relations among the sentences. By linking sentences and ideas with coordinating conjunctions or conjunctive adverbs, a writer can help readers see the relations more easily. Compare the following passages.

> We should not rely so heavily on coal, oil, and uranium. We have a substantial energy resource in the moving waters of our rivers. Smaller streams add to the total volume of water. The resource renews itself. Coal and oil are irreplaceable. Uranium is also irreplaceable. The cost of water does not increase much over time. The costs of coal, oil, and uranium rise dramatically.

> We should not rely so heavily on coal, oil, and uranium, for we have a substantial energy resource in the moving waters of our rivers and streams. Coal, oil, and uranium are irreplaceable and thus subject to dramatic cost increases; water, however, is self-renewing and more stable in cost.

The information in both passages is essentially the same, but the second is shorter and considerably easier to read and understand. Whereas the first passage strings ideas together in short, simple sentences without relating them to each other, the second passage builds connections among coordinate ideas: the availability of water in rivers and streams (first sentence); the relation between renewal and cost (second sentence); and the contrast between water and the other resources (both sentences).

Punctuating coordinated words, phrases, and clauses

Most coordinated words, phrases, and subordinate clauses are not punctuated with commas (see 21j-2). The exceptions are items in a series and coordinate adjectives.

> We rely heavily on *coal, oil, and uranium.* [A series; see 21f-1.]

> *Dusty, dog-eared* books littered his rooms. [Coordinate adjectives; see 21f-2.]

In a sentence consisting of two main clauses, punctuation depends on whether a coordinating conjunction, a conjunctive adverb, or no connecting word links the clauses.

> Oil is irreplaceable, *but* water is self-renewing. [See 21a.]
> Oil is irreplaceable; *however,* water is self-renewing. [See 22b.]
> Oil is irreplaceable; water is self-renewing. [See 22a.]

1 Avoiding faulty coordination

Faulty coordination occurs when no logical connection seems to exist between two coordinated statements or when the connection expressed by the coordinating conjunction contradicts common sense.

Faulty Forecasters had predicted a mild winter, and temperatures were lower than normal.

Revised Forecasters had predicted a mild winter, *but* temperatures were lower than normal.

Sometimes faulty coordination occurs because the writer omits necessary information, as in the following example.

Faulty Julie is a hairdresser, and she has developed a skin allergy.

Revised As a hairdresser, Julie *must use products containing strong chemicals; consequently,* she has developed a skin allergy.

Revised *Because* her work as a hairdresser *requires that she use products containing strong chemicals,* Julie has developed a skin allergy.

Often, as the second revision shows, the intended relation between clauses can be clarified by subordinating one of the ideas if it modifies or explains the other one. Here is another example.

Faulty John Stuart Mill was a utilitarian, and he believed that actions should be judged by their usefulness or by the happiness they cause.

Revised John Stuart Mill, *a utilitarian,* believed that actions should be judged by their usefulness or by the happiness they cause.

2 Avoiding excessive coordination

A stringy compound sentence—a sequence of main clauses linked with coordinating conjunctions—creates the same effect as a series of simple sentences: it obscures the relative importance of ideas and details.

Excessive coordination We were near the end of the trip, and the storm kept getting worse, and the snow and ice covered the windshield, and I could hardly see the road ahead, and I knew I should stop, but I kept on driving, and once I barely missed a truck.

This sentence contains two main assertions: *the storm kept getting worse* and *I kept on driving.* All the rest is detail elaborating on these simple statements. The information in the sentence needs to be recombined using subordination so that the main assertions and supporting detail are clearly distinguished for the reader.

REVISED As we neared the end of the trip, *the storm kept getting worse,* covering the windshield with snow and ice until I could barely see the road ahead. Even though I knew I should stop, *I kept on driving,* once barely missing a truck.

Be careful not to overuse *so* as a connector.

EXCESSIVE COORDINATION Jim had an examination that day, so he came home late, so he missed seeing the fire, so he was not able to describe it to us.

As with other varieties of excessive coordination, the best way to revise such sentences is to separate the main statement from dependent details.

REVISED *Jim was not able to describe the fire to us* because he had an examination that day and arrived home too late to see the fire.

Excessive coordination is not always as obvious as it is in the two preceding examples. The following passage contains only two compound sentences, but they still connect facts so loosely that the reader is left to distinguish their importance.

EXCESSIVE COORDINATION A man came out of the liquor store. He wore a pair of frayed corduroy pants, and he wore a brown sweater. He started toward a blue car, and the police arrested him.

In revising this passage, a writer might use subordination to show which ideas are important and which less important. The essential fact that the police arrested the man could become the main clause and all other details part of a single subordinate *when* clause.

REVISED When a man wearing frayed corduroy pants and a brown sweater came out of the liquor store and started toward a blue car, *the police arrested him.*

EXERCISE 1

Combine sentences in the following passages to coordinate related ideas in the way that seems most effective to you. You will have to supply coordinating conjunctions or conjunctive adverbs and the appropriate punctuation.

1. Many chronic misspellers do not have the time to master spelling rules. They may not have the motivation. They rely on dictionaries to catch misspellings. Most dictionaries list words under their correct spellings. One kind of dictionary is designed for chronic misspellers. It lists each word under its common *mis*spellings. It then provides the correct spelling. It also provides the definition.

2. Henry Hudson was an English explorer. He captained ships for the Dutch East India Company. On a voyage in 1610 he passed by Greenland. He sailed into a great bay in today's northern Canada. He thought he and his sailors could winter there. The cold was terrible. Food ran out. The sailors mutinied. The sailors cast Hudson adrift in a small boat. Eight others were also in the boat. Hudson and his companions perished.

EXERCISE 2

Revise the following sentences to eliminate faulty or excessive coordination. Relate ideas effectively by adding or subordinating information or by forming more than one sentence. Each item has more than one possible answer.

Example:

My dog barks, and I have to move out of my apartment.

Because my dog's barking *disturbs my neighbors,* I have to move out of my apartment.

1. The candidate was an Independent, and she disagreed with both the Republican and the Democrat.
2. He is almost always cheerful, and he has few friends.
3. The dean was furious, and she let the police know it, but they refused to listen, and they began patrolling the campus anyway.
4. The dogs escaped from the pen because the keeper forgot to secure the latch, and the dogs wanted freedom, and they got it by running away, and it took the rest of the day to find them.
5. The weather in March is cold and rainy, but sometimes it is warm and sunny, and the inconsistency makes it impossible to plan outdoor activities, yet everyone wants to be outdoors after the long winter.
6. The gun sounded, and I froze, but an instant later I was running with a smooth, pumping motion, and I knew I would win the race.
7. The citizens of Vermont are determined to preserve their environment, and they have some of the nation's toughest antipollution laws.
8. Two days last month were legal holidays, and the school held classes as usual.
9. Registering for classes the first time is confusing, and you have to find your way around, and you have to deal with strangers.
10. Air traffic in and out of major cities increases yearly, and the congestion is becoming dangerous, but the current regulations are inadequate, and they cannot control even the present traffic.

16b
Subordinating to distinguish main ideas

Like paragraphs, many sentences consist of a main idea amplified and supported by details. In a paragraph the main idea often appears in a topic sentence, and the details appear in the remaining sentences (see 3a). In a sentence you may choose to present the main idea in the main clause and the details in subordinate structures such as phrases or subordinate clauses. This arrangement helps readers distinguish principal ideas from supporting information. In the following sentence the writer does not provide such assistance.

> In recent years computer prices have dropped, and production costs have dropped more slowly, and computer manufacturers have had to contend with shrinking profits.

The writer gives three facts: computer prices have decreased, production costs have decreased, and profits have shrunk. By loosely coordinating these three facts, the writer suggests some relation among them. But *in recent years* and *more slowly* provide the only explicit relations. We do not know which fact the writer considers most important or how the others qualify or support it. Look at the improvement in these revisions.

> *Because* production costs have dropped more slowly than computer prices in recent years, computer manufacturers have had to contend with shrinking profits.
>
> In recent years computer manufacturers have had to contend with shrinking profits *on account of* a slower drop in production costs than in computer prices.
>
> *Faced with* a slower drop in production costs than in computer prices, computer manufacturers have had to contend with shrinking profits in recent years.

In these revisions the words *because, on account of,* and *faced with* indicate specific cause-and-effect relations among the three facts. Each sentence makes clear that computer manufacturers' profits decline when prices fall more quickly than production costs, but the emphasis varies from one version to another.

No rules can specify what information in a sentence you should make primary and what you should subordinate; the decision will depend on your meaning. But, in general, you should consider using subordinate structures for details of time, cause, condition, concession, purpose, and identification (size, location, and the like). Consider the use of subordinate clauses in the following pairs of examples. (Some appropriate subordinating conjunctions and relative pronouns are listed in parentheses.)

Time (*after, before, since, until, when, while*)

The mine explosion killed six workers. The owners adopted safety measures.

After the mine explosion killed six workers, the owners adopted safety measures.

Cause (*because, since*)

Jones has been without work for six months. He is having trouble paying his bills.

Because Jones has been without work for six months, he is having trouble paying his bills.

Condition (*if, provided, since, unless*)

Mike attends no lectures and studies infrequently. He has little chance of passing his biology examination.

Since Mike attends no lectures and studies infrequently, he has little chance of passing his biology examination.

Concession (*although, as if, even though, though*)

The horse looked gentle. It proved high-spirited and hard to manage.

Although the horse looked gentle, it proved high-spirited and hard to manage.

Purpose (*in order that, so that, that*)

Congress passed new immigration laws. Many Vietnamese refugees could enter the United States.

Congress passed new immigration laws *so that* many Vietnamese refugees could enter the United States.

Identification (*that, when, where, which, who*)

The old factory now manufactures automobile transmissions. It stands on the south side of town and covers three acres.

The old factory, *which* stands on the south side of town and covers three acres, now manufactures automobile transmissions.

Using subordinate clauses to distinguish main ideas from supporting information is an important strategy for creating effective sentences. But you can use other grammatical constructions as well to indicate the subordinate role of certain statements or information. A verbal or prepositional phrase, an appositive, an absolute phrase, or even a single-word modifier will often be the appropriate choice. In general, a subordinate clause places greatest emphasis on the subordinate information; verbal phrases, appositives, and absolute phrases give less weight; prepositional phrases still less; and single words the least. The following examples illustrate the differences among subordinate constructions.

Old barns are common in New England. They are often painted red. [Separate sentences.]

Old barns, *which are often painted red,* are common in New England. [Subordinate clause.]

Old barns, *often painted red,* are common in New England. [Verbal phrase.]

Old *red* barns are common in New England. [Single word.]

In the following examples notice how different grammatical constructions give different weight to the information in some of the sentence pairs we looked at earlier.

Jones has been without work for six months. He is having trouble paying his bills. [Separate sentences.]

Because Jones has been without work for six months, he is having trouble paying his bills. [Subordinate clause.]

Having been without work for six months, Jones is having trouble paying his bills. [Verbal phrase.]

Out of work for six months, Jones is having trouble paying his bills. [Prepositional phrase.]

The horse looked gentle. It proved high-spirited and hard to manage. [Separate sentences.]

Although the horse looked gentle, it proved high-spirited and hard to manage. [Subordinate clause.]

The horse, *a gentle-looking animal,* proved high-spirited and hard to manage. [Appositive.]

The *gentle-looking* horse proved high-spirited and hard to manage. [Single word.]

The old factory now manufactures automobile transmissions. It stands on the south side of town and covers three acres. [Separate sentences.]

The old factory, *which stands on the south side of town and covers three acres,* now manufactures automobile transmissions. [Subordinate clause.]

The *three-acre* factory *on the south side of town* now manufactures automobile transmissions. [Single word and prepositional phrase.]

Punctuating subordinate constructions

A modifying word, phrase, or clause that introduces a sentence is usually set off from the rest of the sentence with a comma (see 21b).

Fortunately, I got the job.
In a little over six months, the company will open a new plant.

sub
16b

Buffeted by the wind, the boat drifted out to sea.
When the crisis passed, everyone was relieved.

A modifier that interrupts or concludes a main clause is *not* set off with punctuation when it restricts the meaning of a word or words in the clause (see 21c).

Her article *about a bank failure* won a prize.

The article *that won the prize* appeared in the local newspaper.

She wrote the article *because the bank failure affected many residents of the town.*

When an interrupting or concluding modifier does *not* restrict meaning, but simply adds information to the sentence, it *is* set off with punctuation, usually a comma or commas (see 21c).

The bank, *over forty years old*, never reopened.

The bank managers, *who were cleared of any wrongdoing*, all found new jobs.

The customers of the bank never recovered all their money, *although most of them tried to do so.*

Like a modifier, an appositive is set off with punctuation (usually a comma or commas) only when it does *not* restrict the meaning of the word it refers to (see 21c-2).

The movie, *a science-fiction adventure*, was a huge success.
The movie *Star Wars* was directed by George Lucas.

A dash or dashes may also be used to set off a nonrestrictive appositive, particularly when it contains commas (see 25b-2). A concluding appositive is sometimes set off with a colon (see 25a-1).

1 Avoiding faulty subordination

Faulty subordination occurs when a writer uses a subordinate clause or other subordinate structure for what seems clearly to be the most important idea in the sentence. Often, faulty subordination merely reverses the dependent relation the reader expects.

FAULTY	Ms. Angelo was in her first year of teaching, although she was a better instructor than others with many years of experience. [The sentence suggests that Ms. Angelo's inexperience is the main idea, whereas the writer almost certainly intended to stress her skill *despite* her inexperience.]
REVISED	Although Ms. Angelo was in her first year of teaching, *she was a better instructor than others with many years of experience.*

Faulty Marty's final interview that was to determine his admission to law school began at two o'clock. [Common sense says that the important fact is the interview's purpose, not its time.]

Revised *Marty's final interview,* which began at two o'clock, *was to determine his admission to law school.*

2
Avoiding excessive subordination

Excessive subordination sometimes occurs when a writer tries to cram too much loosely related information into one long sentence.

Overloaded The boats that were moored at the dock when the hurricane, which was one of the worst in three decades, struck were ripped from their moorings, because the owners had not been adequately prepared, since the weather service had predicted the storm would blow out to sea, which they do at this time of year.

sub
16b

Since such sentences usually have more than one idea that deserves a main clause, they are best revised by sorting their details into more than one sentence.

Revised Struck by one of the worst hurricanes in three decades, *the boats at the dock were ripped from their moorings. The owners were unprepared* because the weather service had said that hurricanes at this time of year blow out to sea.

A common form of excessive subordination occurs with a string of adjective clauses beginning *which, who,* or *that,* as in the following:

String of adjective clauses Every Christmas we all try to go to my grandfather's house, which is near Louisville, which is an attractive city where my parents now live.

To revise such sentences, consider recasting some of the subordinate clauses as other kinds of modifying structures. In the following revision, for example, the clause *which is near Louisville* has been reduced to a simple modifier, and the clause *which is an attractive city* has been changed to an appositive.

Revised Every Christmas we all try to go to my grandfather's house *near Louisville, an attractive city* where my parents now live.

sub
16b

EXERCISE 3

Combine each of the following pairs of sentences twice, each time using one of the subordinate structures in parentheses to make a single sentence. You will have to add, delete, change, and rearrange words.

Example:

During the late eighteenth century, workers carried beverages in brightly colored bottles. The bottles had cork stoppers. (*Clause beginning that. Phrase beginning with.*)

During the late eighteenth century, workers carried beverages in brightly colored bottles *that had cork stoppers.*

During the late eighteenth century, workers carried beverages in brightly colored bottles *with cork stoppers.*

1. Harrods in London is the largest department store in the world. It consists of over 250 departments. (*Phrase beginning consisting. Phrase beginning with.*)
2. The man saw a ship approaching. He fell to his knees. (*Clause beginning when. Phrase beginning seeing.*)
3. Route 93 is the most direct route to school. It is under construction. (*Clause beginning although. Appositive beginning the most.*)
4. Frances Perkins was the first female cabinet member in the U.S. She was dedicated to social reform. (*Phrase beginning dedicated. Appositive beginning the first.*)
5. James Joyce is one of the century's most controversial writers. He has been praised as the greatest writer since Milton and condemned as a writer of "latrine literature." (*Clause beginning who. Phrase beginning praised.*)
6. The Amish live peaceful but austere lives. Most of them refuse to use modern technology. (*Absolute phrase beginning most. Phrase beginning living.*)
7. Hernando de Soto is the legendary European discoverer of the Mississippi River. He supposedly died on the river's banks. (*Clause beginning who. Appositive beginning the legendary.*)
8. Computerized newspaper operations speed up and simplify copy preparation. They are favored by editors and reporters. (*Clause beginning because. Phrase beginning favored.*)
9. Andrew Bradford began the American magazine industry. He first published *American Magazine* in 1741. (*Clause beginning who. Clause beginning when.*)
10. In World War I, German forces set out to capture Verdun. Verdun was a fortress in northeastern France. (*Clause beginning which. Appositive beginning a fortress.*)

EXERCISE 4

Rewrite the following paragraph in the way you think most effective to subordinate the less important ideas to the more important ones. Use subordinate clauses or other subordinate constructions as appropriate.

Many students today are no longer majoring in the liberal arts. I mean by "liberal arts" such subjects as history, English, and the social sciences. Students think a liberal arts degree will not help them get jobs. They are wrong. They may not get practical, job-related experience from the liberal arts, but they will get a broad education, and it will never again be available to them. Many employers look for more than a technical, professional education. They think such an education can make an employee's views too narrow. The employers want open-minded employees. They want employees to think about problems from many angles. The liberal arts curriculum instills such flexibility. The flexibility is vital to the health of our society.

EXERCISE 5

Revise the following sentences to eliminate faulty or excessive subordination by reversing main and subordinate ideas, by coordinating ideas, or by making separate sentences. Some items have more than one possible answer.

Example:

Terrified to return home, he had driven his mother's car into a corn field.

Having driven his mother's car into a corn field, he was terrified to return home.

1. The National Theatre in London is government funded, which means that stand-by and discounted tickets are available for every performance.
2. He had experienced two near air disasters, although he continued to fly.
3. The car that my boss parked in front of the store, which rolled into my bike, was the car that he had just bought.
4. A woman who wants a career in the armed forces is better off now than she used to be because reasonable people no longer think that there's anything wrong with women who want to become career officers, which used to be a problem.
5. The speaker from the Sierra Club, whom we had invited on short notice when our planned speaker canceled, nonetheless gave an informative talk about the need to preserve our wilderness areas, which he said were in danger of extinction.

16c
Choosing clear connectors

Most connecting words signal specific and unambiguous relations; for instance, the coordinating conjunction *but* clearly indicates contrast, and the subordinating conjunction *because* clearly indicates cause. A few connectors, however, require careful use, either because they are ambiguous in many contexts and may therefore confuse the reader or because they are often misused in current English.

1 Avoiding ambiguous connectors: *as* and *while*

The subordinating conjunction *as* can indicate several kinds of adverbial relations, including comparison and time.

Comparison	He was working *as* rapidly as he could.
Time	The instructor finally arrived *as* the class was leaving.

As is sometimes used to indicate cause, but in that sense it is often ambiguous and should be avoided.

Ambiguous	*As* I was in town, I visited some old friends. [Time or cause intended?]
Clear	*When* I was in town, I visited some old friends. [Time.]
Clear	*Because* I was in town, I visited some old friends. [Cause.]

The subordinating conjunction *while* can indicate either time or concession. Unless the context makes the meaning of *while* unmistakably clear, choose a more exact connector.

Ambiguous	*While* we were working nearby, we did not hear the burglars enter. [Time or concession?]
Clear	*When* we were working nearby, we did not hear the burglars enter. [Time.]
Clear	*Although* we were working nearby, we did not hear the burglars enter. [Concession.]

2 Avoiding misused connectors: *as, like,* and *while*

The use of *as* as a substitute for *whether* or *that* is nonstandard — that is, it violates the conventions of spoken and written standard English.

Nonstandard	He was not sure *as* he could come.
Revised	He was not sure *whether* (or *that*) he could come.

Although the preposition *like* is often used as a conjunction in informal speech and in advertising (*Dirt-Away works like a soap should*), writing and formal speech generally require the conjunction *as, as if,* or *as though.*

Informal speech	It seemed *like* the examination would never end.
Writing	It seemed *as if* (*as though*) the examination would never end.

The subordinating conjunction *while* is sometimes carelessly used in the sense of *and* or *but,* creating false subordination.

Faulty	My sister wants to study medicine *while* I want to study law.
Revised	My sister wants to study medicine, *and* I want to study law.

EXERCISE 6

Substitute a clear or correct connector in the following sentences where *as, while,* and *like* are ambiguous or misused.

Example:

He looked to me like he had slept in his clothes.
He looked to me *as if* he had slept in his clothes.

1. The poet looked like he had never read in public before.
2. Many writers use *he* to denote both males and females, while others avoid the usage.
3. As I was going home for Thanksgiving, my mother cooked a squash pie for me.
4. Some banks now charge for each transaction, like the monthly charge weren't enough of a burden for customers.
5. As teachers and legislators worry about the literacy of high school students, the situation may improve.

sub **16c**

EXERCISE 7

The following paragraph contains instances of faulty, excessive, or ineffective coordination or subordination. Rewrite the paragraph in the way you think most effective to emphasize main ideas.

Sir Walter Raleigh personified the Elizabethan Age, which was the period during which Elizabeth I ruled England, which occurred in the last half of the sixteenth century. Raleigh was a courtier and poet. He was also an explorer and entrepreneur. Supposedly, he gained Queen Elizabeth's favor by throwing his cloak beneath her feet at the right moment. She was just about to step over a puddle. There is no evidence for this story, although it illustrates Raleigh's dramatic and dynamic personality. His energy drew others to him. He was one of Elizabeth's favorites. She supported him. She also dispensed favors to him. However, he lost his queen's good will. Without her permission he seduced one of her maids of honor. He eventually married the maid of honor. Elizabeth died. Then her successor imprisoned Raleigh in the Tower of London. Her successor was James I. Raleigh was charged falsely with treason. He was released after thirteen years. He was arrested again two years later on the old treason charges. At the age of sixty-six he was beheaded.

17
Using Parallelism

Parallelism is a similarity of grammatical form between two or more coordinated elements.

The air is dirtied by	factories	belching	smoke
and	cars	spewing	exhaust.

Parallel structure reinforces and highlights a close relation or a contrast between compound sentence elements, whether they be words, phrases, or entire clauses.

The principle underlying parallelism is that form should reflect meaning: since the parts of compound constructions have the same function and importance, they should have the same grammatical form. For the writer, parallelism is both a way to emphasize related ideas and a grammatical requirement to be observed in constructing sentences. In the following sections we will look at both roles of parallelism.

17a
Using parallelism for coordinate elements

Parallel structure is necessary wherever coordination exists: wherever elements are connected by coordinating conjunctions or by correlative conjunctions, wherever elements are compared or contrasted, and wherever items are arranged in a list or outline. The elements should match each other in structure, though they need not match word for word, as the previous sentence of this paragraph illustrates. In the following sentence the coordinate prepositional phrases are parallel even though the second phrase contains more words.

We passed *through the town* and *into the vast, unpopulated desert.*

1
Using parallelism for elements linked by coordinating conjunctions

The coordinating conjunctions *and, but, or, nor,* and *yet* always signal a need for parallelism, as the following sentences show.

> Miracle Grill will cook your food *in the kitchen* or *on the patio.*
>
> Political candidates *often explain what they intend to do* but *rarely explain how they are going to do it.*
>
> In Melanie's home, children had to account for *where they had been* and *what they had been doing.*

Sentence elements linked by coordinating conjunctions should be parallel in structure; otherwise, their coordination will be weakened and the reader distracted.

Faulty Three reasons why steel companies keep losing money are that their plants are inefficient, high labor costs, and foreign competition is increasing.

Revised Three reasons why steel companies keep losing money are inefficient plants, high labor costs, and increasing foreign competition.

When idiom or grammar requires different words in compound constructions, the different words must be included (see also 15c).

Faulty The boy demonstrated an interest and a talent for writing.

Revised The boy demonstrated an interest *in* and a talent for writing. [Idiom dictates different prepositions with *interest* and *talent.*]

Faulty The thieves were careless and apprehended.

Revised The thieves were careless and *were* apprehended. [Each *were* serves a different grammatical function—the first as a linking verb, the second as a helping verb.]

Often, the same word must be repeated to avoid confusion.

Confusing Thoreau stood up for his principles *by not paying* his taxes and *spending* a night in jail. [Did he spend a night in jail or not?]

Revised Thoreau stood up for his principles *by not paying* his taxes and *by spending* a night in jail.

Be sure that clauses beginning *and who* or *and which* are coordinated only with preceding *who* and *which* clauses.

Faulty	Marie is a young woman *of great ability* and *who wants* to be a lawyer.
Revised	Marie is a young woman *who has* great ability and *who wants* to be a lawyer.
Revised	Marie is a young woman *of great ability who wants* to be a lawyer.

2 Using parallelism for elements linked by correlative conjunctions

Correlative conjunctions are pairs of connectors such as *both . . . and, not only . . . but also,* and *either . . . or* (see 5d-1). They stress equality and balance and thus emphasize the relation between elements, even long phrases and clauses. The elements should be parallel to confirm their relation.

> Off-road vehicles are both *interrupting the peacefulness of the desert* and *destroying its vegetation.*
>
> At the end of the novel, Huck Finn not only *rejects society's values by turning down money and a home* but also *affirms his own values by setting out for "the territory."*

Most errors in parallelism with correlative conjunctions occur when the element after the second connector does not match the element after the first connector.

Nonparallel	He told the boy either *to brush* the horse or *feed* the chickens.
Revised	He told the boy either *to brush* the horse or *to feed* the chickens.
Nonparallel	We were warned that we must either *pay* our rent or *we must vacate* the apartment.
Revised	We were warned that we must either *pay* our rent or *vacate* the apartment.

3 Using parallelism for elements being compared or contrasted

Elements being compared or contrasted should ordinarily be cast in the same grammatical form.

> It is better *to live rich* than *to die rich.* – Samuel Johnson

Weak	Jody wanted *a job* rather than *to apply for welfare.*
Revised	Jody wanted *a job* rather than *welfare payments.*
Revised	Jody wanted *to find a job* rather than *to apply for welfare.*

4
Using parallelism for items in lists or outlines

The elements of a list or outline that divides a larger subject are coordinate and should be parallel in structure. (See also 1h-2 on outlining.)

FAULTY	IMPROVED
The Renaissance in England was marked by	The Renaissance in England was marked by
1. an extension of trade routes	1. the extension of trade routes
2. merchant class became more powerful	2. the increasing power of the merchant class
3. the death of feudalism	3. the death of feudalism
4. upsurging of the arts	4. the upsurge of the arts
5. the sciences were encouraged	5. the encouragement of the sciences
6. religious quarrels began	6. the rise of religious quarrels

EXERCISE 1

Identify the parallel elements in the following sentences. How does parallelism contribute to the effectiveness of each sentence?

1. This apparent amnesia, which Freud labelled infantile or childhood amnesia, applies only to our memories about the self, not to our memory for words learned or objects and people recognized. – PATRICK HUYGHE
2. The faster the plane, the narrower the seats. – JOHN H. DURRELL
3. They [pioneer women] rolled out dough on the wagon seats, cooked with fires made out of buffalo chips, tended the sick, and marked the graves of their children, husbands and each other. – ELLEN GOODMAN
4. The mornings are the pleasantest times in the apartment, exhaustion having set in, the sated mosquitoes at rest on ceiling and walls, sleeping it off, the room a swirl of tortured bedclothes and abandoned garments, the vines in their full leafiness filtering the hard light of day, the air conditioner silent at last, like the mosquitoes. – E. B. WHITE
5. Aging paints every action gray, lies heavy on every movement, imprisons every thought. – SHARON CURTIN

EXERCISE 2

Revise the following sentences to make coordinate, compared, or listed elements parallel in structure. Add or delete words or rephrase as necessary to increase the effectiveness of each sentence.

Example:

After emptying her bag, searching the apartment, and having called the library, Jennifer realized she had lost the book.

After emptying her bag, searching the apartment, and *calling* the library, Jennifer realized she had lost the book.

1. The reviews of the play were uniformly positive: unstinting praise for the actors; the director's interpretation was acclaimed; and the reviews applauded the playwright's technique.
2. Her tennis coach taught her how to serve and rushing the net and winning the point.
3. The unprepared student wishes for either a blizzard or to have a blackout on the examination day.
4. Working last summer as a waitress, I learned about choosing wine, how to serve wine, and making small talk while wrestling the cork from the bottle.
5. My favorite winter activities are skiing, reading, and to drink herbal tea by the fire.
6. To receive an A in that class, one must have both a perfect attendance record and academic record.
7. In moving from Vermont to California, I was bothered less by the distance than to experience the climate change and especially that Christmases are warm and snowless.
8. After a week on a construction job, Leon felt not so much exhausted as that he was invigorated by the physical labor.
9. To lose weight, cut down on what you eat, eat fewer calories in the food you do consume, and you should exercise regularly.
10. Her generosity, sympathetic nature, and the fact that she is able to motivate employees make her an excellent supervisor.

17b
Using parallelism to increase coherence

Parallelism not only ensures similarity of form for coordinated structures but also enhances coherence by clearly relating paired or opposed units. Consider this sentence:

NONPARALLEL During the early weeks of the semester, the course reviews fundamentals, but little emphasis is placed on new material or more advanced concepts.

Here "the course" is doing two things—or doing one thing and not doing the other—and these are opposites. But the nonparallel construction of the sentence (*the course reviews . . . little emphasis is placed*) does not help the reader see the connection quickly.

REVISED — During the early weeks of the semester, the course *reviews fundamentals* but *places little emphasis* on new material or more advanced concepts.

Effective parallelism will enable you to combine in a single, well-ordered sentence related ideas that you might have expressed in two or three separate sentences. Compare the following three sentences with the original single sentence written by H. L. Mencken.

> Slang originates in the effort of ingenious individuals to make language more pungent and picturesque. They increase the store of terse and striking words or widen the boundaries of metaphor. Thus a vocabulary for new shades and differences in meaning is provided by slang.

> Slang originates in the effort of ingenious individuals to make the language more pungent and picturesque—to increase the store of terse and striking words, to widen the boundaries of metaphor, and to provide a vocabulary for new shades and differences in meaning.
> – H. L. MENCKEN

Parallel structure works as well to emphasize the connections among related sentences in a paragraph (see 3b-2).

> Style is an extraordinary thing. It is one of the subtlest secrets of all art. . . . *In painting, it is* composition, colour-sense, and brushwork. *In sculpture, it is* the treatment of depths and surfaces and the choice of stones and metals. *In music, it is* surely the melodic line, the tone-colour, and the shape of the phrase. . . . *In prose and poetry, it is* the choice of words, their placing, and the rhythms and melodies of sentence and paragraph.
> – GILBERT HIGHET

Here, Highet clarifies and emphasizes his assertion that style is common to all forms of art by casting four successive sentences in the same structure (*In . . . , it is . . .*).

EXERCISE 3

Combine each group of sentences below into one concise sentence in which parallel elements appear in parallel structures. You will have to add, delete, change, and rearrange words. Each item has more than one possible answer.

Example:

Christin sorted the books neatly into piles. She was efficient about it, too.

Christin sorted the books neatly *and efficiently* into piles.

1. The professor spoke rapidly. Moreover, his voice was almost inaudible.
2. The cyclists finally arrived at their destination. They arrived

after riding uphill most of the day. They had also endured a hailstorm.

3. I go to jazz class on Wednesday evenings. Sometimes I attend on Friday afternoons.
4. Finding an apartment requires expenditures of time and energy. It requires paying close attention to newspaper advertisements. It also requires that one learn the city's neighborhoods.
5. After making several costly mistakes, he stopped to consider the jobs available to him. He thought about his goals for a job.
6. To make a good stew, marinate the meat. There should be plenty of vegetables added. Wine should be included for flavor. Simmer the whole thing for at least two hours.
7. Carlone had three desires. First, he wanted money. Second, he wanted to be famous. The third desire was for happiness.
8. The sun looks small at its zenith. But it looks large when it reaches the horizon.
9. Most people who saw the movie were unimpressed with the acting. Or they frankly criticized the acting.
10. We returned from camping very tired. We were dirty. Mosquito bites covered us.

EXERCISE 4

Revise the following paragraph to create parallelism wherever it is required for grammar or for coherence.

The great white shark has an undeserved bad reputation. Many people consider the great white not only swift and powerful but also to be a cunning and cruel predator on humans. However, scientists claim that the great white attacks humans not by choice but as a result of chance. To a shark, our behavior in the water is similiar to that of porpoises, seals, and sea lions—the shark's favorite foods. These sea mammals are both agile enough and can move fast enough to evade the shark. Thus the shark must attack with swiftness and noiselessly to surprise the prey and giving it little chance to escape. Humans become the shark's victims not because the shark has any preference or hatred of humans but because humans can neither outswim nor can they outmaneuver the shark. If the fish were truly a cruel human-eater, it would prolong the terror of its attacks, perhaps by circling or bumping into its intended victims before they were attacked.

18
Emphasizing Main Ideas

Effective writing uses coordination, subordination, and parallelism to help readers understand the relationship of ideas and details. It also emphasizes important information by making it readily apparent to readers.

18a
Arranging ideas effectively

In arranging ideas within sentences for emphasis, you should keep two principles in mind. First, the beginnings and endings of sentences are the most emphatic positions, and endings are generally more emphatic than beginnings. Second, a parallel series of words, phrases, or clauses will be most emphatic if the elements appear in order of increasing importance.

1
Using sentence beginnings and endings

The basic sentence in English consists of two parts: a subject that names a topic and a predicate that makes a comment on the topic with a verb and any objects or complements (see 5a). Readers automatically look to the basic sentence for the writer's principal meaning, even when words, phrases, or clauses modify parts or all of the basic sentence or add important information to it. By controlling the position of the basic sentence in relation to other elements, you can help readers focus on ideas or information in a way that best suits your purpose.

Just as in speech we stress the beginning and the ending of a sentence, so in reading we expect the beginning and the ending to contain important information. Thus the most effective way to call attention to information is to place it first or last in the sentence, reserving the middle for incidentals.

Unemphatic	Education remains the most important single means of economic advancement, in spite of all its shortcomings.
Revised	In spite of all its shortcomings, education remains the most important single means of economic advancement.
Revised	Education remains, in spite of all its shortcomings, the most important single means of economic advancement.

The topic (*education*), the comment (*remains . . . advancement*), and the modifier (*in spite . . . shortcomings*) remain the same, word for word. However, changes in their positions affect the way we interpret the meaning of each sentence. In the first sentence our final attention rests on education's shortcomings rather than on its importance, even though the importance is clearly what the writer wished to emphasize. The first revision stresses the qualifying phrase a bit by placing it at the beginning but emphasizes education's importance by reserving it for the end. The second revision de-emphasizes the qualification by placing it in the middle, leaving both education and its importance in emphatic positions.

emph
18a

Many sentences begin with the subject and predicate plus their modifiers and then add more modifiers at the end. Such sentences are called **cumulative** (because they accumulate information as they proceed) or **loose** (because they are not tightly structured).

Cumulative	Jim staggered through the doorway, his pants torn, his shirt ripped open, his cheeks greasy and bleeding.
Cumulative	Most of the Great American Desert is made up of bare rock, rugged cliffs, mesas, canyons, mountains, separated from one another by broad flat basins covered with sun-baked mud and alkali, supporting a sparse and measured growth of sagebrush or creosote or saltbush, depending on location and elevation. – Edward Abbey

As these examples illustrate, a cumulative sentence completes its main statement (topic and comment) and then explains, amplifies, or illustrates it. The primary emphasis lies on the opening main clause, but the sentence continues to provide new information.

The opposite kind of sentence, called **periodic,** saves the main clause until just before the end (the period) of the sentence. Everything before the main clause points toward it by telling the reader how to interpret it.

Periodic	Though his lawyer defended him eloquently and he himself begged for leniency in a moving plea, the jury found him guilty.
Periodic	In the Mason jars stacked up dusty and fly-specked on the side shelves, in the broken-webbed snowshoes hung there, the heap of rusty hinged traps waiting this long to be oiled and set to catch something in the night, was the visible imprint of the past we were rooted in. – Joan Chase

A variation of the periodic sentence names the subject at the beginning, follows it with a modifier, and then fills in the predicate.

> Thirty-eight-year-old Dick Hayne, who works in jeans and loafers and likes to let a question cure in the air for a while before answering it, bears all the markings of what his generation used to call a laid-back kind of guy. – George Rush

Whether the subject comes first or is delayed along with the predicate, the periodic sentence creates suspense for the reader by reserving the important information of the main clause for the end.

Here, for comparison, are cumulative and periodic revisions of an unemphatic sentence.

Unemphatic	Under half steam and spewing black smoke, the ship finally reached port with its hull battered and a hole punched in its bow.
Cumulative	The ship finally reached port under half steam and spewing black smoke, with its hull battered and a hole punched in its bow.
Periodic	Under half steam and spewing black smoke, with its hull battered and a hole punched in its bow, the ship finally reached port.

The cumulative sentence parallels the way we naturally think (by accumulating information), and it does not tax the memory of readers. The periodic sentence is more contrived, and it requires careful planning so that the reader can remember all the information leading up to the main clause. You should save the periodic sentence for when your purpose demands climactic emphasis.

2 Arranging parallel elements effectively

Series

Parallelism requires that you express coordinate ideas in similar grammatical structures (see Chapter 17). In addition, you should arrange the coordinate ideas in order of importance. A series of grammatically parallel elements can be weak if you arrange the elements randomly.

> **Unemphatic** The storm ripped the roofs off several buildings, killed ten people, and knocked down many trees in town.

In this sentence the least serious damage (*knocked down many trees*) concludes the series, and the most serious damage (*killed ten people*) is buried in the middle. The revised sentence below presents the items in order of increasing importance.

> **Emphatic** The storm knocked down many trees in town, ripped the roofs off several buildings, and killed ten people.

You may want to use an unexpected item at the end of a series for humor or for another special effect.

> Early to bed and early to rise makes a man healthy, wealthy, and dead.
> – James Thurber

But be careful not to use such a series unintentionally. The following series seems thoughtlessly random rather than intentionally humorous.

> **Unemphatic** The painting has subdued tone, great feeling, and a length of about three feet.
>
> **Emphatic** The painting, about three feet long, has subdued tone and great feeling.

Balanced sentences

When the clauses of a compound or complex sentence are parallel, the sentence is **balanced.**

> The fickleness of the women I love is equalled only by the infernal constancy of the women who love me.
> – George Bernard Shaw

In a pure balanced sentence two main clauses are exactly parallel: they match item for item.

> The love of liberty is the love of others; the love of power is the love of ourselves.
> – William Hazlitt

But the term is commonly applied to sentences that are only approximately parallel or that have only some parallel parts.

> If thought corrupts language, language can also corrupt thought.
> – George Orwell

> The secret of learning to act lies not in the study of methods but in the close observation of those who have already learned.

Balanced sentences are heavily emphatic but require thoughtful planning. When used carefully, they can be an especially effective way to alert readers to a strong contrast between two ideas.

EXERCISE 1

Underline the main clause in each sentence below, and identify the sentence as cumulative or periodic. Then rewrite each cumulative sentence as a periodic one and each periodic sentence as a cumulative one.

1. One of the most disastrous cultural influences ever to hit America was Walt Disney's Mickey Mouse, that idiot optimist who each week marched forth in Technicolor against a battalion of cats, invariably humiliating them with one clever trick after another. – JAMES A. MICHENER
2. At length, in the beginning of May, with the help of some of my acquaintances, rather to improve so good an occasion for neighborliness than from any necessity, I set up the frame of my house. – HENRY DAVID THOREAU
3. Thirty years later, when the country was aroused by a rash of political assassinations—the Kennedys, King, Malcolm X—Congress passed the Gun Control Act of 1968. – JERVIS ANDERSON
4. Matthew's children worked two years to get him out of jail—writing letters, seeing lawyers, attending meetings—because they knew him to be honest and believed him to be innocent.
5. Aspiring writers can learn much from waiting on tables, eavesdropping on conversations to sharpen their ear for dialogue and to pick up promising story material.

emph
18a

EXERCISE 2

Combine each group of sentences below into a single cumulative sentence and then into a single periodic sentence. You will have to add, delete, change, and rearrange words. Each item has more than two possible answers. Does the cumulative or the periodic sentence seem more effective to you?

Example:

The woman refused any treatment. She felt that her life was completed. She wished to die.

Cumulative: The woman refused any treatment, feeling that her life was completed and wishing to die.

Periodic: Feeling that her life was completed and wishing to die, the woman refused any treatment.

1. The lead singer aroused the audience. He was spinning around the stage. He was dancing with the microphone stand.
2. Many writers now use computerized word processors. The machines make both revising and editing easier and faster.

3. The swan took flight. Its wings beat against the water. Its neck stretched forward.
4. The abandoned car was a neighborhood eyesore. Its windows were smashed. Its body was rusted and dented.
5. Carl walked with his back straight. He held his head high. He stared straight ahead. He hid his shame.

EXERCISE 3

Revise the following sentences so that elements in a series or balanced elements are arranged to give maximum emphasis to main ideas.

Example:

The campers were stranded without matches, without food or water, and without a tent.

The campers were stranded without matches, without a tent, and without food or water.

1. Remembering summers at my grandmother's makes me happy, but I get angry when I remember later summers that I spent at camp.
2. Good scientists seek the truth regardless of personal success, whereas for bad scientists personal success is more important than the truth.
3. The car had several problems: the upholstery was torn, the engine was missing, and the left rear window would not open.
4. The explosion at the chemical factory blew up half a city block, killed six workers, and started a fire in a building.
5. In the 1950s Americans wanted to keep up with the Joneses; keeping up with change is what America wants in the 1980s.

18b
Repeating ideas

Although careless repetition results in weak and wordy sentences, judicious repetition of key words and phrases can be an effective means of emphasis. Such repetition often combines with parallelism. It may occur in a series of sentences within a paragraph (see 3b-3). Or it may occur in a series of words, phrases, or clauses within a sentence, as in the following examples.

> We have the tools, all the tools—we are suffocating in tools—but we cannot find the actual wood to work or even the actual hand to work it. – ARCHIBALD MACLEISH

> Government comes from below, not above; government comes from men, not from kings or lords or military masters; government looks to the source of all power in the consent of men. – HENRY STEELE COMMAGER

18c
Separating ideas

When you save important information for the end of a sentence, you can emphasize it even more by setting it off from the rest of the sentence. The second example below illustrates how putting an important idea in a separate sentence can highlight it.

> Boys are wild animals, rich in the treasures of sense, but the New England boy had a wider range of emotions than boys of more equable climates because he felt his nature crudely, as it was meant.
>
> Boys are wild animals, rich in the treasures of sense, but the New England boy had a wider range of emotions than boys of more equable climates. He felt his nature crudely, as it was meant.
>
> – Henry Adams

You can vary the degree of emphasis by varying the extent to which you separate one idea from the others. A semicolon provides more separation than a comma, and a period provides still more separation. Compare the following sentences.

> Most of the reading which is praised for itself is neither literary nor intellectual**,** but narcotic.
>
> Most of the reading which is praised for itself is neither literary nor intellectual**;** it is narcotic.
>
> Most of the reading which is praised for itself is neither literary nor intellectual**.** It is narcotic. – Donald Hall

Sometimes a dash or a pair of dashes will isolate and thus emphasize a part of a statement (see also 25b).

> His schemes were always elaborate, ingenious, and exciting—and wholly impractical.
>
> Athletics—that is, winning athletics—have become a profitable university operation.

EXERCISE 4

Emphasize the main idea in each sentence or group of sentences below by following the instructions in parentheses: either combine sentences so that parallelism and repetition stress the main idea or place the main idea in a separate sentence. Each item has more than one possible answer.

Example:

I try to listen to other people's opinions. When my mind is closed, I find that other opinions open it. And they can change my mind when it is wrong. (*Parallelism and repetition.*)

I try to listen to other people's opinions, for they can open my mind when it is closed and they can change my mind when it is wrong.

1. Without funding, the center will close. The counseling program will end if funding stops. (*Parallelism and repetition.*)
2. Roger worked harder than usual to win the chemistry prize that his father had won before him, for he could not let his father down. (*Separation.*)
3. One of the few worthwhile habits is daily reading. One can read for information. One can read for entertainment. Reading can give one a broader view of the world. (*Parallelism and repetition.*)
4. My parents fear change. They fear change in morals. They are afraid their neighborhood will change. They are afraid of change in their own children. (*Parallelism and repetition.*)
5. By the time the rescuers reached the crash site, the wind had nearly covered the small plane with snow and no one had survived. (*Separation.*)

18d
Preferring the active voice

In the active voice the subject acts (*I peeled the onions*). In the passive voice the subject is acted upon and the actor is either relegated to a phrase (*The onions were peeled by me*) or omitted entirely (*The onions were peeled*). (See Chapter 7, p. 194.) The passive voice is thus indirect because it obscures or removes the actor. The active voice is more direct, vigorous, and emphatic. Further, all sentences turn on their verbs, which give sentences their motion, pushing them along. And active verbs push harder than passive ones.

Passive	For energy conservation it is urged that all lights be turned off when not being used. [Who is urging? Who is to turn the lights off?]
Active	To save energy, students should turn off all lights they are not using.
Passive	The new outpatient clinic was opened by the hospital administration so that the costs of nonemergency medical care would be reduced.
Active	The hospital administration opened the new outpatient clinic to reduce the costs of nonemergency medical care.

Sometimes the subject of an active statement is unknown or unimportant, and then the passive voice can be useful.

The flight was canceled.
Wellington was called the "Iron Duke."
Thousands of people are killed annually in highway accidents.

Except in these situations, however, rely on the active voice. It is economical and creates movement. (See also 31c-3.)

18e
Being concise

Conciseness—brevity of expression—aids emphasis no matter what the sentence structure. Unnecessary words detract from necessary words. They clutter sentences and obscure ideas.

One common structure that may contribute to wordiness is the expletive construction, which inverts the normal subject-verb order by beginning a sentence with *there* or *it* and a form of the verb *be* (see 5e-4).

Weak	*There are* likely to be thousands of people attending the rally against nuclear arms.
Emphatic	*Thousands of people will* likely attend the rally against nuclear arms.

Some frequently used qualifying phrases such as *in my opinion, more or less,* and *for the most part* are also unnecessarily wordy. They can always be reworded more concisely and can often be omitted entirely.

Weak	*In my opinion,* the competition for grades distracts many students from their goal of obtaining a good education.
Emphatic	*I think* the competition for grades distracts many students from their main goal of obtaining a good education.
More emphatic	The competition for grades distracts many students from their goal of obtaining a good education.

(See 31c for further discussion of strengthening sentences through conciseness.)

EXERCISE 5

Revise the following sentences to make them more emphatic by converting passive voice to active voice, by eliminating expletive constructions, or by condensing or eliminating wordy phrases.

(For additional exercises with the passive voice, see pp. 167, 196, and 420.)

Example:

The problem in this particular situation is that we owe more money than we can afford under present circumstances.

The *problem is* that we owe more money than we can afford.

1. As far as I am concerned, the major weakness of the restaurant in question is that the service is surly, in a manner of speaking.
2. The contestant was seated behind a screen so that she could not be seen by the judges while her performance was heard.
3. After all these years there is still something calling me back to the town where I lived as a child.
4. The protesters were ordered by the police to clear the sidewalk when the motorcade was approaching.
5. There must have been some reason why he acted as he did, whether conscious or unconscious.

EXERCISE 6

Drawing on the advice in this chapter, rewrite the following paragraph to emphasize main ideas and to de-emphasize less important information.

In preparing pasta, there is a requirement for common sense and imagination rather than for complicated recipes. The key to success in this area is fresh ingredients for the sauce and perfectly cooked pasta. The sauce may be made with just about any fresh fish, meat, cheese, herb, or vegetable. As for the pasta itself, it may be dried or fresh, although fresh pasta is usually more delicate and flavorful, as many experienced cooks have found. Dried pasta is fine with zesty sauces; with light oil and cream sauces fresh pasta is best used. There is a difference in the cooking time for dried and fresh pasta, with dried pasta taking longer. It is important that the package directions be followed by the cook and that the pasta be tested before the cooking time is up. The pasta is done when the texture is neither tough nor mushy but *al dente,* or "firm to the bite," according to the Italians, who ought to know.

19
Achieving Variety

In a paragraph or an essay, sentences do not stand one by one. Rather, each stands in relation to those before and after it. To make sentences work together effectively, the writer must vary their length, their emphasis, and their word order to reflect the importance and complexity of ideas. Although experienced writers generally find that variety takes care of itself as they commit ideas to paper, inexperienced writers often have difficulty achieving variety without guidance and practice.

A series of similar sentences will prove monotonous and ineffective, as this passage illustrates:

> Ulysses S. Grant and Robert E. Lee met on April 9, 1865. Their meeting place was the parlor of a modest house at Appomattox Court House, Virginia. They met to work out the terms for the surrender of Lee's Army of Northern Virginia. One great chapter of American life ended with their meeting, and another began. Grant and Lee were bringing the Civil War to its virtual finish. Other armies still had to surrender, and the fugitive Confederate government would struggle desperately and vainly. It would try to find some way to go on living with its chief support gone. Grant and Lee had signed the papers, however, and it was all over in effect.

Individually, these eight sentences are perfectly clear and adequately detailed. But together they do not make pleasant reading, and their relative importance is obscure. Their lengths are roughly the same, they are about equally detailed, and they all consist of one or two main clauses beginning with the subject. At the end of the passage we have a sense of names, dates, and events but no sure sense of how they relate.

Now compare the preceding passage with the actual passage written by Bruce Catton.

> When Ulysses S. Grant and Robert E. Lee met in the parlor of a modest house at Appomattox Court House, Virginia, on April 9, 1865, to work out the terms for the surrender of Lee's Army of Northern Virginia, a great chapter in American life came to a close, and a great new chapter began.
>
> These men were bringing the Civil War to its virtual finish. To be sure, other armies had yet to surrender, and for a few days the fugitive Confederate government would struggle desperately and vainly, trying to find some way to go on living now that its chief support was gone. But in effect it was all over when Grant and Lee signed the papers. – BRUCE CATTON, "Grant and Lee"

The information in these two passages is almost identical. The differences lie chiefly in the sentence variety of the second and the sharp focus on the end of war which that variety underscores. Catton's four sentences range from eleven to fifty-five words, and only one of the sentences begins with its subject. The first sentence brings together in one long *when* clause all the details of place, time, and cause contained in the first three sentences of the first passage. The sentence is periodic (see 18a-1), and the suspense it creates forces us to focus on the significance of the meeting described in the two main clauses at the end. The very brief second sentence, contrasting sharply with the one before it, quickly recapitulates the reason for the meeting. The third sentence, a long, cumulative one (see 18a-1), reflects the lingering obstacles to peace. And the fourth sentence, another short one, tersely indicates the futility of future struggle. Together, the four sentences clearly, even dramatically, convey that the meeting ended the war and marked a turning point in American history. The rest of this chapter suggests some ways you can vary your sentences to achieve such effectiveness.

19a
Varying sentence length and emphasis

The sentences of a stylistically effective essay will differ most obviously in their length. Further, some sentences will consist only of one main clause with modifiers, others of two main clauses; some will be cumulative, and a few perhaps will be periodic. (See 18a-1.) This variation in length and emphasis marks mature writing, making it both readable and clear.

Neither short sentences nor long sentences are intrinsically better. But in most contemporary writing, sentences tend to vary from about ten words on the short side to about forty words on the long, with an average of between fifteen and twenty-five words, depending on the writer's purpose and style. Your sentences generally should not be all at one extreme or the other, for if they are your readers may have difficulty focusing on main ideas and seeing the relations among them. If most of your sentences contain thirty-five words or more, you probably need to break some up into shorter, simpler sentences. If most of your sentences contain fewer than ten or fifteen words, you probably need to add details to them or combine them through coordination and subordination. Examine your writing particularly for a common problem: strings of main clauses, subjects first, in either simple or compound sentences.

1
Avoiding strings of brief and simple sentences

A series of brief and simple sentences is both monotonous and hard to understand because it forces the reader to sort out relations among ideas. If you find that you depend on brief, simple sentences, work to increase variety by combining some of them into longer units that emphasize and link new and important ideas while de-emphasizing old or incidental information. (See 16a, 16b, and 18a.)

The following example shows how a string of simple sentences can be revised into an effective piece of writing.

Weak

The moon is now drifting away from the earth. It moves away at the rate of about one inch a year. Our days on earth are getting longer. They grow a thousandth of a second longer every century. A month might become forty-seven of our present days long. We might eventually lose the moon altogether. Such great planetary movement rightly concerns astronomers. It need not worry us. The movement will take 50 million years.

Revised

The moon is now drifting away from the earth, moving at the rate of about one inch a year. And at the rate of a thousandth of a second or so every century, our days on earth are getting longer. Someday, a month will be forty-seven of our present days long, if we don't eventually lose the moon altogether. Such great planetary movement rightly concerns astronomers, but it need not concern us. It will take 50 million years.

In the first passage the choppy movement of the nine successive simple sentences leaves the reader with nine independent facts and a lame conclusion. The revision retains all the facts of the original but compresses them into five sentences that are structured to emphasize main ideas and to show relations among them. The three most important facts of the passage—the moon's movement (sentence 1), our lengthening days (sentence 2), and the enormous span of time involved (sentence 5)—appear, respectively, in the opening main clause of a cumulative sentence, in the ending main clause of a periodic sentence, and in a terse simple sentence. The arrangement of the third sentence stresses the dramatic possibility that we may lose the moon. And the coordination of the fourth sentence accentuates with *but* the contrast between the astronomers' concerns and ours, thus preparing the way for the highly emphatic brief sentence at the end.

2
Avoiding excessive compounding

Because compound sentences are usually just simple sentences linked with conjunctions, a series of them will be as weak as a series of brief simple sentences, especially if the clauses of the compound sentences are all about the same length.

Weak

The hotel beach faces the south, and the main street runs along the north side of the hotel. The main street is heavily traveled and often noisy, but the beach is always quiet and sunny. It was Sunday afternoon, and we were on the hotel beach. We lay stretched out on the sand, and the sun poured down on us.

Revised

The main street, heavily traveled and often noisy, runs along the north side of the hotel. But on the south side the hotel beach is always quiet and sunny. On Sunday we lay there stretched out on the sand, letting the sun pour down on us.

The first passage creates a seesaw effect. The revision, with some main clauses changed into modifiers and repositioned, is both clearer and more emphatic. (See 16a-2 for additional discussion of how to avoid excessive coordination within sentences.)

EXERCISE 1

Rewrite the following paragraphs to increase variety so that important ideas receive greater emphasis than supporting information. You will have to change some main clauses into modifiers and then combine and reposition the modifiers and the remaining main clauses.

1. Charlotte Perkins Gilman was a leading intellectual in the women's movement during the first decades of this century. She wrote *Women and Economics*. This book challenged Victorian assumptions about differences between the sexes. It explored the economic roots of women's oppression. Gilman wrote little about gaining the vote for women. Many feminists were then preoccupied with this issue. Historians have since focused their anal-

yses on this issue. As a result, Gilman's contribution to today's women's movement has often been overlooked.

2. Nathaniel Hawthorne was one of America's first great writers, and he was descended from a judge. The judge had presided at some of the Salem witch trials, and he had condemned some men and women to death. Hawthorne could never forget this piece of family history, and he always felt guilty about it. He never wrote about his ancestor directly, but he did write about the darkness of the human heart. He wrote *The Scarlet Letter* and *The House of the Seven Gables*, and in those books he demonstrated his favorite theme of a secret sin.

19b
Varying sentence beginnings

var
19b

Most English sentences begin with their subjects.

The defendant's lawyer relentlessly cross-examined the stubborn witness for two successive days.

However, an unbroken sequence of sentences beginning with the subject quickly becomes monotonous, as shown by the altered passage on Grant and Lee at the start of this chapter (p. 300). Your final arrangement of sentence elements should always depend on two concerns: the relation of a sentence to those preceding and following it and the emphasis required by your meaning. When you do choose to vary the subject-first pattern, you have several options.

Adverb modifiers can often be placed at a variety of spots in a sentence. Consider the different emphases created by moving the adverbs in the basic sentence above.

For two successive days, the defendant's lawyer *relentlessly* cross-examined the stubborn witness.

Relentlessly, the defendant's lawyer cross-examined the stubborn witness *for two successive days*.

Relentlessly, for two successive days, the defendant's lawyer cross-examined the stubborn witness.

Notice that the last sentence, with both modifiers at the beginning, is periodic and thus highly emphatic (see 18a-1).

Beginning a sentence with a participial phrase also postpones the subject and sometimes creates a periodic sentence.

The lawyer thoroughly cross-examined the witness and then called the defendant herself to testify.

Having thoroughly cross-examined the witness, the lawyer called the defendant herself to testify.

When the relation between two successive sentences demands, you may begin the second with a coordinating conjunction or with a transitional expression such as *first, for instance, however, in addition, moreover,* or *therefore.* (See 3b-6 for a list of transitional expressions.)

> The witness expected to be dismissed after his first long day of cross-examination. He was not; the defendant's lawyer called him again the second day.
>
> The witness expected to be dismissed after his first long day of cross-examination. *But* he was not; the defendant's lawyer called him again the second day.

> The prices of clothes have risen astronomically in recent years. The cotton shirt that once cost $6.00 and now costs $25.00 is an example.
>
> The prices of clothes have risen astronomically in recent years. *For example,* a cotton shirt that once cost $6.00 now costs $25.00.

Occasionally, an expletive construction—*it* or *there* plus a form of *be*—may be useful to delay and thus emphasize the subject of the sentence.

> His judgment seems questionable, not his desire.
> *It is* his judgment that seems questionable, not his desire.

However, expletive constructions are more likely to harm writing by adding extra words. You should use them rarely, only when you can justify doing so. (See also 18e.)

EXERCISE 2

Revise each pair of sentences below, following the instructions in parentheses to make a single sentence that begins with an adverb modifier or a participial phrase, or to make one of the two sentences begin with an appropriate coordinating conjunction or transitional expression.

> *Example:*
>
> The *Seabird* left to take its place in the race. It moved quickly in the wind. (*One sentence with participial phrase beginning moving.*)
>
> *Moving quickly in the wind,* the *Seabird* left to take its place in the race.

1. The loan application was denied by the bank. The business had to close its doors. (*Two sentences with transitional expression.*)
2. The school may build a new athletic complex. It will tear down the old field house. (*One sentence with adverb modifier beginning if.*)
3. Voting rights for women seemed a possibility in the 1860s. Women were not actually given the vote for nearly sixty years. (*Two sentences with coordinating conjunction.*)

4. Robert had orders to stay in bed. He returned to work immediately. (*One sentence with adverb modifier beginning although.*)
5. The rescuers were careful as they handled the ropes. They lowered the frightened climber from the ledge. (*One sentence with participial phrase beginning carefully.*)

EXERCISE 3

Revise the following paragraph to vary sentence beginnings by using each of the following at least once: an adverb modifier, a participial phrase, a coordinating conjunction, and a transitional expression.

The instructor found himself in class alone. He waited patiently for his students to arrive. He went over his lecture notes. He read yesterday's newspaper. No one arrived. He noticed an article on the front page of the paper instructing readers to turn their clocks back one hour. He realized his mistake. He smiled.

19c
Inverting the normal word order

Inverted sentences such as *Up came the dawn* and *Mutton he didn't like* are infrequent in modern prose. Because the word order of subject, verb, and object or complement is so strongly fixed in English, an inverted sentence can be emphatic.

> Harry had once been a dog lover. Then his neighbors' barking dogs twice raced through his garden. Now Harry detests all dogs, especially barking dogs.

> Harry had once been a dog lover. Then his neighbors' barking dogs twice raced through his garden. Now *all dogs,* especially barking dogs, *Harry detests.*

Inverting the normal order of subject, verb, and complement can be useful in two successive sentences when the second expands on the first.

> Critics have not been kind to Presidents who have tried to apply the ways of private business to public affairs. Particularly *explicit was the curt verdict* of one critic of President Hoover: Mr. Hoover was never President of the United States; he was four years chairman of the board. – Adapted from EMMET JOHN HUGHES, "The Presidency vs. Jimmy Carter"

Inverted sentences used without need are artificial. Avoid descriptive sentences such as *Up came Larry and down went Cindy's spirits.*

19d

Mixing types of sentences

Most written sentences make statements. Occasionally, however, questions, commands, or, more rarely, exclamations may enhance variety. Questions may set the direction of a paragraph, as in *What does a detective do?* or *How is the percentage of unemployed workers calculated?* More often, though, the questions used in exposition or argumentation do not require answers but simply emphasize ideas that readers can be expected to agree with. These **rhetorical questions** are illustrated in the following passage.

> Another word that has ceased to have meaning due to overuse is *attractive. Attractive* has become verbal chaff. Who, by some stretch of language and imagination, cannot be described as attractive? And just what is it that attractive individuals are attracting? – DIANE WHITE

Imperative sentences occur frequently in an explanation of a process, particularly in directions, as this passage on freewriting illustrates.

> The idea is simply to write for ten minutes (later on, perhaps fifteen or twenty). Don't stop for anything. Go quickly without rushing. Never stop to look back, to cross something out, to wonder how to spell something, to wonder what word or thought to use, or to think about what you are doing. – PETER ELBOW

Notice that the authors of these examples use questions and commands not merely to vary their sentences but to achieve some special purpose. Variety occurs because a particular sentence type is effective for the context, not because the writer set out to achieve variety for its own sake.

EXERCISE 4

Imagine that you are writing an essay either on the parking problem at your school or on the problems of living in a dormitory. Practice varying sentences by composing a sentence or passage to serve each purpose listed below.

1. Write a question that could open the essay.
2. Write a command that could open the essay.
3. Write an exclamation that could open the essay.
4. For the body of the essay, write an appropriately varied paragraph of at least five sentences, including at least one short and one long sentence beginning with the subject; at least one sentence beginning with an adverb modifier; at least one sentence beginning with a coordinating conjunction or transitional expression; and one rhetorical question or command.

EXERCISE 5

Examine the following paragraphs for sentence variety. By analyzing your own response to each sentence, try to explain why the author wrote each short or long sentence, each cumulative or periodic sentence, each sentence beginning with its subject or beginning some other way, and each question.

1. There is something uneasy in the Los Angeles air this afternoon, some unnatural stillness, some tension. What it means is that tonight a Santa Ana will begin to blow, a hot wind from the northeast whining down through the Cajon and San Gorgonio Passes, blowing up sandstorms out along Route 66, drying the hills and the nerves to the flash point. For a few days now we will see smoke back in the canyons, and hear sirens in the night. I have neither heard nor read that a Santa Ana is due, but I know it, and almost everyone I have seen today knows it too. We know it because we feel it. The baby frets. The maid sulks. I rekindle a waning argument with the telephone company, then cut my losses and lie down, given over to whatever it is in the air. To live with the Santa Ana is to accept, consciously or unconsciously, a deeply mechanistic view of human behavior.

– JOAN DIDION, "Los Angeles Notebook"

2. That night in my rented room, while letting the hot water run over my can of pork and beans in the sink, I opened [H. L. Mencken's] *A Book of Prefaces* and began to read. I was jarred and shocked by the style, the clear, clean, sweeping sentences. Why did he write like that? And how did one write like that? I pictured the man as a raging demon, slashing with his pen, consumed with hate, denouncing everything American, extolling everything European or German, laughing at the weaknesses of people, mocking God, authority. What was this? I stood up, trying to realize what reality lay behind the meaning of the words. Yes, this man was fighting, fighting with words. He was using words as a weapon, using them as one would use a club. Could words be weapons? Well, yes, for here they were. Then, maybe, perhaps, I could use them as a weapon? No. It frightened me. I read on and what amazed me was not what he said, but how on earth anybody had the courage to say it. – RICHARD WRIGHT, *Black Boy*

V
Punctuation

MAJOR INTERNAL SENTENCE PUNCTUATION
Commas, Semicolons, Colons, Dashes, and Parentheses

(For explanations, consult the sections in parentheses.)

Sentences with two main clauses

The bus stopped, *but* no one got off. (21a)
The bus stopped; no one got off. (22a)
The bus stopped; *however,* no one got off. (22b)
The mechanic replaced the battery, the distributor cap, and the starter; *but* still the car would not start. (22c)
His duty was clear: he had to report the theft. (25a-1)

Introductory elements

MODIFIERS (21b)

After the argument was over, we laughed at ourselves.
Racing over the plain, the gazelle escaped the lion.
To dance in the contest, he had to tape his knee.
Suddenly, the door flew open.
With 125 passengers aboard, the plane was half full.
In 1983 he won the Nobel Prize.

ABSOLUTE PHRASES (21d)

Its wing broken, the bird hopped about on the ground.

p

Interrupting and concluding elements

NONRESTRICTIVE MODIFIERS (21c-1)

Jim's car, *which barely runs*, has been impounded.
We consulted the dean, *who had promised to help us.*
The boy, *like his sister*, wants to be a pilot.
They moved across the desert, *shielding their eyes from the sun.*
The men do not speak to each other, *although they share a car.*

NONRESTRICTIVE APPOSITIVES

Bergen's daughter, *Candice*, became an actress. (21c-2)
The residents of three counties—*Suffolk, Springfield, and Morrison*—were urged to evacuate. (25b-2)
Our father demanded one promise: *that we not lie to him.* (25a-1)

RESTRICTIVE MODIFIERS (21j-3)

The car *that hit mine* was uninsured.
We consulted a teacher *who had promised to help us.*
The boy *in the black hat* is my cousin.
They were surprised to find the desert *teeming with life.*
The men do not speak to each other *because they are feuding.*

Restrictive appositives (21j-3)

Shaw's play *Saint Joan* was performed last year.
Their sons *Tony, William, and Steve* all chose military careers, leaving only Joe to run the family business.

Parenthetical expressions

We suspect, *however*, that he will not come. (21c-3)
Jan is respected by many people—*including me.* (25b-2)
George Balanchine (*1904–1983*) was a brilliant choreographer. (25c-1)

Absolute phrases (21d)

The bird, *its wing broken*, hopped about on the ground.
The bird hopped about on the ground, *its wing broken.*

Phrases expressing contrast (21e)

The humidity, *not just the heat*, gives me headaches.
My headaches are caused by the humidity, *not just the heat.*

Concluding summaries and explanations

The movie opened to bad notices: *the characters were judged shallow and unrealistic.* (25a-1)
We dined on gumbo, blackened fish, and jambalaya—*a Cajun feast.* (25b-3)

Items in a series

Three or more items

Chimpanzees, gorillas, orangutans, and gibbons are all apes. (21f-1)
The cities singled out for praise were *Birmingham, Alabama; Lincoln, Nebraska; Austin, Texas; and Madison, Wisconsin.* (22d)

Two or more adjectives before a noun or pronoun (21f-2)

Dingy, smelly clothes decorated their room.
The luncheon consisted of *one tiny watercress* sandwich.

Introductory series (25b-3)

Appropriateness, accuracy, and necessity—these criteria should govern your selection of words.

Concluding series

Every word should be *appropriate, accurate, and necessary.* (25a-3)
Every word should meet three criteria: *appropriateness, accuracy, and necessity.* (25a-1)
Pay attention to your words—*to their appropriateness, their accuracy, and their necessity.* (25b-3)

p

20
End Punctuation

THE PERIOD

20a
Use the period to end sentences that are statements, mild commands, or indirect questions.

STATEMENTS

These are exciting and trying times.
The airline went bankrupt.
The violins played quietly in the background.

MILD COMMANDS

Please do not smoke.
Think of the possibilities.
Turn to page 146.

If you are unsure whether to use an exclamation point or a period after a command, use a period. The exclamation point should be used only rarely (see 20f).

An **indirect question** reports what someone has asked but not in the original speaker's own words.

INDIRECT QUESTIONS

The judge asked why I had been driving with my lights off.

Students sometimes wonder whether their teachers read the papers they write.

Abused children eventually stop asking why they are being punished.

20b

Use periods with most abbreviations.

Ordinarily, use periods with abbreviations.

p.	B.A.	A.D.	Mr.
D.C.	Ph.D.	A.M., a.m.	Mrs.
M.D.	e.g.	P.M., p.m.	Ms.
Dr.	B.C.		

When an abbreviation falls at the end of a sentence, use only one period: *Government, not industry, is the business of Washington, D.C.*

Periods are usually dropped from abbreviations for organizations, corporations, and government agencies when more than two words are abbreviated. For example:

IBM	USMC	NFL	AFL-CIO

Check a dictionary for the preferred form of such abbreviations, and see Chapter 28 on abbreviations.

Note that **acronyms**—pronounceable words, such as UNESCO, NATO, VISTA, and WHO, formed from the initial letters of the words in a name—never require periods (see 28b).

EXERCISE 1

Revise the following sentences so that periods are used correctly.

Example:

Several times I wrote to ask when my subscription ended?
Several times I wrote to ask when my subscription ended.

1. Cut the flowers and put them in the vase
2. The office manager asked whose typewriter was broken?
3. The championship game begins at 7:30 PM sharp.
4. The area of the new athletic complex is almost 8200 sq ft.
5. Plato wrote *Republic* in about 370 BC..

? 20c

THE QUESTION MARK

20c

Use the question mark after direct questions.

DIRECT QUESTIONS

Who will follow her?
What is the difference between these two people?
Will economists ever really understand the economy?

After indirect questions, use a period: *My mother asked why I came in so late.* (See 20a.)

Questions in a series are each followed by a question mark.

> The officer asked how many times the suspect had been arrested. Three times? Four times? More than that?

The use of capital letters for questions in a series is optional (see 26a).

Note: Question marks are never combined with other question marks, exclamation points, periods, or commas.

Faulty	I finally asked myself, "Why are you working at a job you hate?."
Revised	I finally asked myself, "Why are you working at a job you hate?"

20d

Use a question mark within parentheses to indicate doubt about the correctness of a number or date.

> The Greek philosopher Socrates was born in 470 (?) B.C. and died in 399 B.C. from drinking poison after having been condemned to death.

? 20d

Note: Don't use a question mark within parentheses to express sarcasm or irony. Express these attitudes through sentence structure and diction. (See Chapters 18 and 31.)

Faulty	Her friendly (?) criticism did not escape notice.
Revised	Her criticism, *too rough to be genuinely friendly,* did not escape notice.

EXERCISE 2

Revise the following sentences so that question marks (along with other punctuation marks) are used correctly.

Example:

"When will it end?," cried the man dressed in rags.
"When will it end?" cried the man dressed in rags.

1. I often wonder whether I will remember any of my French when I'm sitting in a café in Paris?
2. Why does the poem end with the question "How long?"?
3. "What does *ontogeny* mean?," the biology instructor asked?
4. The candidate for Congress asked whether there was anything he could do to help us?
5. Ulysses and his mariners took seven years to travel from Troy to Ithaca. Or was it six. Or eight?

THE EXCLAMATION POINT

20e

Use the exclamation point after emphatic statements and interjections and after strong commands.

No! We must not lose this election!
When she saw her rain-soaked term paper, she gasped, "Oh, no!"
Come here immediately!
"Stop!" he yelled.

Follow mild interjections and commands with commas or periods, as appropriate.

No, the response was not terrific.
To prolong your car's life, change its oil regularly.

Note: Exclamation points are never combined with other exclamation points, question marks, periods, or commas.

Faulty	My father was most emphatic. "I will not give you any more money!," he roared.
Revised	My father was most emphatic. "I will not give you any more money!" he roared.

20f

Avoid overusing exclamation points.

Don't express sarcasm, irony, or amazement with the exclamation point. Rely on sentence structure and diction to express these attitudes. (See Chapters 18 and 31.)

Faulty	After traveling 1.24 billion miles through space, *Voyager 2* missed its target by 41 miles (!).
Revised	After traveling 1.24 billion miles through space, *Voyager 2* missed its target by *a mere* 41 miles.

Relying on the exclamation point for emphasis is like crying wolf: the mark loses its power to impress the reader. Frequent exclamation points can also make writing sound overemotional. In the following passage, the writer could have conveyed her ideas more effectively by punctuating sentences with periods.

> Our city government is a mess! After just six months in office, the mayor has had to fire four city officials! In the same period the city councilors have done nothing but argue! And city services decline with each passing day!

EXERCISE 3

Revise the following sentences so that exclamation points (along with other punctuation marks) are used correctly. If a sentence is punctuated correctly as given, circle the number preceding it.

Example:

What a shock it was to hear her scream, "Stop"
What a shock it was to hear her scream, "Stop!"

1. I was so late returning from lunch that I missed the three o'clock meeting!
2. Look both ways before you cross the street.
3. "Well, now!," he said loudly.
4. The child's cries could be heard next door: "Don't go. Don't go."
5. As the fire fighters moved their equipment into place, police walked through the crowd shouting, "Move back!."

EXERCISE 4

Insert appropriate punctuation (periods, question marks, or exclamation points) where needed in the following paragraph.

When Maureen approached Jesse with her idea for a class gift to the school, he asked if she knew how much it would cost "Forget it if it's over $200," he said "Do you think the class can come up with even that much" Both of them knew the committee treasury contained only the $100 given by Dr Wheeler Maureen said that she thought they could raise the rest with a talent show "That's ridiculous" exclaimed Jesse "What talent Dr Wheeler's Whose" But he softened when Maureen asked him if he would perform his animal imitations Jesse loved to do animal imitations.

! 20f

NOTE: See page 376 for a punctuation exercise combining periods with other marks of punctuation such as commas and semicolons.

21
The Comma

The comma is the most frequently used—and misused—mark of internal punctuation. In general, commas function within sentences to indicate pauses and to separate elements; they also have several conventional uses, as in dates. Omitting needed commas or inserting needless ones can confuse the reader, as the following sentences show.

Comma needed	Though very tall Abraham Lincoln was not an overbearing man.
Revised	Though very tall, Abraham Lincoln was not an overbearing man.
Unneeded commas	The hectic pace of Beirut, broke suddenly into frightening chaos when the city became, the focus of civil war.
Revised	The hectic pace of Beirut broke suddenly into frightening chaos when the city became the focus of civil war.

21a
Use a comma before a coordinating conjunction linking main clauses.

The coordinating conjunctions are *and, but, or, nor,* and sometimes *for, yet,* and *so.* Words or phrases joined by a coordinating conjunction are *not* separated by a comma: *Bill plays and sings Irish and English folk songs* (see 21j-2). However, main clauses joined by a coordinating conjunction *are* separated by a comma. Main clauses are those with a subject and predicate (and without a subordinating word at the beginning) that make complete statements (see 5c).

> She was perfectly at home in what she knew, *and* what she knew has remained what all of us want to know.
> – EUDORA WELTY on Jane Austen

> He would have turned around again without a word, *but* I seized him.
> – FYODOR DOSTOYEVSKY

> Seventeen years ago this month I quit work, *or,* if you prefer, I retired from business.
> – F. SCOTT FITZGERALD

> They made their decision with some uneasiness, *for* they knew that in such places any failure to conform could cause trouble.
> – RICHARD HARRIS

> In putting on trousers a man always inserts the same old leg first. . . . All men do it, *yet* no man thought it out and adopted it of set purpose.
> – MARK TWAIN

> Near evening I was too jittery to attend to chores, *so* Bailey volunteered to do all before his bath.
> – MAYA ANGELOU

EXCEPTIONS: Some writers prefer to use a semicolon before *so* and *yet.*

> Many people say that the institution of marriage is in decline; *yet* recent evidence suggests that the institution is at least holding steady.

21a

When the main clauses in a sentence are very long or grammatically complicated, or when they contain internal punctuation, a semicolon before the coordinating conjunction will clarify the division between clauses (see 22c).

> Life would be dull without its seamier side, its violence, filth, and hatred; *for* otherwise how could we appreciate the joys?
> – ELLEN STEPIK

When main clauses are very short and closely related in meaning, you may omit the comma between them as long as the resulting sentence is clear.

> She opened her mouth *but* no sound came out of it.
> – FLANNERY O'CONNOR

> My heart raced *and* I felt ill.

If you are in doubt about whether to use a comma in such sentences, use it. It will always be correct.

EXERCISE 1

Insert a comma before each coordinating conjunction that links main clauses in the following sentences.

Example:

I would have attended the concert but I had to baby-sit for my niece.

I would have attended the concert, but I had to baby-sit for my niece.

1. I have auditioned for many lead roles but I have been offered only one minor speaking part and two walk-on parts.
2. Videocassette recorders continue to come down in price so more people are buying them.
3. Kampala is Uganda's capital and largest city and it serves as the nation's social and economic center.
4. He wanted to wear his black leather jacket but his roommate had borrowed it.
5. We had driven all night and all day to get to the town and we were too tired to sightsee or search for a cozy inn.

EXERCISE 2

Combine each pair of sentences below into one sentence that uses a comma between main clauses connected by the coordinating conjunction in parentheses.

Example:

The circus had just come to town. Everyone wanted to see it. (*and*)

The circus had just come to town, *and* everyone wanted to see it.

1. The police must have based the accusation on the polygraph test. They would not have made it at all. (*or*)
2. We once thought computers were an unmitigated blessing. Now we know they can create unexpected problems. (*but*)
3. We caught Bobby in his lie. He refused to tell the truth. (*yet*)
4. His father sometimes hit him. The boy sometimes hit his little sister. (*so*)
5. In many bird species the female builds the nest. The male defends it. (*and*)

21b

Use a comma to set off most introductory elements.

Introductory elements modify a word or words in the main clause that follows. They include subordinate clauses serving as adverbs (5c-4); participles, infinitives, and participial and infinitive phrases serving as adjectives and adverbs (5c-2); prepositional phrases (5c-1); and sentence modifiers such as *unfortunately, cer-*

tainly, and *of course*. These elements are usually set off from the rest of the sentence with a comma.

> *If Ernest Hemingway had written comic books*, they would have been just as good as his novels. [Subordinate clause.]
>
> – Stan Lee
>
> *Exhausted*, the runner collapsed at the finish line. [Participle.]
>
> *To win the most important race of her career*, she had nearly killed herself. [Infinitive phrase.]
>
> *From Columbus and Sir Walter Raleigh onward*, America has been traveling the road west. [Prepositional phrase.]
>
> – Peter Davison
>
> *Unfortunately*, the diamond was fake. [Sentence modifier.]

The comma may be omitted following short introductory prepositional and infinitive phrases and subordinate clauses if its omission does not create confusion. (If you are in doubt, however, the comma is always correct.)

Clear	*By the year 2000* the world population will be more than 6 billion. [Prepositional phrase.]
Clear	*To write clearly* one must think clearly. [Infinitive phrase.]
Clear	*When snow falls* the city collapses. [Subordinate clause.]
Confusing	At eighteen people are considered young adults.
Revised	At eighteen, people are considered young adults.

21b

Note: Take care to distinguish verbals used as modifiers from verbals used as subjects. The former almost always take a comma; the latter never do.

> *Jogging through the park*, I was unexpectedly caught in a downpour. [Participial phrase used as modifier.]
>
> *Jogging through the park* has become a popular form of recreation for city dwellers. [Gerund phrase used as subject.]
>
> *To dance professionally*, he trained for years. [Infinitive phrase used as modifier.]
>
> *To dance professionally* is his one desire. [Infinitive phrase used as subject.]

In addition, do not use a comma to separate a verbal from the noun or pronoun it modifies when it restricts the meaning of the noun or pronoun (see also 21c).

> *Shuttered houses* lined the street. [*Shuttered* restricts *houses*.]
>
> *Shuttered*, the houses were protected from the elements. [*Shuttered* does not restrict *houses*.]

EXERCISE 3

Insert commas where needed after introductory elements in the following sentences. If a sentence is punctuated correctly as given, circle the number preceding it.

Example:

After the new library opened the old one became a student union.

After the new library opened, the old one became a student union.

1. Giggling to themselves the children ran behind the barn.
2. Before you proceed to your argument state your thesis.
3. Juggling two jobs while attending school proved too much for Helen.
4. When young Michael craved avocados.
5. Running water is a luxury in some of the villages.
6. Even when employees have been laid off they may still be entitled to health insurance from the company.
7. Predictably the lawyer was late for the deposition.
8. Gasping for breath the fire fighters staggered out of the burning building.
9. Because of the late morning rain the baseball game had to be canceled.
10. Without so much as nodding her head Phyllis slammed the door and left.

EXERCISE 4

Combine each pair of sentences below into one sentence that begins with an introductory phrase or clause as specified in parentheses. Follow the introductory element with a comma. You will have to add, delete, change, and rearrange words.

Example:

The girl was humming to herself. She walked upstairs. (*Phrase beginning Humming.*)

Humming to herself, the girl walked up the stairs.

1. The government cut back its student loan program. Students and their parents have had to rely more on banks. (*Clause beginning Since.*)
2. More than five hundred people signed the petition. The mayor did not respond. (*Clause beginning Although.*)
3. One needs information to vote wisely. One needs objective information about the candidates' backgrounds and opinions. (*Phrase beginning To.*)
4. The flags were snapping in the wind. They made the speaker's message seem even more urgent. (*Phrase beginning Snapping.*)
5. Vatican City has only 108 acres. It is the smallest sovereign state in the world. (*Phrase beginning With.*)

21c

Use a comma or commas to set off nonrestrictive elements.

Restrictive and nonrestrictive sentence elements contribute differently to meaning and require different punctuation. A **restrictive element** limits, or restricts, the meaning of the word or words it applies to. Thus it is essential to the meaning of the sentence and cannot be omitted without significantly changing that meaning. Restrictive elements are never set off with punctuation.

RESTRICTIVE ELEMENT

Employees *who work hard* will receive raises.

A **nonrestrictive element** gives added information about the word or words it applies to, but it does not limit the word or words. It can be omitted from the sentence without changing the essential meaning. Nonrestrictive elements are always set off with punctuation.

NONRESTRICTIVE ELEMENT

Molly Berman, *who lives next door*, got a raise.

Commas are most commonly used to set off nonrestrictive elements, although dashes or parentheses are sometimes used to emphasize or de-emphasize them (see 25b-2 and 25c-1, respectively). Whatever punctuation mark you select, be sure to use a pair if the nonrestrictive element falls in the middle of a sentence—one *before* and another *after* the element.

A test can help you determine whether a sentence element is restrictive or nonrestrictive: does the meaning of the sentence change when the element is removed? It does in the restrictive example above, for *Employees will receive raises* does not provide the same information about employees as the original sentence did. The employees are no longer defined or limited to a specific group, the ones who work hard, but instead include all employees, whatever their work habits. Conversely, *Molly Berman got a raise* has essentially the same meaning as the original nonrestrictive example. Not knowing where Molly Berman lives does not change our understanding of the sentence: no matter where she lives, she still got the raise.

The presence or absence of commas around a sentence element can change the meaning of a single sentence, as the following examples illustrate.

The band *playing old music* held the audience's attention.
The band, *playing old music*, held the audience's attention.

In the first sentence the absence of commas restricts the subject to a particular band, the one playing old music, and thus implies that more than one band played more than one kind of music. In the second sentence, however, the commas setting off the phrase imply that only one band played because the phrase does not restrict the subject to a particular band. Which punctuation is correct depends on the writer's intended meaning and on the context in which the sentence appears. For example:

Restrictive

Not all the bands were equally well received, however. The band *playing old music* held the audience's attention. The other groups created much less excitement.

Nonrestrictive

A new band called Fats made its debut on Saturday night. The band, *playing old music*, held the audience's attention. If this performance is typical, the group has a bright future.

1

Use a comma or commas to set off nonrestrictive clauses and phrases.

Clauses and phrases serving as adjectives and adverbs may be either nonrestrictive or restrictive. Only nonrestrictive clauses and phrases are set off with punctuation, as the following examples illustrate.

Nonrestrictive clauses

Carl O'Hara, *who used to raise funds for public radio*, has joined a commercial television network. [Compare *Carl O'Hara has joined a commercial television network.* O'Hara's background does not alter the fact that he now works in commercial television.]

Three-year-old Nancy, *whose blue eyes shone with mischief*, had to be rescued more than once from her adventures. [Compare *Three-year-old Nancy had to be rescued more than once from her adventures.* The look of the child's eyes does not restrict the meaning.]

The American farming system, *which is the envy of the world*, is the despair of the American farmer. [Compare *The American farming system is the despair of the American farmer.* The meaning of the subject is unchanged.] – Charles Kuralt

Puerto Rico was a Spanish colony until 1898, *when it was ceded to the United States.* [Compare *Puerto Rico was a Spanish colony until 1898.* The meaning of the main clause remains the same.]

Note: Most subordinate clauses serving as adverbs are restrictive because they describe conditions necessary to the main clause.

They are set off by a comma only when they introduce sentences (see 21b) and when they are truly nonrestrictive, adding incidental information (as in the last example above) or expressing a contrast beginning *although, even though, whereas,* and the like.

Nonrestrictive phrases

The dog, *seeking a bone,* jumped on the boy's lap. [Compare *The dog jumped on the boy's lap.* Assuming that only one dog is present, then the dog's goal does not restrict it to a specific dog.]

The Capitol Building, *at one end of Independence Mall,* is an imposing sight. [Compare *The Capitol Building is an imposing sight.* The building's name identifies it; its location does not supply further restriction.]

The library's most valuable book, *bought at auction in 1962,* is a thirteenth-century Bible. [Compare *The library's most valuable book is a thirteenth-century Bible.* Assuming that the Bible is the most valuable book in the library's entire collection, the details of its purchase do not restrict it further.]

He beat the other runners, *reaching the finish line in record time.* [Compare *He beat the other runners.* The meaning of the main clause remains the same.]

Note: When a participial phrase is separated from the noun or pronoun it modifies, as in the last example above, a comma is essential to clarify that the phrase does not modify the word closest to it. Without the comma, the reader automatically connects the phrase to *runners: He beat the other runners reaching the finish line in record time.*

Restrictive clauses

The person *who vandalized the dormitory* was never caught. [Compare *The person was never caught,* which does not identify the person.]

Every question *that has a reasonable answer* is justifiable. [Compare *Every question is justifiable,* which clearly alters the writer's meaning.] – Konrad Lorenz

He wore the look of one *who knows he is the victim of a terrible disease and understands his helplessness.* [Compare *He wore the look of one.* Without its modifying clause, *one* is meaningless.] – Stephen Crane

Books fall apart *when they are not well bound.* [Compare *Books fall apart,* which omits the limiting circumstances and thus implies that all books always fall apart. See the note above on adverb clauses.]

Restrictive phrases

A student *seeking an easy course* should not enroll *in History 101.* [Compare *A student should not enroll,* which fails to limit the kind of student who should not enroll and does not specify the course to be avoided.]

The ongoing taboo *against women dating men shorter than themselves* is among the strictest of this society. [Compare *The ongoing taboo is among the strictest of this society,* which no longer specifies what taboo.] – Ralph Keyes

The sealed crates *containing the records of my past* were drawn from storage and opened. [Compare *The sealed crates were drawn from storage and opened.* The crates are no longer limited by their contents.] – John Gregory Dunne

Note: Whereas both nonrestrictive and restrictive clauses may begin with *which,* only restrictive clauses begin with *that.* Some writers prefer *that* exclusively for restrictive clauses and *which* exclusively for nonrestrictive clauses. See the Glossary of Usage, page 601, for advice on the use of *that* and *which.*

2
Use a comma or commas to set off nonrestrictive appositives.

An **appositive** is a noun or noun substitute that renames and could substitute for another noun immediately preceding it. (See 5c-5.) Many appositives are nonrestrictive; thus they are set off, usually with commas. Take care *not* to set off restrictive appositives; like restrictive phrases and clauses, they limit or define the noun or nouns they refer to.

Nonrestrictive appositives

The Chapman lighthouse, *a three-legged thing erect on a mud-flat,* shone strongly. [Compare *The Chapman lighthouse shone strongly.*] – Joseph Conrad

John Kennedy Toole's only novel, *A Confederacy of Dunces,* won the Pulitzer Prize. [Compare *John Kennedy Toole's only novel won the Pulitzer Prize.*]

Restrictive appositives

Paul Scott's novel *The Jewel in the Crown* is about India under British rule. [Compare *Paul Scott's novel is about India under British rule,* which implies wrongly that Scott wrote only one novel.]

The philosopher *Alfred North Whitehead* once wrote that the history of philosophy was a series of footnotes to Plato. [Compare *The philosopher once wrote that the history of philosophy was a series of footnotes to Plato.*]

Our language has adopted the words *garage, panache, and fanfare* from French. [Compare *Our language has adopted the words from French.*]

3
Use a comma or commas to set off parenthetical expressions.

Parenthetical expressions are explanatory, supplementary, or transitional words or phrases. (Transitional expressions include *however, indeed, consequently, as a result, of course, for example,* and *in fact;* see 3b-6 for a more complete list.) Parenthetical expressions are usually set off by a comma or commas.

> The Cubist painters, *for example,* were obviously inspired by the families of crystals. – JACOB BRONOWSKI
>
> The only option, *besides locking him up,* was to release him to his parents' custody.
>
> The film is one of Redford's best, *according to the critics.*
>
> Any writer, *I suppose,* feels that the world into which he was born is nothing less than a conspiracy against the cultivation of his talent. – JAMES BALDWIN

(Dashes and parentheses may also set off parenthetical elements. See 25b-2 and 25c-1, respectively.)

4
Use a comma or commas to set off *yes* and *no,* tag questions, words of direct address, and mild interjections.

21c

YES AND NO

Yes, the editorial did have a point.
No, that can never be.

TAG QUESTIONS

Jones should be allowed to vote, *should he not?*
They don't stop to consider others, *do they?*

DIRECT ADDRESS

Cody, please bring me the newspaper.
With all due respect, *sir,* I will not do that.

MILD INTERJECTIONS

Well, you will never know who did it.
Oh, they forgot all about the baby.

(You may want to use exclamation points to set off forceful interjections. See 20e.)

EXERCISE 5

Insert commas in the following sentences to set off nonrestrictive elements, and delete any commas that incorrectly set off restrictive elements. If a sentence is correct as given, circle the number preceding it.

Example:

Elizabeth Blackwell who attended medical school in the 1840s was the first American woman to receive a medical degree.

Elizabeth Blackwell, who attended medical school in the 1840s, was the first American woman to receive a medical degree.

1. *The Time Machine* a novel by H. G. Wells is a haunting portrayal of Darwin's evolutionary theory carried to a terrible conclusion.
2. The report concluded that Americans who pay property taxes are the most disgruntled citizens.
3. We will not come unless you apologize.
4. All people, over six feet tall, can join the Boston Beanstalks Club.
5. *The Fantasticks* which has been playing in New York for more than a quarter century is America's longest-running musical.
6. The Temptations and the Four Tops, two veteran soul groups, will perform in the city this year.
7. Our modern ideas about civil liberties can be traced back to the Magna Carta which was written in 1215.
8. Please listen fellow voters while I explain my position.
9. Jarratt studies the eating disorder bulimia researching its causes and treatment.
10. Those of us, who hadn't seen the concert, felt we had missed something.

21c

EXERCISE 6

Combine each pair of sentences below into one sentence that uses the element described in parentheses. Insert commas as appropriate. You will have to add, delete, and rearrange words. Some items have more than one possible answer.

Example:

Mr. Ward's oldest sister helped keep him alive. She was a nurse in the hospital. (*Nonrestrictive clause beginning who.*)

Mr. Ward's oldest sister, *who was a nurse in the hospital,* helped keep him alive.

1. A house is on Langdon Street. It is rumored to be haunted by the ghost of a sea captain. (*Restrictive phrase beginning on.*)
2. The senator is William de Silva. He is a native of this city. (*Nonrestrictive appositive.*)
3. The juror voted not guilty. He caused a hung jury. (*Restrictive phrase beginning voting.*)
4. Joan Silver was leading the runners. She was the first to come in view. (*Nonrestrictive phrase beginning leading.*)

5. Men and women signed up for the exercise class. They are interested in toning their muscles. (*Restrictive clause beginning who.*)
6. Winter is the best of seasons. It is a time of dazzling snows and toasty fires. (*Nonrestrictive appositive.*)
7. The demonstrators were arrested. They refused to leave the building. (*Restrictive clause beginning because.*)
8. The island is in the middle of the river. It is a perfect hideaway. (*Nonrestrictive phrase beginning in.*)
9. Psychologists say that children have difficulty evaluating their own performances. They need the constant support of their parents. (*Nonrestrictive clause beginning who.*)
10. Some courses sharpen communications skills. They should be required of medical and nursing students. (*Restrictive clause beginning that.*)

21d

Use a comma or commas to set off absolute phrases.

21d

An **absolute phrase** modifies a whole main clause rather than any word or word group in the clause; it is not connected to the rest of the sentence by a conjunction, preposition, or relative pronoun. (See 5c-3.) Absolute phrases usually consist of at least a participle and its subject (a noun or pronoun), as in the following:

Their work finished, the men quit for the day.

Absolute constructions can occur at almost any point in the sentence. Whatever their position, they are always set off by a comma or commas.

Their homework done, the children may watch whatever they want on television.

After reaching Eagle Rock, we pointed our canoes toward shore, *the rapids ahead being rough.*

His clothes, *the fabric tattered and the seams ripped open*, looked like Salvation Army rejects.

EXERCISE 7

Insert commas in the following sentences to set off absolute constructions.

Example:

The recording contract was canceled the band having broken up.

The recording contract was canceled, the band having broken up.

1. His errands finished he settled down to read the paper.

2. They viewed the Atlantic wearily their cross-country drive completed.
3. All her customers served the waitress took a break.
4. The negotiations having started the doors were closed to the public.
5. Their boss having left early the employees extended their afternoon coffee breaks.
6. Spring coming nearer the ground felt damp and the air smelled fresh.
7. The governor had a chance the legislature being in recess to enhance his position with the voters.
8. The case was finally closed the only suspect having died.
9. Children their imaginations being vivid often suffer from terrifying nightmares.
10. Prices having risen steadily the government contemplated a price freeze.

21e

Use a comma or commas to set off phrases expressing contrast.

It was Saturday when the burglary occurred, *not Sunday as the newspaper reported.*

His generosity, *not his good looks,* won him friends.

Style is the manner of a sentence, *not its matter.* – DONALD HALL

It is not light that is needed, *but fire;* it is not the gentle shower, *but thunder.* – FREDERICK DOUGLASS

NOTE: Writers often omit commas around contrasting phrases beginning *but.*

His life was long *but sadly empty.* – HERMAN CRATSLEY

EXERCISE 8

Insert commas in the following sentences to set off phrases that express contrast.

Example:

Susan not her sister was the one who attended college in Michigan.

Susan, not her sister, was the one who attended college in Michigan.

1. The expense of heating homes not just the cold makes the winter months difficult in Maine.
2. We vacationed in Arizona not in New Mexico as we had planned.
3. It was the actress not the director who won an Academy Award.

4. World War II ended with the Japanese surrender not with the German surrender.
5. My family attends church in Cromwell not Durben because we know the minister in Cromwell.

21f

Use commas between items in a series and between coordinate adjectives.

1
Use commas between words, phrases, or clauses forming a series.

Place commas between all elements of a **series**—that is, three or more items of equal importance.

> The names *Belial, Beelzebub, and Lucifer* sound ominous.
>
> He felt cut off from them *by age, by understanding, by sensibility, by technology, and by his need to measure himself against the mirror of other men's appreciation.* – RALPH ELLISON
>
> The ox *was solid black, stood five feet high at the shoulder, had a five-foot span of horns, and must have weighed 1,200 pounds on the hoof.* – RICHARD B. LEE

Though some writers omit the comma before the coordinating conjunction in a series (*Breakfast consisted of coffee, eggs and kippers*), the final comma is never wrong and it always helps the reader see the last two items as separate. Use it consistently and your writing will be clearer, as the following example shows.

CONFUSING	The job involves typing, answering the phone, filing and reading manuscripts.
CLEAR	The job involves typing, answering the phone, filing, and reading manuscripts.

EXCEPTION: When items in a series are long and grammatically complicated, composed of clauses or phrases with modifiers, they may be separated by semicolons. When the items contain commas, they must, for clarity, be separated by semicolons. (See 22d.)

2
Use commas between coordinate adjectives not linked by conjunctions.

Coordinate adjectives are two or more adjectives that modify equally the same noun or pronoun. The individual adjectives are separated either by coordinating conjunctions or by commas.

The *sleek* and *shiny* car was a credit to the neighborhood.

The *dirty*, *rusty*, *dented* car was an eyesore.

Nothing is more essential to *intelligent*, *profitable* reading than sensitivity to connotation. – RICHARD ALTICK

Adjectives are not coordinate—and should *not* be separated by commas—when the one nearer the noun is more closely related to the noun in meaning.

The house overflowed with *ornate electric* fixtures. [*Ornate* modifies *electric fixtures.*]

The museum's most valuable object is a *sparkling diamond necklace.* [*Sparkling* modifies *diamond necklace.*]

Two tests will help you determine whether adjectives are coordinate: (1) Can the adjectives be rearranged without changing the meaning? (2) Can the word *and* be inserted between the adjectives without changing the meaning? In the sentence *They are dedicated medical students,* the adjectives cannot be rearranged (*medical dedicated students*) or separated by *and* (*dedicated and medical students*). Thus the adjectives are not coordinate, and no comma belongs between them. However, in the sentence *She was a faithful sincere friend,* the adjectives can be rearranged (*sincere faithful friend*), and they can be separated by *and* (*faithful and sincere friend*). Thus the adjectives are coordinate, and a comma belongs between them: *She was a faithful, sincere friend.*

21f

Notice that numbers are not coordinate with other adjectives.

FAULTY	Among the junk in the attic was *one, lovely* vase.
REVISED	Among the junk in the attic was *one lovely* vase.

Do not use a comma between the final coordinate adjective and the noun.

FAULTY	Spring evenings in the South are *warm, sensuous,* experiences.
REVISED	Spring evenings in the South are *warm, sensuous* experiences.

EXERCISE 9

Insert commas in the following sentences to separate coordinate adjectives or elements in series. Circle the number preceding each sentence whose punctuation is already correct.

Example:

Although quiet by day, the club became a noisy smoky dive at night.

Although quiet by day, the club became a noisy, smoky dive at night.

1. The tedious work absence of people her own age and paltry salary depressed Debra.
2. The manager bought new pine bar stools for the restaurant.
3. She was a Miamian by birth a farmer by temperament and a worker to the day she died.
4. The first boats were probably crude heavy canoes made from hollowed-out logs.
5. The child was dragged kicking crying and screaming into the classroom.
6. Somebody left a turquoise paperback book in my car yesterday.
7. As funny exciting and happy as it seemed, the dream frightened him terribly.
8. For his second birthday I'd like to buy my son a plastic hammer a punching bag and a leash.
9. Television newscasters rarely work full-time as reporters investigate only light stories if any and rarely write the copy they read on the air.
10. I called the police when I received the third crank phone call of the evening.

21g

Use commas according to convention in dates, addresses, place names, and long numbers.

The items in a date, address, or place name are conventionally separated with commas, as illustrated below. When they appear within sentences, dates, addresses, and place names punctuated with commas are also ended with commas.

Dates

July 4, 1776, was the day the Declaration of Independence was signed.

The bombing of Pearl Harbor on December 7, 1941, prompted American entry into World War II.

Commas are not used between the parts of a date in inverted order: *Their anniversary on 15 December 1982 was their fiftieth.* Commas need not be used in dates consisting of a month or season and a year: *For the United States the war began December 1941 and ended August 1945.*

Addresses and place names

Use the address 5262 Laurie Lane, Memphis, Tennessee, for all correspondence.

Send inquiries to Box 3862, Pasadena, California.

Columbus, Ohio, is the location of Ohio State University.

The population of Garden City, Long Island, New York, is 30,000.

Commas are not used between state names and zip codes in addresses: *Berkeley, California 94720, is the place of my birth.*

Long numbers

Use the comma to separate the figures in long numbers into groups of three, counting from the right. The comma with numbers of four digits is optional.

A kilometer is 3,281 feet (*or* 3281 feet).

Russia's 8,649,490 square miles make it the largest country in the world.

EXERCISE 10

Insert commas as needed in the following sentences.

Example:

The house cost $27000 fifteen years ago.
The house cost $27,000 fifteen years ago.

1. The novel opens on February 18 2054 in Montana.
2. The world's population exceeds 4762000000.
3. Boulder Colorado sits at the base of the Rocky Mountains.
4. Whoever writes P.O. Box 725 Asheville North Carolina 28803 will get a quick response.
5. The police discovered that the call was made on September 28 1985 from Ames Iowa.

21h

Use commas with quotations according to standard practice.

The words used to explain a quotation (*he said, she replied,* and so on) may come before, after, or in the middle of the quotation. They must always be separated from the quotation by punctuation, usually a comma or commas.

1

Ordinarily, use a comma to separate introductory and concluding explanatory words from quotations.

General Sherman summed up the attitude of all thoughtful soldiers when he said, "War is hell."

"Knowledge is power," wrote Francis Bacon.

Exceptions: Do not use a comma when a quotation followed by explanatory words ends in an exclamation point or a question mark (see 20c and 20e).

"Claude!" Mrs. Harrison called.

"Why must I come home?" he asked.

Do not use commas with a quotation introduced by *that* or with a short quotation in a sentence that does more than merely introduce or explain the quotation.

The warning that "cigarette smoking is dangerous to your health" has fallen on many deaf ears.

People should always say "Excuse me" when they bump into fellow pedestrians.

Use a colon instead of a comma to separate explanatory words from a quotation when there is an emphatic break between them in meaning or in grammar or when the quotation is very formal or longer than a sentence. (See also 25a.) For instance:

The Bill of Rights is unambiguous: "Congress shall make no law respecting an establishment of religion, or prohibiting the free exercise thereof."

2

Use a comma after the first part of a quotation interrupted by explanatory words. Follow the explanatory words with the punctuation required by the quotation.

Quotation

"When you got nothin', you got nothin' to lose."

Explanatory words

"When you got nothin'," Kris Kristofferson sings, "you got nothin' to lose." [The explanatory words interrupt the quotation at a comma and thus end with a comma.]

Quotation

"That part of my life was over; his words had sealed it shut."

Explanatory words

"That part of my life was over," she wrote; "his words had sealed it shut." [The explanatory words interrupt the quotation at a semicolon and thus end with a semicolon.]

Quotation

"This is the faith with which I return to the South. With this new faith we will be able to hew out of the mountain of despair a stone of hope."

Explanatory words

"This is the faith with which I return to the South," Martin Luther King, Jr., proclaimed. "With this new faith we will be able to hew out of the mountain of despair a stone of hope." [The explanatory words interrupt the quotation at the end of a sentence and thus end with a period.]

Note: Using a comma instead of a semicolon or a period in the last two examples would result in the error called a comma splice: two main clauses separated only by a comma, without a linking coordinating conjunction. (See 11a.)

3
Place commas that follow quotations within quotation marks.

"That's my seat," she said coldly.

"You gave it up," I replied evenly, "so you have no right to it."

(For further discussion of punctuating quotations, see 24g.)

EXERCISE 11

Insert commas or semicolons in the following sentences to correct punctuation with quotations. Circle the number preceding any sentence whose punctuation is already correct.

Example:

When asked to open her bag, the shoplifter said "I didn't steal anything."

When asked to open her bag, the shoplifter said, "I didn't steal anything."

1. My grandfather's adage that "the things you worry about never happen" has so far proved to be true.
2. "Having the chicken pox as an adult" the doctor explained "is much more serious than having them as a child."
3. "We are not only a Latin-American nation" Fidel Castro said in 1977 "we are also an Afro-American nation."
4. "The mass of men lead lives of quiet desperation" Henry David Thoreau wrote in *Walden*.
5. "I'll be on the next bus for Cleveland" the woman promised.

21i
Use commas to prevent misreading.

The comma tells the reader to pause slightly before moving on. In some sentences words may run together in unintended and confusing ways unless a comma separates them. Use a comma in such sentences even though no rule requires one.

Confusing Soon after she left town for good. [A short introductory phrase does not require a comma, but clarity requires it in this sentence.]

Revised	Soon after, she left town for good.
Confusing	The students who can usually give some money to the United Fund. [Without a comma the sentence seems incomplete.]
Revised	The students who can, usually give some money to the United Fund.

EXERCISE 12

Insert commas in the following sentences to prevent misreading.

Example:

To Laura Ann symbolized decadence.
To Laura, Ann symbolized decadence.

1. Beginning next Saturday night games will cost more than day games.
2. Though happy people will still have moments of self-doubt.
3. Of the fifty eight accepted admission to the program.
4. However crude the invention is promising.
5. Those who can't regret it.

no ↟ 21j

21j
Avoid misusing or overusing the comma.

Although commas are useful and often necessary to signal pauses in sentences, they can make sentences choppy and even confusing if they are used more often than needed or in violation of rules 21a through 21h. Examine every sentence you write to be sure you have used commas appropriately.

1
Don't use a comma to separate a subject from its verb, or a verb or a preposition from its object, unless the words between them require punctuation.

Faulty	The returning *soliders, expected* a warmer welcome than they received. [Separation of subject and verb.]
Revised	The returning *soldiers expected* a warmer welcome than they received.
Faulty	After deciding that she could do one but not both, my sister *chose, to have children* rather than pursue a career. [Separation of verb and object.]
Revised	After deciding that she could do one but not both, my sister *chose to have children* rather than pursue a career.

FAULTY	Amazingly, the refund arrived *after, only three weeks.* [Separation of preposition and object.]
REVISED	Amazingly, the refund arrived *after only three weeks.*

In the following sentence, commas are needed to set off the nonrestrictive clause that interrupts subject and verb.

> Americans, who are preoccupied with other sports, have not developed a strong interest in professional soccer.

2

Don't use a comma to separate words or phrases joined by coordinating conjunctions.

FAULTY	*The defense attorney, and the presiding judge* disagreed with the verdict. [Compound subject.]
REVISED	*The defense attorney and the presiding judge* disagreed with the verdict.
FAULTY	Television advertising is *expensive, and sometimes very effective.* [Compound complement.]
REVISED	Television advertising is *expensive and sometimes very effective.*
FAULTY	The sale of *handguns, and other weapons* is increasing alarmingly. [Compound object of a preposition.]
REVISED	The sale of *handguns and other weapons* is increasing alarmingly.
FAULTY	The boys *hiked up the mountain, and camped for the night* on the summit. [Compound predicate.]
REVISED	The boys *hiked up the mountain and camped for the night* on the summit.
FAULTY	Banks *could, and should* help older people manage their money. [Compound helping verb.]
REVISED	Banks *could and should* help older people manage their money.

(See 21a and 21f-1, respectively, for the appropriate use of commas with coordinating conjunctions between main clauses and with elements in a series.)

no ,
21j

3

Don't use commas to set off restrictive elements.

FAULTY	The land, *that both families claim as theirs,* is mostly swamp. [The clause beginning *that* restricts the meaning of the subject *land.*]

Revised The land *that both families claim as theirs* is mostly swamp.

Faulty Hawthorne's work, *The Scarlet Letter,* was the first major American novel. [The title of the novel is essential to distinguish the novel from the rest of Hawthorne's work.]

Revised Hawthorne's work *The Scarlet Letter* was the first major American novel.

Faulty Birds, *heading south,* signal the end, *of summer.* [*Heading south* limits *birds,* and *of summer* limits *end.*]

Revised Birds *heading south* signal the end *of summer.*

Faulty Buckle your seat belt, *whenever you travel by car.* [The clause specifies when to buckle up.]

Revised Buckle your seat belt *whenever you travel by car.*

(See 21c for further discussion of identifying and punctuating nonrestrictive and restrictive elements in sentences.)

no ,
21j

4

Don't use a comma before the first or after the last item in a series unless a rule requires it.

Faulty The *forsythia, daffodils, and tulips,* turned the garden into a rush of color. [The comma after *tulips* separates subject and verb.]

Revised The *forsythia, daffodils, and tulips* turned the garden into a rush of color.

Faulty Among other things, the Europeans brought to the New World, *horses, advanced technology, and new disease.* [The comma after *World* separates verb and object.]

Revised Among other things, the Europeans brought to the New World *horses, advanced technology, and new disease.*

In the following sentence the commas before and after the series are appropriate because the series is an appositive.

> The three major television networks, *ABC, CBS, and NBC,* face fierce competition from the cable networks.

However, many writers prefer to use dashes rather than commas to set off series functioning as appositives (see 25b-2).

(See 21f for further discussion of punctuating series.)

5
Don't use commas to set off an indirect quotation or a single word unless it is a nonrestrictive appositive.

INDIRECT QUOTATION

FAULTY The students asked, why they had to take a test the day before vacation.

REVISED The students asked why they had to take a test the day before vacation.

QUOTED OR ITALICIZED WORD

FAULTY James Joyce's story, "Araby," was assigned last year, too. [The story title is a restrictive appositive. The commas imply wrongly that Joyce wrote only one story.]

REVISED James Joyce's story "Araby" was assigned last year, too.

FAULTY The word, *open,* can be both a verb and an adjective. [*Open* is a restrictive appositive.]

REVISED The word *open* can be both a verb and an adjective.

The following sentence requires commas because the quoted title is a nonrestrictive appositive.

Her only poem about death, "Mourning," was printed in *The New Yorker.*

(See 21c-2 for more on punctuating appositives.)

EXERCISE 13

Revise the following sentences to eliminate needless or misused commas. Circle the number preceding each sentence that is already punctuated correctly.

Example:

The portrait of the founder, that hung in the dining hall, was stolen by pranksters.

The portrait of the founder that hung in the dining hall was stolen by pranksters.

1. Classes were canceled, for five days, because of the heat.
2. My sister was furious, when I dragged her out of bed.
3. The radio is the size of a credit card, and just a little heavier.
4. The students, having finished their exams, drove home for the holidays.
5. The mechanic wore a dirty, brown, coffee-stained, shirt.

6. His guidebook suggested a visit to the Smithsonian, and to the Kennedy Center.
7. The 5 percent rent decrease for all rent-controlled units, reflects this year's lower property taxes.
8. After the laboratory test, determines the level of hemoglobin in the bloodstream, the doctor prescribes an appropriate medication.
9. Charles Dickens's novel, *David Copperfield,* is still a favorite of generations of readers.
10. The coach said, that next year the team would have a winning season.
11. The tennis term, *love,* meaning, "zero," comes from the French word, *l'oeuf,* meaning, "the egg."
12. Cheese, eggs, and milk, are high in cholesterol.
13. Mary bought some of her course books at a used-book store, and borrowed the rest.
14. The point, of many of F. Scott Fitzgerald's stories, is that having money does not guarantee happiness.
15. Forest fires are destructive, although they sometimes benefit the woods they burn.

EXERCISE 14

Insert commas in the following paragraphs wherever they are needed, and eliminate any misused or needless commas.

Ellis Island New York has reopened for business but now the customers are tourists not immigrants. This spot which lies in New York Harbor was the first American soil seen, or touched by many of the nation's immigrants. Though other places also served as ports of entry for foreigners none has the symbolic power of, Ellis Island. Between its opening in 1892 and its closing in 1954, over 20 million people about two-thirds of all immigrants were detained there before taking up their new lives in the United States. Ellis Island processed over 2000 newcomers a day when immigration was at its peak between 1900 and 1920.

As the end of a long voyage and the introduction to the New World Ellis Island must have left something to be desired. The "huddled masses" as the Statue of Liberty calls them indeed were huddled. New arrivals were herded about kept standing in lines for hours or days yelled at and abused. Assigned numbers they submitted their bodies to the pokings and proddings of the silent nurses and doctors, who were charged with ferreting out the slightest sign of sickness, disability or insanity. That test having been passed the immigrants faced interrogation by an official through an interpreter. Those, with names deemed inconveniently long or difficult to pronounce, often found themselves permanently labeled with abbreviations, of their names, or with the names, of their hometowns. But of course millions survived the examination humiliation and confusion, to take the last short boat ride to New York City. For many of them and especially for their descendants Ellis Island eventually became not a nightmare but the place where life began.

Note: See page 376 for a punctuation exercise combining commas with other marks of punctuation such as semicolons and colons.

22
The Semicolon

22a

Use a semicolon to separate main clauses not joined by a coordinating conjunction.

Main clauses contain a subject and a predicate and do not begin with a subordinating word (see 5c). They may be linked by a coordinating conjunction such as *and* or *but* and then separated by a comma (see 21a). But when no coordinating conjunction is present, the clauses should be separated with a semicolon.

> I was not led to the university by conventional middle-class ambitions; my grip on the middle class was more tenuous than that on the school system. – Robin Fox

A semicolon provides less separation between main clauses than a period does and more separation than a comma and coordinating conjunction do. Generally, the semicolon is most appropriate when the first clause creates some suspense—some expectation in the reader that an equally important and complementary statement is coming. The semicolon then provides a pause before the second clause fulfills the expectation.

> Directing movies was only one of his ambitions; he also wanted to direct theatrical productions of Shakespeare's plays.

Note: If you do not link main clauses with a coordinating conjunction and you separate them only with a comma or with no punctuation at all, you will produce a comma splice or a fused sentence. See Chapter 11.

Exception: Writers sometimes use a comma instead of a semicolon between very short and closely parallel main clauses.

The poor live, the rich just exist.

But a semicolon is safer, and it is always correct.

EXERCISE 1

Insert semicolons or substitute them for commas to separate main clauses in the following sentences.

Example:

One man at the auction bid prudently another did not.
One man at the auction bid prudently; another did not.

1. Steve spent an evening writing the paper he spent an entire day typing it.
2. Hula hoops and bongo boards were once immensely popular today they are forgotten objects.
3. Karate is not just a technique for self-defense, like a religion, it teaches inner calm.
4. The Himalayas are the world's loftiest mountain range, they culminate in the world's highest mountain, Mount Everest.
5. Subways in New York City are noisy, dirty, and dangerous they are also a superbly efficient means of transportation.

; 22a

EXERCISE 2

Combine each set of three sentences below into one sentence containing only two main clauses, and insert a semicolon between the clauses. You will have to add, delete, change, and rearrange words. Each item has more than one possible answer.

Example:

The painter Andrew Wyeth is widely admired. He is not universally admired. Some critics view his work as sentimental.

The painter Andrew Wyeth is widely but not universally admired; some critics view his work as sentimental.

1. Coca-Cola offered a new flavor. The new flavor was sweeter. It was more like that of Pepsi.
2. The cartoonist gave in to pressure from the public. He also gave in to pressure from newspaper editors. He changed the image of the objectionable character in his comic strip.
3. Indian rugs are deceptively decorative. Their designs have religious meanings. The colors also have religious meanings.
4. The storm blew down trees. It blew down all the trees but the poplars. They stood in a row, undamaged.
5. The legend is that Betsy Ross designed the first American flag. The legend is probably untrue. Historians have never found any evidence to support it.

22b

Use a semicolon to separate main clauses joined by a conjunctive adverb.

Conjunctive adverbs include *consequently, hence, however, indeed, instead, nonetheless, otherwise, still, then, therefore,* and *thus.* (See 5d-2.) When a conjunctive adverb links two main clauses, the clauses should be separated by a semicolon.

> The Labor Department lawyers will be here in a month; *therefore,* the grievance committee should meet as soon as possible.
>
> For the first time in twenty years, the accident rate in St. Louis did not rise; *indeed,* it actually declined.

The position of the semicolon between main clauses never changes, but the conjunctive adverb may appear in several positions within a clause. The adverb is usually set off with a comma or commas.

> Blue jeans have become fashionable all over the world; *however*, the American originators still wear more jeans than anyone else.
>
> Blue jeans have become fashionable all over the world; the American originators, *however*, still wear more jeans than anyone else.
>
> Blue jeans have become fashionable all over the world; the American originators still wear more jeans than anyone else, *however.*

Commas are optional with *thus, hence,* and some other one-syllable conjunctive adverbs; and commas are usually omitted when *therefore, instead,* and a few other adverbs fall inside or at the ends of clauses.

> She skipped first grade; *thus* she is younger than her classmates.
>
> She skipped first grade; she is *therefore* younger than her classmates.
>
> I did not buy the book; I borrowed it *instead.*

Note: If you use a comma or no punctuation at all between main clauses connected by a conjunctive adverb, you will produce a comma splice or a fused sentence. See Chapter 11.

EXERCISE 3

Insert a semicolon in each sentence below to separate main clauses linked by a conjunctive adverb, and insert a comma or commas to set off the adverb.

Example:

He knew that tickets for the concert would be scarce therefore he arrived at the box office hours before it opened.

He knew that tickets for the concert would be scarce; therefore, he arrived at the box office hours before it opened.

1. Door-to-door salespeople are less common than they once were they still turn up from time to time however.
2. It was 11 P.M. on his twentieth birthday still his family had not acknowledged the day.
3. The jukebox suddenly went quiet consequently everyone could hear their argument.
4. The elevator shakes when it goes down the inspector says it is safe however.
5. We must cut down on our fuel consumption otherwise we'll find ourselves with *no* fuel, not just less.

EXERCISE 4

Combine each set of three sentences below into one sentence containing only two main clauses. Connect the clauses with the conjunctive adverb in parentheses, and separate them with a semicolon. (Be sure conjunctive adverbs are punctuated appropriately.) You will have to add, delete, and rearrange words. Each item has more than one possible answer.

Example:

The Russians censor their news. We get little news from them. And what we get is unreliable. (*therefore*)

The Russians censor their news; *therefore*, the little news we get from them is unreliable.

1. She was disappointed with the conclusion of the novel. It seemed anticlimactic. She went on to read the author's other two books. (*nonetheless*)
2. Most young children did not enjoy the movie. The jokes went over their heads. The characters' adventures frightened them. (*furthermore*)
3. My grandfather grew up in Italy. But he never spoke Italian in the United States. He always spoke English. (*instead*)
4. Peanuts thrive in light, sandy soil. They are an ideal crop for the South. In the South such soil is common. (*thus*)
5. The speaker's nervousness showed in his damp brow. His trembling voice also indicated nervousness. His hands shook so badly that he could barely hold his notes. (*moreover*)

22c

Use a semicolon to separate main clauses if they are very long and complex or if they contain commas, even when they are joined by a coordinating conjunction.

You would normally use a comma with the coordinating conjunctions *and, but, or, nor,* and *for* between main clauses. But placing semicolons between clauses punctuated with commas or between long and grammatically complicated clauses makes a sentence easier to read.

> Lewis and Clark led the men of their party with consummate skill, inspiring and encouraging them, doctoring and caring for them**;** *and* they kept voluminous notes and journals. – PAGE SMITH

> By a conscious effort of the mind, we can stand aloof from actions and their consequences**;** *and* all things, good and bad, go by us like a torrent. – HENRY DAVID THOREAU

Many writers prefer to use a semicolon instead of a comma between main clauses joined by the coordinating conjunctions *so* and *yet,* even when the clauses are not complicated or internally punctuated.

> The day was rainy and blustery**;** *so* the food vendors kept their fruits and vegetables indoors.

> Three truckloads of supplies arrived at the construction site**;** *yet* we still did not have enough cement.

; 22c

EXERCISE 5

Substitute semicolons for commas in the following sentences to separate main clauses that are long or grammatically complicated or that are internally punctuated.

Example:

She enjoyed dancing to popular music, often joined a group for square dancing, and even danced the fox trot with her father and brothers, but she preferred ballet.

She enjoyed dancing to rock music, often joined a group for square dancing, and even danced the fox trot with her father and brothers**;** but she preferred ballet.

1. The ushers had been instructed to clear the movie theater of popcorn boxes, candy wrappers, and beverage containers, yet we found trash all over the floor when we took our seats.
2. Seeking a change after the long, arduous trial, Judge Demme rented a cottage on a remote, uncrowded island, and there he found the serenity he needed.
3. By evening, having looked at every house on the realtor's list, the Morianis were exhausted and crabby, but they still hadn't found anything they could afford to buy.
4. James did whatever he wanted, without regard for the feelings or welfare of those around him or for the harm he was doing to himself, and eventually he got in trouble.
5. She had a challenging job, a decent income, and good prospects for the future, but she remained miserable.

EXERCISE 6

Combine each set of sentences below into one sentence containing only two main clauses. Link the clauses with the coordinating conjunction in parentheses, and separate them with a semicolon. You will have to add, delete, and rearrange words. Each item has more than one possible answer.

Example:

The election will be very close. Perhaps it will even be a tie. The nominees have hardly campaigned. They do not seem concerned. (*but*)

The election will be very close, perhaps even a tie**;** *but* the nominees have hardly campaigned and do not seem concerned.

1. The reform movements of the 1830s had a variety of goals. The goals included abolition of slavery. They also included equal rights for women. Few of the goals were realized until later. (*but*)
2. Scientists cannot count the stars, planets, and moons in the universe. They do not have the means. They must rely on estimates. (*so*)
3. Legends of the towns of the Old West create a lively picture. The picture consists of constant saloon brawls, bank robberies, and gunfights. The picture is inaccurate. (*but*)
4. Most Americans believe that the Internal Revenue Service reads their tax returns carefully. They believe that the IRS checks and double-checks all the information they provide. The IRS counts on this belief to keep taxpayers honest. (*and*)
5. In the office Mrs. Brown was a tyrant. She expected her subordinates to do exactly as she said. At home she was a pushover. She let her children do whatever they pleased. (*yet*)

22d

Use semicolons to separate items in a series if they are long or contain commas.

You normally use commas to separate items in a series (see 21f-1). But use semicolons instead when the items are long or internally punctuated. The semicolons help the reader identify the items.

The custody case involved Amy Dalton, the child**;** Ellen and Mark Dalton, the parents**;** and Ruth and Hal Blum, the grandparents.

One may even reasonably advance the claim that the sort of communication that really counts, and is therefore embodied into permanent records, is primarily written**;** that "words fly away, but written messages endure," as the Latin saying put it two

thousand years ago; and that there is no basic significance to at least fifty per cent of the oral interchange that goes on among all sorts of persons, high and low.
– Mario Pei

EXERCISE 7

Substitute semicolons for commas in the following sentences to separate long or internally punctuated items in a series.

Example:

After graduation he debated whether to settle in San Francisco, which was temperate but far from his parents, New York City, which was exciting but expensive, or Atlanta, which was close to home but already familiar.

After graduation he debated whether to settle in San Francisco, which was temperate but far from his parents; New York City, which was exciting but expensive; or Atlanta, which was close to home but already familiar.

1. The judge is known for her efficiency, her tight control over feisty, overzealous attorneys, and her ability to explain a difficult, complicated case to a jury.
2. The picnic was a disaster from the start because Brian forgot the beach blankets and chairs, Julie forgot the beer, potato salad, and hot dogs, and Sam forgot his bathing suit.
3. We have a cat that is the size of a cocker spaniel, with a bark to match, a dog that is so big we can't trust him in the house, and neighbors who, for some reason, won't speak to us.
4. The car swerved into oncoming traffic, narrowly missed a large, loaded oil truck, and headed nose first into a deep, muddy ditch.
5. The farm we visited has a clear, fast-moving brook, a shallow but clear pond, and trees, hundreds of trees that keep the waters and the house delightfully cool.

EXERCISE 8

Combine each set of sentences below into one sentence that includes a series punctuated with semicolons. You will have to add, delete, and rearrange words. Each item has more than one possible answer.

Example:

He lived in a dream world. It was populated by chauffeurs who drove him about in expensive, fast cars. Servants fulfilled his every wish. Politicians sought his favors.

He lived in a dream world populated by chauffeurs who drove him about in expensive, fast cars; servants who fulfilled his every wish; and politicians who sought his favors.

1. The facade of the building is an architectural nightmare. It consists of horizontal black and blue stripes and red, almost hot pink, vertical slashes. Also, it consists of round, bottle-green windows.
2. Driving west from Pennsylvania, we saw vast expanses of tall corn and shorter soybean plants. We saw many cows, some horses, and a few sheep grazing in rolling pastures. And sturdy, well-kept houses appeared with matching barns.
3. The campaign took an unexpected turn when the Republican had to undergo an operation that kept her in the hospital for two weeks. Also, the Democrat's wife gave birth to twins, a boy and a girl. And an independent candidate accused the other two of graft.
4. California's Fresno County, the nation's leading county in farm production, produces vegetables such as potatoes and tomatoes. It produces fruits such as figs, peaches, and nectarines. It produces seed crops such as alfalfa, barley, and cotton.
5. We Americans should be familiar with the basic metric weights and measures. These include the meter, about 39 inches. They also include the kilogram, about 2.2 pounds, and the liter, about 1.06 quarts.

22e

Avoid misusing or overusing the semicolon.

1

Don't use a semicolon to separate a subordinate clause or a phrase from a main clause.

The semicolon separates only equal sentence parts: main clauses and sometimes items in series. It does not separate unequal parts: subordinate clauses and main clauses, or phrases and main clauses.

Faulty	According to African authorities; only about 35,000 Pygmies exist today.
Revised	According to African authorities, only about 35,000 Pygmies exist today.
Faulty	The world would be less interesting; if clothes were standardized.
Revised	The world would be less interesting if clothes were standardized.

Many readers regard a phrase or subordinate clause set off with a semicolon as a sentence fragment. See Chapter 10.

2
Don't use a semicolon to introduce a series.

Colons and dashes, not semicolons, introduce explanations, series, and so forth. (See 25a and 25b.)

Faulty	The teacher had heard all the students' reasons for doing poorly; psychological problems, family illness, too much work, too little time.
Revised	The teacher had heard all the students' reasons for doing poorly**:** psychological problems, family illness, too much work, too little time.
Revised	The teacher had heard all the students' reasons for doing poorly—psychological problems, family illness, too much work, too little time.

3
Don't overuse the semicolon.

; 22e

Use the semicolon only occasionally and only when required by a rule. Too many semicolons, even when they are required by rule, often indicate repetitive sentence structure. Compare these two versions of the same passage. The first overuses the semicolon. The second, with only one semicolon, is clearer and contains more varied sentences.

> The Make-a-Wish Foundation helps sick children; it grants the wishes of children who are terminally ill. The foundation learns of a child's wish; the information usually comes from parents, friends, or hospital attendants; the wish may be for anything from a special toy to a visit to Disneyland. The foundation grants some wishes with its own funds; for other wishes it enlists the help of those who make or own what the child desires.

> The Make-a-Wish Foundation grants the wishes of children who are terminally ill. From parents, friends, or hospital attendants, the foundation learns of a child's wish for anything from a special toy to a visit to Disneyland. It grants some wishes with its own funds; for other wishes it enlists the help of those who make or own what the child desires.

EXERCISE 9

Revise the following sentences or groups of sentences to eliminate misused or overused semicolons, substituting other punctuation as appropriate.

Example:

The doctor gave all his patients the same advice; cut back on salt and fats, don't smoke, and, exercise regularly.

The doctor gave all his patients the same advice: cut back on salt and fats, don't smoke, and exercise regularly.

1. Walking all afternoon on hot sidewalks in chic plastic shoes; Marie burned her feet.
2. Although adventure films do vary, most of them have common elements; heroes and heroines, conflicts between good and evil, and elaborate special effects.
3. The bus line finally went out of business; because more and more students drove themselves to school.
4. Even though the National League wins the All-Star Game more often; I think the American League is superior.
5. Walking is great fun; we don't do enough of it. You see things when you're walking that you don't see when you're driving; you can smell and feel different things, too. Walking makes you a part of life; driving just races you through it.

EXERCISE 10

Insert semicolons in the following paragraph wherever they are needed. Eliminate any misused or needless semicolons, substituting other punctuation as appropriate.

The set, sounds, and actors in the movie captured the essence of horror films. The set was ideal; dark, deserted streets, trees dipping their branches over the sidewalks, mist hugging the ground and creeping up to meet the trees, looming shadows of unlighted, turreted houses. The sounds, too, were appropriate, especially terrifying was the hard, hollow sound of footsteps echoing throughout the film. But the best feature of the movie was its actors; all of them tall, pale, and thin to the point of emaciation. With one exception, they were dressed uniformly in gray and had gray hair. The exception was an actress who dressed only in black; as if to set off her pale yellow, nearly white, long hair; the only color in the film. The glinting black eyes of another actor stole almost every scene, indeed, they were the source of all the film's mischief.

Note: See page 376 for a punctuation exercise combining semicolons with other marks of punctuation such as commas and colons.

23
The Apostrophe

The apostrophe is used to form the possessive case of nouns and indefinite pronouns (23a); to indicate omissions in contractions such as *won't* (23c); and to form plurals of letters, numbers, and words named as words (23d). The apostrophe is *not* used to form plurals of nouns or the possessive case of personal pronouns (23b).

23a

Use the apostrophe to indicate the possessive case for nouns and indefinite pronouns.

The **possessive case** shows ownership or possession of one person or thing by another (see Chapter 6). Possession may be shown with an *of* phrase (*the hair of the dog*); or it may be shown with the addition of an apostrophe and, usually, an *-s* (*the dog's hair*).

1

Add *-'s* to form the possessive case of singular or plural nouns or indefinite pronouns that do *not* end in *-s*.

The *cat's* eyes were pale blue.
Bill *Boughton's* skillful card tricks amaze his friends.
The *children's* parents performed *Snow White.*
Laura felt she was *no one's* friend.

2

Add *-'s* to form the possessive case of singular words ending in *-s*.

Henry *James's* novels reward the patient reader.
Doris's term paper was read aloud in our English class.
The *business's* customers filed suit.

Exception: We typically do not pronounce the possessive *-s* of a few singular nouns ending in an *s* or *z* sound, especially names with more than one *s* sound (*Moses*), names that sound like plurals (*Rivers, Bridges*), and other nouns when they are followed by a word beginning in *s*. In these cases, many writers add only the apostrophe to indicate possession.

Moses' mother concealed him in the bulrushes.
Joan *Rivers'* jokes offend many people.
For *conscience'* sake she confessed her lie.

However, usage varies widely, and the final *-s* is not wrong with words like these (*Moses's, Rivers's, conscience's*).

3
Add only an apostrophe to form the possessive case of plural words ending in *-s*.

The *teachers'* association called a strike.

Workers' incomes have risen over the past decade, but not fast enough.

She took two *years'* leave from school.

The *Murphys'* car was stolen.

4
Add *-'s* only to the last word to form the possessive case of compound words or word groups.

My *father-in-law's* birthday was yesterday.
The *council president's* address was a bore.
Go bang on *somebody else's* door.

5
When two or more words show individual possession, add *-'s* to them all. If they show joint possession, add *-'s* only to the last word.

Individual possession

Harry's and Gerry's dentists both use hypnotism. [Harry and Gerry have different dentists.]

Joint possession

That living room is an example of *John and Martha's* bad taste. [John and Martha are jointly responsible for the living room.]

EXERCISE 1

Form the possessive case of each word or word group in parentheses.

Example:

The (*men*) blood pressures were higher than the (*women*).
The *men's* blood pressures were higher than the *women's*.

1. The (*treasurer*) resignation was expected.
2. My (*brother-in-law*) attitude was predictable.
3. The (*Smiths*) car alarm went off at midnight.
4. (*Laura and Jane*) landlord was totally unreasonable.
5. They visited (*Keats*) house on Hampstead Heath.
6. An (*hour*) exercise was plenty.
7. She studied the (*goddesses*) roles in Greek myths.
8. Higher pay and three (*weeks*) vacation were the focus of the (*garbage collectors*) strike.
9. John (*Adams*) letters to his wife illuminate his character.
10. (*Everyone*) books were stolen from the gym.
11. (*Children*) clothes are ridiculously expensive.
12. (*Susan and Sarah*) husbands are both out of work.
13. The (*utility companies*) recent price increases are unlawful.
14. Sam (*Prince*) speech won special praise.
15. The (*Hickses*) decision to move upset their children.

23b

Don't use the apostrophe to form the plurals of nouns or the possessive case of personal pronouns.

The plurals of nouns are generally formed by adding *-s* or *-es* (*boys, Smiths, families, Joneses*). Don't mistakenly add an apostrophe to form the plural.

Faulty	The unleashed *dog's* began traveling in a pack.
Revised	The unleashed *dogs* began traveling in a pack.
Faulty	The *Jones'* and *Bass'* are feuding.
Revised	The *Joneses* and *Basses* are feuding.

His, hers, its, ours, yours, theirs, and *whose* are possessive forms of the personal pronouns. They do not need apostrophes.

Faulty	Credit for discovering the house is really *her's*.
Revised	Credit for discovering the house is really *hers*.

The personal pronouns are often confused with contractions. See 23c below.

EXERCISE 2

Revise the following sentences to correct mistakes in the formation of plurals or of the possessive case of personal pronouns. Circle the number preceding any sentence that is already correct.

Example:

Was the raincoat her's?
Was the raincoat *hers?*

1. Radio talk-show host's all sound the same.
2. Its unfairness was clear.
3. We could hear the shouts of the boys playing basketball down the street.
4. The Hawaiian shirt's, each with it's own loud design, went on sale Tuesday.
5. The responsibility was your's.
6. The Russian's high prices make our's seem reasonable.
7. Its shocking color made the car easy to spot.
8. Theirs was far messier.
9. Book's can be good friend's.
10. Street crime was a particular focus of their's.

23c

Use an apostrophe to indicate the omission of one or more letters, numbers, or words in a standard contraction.

23c

it is	it's	does not	doesn't
they are	they're	were not	weren't
you are	you're	class of 1987	class of '87
who is	who's	of the clock	o'clock
cannot	can't	madam	ma'am

Contractions of verb phrases (*don't, weren't, isn't*) and of pronoun-verb pairs (*I'll, we're, she's*) are common in speech and in informal writing. They may also be used to relax style in more formal kinds of writing, as they are in this handbook. But be aware that many people disapprove of contractions in any kind of formal writing.

Note: Don't confuse the personal pronouns *its, their, your,* and *whose* with the contractions *it's, they're, you're,* and *who's.*

Faulty	*It's* messiness is not *you're* problem or *they're* problem. But *whose* going to clean up?
Revised	*Its* messiness is not *your* problem or *their* problem. But *who's* going to clean up?

EXERCISE 3

Form contractions from each set of words below. Use each contraction in a complete sentence.

Example:

we are
we're
We're open to ideas.

1. she would
2. could not
3. they are
4. he is
5. do not
6. she will
7. hurricane of 1962
8. is not
9. we would
10. will not

EXERCISE 4

Revise the following sentences to correct mistakes in the use of contractions and personal pronouns. Circle the number preceding any sentence that is already correct.

Example:

The company gives it's employees their birthdays off.
The company gives *its* employees their birthdays off.

1. They're reasons for the merger were questioned.
2. Its important to review you're notes before taking an exam.
3. I can begin work whenever your ready for me.
4. After spending two weeks on vacation, their now looking for jobs.
5. When it's team won the championship, the city celebrated.
6. The investigators wondered whose gun it was.
7. Its a wonder that any rivers remain unspoiled.
8. Business is a good major because it's certain that corporations will always need competent managers.
9. The Soltis, who's daughter was married last year, retired to Florida.
10. The only way of avoiding a fine is to pay you're taxes on time.

23d

Use an apostrophe plus -*s* to form the plurals of letters, numbers, and words named as words.

That sentence has too many *but*'s.

At the end of each chapter the author had written two *3*'s.

Remember to dot your *i*'s and cross your *t*'s, or your readers may not be able to distinguish them from *e*'s and *l*'s.

Notice that the letters, numbers, and words are italicized (underlined in typed or handwritten copy) but that the apostrophe and added *-s* are not. (See 27d on this use of italics or underlining.)

Exception: References to the years in a decade are not italicized and often omit the apostrophe. Thus either *1960's* or *1960s* is acceptable as long as usage is consistent.

EXERCISE 5

Form the plural of each letter, number, or word by using an apostrophe and *-s* and by underlining (italicizing) appropriately. Use the new plural in a complete sentence.

Example: x

Erase or white out typing mistakes. Do not use *x*'s.

1. 7
2. q
3. if
4. and
5. stop

EXERCISE 6

Correct any mistakes in the use of the apostrophe or any confusion between personal pronouns and contractions in the following paragraph.

Landlocked Chad is among the worlds most troubled countries. The people's of Chad are poor: they're average per capita income equals $73 a year. No more than 15 percent of Chads population is literate, and every thousand people must share only two teacher's. The natural resources of the nation have never been plentiful, and now, as it's slowly being absorbed into the growing Sahara Desert, even water is scarce. Chads political conflicts go back beyond the turn of the century, when the French colonized the land by brutally subduing it's people. The rule of the French—who's inept government of the colony did nothing to ease tensions among racial, tribal, and religious group's—ended with independence in 1960. But since then the Chadians experience has been one of civil war and oppression, and now their threatened with invasions from they're neighbors.

Note: See page 376 for a punctuation exercise involving apostrophes along with other marks of punctuation.

24
Quotation Marks

The principal function of quotation marks—either double (" ") or single (' ')—is to enclose direct quotations from speech and from writing. Always use quotation marks in pairs, one at the beginning of a quotation and one at the end.

(Several quotation practices are discussed in the appropriate sections of this book. See 25d for the use of brackets within quotations to separate your own comments from the words of the author you quote. See 25e for the use of the ellipsis mark [. . .] to indicate an omission from a quotation. And see 35g-2 for information on integrating quotations into your own writing.)

24a
Use double quotation marks to enclose direct quotations.

Direct quotations report what someone has said or written in the exact words of the original. Always enclose direct quotations in quotation marks.

> "If a sentence does not illuminate your subject in some new and useful way," says Kurt Vonnegut, "scratch it out."

Indirect quotations report what has been said or written, but not in the exact words of the person being quoted. Indirect quotations are *not* enclosed in quotation marks.

> Kurt Vonnegut advises inexperienced writers to scratch out any sentence that does not illuminate their subject in some new and useful way.

24b

Use single quotation marks to enclose a quotation within a quotation.

When you quote a writer or speaker, use double quotation marks (see 24a). When the material you quote contains yet another quotation, enclose the second quotation in single quotation marks.

> "In formulating any philosophy," Woody Allen writes, "the first consideration must always be: What can we know? . . . Descartes hinted at the problem when he wrote, 'My mind can never know my body, although it has become quite friendly with my legs.' "

Notice that two different quotation marks appear at the end of the sentence—one single (to finish the interior quotation) and one double (to finish the main quotation).

EXERCISE 1

Insert single and double quotation marks as needed in the following sentences. Circle the number preceding each sentence that is already correct.

Example:

The phrase Feed a cold, starve a fever, Ms. Coyne explained, actually originated as Feed a cold, die of fever during a plague in London in the Middle Ages.

"The phrase 'Feed a cold, starve a fever,' " Ms. Coyne explained, "actually originated as 'Feed a cold, die of fever' during a plague in London in the Middle Ages."

1. Many people sneer at the friendly line Have a nice day.
2. She tells us, Dance is poetry, Marsha said, but I don't understand what she means.
3. Mark Twain quipped, Reports of my death are greatly exaggerated.
4. We shall overcome, sang the civil rights workers of the 1960s. I think we should still be singing those words.
5. After a long pause he said that the man in the red shirt had stolen the car.

24c

Set off quotations of dialogue, poetry, and long prose passages according to standard practice.

Dialogue

When quoting conversations, begin a new paragraph for each speaker.

> "Say something, son," the detective said.
> "I didn't hold this guy up," said the suspect in a dead voice.
> – BERNARD MALAMUD

NOTE: When you quote a single speaker for more than one paragraph, put quotation marks at the beginning of each paragraph but at the end of only the last paragraph. The absence of quotation marks at the end of each paragraph but the last tells readers that the speech is continuing.

Poetry

When you quote a single line from a poem, song, or verse play, place the line in the running text and enclose it in quotation marks.

> Dylan Thomas remembered childhood as an idyllic time, "About the lilting house and happy as the grass was green."

Poetry quotations of two or three lines may be placed in the text or displayed separately. If you place such a quotation in the text, enclose it in quotation marks and separate the lines with a slash surrounded by space (see 25f).

> Robert Frost's incisiveness shows in two lines from "Death of the Hired Man": "Home is the place where, when you have to go there, / They have to take you in."

" "
24c

Quotations of more than three lines of poetry should always be separated from the text with space and an indention. Do not add quotation marks.

> Emily Dickinson rarely needed more than a few lines to express her complex thoughts:
>
> To wait an Hour–is long–
> If Love be just beyond–
> To wait Eternity–is short–
> If Love reward the end–

The *MLA Handbook,* the standard guide to manuscript format in English and some other disciplines, recommends the following spacings for displayed quotations: double-space above and below the quotation, indent it ten spaces from the left margin, and double-space the quoted lines. Unless your instructor specifies otherwise, follow these guidelines for your papers, whether typewritten or handwritten. (See Chapter 35, p. 532, for an example of a displayed quotation in a typed paper.)

NOTE: Be careful when quoting poetry to reproduce faithfully all line indentions, space between lines, spelling, capitalization, and punctuation, such as the capitals and dashes in the Dickinson poem above.

Long prose passages

Separate a prose quotation of more than four typed or handwritten lines from the body of your paper. Following the guidelines of the *MLA Handbook* (see above), double-space above and below the quotation, indent it ten spaces from the left margin, and double-space the quoted lines. Do not add quotation marks.

> While deploring the effects of the social sciences on English prose style, Malcolm Cowley can still use his sense of humor:
>
> > Considering this degradation of the verb, I have wondered how one of Julius Caesar's boasts could be translated into Socspeak. What Caesar wrote was *"Veni, vidi, vici"*—only three words, all of them verbs. The English translation is in six words: "I came, I saw, I conquered," and three of the words are first-personal pronouns, which the sociologist is taught to avoid. I suspect that he would have to write: "Upon the advent of the investigator, his hegemony became minimally coextensive with the areal unit rendered visible by his successive displacements in space."

Do not use a paragraph indention when quoting a single complete paragraph or a part of a paragraph. Use paragraph indentions only when quoting two or more complete paragraphs.

EXERCISE 2

Practice using quotation marks in quoted dialogue, poetry, and long prose passages by completing each of the exercises below.

1. Write a short sketch of dialogue between two people.
2. Write a sentence that quotes a single line of poetry.
3. Write two sentences, each quoting the same two lines of poetry. In one, place the poetry lines in the text. In the other, separate the two lines from the text.
4. Write a sentence introducing a prose passage of more than four lines, and then set up the quotation appropriately.

24d

Put quotation marks around titles according to standard practice.

Use quotation marks to enclose the titles of songs, short poems, articles in periodicals, short stories, essays, episodes of television and radio programs, and the subdivisions of books. For all other titles, use italics (underlining); see 27a.

Songs

"Lucy in the Sky with Diamonds"
"Mr. Bojangles"

Short poems

"Stopping by Woods on a Snowy Evening"
"Sunday Morning"

Articles in periodicals

"Comedy and Tragedy Transposed" (in *The Yale Review*)
"Does 'Scaring' Work?" (in *Newsweek*)

Short stories

"The Battler"
"The Gift of the Magi"

Essays

"Politics and the English Language"
"Joey: A 'Mechanical Boy'"

Episodes of television and radio programs

"The Mexican Connection" (on *60 Minutes*)
"Cooking with Clams" (on *Eating In*)

Subdivisions of books

"Voyage to the Houyhnhnms" (Part IV of *Gulliver's Travels*)
"The Mast Head" (Chapter 35 of *Moby Dick*)

See 26b for guidelines on the use of capital letters in titles.

24e

Occasionally, quotation marks may be used to enclose defined words and words used in a special sense.

By "charity," I mean the love of one's neighbor as oneself.
An architect refers to one view of a building as its "aspect."
Pardon my pun, but I find that lawyer "appealing."

Note: In definitions, italics (or underlining) are more common than quotation marks (see 27d).

By *charity,* I mean the love of one's neighbor as oneself.
An architect refers to one view of a building as its *aspect.*

EXERCISE 3

Insert quotation marks as needed for titles and words in the following sentences. If quotation marks should be used instead of italics, insert them.

Example:

The students forget to call her professor because she is the same age they are.

The students forget to call her "professor" because she is the same age they are.

1. In Chapter 8, titled *How to Be Interesting*, the author explains the art of conversation.
2. The Beatles' Let It Be reminds him of his uncle.
3. Doom means simply judgment as well as unhappy destiny.
4. The article that appeared in *Mental Health* was titled *Children of Divorce Ask, "Why?"*
5. In my encyclopedia the discussion under Modern Art fills less than a column.

24f

Avoid using quotation marks where they are not required.

Don't use quotation marks in the titles of your papers unless they contain or are themselves direct quotations.

Not	"The Death Wish in One Poem by Robert Frost"
But	The Death Wish in One Poem by Robert Frost
Or	The Death Wish in "Stopping by Woods on a Snowy Evening"

" " 24f

Don't use quotation marks to enclose common nicknames or technical terms that are not being defined.

Not	Even as President, "Jimmy" Carter preferred to use his nickname.
But	Even as President, Jimmy Carter preferred to use his nickname.
Not	"Mitosis" in a cell is fascinating to watch.
But	Mitosis in a cell is fascinating to watch.

Don't use quotation marks in an attempt to justify or apologize for slang and trite expressions that are inappropriate to your writing. If slang is appropriate, use it without quotation marks.

Not	It "rained cats and dogs" for the whole week, so we did not make any "bread" in our temporary construction jobs.
But	It rained hard for the whole week, so we did not make any money in our temporary construction jobs.

(See 31a-1 and 31b-5 for a discussion of slang and trite expressions.)

24g

Place other marks of punctuation inside or outside quotation marks according to standard practice.

1

Place commas and periods inside quotation marks.

"Your first check will come next month," the social worker said.
Without pausing he pointed and said, "That's the man."
Swift uses irony in his essay "A Modest Proposal."

(See 21h for the use of commas to separate quotations from words used to introduce or explain them.)

2

Place colons and semicolons outside quotation marks.

A few years ago the slogan in elementary education was "learning by playing"; now educators are concerned with teaching basic skills.

We all know what is meant by "inflation": more money buys less.

3

Place dashes, question marks, and exclamation points inside quotation marks only if they belong to the quotation.

When a dash, question mark, or exclamation point is part of the quotation, put it *inside* quotation marks.

"But must you—" Marcia hesitated, afraid of the answer.

Did you say, "Who is she?"

"Go away!" I yelled.

When a dash, question mark, or exclamation point applies only to the larger sentence, not to the quotation, place it *outside* quotation marks.

One of the most evocative lines in English poetry—"After many a summer dies the swan"—was written by Alfred, Lord Tennyson.

Who said, "Now cracks a noble heart"?

That woman called me "stupid"!

EXERCISE 4

Revise the following sentences for the proper use of quotation marks. Insert quotation marks where they are needed, remove them where they are not needed, and be sure that other marks of punctuation are correctly placed inside or outside the quotation marks. Circle the number preceding any sentence that is already punctuated correctly.

Example:

The award-winning story was titled How to Say I'm Sorry to a Child.

The award-winning story was titled "How to Say 'I'm Sorry' to a Child."

1. The course reading included Virginia Woolf's essay The Anatomy of Fiction.
2. No smoking on this bus! the driver shouted.
3. The commercial says, Lite Beer is a third less filling than your regular beer; but how do they measure that?
4. Wearing calico and lace, she looked like a "down-home girl."
5. How can we answer children who ask, Will there be a nuclear war?
6. In America the signs say, Keep off the grass; in England they say, Please refrain from stepping on the lawn.
7. In *King Richard II* Shakespeare calls England This precious stone set in the silver sea.
8. The doctors gave my father an "electrocardiogram" but found nothing wrong.
9. Our forests—in Longfellow's words, "The murmuring pines and the hemlocks"—are slowly succumbing to land development.
10. Must we regard the future with what Kierkegaard called fear and trembling?

EXERCISE 5

Insert quotation marks as needed in the following paragraph.

In one class we talked about two lines from Shakespeare's Sonnet 55:

> Not marble, nor the gilded monuments
> Of princes, shall outlive this powerful rime.

Why is this true? the teacher asked. Why does Shakespeare's powerful rime indeed live longer than the gilded monuments / Of princes? She then asked if the lines were protected only by Shakespeare's status as our greatest writer. No, said one student. It has more to do with the power of the language. Then another student added, Even though paper is less durable than stone, ideas are more durable than monuments to dead princes. The whole discussion was an eye opener for those of us (including me) who had never given much credit to rhymes or the words that made them.

Note: See page 376 for a punctuation exercise involving quotation marks along with other marks of punctuation.

25
Other Punctuation Marks

THE COLON

25a

Use the colon to introduce and to separate.

1

Use a colon to introduce summaries, explanations, series, appositives ending sentences, long or formal quotations, and statements introduced by *the following* or *as follows*.

The colon is primarily a mark of introduction: it signals that the preceding statement is about to be explained, amplified, or summarized; or it signals that a series or quotation follows. A colon is always preceded by a complete main clause, but it need not be followed by a main clause. Thus the colon differs from the semicolon, whose primary function is to separate main clauses expressing complementary and equally important ideas (see 22a). The colon is often interchangeable with the dash, though the dash is more informal and more abrupt (see 25b).

Summary

They cannot pay their children's college costs because their money is tied up in their house and antique furniture**:** they are possession-rich and cash-poor.

Explanation

It is a good thing to be old early**:** to have the fragility and sensitivity of the old, and a bit of wisdom, before the years of planning and building have run out. – Martin Gumbert

SERIES

It is impossible to dissociate language from science or science from language, because every natural science always involves three things: the sequence of phenomena on which the science is based; the abstract concepts which call these phenomena to mind; and the words in which the concepts are expressed.
— ANTOINE LAVOISIER

FINAL APPOSITIVE

Two chief elements make work interesting: first, the exercise of skill, and second, construction. — BERTRAND RUSSELL

LONG OR FORMAL QUOTATION

He concluded with an ultimatum: "Either improve the mass transit system or anticipate further decay in your downtown area."

STATEMENT INTRODUCED BY *THE FOLLOWING* OR *AS FOLLOWS*

The relation between leisure and income is as follows: the quality of play depends on the quantity of pay.

NOTE: A complete sentence following a colon may begin with a capital letter or a small letter.

2

Use a colon to separate titles and subtitles, the subdivisions of time, and the parts of biblical citations.

: 25a

TITLES AND SUBTITLES

Charles Dickens: An Introduction to His Novels
Eros and Civilization: A Philosophical Inquiry into Freud

TIME	BIBLICAL CITATIONS
1:30	Isaiah 28:1–6
12:26	1 Corinthians 3:6–7

3

Avoid misusing the colon.

Use the colon only at the end of a main clause. Avoid using it between a verb and its object or between a preposition and its object.

NOT	Two entertaining movies directed by Stephen Spielberg are: *E.T.* and *Raiders of the Lost Ark.*
BUT	Two entertaining movies directed by Stephen Spielberg are *E.T.* and *Raiders of the Lost Ark.*

Not Shakespeare showed the qualities of a Renaissance man, such as: humanism and a deep interest in classical Greek and Roman literature.

But Shakespeare showed the qualities of a Renaissance man, such as humanism and a deep interest in classical Greek and Roman literature.

EXERCISE 1

Insert colons as needed in the following sentences, or delete colons that are misused.

Example:

Mix the ingredients as follows sift the flour and salt together, add the milk, and slowly beat in the egg yolk.

Mix the ingredients as follows: sift the flour and salt together, add the milk, and slowly beat in the egg yolk.

1. During the interview she detailed: her impressions of the job, her own qualifications, and her career hopes.
2. He concluded with a threat "Either rehire me, or I will go to the labor board."
3. He based his prediction of the Second Coming on John 21 17–30.
4. She left her cottage at 8:00 in the morning with only one goal in mind to murder the man who was blackmailing her.
5. The Pilgrims had one major reason for coming to the New World they sought religious freedom.

— 25b

THE DASH

25b

Use a dash or dashes to indicate sudden changes in tone or thought and to set off some sentence elements.

1

Use a dash or dashes to indicate sudden shifts in tone, new or unfinished thoughts, and hesitation in dialogue.

Shift in tone

He tells us—does he really mean it?—that he will speak the truth from now on.

Unfinished thought

If she found out—he did not want to think what she would do.

Hesitation in dialogue

"I was worried you might think I had stayed away because I was influenced by—" he stopped and lowered his eyes.

Astonished, Howe said, "Influenced by what?"

"Well, by—" Blackburn hesitated and for answer pointed to the table. – Lionel Trilling

2 Use a dash or dashes to emphasize appositives and parenthetical expressions.

Dashes may be used in place of commas (21c-3) or parentheses (25c-1) to set off and emphasize appositives and parenthetical expressions. Dashes are especially useful when these elements are internally punctuated. Be sure to use a pair of dashes when the element interrupts a main clause.

Appositive

The qualities Monet painted—sunlight, rich shadows, deep colors—abounded near the rivers and gardens he used as subjects.

Parenthetical expressions

Though they are close together—separated by only a few blocks—the two neighborhoods could be in different countries.

At any given time there exists an inventory of undiscovered embezzlement in—or more precisely not in—the country's businesses and banks. – John Kenneth Galbraith

3 Use a dash to set off introductory series and concluding series and explanations.

Introductory series

Shortness of breath, skin discoloration or the sudden appearance of moles, persistent indigestion, the presence of small lumps—all these may signify cancer.

A dash sets off concluding series and explanations more informally and more abruptly than a colon does (see 25a-1).

Concluding series

We packed our camping gear—tent, sleeping bags, stove, and cooler.

Concluding explanation

The country was the most beautiful he had seen—green, rolling hills dotted with stands of dark pine and etched with stone walls.

4
Avoid misusing or overusing the dash.

Don't use the dash when commas, semicolons, and periods are more appropriate. And don't use too many dashes. They can create a jumpy or breathy quality in writing.

NOT	In all his life—eighty-seven years—my great-grandfather never allowed his picture to be taken—not even once. He claimed the "black box"—the camera—would steal his soul.
BUT	In all his eighty-seven years my great-grandfather did not allow his picture to be taken even once. He claimed the "black box"—the camera—would steal his soul.

EXERCISE 2

Insert dashes as needed in the following sentences.

Example:

What would we do if someone like Adolf Hitler that monster appeared among us?

What would we do if someone like Adolf Hitler— that monster— appeared among us?

1. The exuberant I should say lunatic quality of his ravings electrified the crowd.
2. The two brothers one tall and thin, the other short and stout look nothing alike.
3. The difficulties of city living they hardly need enumerating can undermine the most cheerful spirit.
4. "The dream just" she hesitated slightly and then continued. "Actually, it terrifies me."
5. To feed, clothe, and find shelter for the needy these are real achievements.

( )
25c

PARENTHESES

25c
Use parentheses to enclose nonessential elements within sentences.

1
Use parentheses to enclose parenthetical expressions.

Parenthetical expressions include explanations, facts, minor digressions, and examples that may aid understanding but are not essential to meaning. They are emphasized least when set off with a pair of parentheses. Commas (21c-3) and dashes (25b-2) give them greater emphasis.

> He drove trucks (tractor-trailers, actually) to earn money for college tuition.
>
> The population of Philadelphia (now about 1.7 million) has declined since 1950.
>
> Unlike the creatures (some insects, for instance) that have been unchanged for five, ten, even fifty million years, man has changed over this time-scale out of all recognition. – JACOB BRONOWSKI

NOTE: Don't put a comma before a parenthetical expression enclosed in parentheses.

NOT	The dungeon, (really the basement) haunted us.
BUT	The dungeon (really the basement) haunted us.

A comma or period falling after a parenthetical expression should be placed outside the closing parenthesis.

> We received numerous complaints (125 to be exact), but most harped on the same old theme (namely, high prices).

When it falls between other complete sentences, a complete sentence enclosed in parentheses has a capital letter and end punctuation.

> In general, coaches will tell you that scouts are just guys who can't coach. (But then, so are brain surgeons.) – ROY BLOUNT, JR.

( )
25c

2
Use parentheses to enclose letters and figures labeling items in lists within sentences.

> My father could not, for his own special reasons, even *like* me. He spent the first twenty-five years of my life acting out that painful fact. Then he arrived at two points in his own life: (1) his last years, and (2) the realization that he had made a tragic mistake.
> – RAY WEATHERLY

When lists are set off from the text, the numbers or letters labeling them are usually not enclosed in parentheses.

EXERCISE 3

Insert parentheses as needed in the following sentences.

Example:

Students can find good-quality, inexpensive furniture for example, desks, tables, chairs, sofas, even beds in junk stores.

Students can find good-quality, inexpensive furniture (for example, desks, tables, chairs, sofas, even beds) in junk stores.

1. T. S. Eliot's *The Waste Land* 1922 is one of the most analyzed poems in the English language.
2. The Golden Gate Bridge actually it's closer to red is a famous landmark of San Francisco.
3. Our present careless use of coal and oil will lead to a series of unpleasant events: 1 all of us will have to cut back drastically on our use of resources; 2 only the rich will have access to these resources; and 3 no one will have access to them for they will be exhausted.
4. Some exotic pets monkeys and fragile breeds of dog require too much care to be enjoyable.
5. The Hundred Years' War 1337–1453 between England and France was actually a series of widely spaced battles, not a continuous war.

BRACKETS

[ ]
25d

25d

Use brackets only within quotations to separate your own comments from the words of the writer you quote.

If you need to explain, clarify, or correct the words of the writer you quote, place your additions in a pair of brackets.

"That Texaco station [just outside Chicago] is one of the busiest in the nation," said a company spokesman.

You may also use a bracketed word or words to substitute for parts of the original quotation that would otherwise be unclear. In the sentence below, the bracketed word substitutes for *they* in the original.

"Despite considerable achievements in other areas, [humans] still cannot control the weather and probably will never be able to do so."

The word *sic* (Latin for "in this manner") in brackets indicates that an error in the quotation appeared in the original and was not made by you.

According to the newspaper report, "The car slammed thru [*sic*] the railing and into oncoming traffic."

But don't use *sic* to make fun of a writer or to note errors in a passage that is clearly nonstandard or illiterate.

THE ELLIPSIS MARK

25e

Use the ellipsis mark to indicate omissions within quotations.

The **ellipsis mark** consists of three spaced periods (. . .). It is used most often to indicate an omission from a quotation.

ORIGINAL QUOTATION

"It took four years for Bernice Gera to walk onto that ball field, four years of legal battles for the right to stand in the shadow of an 'Enjoy Silver Floss Sauerkraut' sign while the crowd cheered and young girls waved sheets reading 'Right On, Bernice!' and the manager of the Geneva Phillies welcomed her to the game. 'On behalf of professional baseball,' he said, 'we say good luck and God bless you in your chosen profession.' And the band played and the spotlights shone and all three networks recorded the event. Bernice Gera had become the first woman in the 133-year history of the sport to umpire a professional baseball game."

– NORA EPHRON

OMISSION OF PART OF A SENTENCE

"Bernice Gera had become the first woman . . . to umpire a professional baseball game."

OMISSION OF ONE OR MORE SENTENCES

"It took four years for Bernice Gera to walk onto that ball field, four years of legal battles for the right to stand in the shadow of an 'Enjoy Silver Floss Sauerkraut' sign while the crowd cheered and young girls waved sheets reading 'Right On, Bernice!' and the manager of the Geneva Phillies welcomed her to the game. . . . Bernice Gera had become the first woman in the 133-year history of the sport to umpire a professional baseball game."

Notice that when the ellipsis mark follows a sentence, as in the example immediately above, four equally spaced periods result: the sentence period (closed up to the last word of the sentence) and the three periods of the ellipsis mark. Notice also that although Ephron's essay goes on after the quoted paragraph, an ellipsis mark is not used at the end of the quotation.

If you omit one or more lines of poetry or paragraphs of prose from a quotation, use a separate line of ellipsis marks across the full width of the quotation to show the omission.

NOTE: Pauses and unfinished statements in quoted speech may be indicated with the ellipsis mark. (See 25b-1 for the use of the dash for this purpose.)

"I wish. . . " His voice trailed off.

EXERCISE 4

To practice using ellipsis marks to show omissions from quotations, follow each instruction below, using the following paragraph by Stewart Udall.

> The most common trait of all primitive peoples is a reverence for the life-giving earth, and the native American shared this elemental ethic: the land was alive to his loving touch, and he, its son, was brother to all creatures. His feelings were made visible in medicine bundles and dance rhythms for rain, and all of his religious rites and land attitudes savored the inseparable world of nature and God, the master of life. During the long Indian tenure the land remained undefiled save for scars no deeper than the scratches of cornfield clearings or the farming canals of the Hohokams on the Arizona desert. – STEWART UDALL

1. Quote the first sentence from the paragraph, but omit the words *its son* (and punctuation as necessary). Show the omission with an ellipsis mark.
2. Quote the paragraph, but omit the second sentence. Show the omission with an ellipsis mark.

THE SLASH

/ 25f

25f

Use the slash between options and to separate lines of poetry that are run in to the text.

OPTION

I don't know why some teachers oppose pass/fail courses.

When used between options, the slash is not surrounded by extra space.

NOTE: The options *and/or* and *he/she* should be avoided. (See the Glossary of Usage, pp. 588 and 594.)

POETRY

More than fifty years after its introduction, people are still baffled by E. E. Cummings's unique form of expression, such as in the lines "next to of course god america i / love you land of the pilgrims' and so forth oh."

When used to separate lines of poetry, the slash is surrounded by space. (See 24c for more on quoting poetry.)

EXERCISE 5

Insert colons, dashes, parentheses, brackets, ellipsis marks, or slashes as needed in the following sentences, or remove them where they are not needed. When different marks would be appropriate in the same place, be able to defend the choice you make. Circle the number preceding any sentence that is already correct.

Example:

The residents of the neighborhood including many who grew up there signed a petition against further development.

The residents of the neighborhood—including many who grew up there—signed a petition against further development. [The dashes emphasize the parenthetical expression.]

1. Year-round warmth, lush vegetation, Mexican food these are her favorite things about San Diego.
2. I read about Emma Goldman (or Red Emma), an American anarchist who died in 1940.
3. He has all the qualities of a fine cook he shops patiently for the freshest ingredients, he prepares the food with imagination and care, and he serves the meal elegantly.
4. From the reviewer's sentence "The acting is amazingly incompetent, given that these actors can be powerful," the advertisement extracted praise by using an ellipsis mark: "The acting is amazingly powerful."
5. The bikers—tattooed and draped in chains look more threatening than they really are.
6. "Buy the new Universal Dictionery *sic*," the ad said. But how could anybody buy a dictionary that can't spell *dictionary?*
7. James Joyce's *Ulysses* first published in 1922 is a beautiful, shocking novel.
8. In the letter he quoted two lines of poetry that John Donne once wrote in a letter of his own "Sir, more than kisses, letters mingle souls; For thus friends absent speak."
9. Paying taxes one of life's certainties is only a little less painful than the other certainty.
10. The book is filled with behind-the-scenes anecdotes about some of the all-time most popular television shows, including *I Love Lucy, Gunsmoke, All in the Family,* and *Dallas.*

/ 25f

Note: See the next page for a punctuation exercise combining colons, dashes, and parentheses with other marks of punctuation such as commas and semicolons.

EXERCISE ON CHAPTERS 20–25
Periods, Commas, Semicolons, Apostrophes, Quotation Marks, Colons, Dashes, and Parentheses

The following paragraphs are unpunctuated except for end-of-sentence periods. Insert the appropriate punctuation marks where they are required. When different marks would be appropriate in the same place, be able to defend the choice you make.

Brewed coffee is the most widely consumed beverage in the world. The trade in coffee beans alone amounts to well over $6000000000 a year and the total volume of beans traded exceeds 4250000 tons a year. Its believed that the beverage was introduced into Arabia in the fifteenth century AD probably by Ethiopians. By the middle or late sixteenth century the Arabs had introduced the beverage to the Europeans who at first resisted it because of its strong flavor and effect as a mild stimulant. The French Italians and other Europeans incorporated coffee into their diets by the seventeenth century the English however preferred tea which they were then importing from India. Since America was colonized primarily by the English Americans also preferred tea. Only after the Boston Tea Party 1773 did Americans begin drinking coffee in large quantities. Now though the US is one of the top coffee-consuming countries consumption having been spurred on by familiar advertising claims Good till the last drop Rich hearty aroma Always rich never bitter.

Produced from the fruit of an evergreen tree coffee is grown primarily in Latin America southern Asia and Africa. Coffee trees require a hot climate high humidity rich soil with good drainage and partial shade consequently they thrive on the east or west slopes of tropical volcanic mountains where the soil is laced with potash and drains easily. The coffee beans actually seeds grow inside bright red berries. The berries are picked by hand and the beans are extracted by machine leaving a pulpy fruit residue that can be used for fertilizer. The beans are usually roasted in ovens a chemical process that releases the beans essential oil caffeol which gives coffee its distinctive aroma. Over a hundred different varieties of beans are produced in the world each with a different flavor attributable to three factors the species of plant *Coffea arabia* and *Coffea robusta* are the most common and the soil and climate where the variety was grown.

p

VI
Mechanics

26
Capitals

Experienced writers generally agree on when to use capitals, but the conventions are constantly changing. Consult a recent dictionary if you have any doubt about whether a particular word should be capitalized.

26a
Capitalize the first word of every sentence.

Every writer should own a good dictionary.
Will this rain ever stop?
Watch out!

When quoting other writers, you must reproduce the capital letters beginning their sentences or indicate that you have altered the source. Whenever possible, integrate the quotation into your own sentence so that its capitalization coincides with yours.

> "Psychotherapists often overlook the benefits of self-deception," the author argues.
>
> The author argues that "the benefits of self-deception" are not always recognized by psychotherapists.

If you need to alter the capitalization in the source, indicate the change with brackets (see 25d).

> "[T]he benefits of self-deception" are not always recognized by psychotherapists, the author argues.
>
> The author argues that "[p]sychotherapists often overlook the benefits of self-deception."

NOTE: Capitalization of questions in a series is optional. Both of the following examples are correct.

Is the ideal population for a city a hundred thousand? Half a million? Over a million?

Is the ideal population for a city a hundred thousand? half a million? over a million?

Also optional is capitalization of the first word in a complete sentence after a colon (see 25a).

26b

Capitalize words in the titles of works according to standard practice.

Capitalize all words in the title of a work *except* articles (*a, an, the*) and prepositions and conjunctions of fewer than five letters. Capitalize even these short words when they are the first or last word in a title or when they fall after a colon or semicolon.

The Sound and the Fury
"Courtship Through the Ages"
Merry England; Or, the History of a People
What Do I Live For?
"Once More to the Lake"
Management: A New Approach
"Once Is Not Enough"

NOTE: Always capitalize the prefix or first word in a hyphenated word within a title. Capitalize the second word only if it is a noun or an adjective or is as important as the first word.

"Applying Stage Make-up"
The Pre-Raphaelites
Through the Looking-Glass

26c

Always capitalize the pronoun *I* and the interjection *O*. Don't capitalize *oh* unless is begins a sentence.

I love to stay up at night, but, oh, I hate to get up in the morning.

He who thinks himself wise, O heavens, is a great fool.
– VOLTAIRE

26d

Capitalize proper nouns, proper adjectives, and words used as essential parts of proper nouns.

1

Capitalize proper nouns and proper adjectives.

Proper nouns name specific persons, places, and things: *Shakespeare, California, World War I*. **Proper adjectives** are formed from some proper nouns: *Shakespearean, Californian.* Capitalize all proper nouns and proper adjectives but not the articles (*a, an, the*) that precede them.

Specific persons and things

Stephen King	the Leaning Tower of Pisa
Napoleon Bonaparte	Boulder Dam
Jane Fonda	the Empire State Building

Specific places and geographical regions

New York City	the Mediterranean Sea
China	Lake Victoria
Europe	the Northeast
North America	the Rocky Mountains

Days of the week, months, holidays

Monday	Yom Kippur
May	Christmas
Thanksgiving	Columbus Day

Historical events, documents, periods, movements

World War II	the Middle Ages
the Vietnam War	the Age of Reason
the Boston Tea Party	the Renaissance
the Treaty of Ghent	the Great Depression
the Constitution	the Romantic Movement

Government offices or departments and institutions

House of Representatives	Warren County Hospital
Department of Defense	Northeast Regional High School
Appropriations Committee	Springfield Board of Education
Postal Service	
York Municipal Court	

cap 26d

Political, social, athletic, and other organizations and associations and their members

Democratic Party, Democrats	B'nai B'rith
Communist Party, Communist	Rotary Club, Rotarians
Sierra Club	Eastern Star
Girl Scouts of America, Scout	League of Women Voters
Young Men's Christian Association	Boston Celtics
	Chicago Symphony Orchestra

Races, nationalities, and their languages

Native American	Germans
Afro-American, Negro	Swahili
Caucasian	Italian

But: blacks, whites

RELIGIONS AND THEIR FOLLOWERS

Christianity, Christians	Judaism, Jews
Protestantism, Protestants	Orthodox Judaism, Reform Jew
Catholicism, Catholics	Islam, Moslems *or* Muslims
Hinduism, Hindu	

RELIGIOUS TERMS FOR SACRED PERSONS AND THINGS

God	Buddha
Allah	the Bible (*but* biblical)
Christ	the Koran

NOTE: Capitalization of pronouns referring to God is optional in most contexts, but it is often used in religious texts and should be used where necessary to avoid confusion.

AMBIGUOUS Our minister spoke of God as though *he* loved every member of our congregation.

REVISED Our minister spoke of God as though *He* loved every member of our congregation.

2
Capitalize common nouns used as essential parts of proper nouns.

Common nouns name general classes of persons, places, or things, and they generally are not capitalized. However, capitalize the common nouns *street, avenue, park, river, ocean, lake, company, college, county,* and *memorial* when they are part of proper nouns naming specific places or institutions.

Main Street	Lake Superior
Central Park	Ford Motor Company
Mississippi River	Madison College
Pacific Ocean	George Washington Memorial Park

cap **26d**

3
Capitalize trade names.

Trade names identify individual brands of certain products. When a trade name loses its association with a brand and comes to refer to a product in general, it is not capitalized. Refer to a dictionary for current usage when you are in doubt about a name.

Scotch tape	Xerox
Chevrolet	Bunsen burner

But: nylon, thermos

26e

Capitalize titles when they precede proper names but generally not when they follow proper names or are used alone.

Professor Otto Osborne	Otto Osborne, a professor of English
Doctor Jane Covington	Jane Covington, a medical doctor
Senator Robert Dole	Robert Dole, senator from Kansas
the Reverend Ann Cole	Ann Cole, the minister

Exception: Many writers capitalize a title denoting very high rank even when it follows a proper name or is used alone.

Ronald Reagan, the President of the United States
the Chief Justice of the United States

26f

Avoid unnecessary capitalization.

In general, modern writers capitalize fewer words than earlier writers did. Don't capitalize a word unless a rule says you must.

1

Don't capitalize common nouns used in place of proper nouns.

Unnecessary I am determined to take an Economics course before I graduate from College.

Revised I am determined to take an economics course before I graduate from college.

Revised I am determined to take Economics 101 before I graduate from Madison College.

cap
26f

2

Don't capitalize compass directions unless they refer to specific geographical areas.

The storm blew in from the northeast and then veered south along the coast. [Here *northeast* and *south* refer to general directions.]

Students from the South have trouble adjusting to the Northeast's bitter winters. [Here *South* and *Northeast* refer to specific regions.]

3

Don't capitalize the names of seasons or the names of academic years or terms.

spring	autumn	freshman year
fall	winter quarter	summer term

4
Don't capitalize the names of relationships unless they form part of or substitute for proper names.

my mother
John's brother
the father of my friend

BUT

I remember how Father scolded us.

Aunt Annie, Uncle Jake, and Uncle Irvin died within two months of each other.

EXERCISE

Capitalize words as necessary in the following sentences, or substitute small letters for unnecessary capitals. Consult a dictionary if you are in doubt. If the capitalization in a sentence is already correct, circle the number preceding the sentence.

Example:

The first book on my summer reading list is mark twain's *a connecticut yankee in king arthur's court.*

The first book on my summer reading list is Mark Twain's *A Connecticut Yankee in King Arthur's Court.*

1. The new State House is very imposing. it is made of reflective glass and steel.
2. My Grandmother told me stories about my Father and Uncle Bill.
3. Although Rashid is a moslem, he is very knowledgeable about the bible, especially the old testament.
4. Professor Kellogg recommended that *Sexist and non-sexist language* be a required text for all fall writing courses.
5. The photograph showed senator Ertel shaking hands with the Rabbi of the largest Synagogue in Florida.
6. The grand canyon is in arizona, not too far from phoenix.
7. Colson, the doctor, knew his medicine, but his manner made his patients nervous.
8. Our scavenger-hunt map directed us two blocks Southeast and two blocks Northeast to find an old sink.
9. The Suwannee river rises in the Okefenokee swamp and moves through Georgia and Florida to the gulf of Mexico.
10. The new Saunders theater is an acoustical triumph, but, Oh, it was expensive to build.

27
Italics

Type that slants upward to the right is known as *italic type.* We use italics to distinguish or emphasize certain words and phrases. In your handwritten or typed papers, underline to indicate material that would be italicized if set into type.

27a
Underline titles according to standard practice.

Underline the titles of books, long poems, plays, periodicals, pamphlets, published speeches, long musical works, movies, television and radio programs, and works of visual art. Enclose all other titles in quotation marks (see 24d).

Books

Catch-22
War and Peace
The Promise

Long poems

Beowulf
The Song of Roland
Paradise Lost

Plays

Equus
Hamlet
Summer and Smoke

Periodicals

Time
Philadelphia Inquirer
Yale Law Review

Pamphlets

The Truth About Alcoholism
On the Vindication of the Rights of Women

Published Speeches

Lincoln's *Gettysburg Address*
Pericles's *Funeral Oration*

Long musical works

Tchaikovsky's *Swan Lake*
Bach's *St. Matthew Passion*
The Beatles' *Revolver*

Movies

Gone with the Wind
Star Wars
Invasion of the Body Snatchers

TELEVISION AND RADIO PROGRAMS	**WORKS OF VISUAL ART**
60 Minutes	Michelangelo's *David*
The Shadow	the *Mona Lisa*

NOTE: Be careful to underline marks of punctuation only if they are part of the title: *Did you read* Catch-22? (not Catch-22?). In titles of newspapers underline the name of the city only when it is part of the title.

Manchester *Guardian*
New York Times

When giving the title of a periodical in your text, you do not need to capitalize or underline the article *the,* even if it is part of the title.

She has the *New York Times* delivered to her in Alaska.

Omit the article entirely in bibliographic references (see Chapter 35, p. 486).

EXCEPTIONS: Legal documents, the Bible, and their parts are generally not italicized.

NOT	They registered their *deed.*
BUT	They registered their deed.
NOT	We studied the *Book of Revelation* in the *Bible.*
BUT	We studied the Book of Revelation in the Bible.

27b
Underline the names of ships, aircraft, spacecraft, and trains.

ital
27c

Queen Elizabeth II	*Apollo XI*
Spirit of St. Louis	*Orient Express*

27c
Underline foreign words and phrases that are not part of the English language.

English tends to absorb foreign words and phrases that speakers and writers find useful. The French expression "bon voyage," for example, is now part of our language and need not be underlined. If a foreign word or phrase has not been absorbed into our language, it should be underlined. A dictionary will tell you whether or not the words you wish to use should be underlined.

The scientific name for the brown trout is *Salmo trutta.* [The scientific names for plants and animals are always underlined.]

What a life he led! He was a true *bon vivant.*

The Latin *De gustibus non est disputandum* translates roughly as "There's no accounting for taste."

27d

Underline words, letters, numbers, and phrases named as words.

Some people pronounce *th,* as in *thought,* with a faint *s* or *f* sound.

Carved into the middle of the column, twenty feet up, was a mysterious 7.

Try pronouncing *unique New York* ten times fast.

Italics may also be used instead of quotation marks in definitions (see 24e).

The word *syzygy* refers to a straight line formed by three celestial bodies, as in the alignment of earth, sun, and moon that produces an eclipse.

27e

Occasionally, underlining may be used for emphasis.

Compare these sentences:

ital
27e

I thought you had the key	I *thought* you had the key.
I thought you had the key.	I thought *you* had the key.

In the absence of clues from context, the first sentence doesn't tell us where the emphasis should lie. The three following sentences, however, tell us exactly what word to emphasize, and the different emphases create different meanings. In this way italics (or underlining) can stress an important word or phrase, especially in reporting how someone said something. But such emphasis should be used sparingly. Excessive underlining will make your writing sound immature or hysterical, as the following example illustrates.

The hunters had *no* food and *no* firewood. But they were *too* tired to do anything more than crawl into their *sopping* sleeping bags. Had it been ten degrees colder, *they might have frozen to death.*

If you find that you rely too much on underlining to achieve emphasis, consult Chapter 18 for other techniques to help you accent your writing.

EXERCISE

Underline (italicize) words and phrases as needed in the following sentences, or circle any words or phrases that are italicized unnecessarily.

Example:

Of Hitchcock's movies, Psycho is the scariest.
Of Hitchcock's movies, Psycho is the scariest.

1. The essay contains many puns and jeux de mots.
2. The author's stories have appeared in Redbook, Vogue, and Ms., among other magazines.
3. The director warned the writer that the screenplay for Opiela in Love had better be finished *tout de suite.*
4. The map was *so* out of date that it didn't even show the *town* Tammy lived in, let alone the *street* her *house* was on.
5. According to Publishers Weekly, Markosian's book is out of print.
6. San Francisco's major newspapers are the Chronicle and the Examiner.
7. Both the *Old Testament* and the *New Testament* of the *Bible* offer profound lessons in human nature.
8. No matter how many times I say it, the word euphemism comes out wrong.
9. Homo sapiens has evolved further than any other species.
10. Whether he's watching Masterpiece Theatre, Wide World of Sports, or the silliest situation comedy, Larry is happy in front of the television.

28
Abbreviations

Everyone uses certain standard abbreviations because they are convenient and readily understood. Nevertheless, only a few abbreviations are acceptable in general writing. For a list of abbreviations used in source citations, see Chapter 35, p. 492.

28a
Use standard abbreviations for titles immediately before and after proper names.

Before the name	**After the name**
Dr. James Hsu	James Hsu, M.D.
Mr., Mrs., Ms., Hon.,	D.D.S., D.V.M., Ph.D.,
St., Rev., Msgr., Gen.	Ed.D., O.S.B., S.J., Sr., Jr.

(Note that the title *Ms.* is followed by a period, even though it is not actually an abbreviation: *Ms. Judith Boyer.*)

Use abbreviations such as *Rev., Hon., Prof., Rep., Sen., Dr.,* and *St.* (for *Saint*) only if they appear with a proper name. Spell them out in the absence of a proper name.

Faulty By then my head hurt so badly that I was forced to call the *Dr.*

Revised By then my head hurt so badly that I was forced to call the *doctor.*

Revised By then my head hurt so badly that I was forced to call *Dr. Kaplan.*

The abbreviations for academic degrees—*Ph.D., M.A., B.A.,* and the like—may be used without a proper name.

> My brother took seven years to get his *Ph.D.* It will probably take me just as long to earn my *B.A.*

28b

Familiar abbreviations and acronyms for the names of organizations, corporations, people, and some countries are acceptable in most writing.

An **acronym** is an abbreviation that spells a pronounceable word. *Radar,* which we no longer capitalize, is an acronym for "*ra*dio *d*etecting *a*nd *r*anging." Other acronyms include WHO, UNESCO, and NATO. These abbreviations, written without periods, are acceptable in most writing as long as they are familiar. So are several familiar abbreviations of the names of organizations, corporations, people, and countries. When these abbreviate three or more words, they are usually written without periods.

Organizations	CIA, FBI, YMCA, AFL-CIO
Corporations	IBM, CBS, ITT
People	JFK, LBJ, FDR
Countries	U.S.A. (or USA), U.S.S.R. (or USSR)

(See 20b for more information on when to use periods in abbreviations.)

Note: If a name or term (such as *operating room*) appears often in a piece of writing, then its abbreviation (*O.R.*) can cut down on extra words. Spell out the full term at its first appearance, indicate its abbreviation in parentheses, and use the abbreviation from then on. However, if the term occurs only a few times in a paper, the abbreviation will serve no useful purpose and may even confuse readers. In that case spell out the term each time it occurs.

ab
28c

28c

Use *B.C., A.D., A.M., P.M., no.,* and *$* only with specific dates and numbers.

The abbreviation B.C. ("before Christ") always follows a date, whereas A.D. (*anno Domini,* Latin for "year of the Lord") precedes a date.

44 B.C.	8:05 P.M. (*or* p.m.)	no. 36 (*or* No. 36)
A.D. 1492	11:26 A.M. (*or* a.m.)	$7.41

Faulty	Hospital routine is easier to follow in the A.M. than in the P.M.
Revised	Hospital routine is easier to follow in the *morning* than in the *afternoon or evening.*

NOTE: The capitalized abbreviations above are often set in small capital letters in publications: B.C., A.D., A.M., P.M. In handwriting and typewriting, use B.C. and A.D. and either A.M./P.M. or a.m./p.m. The abbreviation for *number* may be either capitalized or not (No., no.).

28d

Generally, reserve common Latin abbreviations such as *i.e., e.g.,* and *etc.* for use in source citations and comments in parentheses.

i.e.	that is (*id est*)
c.f.	compare (*confer*)
e.g.	for example (*exempli gratia*)
et al.	and others (*et alii*)
etc.	and so forth (*et cetera*)
N.B.	note well (*nota bene*)

He said he would be gone a fortnight (i.e., two weeks).
Bloom et al., editors, *Anthology of Light Verse*
Trees, too, are susceptible to disease (e.g., Dutch elm disease).

(Note that these abbreviations are generally not italicized or underlined.) In formal writing use the appropriate English phrases instead of the Latin abbreviations.

FAULTY	The cabs of some modern farm machines—e.g., combines—look like airplane cockpits.
INFORMAL	The cabs of some modern farm machines (e.g., combines) look like airplane cockpits.
FORMAL	The cabs of some modern farm machines (for example, combines) look like airplane cockpits.
FORMAL	The cabs of some modern farm machines—for example, combines—look like airplane cockpits.

ab 28e

28e

Don't use *Inc., Bros., Co.,* or & (for *and*) except when it is part of the official name of a business firm.

FAULTY	*The Santini bros.* operate a large moving firm in New York City.
REVISED	*The Santini brothers* operate a large moving firm in New York City.
REVISED	*Santini Bros.* is a large moving firm in New York City.

Faulty	As a child I read every story about the Hardy Boys & Nancy Drew.
Revised	As a child I read every story about the Hardy Boys *and* Nancy Drew.

28f

In most writing don't abbreviate units of measurement; geographical names; names of days, months, and holidays; names of people; courses of instruction; and labels for divisions of written works.

Units of measurement

The dog is thirty *inches* (not *in.*) high.
Dig a hole six *feet* (not *ft.*) deep.

Exceptions: Long phrases such as *miles per hour* (m.p.h.) or *cycles per second* (c.p.s.) are conventionally abbreviated and may or may not be punctuated with periods: *The speed limit on that road was once 75 m.p.h.* (or *mph*).

Geographical names

The publisher is in *Massachusetts* (not *Mass.* or *MA*).
He came from Aukland, *New Zealand* (not *N.Z.*).
She lived on Morrissey *Boulevard* (not *Blvd.*).

Exceptions: The United States is often referred to as the U.S.A. (USA) or the U.S., and the Soviet Union as the U.S.S.R. (USSR). In writing of the U.S. capital, we use the abbreviation D.C. for District of Columbia when it follows the city's name: *Washington, D.C.*

Names of days, months, and holidays

The truce was signed on *Tuesday* (not *Tues.*), *January* (not *Jan.*) 16.
The *Christmas* (not *Xmas*) holidays were uneventful.

Names of people

James (not *Jas.*) Bennett ran for that seat.
Robert (not *Robt.*) Frost writes accessible poems.

Courses of instruction

I'm majoring in *political science* (not *poli. sci.*).
Economics (not *Econ.*) is a tough course.

Labels for divisions of written works

The story begins on *page* (not *p.*) 15.
Read *Chapter* (not *Ch.*) 6.
We finally finished *Volume* (not *Vol.*) 1 of our history text.

EXERCISE 1

Revise the following sentences as needed to correct faulty use of abbreviations. Circle the number preceding any sentence in which the abbreviations are already correct as written.

Example:

One prof. spent five class hrs. reading from the textbook.
One *professor* spent five class *hours* reading from the textbook.

1. The kite was flying at about a hundred ft. when the line snapped.
2. Old Louisville, a section of Louisville between Third and Fourth Sts., near Central Pk., has some beautiful Victorian houses.
3. Jet lag—i.e., disruption of sense of time, place, or well-being—often afflicts air travelers.
4. Upon his inauguration on Fri., Jan. 20, 1961, JFK became the first Roman Catholic President in American history.
5. The relationship between the U.S.A. and the U.S.S.R. is one of the most analyzed subjects of the century.
6. Mount Vesuvius erupted in *anno Domini* 79 and buried Pompeii.
7. Mr. and Mrs. Harold Marsh, Jr., donated a new wing for the library.
8. The Lynch bros., Wm. & Robt., went bankrupt in the same year.
9. They asked the rev. to marry them on horseback.
10. There, in the middle of Ch. 6, between pp. 128 & 129, was a leaf my mother had pressed as a child.

ab
28f

EXERCISE 2

Spell out all inappropriate abbreviations in the following paragraph. If an abbreviation is appropriate in its context, leave it as is.

The advantages of a grad. degree are not lost on me. With a Ph.D. I might become a college prof., a job that would allow me to work only in the P.M., so I wouldn't have to get up before 11:00 A.M., and only on Tues., Wed., and Thurs., my favorite days. Or I could get an M.D. and become a dr. Though I might have to work long hrs., I could earn plenty of $ and, by serving on a professional association like the AMA, could have a lot of influence. I know about these advantages because my two older bros. are Prof. Giordano and Dr. Giordano. I also know how hard they had to work for their degrees, so I think I'll stick with poli. sci. courses and look for a nice, safe govt. job after I get my B.A.

29
Numbers

Experienced writers vary in their choice between writing numbers out and using figures. In scientific and technical writing, all numbers are usually written as figures. In business writing, all numbers over ten are usually written as figures. In general writing, numbers are more often spelled out. The following rules give conventions for general writing.

29a
Use figures for numbers that require more than two words to spell out.

The leap year has *366* days.
The population of Minot, North Dakota, is about *32,500*.

Spell out numbers of one or two words. (See also 29b.)

That hotel can accommodate no more than *seventy-five* people.

The first writing we know of was done over *six thousand* years ago.

The collection included almost *twelve hundred* drawings and paintings.

A hyphenated number can be considered one word.

The ball game drew *forty-two thousand* people.

Exception: When you use several numbers together, they should be consistently spelled out or consistently expressed in figures.

Inconsistent Only *ninety-nine* students attended the first lecture, but the audience increased to *126* for the second lecture and *two hundred* for the third.

Revised	Only *99* students attended the first lecture, but the audience increased to *126* for the second lecture and *200* for the third.

29b

Use figures instead of words according to standard practice.

Even when a number requires one or two words to spell out, we conventionally use figures for days and years; pages, chapters, volumes, acts, scenes, and lines; decimals, percentages, and fractions; addresses; scores and statistics; exact amounts of money; and the time of day.

Days and years

June 18, 1985 A.D. 12 456 B.C.

Exception: The day of a month may be expressed in words when it is not followed by a year (*June fifth; October first*).

Pages, chapters, volumes, acts, scenes, lines

Chapter 9, page 123
Encyclopaedia Britannica, Volume 14
Hamlet, Act 5 (*or* V), Scene 3 (*or* iii), lines 35–40

Decimals, percentages, and fractions

22.5
48% (or 48 percent)
3½

Addresses

355 Clinton Avenue
419 Stonewall Street
Washington, D.C. 20036

Scores and statistics

21 to 7
a mean of 26
a ratio of 8 to 1

Exact amounts of money

$4.50
$3.5 million (*or* $3,500,000)
$2,763 (*or* $2763)

The time of day

9:00
3:45
2:30

Exceptions: Round dollar or cent amounts of only a few words may be expressed in words: *seventeen dollars; fifteen hundred dollars; sixty cents.* When the word *o'clock* is used for the time of day, also express the number in words: *two o'clock* (not *2 o'clock*).

num
29c

29c

Always spell out numbers that begin sentences.

We are so accustomed to seeing a capital letter at the beginning of a sentence that a number there can make reading difficult.

Therefore, always spell out any number that begins a sentence. If the number requires more than two words, avoid further awkwardness by rewording the sentence so the number falls later and can be expressed as a figure.

AWKWARD *103* of the opening-night audience asked for a refund.

AWKWARD *One hundred and three* of the opening-night audience asked for a refund.

REVISED Of the opening-night audience, *103* asked for a refund.

EXERCISE

Revise the following sentences to correct the use of numbers. Circle the number preceding any sentence in which numbers are already used appropriately.

Example:

Carol paid one hundred and forty-five dollars for a bridesmaid's dress she would never wear again.

Carol paid $145 for a bridesmaid's dress she would never wear again.

1. 1036 Colgate University students played Twister for three and one-half hours on May fifth, 1984, in the largest game on record.
2. I lost a trivia game because I forgot that sixteen hundred Pennsylvania Avenue is the White House.
3. Only 27 percent of the 350 consumers we polled preferred the new product to the old one.
4. The largest carousel in the United States is 100 feet tall and cost over a million and three-quarters dollars to build.
5. Covering four hundred and two acres, Ankor Wat in Cambodia is the largest religious building ever constructed.
6. A liter is equal to almost one and six-hundredths quarts.
7. Not until page ninety-nine, in the middle of Chapter five, does the author introduce the main character.
8. I was born on May fifteenth, six days after my dog.
9. Peter Minuit bought Manhattan Island from the Indians for twenty-four dollars.
10. Dominating the town's skyline was a sign that stood thirty feet off the ground and measured 112 feet by thirty-seven feet.

30
Word Division

As much as possible, avoid dividing words. If you must divide a word between the end of one line and the beginning of the next, do so only between syllables. Put a hyphen at the end of the first line, never at the beginning of the second. Never divide the last word on a page, because in the act of turning the page the reader may forget the beginning of the word. If you are in doubt about how to break any word into syllables, consult a dictionary. Note, however, that not all syllable breaks are appropriate for word division. Use the following rules to decide when and how to divide words.

30a
Don't make a division that leaves a single letter at the end of a line or fewer than three letters at the beginning of a line.

FAULTY	A newspaper or television editorial for or *a-gainst* a candidate can sway an election.
REVISED	A newspaper or television editorial for or *against* a candidate can sway an election.
FAULTY	Counseling is required for every child *abus-er.*
REVISED	Counseling is required for every child *abuser.*

30b
Don't divide one-syllable words.

Since one-syllable words have no break in pronunciation, they should not be divided.

FAULTY	The shiny, spinning space capsule *drop-ped* suddenly from the clouds.
REVISED	The shiny, spinning space capsule *dropped* suddenly from the clouds.

30c

Divide compound words only between the words that form them or at fixed hyphens.

Compound words are made up of two or more words (*draw-back, homecoming*). Their component words may be separated by a hyphen (*well-paying, cross-reference*), in which case the hyphen is called **fixed.** Compound words should be divided only between their component words and at fixed hyphens.

FAULTY	If you want to have friends, be *good-na-tured.*
REVISED	If you want to have friends, be *good-natured.*
FAULTY	Sherlock Holmes exemplifies the *mas-termind.*
REVISED	Sherlock Holmes exemplifies the *master-mind.*

(See 34d for guidelines on when to use hyphens in spelling compound words.)

div **30d**

30d

Avoid confusing word divisions.

Some word divisions may momentarily confuse the reader because the first or second part by itself forms a pronounceable (or unpronounceable) unit that does not fit with the whole. For example: *poi-gnant, read-dress, in-dict.* Avoid word divisions like these.

CONFUSING	Her walking out of class was an act of *her-oism.*
CLEAR	Her walking out of class was an act of *hero-ism.*
CONFUSING	He claims that stealing never bothered his *con-science.*
CLEAR	He claims that stealing never bothered his *conscience.*

EXERCISE

Revise the following sentences to repair any incorrect word divisions. Consult a dictionary if necessary. Circle the number preceding any sentence in which word division is already correct.

Example:

I thought Harry's joke was sidesplit-
ting, but no one else even smiled.

I thought Harry's joke was *side-*
splitting, but no one else even smiled.

1. After my cousin graduated, she joined the army as an officer.
2. A travel agent booked a seat for me on a char-
ter flight.
3. The tarantella is a vivacious folk dance of southern Italy.
4. He took bad advice from several well-mean-
ing friends.
5. The product inspector detects any surfaces that are not smoothly sanded.
6. Last year I completely forgot to call my father on Father's Day.
7. Each of the twenty-three apartments he looked at was rented before he could make a deposit on it.
8. Americans find any number of ways to keep from feeling mid-
dle-aged.
9. While the photographers snapped pictures, Dan blush-
ed with embarrassment.
10. After the lecture Dotty felt she knew e-
nough about the subject to pass the test.

VII
Effective Words

31
Controlling Diction

Diction is the choice and use of words. Controlling your diction is essential because the substance and effect of what you say will depend finally on the words you choose. You should select words that fit your purpose and express your meaning accurately, and you should prune those that fail to make your writing more exact or forceful. The following sections offer some guidelines for choosing words. No firm rules dictate the proper words for every situation, however; in many instances you must rely on your own judgment to choose words that suit your subject, your purpose, and your audience. The most useful advice, perhaps, is to suspect the first word that comes to mind and to be willing to search for another word with a shade of meaning closer to your intention.

31a
Choosing the appropriate word

Words are appropriate when they suit your subject and the purpose of your writing, the role you are assuming, the attitude you want to project, and the readers you are writing for. We all use various kinds of language—various sets of words—depending on the context in which we are speaking or writing. Talking to friends, for example, you might say, *My sister decided to bag therapy because her shrink seemed even more strung out than she was.* Writing for a general audience, however, you would convey the same information quite differently, perhaps writing, *My sister decided to abandon therapy because her psychiatrist seemed even more disturbed than she was.* In each case the diction fits the occasion: when you talk to people you know well and share experiences with, you can relax into informal or slang expressions such as *bag, shrink,* and *strung out;* when you write for a general audience, you must be more formal, using more widely understood words such as *abandon, psychiatrist,* and *disturbed.*

Most of your writing in college and after will be analyzing, explaining, and sometimes defending your understanding and interpretation of facts, events, and ideas. The words appropriate to such writing, like the conventions of grammar and usage described earlier in this handbook, are those which educated readers and writers normally expect. The huge vocabulary in what is called standard or educated English excludes words that only limited groups of people use and understand: slang, colloquial language, regional words and expressions, nonstandard language, obsolete words, technical terms, euphemisms, and pretentious words. These more limited vocabularies, discussed below, should be avoided altogether or used cautiously and in special contexts—for example, when aiming for a special effect with an audience you know will appreciate it. Whenever you doubt a word's status, consult a dictionary (see 32b-2).

1
Avoiding slang

All groups of people—from musicians and computer scientists to vegetarians and golfers—create **slang,** novel and colorful expressions that reflect the group's special experiences and set it off from others. Slang displays endless inventiveness. Some of it gives new meanings to old words. For example, several decades ago the word *cool* gained a meaning of "pleasing, excellent" (*The movie was cool*), and during the 1970s *into* came to describe personal commitment (*I'm really into plants*). More recently, the word *hacker* has been applied to computer buffs (*Enthusiastic hackers have produced innovative computer games*). Some slang comes from other languages: our word *chow* ("food" or "a meal") comes from the Chinese *chao,* meaning "to stir or fry"; and *schlep* ("to lug" or "a clumsy person") comes from the Yiddish *schleppen,* "to drag." Sometimes the slang of a particular ethnic group is widely adopted by the rest of the population. *Out to lunch, put on ice,* and *funky,* for example, are contributions of black slang.

Among those who understand it, slang may be vivid and forceful. It often occurs in dialog, and an occasional slang expression can enliven an informal essay. Some slang, such as *dropout* (*She was a high school dropout*), has proved so useful that it has passed into the general vocabulary.

However, most slang is too flippant and imprecise for effective communication, and it is generally inappropriate for college or business writing. The writer who says that *many students start out pretty straight but then get weird* deprives her writing of seriousness while failing to specify what happens to the students. Avoiding imprecise slang and including specific, informative language would strengthen the sentence.

2 Using colloquial language with care

Colloquial language designates the words and expressions appropriate to everyday spoken language. Regardless of our backgrounds and how we live, we all try to *get along with* each other. We sometimes *get together with* our neighbors. We play with *kids, go crazy* about one thing, *crab* about something else, and in our worst moments try to *get back at* someone who has made us do the *dirty work.* These italicized words and expressions are not "wrong"; quite the contrary, more formal language might sound stilted and pompous in casual conversation and in some kinds of writing.

When you write informally, colloquial language may be appropriate to achieve the casual, relaxed effect of conversation. An occasional colloquial word dropped into otherwise more formal writing can also help you achieve a desired emphasis. And some formerly colloquial words (*rambunctious, trigger* as a verb) have gained acceptance in standard English. But colloquial language does not provide the exactness needed in more formal college, business, and professional writing. In such writing you should generally avoid any words and expressions labeled "informal" or "colloquial" in your dictionary. Take special care to avoid **mixed diction,** a combination of standard and colloquial words.

MIXED DICTION	According to a Native American myth, the Great Creator *had a dog hanging around with him* when he created the earth.
CONSISTENT	According to a Native American myth, the Great Creator *was accompanied by a dog* when he created the earth.

appr
31a

3 Avoiding regional words and expressions

Most national languages vary slightly from one geographical area to another. In American English, regional differences are most marked in pronunciation: a Texan overhearing a conversation between a New Yorker and a Georgian will not mistake either for a fellow Texan. But regional vocabularies differ somewhat, too. Southerners may say they *reckon,* meaning "think" or "suppose." People in Maine invite their Boston friends to come *down* rather than *up* (north) to visit. In the Northeast, people *catch a cold* and *get sick,* but in some other parts of the country they *take a cold* and *take sick.* Regional expressions are appropriate in writing addressed to local readers and may lend realism to regional description, but they should be avoided in writing intended for a general audience.

REGIONAL	The house where I spent my childhood was *down the road a piece* from a federal prison.
GENERAL	The house where I spent my childhood was *a short distance* from a federal prison.

4 Avoiding nonstandard language

Words and grammatical forms called **nonstandard,** though spoken by many intelligent people, are never acceptable in standard written English. Examples include *nowheres;* such pronoun forms as *hisn, hern, hisself,* and *theirselves; them* as an adjective, as in *them dishes, them courses;* the expressions *this here* and *that there,* as in *that there elevator;* verb forms such as *knowed, throwed, hadn't ought,* and *could of;* and double negatives such as *didn't never* and *haven't no.* Dictionaries label such expressions "nonstandard," "illiterate," or "substandard." Avoid all nonstandard expressions in speech and especially in writing.

5 Avoiding obsolete or archaic words and neologisms

Since our surroundings and our lives are constantly changing, some words pass out of use and others appear to fill new needs. **Obsolete** and **archaic** are dictionary labels for words or meanings of words that we never or rarely use but that appear in older documents and literature still read today. Obsolete words or meanings are no longer used at all—for example, *enwheel* ("to encircle") and *cote* ("to pass"). Archaic words or meanings occur now only in special contexts such as poetry—for example, *fast* ("near," as in *fast by the road*) and *belike* ("perhaps").

Neologisms are words created (or coined) so recently that they have not come into established use. Some neologisms do become accepted as part of our general vocabulary. *Motel,* coined from *motor* and *hotel,* and *brunch,* meaning a combination of breakfast and lunch, are examples. But most neologisms pass quickly from the language. In the late 1970s newsmagazines coined the words *equalimony* and *palimony* to refer to changing attitudes and court interpretations of alimony rights, but these words did not gain much wider use. Unless such words serve a special purpose in your writing and are sure to be understood and appreciated by your readers, you should avoid them.

6
Using technical words with care

All disciplines and professions rely on special words or give common words special meanings. Chemists speak of *esters* and *phosphatides,* geographers and mapmakers refer to *isobars* and *isotherms,* and literary critics write about *motifs* and *subtexts.* Printers use common words like *cut, foul,* and *slug* in special senses. Such technical language allows specialists to communicate precisely and economically with other specialists who share their vocabulary. But without explanation these words are meaningless to the nonspecialist. When you are writing for a general audience, avoid unnecessary technical terms. If your subject requires words the reader may not understand, be careful to define them. (See also 31c-4 for a discussion of jargon and overly technical and inflated language.)

7
Avoiding euphemisms and pretentious writing

A **euphemism** is a presumably inoffensive word that a writer or speaker substitutes for a word deemed potentially offensive or too blunt. We speak euphemistically when we say that someone *passed on* rather than *died.* Government officials use euphemism when they describe an effort to cut waste in military spending as an *acquisitions-improvement program* or when they call nuclear war *nuclear engagement.* Because euphemisms conceal meaning instead of clarifying it, use them only when you know that blunt, truthful words would needlessly offend members of your audience.

People who write euphemistically also tend to decorate their prose with ornate phrases. Any writing that is more elaborate than its subject requires will sound pretentious or excessively showy. Good writers choose their words for their exactness and economy. Pretentious writers choose them in the belief that fancy words will impress readers. They rarely will.

appr
31a

Pretentious	Many institutions of higher education recognize the need for youth at the threshold of maturity to confront the choice of life's endeavor and thus require students to select a field of concentration.
Revised	Many colleges and universities force students to make decisions about their careers by requiring them to select a major.

When either of two words will say what you mean, prefer the small word to the big one, the common word to the uncommon one. If you want to say *It has begun to rain,* say so. Don't say *I perceive that moisture has commenced to precipitate earthward.*

EXERCISE 1

Insert words appropriate for standard written English in the following sentences to replace slang, colloquialisms, regionalisms, nonstandard expressions, obsolete or archaic words, neologisms, technical words, euphemisms, or pretentious expressions. Consult a dictionary as needed to determine a word's appropriateness and to find suitable substitutes.

Example:

If negotiators get hyper during contract discussions, they may mess up chances for a settlement.

If negotiators *become excited or upset* during contract discussions, they may *harm* chances for a settlement.

1. The food shortages in some parts of Africa are so severe that tens of thousands of people have met their demise.
2. A few stockholders have been down on the company ever since it refused to stop conducting business in South Africa.
3. The most stubborn members of the administration still will not hearken to our pleas for a voice in college doings.
4. They bought a beaut of a Victorian house in a ritzy neighborhood.
5. I almost failed Western Civ because the creep who borrowed my notes lost them.
6. During your first three months on the job, stifle your gripes and showcase your abilities for your boss.
7. Her arm often aches, but she says it doesn't bother her none.
8. Because he understands the finest intricacies of democratic management and can thus covertly persuade the most recalcitrant legislator to do his every bidding, we should return the governor to his position as chief executive of our fair state.
9. Too many Little League coaches know lots about baseball but not an awful lot about kids.
10. After every concert the cops hang around the parking lot until all the kids have taken off.

31b
Choosing the exact word

Good writers labor to find the words within the large vocabulary of standard English that fit their meaning exactly, with precisely the overtones they intend. Inexact words—wrong, vague, unspecific, or trite—weaken writing and often confuse readers.

1
Using the right word for your meaning

The precise expression of meaning requires understanding both the denotations and connotations of words. A word's **denota-**

tion is the thing or idea it refers to, the meaning listed in the dictionary without reference to the emotional associations it may arouse in a reader. Using words according to their established denotations is essential if readers are to grasp your meaning. The person who writes *My dog is inflicted with fleas* or *Older people must often endure infirmaries* has mistaken *inflicted* for *afflicted* and *infirmaries* for *infirmities.* In using the wrong word, the writer says something different from what he or she intended, thus either amusing or confusing the reader. The writer who says *The divergence between the estimate and the actual cost is surprising* has also missed the mark, though not as widely. The word needed is *discrepancy,* not *divergence.* The two words are second cousins, but they are not interchangeable. Some mistakes in diction occur because of confusion of **homonyms,** words such as *principle/principal* or *rain/reign/rein* that sound alike but have different spellings and meanings. (See 34a-1 for a list of commonly confused homonyms.) Whenever you are unsure of a word's exact meaning, consult your dictionary.

Writers miss the right word more often by misjudging its connotation than by mistaking its denotation. **Connotation** refers to the associations a word carries with it. Some connotations are personal, deriving from one's particular experiences. A person whose only experience with dogs was being bitten three times will have a different reaction to the word *dog* than will someone who lives with the warm memories of a childhood pet. Such personal associations aside, however, most people agree about the favorable or unfavorable connotations of words. To most readers, the connotations of *love, home,* and *peace* are favorable, whereas those of *lust, shack,* and *war* are unfavorable. Most of us prefer to hear our tastes described as *inexpensive* rather than *cheap.*

Understanding connotation is especially important in choosing among **synonyms,** words with approximately, but often not exactly, the same meanings. *Cry* and *weep* are similar, both denoting the shedding of tears; but *cry* more than *weep* connotes a sobbing sound accompanying the tears. *Sob* itself connotes broken, gasping crying, with tears, whereas *wail* connotes sustained sound, rising and falling in pitch, perhaps without tears. Used in the blank in the sentence *We were disturbed by his ______ing,* each of these words would evoke different sounds and images. Tracking down the word whose connotation is exactly what you want can take time and effort. The most convenient resource is a dictionary, particularly the discussions of synonyms and their shades of meaning at the ends of many entries (see 32b-2 and 33c-2 for samples). Other useful resources are a thesaurus, which lists groups of synonyms, and a dictionary of synonyms, which both lists and defines them. (See 32a-3 for specific titles.)

EXERCISE 2

Revise the following sentences to replace any italicized word that is not used according to its established denotation. If the italicized word in a sentence is used correctly, circle the number preceding the sentence. Consult a dictionary if you are uncertain of a word's precise meaning.

Example:

Sam and Dave are going to Bermuda and Hauppauge, *respectfully,* for spring vacation.

Sam and Dave are going to Bermuda and Hauppauge, *respectively,* for spring vacation.

1. The *enormity* of the beached whale—and its horrible stench—both amazed and repelled us.
2. Burning solid waste is not an *economic* way to generate power, but it eliminates the need for new dumping grounds.
3. The jury did not find the defendant's testimony *credible* and so convicted her.
4. Hospital personnel must wear protective clothing when tending a patient with a highly *communicative* disease.
5. I did not attend the lecture on artificial intelligence because I am *disinterested* in computers.
6. We've been without furniture for days, but now the movers are due to arrive *momentously.*
7. To support her argument she *sited* Mead's conclusion that schooling must challenge conventional views of the world.
8. After trying *continually* for two weeks to see my teacher, I finally complained to the dean.
9. One *affect* of the report is that doctors are less willing to order expensive tests for their patients.
10. Having been *deferred* from acting on impulse, she felt paralyzed by indecision.

EXERCISE 3

Describe how the connotation of each italicized word in the following sentences contributes to the writer's meaning. Give at least one synonym or related word that the writer could have used instead of the italicized word, and describe how the new word would alter the meaning. Consult a dictionary or thesaurus as necessary.

1. [The river] *slumbers* between broad prairies, *kissing* the long meadow grass, and *bathes* the overhanging boughs of elder bushes and willows or the roots of elms and ash trees and clumps of maples. – NATHANIEL HAWTHORNE
2. The new earth, freshly *torn* from its parent sun, was a ball of *whirling* gases, *intensely* hot, *rushing* through the black spaces

of the universe on a path and a speed controlled by *immense* forces. – RACHEL CARSON

3. When the country loved it with a passion, baseball was boyhood eternal, all *bluster,* innocence, and *bravado flashing* across green *meadows* in the sunlight. – RUSSELL BAKER
4. I think all theories are suspect, that the finest principles may have to be *modified,* or may even be *pulverized* by the demands of life, and that one must find, therefore, one's own moral *center* and move through the world hoping that this center will guide one aright. – JAMES BALDWIN
5. After a long straight *swoop* across the pancakeflat prairies, hour after hour of harvested land *streaked* with yellow *wheat-stubble* to the horizon, it's exciting to see hills ahead, *dark* hills under clouds against the west. – JOHN DOS PASSOS

2
Balancing the abstract and concrete, the general and specific

To understand a subject as you understand it, to experience it as you experience it, your readers need ample guidance from your words. When you describe a building as beautiful and nothing more, you force readers to provide their own conceptions of the features that make a building beautiful. If readers trouble to do the work you have assigned them—and they may not—they will call up diverse images of the many beautiful buildings they have seen, not a coherent image of the one you have seen. In evading your responsibility to be exact, you will have failed to communicate your meaning. Effective writing demands that abstract and general words like *beautiful* and *building,* which convey the broad outlines of ideas and objects, be balanced by concrete and specific words that make the ideas and objects sharp and firm. For instance, you might describe a *Victorian brick courthouse faced with stately arched windows and trimmed with ornate sandstone carvings.*

exact **31b**

Abstract words name qualities and ideas: *beauty, inflation, depression, labor, management, truth, culture, network, liberal, conservative.* **Concrete words** name things we can know by our senses: *brick, sandstone, arched, bacon, apple, sticky, crisp, hard.*

General words name classes or groups of things, such as *buildings, weather, birds,* or *professional people,* and include all the varieties of the class. **Specific words** limit a general class like *buildings* by naming one of its varieties, such as *Victorian courthouse, office tower,* or *hut. Professional people* include *doctors, scientists, teachers,* or *public accountants. Weather* includes *sunshine, drought, rain, windstorm,* and *cyclone. Birds* include *sparrows, eagles, geese, parrots, bobolinks,* and *vultures.* But *general* and *specific* are relative terms. *Doctor* becomes a general word in relation to *radiologist* and *surgeon,* and *surgeon* is general in relation to *neurosurgeon* and *orthopedic surgeon. Rain* is the general class for *drizzle, sprinkle,* and *downpour,* and *downpours* can be *continuous* or *sudden.* You become more and more specific as you move from a general class to a unique item, from *bird* to *pet bird* to *parrot* to *my parrot Moyshe.*

Abstract and general words are useful in the broad statements that set the course for your writing and tell readers what to expect.

> The wild horse in America has a *romantic* history.
>
> We must be *free* from *government interference* in our *affairs.*
>
> *Relations* between the sexes today are only a *little* more *relaxed* than they were in the past.

But statements like these, which rely heavily on abstract and general words, must be developed and supported by concrete and specific detail. Writing seldom fails because it lacks abstraction and generality. It often fails because it lacks concrete and specific words to nail down meaning and make the writing vivid, real, and clear. In your own writing choose the concrete and specific word over the general and abstract. When your meaning does call for an abstract or general word, make sure you define it, explain it, and narrow it with the concrete and specific words that most precisely reflect your knowledge and experience. Look at how concrete and specific information turns vague sentences into exact ones in the examples below.

Vague	The size of his hands made his smallness real. [How big were his hands? How small was he?]
Exact	Not until I saw his white, doll-like hands did I realize that he stood at least a full head shorter than most other men.
Vague	The long flood caused a lot of awful destruction in the town. [How long did the flood last? What destruction did it cause, and why was the destruction awful?]
Exact	The flood waters, which rose swiftly and then stayed stubbornly high for days, killed at least six townspeople and made life a misery for the hundreds who had to evacuate their ruined homes and stores.

EXERCISE 4

Make the following paragraph vivid by expanding the sentences with appropriate details of your own choosing. Concentrate especially on substituting concrete and specific words for the abstract and general ones in italics.

I remember *clearly* how *awful* I felt the first time I *attended* Mrs. Murphy's second grade class. I had *recently* moved from a *small* town in Missouri to a *crowded* suburb of Chicago. My new school looked *big* from the outside and seemed *dark* inside as I *walked* down the *long* corridor toward the classroom. The class was *noisy* as I neared the door; but when I *entered, everyone* became *quiet* and *looked* at me. I felt *uncomfortable* and *wanted* a place to hide. However, in a *loud* voice Mrs. Murphy *directed* me to the front of the room to introduce myself.

EXERCISE 5

For each abstract or general word below, give at least two other words or phrases that illustrate increasing specificity or concreteness. Consult a dictionary as needed. Use the most specific or concrete word from each group in a sentence of your own.

Example:

tired, *sleepy, droopy-eyed*

We stopped for the night when I became so *droopy-eyed* that the road blurred.

1. fabric
2. delicious
3. car
4. narrow-minded
5. reach (*verb*)
6. green
7. walk (*verb*)
8. flower
9. serious
10. pretty
11. teacher
12. nice
13. virtue
14. angry
15. crime
16. smile (*verb*)
17. sick
18. desire (*verb*)
19. candy
20. misfortune

3 Using idioms

Idioms are expressions in any language whose meanings cannot be determined simply from the words in them or whose component words cannot be predicted by any rule of grammar; often, they violate conventional grammar. Examples of English idioms include *put up with, plug away at,* and *make off with.* Because they are not governed by rules, idioms usually cause particular difficulty for people learning to speak and write a new language. For instance, those learning English as a second language find it easy to confuse certain prepositions such as *at/in/on* and *of/for.* But English prepositions can cause problems for native speakers of English, too, especially when a preposition is combined with an adjective or a verb. Some typical idioms with prepositions are listed below for reference. Check a dictionary if you are unsure of what preposition to use with an idiom (see 32b-2).

accords *with*
according *to*
accuse *of* a crime
agree *with* a person
agree *to* a proposal
agree *on* a plan

angry *with*

capable *of*

charge *for* a purchase
charge *with* a crime

compare *to* something in a different class
compare *with* something in the same class

concur *with* a person
concur *in* an opinion

contend *with* a person
contend *for* a principle

differ *with* a person
differ *from* in appearance
differ *about* or *over* a question

independent *of*

impatient *at* her conduct
impatient *of* restraint

impatient *for* a raise
impatient *with* a person

inferior *to*

infer *from*

occupied *by* a person
occupied *in* study
occupied *with* a thing

part *from* a person
part *with* a possession

prior *to*

rewarded *by* the judge
rewarded *for* something done
rewarded *with* a gift

superior *to*

wait *at* a place
wait *for* a train, a person
wait *on* a customer

EXERCISE 6

Insert the preposition that correctly completes each idiom in the following sentences. Consult the preceding list or a dictionary as needed.

Example:

I disagree _______ many feminists who say women should not be homemakers.

I disagree *with* many feminists who say women should not be homemakers.

1. He had waited for years, growing impatient _______ her demands and _______ the money that she would leave to him.
2. The writer compared gorilla society _______ human society.
3. They agreed _______ most things, but they differed consistently _______ how to raise their child.
4. I was rewarded _______ my persistence _______ an opportunity to meet the senator.
5. He would sooner part _______ his friends than part _______ his Corvette.

exact
31b

4
Using figurative language

Figurative language expresses or implies comparisons between different ideas or objects. The sentence *As I try to write, I can think of nothing to say* is literal. The sentence *As I try to write, my* *mind is a blank slab of black asphalt* is figurative. The abstract concept of having nothing to say has become concrete, something the reader can visualize. The blank slab of black asphalt is bare, hard, and unyielding, just as the frustrated writer's mind seems bare, resisting all attempts at writing.

Figurative language is commonplace. We sprinkle our conversation with figures: having *slept like a log,* we get up to find it *raining cats and dogs* but have to *pluck up our courage* and *battle the storm.* The sports pages abound in figurative language: the Yankees *shell* the Royals, the Cowboys *embark* on another season, and basketball players make *barrels* of money. Slang, too, is largely figurative: you may think chemistry *rots,* but you can *get into* physics.

The rapid exchange of speech leaves little time for inventiveness, and most figures of daily conversation, like hastily written news stories, are worn and hackneyed. But writing gives you time to reject the tired figure and to search out the fresh words and phrases that will carry meaning concretely and vividly.

The two most common figures of speech are the **simile** and the **metaphor.** Both compare two things of different classes, often one abstract and the other concrete. A simile makes the comparison explicit and usually begins with *like* or *as.*

> We force their [children's] growth as if they were chicks in a poultry factory. — ARNOLD TOYNBEE

> To hold America in one's thoughts is like holding a love letter in one's hand—it has so special a meaning. — E. B. WHITE

Instead of stating a comparison, the metaphor implies it, omitting such words as *like* or *as.*

> I refuse to accept the notion that nation after nation must spiral down a militaristic stairway into the hell of nuclear war. — MARTIN LUTHER KING, JR.

> A school is a hopper into which children are heaved while they are young and tender; therein they are pressed into certain standard shapes and covered from head to heels with official rubber stamps. — H. L. MENCKEN

exact 31b

Two other figures of speech, **personification** and **hyperbole,** are less common than metaphor and simile. Personification treats ideas and objects as if they were human.

> The economy consumes my money and gives me little in return.

> I could hear the whisper of snowflakes, nudging each other as they fell.

Hyperbole deliberately exaggerates.

> She appeared in a mile of billowing chiffon, flashing a rhinestone as big as an ostrich egg.

I'm going to cut him up in small cubes and fry him in deep fat.

To be successful, figurative language must be fresh and unstrained, calling attention not to itself but to the writer's meaning. If readers reject your language as trite or overblown, they may reject your message. One kind of figurative language gone wrong is the **mixed metaphor,** in which the writer combines two or more incompatible figures.

MIXED He often hatched new ideas, using them to unlock the doors of opportunity.

Since metaphors often generate visual images in the mind of the reader, a mixed metaphor can create a ludicrous scene.

MIXED Various thorny problems that one would prefer to sweep under the rug continue to bob up all the same.

To revise a mixed metaphor, follow through consistently with just one image.

IMPROVED Various thorny problems that one would prefer to weed out continue to sprout up all the same.

EXERCISE 7

Identify each figure of speech in the following sentences as a simile or a metaphor and analyze how it contributes to the writer's meaning.

1. All artists quiver under the lash of adverse criticism.
   – CATHERINE DRINKER BOWEN
2. Louisa spends the entire day in blue, limpid boredom. The caressing sting of it appears to be, for her, like the pleasure of lemon, or the coldness of salt water.
   – ELIZABETH HARDWICK
3. Every writer, in a roomful of writers, wants to be the best, and the judge, or umpire, or referee is soon overwhelmed and shouted down like a chickadee trying to take charge of a caucus of crows. – JAMES THURBER
4. And meanwhile, like enormous, irresistible, gleaming and spinning toys, there are the missiles and their warheads, each one more destructive than one thousand Hiroshima bombs, loaded with magnificent navigational equipment more fun to play with than anything else on earth or in space.
   – LEWIS THOMAS
5. At best today it [the railroad in America] resembles a fabled ruin, a vast fallen empire. More commonly it suggests a stodgy and even dirtier-looking subway; a sprawling anachronism

> that conveys not ruin but mess, not age but senility, not something speeding across continents but stalled between stations.
> – LOUIS KRONENBERGER

EXERCISE 8

Invent appropriate figurative language of your own (simile, metaphor, hyperbole, or personification) to describe each scene or quality below, and use the figure effectively in a sentence.

Example:

the attraction of a lake on a hot day
The small waves *like fingers beckoned* us irresistibly.

1. the sound of a kindergarten classroom
2. people waiting in line to buy tickets to a rock concert
3. the politeness of strangers meeting for the first time
4. a streetlight seen through dense fog
5. the effect of watching television for ten hours straight

5
Avoiding trite expressions

Trite expressions, or **clichés,** are phrases so old and so often repeated that they become stale. They include worn figures of speech, such as *heavy as lead, thin as a rail, wise as an owl;* stale scraps from literature, such as *to be or not to be, trip the light fantastic, gone with the wind;* adjectives and nouns that have become inseparable, such as *acid test, crushing blow, ripe old age;* and simply overused phrases, such as *point with pride, easier said than done, better late than never.* Many of these expressions were probably once fresh and forceful, but constant use has dulled them. They can slide almost automatically into your writing unless you are alert to them. If you let a few slip through, they will weaken your writing by suggesting that you have not thought about what you are saying and have used the easiest expression.

The following list contains just a few of the dozens of trite expressions.

add insult to injury
beyond the shadow of a doubt
brought back to reality
cool, calm, and collected
dyed in the wool
face the music
gentle as a lamb
hard as a rock
hit the nail on the head
hour of need
ladder of success
moving experience
needle in a haystack
sadder but wiser
sneaking suspicion
sober as a judge
stand in awe
strong as an ox
tired but happy
tried and true

You can avoid such expressions by substituting fresh words of your own or by restating the idea in plain language.

Trite	A *motley crowd* of the singer's *ardent admirers* awaited her arrival in *breathless silence.*
Revised	*Dressed in wild, colorful costumes,* a crowd of the singer's *fans* awaited her arrival in *eager silence.*

EXERCISE 9

Revise the following sentences to eliminate trite expressions.

Example:

The basketball team had almost seized victory, but it faced the test of truth in the last quarter of the game.

The basketball team *seemed about to win,* but the *real test* came in the last quarter of the game.

1. These disastrous consequences of the war have shaken the small nation to its roots.
2. Some say that liberal arts majors face an uphill climb getting jobs in business; others observe that corporations have been looking high and low for liberal arts students.
3. When my father retired from the gas company after thirty long years, he was honored to receive a large clock in recognition of his valued service.
4. Sam shouldered his way through the crowd, hoping to catch a glimpse of the actress who had become the woman of his dreams.
5. My new car was supposed to be a technological triumph, but the catalytic converter started smelling to high heaven after only 500 miles.

31c
Avoiding wordiness

w **31c**

Avoiding wordiness means cutting whatever adds nothing to your meaning or the freshness of your writing. In editing your sentences, search for forceful and exact words and details that are essential to your meaning. Cross out all the empty words; cut out repetition that neither clarifies nor emphasizes your meaning; and be sure you have used the most direct grammatical form to express your ideas. Don't sacrifice necessary detail or original expression for mere brevity, however. Concise writing does not waste words but still includes the concrete and specific details that make meaning clear. In concise writing the length of an expression is appropriate to the thought.

1
Cutting empty words and phrases

Writers sometimes resort to empty words and phrases, either thinking that they sound authoritative or leaning on them when solid words will not come. But empty expressions simply fill space, and they should be eliminated in revision.

Filler phrases say in several words what a single word can say as well.

For	Substitute
at all times	always
at the present time	now
at this point in time	now
in the nature of	like
for the purpose of	for
in order to	to
until such time as	until
for the reason that	because
due to the fact that	because
because of the fact that	because
by virtue of the fact that	because
in the event that	if
by means of	by
in the final analysis	finally

Some filler phrases—such as *all things considered, as far as I'm concerned,* and *for all intents and purposes*—can be cut entirely with no loss in meaning.

WORDY — *For all intents and purposes,* few women have yet achieved equal pay for equal work.

CONCISE — Few women have yet achieved equal pay for equal work.

w
31c

All-purpose words, as their name implies, could mean almost anything. They include *angle, area, aspect, case, character, factor, field, kind, situation, thing,* and *type.* Because all-purpose words convey so little information, they almost always clutter and complicate the sentences they appear in.

WORDY — Because I chose the *field* of chemistry as my major, the whole *character* of my attitude toward the *area* of learning has changed.

CONCISE — Majoring in chemistry has changed my attitude toward learning.

WORDY — The *type* of large expenditures on advertising that manufacturers must make is a very important *aspect* of the cost of detergent cleansers.

CONCISE Manufacturers' large advertising expenditures increase the cost of detergents.

EXERCISE 10

Revise the following sentences as necessary to achieve conciseness. Concentrate on cutting filler phrases and all-purpose words.

Example:

I came to college because of many factors, but most of all because of the fact that I want a career in medicine.

I came to college *primarily because* I want a career in medicine.

1. Some lawyers still believe that advertising is a thing that will damage their profession.
2. The fact is that most people are too absorbed in their own lives to care much about the situations of others.
3. The baseball situation I like best is when the game seems to be over, for all intents and purposes, and the home team's slugger hits the winning run out of the park.
4. By virtue of their athletic abilities, a few lucky teenagers are able to escape the types of pressures that living in a poverty situation can create.
5. One aspect of majoring in Asian studies is a distinct drawback: except for a few rare teaching and curatorial positions, jobs are not available now and probably will not be available for some time to come.

2 Avoiding unnecessary repetition

Deliberately repeating words for parallelism or emphasis may clarify meaning and enhance coherence (see 17b and 18b). But unnecessary repetition weakens sentences. Avoid flabby repetition like that illustrated in the following example.

w **31c**

WORDY The machine *crushes* the *ore* into fine bits and dumps the *crushed ore* into a bin.

CONCISE The machine pulverizes the ore and then dumps it into a bin.

Notice that using one word two different ways within a sentence is especially confusing.

CONFUSING Preschool instructors play a *role* in the child's understanding of male and female *roles.*

CLEAR Preschool instructors contribute to the child's understanding of male and female roles.

The simplest kind of useless repetition is the **redundant phrase,** a phrase that says the same thing twice, such as *few in number* and *large in size.* Some of the most common redundant phrases are listed below. (The unneeded words are italicized.)

biography *of his life*	*important* (*basic*) essentials
consensus *of opinion*	puzzling *in nature*
cooperate *together*	repeat *again*
final completion	return *again*
frank and honest exchange	square (round) *in shape*
habitual custom	*surrounding* circumstances

A related form of redundancy is repetition of the same idea in slightly different words. In the following sentences, the unneeded phrases are italicized.

WORDY Theodore Fontane began his writing career late in life *at a relatively old age.*

WORDY Many unskilled workers *without training in a particular job* are unemployed *and don't have any work.*

EXERCISE 11

Revise the following sentences to achieve conciseness. Concentrate on eliminating unnecessary or confusing repetition and redundancy.

Example:

Because the circumstances surrounding the cancellation of classes were murky and unclear, the editor of the student newspaper assigned a staff reporter to investigate and file a report on the circumstances.

Because the circumstances leading to the cancellation of classes were unclear, the editor of the student newspaper assigned a staffer to investigate and report the story.

1. In today's world in the last quarter of the twentieth century, security has become a more compelling goal than social reform.
2. Deadly nightshade is aptly named. It has small white flowers and deep black fruit. The fruit looks like night, and it also looks like death. The fruit does happen to be poisonous, too.
3. As they embark on the beginning of an operation, all these specialists—the surgeon, the anesthetist, and the operating-room nurses—have specialized tasks to perform.
4. The disastrous drought was devastating to crops, but the farmers cooperated together to help each other out.
5. In deciding whether to choose a career in the field of dentistry, remember that some experts predict a future decline in the incomes of all health professionals.

3 Simplifying word groups and sentences

Choose the simplest and most direct grammatical construction that fits your meaning. Don't use a clause if a phrase will do; don't use a phrase if a word will do. *The strength that the panther has, the strength of the panther,* and *the panther's strength* mean the same thing. But the first takes six words, the last only three.

Wordy	The figurine, which was carved from a piece of ivory, measured three inches.
Revised	The figurine, carved of ivory, measured three inches.
Concise	The carved ivory figurine measured three inches.
Wordy	People with jobs that are low in pay are more likely to develop problems in their health.
Concise	People with low-paying jobs are more likely to develop health problems.

(See 16b for advice on the ways to subordinate information.)

You can streamline and strengthen sentences by choosing strong verbs that advance the action rather than weak verbs that merely mark time. Weak verbs and their baggage of extra words flatten sentences just where they should be liveliest and pad them needlessly.

Wordy	The painting *is a glorification of* Queen Victoria.
Concise	The painting *glorifies* Queen Victoria.

The first sentence takes three more words than the second to convey the same information. In the second sentence the direct, evocative verb *glorifies* substitutes for the colorless verb *is,* the long noun *glorification,* and the preposition *of.* Wordy constructions of a weak verb such as *is, has,* or *make* plus an adjective or noun commonly clutter writing.

Wordy	I *am desirous* of teaching music to children.
Concise	I *want* to teach music to children.
Wordy	He *had the sense* that she would die.
Concise	He *sensed* that she would die.
Wordy	Though they *made some advancement* in the next hours, they still failed to reach camp.
Concise	Though they *advanced* in the next hours, they still failed to reach camp.

Passive constructions usually contain more words (and much more indirectness) than active constructions. Revise passive constructions by shifting their verbs to the active voice and positioning the actor as the subject. (See also 7h and 18d.)

Wordy	*The building had been designed by the architects* six years earlier, and *the plans had been reviewed by no one* before *construction was begun.*
Concise	*The architects had designed the building* six years earlier, and *no one had reviewed the plans* before *construction began.*

Whenever possible, avoid sentences beginning with the expletive constructions *there is* and *there are.* Revise such constructions by removing *there,* moving the subject to the beginning of the sentence, and substituting a strong verb for *is* or *are.* (See also 18e.)

Wordy	*There are several plots that are repeated* in television drama.
Concise	*Several plots occur repeatedly* in television drama.

EXERCISE 12

Make the following sentences as concise as possible. Simplify grammatical structures, replace weak verbs with strong ones, and eliminate passive and expletive constructions.

Example:

He was taking some exercise in the park when several thugs were suddenly ahead in his path.

He was *exercising* (or *jogging* or *strolling* or *doing calisthenics*) in the park when several thugs suddenly *loomed* in his path.

1. The new goal posts were torn down by vandals before the first game, and the science building windows were broken.
2. The house on Hedron Street that is brightly lighted belongs to a woman who was once a madam.
3. I am aware that most people of about my age are bored by politics, but I myself am becoming more and more interested in the subject.
4. When a social reform is taking root, such as affirmative action in education and business, it is followed by backlash from those for whom the reform is not directly beneficial.
5. The attendance at the conference was lower than we expected, but there is evidence that the results of the meeting have been spread by word of mouth.

4 Avoiding jargon

Jargon is the special vocabulary of any discipline or profession—the terminology that permits doctors, economists, art historians, and others to communicate clearly and efficiently with their colleagues (see 31a-6). But *jargon* also commonly describes any vague, inflated language that states relatively simple ideas in unnecessarily complicated ways. The directions for using a shower head tell us that *this spray system will allow the user to reduce the mean diameter of the spray spectrum* instead of simply saying that *the nozzle will concentrate the spray*. Jargon often sounds as if the writer studied all the guidelines for being exact and concise and then set out to violate every one.

JARGON	The necessity for the individual to become a separate entity in his own right may impel a child to engage in open rebelliousness against parental authority or against sibling influence, with resultant confusion of those being rebelled against.
TRANSLATION	A child's natural desire to become himself may make him rebel against bewildered parents or siblings.
JARGON	The weekly social gatherings stimulate networking among members of management from various divisions, with the aim of developing contacts and maximizing the flow of creative information.
TRANSLATION	The weekly parties give managers from different divisions a chance to meet and to share ideas.

EXERCISE 13

Make the following passage as concise as possible. Eliminate jargon by cutting unneeded or repeated words and by simplifying both words and grammatical structures. Consult a dictionary as needed. Be merciless.

Example:

The nursery school teacher education training sessions involve active interfacing with preschool children of the appropriate age as well as intensive peer interaction in the form of role plays.

Training for nursery school teachers involves *interaction* with *preschoolers* and *role playing with peers.*

At the end of a lengthy line of reasoning, he came to the conclusion that the situation with carcinogens [cancer-causing substances] should be regarded as analogous to the situation with the automobile. Rather than giving in to an irrational fear of cancer, we should consider all aspects of the problem in a balanced and dispassionate frame of mind, making a total of the benefits received from potential carcinogens (plastics, pesticides, and other similar products) and measuring said total against the damage

w **31c**

done by such products. This is the nature of most discussions about the automobile. Rather than responding irrationally to the visual, aural, and oral pollution caused by automobiles, we have decided to live with them (while simultaneously working to improve on them) for the benefits brought to society as a whole.

32 *Using the Dictionary*

Consulting a dictionary can strengthen your choice of words. It can show you what words fit your needs (see Chapter 31); it can help you build your vocabulary (see Chapter 33); and it can show you how to spell words (see Chapter 34). It can answer most of the questions about words you may ask. This chapter will show you how to choose a dictionary that suits your purpose, how to read a dictionary without difficulty, and how to work with a dictionary as a flexible, compact, and thorough word reference.

An ordinary dictionary records in an alphabetical list the current usage and meaning of the words of a language. To do this, it includes a word's spelling, syllables, pronunciation, origin, meanings, grammatical functions, and grammatical forms. For some words the dictionary may provide a label indicating the status of the word according to geography, time, style, or subject matter. It may also list other words closely related in meaning and explain the distinctions among them. Some dictionaries include quotations illustrating a word's history or special uses. Many dictionaries include additional reference information, such as an essay on the history of English, rules for punctuation and spelling, a vocabulary of rhymes, names and locations of colleges, and tables of weights and measures.

32a Choosing a dictionary

1 Abridged dictionaries

Abridged dictionaries are the most practical for everyday use. Often called desk dictionaries because of their convenient size, they usually list 100,000 to 150,000 words and concentrate on fairly common words and meanings. Though you may sometimes need to consult an unabridged or a more specialized dictionary, a good abridged dictionary will serve most reference needs for writing and reading. Any of the following abridged dictionaries, listed alphabetically, is dependable.

The American Heritage Dictionary. 2nd coll. ed. Boston: Houghton, 1982. This dictionary's most obvious feature is its wealth of illustrations: more than 3000 photographs, drawings, and maps. The dictionary includes foreign words among the main entries and has separate sections on abbreviations and geographical and biographical names. The definitions are arranged in clusters of related meanings, with the most common meaning generally first. Usage labels (*slang, informal,* and so on) are applied liberally. Many words are followed by usage notes, which reflect the consensus of a panel of over 150 writers, editors, and teachers. The dictionary uses as few abbreviations and symbols as practicable. It includes guides to usage, grammar, spelling, and punctuation.

Oxford American Dictionary. New York: Oxford UP, 1980. A descendant of the unabridged *Oxford English Dictionary* (see below), this abridged dictionary is somewhat briefer than any of the others listed here. Its pronunciation symbols are particularly straightforward and easy to use. Its word meanings, arranged according to the frequency of their use, are short and simple. The dictionary emphasizes correct American usage, applies usage labels frequently, and includes over 600 usage notes. Unlike most other abridged dictionaries, this one contains no special appendixes and no etymologies, or word histories.

The Random House College Dictionary. Rev. ed. New York: Random, 1980. Based on the unabridged *Random House Dictionary* (see below), this dictionary includes abbreviations and biographical and geographical names in the main alphabetical listing. Its list of words is particularly up to date. Appendixes include a manual of style.

32a

Webster's Ninth New Collegiate Dictionary. Springfield: Merriam, 1983. This dictionary, based on the unabridged *Webster's Third New International Dictionary* (see below), concentrates on standard English and applies usage labels (such as *slang*) less frequently than do other dictionaries. Word definitions are listed in chronological order of their appearance in the language. The main alphabetical listing includes abbreviations. Geographical names and foreign words and phrases appear in appendixes, as does a manual of style.

Webster's New World Dictionary of the American Language. 2nd coll. ed. New York: Simon, 1982. This dictionary includes foreign words, abbreviations, and geographical and biographical names in the main alphabetical listing. The definitions of words are arranged in chronological order. Usage labels (*colloquial, slang,* and so on) are applied liberally, and words and phrases of American origin are starred. Appendixes on punctuation and mechanics and on manuscript form are included.

2 Unabridged dictionaries

Unabridged dictionaries are the most scholarly and comprehensive of all dictionaries, sometimes consisting of several volumes. They emphasize the history of words and the variety of their uses. An unabridged dictionary is useful when you are studying a word in depth, reading or writing about the literature of another century, or looking for a quotation containing a particular word. The following unabridged dictionaries are available at most libraries.

The Oxford English Dictionary. 13 volumes plus 4 supplements (in progress). New York: Oxford UP, 1933, 1972, 1976. Also available in a compact, photographically reduced, two-volume edition, 1971. This is the greatest dictionary of our language. Its purpose is to show the histories and current meanings of all words. Its entries illustrate the changes in a word's spelling, pronunciation, and meaning with quotations from writers of every century. Some entries span pages. The main dictionary focuses on British words and meanings, but the supplements include American words and meanings.

The Random House Dictionary of the English Language. New York: Random, 1980. This dictionary is smaller (and less expensive) than many unabridged dictionaries (it has 260,000 entries compared to 450,000 in *Webster's Third New International*). Its entries and definitions are especially up to date. Its appendixes include short dictionaries of French, Spanish, Italian, and German; a list of reference books; a manual of style; a brief atlas with color maps; and a list of major dates in history.

Webster's Third New International Dictionary of the English Language. Springfield: Merriam, 1981. This dictionary attempts to record our language more as it *is* used than as it *should be* used. Therefore, usage labels (such as *slang*) are minimal. Definitions are given in chronological order of their appearance in the language. Most acceptable spellings and pronunciations are provided. Plentiful illustrative quotations show variations in the uses of words. The dictionary is unusually strong in new scientific and technical terms.

3 Special dictionaries

Special dictionaries limit their attention to a single class of word (for example, slang, engineering terms, abbreviations), to a single kind of information (synonyms, usage, word origins), or to a specific subject (black culture, biography, history). Thus special dictionaries provide more extensive and complete information about their topics than general dictionaries do.

Special dictionaries on slang or word origins not only can help you locate uncommon information but also can give you a sense of the great richness and variety of language. They often make entertaining reading.

For information on slang

Partridge, Eric. *A Dictionary of Slang and Unconventional English.* 8th ed. Ed. Paul Beale. New York: Macmillan, 1984.

Wentworth, Harold, and Stuart Berg Flexner. *Dictionary of American Slang.* 2nd supp. ed. New York: Crowell, 1975.

For the origins of words

Oxford Dictionary of English Etymology. Ed. Charles T. Onions et al. New York: Oxford UP, 1966.

Partridge, Eric. *Origins: A Short Etymological Dictionary of Modern English.* 4th ed. New York: Macmillan, 1966.

Two kinds of special dictionaries—a usage dictionary and a dictionary of synonyms—are such useful references for everyday writing that you may want one of each on your own reference shelf. A dictionary of usage contains extensive entries for the words, phrases, and constructions that most frequently cause problems and controversy.

For guidance on English usage

Follett, Wilson. *Modern American Usage.* Ed. Jacques Barzun. New York: Hill, 1966.

Fowler, H. W. *A Dictionary of Modern English Usage.* 2nd ed. Rev. and ed. Sir Ernest Gowers. New York: Oxford UP, 1965.

Morris, William, and Mary Morris. *Harper Dictionary of Contemporary Usage.* 2nd ed. New York: Harper, 1985.

A dictionary of synonyms provides lists of words with closely related meanings. The lists are much more extensive than the usage notes in a general dictionary. Some dictionaries of synonyms contain extended discussions and illustrations of various shades of meaning.

For information about synonyms

Lewis, Norman. *The New Roget's Thesaurus of the English Language in Dictionary Form.* New York: Putnam's, 1964.

Webster's New Dictionary of Synonyms. Springfield: Merriam, 1973.

See 35b for an extensive list of special dictionaries in fields such as literature, business, history, psychology, and science.

32b
Working with a dictionary's contents

1
Finding general information

The dictionary is a convenient reference for information of every sort. Most abridged dictionaries will tell you the atomic weight of oxygen, Napoleon's birth and death dates, the location of Fort Knox, the population of Gambia, what the Conestoga wagon of the Old West looked like, the origin and nature of surrealism, or the number of cups in a quart. Finding such information may require a little work—for instance, checking the entry *periodic table* or *element* as well as *oxygen,* or consulting an appendix of biographical names to find Napoleon. But a dictionary is often the quickest and most accessible reference for general information when an encyclopedia, textbook, or other reference book is unavailable or inconvenient to use.

2
Answering specific questions

Dictionaries use abbreviations and symbols to squeeze a lot of information into a relatively small book. This system of condensed information may at first seem difficult to read. But all dictionaries include in their opening pages detailed information on the arrangement of entries, pronunciation symbols, and abbreviations. And the format is quite similar from one dictionary to another, so becoming familiar with the abbreviations and symbols in one dictionary makes reading any dictionary an easy routine. The labeled parts of the two entries below—*conjecture* from the *American Heritage Dictionary* (referred to from now on as *AHD*) and *reckon* from *Webster's Ninth New Collegiate Dictionary*—are discussed in the following sections.

Spelling and word division · Pronunciation · Meanings · Etymology · Grammatical functions and forms · Synonyms · Quotation

con·jec·ture (kən-jĕk'chər) *n.* **1.** Inference based on inconclusive or incomplete evidence. **2.** A statement, opinion, or conclusion based on inference. —*v.* **-tured, -tur·ing, -tures.** —*tr.* To infer from inconclusive evidence; guess. —*intr.* To make a conjecture. [ME < Lat. *conjectura* < *conicere*, to infer : *com-*, together + *jacere*, to throw.] —**con·jec'tur·a·ble** *adj.* —**con·jec'tur·a·bly** *adv.* —**con·jec'tur·er** *n.*

Synonyms: *conjecture, surmise, guess, speculate, presume, infer.* These verbs mean to reach a conclusion or judgment. *Conjecture* implies that a conclusion is based on incomplete evidence. *Surmise* suggests a conclusion reached by intuition or by interpretation of slender evidence. *Guess,* in formal usage, implies a haphazard attempt to answer or solve a problem and suggests substantial grounds for doubt. Informally the term implies a tentative conclusion reached in the absence of alternatives: *I guess I'll go to the movies.* *Speculate* implies an orderly process of reasoning based on inconclusive evidence, and is often interchangeable with *conjecture.* *Presume* and *infer* apply to conclusions about which less doubt is implied. *Presume* involves taking a conclusion for granted. In careful usage it is limited to what is considered worthy of trust; thus the term implies assumption based on experience or knowledge. *Infer* involves reaching a conclusion by reasoning from evidence about which no doubt is necessarily suggested.

Spelling and word division · Pronunciation · Etymology · Grammatical functions and forms · Quotation and source · Label · Idioms

reck·on \'rek-ən\ *vb* **reck·oned; reck·on·ing** \-(ə-)niŋ\ [ME *rekenen,* fr. OE *-recenian* (as in *gerecenian* to narrate); akin to OE *reccan*] *vt* (13c) **1 a :** COUNT ⟨~ the days till Christmas⟩ **b :** ESTIMATE, COMPUTE ⟨~ the height of a building⟩ **c :** to determine by reference to a fixed basis ⟨the existence of the U.S. is ~*ed* from the Declaration of Independence⟩ **2 :** to regard or think of as : CONSIDER **3** *chiefly dial* : THINK, SUPPOSE ⟨I ~ I've outlived my time —Ellen Glasgow⟩ ~ *vi* **1 :** to settle accounts **2 :** to make a calculation **3 a :** JUDGE **b** *chiefly dial* : SUPPOSE, THINK **4 :** to accept something as certain : place reliance ⟨I ~ on your promise to help⟩ — **reckon with :** to take into consideration — **reckon without :** to fail to consider : IGNORE

Spelling and word division

32b

The small initial letters for both *conjecture* and *reckon* indicate that these words are not normally capitalized. (In contrast, *Franklin stove* is capitalized in both the *AHD* and *Webster's Collegiate* because *Franklin* is a proper noun.)

The centered periods in **con·jec·ture** and **reck·on** show the divisions of these words into syllables. If you are writing or typing a word of more than one syllable and need to break it at the end of a line, follow the dictionary's division of the word into syllables. (See also Chapter 30 for general rules about word division.)

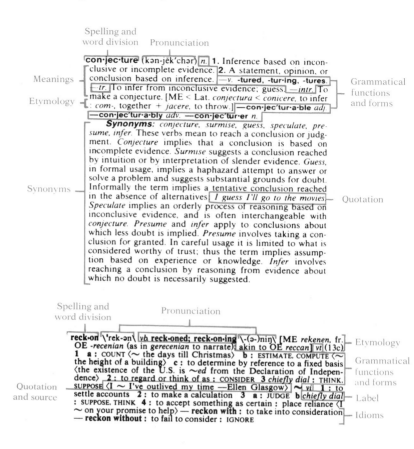

If a word is a hyphenated compound word, such as *cross-reference,* a dictionary shows the hyphen as part of the spelling: **cross-ref·er·ence.** The treatment of foreign words such as *joie de vivre* or *ex post facto,* which are normally italicized (or underlined) in writing, is more varied. *Webster's New World Dictionary* places a special symbol (‡) before each one. The *AHD* simply designates them as *French* and *Latin*, respectively, thereby indicating they should be italicized.

Dictionaries provide any variant spellings of a word at the beginning of an entry. Thus, for the word *dexterous*, *Webster's Collegiate* has "**dex·ter·ous** *or* **dex·trous**," indicating that either spelling is acceptable.

EXERCISE 1

Check the spelling of the following words in a dictionary. Correct any incorrect spellings, and divide all the words into syllables.

1. England
2. innoculate
3. reccommend
4. methodical
5. inheritence
6. over-estimate
7. depreciation
8. excruciating
9. grievance
10. secretery
11. trans-Atlantic
12. crossreference

Pronunciation

Dictionaries use symbols to indicate how to pronounce a word because the alphabet itself does not record all the sounds in the language. (Listen, for example, to the different sounds of *a* in only three words: *far*, *make*, and *answer*.) Most dictionaries provide a key to the pronunciation symbols at the foot of each page or every two facing pages.

The entries for *conjecture* and *reckon* show two slightly different pronunciation systems. In the *AHD*'s *conjecture* the pronunciation appears in parentheses; in *Webster's Collegiate* it appears in reversed slashes (\ \ ). In both entries the stressed syllable is indicated by an accent mark (′ and ˈ); but in the *AHD* the mark follows the stressed syllable (kən-jĕk′chər), whereas in *Webster's Collegiate* it precedes the stressed syllable (ˈrek-ən).

Most unabridged and some abridged dictionaries provide variant pronunciations, including regional differences. The *AHD*, for example, provides two pronunciations for the last syllable of *licorice*, indicating that the word may be pronounced either of two ways: "lĭk′ər-ĭs, -ĭsh."

32b

EXERCISE 2

Consult a dictionary for the correct pronunciation of the following words. Write out the pronunciation as given, using the dictionary's symbols. (If more than one pronunciation is given, write them all out.)

1. crucifixion
2. mnemonics
3. timorous
4. utilitarian
5. bathos
6. epitome
7. miserable
8. obelisk
9. polemic
10. yacht
11. promenade
12. insouciance

Grammatical functions and forms

Dictionaries give helpful information about a word's function and forms. The *Webster's Collegiate* entry for *reckon* shows the word to be a verb (*vb*), with the past tense and past participle *reckoned* and the present participle *reckoning*, and with both transitive (*vt*) and intransitive (*vi*) meanings. The *AHD* entry for *conjecture* shows it to be an even more versatile word. It is a noun (*n.*), with separate meanings in that function. And it is also a verb (*v.*): past tense and past participle *conjectured*, present participle *conjecturing*, and third-person singular present tense *conjectures*. The verb has both transitive (*tr.*) and intransitive (*intr.*) meanings.

Most dictionaries provide not only the principal forms of regular and irregular verbs but also the plural forms of irregular nouns and the comparative and superlative forms of adjectives and adverbs that commonly show degree with *-er* and *-est*. An adjective or adverb without *-er* and *-est* forms in the dictionary requires the addition of *more* and *most* to show the comparative and superlative.

When other parts of speech are formed from the word being defined and have related meanings, those words are grouped at the end of the entry, where they are spelled, divided, accented, and identified by part of speech but not defined. Several of these so-called derivative forms are provided at the end of the *AHD* entry for *conjecture: conjecturable* (*adj.*), *conjecturably* (*adv.*), and *conjecturer* (*n.*).

The *Webster's Collegiate* entry for *reckon* ends with two uses of the word in idiomatic expressions (*reckon with* and *reckon without*). These phrases are defined (unlike the related parts of speech of *conjecture*) because, as with all idioms, their meanings cannot be inferred simply from the words they consist of (see 31b-3).

32b

EXERCISE 3

Consult a dictionary to determine the part of speech of each of the following words. If the word functions as more than one part of speech, list them all. If the word is a verb, list its principal parts; if a noun, its plural form; if an adjective or adverb, its comparative and superlative.

1. little
2. that
3. study
4. happen
5. machine
6. orient
7. roof
8. ring
9. upset
10. steal
11. manifest
12. firm

Etymology

Dictionaries provide the **etymology** of a word (its history) to indicate its origin and the evolution of its meanings and forms. The dictionary can compress much information about a word into a small space through symbols, abbreviations, and different typefaces. An explanation of these systems appears in the dictionary's opening pages. The *AHD* traces *conjecture* first to Middle English (ME) (twelfth to fifteenth centuries) and then back to Latin (Lat.). As the entry in *Webster's Collegiate* shows, *reckon* came to English by a different route, arriving from Old English (OE) by way of Middle English (ME). The notation "(13c)" at the end of the second line indicates that the first recorded use of *reckon* to mean "count" occurred in the thirteenth century. (See 33a for a brief history of the English language.)

Sometimes dictionaries do not give the etymology for a word. Their practices differ (and are explained in their opening pages), but in general they omit etymology when it is obvious, unknown, or available elsewhere in the dictionary.

EXERCISE 4

Consult a dictionary for the etymologies of the following words. Use the dictionary's own explanations of abbreviations and symbols to get the fullest history of the word, and write out that history in your own words.

1. grammar
2. engage
3. leaf
4. moon
5. penetrate
6. promote
7. retrieve
8. toxic
9. calico
10. chauvinism
11. assassin
12. water

Meanings

Dictionaries divide the general meaning of a word into particular meanings on the basis of how the word is or has been actually used. They arrange a word's meanings differently, however, explaining the basis of their arrangement in their opening pages. *Webster's Collegiate* and *Webster's New World* list meanings in order of their appearance in the language, earliest first. The *AHD, Oxford American,* and abridged *Random House,* in contrast, usually place the word's most basic or common meaning first and follow it with the other meanings. These different policies will result in roughly the same arrangement of meanings only when the oldest meaning of a word is also the most common. Thus you should be sure you know the system of arrangement used by any dictionary you are consulting. Then read through the entire entry before settling on the meaning that most closely fits the context of what you're reading or writing.

Most dictionaries provide any special technical and scientific meanings of a word in separately numbered entries that are usually labeled. These labels are discussed on the next page.

EXERCISE 5

Consult a dictionary for the meanings of the following words. How many distinct meanings does each word have? How does the dictionary list meanings, chronologically or in order of importance? If chronologically, is the oldest meaning also the most common? What changes have occurred in each word's use over time?

1. weight
2. recipe
3. color
4. condition
5. order
6. apt
7. astrology
8. offered
9. prefer
10. quit
11. spring
12. sue

Synonyms and antonyms

Synonyms are words whose meanings are approximately the same, such as *small* and *little.* **Antonyms** are words whose meanings are approximately opposite, such as *small* and *big.* When a word has many closely related synonyms that are hard to distinguish, an abridged dictionary may devote a separate paragraph to them. The *AHD* does so in distinguishing the verb *conjecture* from the verbs *surmise, guess, speculate, presume,* and *infer,* each of which can also be looked up in its alphabetical place. *Webster's Collegiate* defines *reckon* with some words in small capital letters (COUNT, ESTIMATE, COMPUTE, and so on). These are both synonyms and cross-references, in that each word may be looked up in its alphabetical place. Dictionaries specify antonyms less often than synonyms, usually with a boldface **ant** at the end of the entry.

32b

Reading through the lists and discussions of synonyms and antonyms for a word can help you locate its meaning in a given context more exactly. (See 33c-2 for a discussion of how to use the synonyms provided by a dictionary to increase your vocabulary.)

EXERCISE 6

Consult a dictionary for the synonyms and antonyms of the following words. Use the word itself and each synonym and antonym appropriately in a sentence of your own.

1. suggest
2. plain (*adj.*)
3. high (*adj.*)
4. discover
5. change (*v.*)
6. beautiful
7. kind (*adj.*)
8. memory
9. serious

Labels

Dictionaries apply labels to words or to particular meanings that have a special status or use. The labels are usually of four kinds: subject, style, region, and time.

Subject labels tell us that a word or one of its meanings has a special use in a field of knowledge or a profession. In its entry for *relaxation,* for instance, the *AHD* presents specialized meanings with the subject labels *physiology, physics,* and *mathematics.*

Style labels restrict a word or one of its meanings to a particular level of usage, such as *slang, colloquial* or *informal, nonstandard* or *substandard, vulgar,* and *poetic* or *literary.* The label *slang* indicates that a word should be used in writing only for a special effect. For example, all the abridged dictionaries label *crumb* as slang when it means "a worthless or despicable person." The label *informal* or *colloquial* is applied to words that are appropriate for conversation and informal writing but not for formal writing. For instance, the *AHD* labels as informal the use of *sure* in the sentence *We sure need that money* (the more formal word is *surely*). The label *nonstandard* or *substandard* is applied to words or their meanings that are considered inappropriate for standard speech and writing. The *AHD* labels all uses of *ain't* as nonstandard, whereas *Webster's Collegiate* remarks that *ain't* is "disapproved by many" but labels expressions like *I ain't got* as substandard. The label *vulgar,* or sometimes *vulgar slang,* is applied to words or their meanings that are normally considered offensive in speech and writing. The label *poetic* or *literary* designates words or their meanings (such as *eve* for *evening* and *o'er* for *over*) used only in poetry or the most formal writing.

Region labels indicate that a particular spelling, pronunciation, or meaning of a word is not national but limited to some area. A regional difference may be indicated by the label *dialect. Webster's Collegiate* labels as dialect (*dial*) the uses of *reckon* to mean "suppose" or "think" (as in *I reckon I'll do that*). More specific region labels may designate areas of the United States or other countries. The word *bloke* (meaning "fellow") is labeled as British by most dictionaries. And the *AHD* labels *arroyo,* "a deep gully" or "a dry gulch," as Southwestern U.S.

Time labels indicate words or their meanings that the language, in evolving, has discarded. These words and meanings are included in the dictionary primarily to help readers of some older texts that contain them. The label *obsolete* designates words or specific meanings that are no longer used, whereas the label *archaic* designates words or specific meanings that are out of date though still in occasional use.

See 31a for further discussion of levels of usage and their appropriateness in your writing.

EXERCISE 7

Consult at least two dictionaries to determine the status of each of the following words or any one of their meanings according to subject, style, region, or time.

1. impulse	5. goof	9. mad
2. OK	6. goober	10. sing
3. irregardless	7. lift	11. brief (*n.*)
4. neath	8. potlatch	12. joint

Illustrative quotations

Dictionaries are made by collecting quotations showing actual uses of words in all kinds of speech and writing. Some of these quotations, or others that the dictionary makers invent, may appear in the dictionary's entries as illustrations of how a word may be used. Unabridged dictionaries usually provide many such examples, not only to illustrate a word's current uses but also to show the changes in its meanings over time. Abridged dictionaries use quotations more selectively: to illustrate an unusual meaning of the word, to help distinguish between two closely related meanings of the same word, or to show the differences between synonyms. The *AHD* entry for *conjecture* and the *Webster's Collegiate* entry for *reckon* both employ quotation.

EXERCISE 8

Consult a dictionary to find a quotation illustrating at least one meaning of each word below. Then write an illustrative sentence of your own for each word.

1. jolt	4. ceremonial	7. legitimate
2. articulate	5. sensuous	8. inquire
3. discreet	6. tremble	9. nether

33
Improving Your Vocabulary

A precise and versatile vocabulary is essential to effective communication. As you gain experience writing, you will want to improve the precision with which you use familiar words (see Chapter 31) and increase the number of words you can use appropriately. To a great extent, you can improve your vocabulary by frequent and inquisitive reading, by troubling to notice and learn the interesting or unfamiliar words used by other writers.

This chapter briefly describes the development of English and explains how words are formed. Then it offers some advice for learning to use new words. The chapter has a twofold purpose: to provide a sense of the potential of English by acquainting you with its history and range of words; and to help you increase the range, versatility, and precision of your own vocabulary.

33a
Understanding the sources of English

People change their language as they and their surroundings change. They revise spellings, pronunciation, and syntax, alter meanings, and even add or drop words to keep the language fresh and useful. English changes continuously, but its subtle and complex character stays the same.

English has over 500,000 words, probably more than any other language. This exceptional vocabulary and the power and range of expression that accompany it derive from its special mix of word sources. Unlike many other languages, English has borrowed a large number of words.

How English drew on its several sources and acquired its large vocabulary is the story of historical changes. The ancestor of

English, Indo-European, was spoken (but not written) perhaps as far back as 500 B.C., and it eventually spread to cover the area from India west to the British Isles. In what is now England, an Indo-European offshoot called Celtic was spoken extensively until the fifth century A.D. But over the next few centuries invaders from the European continent, speaking a dialect of another Indo-European language, Germanic, overran the native Britons. The Germanic dialect became the original source of English.

Old English, spoken from the eighth to the twelfth century, was a rugged, guttural language. It used a slightly different alphabet from ours (including the characters ð and þ for *th*), which has been transcribed in the sample below. The sample shows the opening lines of the Lord's Prayer: "Our father, who art in heaven, hallowed be thy name. Thy kingdom come. Thy will be done on earth as it is in heaven."

> Fæder ure thu the eart on heofonum, si thin nama gehalgod. Tobecume thin rice. Gewurthe thin willa on eorthan swa swa on heofonum.

Many of our nouns, such as *stone, word, gift,* and *foot,* come from Old English. So do most of our pronouns, prepositions, and conjunctions, some (such as *he, under,* and *to*) without any change in spelling. Other Germanic tribes, using a similar dialect but settling on the European continent instead of in England, fostered two other languages, Dutch and German. As a result, Dutch, German, and English are related languages with some similar traits.

In 1066 the Normans, under William the Conqueror, invaded England. The Normans were originally Vikings who had settled in northern France and had forsaken Old Norse for their own dialect of Old French. They made Norman French the language of law, literature, and the ruling class in England. As a result, English acquired many French words, including many military and governmental words such as *authority, mayor, crime, army,* and *guard.* The common English people kept English alive during the Norman occupation, but they adopted many French words intact (*air, point, place, age*). Eventually, the French influence caused the language to shift from Old to Middle English, which lasted from the twelfth through the fifteenth centuries. During this time a great many Latin words also entered English, for Latin formed the background of Norman French, and it was the language of the Church and of scholars. English words that entered Middle English directly from Latin or from Latin through French include *language, luminous, memory, liberal,* and *sober.*

Middle English, as the following passage from Geoffrey Chaucer's *Canterbury Tales* shows, was much closer to our own language than to Old English.

A clerk there was of Oxenford also,
That unto logyk hadde longe ygo.
As leene was his hors as is a rake,
And he nas nat right fat, I undertake,
But looked holwe, and therto sobrely.

Modern English evolved in the fourteenth and fifteenth centuries as the language's sound and spellings changed. This was the time of the Renaissance in Europe. Ancient Latin and Greek art, learning, and literature were revived, first in Italy and then throughout the continent. English vocabulary expanded rapidly, not only with more Latin and many Greek words (such as *democracy* and *physics*) but also with words from Italian and French. Advances in printing, beginning in the fifteenth century, made publications widely available to an increasingly literate audience. The Modern English of twentieth-century America is four centuries and an ocean removed from the Modern English of sixteenth-century England, but the two are fundamentally the same. The differences and the similarities are evident in this passage from the King James Bible, published in 1611:

> And the Lord God commanded the man, saying, Of euery tree of the garden thou mayest freely eate. But of the tree of the knowledge of good and euill, thou shalt not eate of it: for in the day that thou eatest thereof, thou shalt surely die.

33b
Learning the composition of words

Words can often be divided into meaningful parts. A *handbook,* for instance, is a book you keep at hand (for reference). A *shepherd* herds sheep (or other animals). Knowing what the parts of a word mean by themselves, as you do here, can often help you infer approximately what they mean when combined.

The following explanations of roots, prefixes, and suffixes provide information that can open up the meanings of words whose parts may not be familiar or easy to see. For more information, refer to a dictionary's etymologies, which provide the histories of words (see 32b).

1
Learning roots

A **root** is the unchanging component of words related in origin and usually in meaning. Both *illiterate* ("unable to read and write") and *literal* ("sticking to the facts or to the first and most obvious meaning of an idea") share the root *liter,* derived from *littera,* a Latin word meaning "letter." A person who cannot understand the letters that make up writing is *illiterate.* A person who wants to understand the primary meaning of the letters (the words) in a contract is seeking the *literal* meaning of that contract.

At least half our words come from Latin and Greek. The list below includes some common Latin and Greek roots, their meanings, and examples of English words containing them.

Root (source)	Meaning	English words
aster, astr (G)	star	astronomy, astrology
audi (L)	to hear	audible, audience
bene (L)	good, well	benefit, benevolent
bio (G)	life	biology, autobiography
dic, dict (L)	to speak	dictator, dictionary
fer (L)	to carry	transfer, referral
fix (L)	to fasten	fix, suffix, prefix
geo (G)	earth	geography, geology
graph (G)	to write	geography, photography
jur, jus (L)	law	jury, justice
log, logue (G)	word, thought, speech	astrology, biology, neologism
luc (L)	light	lucid, translucent
manu (L)	hand	manual, manuscript
meter, metr (G)	measure	metric, thermometer
op, oper (L)	work	operation, operator
path (G)	feeling	pathetic, sympathy
ped (G)	child	pediatrics
phil (G)	love	philosophy, Anglophile
phys (G)	body, nature	physical, physics
psych (G)	soul	psychic, psychology
scrib, script (L)	to write	scribble, manuscript
tele (G)	far off	telephone, television
ter, terr (L)	earth	territory, extraterrestrial
vac (L)	empty	vacant, vacuum, evacuate
verb (L)	word	verbal, verbose
vid, vis (L)	to see	video, vision, television

EXERCISE 1

Define the following italicized words, using the list of roots above and any clues given by the rest of the sentence. Check the accuracy of your meanings in a dictionary.

1. After guiding me through college, my *benefactor* will help me start a career.
2. Always afraid of leading a *vacuous* life, the heiress immersed herself in volunteer work.
3. The posters *affixed* to the construction wall advertised a pornographic movie.

4. After his *auditory* nerve was damaged, he had trouble catching people's words.
5. The child *empathized* so completely with his mother that he felt pain when she broke her arm.

2
Learning prefixes

Prefixes are standard syllables fastened to the front of a word to modify its meaning. For example, the word *prehistory* is a combination of the word *history,* meaning "based on a written record explaining past events," and the prefix *pre-,* meaning "before." Together, prefix and word mean "before a written record explaining past events," or before events were recorded. Learning standard prefixes can help you improve vocabulary and spelling just as learning word roots can. The following lists group prefixes according to sense so that they are easier to remember. When two or more prefixes have very different spellings but the same meaning, they usually derive from different languages, most often Latin and Greek.

Prefixes showing quantity

Meaning	Prefixes in English words
half	*semi*annual; *hemi*sphere
one	*uni*cycle; *mon*arch, *mono*rail
two	*bi*nary, *bi*monthly; *di*lemma, *dicho*tomy
three	*tri*angle, *tri*logy
four	*quadr*angle, *quar*tet
five	*quint*et; *penta*gon
six	*sex*tuplets; *hexa*meter
seven	*sept*uagenarian; *hept*archy
eight	*oct*ave, *octo*pus
nine	*nona*genarian
ten	*dec*ade, *deca*thlon
hundred	*cent*ury; *hecto*liter
thousand	*milli*meter; *kilo*cycle

33b

Prefixes showing negation

Meaning	Prefixes in English words
without, no, not	*a*sexual; *il*legal, *im*moral, *in*valid, *ir*reverent; *un*skilled
not, absence of, opposing, against	*non*breakable; *ant*acid, *anti*pathy *contra*dict
opposite to, complement to	*counter*clockwise, *counter*weight

Meaning	Prefixes in English words
do the opposite of, remove, reduce	*de*horn, *de*vitalize, *de*value
do the opposite of, deprive of	*dis*establish, *dis*arm
wrongly, bad	*mis*judge, *mis*deed

Prefixes showing time

Meaning	Prefixes in English words
before	*ante*cedent; *fore*cast; *pre*cede; *pro*logue
after	*post*war
again	*re*write

Prefixes showing direction or position

Meaning	Prefixes in English words
above, over	*super*vise
across, over	*trans*port
below, under	*infra*sonic; *sub*terranean; *hypo*dermic
in front of	*pro*ceed; *pre*fix
behind	*re*cede
out of	*e*rupt, *ex*plicit; *ec*stasy
into	*in*jection, *im*merse; *en*courage, *em*power
around	*circum*ference; *peri*meter
with	*co*exist, *col*loquial, *com*municate, *con*sequence, *cor*respond; *sym*pathy, *syn*chronize

EXERCISE 2

Provide meanings for the following italicized words, using the lists of prefixes and any clues given by the rest of the sentence. Check the accuracy of your meanings in a dictionary.

1. In the twenty-first century some of our oldest cities will celebrate their *quadricentennials.*
2. Most poems called sonnets consist of fourteen lines divided into an *octave* and a *sestet.*
3. When the Congress seemed ready to cut Social Security benefits again, some representatives proposed the *countermeasure* of increasing Medicare payments.
4. By increasing Medicare payments, the representatives hoped to *forestall* the inevitable financial squeeze on the elderly.
5. Ferdinand Magellan, a Portuguese sailor, commanded the first expedition to *circumnavigate* the globe.

3
Learning suffixes

Suffixes are standard syllables fastened to the end of a word to modify its meaning and usually its part of speech. The word *popular* is an adjective. With different suffixes, it becomes a different adjective, an adverb, a noun, and two different verbs.

ADJECTIVE	popular	NOUN	popul*ation*
	popul*ous*	VERB	popul*ate*
ADVERB	popul*arly*		popul*arize*

Many words change suffixes in the same way. In fact, suffixes help us recognize what parts of speech many words are, as the following examples show.

Noun suffixes

mis*ery*	min*er*	intern*ship*	random*ness*
refer*ence*	base*ment*	presid*ency*	brother*hood*
relev*ance*	national*ist*	discus*sion*	king*dom*
operat*or*	national*ism*	agita*tion*	

Verb suffixes

hard*en*	pur*ify*
national*ize*	agit*ate*

Adjective suffixes

miser*able*	president*ial*	wonder*ful*	use*less*
ed*ible*	gigant*ic*	fibr*ous*	self*ish*
nation*al*	friend*ly*	adopt*ive*	flatu*lent*

The only suffix regularly applied to adverbs is *-ly: openly, selfishly.*

NOTE: Inflectional endings, such as the plural *-s,* the possessive *-'s,* the past tense *-ed,* and the comparative *-er* or *-est,* appear at the ends of words but do not change a word's grammatical function.

33b

EXERCISE 3

Identify the part of speech of each word below, and then change it to the part or parts of speech in parentheses by deleting, adding, or changing a suffix. Use the given word and each created word in a sentence. Check a dictionary if necessary to be sure suffixes and spellings are correct.

1. magic (*adjective*)
2. durable (*noun; adverb*)
3. refrigerator (*verb*)
4. self-critical (*noun*)
5. differ (*noun; adjective*)
6. equal (*noun; adverb*)
7. conversion (*verb; adjective*)
8. strictly (*adjective; noun*)
9. assist (*noun*)
10. qualification (*verb; adjective*)

33c
Learning to use new words

You can learn a new word not only by understanding its composition but also by examining the context in which it appears and by looking it up in a dictionary—both ways to increase your vocabulary by multiplying and varying your experience with language.

1
Examining context

Most people guess the meaning of an unfamiliar word by looking at familiar words around it. Imagine, for example, that you read the following:

> I was so tired I didn't bother with a real bed. I just lay down on the liclac in the living room. As soon as my feet rested at one end and my head at the other, I fell asleep. In the morning I was cramped from pushing against the back of the liclac.

To guess what *liclac* means, you could examine all the familiar words and learn that (1) a liclac isn't a bed, but you can lie on it; (2) it's part of a living room; (3) it's the length of a person; (4) it's narrow and has a back. From these clues you might guess that the nonsense word *liclac* represents a piece of living room furniture similar to a couch or sofa.

Parallelism shows you which ideas line up or go together and can often suggest the meaning of a new word. Watch for parallel ideas in the following sentence.

> The kittens see their mother hunt and kill, and they in turn take up *predatory* behavior.

If you did not know the word *predatory*, you could put together clues from the context: parallel construction (*kittens see . . . and they . . . take up*); the tip-off phrase *in turn;* and the suggested idea of imitation (kittens watching their mother and taking up her behavior). These clues produce the correct assumption that predatory behavior consists of hunting and killing.

The phrase *is called* or the word *is* often signals a definition.

> The point where the light rays come together is called the *focus* of the lens.

Sometimes definitions are enclosed in parentheses or set off by commas or dashes.

> In early childhood these tendencies lead to the development of *schemes* (organized patterns of behavior).
>
> Many Chinese practice *Tai Chi,* an ancient method of self-defense performed as exercise in slow, graceful motions.
>
> At *burnout*—the instant a rocket stops firing—the satellite's path is fixed.

Noticing examples can also help you infer the meaning of a word. The expressions *such as, for example, for instance, to illustrate,* and *including* often precede examples.

> Society often has difficulty understanding *nonconformists* such as criminals, inventors, artists, saints, and political protesters.

The parallel examples help explain *nonconformist* because they all seem to be exceptions, people who go beyond the average or beyond the rules. This is close to an understanding of *nonconformists* as people who do not adapt themselves to the usual standards and customs of society.

Sometimes an example that reveals the meaning of an unfamiliar word is spread throughout the sentence or paragraph and is not announced by a phrase.

> During the first weeks of *rehabilitation,* Brian exercised as best he could, took his medicine daily, and thought constantly about the physical condition he once possessed.

Guessing the meaning of *rehabilitation* requires considering what occurred during it: (1) exercising "as best he could," as if Brian had some kind of handicap; (2) taking medicine, as if Brian were ill; and (3) thinking about his past physical condition, as if Brian were wishing for the good shape he used to be in. Putting these examples together suggests that *rehabilitation* is returning to a healthy condition, which is one of its meanings. (The more precise definition is "restoring a former capacity"; and that idea includes reviving a skill as well as recuperating from a sickness.)

EXERCISE 4

Use context to determine the meanings of the words italicized below (not including titles). Check the accuracy of your guess by consulting a dictionary.

1. Like America, Michael [Corleone, in *The Godfather*] began as a clean, brilliant young man *endowed* with incredible resources and believing in a humanistic idealism. Like America, Michael was an innocent who had tried to correct the ills and injustices of his *progenitors*. – FRANCIS FORD COPPOLA
2. Everything about man is a *paradox*. The *magnanimous* man grown rich becomes mean. The creative artist for whom everything is made easy nods. Every doctrine swears that it will breed men, but none can tell us in advance what sort of men it will breed. – ANTOINE DE SAINT-EXUPÉRY
3. "And this, too, shall pass away." How much [this sentence] expresses! How *chastening* in the hour of pride! How *consoling* in the depths of *affliction!* – ABRAHAM LINCOLN
4. As long as there is one upright man, as long as there is one compassionate woman, the *contagion* may spread and the scene is not *desolate*. Hope is the thing that is left to us in a bad time. – E. B. WHITE
5. In a community where public services have failed to keep *abreast* of private consumption, ... in an atmosphere of private *opulence* and public *squalor*, the private goods have full sway. – JOHN KENNETH GALBRAITH

2
Using the dictionary

The dictionary is a quick reference for the meaning of words (see 32b). It can give the precise meaning of a word whose general meaning you have guessed by examining the word's context. It can also help you fix the word in your memory by showing its spelling, pronunciation, grammatical functions and forms, etymology, and synonyms and antonyms.

For example, suppose you did not understand the word *homogeneous* in the following sentence:

> Its homogeneous population makes the town stable but dull.

33c

The dictionary gives the meanings of the word: "of the same kind," "of similar composition throughout." Thus the town's population is made up of similar kinds of people. *Homogeneous* comes from the Greek words *hom,* meaning "same," and *genos,* meaning "kind, type." Obviously, the composition of the word reinforces its definitions. Looking down the dictionary's column under *homogeneous,* you would find a related word, *homogenize,* which might be more familiar because of the common phrase *homogenized milk.* To *homogenize* means "to blend into a smooth mixture" and "to break up the fat globules of milk by forcing them through minute openings." The relation between this familiar word and the other, less familiar one gives added meaning to both words. A similar expansion of meaning could come from examining an antonym of *homogeneous,* such as *heterogeneous,* meaning "consisting of dissimilar ingredients." Thinking of the two opposite words together might fix them both in your memory.

A dictionary of synonyms is the best source for the precise meanings of similar words (see 32a-3). But even an abridged dictionary will supply much information about synonyms (see 32a-1). Most abridged dictionaries list a word's common synonyms and either direct you to the entries for the synonyms or distinguish among them in one place. An example of the latter format is the paragraph below, which follows the main entry for the word *real* in *The American Heritage Dictionary of the English Language.* By drawing on this information as you write, you can avoid overreliance on the word *real* when a more precise word is appropriate.

> ***Synonyms:*** *real, actual, true, authentic, concrete, existent, genuine, tangible, veritable. Real,* although frequently used interchangeably with the terms that follow, pertains basically to that which is not imaginary but is existent and identifiable as a thing, state, or quality. *Actual* connotes that which is demonstrable. *True* implies belief in that which conforms to fact. *Authentic* implies acceptance of historical or attributable reliability rather than visible proof. *Concrete* implies the reality of actual things. *Existent* applies to concepts or objects existing either in time or space: *existent tensions. Genuine* presupposes evidence or belief that a thing or object is what it is claimed to be. *Tangible* stresses the mind's acceptance of that which can be touched or seen. *Veritable,* which should be used sparingly, applies to persons and things having all the qualities claimed for them.

EXERCISE 5

The dictionary entry above lists the following words as synonyms for *real: actual, true, authentic, concrete, existent, genuine, tangible,* and *veritable.* Using this entry and consulting another dictionary if necessary, write nine sentences that make precise use of *real* and each of its eight synonyms.

34
Spelling

Because of the history and complexity of English, spelling English words according to standard usage requires consistent attention. However, learning to spell well is worth the effort because misspelling can make writing seem incompetent or lazy. This chapter will show you how to recognize typical spelling problems, how to follow a handful of rules as a guide to spelling, and how to develop spelling skills through conscious effort.

34a
Avoiding typical spelling problems

Spelling well involves recognizing situations that commonly lead to misspelling: pronunciation can mislead you in several ways; different forms of the same word may have different spellings; and some words have more than one acceptable spelling. Watching for the errors these situations encourage will prevent many spelling mistakes.

1
Avoiding excessive reliance on pronunciation

In English, unlike some languages, pronunciation of words is an unreliable guide to their spelling. The same letter or combination of letters may have different sounds in the pronunciation of different words. For an example, say aloud these different ways of pronouncing the letters *ough: tough, dough, cough, through, bough*. And say aloud these ways of pronouncing *ea: beat, tread, pear, search, fear*. Another problem is that some words contain letters that are not pronounced clearly or at all, such as the *ed* in *asked*, the silent *e* in *swipe*, or the unpronounced *gh* in *tight*.

Pronunciation is a particularly unreliable guide to the spelling of **homonyms,** words pronounced the same though they have different spellings and meanings: for example, *great/grate, to/too/two, threw/through, horse/hoarse, board/bored, break/brake.* Homonyms and words with very similar pronunciations, such as *gorilla/guerrilla* and *accept/except,* are common sources of spelling errors. Studying the following list of homonyms and similar-sounding words will help you avoid spelling errors caused by word sounds. (See 34c-3 for some tips on how to use spelling lists.)

accept (to receive)
except (other than)

affect (to have an influence on)
effect (result)

all ready (prepared)
already (by this time)

allude (to refer to indirectly)
elude (to avoid)

allusion (indirect reference)
illusion (erroneous belief or perception)

ascent (a movement up)
assent (agreement)

bare (unclothed)
bear (to carry, or an animal)

board (a plank of wood)
bored (uninterested)

born (brought into life)
borne (carried)

brake (stop)
break (smash)

buy (purchase)
by (next to)

capital (the seat of a government)
capitol (the building where a legislature meets)

cite (to quote an authority)
sight (the ability to see)
site (a place)

descent (a movement down)
dissent (disagreement)

desert (to abandon)
dessert (after-dinner course)

discreet (reserved, respectful)
discrete (individual or distinct)

elicit (to bring out)
illicit (illegal)

fair (average, or lovely)
fare (a fee for transportation)

formally (conventionally)
formerly (in the past)

forth (forward)
fourth (after *third*)

gorilla (a large primate)
guerrilla (a kind of soldier)

hear (to perceive by ear)
here (in this place)

heard (past tense of *hear*)
herd (a group of animals)

hole (an opening)
whole (complete)

its (possessive of *it*)
it's (contraction of *it is*)

lead (heavy metal)
led (past tense of *lead*)

lessen (to make less)
lesson (something learned)

meat (flesh)
meet (encounter)

no (the opposite of *yes*)
know (to be certain)

passed (past tense of *pass*)
past (after, or a time gone by)

patience (forbearance)
patients (persons under medical care)

peace (the absence of war)
piece (a portion of something)

plain (clear)
plane (a carpenter's tool, or an airborne vehicle)

presence (the state of being at hand)
presents (gifts)

principal (most important, or the head of a school)
principle (a basic truth or law)

rain (precipitation)
reign (to rule)
rein (a strap for controlling an animal)

raise (to build up)
raze (to tear down)

right (correct)
rite (a religious ceremony)
write (to make letters)

road (a surface for driving)
rode (past tense of *ride*)

scene (where an action occurs)
seen (past participle of *see*)

stationary (unmoving)
stationery (writing paper)

straight (unbending)
strait (a water passageway)

their (possessive of *they*)
there (opposite of *here*)
they're (contraction of *they are*)

to (toward)
too (also)
two (following *one*)

waist (the middle of the body)
waste (discarded material)

weak (not strong)
week (Sunday through Saturday)

which (one of a group)
witch (a sorcerer)

who's (contraction of *who is*)
whose (possessive of *who*)

your (possessive of *you*)
you're (contraction of *you are*)

2
Distinguishing between different forms of the same word

sp
34a

Other spelling problems occur when the noun form and the verb form of the same word are spelled differently. For example:

Verb	Noun	Verb	Noun
advise	advice	enter	entrance
argue	argument	marry	marriage
describe	description	omit	omission

Sometimes the noun and the adjective forms of the same word differ.

Noun	Adjective	Noun	Adjective
comedy	comic	height	high
courtesy	courteous	Britain	British
generosity	generous		

The principal parts of irregular verbs are usually spelled differently.

begin, began, begun	know, knew, known
break, broke, broken	ride, rode, ridden
do, did, done	ring, rang, run

Irregular nouns change spelling from singular to plural.

child, children	shelf, shelves
goose, geese	tooth, teeth
mouse, mice	woman, women

Notice, too, that the stem of a word may change its spelling in different forms.

four, forty	thief, theft

3
Using preferred spellings

Many words have variant spellings as well as preferred spellings (see 32b-2). Since the variant spellings listed in an American dictionary are often British spellings, you should know the main differences between American and British spellings.

American	**British**
encyclop*e*dia	encyclop*ae*dia
col*or*, hum*or*	col*our*, hum*our*
theat*er*, cent*er*	theat*re*, cent*re*
cance*l*ed, trave*l*ed	cance*ll*ed, trave*ll*ed
judgment	judg*e*ment
reali*z*e	reali*s*e

34b
Following spelling rules

Misspelling is often a matter of misspelling a syllable rather than the whole word. The following general rules focus on troublesome syllables, with notes for the occasional exceptions.

1
Distinguishing between *ie* and *ei*

Words like *believe* and *receive* sound alike in the second syllable, but the syllable is spelled differently. How do you know which word should have *ie* and which one *ei*? The answer is in the familiar jingle:

I before *e*, except after *c*, or when pronounced "ay" as in *neighbor* and *weigh*.

i BEFORE *e*	believe grief chief	bier thief fiend	hygiene friend
ei AFTER *c*	ceiling receive	conceive deceit	perceive conceit
ei SOUNDED AS "AY"	neighbor sleigh weight	freight eight vein	beige heinous

EXCEPTIONS: Some words are spelled with an *ei* combination even though it doesn't follow *c* and isn't pronounced "ay." These words include *either, neither, foreign, forfeit, height, leisure, weird, seize,* and *seizure*. This sentence might help you remember some of them:

The weird foreigner neither seizes leisure nor forfeits height.

EXERCISE 1

Insert *ie* or *ei* in the words below. Check doubtful spellings in a dictionary.

1. br__f
2. dec__ve
3. rec__pt
4. s__ze
5. for__gn
6. pr__st
7. gr__vance
8. f__nd
9. l__surely
10. ach__ve
11. pat__nce
12. p__rce
13. h__ght
14. fr__ght
15. f__nt

2
Keeping or dropping a final *e*

sp 34b

Many words end with an unpronounced or silent *e*: for instance, *move, brave, late, rinse*. When adding endings like *-ing* or *-ly* to these words, do you keep the final *e* or drop it? You drop it if the ending begins with a vowel.

advise + able = advisable
force + ible = forcible
surprise + ing = surprising

You keep the final, silent *e* if the ending begins with a consonant.

advance + ment = advancement
accurate + ly = accurately
care + ful = careful

Exceptions: The silent *e* is sometimes retained before an ending beginning with a vowel. It is kept when *dye* becomes *dyeing*, to avoid confusion with *dying*. It is kept to prevent mispronunciation of words like *shoeing* (not *shoing*) and *mileage* (not *milage*). And the final *e* is often retained after a soft *c* or *g*, to keep the sound of the consonant soft rather than hard.

courageous	changeable	noticeable
outrageous	manageable	embraceable

The silent *e* is also sometimes *dropped* before an ending beginning with a consonant, when the *e* is preceded by another vowel.

argue + ment = argument
true + ly = truly
due + ly = duly

EXERCISE 2

Combine the following words and endings, keeping or dropping final *e*'s as necesary to make correctly spelled words. Check doubtful spellings in a dictionary.

1. malice + ious
2. love + able
3. service + able
4. retire + ment
5. sue + ing
6. virtue + ous
7. note + able
8. battle + ing
9. suspense + ion
10. astute + ness

3
Keeping or dropping a final *y*

Words ending in *y* often change their spelling when an ending is added to them. The basic rule is to change the *y* to *i* when it follows a consonant.

beauty, beauties	worry, worried	supply, supplier
folly, follies	merry, merrier	deputy, deputize

But keep the *y* when it follows a vowel; when the ending is *-ing;* or when it ends a proper name.

day, days	cry, crying	May, Mays
obey, obeyed	study, studying	Minsky, Minskys
key, keyed	marry, marrying	

sp **34b**

EXERCISE 3

Combine the following words and endings, changing or keeping final *y*'s as necessary to make correctly spelled words. Check doubtful spellings in a dictionary.

1. imply + s
2. messy + er
3. apply + ing
4. delay + ing
5. defy + ance
6. say + s
7. solidify + s
8. Murphy + s
9. misty + er
10. supply + ed

4
Doubling Consonants

Words ending in a consonant sometimes double the consonant when adding an ending. Whether to double the final consonant depends on the number of syllables in the word, on the letters preceding the final consonant, and on which syllable is stressed in pronunciation.

In one-syllable words, double the final consonant when a single vowel precedes the final consonant.

slap, slapping	flat, flatter
tip, tipped	pit, pitted

However, *don't* double the final consonant when two vowels or a vowel and another consonant precede the final consonant.

pair, paired	park, parking
real, realize	rent, rented

In words of more than one syllable, double the final consonant when a single vowel precedes the final consonant and the stress falls on the last syllable of the stem once the ending is added.

submit, submitted	refer, referring
occur, occurred	begin, beginning

But *don't* double the final consonant when it is preceded by two vowels or by a vowel and another consonant, or when the stress falls on other than the stem's last syllable once the ending is added.

refer, reference	despair, despairing
relent, relented	beckon, beckoned

EXERCISE 4

Combine the following words and endings, doubling final consonants as necessary to make correctly spelled words. Check doubtful spellings in a dictionary.

1. repair + ing
2. admit + ance
3. benefit + ed
4. shop + ed
5. fear + ing
6. conceal + ed
7. allot + ed
8. drip + ing
9. declaim + ed
10. parallel + ing

5 Attaching prefixes

Adding prefixes such as *dis-*, *mis-*, and *un-* does not change the spelling of the word. When adding a prefix, do not drop a letter from or add a letter to the original word.

uneasy	disappoint	misinform
unnecessary	dissatisfied	misstate
antifreeze	defuse	misspell
anti-intellectual	de-emphasize	

(See also 34d-4 on when to use hyphens with prefixes.)

6 Forming plurals

Nouns

Most nouns form plurals by adding *-s* to the singular form.

boy, boys	table, tables	carnival, carnivals

Some nouns ending in *f* or *fe* form the plural by changing the ending to *ve* before adding *-s*.

leaf, leaves	life, lives	yourself, yourselves

Singular nouns ending in *-s, -sh, -ch,* or *-x* form the plural by adding *-es.*

kiss, kisses	church, churches
wish, wishes	fox, foxes

(Notice that verbs ending in *-s, -sh, -ch,* or *-x* form the third-person singular in the same way. *Taxes* and *lurches* are examples.)

Nouns ending in *o* preceded by a vowel usually form the plural by adding *-s.*

ratio, ratios	zoo, zoos

Nouns ending in *o* preceded by a consonant usually form the plural by adding *-es.*

hero, heroes	tomato, tomatoes

Some English nouns that were originally Italian, Greek, Latin, or French form the plural according to their original language: *piano, pianos; medium, media; datum, data; alumnus, alumni; alumna, alumnae.*

Compound nouns

Compound nouns form plurals in two ways. An *-s* is added to the last word when the component words are roughly equal in importance, whether or not they are hyphenated.

city-states	bucket seats	breakthroughs
painter-sculptors	booby traps	

When the parts of the compound word are not equal—especially when a noun is combined with other parts of speech—then *s* is added to the noun.

fathers-in-law passersby

Note, however, that most modern dictionaries give the plural of *spoonful* as *spoonfuls.*

EXERCISE 5

Make correct plurals of the following words. Check doubtful spellings in a dictionary.

1. pile
2. donkey
3. beach
4. summary
5. thief
6. box
7. switch
8. rodeo
9. criterion
10. cupful
11. libretto
12. sister-in-law
13. mile-per-hour
14. cargo
15. hiss

34c
Developing spelling skills

sp **34c**

You should habitually consult a dictionary for spellings you are unsure of (see Chapter 32). Start by looking up the word as you think it is spelled. Then try different variations based on the pronunciation of the word. Once you think you have found the correct spelling, check the definition to make sure you have the word you want. In addition to consulting the dictionary regularly, you can improve spelling in several other ways: by pronouncing words carefully; by inventing tricks to help you remember troublesome words; and by memorizing the spellings of words that cause problems for many people.

1
Pronouncing carefully

Pronunciation will not always work to tell you how to spell because, as we observed in 34a, accurate pronunciation may not give you all the information you need. In addition, speakers of some English dialects pronounce words differently from the way they are spelled. Nevertheless, careful pronunciation can help you spell many words in which sounds are frequently added, omitted, or reversed in pronunciation.

athletics (not ath*e*letics)	lib*r*ary (not libary)
disastrous (not disast*e*rous)	mischievous (not mischiev*i*ous)
recognize (not reconize)	stric*t*ly (not stricly)
lightning (not light*e*ning)	gover*n*ment (not goverment)
height (not heigh*th*)	hist*o*ry (not histry)
irrelevant (not irre*vel*ant)	temper*a*ment (not temperment)
perform (not p*re*form)	represent*at*ive (not representive)
nuclear (not nuc*ula*r)	

2
Using mnemonics

Mnemonics (pronounced with an initial "*n*" sound) are techniques for assisting your memory. The *er* in *letter* and *paper* can remind you that *stationery* (meaning "writing paper") has an *er* near the end; *stationary* with an *a* means "st*a*nding in place." Or the word *dome* with its long *o* sound can remind you that the building in which the legislature meets is spelled *capitol,* with an *o*. The *capital* city is spelled with *al* like *Albany,* the capital of New York. If you identify the words you have trouble spelling, you can take a few minutes to think of your own mnemonics, which may work better for you than someone else's.

3
Studying spelling lists

Learning to spell commonly misspelled words will reduce your spelling errors. As you work with the following list, study only a small group of words at a time. (Learning tests have demonstrated that seven items is a good number to work with.) Be sure you understand the meaning of the word before you try to memorize its spelling. Look it up in a dictionary if you are uncertain, and try using it in a sentence. Pronounce the word out loud, syllable by syllable, and write the word out. (Additional words that are commonly misspelled appear in the list of similar-sounding words in 34a. That list should be considered an extension of the one below.)

absence	accidentally	acknowledge	address
absorption	accommodate	acquaintance	admission
abundance	accuracy	acquire	adolescent
acceptable	accustomed	across	advice
accessible	achieve	actually	advising

against
aggravate
aggressive
all right
all together
almost
although
altogether
amateur
analysis
analyze
angel
annihilate
annual
answer
apology
apparent
appearance
appetite
appreciate
appropriate
approximately
argument
arrest
ascend
assassinate
assistance
associate
atheist
athlete
attendance
audience
auxiliary
average

bargain
basically
beginning
belief
believe
beneficial
benefited
boundary
breath
breathe
Britain
bureaucracy
burial
business

calculator
calendar
carrying
category
cede
cemetery
certain
changeable
changing
characteristic
chief
chocolate
choose
chose
climbed
coarse
column
coming
commercial
commitment
committed
committee
competent
competition
complement
compliment
conceit
conceive
concentrate
concert
condemn
conquer
conscience
conscientious
conscious
consistency
consistent
continuous
controlled
controversial
convenience
convenient
coolly
council
counsel
course
courteous
criticism
criticize

crowd
cruelty
curiosity
curious

deceive
deception
decide
decision
definitely
degree
dependent
descend
descendant
describe
description
desirable
despair
desperate
destroy
determine
develop
device
devise
dictionary
difference
dining
disagree
disappear
disappoint
disapprove
disastrous
discipline
discriminate
discussion
disease
dispel
dissatisfied
distinction
divide
divine
division
doctor
drawer
drunkenness

easily
ecstasy
efficiency
efficient
eighth
either
eligible
embarrass
emphasize
empty
enemy
entirely
environment
equipped
especially
essential
every
exaggerate
exceed
excellent
exercise
exhaust
existence
expense
experience
experiment
explanation
extremely

familiar
fascinate
favorite
February
finally
financially
forcibly
foreign
foresee
forty
forward
friend
frightening
fulfill

gauge
generally
government
grammar
grief
guarantee
guard
guidance

happily
harass
height
heroes
hideous
humorous
hungry
hurriedly
hurrying
hypocrisy
hypocrite

ideally
illogical
imaginary
imagine
imitation
immediately
immigrant
incidentally
incredible
independence
independent
indispensable
individually
inevitably
influential
initiate
innocuous
inoculate
insistent
integrate
intelligence
interest
interference
interpret
irrelevant
irresistible
irritable
island

jealousy
judgment

knowledge

laboratory
leisure
length
lenient
library
license
lightning
likelihood
literally
livelihood
loneliness
loose
lose
luxury
lying

magazine
maintenance
manageable
maneuver
marriage
mathematics
meant
medicine
miniature
minor
minutes
mirror
mischievous
missile
misspelled
morale
morals
mournful
muscle
mysterious

naturally
necessary
neighbor
neither
nickel
niece
ninety
ninth
noticeable
nuclear
nuisance
numerous

obstacle
occasion
occasionally
occur
occurrence
official
omission
omit
omitted
opponent
opportunity
opposite
ordinarily
originally

paid
panicky
paralleled
particularly
pastime
peaceable
peculiar
pedal
perceive
perception
performance
permanent
permissible
persevere
persistence
personnel
perspiration
persuade
persuasion
petal
physical
pitiful
planning
pleasant
poison
politician
pollute
possession
possibly
practically
practice
prairie
precede
preference
preferred
prejudice
preparation
prevalent
primitive
privilege
probably
procedure
proceed
process
professor
prominent
pronunciation
prophecy
prophesy
psychology
purpose
pursue
pursuit

quandary
quantity
quiet
quizzes

realistically
realize
really
rebel
rebelled
recede
receipt
receive
recognize
recommend
reference
referred
relief
relieve
religious
remembrance
reminisce
renown
repetition
representative
resemblance
resistance
restaurant
rhythm
ridiculous
roommate

sacrifice
sacrilegious
safety
satellite
scarcity
schedule
science
secretary
seize
separate
sergeant
several
sheriff
shining
shoulder
significance
similar
sincerely
sophomore
source

speak
speech
sponsor
stopping
strategy
strength
strenuous
stretch
strict
studying
succeed
successful
sufficient
summary
superintendent
supersede
suppress
surely
surprise
suspicious

technical
technique
temperature
tendency
than
then
thorough
though
throughout
together
tomorrow
tragedy
transferred
truly
twelfth
tyranny

unanimous
unconscious
undoubtedly
unnecessary
until
usually

vacuum
vegetable
vengeance
vicious
villain
visible

weather
Wednesday
weird
wherever
whether
wholly
woman
women
writing

34d
Using the hyphen to form compound words

The hyphen (-) is a mark of punctuation used either to divide a word or to form a compound word. Always use a hyphen to divide a word at the end of a line and continue it on the next line as explained in Chapter 30 on word division. Using a hyphen to form compound words is somewhat more complicated.

Compound words express a combination of ideas. They may be written as a single word, like the noun *breakthrough;* as two words, like the noun *decision making;* or as a hyphenated word, like the noun *cave-in.* Sometimes compound words using the same element are spelled differently—for example, *cross-reference, cross section,* and *crosswalk.* Because of the variations in spelling compound words, you should check a recent edition of a dictionary for current standard spelling. However, several reliable generalizations can be made about using the hyphen for compound adjectives, for fractions and compound numbers, for coined compounds, for certain prefixes and suffixes, and for clarity.

1
Forming compound adjectives

When two or more words serve together as a single modifier before a noun, a hyphen or hyphens form the modifying words clearly into a unit.

She is a *well-known* actor.
The conclusions are based on *out-of-date* statistics.
No *English-speaking* people were in the room.

When the same compound adjectives follow the noun, hyphens are unnecessary and are usually left out.

The actor is *well known.*
The statistics were *out of date.*
Those people are *English speaking.*

Hyphens are also unnecessary in compound modifiers containing an *-ly* adverb, even when these fall before the noun. In a phrase like *clearly defined terms,* the *-ly* in *clearly* serves as a sufficient link between the two parts of the modifier.

When the main part of a compound adjective appears only once in a pair or a series of parallel compound adjectives, hyphens indicate which words the reader should mentally join with the main part.

School-age children should have eight- or nine-o'clock bedtimes.

2 Writing fractions and compound numbers

Hyphens join the numerator and denominator of fractions.

three-fourths
one-half

The whole numbers twenty-one to ninety-nine are always hyphenated regardless of their function or of their position in relation to the noun or verb.

Eighteen girls and twenty-four boys took the bus.
The total is eighty-seven.

3 Forming coined compounds

Writers sometimes create (coin) temporary compounds and join the words with hyphens.

Muhammad Ali gave his opponent a classic come-on-over-here-and-get-me look.

4 Attaching some prefixes and suffixes

Prefixes are usually attached to word stems without hyphens: *predetermine, unnatural, disengage.* However, when the prefix precedes a capitalized word or when a capital letter is combined with a word, a hyphen usually separates the two: *un-American, pre-Eisenhower, non-European, A-frame.* And some prefixes, such as *self-, all-,* and *ex-* (meaning "formerly"), usually require hyphens whether or not they precede capitalized words: *self-control, all-inclusive, ex-student.* The only suffix that regularly requires a hyphen is *-elect,* as in *president-elect.*

A hyphen is sometimes necessary to prevent misreading, especially when a prefix and stem place the same two vowels together or when a stem and suffix place the same three consonants together.

deemphasize, de-emphasize
antiintellectual, anti-intellectual
trilllike, trill-like

Check a recent dictionary for the current form, particularly for words that join two *e*'s or *i*'s. If a word joining two vowels does not appear in the dictionary (either with or without a hyphen), you may assume that it should be hyphenated.

5 Avoiding confusion

If you wrote the sentence *Doonesbury is a comic strip character,* the reader might stumble briefly over your meaning. Is Doonesbury a character in a comic strip or a comic (funny) character who strips? Presumably you would mean the former, but a hyphen would prevent any possible confusion: *Doonesbury is a comic-strip character.*

Adding prefixes to words can sometimes create ambiguity. *Recreation* (*creation* with the prefix *re-*) could mean either "a new creation" or "diverting, pleasurable activity." Using a hyphen, *re-creation,* limits the word to the first meaning. Without a hyphen the word suggests the second meaning.

sp
34d

EXERCISE 6

Insert hyphens as needed in the following compounds. Circle all compounds that are correct as given. Consult a dictionary as needed.

1. reimburse
2. deescalate
3. forty odd soldiers
4. little known bar
5. seven eighths
6. seventy eight
7. happy go lucky
8. preexisting
9. senator elect
10. postwar
11. two and six person cars
12. ex songwriter
13. V shaped
14. reeducate

VIII
Special Writing Assignments

35 *Writing a Research Paper*

A **research paper** is a composition based on investigation and assessment of other people's work rather than solely on your own experiences or observations. Many of the activities in planning and writing a research paper—such as limiting a subject, developing a thesis, and organizing material—are the same as those you follow in writing other kinds of essays (see Chapter 1). But the research paper takes you further, allowing you to study a topic in depth, pursuing your special interest, as you locate, assess, and present what others have written about it.

In preparing a research paper, you will not only add to your store of knowledge but also master several important and practical skills such as using the resources of a library, evaluating sources, drawing on sources to refine and support your opinions, and acknowledging the use you make of others' facts and opinions. In college these skills are essential for the many courses that require research papers. In most kinds of work research skills will help you in the daily activities of investigating and solving problems. And in life outside work, research skills will help you resolve anything from a consumer complaint to a tax question.

Your role in writing a research paper will depend on whether you are assigned a report, an interpretive report, or an analysis. In writing a **report**, you survey, organize, and present the available facts and opinions about a topic (for instance, how lobbyists influence legislators' votes or how a multinational corporation is organized). In writing an **interpretive report**, you examine a range of views on a topic in order to draw your own conclusions (for instance, the ethical dilemmas in using humans as experimental subjects), or you search in varied sources for facts and opinions relevant to your thesis (for instance, that adopted children should, or should not, have access to their birth records). In writing an **analysis**, you isolate an unsolved problem or unanswered question (for instance, the failure of an economics theory to explain a change in the economy or the significance of a repeated image in the work of a poet), and then you attempt to reach a solution or answer through critical evaluation (or analysis) of relevant scholarly sources or of texts such as literary works or historical documents.

As distinct as they are, a report, an interpretive report, and an analysis each contain elements of the other two. To prepare a report on how lobbyists influence legislators' votes, you would have to interpret the facts and analyze the opinions of others to determine their relevance and importance. To prepare an interpretive report on the ethical dilemmas in using humans as experimental subjects, you would have to survey and analyze a range of views to arrive at your own conclusion. And to prepare an analysis of a repeated image in a poet's work, you would have to survey and interpret a range of poems and pertinent critical works by others.

Because the three kinds of papers overlap, the research and writing process described in this chapter can generally be applied to any one of them. Throughout the chapter we will follow the development of research papers by two students, Paul Fuller and Ann Weiss. Fuller's work, on an interpretive report, receives somewhat more attention; Weiss's work, on an analysis, enters the discussion whenever her process differed significantly from Fuller's. Both students followed the same basic process, however. Broken down into stages, the process unfolds as follows:

1. Find and limit a researchable topic (p. 464).
2. Find information on the topic and read to refine the topic further (p. 467).
3. Make a working bibliography (p. 480).
4. Read to strengthen your overview of the topic and work up a tentative thesis sentence and outline (p. 493).
5. Take detailed notes (p. 497).
6. Revise the thesis sentence and write a formal outline (p. 502).
7. Write and revise the paper (p. 505).
8. Prepare the list of works cited (p. 510).
9. Cite your sources (p. 511).

As this list implies, a research paper, like any other essay, evolves gradually. While you do research, your reading leads you to organize ideas. And while you organize ideas, you discover where you need to do more research. You begin to limit your topic as soon as you have chosen it, and you continue to limit it as you progress. The working thesis and outline you develop must later be refined. If you anticipate changes like these and allow time for them within the span of your assignment of perhaps four to six weeks, writing a research paper will be straightforward and rewarding.

35a

Finding and limiting a researchable topic

Before reading this section, you may want to review the suggestions for finding and limiting an essay topic described in Chapter 1. Generally, the same procedure applies to writing any kind of research paper: take a subject assigned to you, or think of one that interests you, and narrow it to manageable dimensions by making it specific. However, as this section will show, selecting and limiting a topic for a research paper does present special opportunities and problems.

Paul Fuller and Ann Weiss took slightly different approaches to finding and limiting their topics. For a composition course, Fuller's instructor assigned an interpretive report on any topic of particular interest to the writer. Since he was currently enjoying a course in marketing, Fuller decided to take that broad subject as his starting point. He first divided the subject into several others that also interested him: product development, advertising, wholesaling, and retail sales. He asked himself questions about each of these —such as who performs each function and what its goals and methods are—to arrive at the one function that he most wanted to learn about. Choosing advertising, he then listed several topics suggested by his questions, such as advertising's use of the mass media, the role of advertising agencies, the effect of advertising on consumers, and the case history of a single advertising campaign. Again, Fuller asked himself questions about each of these to narrow his focus and thus choose a specific path for investigation. Some of the questions he posed about advertising and consumers seemed promising: "Do commercials give a product a recognizable personality?" "How do advertisers persuade consumers?" "What do consumers think of commercials?" He finally settled on the second—"How do advertisers persuade consumers?"—as the topic with which to begin his research. Diagrammed, Fuller's narrowing of his subject looks like this:

- *Marketing*
  - Product development
  - *Advertising*
    - Using mass media
    - Advertising agencies
    - *Effect of advertising on consumers*
      - Do commercials give a product a recognizable personality?
      - *How do advertisers persuade consumers?*
      - What do consumers think of commercials?
    - An advertising campaign
  - Wholesaling
  - Retail sales

In developing a topic for an analysis paper assigned in a composition course, Ann Weiss followed a somewhat different procedure. Instead of starting with a general subject, as Fuller did, Weiss began by looking for an unresolved question, interesting problem, or disagreement among the experts in some field of study. She remembered a chapter on the evolution of the Declaration of Independence in an anthology used in her composition class (*Readings in the Arts and Sciences,* edited by Elaine P. Maimon et al.). The chapter mentioned disagreement among historians about the sources of Thomas Jefferson's ideas in his draft of the Declaration, and Weiss decided to pursue this dispute by consulting one of the recent books mentioned as a source in the chapter. Scanning this book, she discovered an additional disagreement over whether Jefferson's draft of the Declaration was improved as it underwent extensive revision in the Continental Congress before it was signed. This issue was more interesting to Weiss than the one about Jefferson's sources, in part because it gave her a chance to analyze the revisions of the Declaration in more detail than had been possible in her composition class. Like Fuller, Weiss framed the issue as a question that would guide her research: "Was Jefferson's Declaration improved by the Continental Congress?"

Though their approaches differed, both Fuller and Weiss arrived at topics that satisfied four main requirements of a topic for a research paper. First, both students could expect to find ample published sources of information. The topics were not too recent, as the latest medical breakthrough or yesterday's news item would be, so others would have had a chance to produce evidence, weigh it, and publish their conclusions. Nor were the topics so removed geographically that the sources on it would be inaccessible, as they might be for someone in Ohio writing about a minor event in California history.

Second, each topic was suited to the kind of paper assigned. Fuller could research his topic in a variety of sources to present the range of facts and opinions necessary for an interpretive report. And Weiss could do the close reading of sources (historians' works as well as the Declaration itself) required for an analysis. In contrast, topics that require only personal opinion and experience, such as "How I see housewives being depicted in detergent commercials," might be suitable for a personal essay but not for any kind of research paper. Nor is a topic suitable if it requires research in only one source. For this reason straight factual biographies of well-known people and how-to topics such as "Making lenses for eyeglasses" generally make poor research subjects. (The only exception is the literary paper in which you analyze a single work such as a novel. But most literary *research* papers require consulting the published opinions of other critics as well.)

The third requirement satisfied by Fuller's and Weiss's topics is that they promised to foster the objective assessment of sources that would lead to defensible conclusions. Even when a research paper is intended to be argumentative, the success of the argument will depend on the balanced presentation of all points of view. Controversial topics that rest on belief, dogma, or prejudice—such as "When human life begins" or "Why women (or men) are superior"—are certainly arguable, but they are risky because the writer's preconceptions can easily slant either the research itself or the conclusions.

Fourth, and finally, Fuller's and Weiss's topics suited the length of papers they were assigned (1500 to 2000 words, or about six to eight pages) and the amount of time they were given to prepare the papers (four weeks). In six to eight pages Fuller could not have covered one of his broader topics, such as "The effect of advertising on consumers," because he would have needed to deal with so many aspects of the relation (as suggested by the three questions he came up with) that he could not have explored any one aspect fully. Such a broad topic would also have required research in so many sources (including the writings not only of advertising specialists and psychologists but also of consumers and consumer representatives) that Fuller might have needed months, not weeks, to complete his research. The same would be true of the topic Weiss originally considered: the sources of Jefferson's ideas in his draft of the Declaration. To treat this topic, Weiss would have had to analyze not only the conflicting opinions of historians but also the actual works they named as Jefferson's sources.

EXERCISE 1

Choose three of the following subjects and narrow each one to at least one topic suitable for beginning library work on a research paper. Or list and then limit three subjects of your own that you would enjoy investigating. (This exercise can be the first step in a research paper project that continues through Exercises 2, 5, 6, 9, 11, 13, 14, and 15.)

1. the United States and Latin America
2. the Opium War
3. dance in America
4. the history of women's suffrage
5. food additives
6. illegal aliens in the United States
7. exploration of outer space
8. the nuclear protest movement
9. the effect of television on professional sports
10. child abuse
11. the modern automobile engine
12. recent developments in cancer research
13. computer piracy
14. Social Security

15. the European exploration of North America before Columbus
16. hazardous substances in the workplace
17. the tax-exempt status of religious organizations
18. science fiction
19. irrigation rights
20. water pollution
21. women writers
22. the history of child labor practices
23. comic film actors
24. the best work of a prominent writer
25. genetic engineering
26. heroes and heroines in modern fiction
27. computers and the privacy of the individual
28. gothic or romance novels in the nineteenth and twentieth centuries
29. the social responsibility of business
30. trends in popular music

35b

Finding information on the topic and reading to refine the topic further

When you go to the library with a topic to investigate, you will have access to three main kinds of sources, all discussed in this section: reference books, periodicals, and general books. Reference books are good sources for either a summary of a topic or information on where to find out about the topic (see below). Periodicals (magazines, journals, and newspapers) contain articles that usually provide detailed and current information on the topic (see p. 474). General books, which constitute the bulk of a library's collection and are usually available for circulation, include literary works, nonfiction surveys, and in-depth studies of a vast range of subjects (see p. 477). Your library may also provide computerized indexes that simplify the search for sources (see p. 479). If you are unsure of how to locate or use your library's resources, ask a reference librarian. A reference librarian is very familiar with all the library's resources and with general and specialized research techniques, and it is his or her job to help you and others with research. Even very experienced researchers often consult reference librarians.

Much information for a brief research paper will appear in **secondary sources,** works that report and analyze information drawn from other sources. Whenever possible, however, you should also seek **primary sources,** which include works of literature as well as historical documents (letters, diaries, speeches, and the like) that provide eyewitness accounts of an issue, event, or period. Primary sources may also include your own interviews, experiments, observations, or correspondence. (Both Ann Weiss and Paul Fuller were able to use primary sources in their research papers. Weiss used a paragraph of the Declaration of Independence showing the editing of Jefferson's draft, which she found in Jefferson's notes on the proceedings in the Continental Congress. See p. 552. Fuller used his own survey of magazine advertisements. See p. 540.)

1
Using reference books

Reference books available in the library include encyclopedias, dictionaries, digests, bibliographies, indexes, atlases, almanacs, and handbooks. Although your research must go beyond these sources, they can help you decide whether your topic really interests you and whether it meets the requirements for a research paper (pp. 465–66). Preliminary research in reference books will also direct you to more detailed sources on your topic. For an analysis paper, a specialized encyclopedia or bibliography can identify the controversies in a field, the main issues involved, and the proponents of each side.

Paul Fuller's use of reference books illustrates how helpful such sources can be as a starting point. Fuller first consulted a general encyclopedia and skimmed the article on advertising. He learned that most advertisements are meant not so much to persuade consumers to buy as to make them aware that products exist. The article also mentioned that consumers often buy for irrational reasons and that advertisers' research into motivation has taught them to include in their ads scientific-sounding claims and symbols of comfort, sex, love of family, and so on. Fuller decided he could narrow his topic to the use of such nonrational, emotional appeals in advertising. He then consulted the *Encyclopedia of Advertising,* where he found references to several books, including *The Hidden Persuaders* and *Motivation in Advertising,* whose titles made them seem promising sources for his topic.

The following list gives the types of reference works and suggests when each may be profitable. Once you have a topic, you can scan this list for a reference book with which to start. If you want a more comprehensive catalog and explanation of reference works, consult Eugene P. Sheehy, *Guide to Reference Books,* 9th ed. (Chicago: American Library Assn., 1976; supplement 1980).

General encyclopedias

General encyclopedias give brief overviews and brief bibliographies. Because they try to cover all fields, they are a convenient, but very limited, starting point. Be sure to consult the most recent edition.

Collier's Encyclopedia. 24 vols. New York: Macmillan, 1981.
Encyclopedia Americana. 30 vols. New York: Grolier, 1983.
Encyclopedia International. 20 vols. New York: Grolier, 1982.
The New Columbia Encyclopedia. New York: Columbia UP, 1975.
The New Encyclopaedia Britannica. 30 vols. Chicago: Encyclopaedia Britannica, 1985.
Random House Encyclopedia. Rev. ed. New York: Random, 1983.

Specialized encyclopedias, dictionaries, bibliographies

A specialized encyclopedia, dictionary, or bibliography generally covers an entire field or subject. These works will give you more detailed and more technical information than a general reference book will, and many of them (especially bibliographies) will direct you to particular books and articles on your subject. One general reference work providing information on sources in many of the fields below is the *Essay and General Literature Index* (New York: Wilson, published since 1900 and now updated semiannually). It lists tens of thousands of articles and essays that appear in books (rather than periodicals) and that might not be listed in other bibliographies and indexes.

Music and the visual arts

Apel, Willi. *The Harvard Dictionary of Music*. 2nd rev. ed. Cambridge: Harvard UP, 1969.
Chujoy, Anatole, and P. W. Manchester. *The Dance Encyclopedia*. New York: Simon, 1978.
Encyclopedia of World Art. 15 vols. New York: McGraw, 1959–68.
Maillard, Robert, ed. *New Dictionary of Modern Sculpture*. Trans. Bettina Wadia. New York: Tudor, 1971.
Moore, Frank L. *Crowell's Handbook of World Opera*. Westport: Greenwood, 1974.
Sadie, Stanley, ed. *The New Grove Dictionary of Music and Musicians*. 20 vols. London: Macmillan, 1980.
Stambler, Irwin. *Encyclopedia of Pop, Rock, and Soul*. New York: St. Martin's, 1977.
Stierlin, Henri. *Encyclopedia of World Architecture*. 2nd ed. New York: Van Nostrand, 1982.
Thompson, Oscar. *International Cyclopedia of Music and Musicians*. 10th ed. Ed. Bruce Bohle. New York: Dodd, 1975.

Business and economics

Buell, Victor P., ed. *Handbook of Modern Marketing*. New York: McGraw, 1970.
Graham, Irvin. *Encyclopedia of Advertising*. 2nd ed. New York: Fairchild, 1969.
Greenwald, Douglas. *The McGraw-Hill Dictionary of Modern Economics*. 3rd ed. New York: McGraw, 1984.

Heyel, Carl. *The Encyclopedia of Management.* 3rd ed. New York: Van Nostrand, 1982.

Munn, Glenn G. *Encyclopedia of Banking and Finance.* 8th ed. Ed. Ferdinand L. Garcia. Boston: Bankers, 1983.

Seidler, Lee J., and Douglas R. Carmichael. *Accountant's Handbook.* 6th ed. 2 vols. New York: Wiley, 1981.

Sloan, Harold S., and Arnold Zurcher. *A Dictionary of Economics.* 5th ed. New York: Barnes, 1970.

History

American Historical Association. *Guide to Historical Literature.* New York: Macmillan, 1961.

Binder, Leonard, ed. *The Study of the Middle East: Research and Scholarship in the Humanities and Social Sciences.* New York: Wiley, 1976.

Cambridge Ancient History. 12 vols. London: Cambridge UP, 1923–39. Revision in progress.

Cambridge Mediaeval History. 9 vols. London: Cambridge UP, 1911–36. Revision in progress.

Fairbank, John K., and Denis Twitchett. *Cambridge History of China.* 14 vols. London: Cambridge UP, 1978–. In progress.

Freidel, Frank, and Richard K. Showman, eds. *Harvard Guide to American History.* Rev. ed. 2 vols. Cambridge: Belknap-Harvard UP, 1974.

Hammond, N. G. L., and H. H. Scullard. *Oxford Classical Dictionary.* 2nd ed. New York: Oxford UP, 1970.

Martin, Michael R., et al. *An Encyclopedia of Latin-American History.* Rev. ed. Westport: Greenwood, 1981.

Miller, Elizabeth W., and Mary Fisher, eds. *The Negro in America: A Bibliography.* Cambridge: Harvard UP, 1970.

New Cambridge Modern History. 14 vols. London: Cambridge UP, 1957–80.

Prucha, Francis P. *A Bibliographical Guide to the History of Indian-White Relations in the United States.* Chicago: U of Chicago P, 1977.

Literature, theater, film, and television

Aaronson, C. S., ed. *International Television Almanac.* New York: Quigley, published annually since 1956.

Adelman, Irving, and R. Dworkin. *Modern Drama: A Checklist of Critical Literature on Twentieth Century Plays.* Metuchen: Scarecrow, 1967.

Benét, William Rose. *The Reader's Encyclopedia.* 2nd ed. New York: Crowell, 1965.

Bukalski, Peter J. *Film Research: A Critical Bibliography with Annotations and Essays.* Boston: Hall, 1972.

Hart, James D., ed. *The Oxford Companion to American Literature.* 5th ed. New York: Oxford UP, 1983.

Hartnoll, Phyllis, ed. *The Oxford Companion to the Theatre.* 4th ed. New York: Oxford UP, 1983.

Harvey, Paul, and Dorothy Eagle, eds. *The Oxford Companion to English Literature.* 4th ed. New York: Oxford UP, 1967.

Holman, C. Hugh. *A Handbook to Literature.* 4th ed. Indianapolis: Bobbs, 1980.

MLA International Bibliography of Books and Articles on the Modern Languages and Literatures. New York: Mod. Lang. Assn., published annually since 1922.

Schweik, Robert C., and Dieter Riesner. *Reference Sources in English and American Literature: An Annotated Bibliography.* New York: Norton, 1977.

Spiller, Robert E. *Literary History of the United States: Bibliography.* New York: Macmillan, 1974.

Trent, W. P., et al. *Cambridge History of American Literature.* New York: Macmillan, 1943.

Ward, A. W., and A. R. Waller, eds. *The Cambridge History of English Literature,* 15 vols. New York: Putnam's, 1907–33.

Watson, G., ed. *New Cambridge Bibliography of English Literature.* 4 vols. New York: Cambridge UP, 1972–76.

Philosophy and religion

Broderick, Robert, ed. *The Catholic Encyclopedia.* New York: Nelson, 1981.

Buttrick, George Arthur, and Keith R. Crim. *The Interpreter's Dictionary of the Bible.* 5 vols. Nashville: Abingdon, 1976.

Cross, F. L., and Elizabeth A. Livingston. *The Oxford Dictionary of the Christian Church.* New York: Oxford UP, 1974.

Edwards, Paul, ed. *The Encyclopedia of Philosophy.* 4 vols. New York: Free, 1973.

Ferm, Vergilius, ed. *An Encyclopedia of Religion.* Westport: Greenwood, 1976.

Rice, Edward. *Eastern Definitions: A Short Encyclopedia of Religions of the Orient.* Garden City: Doubleday, 1978.

Roth, Cecil, ed. *The New Standard Jewish Encyclopedia.* 5th ed. Ed. Geoffrey Wigoder, Garden City: Doubleday, 1977.

Social sciences

Brock, Clifton. *The Literature of Political Science.* New York: Bowker, 1969.

Eysenck, Hans Jurgen, ed. *Encyclopedia of Psychology.* 2nd ed. New York: Continuum, 1979.

Foreign Affairs Bibliography. 5 vols. New York: Bowker, 1960–76.

Leach, Maria, et al., eds. *Funk and Wagnalls Standard Dictionary of Folklore, Mythology and Legend.* 2 vols. New York: Crowell, 1972.

Mitchell, G. Duncan, ed. *A New Dictionary of the Social Sciences.* Chicago: Aldine, 1979.

Mitzel, Harold, ed. *Encyclopedia of Educational Research.* 5th ed. 4 vols. New York: Macmillan, 1982.

Sills, David L., ed. *International Encyclopedia of the Social Sciences.* 8 vols. plus supplement. New York: Free, 1977.

UNESCO International Committee for Social Science Documentation, ed. *International Bibliography of the Social Sciences.* New York: Methuen, 1960–78.

White, Carl M., et al. *Sources of Information in the Social Sciences: A Guide to the Literature.* 2nd ed. Chicago: American Library Assn., 1973.

Winick, Charles. *Dictionary of Anthropology.* Totowa: Littlefield, 1977.

SCIENCES

Belzer, Jack, et al., eds. *Encyclopedia of Computer Science and Technology.* 14 vols. New York: Dekker, 1975–80.

Fairbridge, Rhodes W., ed. *The Encyclopedia of Oceanography.* New York: Academic, 1966.

Gray, Peter. *The Encyclopedia of Biological Sciences.* 2nd ed. Melbourne: Krieger, 1981.

Hampel, Clifford A., and Gessner G. Hawley, eds. *The Encyclopedia of Chemistry.* 3rd ed. New York: Van Nostrand, 1973.

Jobes, Gertrude, and James Jobes. *Outer Space: Myths, Names, Meanings, Calendars.* Metuchen: Scarecrow, 1980.

The Larousse Encyclopedia of Animal Life. London: Hamlyn, 1967.

The McGraw-Hill Encyclopedia of Science and Technology. 5th ed. 15 vols. New York: McGraw, 1982.

Sarton, George. *An Introduction to the History of Science.* 5 vols. Melbourne: Krieger, 1927–75.

Thewlis, J., ed. *Encyclopaedic Dictionary of Physics.* 9 vols. plus supplements. Elmsford: Pergamon, 1961–75.

Unabridged dictionaries and special dictionaries on language

Unabridged dictionaries are more comprehensive than abridged or college dictionaries. Special dictionaries give authoritative information on individual aspects of language. (See Chapter 32 for more on the kinds of dictionaries and how to use them.)

UNABRIDGED DICTIONARIES

Craigie, Sir William, and James R. Hulbert. *A Dictionary of American English on Historical Principles.* 4 vols. Chicago: U of Chicago P, 1938–44.

The Oxford English Dictionary. 13 vols. plus supplements. New York: Oxford UP, 1933–76. *The Compact Edition,* 2 vols., was issued in 1971.

The Random House Dictionary of the English Language. New York: Random, 1981.

Webster's Third New International Dictionary of the English Language. Springfield: Merriam, 1976.

SPECIAL DICTIONARIES

Follett, Wilson. *Modern American Usage.* Ed. Jacques Barzun. New York: Hill, 1966.
Fowler, H. W. *Dictionary of Modern English Usage.* 2nd ed. Rev. and ed. Sir Ernest Gowers. New York: Oxford UP, 1965.
Lewis, Norman. *The New Roget's Thesaurus of the English Language in Dictionary Form.* New York: Putnam's, 1978.
Onions, Charles T., et al., eds. *The Oxford Dictionary of English Etymology.* New York: Oxford UP, 1966.
Partridge, Eric. *A Dictionary of Slang and Unconventional English.* 8th ed. Ed. Paul Beale. New York: Macmillan, 1984.
Partridge, Eric. *Origins: A Short Etymological Dictionary of Modern English.* New York: Macmillan, 1977.
Webster's New Dictionary of Synonyms. Springfield: Merriam, 1984.
Wentworth, Harold, and Stuart Berg Flexner. *Dictionary of American Slang.* 2nd supp. ed. New York: Crowell, 1975.

Biographical reference works

If you want to learn about someone's life, achievements, credentials, or position, or if you want to learn the significance of a name you've come across, consult one of these reference works.

American Men and Women of Science. 15th ed. 7 vols. New York: Bowker, 1982.
Contemporary Authors. 105 vols. Detroit: Gale, 1967–82.
Current Biography. New York: Wilson, published annually since 1940.
Dictionary of American Biography. 16 vols. plus supplements. New York: Scribner's, 1927–81.
Dictionary of Literary Biography. 38 vols. plus supplements. Detroit: Gale, published since 1978 and frequently updated and enlarged.
Dictionary of National Biography (British). 22 vols. plus supplements. New York: Oxford UP, 1882–1972.
James, Edward T., and Janet W. James, eds. *Notable American Women.* 3 vols. Cambridge: Belknap-Harvard UP, 1971–80.
Webster's Biographical Dictionary. Springfield: Merriam, 1972.
Who's Who in America. 2 vols. Chicago: Marquis, published biennially since 1899.

Atlases and gazetteers

Atlases are bound collections of maps; gazetteers are geographical dictionaries.

Columbia Lippincott Gazetteer of the World. New York: Columbia UP, 1962.

Cosmopolitan World Atlas. Chicago: Rand, 1981.
Encyclopaedia Britannica World Atlas International. Chicago: Encyclopaedia Britannica, 1969.
National Geographic Atlas of the World. 5th ed. Washington: National Geographic, 1981.
The Times Atlas of the World. 2nd rev. ed. Boston: Houghton, 1983.

Almanacs and yearbooks

Both almanacs and yearbooks are annual compilations of facts. Yearbooks record information about the previous year. Almanacs give facts and statistics about a variety of fields.

Americana Annual. New York: Americana, published annually since 1923.
Britannica Book of the Year. Chicago: Encyclopaedia Britannica, published annually since 1938.
Facts on File Yearbook. New York: Facts on File, published annually since 1940.
U.S. Bureau of the Census. *Statistical Abstract of the United States*. Washington: GPO, published annually since 1878.
World Almanac and Book of Facts. New York: World-Telegram, published annually since 1868.

2
Using indexes to periodicals

Periodicals—journals, magazines, and newspapers—are invaluable sources of information in research. The difference between journals and magazines lies primarily in their content, readership, frequency of issue, and page numbering. Magazines, such as *Psychology Today, Newsweek*, and *Esquire*, are nonspecialist publications intended for diverse readers. Most magazines appear weekly or monthly. Journals, in contrast, often appear quarterly and contain specialized information intended for readers in a particular field. Examples include *American Anthropologist, Journal of Black Studies*, and *Journal of Chemical Education*. In most magazines the page numbering begins anew with each issue. Many journals also page each issue separately, but others do not. Instead, the issues for an entire year make up an annual volume, and the pages are numbered continuously throughout the volume, so that issue number 3 (the third issue of the year) may open on page 327. (The method of pagination determines how you cite a journal article in a list of works cited and, if you use them, in footnotes or endnotes; see pp. 486 and 522.)

Several guides provide information on the articles in journals, magazines, and newspapers. The contents, formats, and systems of abbreviation in these guides vary widely, and they can be daunting at first glance. But each one includes in its opening pages an introduction and explanation to aid the inexperienced user. (See also p. 479 on using computerized data bases for locating articles in periodicals.)

A typical and general periodical guide is the *Readers' Guide to Periodical Literature,* published since 1900 and updated semimonthly. It lists—by author, title, and subject—articles published each year in more than a hundred popular magazines. For a paper on a current topic you should consult at least several years' *Readers' Guide* volumes. Paul Fuller, checking the volumes as far back as the one for March 1977–February 1978, found one potentially useful article under the main heading "Advertising" and the subheading "Psychological aspects." (Only a quarter of the "Advertising" entries in that volume of the *Readers' Guide* are reproduced here.)

ADVERTISING

Art director who has a way with words also has a book coming from Abrams; publication of The art of advertising; interview, ed by R. Dahlin. G. Lois. Pub W 211:55+ Ja 17 '77

Giving impact to ideas; address, October 11, 1977. L. T. Hagopian. Vital Speeches 44:154-7 D 15 '77

News behind the ads. See alternate issues of Changing times

Preaching in the marketplace. America 136:457 My 21 '77

Selling it. Consumer Rep 42:385, 458, 635 Jl-Ag, N '77

See also

Photography in advertising
Religious advertising
Television advertising
Women in advertising

also subhead Advertising under various subjects, e.g. Books—Advertising

Awards, prizes, etc.

Saturday review's 23rd annual Advertising Awards. C. Tucker. il Sat R 4:34-5 Jl 23 '77

Laws and regulations

Crackdown ahead on advertising: what the government plans next; interview. M. Pertschuk. pors U.S. News 83:70-2 O 17 '77

FTC broadens its attack on ads. Bus W p27-8 Je 20 '77

Moral aspects

See Advertising ethics

Psychological aspects

Art of implying more than you say; work of Richard Harris. S. Bush. Psychol Today 10:36+ My '77

Genderisms; reinforcement of sex role stereotypes. E. Goffman. il Psychol Today 11:60-3 Ag '77

Rates

Challenge to ad discounts; effect on small retailers of rate structure used in newspaper and magazine advertising. il Bus W p 146 S 19 '77

Drop in TV viewing, but not in ad pricing. il Bus W p33-4 Ja 16 '78

Other general indexes to periodicals include the following:

The New York Times Index. New York: New York Times/Bowker, published annually since 1913. This index to the most complete U.S. newspaper can serve as a guide to national and international events and can indicate what issues of unindexed newspapers to consult for local reactions to such events.

Poole's Index to Periodical Literature. Boston: Houghton, 1802–1907. An index by subject to British and American periodicals of the nineteenth century.

Popular Periodicals Index. Camden: Popular Periodicals, published annually since 1973. An index to about twenty-five contemporary, popular periodicals not listed in major indexes.

Many special indexes and indexes to scholarly articles are available in most libraries. The following is a partial list.

America: History and Life. Santa Barbara: ABC-Clio, published three times a year since 1964.

Applied Science and Technology Index. New York: Wilson, published monthly since 1958. From 1913 to 1957 this work was combined with the *Business Periodicals Index* in the *Industrial Arts Index.*

Art Index. New York: Wilson, published quarterly since 1929.

Biological Abstracts. Philadelphia: Biological Abstracts, published semimonthly since 1926.

Biological and Agricultural Index. New York: Wilson, published monthly since 1964. From 1916 to 1963 this work was called the *Agricultural Index.*

Business Periodicals Index. New York: Wilson, published annually since 1958. From 1913 to 1957 this work was combined with the *Applied Science and Technology Index* in the *Industrial Arts Index.*

The Education Index. New York: Wilson, published monthly since 1929.

General Sciences Index. New York: Wilson, published monthly since 1978.

Humanities Index. New York: Wilson, published quarterly since 1974. From 1965 to 1974 this author and subject index was combined with the *Social Sciences Index* in the *Social Sciences and Humanities Index.* From 1907 to 1965 the combined volume was called the *International Index.*

Index Medicus. Washington: National Library of Medicine, published monthly since 1960. From 1927 to 1959 this work was called *Quarterly Cumulative Index Medicus.* From 1899 to 1926 it was *Index Medicus.*

MLA International Bibliography of Books and Articles in the Modern Languages and Literatures. New York: Mod. Lang. Assn., published annually since 1922.

Music Index. Detroit: Information Service, published monthly since 1950.

Philosopher's Index. Bowling Green: Bowling Green U, published quarterly since 1967.

Psychological Abstracts. Washington: American Psychological Assn., published monthly since 1927.

Science Citation Index. Philadelphia: Inst. for Scientific Information, published quarterly since 1961.

Social Sciences Index. New York: Wilson, published quarterly since 1974. From 1965 to 1974 this author and subject index was combined with the *Humanities Index* in the *Social Sciences and Humanities Index.* From 1907 to 1965 the combined volume was called the *International Index.*

Every library lists its complete periodical holdings either in the main catalog (see below) or in a separate catalog. The listing for each periodical tells how far back the issues go and where and in what form the issues are stored. The recent issues of a periodical are usually held in the library's periodical room. Back issues are usually stored elsewhere, in one of three forms: in bound volumes; on **microfilm,** a filmstrip showing pages side by side; or on **microfiche,** a sheet of film with pages arranged in rows and columns. Consulting periodicals stored on microfilm or microfiche requires using a special machine, or "reader," that locates and enlarges the page and projects it on a screen. Any member of the library's staff will show you how to operate the reader.

3
Using guides to books

The library's catalog lists books alphabetically by authors' names, titles of books, and subjects. (In some catalogs authors and titles are alphabetized together and subjects are alphabetized separately.) If you are starting research on a subject you don't know very well, begin by looking under subject headings. If you know of an expert in the field and you want to find his or her books, look under the author's name. If you know the title of a relevant book but not the author's name, look for the title.

The library's card catalog may be the familiar card file, cabinets of drawers containing 3″ × 5″ cards. But to save space and time, many libraries have converted their catalogs to other forms. A printed catalog in bound volumes contains small reproductions of the cards traditionally found in drawers. A catalog on microfilm or microfiche (see above) shows the library's collection on film viewed with a special reader. Increasingly, libraries are computerizing their catalogs: the user gains access to the computer's memory by typing a code onto a keyboard, and a screen displays the requested information. (With many computerized catalogs, the user can conduct a customized search through the library's holdings. See p. 479.)

If you are uncertain about the location, form, or use of your library's catalog, seek help from a member of the library's staff.

Though the storage systems vary, all book catalogs contain similar information and follow a similar organization. By far the most widely used catalog format is that of the Library of Congress card. Here are samples of author, title, and subject cards.

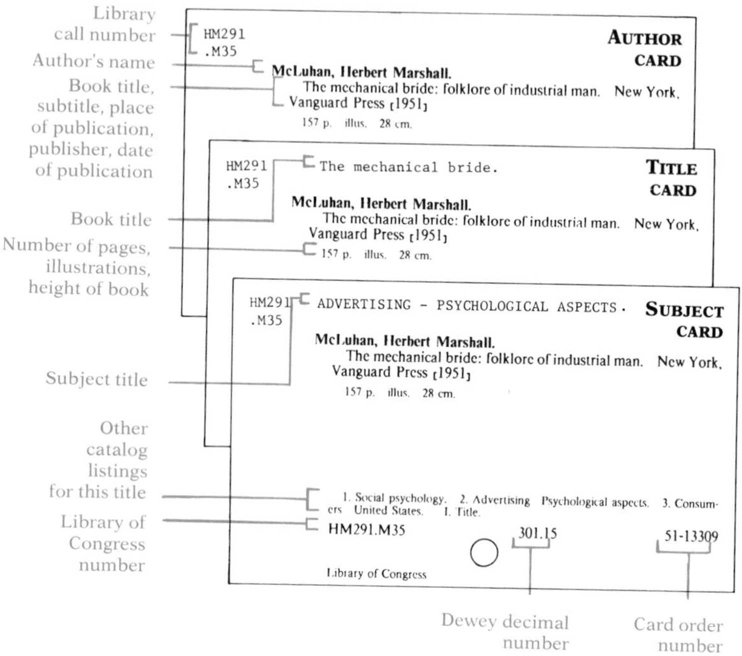

Two types of reference books can help you identify general books that have information about your topic: publishing bibliographies and digests. Publishing bibliographies tell whether a book is still in print, whether a paperback edition is available, what books were published on a certain topic in a certain year, and so on. These bibliographies include the following:

Books in Print. New York: Bowker, published and supplemented annually since 1873. Books indexed by author, title, and subject.

Cumulative Book Index. New York: Wilson, published monthly since 1898.

Paperbound Books in Print. New York: Bowker, published semi-annually since 1955.

You might, for example, want to know if the author of an encyclopedia article has published any relevant books since the date of the encyclopedia. You could look up the author's name in the latest *Books in Print* to find out.

If you want to evaluate a book's relevance to your topic before you search for it, you can consult the *Book Review Digest* (New York: Wilson, published annually since 1905). This digest tells you where to find reviews of current books and summarizes reviews. Another general digest is *Book Review Index* (Detroit: Gale, published annually since 1965). There are also digests for separate subjects, such as *Recent Publications in the Social and Behavioral Sciences* (New York: American Behavioral Scientists, published annually). Again, the reference librarian is the best source of information on the availability and location of sources.

4
Using computerized data bases

Libraries that use computers to store information about their holdings often provide researchers with a quick and effective way to find relevant sources. Either alone or with the aid of a staff member, the researcher gives the computer one or more key words about the topic, and the computer then consults its data base (its entire list of references) to produce a customized list of sources that have been indexed under the key word or words.

The kinds of computerized data bases and the specific search procedures vary widely from library to library. In some libraries only the catalog of general books can be used for a key-word search. The researcher can generally work unaided, following simple instructions on the computer screen. Other libraries have additional, more specialized data bases that index articles in periodicals, government documents, unpublished materials, and other resources. To search these data bases, the researcher often must enlist the help of a staff member, and the library may charge a fee for the service. Ask at your library to learn the resources available to you and the procedures you must follow.

The efficiency and reliability of a data-base search will be determined largely by the key word or words you give the computer. If a term is too general, it may turn up a long list of sources with only a tiny proportion relevant to your topic. If the term is too specific, it may turn up a too-short list or nothing at all. If Paul Fuller searched a computerized book catalog using the general word "advertising," the computer would show him every book in the library indexed under the word—a long list. If, in contrast, he used the specific phrase "persuasion of consumers in advertising," the computer would show him only the few sources (if any) it could find that were indexed under all three important words in the phrase.

Appropriate key words may often be found in the multivolume *Library of Congress Subject Headings,* a list of the various headings under which the Library of Congress catalogs books. Consulting this source and following its system of cross-references and headings at different levels of specificity, Fuller would discover several phrases, including "advertising—psychological aspects," that the computer could match up with likely sources. *Library of Congress Subject Headings* can help with searches in other data bases besides a book catalog, though some data bases have their own indexes as well. Note that *Library of Congress Subject Headings* and some other indexes do not include most proper names of people, places, corporations, associations, government bodies, and the like.

EXERCISE 2

List at least five sources you can consult for further leads on each of the three topics you produced in Exercise 1 (p. 466) or for three other topics. Use the information provided in the preceding section and additional information at your library.

35c

Making a working bibliography

1

Keeping systematic records of sources

Trying to pursue every source lead as you came across it would prove inefficient and probably ineffective. Instead, you'll want to find out what is available before deciding which leads to follow, and that requires systematically keeping track of where information is and what it is. You can keep track of sources by making a working bibliography, a card file of the books, articles, and other sources you believe will help you. When you have a substantial card file of material, you can decide which sources seem most promising and look them up first.

A working bibliography records all the information you need to find the source. Putting each source on an individual 3″ × 5″ card will allow you to arrange your sources alphabetically by author, to discard irrelevant sources without disrupting your list, and later to transfer the information easily to your final list of sources.

bib 35c

Make a bibliography card for each source you think may be useful, whether you find it in the card catalog, in a reference book, or in an index to periodicals. Include all the information you will need for your final list of sources, using standard formats such as those discussed below. Getting all the information the first time will save you from having to retrace your steps later. For sources you find in the catalog of books, list every letter and number of the call number on the bibliography card to save time later. (However, you will not transfer the call number to the final list of sources.) Here are two examples of bibliography cards, the first for a book and the second for a periodical.

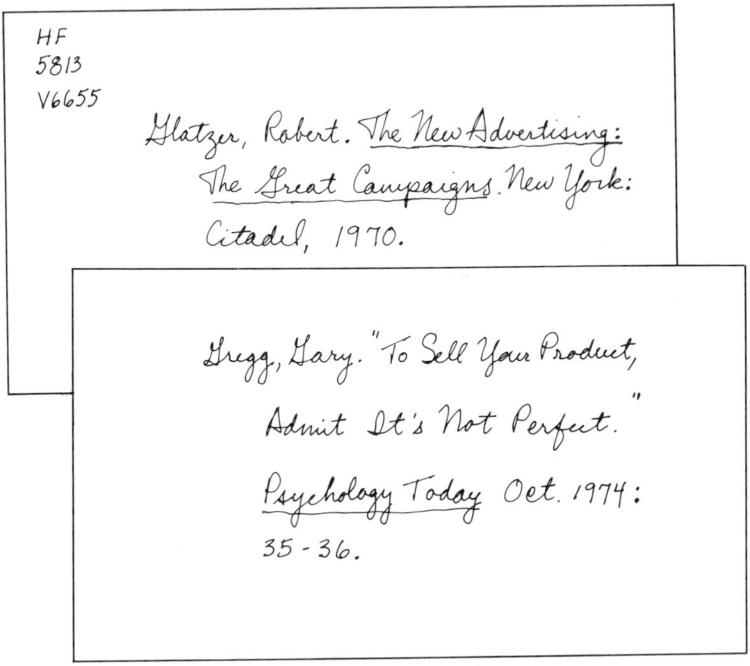
HF
5813
V6655
Glatzer, Robert. The New Advertising: The Great Campaigns. New York: Citadel, 1970.
Gregg, Gary. "To Sell Your Product, Admit It's Not Perfect." Psychology Today Oct. 1974: 35-36.

Listed below are some of the standard guides to the format of bibliographic entries and source citations. Except for the first two general works, each guide is published for a particular academic discipline. All the guides recommend formats that encourage the writer to include all the information needed for someone else to check the source. But the formats differ in the amount, arrangement, and punctuation of information. Your instructor will tell you which guide you should follow.

The Chicago Manual of Style. 13th ed. Chicago: U of Chicago P, 1982.

Turabian, Kate L. *A Manual for Writers of Term Papers, Theses, and Dissertations*. 4th ed. Chicago: U of Chicago P, 1973.

CBE Style Manual. 5th ed. Bethesda: Council of Biology Editors, 1983.

Handbook for Authors. Washington: American Chemical Soc., 1978.

MLA Handbook for Writers of Research Papers. 2nd ed. New York: Mod. Lang. Assn., 1984.

Publication Manual of the American Psychological Association. 3rd ed. Washington: American Psychological Assn., 1983.

Style Manual for Guidance in the Preparation of Papers. 3rd ed. New York: American Inst. of Physics, 1978.

The following sections discuss two standard bibliographic formats: that of the *MLA Handbook* (below) and that of the American Psychological Association (p. 491). A final section lists abbreviations commonly used or found in references to sources (p. 492).

2
Using MLA bibliographic formats

The bibliographic models below are based on the *MLA Handbook*, the standard guide in the study of English and widely accepted in other disciplines as well. Note that models may have to be combined; for example, in citing an article by four authors appearing in a biweekly periodical, you will need to draw on the models below labeled "A book with more than three authors" and "A signed article in a weekly or biweekly periodical."

Books

The basic format for a book includes the following information:

```
  ① [Gilligan, Carol.]   ② [In a Different Voice: Psychological Theory and
      Women's Development.]   ③ [Cambridge: Harvard UP, 1982.]
```

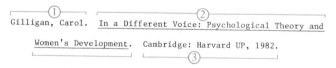

1. The author's full name: the last name first, followed by a comma, and then the first name and any middle name or initial. End the name with a period and two spaces.
2. The full title of the book, including any subtitle. Underline the complete title, capitalize all important words (see 26b), separate the main title and the subtitle with a colon and one space, and end the title with a period and two spaces.
3. The publication information: the city of publication, followed by a colon and one space; then the name of the publisher, followed by a comma; and finally the date of publication, ending with a period. All this information can be found on the title page of the book or on the page after the title page. Shorten most publishers' names—in many cases to a single

word. For instance, use "Knopf" for Alfred A. Knopf and "Little" for Little, Brown. For university presses, use the abbreviation "UP," as in the example above.

When other information is required for a reference, it is generally placed either between the author's name and the title or between the title and the publication information, as specified in the models below.

A BOOK WITH ONE AUTHOR

Gilligan, Carol. In a Different Voice: Psychological Theory and Women's Development. Cambridge: Harvard UP, 1982.

A BOOK WITH TWO OR THREE AUTHORS

Wimsatt, William K., and Cleanth Brooks. Literary Criticism: A Short History. Chicago: U of Chicago P, 1978.

Give the authors' names in the order provided on the title page. Reverse the first and last names of the first author *only,* and separate the authors' names with a comma.

A BOOK WITH MORE THAN THREE AUTHORS

Lopez, Robert S., et al. Civilizations: Western and World. Boston: Little, 1975.

Give the name of the first author only, and follow the name with a comma and the abbreviation "et al." (for the Latin *et alii,* meaning "and others").

A BOOK WITH CORPORATE AUTHORSHIP

Editors of The Progressive. The Crisis of Survival. Glenview: Scott, 1970.

List the name of the corporation, institution, or other body as author.

A LATER EDITION

Bollinger, Dwight L. Aspects of Language. 2nd ed. New York: Harcourt, 1975.

For any edition after the first, place the edition number between the title and the publication information. Use the appropriate designation for editions that are named or dated rather than numbered—for instance "Rev. ed." for "Revised edition."

A REPUBLISHED BOOK

James, Henry. The Golden Bowl. 1904. London: Penguin, 1966.

Place the original date of publication (but not the place of publication or the publisher's name) after the title, and then provide the full publication information for the source you are using.

A WORK IN MORE THAN ONE VOLUME

Lincoln, Abraham. The Collected Works of Abraham Lincoln. Ed. Roy P. Basler. 8 vols. New Brunswick: Rutgers UP, 1953.

Lincoln, Abraham. The Collected Works of Abraham Lincoln. Ed. Roy P. Basler. 8 vols. New Brunswick: Rutgers UP, 1953. Vol. 5.

For a work published in more than one volume, give the total number of volumes regardless of how many you are using. Use an Arabic numeral and the abbreviation "vols.," and place the information after the title (see "8 vols." in the first example). If you use only one volume, add that information at the very end of the entry (see "Vol. 5" in the second example).

A WORK IN A SERIES

Bergman, Ingmar. The Seventh Seal. Modern Film Scripts Series. New York: Simon, 1968.

Place the name of the series (no quotation marks or underlining) after the title.

A BOOK WITH AN EDITOR

Ruitenbeek, Hendrick, ed. Freud as We Knew Him. Detroit: Wayne State UP, 1973.

The abbreviation "ed.," separated from the name by a comma, identifies Ruitenbeek as the editor of the work.

A BOOK WITH AN AUTHOR AND AN EDITOR

Melville, Herman. The Confidence Man: His Masquerade. Ed. Hershel Parker. New York: Norton, 1971.

When citing the work of the author, give his or her name first, and give the editor's name after the title, preceded by "Ed." ("Edited by"). When citing the work of the editor, use the form above for a book with an editor, and give the author's name after the title preceded by "By": "Parker, Hershel, ed. The Confidence Man: His Masquerade. By Herman Melville."

A TRANSLATION

Alighieri, Dante. The Inferno. Trans. John Ciardi. New York: NAL, 1971.

When citing the work of the author, give his or her name first, and give the translator's name after the title, preceded by "Trans." ("Translated by"). When citing the work of the translator, give his or her name first, followed by a comma and "trans.," and give the author's name after the title preceded by "By": "Ciardi, John, trans. The Inferno. By Dante Alighieri."

A SELECTION FROM AN ANTHOLOGY

Twain, Mark. "The War Prayer." The Complete Essays of Mark Twain. Ed. Charles Neider. Garden City: Doubleday, 1963. 679-82.

Give the author and the title of the selection you are citing, placing the title in quotation marks and ending it with a period. Then give the title of the anthology and the name of the editor preceded by "Ed." ("Edited by"). At the end of the entry give the inclusive page numbers for the entire selection, but do not include the abbreviation "pp."

AN ARTICLE OR ESSAY FROM A REPRINTED COLLECTION

Evan, W. M. "Due Process of Law in Military and Industrial Organizations." Administrative Science Quarterly 7 (1962): 187-207. Rpt. in The Managerial Dilemma. Ed. Stephen K. Banks. New York: Interface, 1980. 234-50.

Provide the author and title of the article or essay you are using, placing the title in quotation marks and ending it with a period. Then, unless your instructor specifies otherwise, provide the complete information for the earlier publication of the piece, followed by "Rpt. in" ("Reprinted in") and the information for the source in which you found the piece. If you are not required to provide the earlier publication information, use the format above for a selection from an anthology.

Periodicals: journals, magazines, and newspapers

The basic format for an article from a periodical includes the following information:

```
  ①                  ②
Lever, Janet.  "Sex Differences in the Games Children Play."

     Social Problems 23 (1976): 478-87.
                     ③
```

1. The author's full name: last name first, followed by a comma, and then the first name and any middle name or initial. End the name with a period and two spaces.
2. The full title of the article, including any subtitle. Place the title in quotation marks, capitalize all important words in the title (see 26b), and end the title with a period (inside the final quotation mark) and two spaces.
3. The publication information: the underlined title of the periodical (minus any *A*, *An*, or *The* at the beginning); the volume or issue number (in Arabic numerals); the date of publication, followed by a colon and a space; and the inclusive page numbers of the article (without the abbreviation "pp."). The treatment of volume and issue numbers and publication dates varies depending on the kind of periodical being cited, as the following examples indicate.

A SIGNED ARTICLE IN A JOURNAL WITH CONTINUOUS PAGINATION THROUGHOUT THE ANNUAL VOLUME

Lever, Janet. "Sex Differences in the Games Children Play."
    Social Problems 23 (1976): 478-87.

Give the volume number after the title and place the year of publication in parentheses. (See p. 474 for further explanation of journal pagination.)

A SIGNED ARTICLE IN A JOURNAL THAT PAGES ISSUES SEPARATELY OR THAT NUMBERS ONLY ISSUES, NOT VOLUMES

Boyd, Sarah. "Nuclear Terror." Adaptation to Change 7.4 (1981):
    20-23.

When citing an article in a journal that pages issues separately, use the format above for a journal with continuous pagination, but give the volume number, a period, and the issue number ("7.4"). When citing an article in a journal that numbers only issues, not annual volumes, treat the issue number as if it were a volume number in the preceding format for a journal with continuous pagination. (See p. 474 for further explanation of journal pagination.)

A SIGNED ARTICLE IN A MONTHLY OR BIMONTHLY PERIODICAL

Stein, Harry. "Living with Lies." Esquire Dec. 1981: 23.

Follow the periodical title with the month (abbreviated) and the year of publication. Don't place the date in parentheses, and don't provide a volume or issue number.

A SIGNED ARTICLE IN A WEEKLY OR BIWEEKLY PERIODICAL

Whiteside, Thomas. "Onward and Upward with the Arts (Cable Tele-
vision--Part 1)." New Yorker 20 May 1985: 45-87.

Follow the periodical title with the day, the month (abbreviated), and the year of publication. Don't place the date in parentheses, and don't provide a volume or issue number.

A SIGNED ARTICLE IN A DAILY NEWSPAPER

Gargan, Edward A. "Buffalo Concern Gives Pop Sound to Player
Pianos." New York Times 16 Feb. 1984: B1.

Give the name of the newspaper as it appears on the first page (but without *A, An,* or *The*). Then follow the same format as that above for a weekly or biweekly periodical, with one exception: if the newspaper is divided into lettered or numbered sections, with each section paged separately, provide the section designation before the page number when the newspaper does the same (as in "B1" above), or provide the section designation before the colon when the newspaper does not combine the two in its numbering (as in "sec. 1: 1+" below).

AN UNSIGNED ARTICLE

"The Right to Die." Time 11 Oct. 1976: 101.

"Protests Greet Pope in Holland." Boston Sunday Globe 12 May 1985,
sec. 1: 1+.

Begin the entry for an unsigned article with the title of the article. The page number "1+" indicates that the article does not run on consecutive pages but starts on page 1 and continues later in the issue (in this case, on page 21).

AN EDITORIAL, A LETTER TO THE EDITOR, OR A REVIEW

Ball, George W. "Block That Vietnam Myth." Editorial. New York
Times 19 May 1985: E21.

Don't use quotation marks or underlining for the word "Editorial." For an unsigned editorial, give the title first.

Dowding, Michael. Letter. Economist 5-11 Jan. 1985: 4.

Don't use quotation marks or underlining for the word "Letter."

Dunne, John Gregory. "The Secret of Danny Santiago." Rev. of Famous All over Town, by Danny Santiago. New York Review of Books 16 Aug. 1984: 17-27.

"Rev." is an abbreviation for "Review." The name of the author of the work being reviewed follows the title of the work, a comma, and "by." If the review has no title of its own, then "Rev. of . . ." (without quotation marks) immediately follows the name of the reviewer.

Encyclopedias and almanacs, DICTIONARIES

"Mammoth." The New Columbia Encyclopedia. 1975 ed.

Mark, Herman F. "Polymers." Encyclopaedia Britannica: Macropaedia. 1974.

Give the name of an author only when the article is signed; otherwise, give the title first. If the articles are alphabetized in the reference work, you needn't list the editors of the work itself or any page numbers. For familiar sources like those in the examples, provide only the edition number (if there is one) and the year of publication.

Pamphlets and government documents

Resource Notebook. Washington: Project on Institutional Renewal Through the Improvement of Teaching, 1976.

Most pamphlets can be treated as books. In this example, the pamphlet has no listed author, so the title comes first.

Hawaii. Dept. of Education. Kauai District Schools, Profile 1983-84. Honolulu: Hawaii Dept. of Education, 1983.

United States. Cong. House. Committee on Ways and Means. Medicare Payment for Outpatient Occupational Therapy Services. 98th Cong., 2nd sess. Washington: GPO, 1984.

Unless an author is listed for a government document, give the appropriate agency as author. Provide information in the order illustrated: the name of the government, the name of the agency (which may be abbreviated), and the title and publication information. For a Congressional document (second example), the house and committee involved are given before the title, and the number and session of Congress are given after the title.

Unpublished dissertations and theses

```
Wilson, Stuart M.  "John Stuart Mill as a Literary Critic."
     Diss.  U of Michigan, 1970.
```

The title is quoted rather than underlined. "Diss." stands for "Dissertation." "U of Michigan" is the degree-granting institution.

Musical compositions and works of art

```
Mozart, Wolfgang Amadeus.  Piano Concerto no. 20 in D Minor, K. 466.
```

Don't underline musical compositions identified only by form, number, and key. Do underline titled operas, ballets, and compositions (*Carmen, Sleeping Beauty*).

```
Sargent, John Singer.  Venetian Doorway.  Metropolitan Museum of
     Art, New York.
```

Underline the title of a work of art. Include the name and location of the institution housing the work.

Films and television programs

```
King of America.  Writ. B. J. Merholz.  Music Elizabeth Swados.
     With Larry Atlas, Andreas Katsulas, Barry Miller, and Michael
     Walden.  American Playhouse.  PBS.  WNET, New York.  19 Jan.
     1982.
Allen, Woody, dir.  Manhattan.  With Allen, Diane Keaton, Michael
     Murphy, Meryl Streep, and Anne Byrne.  United Artists, 1979.
```

Generally, place the underlined title first (as in the first example), unless you are citing the work of an individual (second example). After the title, give additional information (writer, lead actors, and so on) as seems appropriate. For a television program, give the series title (if any), the network, and the local station, city, and date. For a film, give the distributor and the date.

Performances

```
Ceremonies in Dark Old Men.  By Lonne Elder.  Dir. Douglas Turner
     Ward.  Theater Four, New York.  15 May 1985.
```

Ozawa, Seiji, cond. Boston Symphony Orch. Concert. Symphony Hall, Boston. 25 Apr. 1982.

As with films and television programs, the title generally comes first unless you are citing the work of an individual (second example). Provide additional information about participants after the title, as well as the theater, city, and date. Note that the orchestra concert in the second example is neither quoted nor underlined.

Recordings

Mitchell, Joni. <u>For the Roses</u>. Asylum, SD 5057, 1972.

Brahms, Johannes. Concerto no. 2 in B-flat, op. 83. Perf. Artur Rubinstein. Cond. Eugene Ormandy. Philadelphia Orch. RCA, RK-1243, 1972.

Begin with the name of the individual whose work you are citing. Then provide the title of the recording (first example) or the title of the work recorded (second example), the names of any artists not already listed, the manufacturer of the recording, the catalog number, and the date.

Interviews

Smithson, Councilman John. Personal interview. 6 Sept. 1985.

Martin, William. Interview. "Give Me That Big Time Religion." <u>Frontline</u>. PBS. WGBH, Boston. 13 Feb. 1984.

Begin with the name of the person interviewed. Then specify "Personal interview" (if you conducted the interview in person), "Telephone interview" (if you conducted the interview over the phone), or "Interview" (if you did not conduct the interview)—without quotation marks or underlining. Finally, provide a date (first example) or other bibliographic information and then a date (second example).

Computer software

bib **35c**

<u>Project Scheduler 5000</u>. Computer software. Scitor, 1984. MS-DOS, 256 KB, disk.

Include the title of the software, the name of the writer (if known), the name of the distributor, and the date. As in this example, you may also provide information about the computer or operating system for which the software is designed, the amount of computer memory it requires, and its format.

3
Using APA or science bibliographic formats

Most of the social sciences and physical sciences employ a bibliographic style that differs from that recommended by the *MLA Handbook*. These other styles differ among themselves, too—for instance, bibliographic entries are sometimes numbered—so you should ask your instructor which one to follow.

The formats recommended by the American Psychological Association (APA), used in many disciplines, are representative of these other styles. Compare the APA models below with those from the *MLA Handbook* on the preceding pages. Note especially differences in the treatment of authors' and publishers' names, the placement and treatment of the date of publication, the capitalization and quotation of titles, and the treatment of volume numbers in journals.

A BOOK WITH ONE AUTHOR

Gilligan, C. (1982). In a different voice: Psychological theory and women's development. Cambridge: Harvard University Press.

A BOOK WITH TWO OR MORE AUTHORS

Lopez, R. S., Barnes, T., Blum, J., & Cameron, R. (1975). Civilizations: Western and world. Boston: Little, Brown.

A LATER EDITION

Bollinger, D. L. (1975). Aspects of language (2nd ed.). New York: Harcourt Brace Jovanovich.

A BOOK WITH AN EDITOR

Ruitenbeek, H. (Ed.). (1973). Freud as we knew him. Detroit: Wayne State University Press.

A SELECTION FROM AN ANTHOLOGY

Twain, M. The war prayer. (1963). In C. Neider (Ed.), The complete essays of Mark Twain. Garden City: Doubleday.

AN ARTICLE IN A JOURNAL

Lever, J. (1976). Sex differences in the games children play. Social Problems, 23, 478-487.

AN ARTICLE IN A MAGAZINE

Stein, H. (1981, December). Living with lies. Esquire, p. 23.

4 Abbreviations

The bibliographic formats illustrated above eliminate many abbreviations. However, they still use some, and you may encounter many more in your reading. The most common abbreviations found in references and source citations appear below.

anon.	anonymous
bk., bks.	book(s)
c., ca.	*circa* ("about"), used with approximate dates
cf.	*confer* ("compare")
ch., chs.	chapter(s)
col., cols.	column(s)
comp., comps.	compiled by, compiler(s)
diss.	dissertation
ed., eds.	edited by, edition(s), editor(s)
et al.	*et alii* ("and others")
ff.	and the following pages, as in pages 17 ff.
ibid.	*ibidem* ("in the same place")
illus.	illustrated by, illustrator, illustration(s)
l., ll.	line(s)
loc. cit.	*loco citato* ("in the place cited")
ms., mss.	manuscript(s)
n., nn.	note(s), as in p. 24, n. 2
n.d.	no date (of publication)
no., nos.	number(s)
n.p.	no place (of publication), no publisher
n. pag.	no pagination
op. cit.	*opere citato* ("in the work cited")
P	Press (UP = University Press)
p., pp.	page(s)
passim	throughout
q.v.	*quod vide* ("which see")
rev.	revised, revision, revised by, review
rpt.	reprint, reprinted
sec.	section
supp., supps.	supplement(s)
trans.	translator, translated by
univ., U	university (UP = University Press)
vol., vols.	volume(s)

bib
35c

EXERCISE 3

Prepare bibliography entries from the following information. Follow the models of the *MLA Handbook* given on pages 482–90 unless your instructor specifies a different style.

1. A book called *Black Voices: An Anthology of Afro-American Literature,* published in 1968 by the New American Library in New York, edited by Abraham Clapham.

2. An article in *Southern Folklore Quarterly*, volume 24, published in 1960. The article is "The New Orleans Voodoo Ritual Dance and Its Twentieth-Century Survivals," written by John Q. Anderson, on pages 135–43. The journal is paged continuously throughout the annual volume.
3. The fifth volume of *The History of Technology*, published in 1958 in London by Oxford University Press, written by Charles Singer, E. J. Holmroyd, A. R. Hall, and Trevor I. Williams.
4. A pamphlet entitled *George Segal*, published in 1979 by the Whitney Museum of American Art in New York.
5. A book by John Bartlett called *Familiar Quotations*, in its fifteenth edition, which was edited by Emily Morison Beck, published in 1980 by Little, Brown and Company in Boston, Massachusetts.

EXERCISE 4

Prepare a working bibliography of at least ten sources for a research paper on one of the following people or on someone of your own choosing. Begin by limiting the subject to a manageable size, focusing on a particular characteristic or achievement of the person. Then consult reference books, periodical indexes, and the library's catalog of books. Record bibliographic information on note cards, using the models of the *MLA Handbook* unless your instructor specifies a different style.

1. John Lennon, or another performer
2. Ronald Reagan, or another politician
3. Emily Dickinson, or another writer
4. Muhammad Ali, or another sports figure
5. Andrew Wyeth, or another artist

EXERCISE 5

Using one of the topics and the possible references for it from Exercise 2 (p. 480), or starting with a different topic and references, prepare a working bibliography of at least ten sources for your developing research paper. List on 3″ × 5″ cards the complete bibliographic information for each source. Use the formats of the *MLA Handbook* unless your instructor specifies a different style.

35d
Reading to strengthen your overview and working up a tentative thesis sentence and outline

When to stop looking for sources and start reading depends, of course, on the assigned length of the paper and on the complexity of your subject. You are probably ready to begin reading when your working bibliography suggests that you have explored most aspects of your topic and have found at least some sources that deal directly with your central concern. For a paper of 1500 to 2000 words, ten to fifteen promising titles should give you a good base.

1 Evaluating sources and reading for ideas

Once you have a satisfactory working bibliography, scan your cards for the sources that are most likely to give you an overview of your topic, and consult those sources first. Paul Fuller, for instance, began by looking at sources on research into motivation as well as more general sources on advertising. Ann Weiss, in contrast, began by looking at some of the sources referred to in the recent book she first consulted when she was searching for her topic. For an analysis paper like Weiss's that examines a disagreement among experts in a field, a recent work by one of the experts often lays out the disagreement and cites the works of others involved in it.

As you glance through your sources, your purpose is to evaluate their usefulness and to shape your thinking, not to collect information. A source is potentially useful to you if it is relevant to your topic and if it is reliable. Scanning the introductions to books and articles and the tables of contents and indexes of books can help you determine whether a source is relevant. Reliability is more difficult to judge. Look for information about the author's background. Once you are satisfied that the author has sufficient expertise in your subject, try to determine whether he or she might be biased. For instance, a book on parapsychology by someone identified as the president of the National Organization of Psychics may contain an authoritative explanation of psychic powers, but the author's view is likely to be biased. It should be balanced by research in other sources whose authors are more skeptical of psychic powers. Determine also whether the source is current and whether it treats the subject responsibly. Look for documentation of the author's sources, ample specific (and convincing) evidence to support general assertions, and a fair presentation of opposing views. If a source lacks any of these features, be sure you have another to balance it or back it up.

Read your sources quickly and selectively to obtain an overview of your topic so that your thesis encompasses the range of available information and represents your informed view. Don't allow yourself to get bogged down in taking very detailed notes at this stage. Without a sense of what information is pertinent, you may not leave time to cover all the potentially relevant sources.

However, do write down general ideas that seem fundamental to your topic. Be especially careful to record ideas of your own, such as a connection between statements by two different writers, because these may not occur to you later.

2
Writing a tentative thesis sentence

When you have a fairly good grasp of the range of views on your topic, the information available, and your own opinion, try to develop a thesis in a tentative thesis sentence. (See 1g.) In your thesis sentence (or sentences, if you need two or three at this stage), you should state your general idea and the perspective you take. Although the sentence is likely to need revision as you gather more information, drafting it early can help keep you focused as you do further research.

For his paper on advertising Paul Fuller wrote the following tentative thesis sentence:

> Advertisers appeal to consumers' emotions, rather than to their reason, because they want to manipulate consumers.

This thesis sentence stated Fuller's central idea (that advertisers appeal to consumers' emotions) and also his view, gathered from his preliminary reading, that advertisers use emotional appeals because they want to manipulate consumers. As we will see, Fuller had to revise his thesis sentence later to reflect his further research and to ensure that it adequately communicated his topic and perspective to readers. But this tentative thesis gave him a focus and a way to organize his work.

To frame a tentative thesis sentence for her paper on the Declaration of Independence, Ann Weiss first had to draw a tentative conclusion about whether Jefferson's draft of the Declaration was improved by the Continental Congress. After skimming the works of the experts who disagreed on this question and closely reading the two versions of the Declaration, she came to believe that the Congress's version was generally more effective. Her tentative thesis sentence indicated that she disagreed with one of the experts:

> Despite one scholar's view that Jefferson's Declaration was damaged in revision, the changes made by the Congress actually improved the document.

Weiss's thesis sentence reflected the state of her knowledge at this stage: she preferred the Congress's version of the Declaration, but she did not have quite enough information to provide concrete reasons for her preference. Getting this information and refining her analysis would be her next goals.

3
Preparing an informal outline

Having written a tentative thesis for your paper, you will be ready to prepare an **informal outline** that will guide your subsequent research. Like the informal outline for an essay (see 1h-2), the outline should show the main divisions of your paper, in the order you think you will cover them, and it should include the important supporting ideas for each division. Fuller's informal outline, below, is probably sufficient. Notice that the organization corresponds to the arrangement of ideas in the thesis sentence: Fuller's central idea comes first, followed by his perspective on it. Notice also that Fuller questions some ideas he has not found evidence for and must research further.

Advertisers appeal to consumers' emotions
- Shows in the ads
  - —full of adventure, humor, sex, status, and other emotional subjects
  - —little information on quality and performance of product or sound reasons to buy
- Advertisers admit they emphasize emotional appeals
  - —they say advertising is communication and therefore emotional
  - —they say consumers choose irrationally
  - —they say sales increase when ads stress emotion

Advertisers appeal to emotions because they want to manipulate consumers
- So say critics: McLuhan, Packard
- Research proves that advertisers use emotional appeals to manipulate (?)
  - —consumers are manipulated by emotional appeals (?)
  - —consumers would respond to rational appeals if they were provided (?)

If you feel that you don't have enough information to complete an informal outline or that one of your ideas lacks support (as Fuller's last idea about research seems to), consult sources in your working bibliography that you skipped before, or reexamine the ones you skimmed. Even if you believe your information is adequate for an outline, you may need to experiment with several arrangements of material to produce one that seems satisfactory. But don't try to construct a detailed, final outline at this stage. Both your organization and your thesis will undoubtedly change as you do more research.

EXERCISE 6

Read through the sources in the working bibliography you made in Exercise 5 (p. 493). Jot down the main ideas related to your topic. Draft a thesis sentence based on those ideas that both states the topic and implies your perspective on it. Finally, construct an informal outline that contains your main divisions and several supporting ideas for each, returning to your sources as needed.

35e
Taking detailed notes

After you have written a thesis sentence and prepared an informal outline, you are ready to gather, interpret, and analyze information. To begin this stage, take detailed notes from your sources to verify and expand your ideas and to record supporting evidence.

Keep a copy of your informal outline with you in the library as a guide to give order to your search. Try to research the headings and subheadings of your outline one at a time. But don't let the outline constrain your thinking. As you learn more about your topic, you will probably revise your outline by changing a heading, by dropping or adding one, or by rearranging headings. Revising is an inevitable, necessary, and beneficial part of research writing.

The most efficient method of reading secondary sources during research is skimming, reading quickly to look for pertinent information. (Primary sources usually need to be read more carefully, especially when they are the focus of your paper.) When skimming, you do not read randomly in hopes of hitting what you want. Rather, you read with a specific question in mind. Consult the table of contents or index to find what you want, and concentrate on headings and main ideas, skipping material unrelated to the specific question you are researching. Then, when you find something relevant, read slowly and carefully to achieve a clear understanding of what the author is saying and to interpret and evaluate the material in the context of your own and others' opinions.

If it is effective, your final paper will show that you have digested and interpreted the information in your sources—work that can be performed most efficiently in note taking. Taking notes is not a mechanical process of copying from books and periodicals. Rather, as you read and take notes you assess and organize the information in your sources according to your thesis and outline. Thus your notes both prompt and preserve your thoughts.

Using a system for taking notes helps simplify the process and later makes writing the paper easier. The most common method involves note cards: 4″ × 6″ cards allow more room than 3″ × 5″. (Using photocopies from sources is discussed on p. 501.) Write only one fact or idea on a card so that you can easily rearrange information when you want to. (Such rearrangement is extremely difficult when notes are combined on sheets of paper.) If the same source gives you more than one idea or fact, make more than one card. At the top of every card, write the author, title, and page number(s) of the source so that you will always know where the note came from. In addition, write the outline heading that this note belongs under so that you can remember what you intended to do with it. This format is illustrated below by several note cards.

You can use four different kinds of notes: summary, paraphrase, direct quotation, and a combination of these methods. When you **summarize,** you condense an extended idea or argument into a sentence or two in your own words. Here, for instance, is a passage from one of Fuller's sources, Pierre Martineau's *Motivation in Advertising* (New York: McGraw, 1971), p. 139:

> Advertising combines forces of both logical thought and emotive, aesthetic thought. Because it is communication from one set of humans to another set of humans, part of the meaning will be rational; but also there will be much meaning conveyed by nonrational symbols.

Compare this passage with Fuller's one-sentence summary, which picks out the kernel of Martineau's idea:

> Advertising as communication
>
> Martineau, Motivation in Advertising, p. 139.
>
> Advertising is both emotional and rational.

Summary is most useful when you want to record the gist of an author's idea without the background or supporting evidence.

When you **paraphrase,** you follow much more closely the author's original presentation, but you still restate it in your own words. Paraphrase is most useful when you want to reconstruct an author's line of reasoning but don't feel the original words merit direct quotation. The note card at the top of the next page shows how Fuller might have paraphrased the passage by Martineau given above. Notice how the paraphrase uses a different sentence structure and different words to express Martineau's idea: *form of human communication* instead of *communication from one set of humans to another set of humans; emotional and rational meanings* instead of *logical thought and emotive, aesthetic thought . . . part of the meaning will be rational; but also there will be much meaning conveyed by nonrational symbols.*

Advertising as communication

Martineau, Motivation in Advertising,
p. 139.

Advertising is a form of human communication, so emotional and rational meanings are communicated at the same time.

As you summarize and paraphrase, be careful not to distort the author's meaning, but don't feel you have to put down in new words the whole passage or all the details. Select what is pertinent and restate only that. In this way you will be developing your thoughts about the topic as you read and take notes. (For more on paraphrasing and summarizing, see Appendix A, p. 570.)

Summary and paraphrase are the methods you will use most often in taking notes from secondary sources. Occasionally, however, you will want to use **direct quotation** from secondary sources when you feel an author's words give a special effect you want to include, when you want to give impact to an expert's opinion, or when you plan to use a graph, table, or diagram from a source. And in a paper analyzing primary sources such as literary works, you will use direct quotation extensively to illustrate and support your analysis. (Ann Weiss used many quotations from her primary source, the Declaration of Independence; see her final paper, pp. 554–56.)

When you quote directly, keep in mind that you can use brackets to show any additional words needed for understanding (see 25d) and ellipsis marks (usually three spaced periods) to show omissions of irrelevant words or sentences (see 25e). The note card at the top of the following page shows how Fuller might have quoted rather than summarized Martineau, using both ellipses and brackets to make the quotation more concise without changing its meaning.

A direct quotation must be completely accurate. Be sure you copy the author's exact wording, spelling, capitalization, and punctuation. Proofread every direct quotation *at least twice,* and be sure you have supplied the quotation marks so that later you won't confuse the direct quotation card with a paraphrase or summary card.

Advertising as communication

Martineau, Motivation in Advertising,
p. 139.

"Advertising combines . . . logical thought and emotive, aesthetic thought. Because it is [human] communication . . . , part of the meaning will be rational; but also there will be much meaning conveyed by nonrational symbols."

Using quotation in combination with summary or paraphrase can help you shape the material to suit your purposes (although you must be careful not to distort the author's meaning). The card below shows how Fuller might have used a combination of quotation and paraphrase to record the statement by Martineau. Notice that the quotation marks are clearly visible and that the quotations are absolutely exact.

Advertising as communication

Martineau, Motivation in Advertising,
p. 139.

One advertiser says, "Advertising combines forces of both logical thought and emotive, aesthetic thought" because of its nature as "communication from one set of humans to another."

If the material you are quoting, summarizing, or paraphrasing runs from one page to the next in the source, make a mark (such as a check mark or a slash) at the exact spot where one page ends and the next begins. When writing your paper, you may want to use only a part of the material (say, the first or second half). The mark will save you from having to go back to your source to find which page the material actually appeared on.

To ensure accuracy of quotations and also to save time, researchers often photocopy sources. (All libraries provide one or more copying machines for this purpose.) But just running pages through a copier does not generate the creative, interpretive, and analytical thinking about sources that is so crucial in taking notes. If you do use a copier, turn to the photocopy soon after you make it, when you still have your hand on the original source and your thoughts about it are still fresh in your mind. At the top of the copy, write a heading from your outline, the author's name, the source title, and the page number as you would on a note card. Then circle or underline the relevant passages and make notes in the margin about their significance to your topic. To make it possible to integrate photocopied notes with your notes on cards, you might want to paste or tape the copy on a notecard of the same size you are using for your handwritten notes. If the photocopy won't fit on one card, cut it apart and paste it on two or more cards. Be sure to write the appropriate source information at the top of each card so that you don't lose track of where the copy, or a part of it, came from.

A note on plagiarism

Plagiarism—presenting someone else's ideas as your own, whether deliberately or accidentally—is a serious offense, and a separate section of this book is devoted entirely to it (see Appendix A). If you use another writer's words or ideas in your final draft without citing a source for them, you will be committing plagiarism. The problem can start in careless note taking. For instance, if you copy even a phrase from a source without using quotation marks, you may, in writing the paper from your notes, assume that the phrase is your own paraphrase or summary and use it without quotation marks. Or if you paraphrase an author's idea and neglect to note the source, you might later forget that the idea was not yours originally but another's. Even though you did not intend to do so, you would be plagiarizing in both cases. Thus be sure your note cards show sources and the exact use you are making of them. And read Appendix A (p. 570).

EXERCISE 7

Prepare two note cards, one containing a summary of the entire paragraph below and the other containing a paraphrase of the first four sentences (ending with the word *autonomy*). Use the format for a note card provided in the preceding section, omitting only the outline heading.

Federal organization [of the United States] has made it possible for the different states to deal with the same problems in many different ways. One consequence of federalism, then, has been that people are treated differently, by law, from state to state. The great strength of this system is that differences from state to state in cultural preferences, moral standards, and levels of wealth can be accommodated. In contrast to a unitary system in which the central government makes all important decisions (as in France), federalism is a powerful arrangement for maximizing regional freedom and autonomy. The great weakness of our federal system, however, is that people in some states receive less than the best or the most advanced or the least expensive services and policies that government can offer. The federal dilemma does not invite easy solutions, for the costs and benefits of the arrangement have tended to balance out.

– PETER K. EISINGER ET AL., *American Politics,* p. 44

EXERCISE 8

Prepare a note card containing a combination of paraphrase or summary and direct quotation that states the major idea of the passage below. Use the format for a note card provided in the preceding section, omitting only the outline heading.

Most speakers unconsciously duel even during seemingly casual conversations, as can often be observed at social gatherings where they show less concern for exchanging information with other guests than for asserting their own dominance. Their verbal dueling often employs very subtle weapons like mumbling, a hostile act which defeats the listener's desire to understand what the speaker claims he is trying to say (but is really not saying because he is mumbling!). Or the verbal dueler may keep talking after someone has passed out of hearing range—which is often an aggressive challenge to the listener to return and acknowledge the dominance of the speaker. – PETER FARB, *Word Play,* p. 107

EXERCISE 9

Continuing from Exercise 5 (p. 493), as the next step in preparing a research paper, make notes of specific information from your sources. Use summary, paraphrase, direct quotation, or a combination as seems appropriate. Mark each card (or photocopy) with the author's name, title, and page number as well as with your outline heading.

35f

35f

Revising the thesis sentence and writing a formal outline

As you take notes, you will almost inevitably find reasons to revise your thesis sentence and informal outline. These revisions are the focus of most of the next stage in writing a research paper.

After investigating your topic thoroughly through reading and note taking, you will want to evaluate your thesis sentence in light of what you now know. In his research, for example, Paul Fuller could not find evidence to support his belief that consumers would make rational choices if they were given advertisements that appealed to reason. (See his informal outline on p. 496). Instead, he found the opposite: consumers choose products emotionally and do not use reason even when they are given the chance. Consequently, he revised his informal outline and his thesis sentence so that his paper would reflect the existing evidence, not the evidence as he imagined it.

Tentative thesis sentence

> Advertisers appeal to consumers' emotions, rather than to their reason, because they want to manipulate consumers.

Revised thesis sentence

> Advertisers appeal to consumers' emotions, rather than to their reason, because consumers choose products irrationally.

Ann Weiss's reading and note taking gave her a much clearer sense of the differences between the two versions of the Declaration of Independence and also of the experts' views on the changes. She was able to sharpen her rather fuzzy tentative thesis sentence with concrete reasons for her preference.

Tentative thesis sentence

> Despite one scholar's view that Jefferson's Declaration was damaged in revision, the changes made by the Congress actually improved the document.

Revised thesis sentence

> Despite one scholar's view that Jefferson's Declaration was damaged in revision, the changes made by the Congress improved the document in tone and strengthened it for the purposes it was intended to serve.

After revising your thesis sentence, you may want or be required to prepare a detailed outline from which to write your paper. This **formal outline,** like the formal outline for a brief essay (see 1h-2), is more complete than an informal outline and arranges ideas in a logical way. Inadequate coverage of the thesis, overlapping ideas, ideas that are not parallel yet are in parallel positions, and imprecise phrasing—all of these can be corrected in the process of writing a formal outline. The goal is to produce an outline that presents your ideas in a sensible and persuasive sequence and that supports ideas at each level with enough explanation and evidence.

Before beginning work on your formal outline, you should group your note cards according to their headings, which are also the headings of your informal outline. You can begin revising your outline by rearranging and retitling cards to reflect your changed ideas and the sense of your revised thesis sentence. Gradually, a complete outline of your thinking will evolve.

A formal outline is usually written either in phrases—a **topic outline**—or in sentences—a **sentence outline.** A complete topic outline is illustrated in Chapter 1, page 34. A complete sentence outline accompanies Paul Fuller's research paper on pages 528–29. Either is suitable for a research paper, though a sentence outline, because it requires complete statements, conveys more information. The example below shows the formal outline's format and schematic content.

I. First main idea
  A. First subordinate idea
    1. First evidence for subordinate idea
      a. First detail of evidence
      b. Second detail of evidence
    2. Second evidence for subordinate idea
  B. Second subordinate idea
II. Second main idea

In this model main ideas are labeled with Roman numerals, the first sublevel with capital letters, the second with Arabic numerals, and the third with small letters. (A fourth sublevel, if needed, is labeled with Arabic numerals enclosed in parentheses.) Each level of the outline is indented farther than the one it supports.

To be an effective organizer for your thoughts, a formal outline should be detailed and should adhere to several principles of logical arrangement, clarity, balance, and completeness. These are discussed in detail and illustrated in Chapter 1, pages 35–36. Briefly: (1) The outline should divide material into groups that indicate which ideas are primary and, under them, which subordinate. A long, undivided list of parallel items probably needs to be subdivided. (2) Parallel headings should represent ideas of parallel importance and should not overlap one another. (3) Single sublevels should be avoided because they illogically imply that something is divided into only one part.

If you compare Paul Fuller's sentence outline on pages 528–29 with his informal outline on page 496, you can see that the formal outline has more information and a tighter, more logical arrangement of ideas and details.

EXERCISE 10

Identify the flaws in the following partial outline for a research paper. Check especially for departures from formal outline form, including illogical subdivision of topics, inconsistent wording of items, and nonparallel placement of ideas of parallel importance.

THESIS SENTENCE

Food additives, which aid in processing foods and in preserving them or improving their appearance, are more useful to us than they are dangerous.

FORMAL OUTLINE

I. Processing, preservation, appearance
   A. Processing
      1. Leavening agents
      2. Antifoaming agents
      3. Emulsifiers
         a. Bind ingredients together
   B. Preservation
      1. Protect from internal destruction
         a. Natural enzymes can cause discoloration or over-ripening
         b. Must remove or disable enzymes
      2. External destruction
         a. Bacteria
         b. Fungus
      3. Environment
         a. Heat, moisture, humidity
         b. Humectants protect foods from excess moisture
   C. Appearance
      1. Glazing agents
      2. Foaming agents cause bubbles to appear in hot chocolate
      3. Firming agents
         a. Keep fruits and vegetables firm in cans
         b. Thickeners
            1. Prevent ice crystal formation, as in ice cream
            2. Improve texture
      4. Sequestrants prevent discoloration

EXERCISE 11

Using the note cards you prepared in Exercise 9 (p. 502), revise the thesis sentence from Exercise 6 (p. 496) and construct a formal sentence or topic outline (as specified by your instructor) from which to write a paper.

35g
Writing and revising the paper

35g

After you have taken notes from your sources, revised your thesis as necessary, and written a formal outline for your paper, you are ready to begin writing the first draft. Take time to organize your notes carefully according to your formal outline. Once you have arranged your notes, go through them slowly, considering which of your ideas each note supports, how you will link the evidence in one note with that in others, and how you will move from one idea and block of evidence to the next.

1 Writing the first draft

Beginning a draft of what will be a relatively long and complicated paper can be difficult. If you can't find a way to begin your paper, skip the introduction and start instead with a section that you feel confident about. Move from there to other sections of the paper, attempting to fit the sections together only after you begin to see the draft take shape.

In writing sections of your draft, remember that a primary reason for doing a research paper is learning how to evaluate and interpret the evidence in sources, draw your own conclusions from the evidence, and weave the two together in a convincing whole. The weaving will be easier if you view each principal idea in your outline as a unit. Depending on the importance of the idea to your scheme, on its complexity, and on the amount of evidence needed to support it, a unit may require a single paragraph or a block of two or three paragraphs.

Begin each unit by stating the idea, which should be a conclusion you have drawn from reading and taking notes. Follow the statement with the specific support from your notes: facts and examples; summaries, paraphrases, or quotations of secondary sources; quotations of passages from primary sources with your analysis; and so on. If your research focuses on or has uncovered a disagreement among experts, present the disagreement fairly and give the evidence that leads you to side with one expert or another. As much as possible, try to remain open to new interpretations or new arrangements of ideas that occur to you.

As you draft your paper, insert the source of each summary, paraphrase, and quotation in parentheses in the text—for instance, "(Martineau 139)," referring to page 139 in a work by Martineau. If you are conscientious about inserting these notes and carrying them through successive drafts, you will be less likely to plagiarize accidentally and you will have little difficulty citing your sources in the final paper. (Citing sources is discussed on pp. 511–25.)

2 Introducing summaries, paraphrases, and quotations

One of your challenges in writing a research paper will be deciding when, where, and how to introduce summaries, paraphrases, and quotations from your sources into your text. Whether you summarize, paraphrase, or quote, make others' facts and opinions serve your ideas; don't allow them to overwhelm your own point of view. Except when you are analyzing literature or other primary sources, favor paraphrases and summaries over quotations. Quote secondary sources only when the original wording is essential to understanding the exact meaning or is particularly succinct, forceful, or otherwise interesting (for instance, a bold statement from an acknowledged authority or an inventive comparison). Keep quotations short by eliminating sentences and phrases that are not essential to the intended meaning and that do not contribute to your purpose. Most papers of six to eight pages should not need more than two or three quotations that are longer than a few lines. More than that may bury rather than enhance your argument.

When using summaries, paraphrases, and quotations, be careful to integrate them into your own sentences and at the same time explain why you are using them. A quotation, summary, or paraphrase that is dumped in readers' laps is unlikely to achieve what you intend it to, as the following example illustrates:

> **A DUMPED QUOTATION**
>
> In short, many news editors and reporters maintain that it is impossible and perhaps not even desirable to keep personal opinions from influencing the selection and presentation of facts. "True, news reporters, like everyone else, form impressions of what they see and hear. However, a good reporter does not fail to separate his opinions from his facts" (Lyman 52).

The writer of this passage provides no clues that the quotation contradicts the first sentence; instead, she forces us to figure that out for ourselves. In addition, she loses an opportunity to explain who Lyman is and why his opinion is worthwhile; consequently, we aren't likely to see the quotation as very strong evidence.

With some rewriting, the quotation above can be smoothly integrated into the writer's sentences so that the contradiction and the reason for quoting Lyman are both clear:

> **AN INTEGRATED QUOTATION**
>
> In short, many news editors and reporters maintain that it is impossible and perhaps not even desirable to keep personal opinions from influencing the selection and presentation of facts. Yet not all authorities agree with this view. Harold Lyman, a newspaper editor for more than forty years, grants that "news reporters, like everyone else, form impressions of what they see and hear." But, Lyman insists, "a good reporter does not fail to separate his opinions from his facts" (52).

In this passage the second sentence and the writer's words *grants, But,* and *insists* tell us what to expect in the quotation. And the phrase identifying Lyman, *a newspaper editor for more than forty years,* tells us why Lyman is quoted and why we should value his opinion.

It is not always necessary to name your sources and indicate their credentials in your running text. In fact, such introductions may get in the way when you are simply establishing facts or weaving together facts and opinions from varied sources. In the following passage from Ann Weiss's paper, the information is more important than the source, so the name of the source is confined to a parenthetical acknowledgment:

> To end the abuses of the British, many colonists were urging three actions: forming a united front, seceding from Britain, and taking control of their own international trade and diplomacy (Wills 325–26).

(See pp. 512–17 for an explanation of the parenthetical form of citation used in this passage and the ones above.)

In papers analyzing literature, historical documents, and other sources, quotations will often be both the target of your analysis and the chief support for your ideas. You may need to quote many brief passages, integrated into your sentences, and then comment on the quotations to clarify your analysis and win readers' agreement with it. An example of such extensive quotation can be seen in Ann Weiss's analysis of the Declaration of Independence, pages 554–56.

If you need guidance in the mechanics of quotation, see 21h (punctuating explanatory words such as *he insists*), 24c (quoting poetry and long prose passages), and 25d and 25e (using brackets and ellipsis marks for additions to and deletions from quotations).

3
Revising and editing the paper

When you have written a first draft, take a break for at least a day so that you can gain some objectivity about your work and read the draft critically when you begin to revise. Then evaluate your first draft according to the advice and revision checklist in 2b (pp. 42–47). Rethink the content and effectiveness of every sentence and of the whole. Ensure that your thesis sentence accurately describes your topic and your perspective and that the paper is unified around it. Be alert for major structural problems that may not have been apparent in your outline: for instance, illogical arrangements of ideas; inadequate emphasis of important points and overemphasis of minor ones; or imbalance between the views of others (support) and your own views (interpretation or analysis). Hunt out irrelevant ideas and facts that crept in just because you had notes on them. Look for and improve places where supporting evidence is weak. Examine your explanations to be sure your readers will understand them, being especially careful to define terms and clarify concepts that readers may be unfamiliar with.

When you complete your revision, retype the new draft if possible so that you have a clean copy to edit. For editing, consult the advice and checklist in 2c (pp. 47–49). Try to read the paper from the point of view of someone who has not spent hours planning and researching but instead has come fresh to the paper. Look for lapses in sense, awkward passages, poor transitions between ideas and evidence, unnecessary repetitions, wrong or misspelled words, errors in grammar or punctuation — in short, anything that is likely to interfere with a reader's understanding of your meaning.

When you finish editing your paper, but before you prepare and proofread the final draft, you need to prepare your list of sources and insert the final source citations into the text. Preparing the list and citing sources are the subjects of the next two sections.

EXERCISE 12

Drawing on the ideas in the following paragraph and using examples from your own observations and experiences, write a paragraph about anxiety. Integrate at least one direct quotation and one paraphrase from the following paragraph into your own sentences. In your paragraph identify the author by name and give his credentials: he is a professor of psychiatry and a practicing psychoanalyst.

> There are so many ways in which man is unique from all the lower forms of animals, and almost all of them make us uniquely susceptible to feelings of anxiousness. Our imagination and reasoning powers facilitate anxiety; the anxious feeling is precipitated not by an absolute impending threat—such as the worry about an examination, a speech, travel—but rather by the symbolic and often unconscious representations. We do not have to be experiencing a potential danger. We can experience something related to it. We can recall, through our incredible memories, the original symbolic sense of vulnerability in childhood and suffer the feeling attached to that. We can even forget the original memory and still be stuck with the emotion—which is then compounded by its seemingly irrational quality at this time. It is not just the fear of death which pains us, but the anticipation of it; or the anniversary of a specific death; or a street, a hospital, a time of day, a color, a flower, a symbol associated with a death.
>
> – WILLARD GAYLIN, "Feeling Anxious," p. 23

EXERCISE 13

Write the research paper you have been preparing in Exercises 1, 2, 5, 6, 9, and 11. Before beginning the first draft, study your notes.

While writing, follow your note cards (Exercise 9) and formal outline (Exercise 11) as closely as you need to, but stay open to new ideas, associations, and arrangements. Then revise and edit thoroughly and carefully, working to improve not only your presentation of ideas but also the ideas themselves if necessary.

35h

Preparing the final list of works cited

When you finish editing your paper, prepare a final list of the sources you used in it. Include in your list all the sources you quoted, paraphrased, or summarized. Unless your instructor requests it, don't include sources you examined but did not actually use in your paper.

If you are following the guidelines of the *MLA Handbook,* title your list of sources "Works Cited." (Use the title "Works Consulted" if your instructor asks you to include all the sources you examined as well as those you actually used.) Type the information about sources in the formats given on pages 482–90, and arrange them in alphabetical order by the last name of the author or, if an author is not given, by the first main word of the title (excluding *A, An,* or *The*). Double-space the entire list (within and between entries), and indent the second and subsequent lines of each entry five spaces from the left. Place the list at the end of your paper. See the lists of works cited in the papers by Paul Fuller (p. 548) and Ann Weiss (p. 557) and the comments opposite Fuller's list (p. 549) for the form to follow in typing this section.

The *MLA Handbook* gives a special format for listing two or more works by the same author:

Gardner, Howard. The Arts and Human Development. New York: Wiley, 1973.

---. The Quest for Mind: Piaget, Lévi-Strauss, and the Structuralist Movement. New York: Knopf, 1973.

The author's name is given only in the first entry. For the second and any subsequent works by the same author, substitute three hyphens for the author's name, followed by a period. Arrange the sources alphabetically by the first main word of the title. Note that the three hyphens stand for *exactly* the same name or names. If the second source above were by Gardner and somebody else, both names would have to be given in full.

The guidelines of the American Psychological Association for the list of sources are slightly different. Title the list "References," and present the information about sources in the appropriate for-

35h

mats (see p. 491 for models). Arrange the entries alphabetically by the author's last name. When citing two or more works by exactly the same author, give the author's name in each entry and arrange the sources in order of their publication dates, earliest first. When citing two or more works by exactly the same author published in the same year, arrange them alphabetically by the first main word of the title and distinguish the sources by adding a letter to the date. For example:

```
Gardner, H.  (1973a).  The arts and human development.  New York:
     Wiley.
Gardner, H.  (1973b).  The quest for mind: Piaget, Lévi-Strauss,
     and the structuralist movement.  New York: Knopf.
```

Both the date and the letter are used in citing the source in the text (see p. 518).

EXERCISE 14

Prepare the final list of works cited for the research paper you wrote and revised in Exercise 13 (p. 509). Follow the *MLA Handbook* models on pages 482–90 unless your instructor specifies a different format.

35i
Citing sources

Every time you borrow the words, facts, or ideas of others, you must acknowledge the source in your text so that readers know you borrowed the material and know where you borrowed it from. You must acknowledge sources of direct quotation as well as of tables and diagrams. You must also acknowledge sources of ideas, facts, or associations between them that you paraphrase or summarize from others. Acknowledge all quotations, summaries, and paraphrases no matter what their length or how often you have already cited the source. You do not need to acknowledge your own ideas or ideas that are considered common knowledge, such as well-known historical and scientific facts, when you express these in your own words. (For a detailed discussion of what to acknowledge and when, see Appendix A on avoiding plagiarism.)

As you read through your paper, check your note cards. Identify each summary, paraphrase, and quotation in the text, proofread every quotation a final time, and then locate the corresponding entry in your list of works cited. The page numbers on your note cards and the information on your list of works cited give you everything you need to write your source citations.

The format of source acknowledgments differs from discipline to discipline. This section explains and illustrates several different formats: the parenthetical style recommended by the *MLA Handbook* (below); the parenthetical style of the American Psychological Association and that of many of the sciences (p. 517); and footnotes or endnotes (p. 519). Your instructor will tell you which format to follow.

1
Using the MLA style of parenthetical reference

The documentation system of the *MLA Handbook* employs brief parenthetical references within the text that direct readers to the list of works cited. For example:

> Only one article mentions this discrepancy (Wolfe 62).

The name Wolfe directs readers to the article by Wolfe in the list of works cited, and the page number 62 specifies the page in the article on which the cited material appears.

The following pages describe this documentation system: what must be included in a reference (below), where to place references (p. 516), and when to use footnotes or endnotes in addition to parenthetical references (p. 516).

What to include in a parenthetical reference

The in-text references to sources must include (1) just enough information for the reader to locate the appropriate source in your list of works cited and (2) just enough information for the reader to locate the place in the source where the borrowed material appears. Usually, you can meet these requirements by providing the author's last name and the page(s) in the source on which the material appears.

> One researcher concludes that "women impose a distinctive construction on moral problems, seeing moral dilemmas in terms of conflicting responsibilities" (Gilligan 105).

cit
35i

With the information provided in parentheses, the reader can find Gilligan's book in the list of works cited and find the quotation in the book itself.

If the author's name is already given in the text, you need not repeat it in the parenthetical reference.

One researcher, Carol Gilligan, concludes that "women impose a distinctive construction on moral problems, seeing moral dilemmas in terms of conflicting responsibilities" (105).

If the source has two or three authors, give all their names in the text or in the reference.

Spradley and McCurdy treat both non-Western and Western cultures as appropriate concerns of cultural anthropology (1-2).

If the source has more than three authors, give only the first author's name followed by "et al." (the abbreviation for the Latin "and others").

Over 100,000 rebels besieged Peking for nearly two months in 1900 before American, European, and Japanese troops broke through and gained control of the city (Lopez et al. 362).

Sometimes the author's name and page number will not provide enough information for the reader. Such cases include references to one of two or more listed works by the same author and references to one volume of a multivolume work. The following models illustrate how to cite these and other sources.

A GENERAL REFERENCE TO AN ENTIRE WORK

When you cite an entire work rather than a part of it, the reference will not include any page number. If the author's name appears in the text, no parenthetical reference is needed at all. Remember, though, that the source must be included in the list of works cited.

Boyd deals with the need to acknowledge and come to terms with our fear of nuclear technology.

A REFERENCE TO AN ARTICLE OR A ONE-VOLUME BOOK

An article:

For women prisoners who wanted "to go home (and stay there, if they had husbands) and to go out partying (if they needed a man)," feminism represented "separatism and . . . misandry, male hating" (Gubar and Hedin 780).

A one-volume book:

Wimsatt and Brooks note the power of Tolstoy's "walloping caricatures of metropolitan fashionable culture" (464).

A REFERENCE TO A MULTIVOLUME WORK

If you used only one volume of a multivolume work, your list of works cited can indicate that by giving the appropriate volume in the entry (see the second entry for Lincoln on p. 484). However, if you used and listed all the volumes in a multivolume work, your parenthetical reference must specify which volume you are referring to.

> After issuing the Emancipation Proclamation, Lincoln said, "What I did, I did after very full deliberation, and under a very heavy and solemn sense of responsibility" (5: 438).

The number 5 indicates the volume from which the quotation was taken; the number 438 indicates the page number in that volume. If you are referring generally to an entire volume of a multivolume work and are not citing specific page numbers, add the abbreviation "vol." before the volume number—for example, "(vol. 5)." Then readers will not misinterpret the volume number as a page number.

A REFERENCE TO ONE WORK BY AN AUTHOR OF TWO OR MORE WORKS

If your list of works cited includes two or more works by the same author, then your reference must tell the reader which of the author's works you are citing. Use the appropriate title or a shortened version of it in the parenthetical reference.

> At about age seven, most children begin to tell stories accurately, describe scenes realistically, and use appropriate gestures to reinforce their story (Gardner, Arts 144-45).

The title *Arts* is shortened from Gardner's full title, *The Arts and Human Development* (see the entry for this book on p. 510). Often, as here, the first main word in the title is enough to direct the reader to the appropriate source.

A REFERENCE TO AN UNSIGNED WORK

Anonymous works are alphabetized by title in the list of works cited. In the text they are referred to by full or shortened title.

> One article notes that a death-row inmate may demand his own execution to achieve a fleeting notoriety ("Right").

cit
35i

This reference is to an unsigned article titled "The Right to Die." A page reference is unnecessary because the article is no longer than a page (see the entry for the article on p. 487).

A REFERENCE TO A GOVERNMENT DOCUMENT OR A WORK WITH A CORPORATE AUTHOR

If the author of the work is listed as a government body or a corporation, cite the work by the name given as the author's. If the name is long, try to work it into the text to avoid an intrusive reference.

> A 1983 report by the Hawaii Department of Education predicts a gradual increase in school enrollments (6).

A REFERENCE TO AN INDIRECT SOURCE

When you quote or paraphrase one source's quotation of another source, your reference must indicate as much. In the following reference "qtd. in" ("quoted in") says that Davino was quoted by Boyd.

> George Davino maintains that children as young as three "are experiencing nightmares about nuclear war" (qtd. in Boyd 22).

A REFERENCE TO A LITERARY WORK

Novels, plays, and poems are often available in many editions, so your instructor may ask you to provide information that will help readers find the passage you cite no matter what edition they consult. For novels, the page number comes first, followed by information on the appropriate part or chapter of the work.

> Toward the end of James's novel, Maggie suddenly feels "the thick breath of the definite--which was the intimate, the immediate, the familiar, as she hadn't had them for so long" (535; pt. 6, ch. 41).

For verse plays and poems, you can omit the page number and instead cite the appropriate part or act (and scene, if any) plus the line number(s). Use Arabic numerals for acts and scenes ("3.4") unless your instructor specifies Roman numerals ("III.iv").

> Later in King Lear Shakespeare has the disguised Edgar say, "The prince of darkness is a gentleman" (3.4.147).

For prose plays, provide the page number followed by the act and scene, if any (see the reference to *Death of a Salesman* on the next page).

A REFERENCE TO MORE THAN ONE WORK

If you use a parenthetical reference to cite more than a single work, separate the citations by a semicolon.

> Two recent articles urge small businesses not to rush to buy a personal computer, even an inexpensive one, on the grounds that a computer badly used is less efficient than no computer at all (Richards 162; Gough and Hall 201).

Since long references in the text can distract the reader, you may choose to cite several or more works in an endnote or footnote rather than in the text. See below.

Where to place parenthetical references

Generally, place a parenthetical reference at the end of the sentence in which you summarize, paraphrase, or quote a work. The reference should follow a closing quotation mark but precede the sentence punctuation. (See the examples in the previous section.) When a reference pertains to only part of a sentence, place the reference after the material being cited and at the least intrusive point—usually at the end of a clause.

> Though Spelling argues that American automobile manufacturers "have done the best that could be expected" in meeting consumer needs (26), not everyone agrees with him.

When a reference appears at the end of a quotation set off from the text, place it two spaces *after* the punctuation ending the quotation.

> In Arthur Miller's Death of a Salesman, the most poignant defense of Willie Loman comes from his wife, Linda:
>
> > He's not the finest character that ever lived. But he's a human being, and a terrible thing is happening to him. So attention must be paid. He's not to be allowed to fall into his grave like an old dog. Attention, attention must finally be paid to such a person. (56; act 1)

(The reference includes the act number as well as the page number. See "A reference to a literary work" on the preceding page.)

See the two sample research papers starting on pages 526 and 550 for further examples of placing parenthetical references.

Using footnotes or endnotes in special circumstances

cit
35i

Occasionally, you may want to use footnotes or endnotes in place of parenthetical references. If you need to cite several sources at once, listing them in a long parenthetical reference could be intrusive. In that case, signal the citation with a numeral raised above the appropriate line of text and write a note with the same numeral to cite the sources:

TEXT At least five subsequent studies have confirmed these results.[1]

NOTE [1] Abbott and Winger 266-68; Casner 27; Hoyenga 78-79; Marino 36; Tripp, Tripp, and Walk 179-83.

You may also use a footnote or endnote to comment on a source or provide information that does not fit easily in the text:

TEXT So far, no one has succeeded in confirming these results.[2]

NOTE [2] Manter reports spending nearly a year trying to replicate the experiment, but he was never able to produce the high temperatures reported by the original experimenters (616).

In a note the raised numeral is indented five spaces and followed by a space. If the note appears as a footnote, place it at the bottom of the page on which the citation appears, set it off from the text with quadruple spacing, and single-space the note itself. If the note appears as an endnote, place it in numerical order with the other endnotes on a page between the text and the list of works cited; double-space all the endnotes. (See pp. 546–47 for an example of an endnote and the format to use in typing a page of endnotes.)

2 Using the APA or science style of parenthetical reference

Most of the social and physical sciences also use parenthetical references, but their styles are different from the style of the *MLA Handbook*. The text reference may consist of the author's last name and the year of the source's publication, together in parentheses, or simply of a number in parentheses or brackets. Your instructor will specify the style you should use.

The style guide of the American Psychological Association (APA) and those in some other disciplines recommend the **name-year style:**

One researcher (Herskowitz, 1974) found that mice fight each other more frequently when they are hungry.

The author's last name (Herskowitz) is followed by a comma and the year of publication of the source being cited. When the author's name already appears in the discussion, you need provide only the date in parentheses immediately after the name.

Herskowitz (1974) found that mice fight each other more frequently when they are hungry.

If a source has two authors, give both last names. If it has three or more authors, give all their last names the first time you cite the source, but in subsequent references give only the first author's name followed by "et al."

> According to Jones and Oman (1979), factory accidents can be dramatically reduced when employees receive periodic instruction in safety.

> A large-scale study of child-rearing patterns (Sears, Maccoby, & Levin, 1957) discovered that highly permissive parents tend to have highly aggressive children.

> This conclusion appears to contradict that of Sears et al. (1957).

Note that the *and* linking authors' names is spelled out when the names appear in the running text (first example). Inside parentheses, however, an ampersand (&) is used instead of *and* (second example).

When you need to identify a page number in a source, place it inside parentheses as well, after the material you are citing. If the author and date of publication are given before the cited material, the page number will appear in a separate parenthetical reference.

> Jacob Bronowski (1973) maintains that an important achievement of twentieth-century physics has been to prove that "the physical world will forever elude our complete understanding." (p. 353).

When your list of sources includes two or more works by the same author published in the same year, the date for each source will be followed by a letter (see p. 511). In the reference give the letter with the date to tell the reader which source you are citing.

> At about age seven, most children begin to tell stories accurately, describe scenes realistically, and use appropriate gestures to reinforce their story (Gardner, 1973a, pp. 144-145).

cit
35i

In the **number style** of source citation, used in many physical sciences, you number the entries in a list of references arranged either alphabetically or in the order of their citation in the text. The text reference then consists of the appropriate number (with or without the author's name, depending on the style) enclosed in parentheses or brackets.

> In an earlier study Herskowitz (15) found that mice also fight when they have been deprived of sleep.

Some researchers (e.g., Philby, 19) doubt that the human brain will ever fully understand itself.

Four studies [9-12] have isolated the virus responsible for the disease.

3
Using footnotes or endnotes to document sources

Until its second edition was published in 1984, the *MLA Handbook* recommended using footnotes and endnotes to cite sources, and the new edition continues to provide an explanation and illustrations of this reference system for those who want or are required to use it.

When you document sources with notes (either footnotes or endnotes), you place a raised numeral ([1]) in the text at the end of the material you are acknowledging, and you number the citations consecutively throughout the paper. The notes themselves then fall in the same order. Footnotes are placed at the bottoms of appropriate pages; endnotes are collected on separate pages between the end of the paper and the list of works cited.

Here is a passage from Paul Fuller's paper showing the use of note numbers in the text.

The critics of advertising stress its manipulativeness and mindlessness. Marshall McLuhan, the philosopher of mass-media culture, says that advertising directs its appeals to the unconscious:

> Ours is the first age in which many thousands of the best-trained individual minds have made it a full-time business to get inside the collective public mind . . . to manipulate, exploit, control. . . . Why not assist the public to observe consciously the drama intended to operate unconsciously?[1]

Vance Packard, who brought national attention to the manipulations of advertisers in his best-selling The Hidden Persuaders, asserts that the methods of advertisers "represent regress rather than progress for man in his long struggle to become a rational and self-guiding being."[2]

For footnotes, begin the first entry four lines below the last line

fn 35i

of text (two double spaces), single-space each footnote, and double-space between notes. For endnotes, double-space within and between notes, as in the following sample:

[1] Herbert Marshall McLuhan, The Mechanical Bride: Folklore of Industrial Man (New York: Vanguard, 1951) v.

[2] Vance Packard, The Hidden Persuaders, rev. ed. (New York: Pocket, 1981) 4.

See pages 546–47 for the heading, spacing, and other elements of a page of endnotes.

The format for a note differs from that for an entry in the list of works cited.

LIST OF WORKS CITED

Wimsatt, William K., and Cleanth Brooks. Literary Criticism: A Short History. Chicago: U of Chicago P, 1978.

NOTE

[2] William K. Wimsatt and Cleanth Brooks, Literary Criticism: A Short History (Chicago: U of Chicago P, 1978) 312.

In the works cited entry you start the first line at the left margin and indent the second and subsequent lines five spaces; but in the note you indent the first line and not the others. The note is intended to be read as a sentence, so a period appears only at the end while the body of the note is punctuated with commas and colons. In the note, unlike the works cited entry, you enclose the publication information (place of publication, publisher, date of publication) in parentheses. Whereas you start the works cited entry with the first author's last name, to make it easier to find the name in an alphabetical listing, in the note you give the author's name in normal order. And in the note you include the specific page number(s) in the source from which the summary, paraphrase, or quotation is taken (but without "p." or "pp.").

The note models below use the same sources as those in the bibliographic models on pages 482–90, and the explanations on those pages point out the special information that must be included for each kind of source. Like bibliographic models, note models may be combined if necessary; for example, the model for a book with an editor may be combined with that for a multivolume book if your source is a multivolume edited work. The following note models are for first reference to a source. When you acknowledge the same source more than once in the same paper, you should use the shortened form of reference described on pages 524–25.

fn
35i

A BOOK WITH ONE AUTHOR

[1] Carol Gilligan, In a Different Voice: Psychological Theory and Women's Development (Cambridge: Harvard UP, 1982) 27.

A BOOK WITH TWO OR THREE AUTHORS

[2] William K. Wimsatt and Cleanth Brooks, Literary Criticism: A Short History (Chicago: U of Chicago P, 1978) 312.

A BOOK WITH MORE THAN THREE AUTHORS

[3] Robert S. Lopez et al., Civilizations: Western and World (Boston: Little, 1975) 281-82.

A BOOK WITH CORPORATE AUTHORSHIP

[4] Editors of The Progressive, The Crisis of Survival (Glenview: Scott, 1970) 61.

A LATER EDITION

[5] Dwight L. Bollinger, Aspects of Language, 2nd ed. (New Yor Harcourt, 1975) 20.

A REPUBLISHED BOOK

[6] Henry James, The Golden Bowl (1904; London: Penguin, 1966) 163.

A WORK IN MORE THAN ONE VOLUME

[7] Abraham Lincoln, The Collected Works of Abraham Lincoln, ed. Roy P. Basler, 8 vols. (New Brunswick: Rutgers UP, 1953) 5: 426-28.

A WORK IN A SERIES

[8] Ingmar Bergman, The Seventh Seal, Modern Film Scripts Series (New York: Simon, 1968) 6.

A BOOK WITH AN EDITOR

[9] Hendrick Ruitenbeek, ed., Freud as We Knew Him (Detroit: Wayne State UP, 1973) 64.

A BOOK WITH AN AUTHOR AND AN EDITOR

[10] Herman Melville, The Confidence Man: His Masquerade, ed. Hershel Parker (New York: Norton, 1971) 49.

A TRANSLATION

[11] Dante Alighieri, The Inferno, trans. John Ciardi (New York: NAL, 1971) 73-74.

A SELECTION FROM AN ANTHOLOGY

[12] Mark Twain, "The War Prayer," The Complete Essays of Mark Twain, ed. Charles Neider (Garden City: Doubleday, 1963) 681.

AN ARTICLE OR ESSAY FROM A REPRINTED COLLECTION

[13] W. M. Evan, "Due Process of Law in Military and Industrial Organizations," Administrative Science Quarterly 7 (1962): 187-207, rpt. in The Managerial Dilemma, ed. Stephen K. Banks (New York: Interface, 1980) 238.

Periodicals: journals, magazines, and newspapers

A SIGNED ARTICLE IN A JOURNAL WITH CONTINUOUS PAGINATION THROUGHOUT THE ANNUAL VOLUME

[14] Janet Lever, "Sex Differences in the Games Children Play," Social Problems 23 (1976): 482.

A SIGNED ARTICLE IN A JOURNAL THAT PAGES ISSUES SEPARATELY OR THAT NUMBERS ONLY ISSUES, NOT VOLUMES

[15] Sarah Boyd, "Nuclear Terror," Adaptation to Change 7.4 (1981): 20-21.

A SIGNED ARTICLE IN A MONTHLY OR BIMONTHLY PERIODICAL

[16] Harry Stein, "Living with Lies," Esquire Dec. 1981: 23.

A SIGNED ARTICLE IN A WEEKLY OR BIWEEKLY PERIODICAL

[17] Thomas Whiteside, "Onward and Upward with the Arts (Cable Television--Part 1)," New Yorker 20 May 1985: 49.

A SIGNED ARTICLE IN A DAILY NEWSPAPER

[18] Edward A. Gargan, "Buffalo Concern Gives Pop Sound to Player Pianos," New York Times 16 Feb. 1984: B1.

AN UNSIGNED ARTICLE

[19] "The Right to Die," Time 11 Oct. 1976: 101.

[20] "Protests Greet Pope in Holland," Boston Sunday Globe 12 May 1985, sec. 1: 21.

AN EDITORIAL, A LETTER TO THE EDITOR, OR A REVIEW

[21] George W. Ball, "Block That Vietnam Myth," editorial, New York Times 19 May 1985: E21.

[22] Michael Dowding, letter, Economist 5-11 Jan. 1985: 4.

[23] John Gregory Dunne, "The Secret of Danny Santiago," rev. of Famous All over Town, by Danny Santiago, New York Review of Books 16 Aug. 1984: 20.

Encyclopedias and almanacs

[24] "Mammoth," The New Columbia Encyclopedia, 1975 ed.

[25] Herman F. Mark, "Polymers," Encyclopaedia Britannica: Macropaedia, 1974.

Pamphlets and government documents

[26] Resource Notebook (Washington: Project on Institutional Renewal Through the Improvement of Teaching, 1976) 17.

[27] Hawaii, Dept. of Education, Kauai District Schools, Profile 1983-84 (Honolulu: Hawaii Dept. of Education, 1983) 2.

[28] United States, Cong., House, Committee on Ways and Means, Medicare Payment for Outpatient Occupational Therapy Services, 98th Cong., 2nd sess. (Washington: GPO, 1984) 3.

Unpublished dissertations and theses

[29] Stuart M. Wilson, "John Stuart Mill as a Literary Critic," diss., U of Michigan, 1970, 7.

Musical compositions and works of art

[30] Wolfgang Amadeus Mozart, Piano Concerto no. 21 in D Minor, K. 466.

[31] John Singer Sargent, Venetian Doorway, Metropolitan Museum of Art, New York.

Films and television programs

[32] King of America, writ. B. J. Merholz, music Elizabeth Swados, with Larry Atlas, Andreas Katsulas, Barry Miller, and Michael Walden, American Playhouse, PBS, WNET, New York, 19 Jan. 1982.

[33] Woody Allen, dir., Manhattan, with Allen, Diane Keaton, Michael Murphy, Meryl Streep, and Anne Byrne, United Artists, 1979.

Performances

[34] Ceremonies in Dark Old Men, by Lonne Elder, dir. Douglas Turner Ward, Theater Four, New York, 15 May 1985.

[35] Seiji Ozawa, cond., Boston Symphony Orch. Concert, Symphony Hall, Boston, 25 Apr. 1982.

Recordings

[36] Joni Mitchell, For the Roses, Asylum, SD 5057, 1972.

[37] Johannes Brahms, Concerto no. 2 in B-flat, op. 83, perf. Artur Rubinstein, cond. Eugene Ormandy, Philadelphia Orch., RCA, RK-1243, 1972.

Interviews

[38] Councilman John Smithson, personal interview, 6 Sept. 1985.

[39] William Martin, interview, "Give Me That Big Time Religion," Frontline, PBS, WGBH, Boston, 13 Feb. 1984.

Computer software

[40] Project Scheduler 5000, computer software, Scitor, 1984, MS-DOS, 256 KB, disk.

fn
35i

Subsequent references to the same source

To minimize clutter in notes and to give readers a quick sense of how often you acknowledge a source, you should use a shortened form for subsequent references to a source you have already cited fully. When you refer to only one source by the author cited (or only one source bearing the title cited if there is no author), the *MLA Handbook* recommends that subsequent references carry only the author's name (or a short form of the title) and the page reference appropriate for the later citation. Here are two examples, preceded by the full citations.

[10] Herman Melville, The Confidence Man: His Masquerade, ed. Hershel Parker (New York: Norton, 1971) 49.

[41] Melville 62.

[19] "The Right to Die," Time 11 Oct. 1976: 101.

[42] "Right" 101.

However, if two of your sources are by the same author, give a shortened form of the appropriate title so there can be no confusion about which work you are citing. For example:

[1] Carol Gilligan, In a Different Voice: Psychological Theory and Women's Development (Cambridge: Harvard UP, 1982) 27.

[43] Carol Gilligan, "Moral Development in the College Years," The Modern American College, ed. A. Chickering (San Francisco: Jossey-Bass, 1981) 286.

[44] Gilligan, "Moral" 288.

Note: The *MLA Handbook* discourages use of the Latin abbreviation "ibid." ("in the same place") as a means of indicating that a citation refers to the source in the preceding note.

EXERCISE 15

Add the final source citations to the research paper you wrote and revised in Exercise 13 (p. 509), using the list of works cited you prepared in Exercise 14 (p. 511). Use the style of parenthetical reference recommended by the *MLA Handbook* (pp. 512–17) unless your instructor specifies a different style.

35j
Examining two sample research papers

The research papers of Paul Fuller and Ann Weiss appear on the following pages (Fuller's begins on the next page, Weiss's on p. 550). Both students used the bibliographic formats and the style of parenthetical reference recommended by the *MLA Handbook*, and both typed their papers following the advice on manuscript format in Appendix B of this handbook. Facing each page of Fuller's paper are comments, keyed by number, that explain the format of his manuscript and some of the decisions he made in moving from research to writing. Comments in the margins of Weiss's paper note the distinctive features of her analysis.

How Advertisers Make Us Buy 1

By

Paul Fuller

English 101, Section A

Mr. R. Macek

March 12, 1984

35j

1. **Title page format.** Provide a separate title page if your instructor requests it or if you are required to submit an outline with your paper. On his title page Fuller includes the title of his paper about a third of the way down the page, his own name (preceded by "By") about an inch below the title, and, starting about an inch below his name, some identifying information requested by his instructor (course number, section label, and instructor's name) and the date. He centers all lines in the width of the page and separates them from each other with at least one line of space. If your instructor does not require a title page for your paper, place your name, the identifying information, and the date on the first page of the paper. See Ann Weiss's paper (p. 550) for this alternative format.

Next two pages

2. **Outline format.** If your instructor asks you to include your final outline, place it between the title page and the text, as Fuller does on the following pages. Number the pages with small Roman numerals (i, ii), and place your name just before the page numbers in case the pages of your paper become separated. Place the heading "Outline" an inch from the top of the first page, and double-space under the heading.
3. **Outline content.** Fuller includes his final thesis sentence as part of his outline so that his instructor can see how the parts relate to the whole.
4. Fuller casts his final outline in full sentences. Some instructors request topic outlines, in which ideas appear in phrases instead of in sentences and do not end with periods.
5. Notice that each main division (numbered with Roman numerals) refers directly to a portion of the thesis sentence and that all the subdivisions relate directly to their main division. Notice, too, the use of parallel phrasing for parallel levels. You need not repeat words such as *advertisers say,* but in this case they help Fuller relate his ideas to each other logically and clearly.

Fuller i

Outline 2

Thesis sentence: Advertisers appeal to consumers' emotions, rather than to their reason, because consumers choose products irrationally. 3

I. Critics of advertising say advertisers deliberately use strong emotional and irrational appeals. 4

   A. Marshall McLuhan says the appeals of advertising are directed to the unconscious.

   B. Vance Packard says the methods of advertisers represent regression for the rational nature of human beings.

   C. David Ogilvy says that most advertising treats consumers as if they were idiots, unable to reason.

II. Advertisers say they appeal to emotion because consumers choose products irrationally. 5

   A. Advertisers say that advertising by its nature as human communication expresses both emotional and rational messages.

   B. Advertisers say human beings choose irrationally.

   C. Advertisers say that appealing to emotion increases sales.

      1. Adding color to products or their advertisements increases sales.

      2. Adding cartoon characters to products or their packages increases sales.

      3. Adding emotional symbols to advertisements increases sales.

Fuller ii

III. Studies of advertising indicate that advertisers do appeal to emotions, as both critics and advertisers claim, and that consumers seem to choose products emotionally, as advertisers claim.

   A. An informal survey of advertisements indicates that the average advertisement uses much more emotional appeal than rational appeal.

   B. Experiments by independent researchers suggest that consumers respond to emotional appeals in advertising and that they do not examine advertisements rationally.

      1. One study showed that consumers make an emotional choice in favor of advertisements that merely sound truthful.

      2. Another study showed that consumers do not examine advertisements rationally but do respond emotionally to a claim that merely sounds rational.

Fuller 1

How Advertisers Make Us Buy 6

Against a background of rolling music and a deep voice 7
speaking of "winning the world," a woman descends from a swirl of sailcloth and clouds. This view widens to take in the whole scene--ship, ocean, sky--in a panorama that seems cosmic. The purpose of this drama is to make a television audience buy some coffee. The advertisement's outsized play for emotional attention and response is typical of contemporary advertising. Critics of such advertising accuse it of ignoring the human capacity for reason, the ability to make purchasing decisions on the basis of a product's performance and quality, while appealing instead to consumers' emotions about humor, sex, status, and adventure and to their unquestioning faith in science. In fact, advertisers do appeal to consumers' emotions, rather than to their reason, because consumers choose products irrationally.

The critics of advertising stress its manipulativeness 8
and mindlessness. Marshall McLuhan, the philosopher of 9
mass-media culture, says that advertising directs its
appeals to the unconscious:

> Ours is the first age in which many thousands of 10
> the best-trained individual minds have made it a
> full-time business to get inside the collective
> public mind . . . to manipulate, exploit, con- 11
> trol. . . . Why not assist the public to observe

6. **Title.** Although a title such as "Appeals to Emotion in Advertising" would reflect Fuller's thesis more accurately, it would also be less forceful. **Paper format.** The margins of the paper are one inch all around. The title appears on the first page of the paper even if a title page is used. The title is typed an inch from the top of the page, and it is neither placed in quotation marks nor underlined. The first line of text is typed four lines (two double spaces) below the title. (See Ann Weiss's paper, p. 550, for the format of the first page when a title page is not required.)
7. **Introduction.** Fuller opens by summarizing a television commercial to demonstrate how illogical advertising can be and to introduce readers to the issues of the thesis. The example is concrete and effective. However, Fuller could have begun his paper without it by omitting everything through the word *coffee* and rephrasing the next sentence: "Outsized plays for emotional attention and response are typical of contemporary advertising." The following sentence elaborates on this idea while also introducing advertising's critics and clarifying two central terms of the thesis sentence and the entire paper: *appeal to reason* and *appeal to emotion.*
8. **Relation to outline.** This paragraph corresponds to part I of Fuller's outline. Part II of the outline begins with the next paragraph and continues until page 5 of the paper.
9. **Introducing quotations.** Fuller effectively introduces his quotations here and on the next two pages: he establishes the credentials of each author in an identifying phrase; he summarizes each author's point of view; and, with the shorter quotation from Packard, he integrates the author's sentence structure into his own. (But see also comment 14, p. 533, on the Ogilvy quotation.)
10. **Format of long quotations.** The McLuhan and Ogilvy quotations on this page and the next exceed four typed lines, so Fuller sets them off from the text. These block quotations are set off by double spacing above and below, are themselves double-spaced, and are indented ten spaces from the left margin.
11. **Editing quotations.** Fuller uses ellipses in the two long quotations to show that he has eliminated irrelevant material (see 25e). All the ellipses consist of three spaced periods; but the second one in the McLuhan quotation is preceded by a sentence period closed up to the last word, and the ellipsis in the Ogilvy quotation is followed by a space and a comma from the original. Fuller's editing of the McLuhan quotation is not entirely successful. The sentence after the ellipsis strays from the idea Fuller wants to capture (that advertising appeals are directed to the unconscious), so he should have omitted it as well.

Fuller 2

> consciously the drama intended to operate unconsciously? (v) 12

Vance Packard, who brought national attention to the manipu- 13
lations of advertisers in his best-selling The Hidden Persuaders, asserts that the methods of advertisers "represent regress rather than progress for man in his long struggle to become a rational and self-guiding being" (4). David Ogilvy, one of advertising's most famous successes, concedes that most advertising treats consumers as if they were unable to reason:

> When I first began making advertisements . . . , I looked at the so-called mass magazines and I was impressed by the extraordinary gap between editorial content and advertising content. I saw that the editors were writing with taste to an intelligent audience, and the advertising writers
> were writing to idiots. (qtd. in Glatzer 85) 14

Advertisers themselves say that ads combine rational 15
and emotional appeals (Bernstein 295). This mixture, they 16
claim, comes from advertising's nature as another form of human communication. Regular conversation illustrates how all human communication, including advertising, works. In regular conversation *how* something is said is often as important as *what* is said. The speaker's voice, gestures, and facial expression carry emotional messages just as important as the rational content of what the speaker says. In printed advertising, art, layout, and typeface carry the emotional messages. In television advertising, the person-

12. **Reference when the author is named in the text.** Fuller has already mentioned McLuhan's name in the text, so he does not repeat it in the reference. Since this is a displayed quotation, the reference falls outside the closing punctuation. In contrast, the reference for Packard in the next sentence falls between the closing quotation mark and the sentence period.
13. **Paragraphing.** Fuller does not begin a new paragraph after the McLuhan quotation because the following material (the Packard and Ogilvy quotations) is directly related. After the Ogilvy quotation, Fuller does begin a new paragraph because he's embarking on a new thought.
14. **Reference to an indirect source.** Fuller's reference indicates that he discovered the Ogilvy quotation in Glatzer's book. **Indirect sources.** Glatzer quotes from Ogilvy's autobiography, a widely available source that Fuller should have consulted directly. A writer should avoid quoting a source secondhand unless the firsthand source cannot be located. In this case, the work of "one of advertising's most famous successes," as Fuller identifies Ogilvy, might have provided significant information. See also comments 31 and 33 on pages 543 and 545.
15. **Diction.** At this point Fuller begins using the informal, clipped form *ads* instead of *advertisements*. In general, the diction in a research paper should be more formal than that appropriate for, say, a personal essay. But Fuller needed to use the words *advertisers* and *advertisements* so often in his paper that he decided *ads* would make the paper more readable.
16. **Reference when the author is not named in the text.** Because Fuller has not used Bernstein's name in the text, he provides it in the reference. **Citing and introducing paraphrases.** Fuller is summarizing Bernstein, so he cites the source as he would the source of a quotation. The rest of this paragraph is a paraphrase from another source cited at the end (next page). Fuller has put the parenthetical reference in the right place, but he has failed to introduce the lengthy paraphrase adequately. As a result, the second sentence ("This mixture, they claim, . . .") appears to be undocumented, and the reference seems to document only the last sentence in the paragraph. Fuller should have introduced the paraphrase in the second sentence and then made it clear that other sentences in the paragraph derive from the same source: "*Advertiser Pierre Martineau claims* that the mixture comes from advertising's nature as another form of human communication. *He notes* that regular conversation. . . ." With Martineau's name in the text, the parenthetical reference would require only page numbers.

Fuller 3

alities of announcers and actors, the music, and the visual imagery become symbols of emotional meaning (Martineau 139-40).

Advertisers maintain that their emotional appeals are 17
appropriate because human beings are essentially irrational.
Car salespeople have noticed that customers on the verge of 18
buying an expensive car for an emotional motive, such as a desire for status, like to talk at the last minute about superior performance in order to make an emotional decision seem rational (Smith 6). Pierre Martineau explains this behavior more generally:

> The entire personality of every individual is built around basic emotional needs, and the whole system of his thinking is determined by these needs, even though superficially the individual defends his point of view on purely rational grounds. Experiments repeatedly show that his rationality is highly selective rationality (or
> in other words, not rational at all). (62; 19
> emphasis added)

Other recent studies confirm the same view of consumers by
advertisers.[1] 20

Advertisers claim many sales successes through appeals 21
to emotion. One technique for increasing the emotional appeal of products is "color engineering." Adding color to an ad or to a product in which color has no practical function increases sales. For example, until the 1920s fountain pens were made of hard black rubber. When colored

35j

17. **Summary statement.** This sentence does not contain a reference because it is Fuller's summary of evidence from the sources cited in the rest of the paragraph.
18. **Paraphrasing.** Fuller paraphrases the example about car salespeople even though his note card contains the exact quotation from the source. He decides not to quote directly because he can reduce several sentences in the original to one of his own, and he does not want two long quotations in a row. Here is the original note card:

> Consumers' irrational choices
>
> Smith, Motivation Research, p. 6.
>
> "Car salesmen joke that their product knowledge—performance statistics, repair record, etc.—doesn't make them a dime. What sells an expensive car is the customer's feeling about luxury, good looks, status. So he does not appear impulsive, the customer may ask about performance just as he is about to sign the papers, but at that moment the salesman could say almost anything without jeopardizing what is essentially an irrational purchase."

19. **Adding emphasis to quotations.** Fuller underlines certain words in the quotation that reinforce his thesis especially clearly. He acknowledges this change inside the parenthetical reference, separated by a semicolon from the page number.
20. **Using an endnote for supplementary information.** Instead of continuing to quote and paraphrase the same view of consumers, Fuller lets readers know that further support is available, and the raised numeral ([1]) signals that he has more to say at a note with the corresponding numeral. See page 546 for the note itself.
21. **Selecting supporting evidence.** In these paragraphs listing sales successes that resulted from appeals to emotion, Fuller has selected from his sources the most dramatic and vivid success stories he found. He provides concrete facts that support his case. And he carefully cites his sources.

Fuller 4

plastic pens were introduced, sales improved "astronomically" (Ketcham 7). Using aluminum paint instead of black on bedsprings improved sales by 25 percent for one manufacturer 22
(Ketcham 8). A Gloucester fish packer increased his sales 33 percent simply by adding color to his advertising circular (Hotchkiss 164). Currently, the emotional appeal of cartoon characters increases sales 10 to 20 percent when the characters are printed on products or their packages (Johnson). 23
Experts disagree on just why color and cartoons have such appeal; for instance, the cartoons may trigger hero worship or nostalgia (Johnson). Clearly, however, the appeal *is* emotional and sales improve because of it.

Two classic advertising campaigns that relied on emotional appeals are Hathaway's and Marlboro's. After ads for 24
Hathaway shirts began to include a well-built, mysterious man with a patch over one eye, sales of the shirts tripled (Martineau 148). The manufacturers of Marlboro cigarettes experienced an even more dramatic increase in sales because of a change in advertising. In 1954 Philip Morris decided to enter one of its worst-selling cigarettes, Marlboro, in the new filter-tip market (Glatzer 122-23). To change the product's image as a woman's cigarette, the advertisers eliminated all women from the ads and substituted virile men. Each new ad emphasized a tattoo on the hand of the man smoking a Marlboro. The tattoos were a symbol that seemed to give the whole ad campaign an emotional unity (Martineau 147). This shift in emotional appeal improved Marlboro's sales drastically: from near zero in 1954 to 6.4 billion in

22. **Going back to sources.** In his first draft Fuller described his examples of sales successes with phrases like "sales increased" and "sales improved" rather than with actual figures, and his assertions lacked force. When he realized he needed to be more specific, he referred to his bibliography cards (showing the call numbers) and to his note cards (showing page numbers) and was able to collect the figures he wanted in a quick trip to the library. In the note card below Fuller has added to the information originally gathered from the article by Johnson.

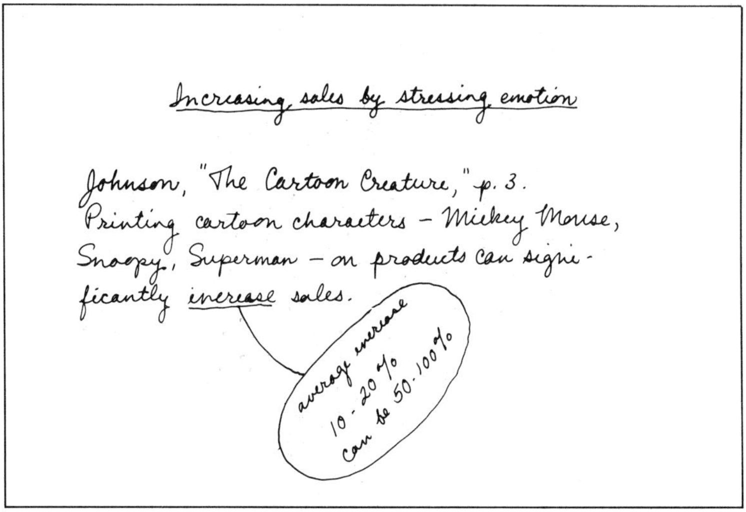

Increasing sales by stressing emotion

Johnson, "The Cartoon Creature," p. 3.
Printing cartoon characters – Mickey Mouse, Snoopy, Superman – on products can significantly increase sales.

average increase 10-20% can be 50-100%

23. **Reference to a one-page article.** Johnson's article appears on only one page of the newspaper it is in, and Fuller gives that page number in the list of works cited (see p. 548). Thus he does not need to repeat the page number in the reference.
24. **Using sources effectively.** In this paragraph Fuller blends material from two sources to make one point about the success of emotional appeals. Instead of merely stringing together other people's ideas, he arranges the material in order of increasing drama and thus shapes his research to express and support his own views. Notice that Fuller's four references (two for each source) indicate clearly which information came from which source.

1955, 14.3 billion in 1956, and 19.5 billion in 1957
(Glatzer 134).

But advertisers' success stories are not the last word. 25
An informal survey and more formal studies of advertising
show that appeals to emotion predominate and that consumers
seem to go out of their way to make choices for emotional
reasons.

My own informal survey of ads in an issue of <u>Newsweek</u> 26
revealed that most of the ads (twenty-six of thirty-eight)
used a predominantly emotional appeal (see Table 1, next 27
page). Only one-fourth of the ads (nine of thirty-eight)
depended on rational appeal as much as 50 percent. Some ads
of products for which rational appeal would be easy or likely
--products such as a newsletter and insurance--barely used
appeals to reason (under 20 percent rational appeal). This
limited (one-reader, one-magazine) study leads to several
conclusions: (1) that most ads appeal primarily to consumers' emotions; (2) that only a tiny fraction of ads (one
of thirty-eight) appeal primarily to reason; and (3) that
no ads use rational appeal 100 percent, although many (twelve
of thirty-eight) use emotional appeal 100 percent.

In an experimental study of advertising, Robert Settle
and Linda Golden found that admitting a product's inferiority
on one or two minor points of comparison was more effective
in advertising than claiming the product's superiority on
all counts. The researchers asked 120 business students to 28
evaluate a series of ads. (The products advertised were
fictitious.) Half the ads claimed that the fictitious

25. **Transitional paragraph and relation to outline.** Here Fuller devotes a paragraph to the transition between part II and part III of the outline, between sales evidence supporting advertisers' claims about consumers and equally supportive studies by nonadvertisers.
26. **Original research.** Because he is a consumer, Fuller feels that his subjective reactions to ads are legitimate responses to evaluate and use. Nevertheless, he wisely admits the limitations of his survey later in the paragraph. **Primary and secondary sources.** Fuller's study of magazine ads is a primary source because it is direct, firsthand information. His other sources are secondary because they contain other people's reports and interpretations of primary or secondary sources. In several instances he relies on secondhand sources when he should have used original sources; see comments 14 (p. 533), 31 (p. 543), and 33 (p. 545).
27. **Reference to illustration.** Here Fuller refers specifically to the table that shows the complete results of his survey.
28. **Reporting studies.** Fuller's descriptions of experiments here are detailed enough to let readers know how the experiments were conducted, yet not so detailed that readers will get bogged down in the experiments and lose track of his ideas. Again, as in presenting the examples of successful advertising campaigns earlier, Fuller arranges material in order of increasing detail and drama. He might have enlivened his description by including more quotations from the studies as well as even more specific information (such as some of the products evaluated in the first study). He had the specific details on his note card but failed to use them.

Research on consumer responses

Gregg, "To Sell Your Product," p. 35.

Repts. study by Robert Settle and Linda Golden in Jnl. of Marketing Research 11 (May 1974).

120 bus. students evaluate fictitious ads for a pen, a watch, a blender, a camera, and a clock radio. Half the ads claimed the product was five ways superior to a well-known competitor; the other half claimed superiority on only three points and inferiority on two points. 80% of the students found ads admitting some inferiority to be more persuasive.

See also comment 31, page 543.

Fuller 6

Table 1 29

Survey of Advertisements in <u>Newsweek</u>, 19 February 1979[a]

Advertisement	Percentages emotional/ rational
Tobacco Institute	100/0
American Forest Institute	50/50
Jeep	80/20
VW	100/0
Winnebago	80/20
Exxon	50/50
Lonestar Building Supplier	80/20
Alcoa aluminum	50/50
Tareyton	100/0
L&M Lights	50/50
Marlboro	100/0
Doral II	90/10
Merit	80/20
Winston Lights	100/0
Salem	100/0
Beechcraft Aviation	80/20
Pan Am	50/50
Pakistan Airlines	80/20
Chivas Regal	90/10
Jameson Irish Whiskey	100/0
Jack Daniels	90/10
Ronrico Rum	90/10
Canadian Club	100/0
Royal copier	60/40
Sharp copier	50/50
Mutual Life Insurance	100/0
Sun Life Insurance	100/0
GE TV	10/90
Vivitar lens	50/50
Book ad	95/5
Famolare shoes	50/50
Trinity missions	100/0
St. Elizabeth Hotel	90/10
Newsletter on new products	80/20
Anderson Windowwalls	50/50
Anacin	50/50
Preparation H	50/50
United Cerebral Palsy	100/0

[a]The method for determining what percentage of an ad appealed to emotion and what percentage to reason involved (1) recording the overall impact of the ad as emotional or rational; (2) evaluating the proportions of space given to different purposes and the effects of layout, color, type, and artwork; (3) thinking of the possible ways to advertise the product without appealing to emotions and evaluating the ad against these; and (4) weighing the observations and assigning percentages to emotional and rational appeals. As an example, the Ronrico Rum ad contains an illustration occupying 80 percent of the space. It shows an upright bottle of rum (label facing out) and the shape of a bottle tilted at 60°, containing a photograph of a couple kissing, palm trees, beautiful water--a scene whose greenness stands out against the mostly white ad and the pale bottle of rum. The angle of the bottle outline suggests it is about to fall and makes the viewer want to reach out and grab it. The ad's brief copy discusses the rum's "authentic" relation with Puerto Rico. Only the words "smooth, light taste" describe a rationally desirable quality of rum. The ad was rated (perhaps generously) 90 percent emotional, 10 percent rational. 30

29. **Table format.** Fuller places the table after the table reference (p. 5 of the paper) and on a separate sheet of paper. He numbers the table with an Arabic numeral (1) and capitalizes the important words in the title. The title tells readers what magazine the advertisements appeared in. His column headings clearly label the information beneath them. Generally, tables like this one should be double-spaced throughout, but Fuller single-spaces his so that it will fit on one page.
30. **Source acknowledgment.** Since the table contains Fuller's original material, no acknowledgment (source note) is needed. If one were, the source would be given immediately after the table and preceded by the word "Source" and a colon. **Explanatory note.** Fuller's table does need an explanation of his method so that readers can judge the value of his survey. The note is keyed as a footnote, but a raised letter ([a]) is used instead of a raised number to prevent possible confusion of any text notes with the table note.

Fuller 7

product was superior to the best-selling and well-known
actual product on five points of comparison. The other half
claimed the fictitious product was superior on only three
counts and inferior on two minor points. The students found
the latter ads, which admitted some inferiority, to be more
successful in persuading them to buy the new (fictitious)
product instead of the best seller (Gregg). They made an
emotional choice in favor of ads that simply sounded truth- 31
ful without having evidence that the claims of truth were in
fact valid.

In another study with experimental ads, Seymour Lieberman had an advertising agency create two television ads for
each of six fictitious products. Each product had one
deceitful ad containing a false or made-up scientific claim
and one truthful ad that did not contain the scientific
claim. For instance, the deceitful ad for a fictitious plant
fertilizer stressed that the fertilizer contained protein
(though in fact protein does not help plants grow), whereas
the truthful ad did not mention protein. The deceitful ad
for a fictitious bunion remedy stated that the remedy contained "four times as much methylglyoxal" (although methyl- 32
glyoxal does not help treat bunions), whereas the truthful
ad did not mention methylglyoxal. Both pairs of ads used
the same actors and the same language; the only difference
was the presence or absence of the scientific claim. After
being asked to say which products interested them, one
hundred middle-income consumers watched the deceitful ads
and another hundred middle-income consumers watched the

31. **Original and secondhand sources.** Fuller's reference here indicates that his information on Settle and Gordon's study comes from Gregg's article. (See the note card below.) Instead of relying on a secondhand report of the study, Fuller should have consulted the original article by Settle and Gordon, not only to ensure the accuracy of his description but also to check for additional information. (Note that Fuller omits page numbers from the Gregg reference because the information appeared on both pages of a two-page article.) **Drawing conclusions.** Fuller places references to Gregg and to the article "Truth Doesn't Sell" (next page of the paper) after his descriptions of the experiments but before the conclusions he draws to support the second part of his thesis (that consumers choose products irrationally). In fact, the experimenters did not use their results for quite the same purposes as Fuller does. For example, a note card on Gregg's article quotes the researchers' conclusion:

> Research on consumer responses - conclusions
>
> Gregg, "To Sell Your Product," Psych. Today, p. 36
>
> Quoting Robert Settle and Linda Golden from their article in Jnl. of Marketing Research 11 (May 1974). "Advertisers [should] disclaim at least one feature of minor importance" rather than "exclude it from the message entirely." They can thus "make advertising claims of superiority more believable."

By separating the studies' results from his own conclusions about the results, Fuller demonstrates the amount of thought he has given his sources, and he hopes to avoid misrepresenting them (always a danger in reporting and interpreting the work of others). However, since Fuller's conclusions are not those of the researchers, he might have mentioned briefly the researchers' goals and conclusions so that his readers could evaluate his use of their results.

32. **Use of quotation.** Fuller's quotation of a key phrase from the study makes his description more concrete and also illustrates how successfully the researchers imitated real ads in their fictitious ones. As noted in comment 28 (p. 539), Fuller might have made greater use of such quotations and details from the studies he cites.

Fuller 8

truthful ads. More consumers showed interest in the deceitful fertilizer ad than showed interest in the truthful ad.
And four times as many consumers showed interest in the
deceitful four-times-as-much methylglyoxal ad for a bunion
remedy as showed interest in the truthful ad. Similar
results occurred with two of the other four pairs of ads
tested ("Truth"). The consumers did not examine the ads' 33
claims rationally. Instead, they gravitated to what sounded
like fact, responding emotionally to claims of scientific
improvements without rationally evaluating the claims.

The critics of advertising accuse advertisers of using 34
emotional appeals deliberately and irresponsibly. They imply
that consumers would make rational decisions about products
if the ads for those products gave them facts about performance and quality on which to base a rational choice. Advertisers freely admit their emphasis on emotional appeals but
maintain that consumers make choices irrationally. As proof,
they offer the sales successes brought about by purely emotional appeals. One informal survey verifies advertisers'
reliance on emotional appeals. And formal experiments suggest that consumers do not require hard information on which
to base decisions but will accept the appearance of truth or
fact as a substitute for the real thing. We may say we
object to the overblown advertisement with no informative content. That is certainly the kind of ad we see most often.
But it also seems to be the kind of ad we deserve.

33. **Reference to an unsigned article.** Here Fuller acknowledges an unsigned article titled "Truth Doesn't Sell" (see the entry for this source on p. 548). Shortening the title to "Truth" provides adequate information for readers to locate the source while keeping the reference as unobtrusive as possible. Fuller draws on information appearing on both pages of the two-page article, so a page number is not needed in the reference. **Original and secondhand sources.** Again, as with the article by Gregg (comment 31, p. 543), Fuller relies on a secondhand report of the study he describes. He should have consulted the original report by Lieberman.
34. **Conclusion.** Fuller's conclusion might be faulted for lack of imagination, but it suits his purpose. He shows that his thesis is valid by summarizing the evidence he has presented in the paper. In his last few sentences he deliberately switches to *we* in a way that emphasizes the relevance of his conclusion for himself and his readers. His last sentence provides a final edge.

Fuller 9

Note 35

[1] See, for example, Engle and Blackwell 58. There the same idea is stated in a complex diagram, the "Complete Model of Consumer Behavior Showing Purchasing Processes and Outcomes." Out of twenty-three boxes of factors only one box, "Evaluative Criteria," seems to represent rationality. 36

35. **Format of notes.** The word "Note" is centered one inch from the top of the page. (The heading would be plural—"Notes"—if Fuller had more than one note.) The note begins two lines (one double space) below the heading. The note itself is double-spaced. The first line is indented five spaces and preceded by a raised number corresponding to the number used in the text. A space separates the number and the note.
36. **Endnote for additional relevant information.** Fuller's single note provides an example of work confirming that advertisers view consumers as irrational. (See p. 534 for the note reference in Fuller's text.) Fuller cites the last names of both authors, and he provides a page number (58) directing readers to the appropriate place in the source.

Fuller 10

Works Cited 37

Bernstein, David. Creative Advertising. London: Longman, 1974. 38

Engel, James F., and Roger D. Blackwell. Consumer Behavior. 4th ed. New York: Dryden, 1982. 39

Glatzer, Robert. The New Advertising: The Great Campaigns. New York: Citadel, 1970.

Gregg, Gary. "To Sell Your Product, Admit It's Not Perfect." Psychology Today Oct. 1974: 35-36. 40

Hotchkiss, George Burton. An Outline of Advertising: Its Philosophy, Science, Art, and Strategy. 3rd ed. New York: Macmillan, 1950.

Johnson, Sharon. "The Cartoon Creature as Salesman." New York Times 11 Feb. 1979, sec. 3: 3. 41

Ketcham, Howard. Color Planning: For Business and Industry. New York: Harper, 1958.

McLuhan, Herbert Marshall. The Mechanical Bride: Folklore of Industrial Man. New York: Vanguard, 1951.

Martineau, Pierre. Motivation in Advertising: Motives That Make People Buy. New York: McGraw, 1971.

Packard, Vance. The Hidden Persuaders. Rev. ed. New York: Pocket, 1981.

Smith, George H. Motivation Research in Advertising and Marketing. Westport: Greenwood, 1971.

"Truth Doesn't Sell." Time 14 May 1973: 96-97. 42

37. **Format of list of works cited.** The heading "Works Cited" is centered one inch from the top of the page. The first entry is typed two lines (one double space) below the heading, and the entire list is double-spaced. The first line of each entry begins at the left margin; subsequent lines of the same entry are indented five spaces. The entries are alphabetized.
38. Typical entry for a **book with one author.**
39. Entry for an **edition other than the first.** Here is Fuller's bibliography card for this source:

HF 541
.2
.E5

Engel, James F., and Roger D. Blackwell.
Consumer Behavior. 4th ed.
New York: Dryden, 1982.

40. Entry for a **signed article in a monthly periodical.**
41. Entry for a **signed article in a daily newspaper.**
42. Entry for an **unsigned article.** Here is Fuller's bibliography card for this source:

"Truth Doesn't Sell." Time
14 May 1973: 96–97.

1

Ann Weiss

Ms. Seaver

April 29, 1985

The Editing of the Declaration of Independence: Better or Worse?

The Declaration of Independence is so widely regarded as a statement of American ideals that its origins in practical politics tend to be forgotten. The document drafted by Thomas Jefferson was intensely debated in the Continental Congress and then substantially revised before being signed. Since then, most historians have agreed that Jefferson's Declaration was improved in the process. But Jefferson himself was disappointed with the result (Boyd 37); and recently his view has received scholarly support. Thus it is an open question whether the Congress improved a flawed document or damaged an inspired one. An answer to the question requires understanding the context in which the Declaration was conceived and examining the document itself.

The Continental Congress in 1776 was attended by representatives of all thirteen colonies. The colonies were ruled more or less separately by Great Britain and had suffered repeated abuses at the hands of King George III, the British parliament, and local appointed governors. To end the abuses of the British, many colonists were urging three actions: forming a united front, seceding from Britain, and taking control of

Format of heading and title when no title page is required

Statement of topic

Focus on the disagreement to be resolved

Statement of how the disagreement will be resolved

Historical background: the context in which the Declaration was conceived (next two paragraphs)

their own international trade and diplomacy (Wills 325-26). They saw the three actions as dependent on each other, and all three were spelled out in a resolution that was proposed in the Congress on June 7, 1776 (Wills 326-27).

The Congress named a five-man committee to prepare a defense of this resolution in order to win the support of reluctant colonists and also to justify secession to potential foreign allies (Malone 219; Wills 330-31). Jefferson, the best writer on the committee, was assigned to draft the document. The other committee members made a few minor changes in his draft before submitting it to the Congress. The Congress made many small and some quite large alterations before finally approving the document on July 4 (Becker 171).

Isolation and summary of the material to be analyzed

The most interesting major change, because of the controversy it ultimately generated, was made in Jefferson's next-to-last paragraph. (See Figure 1 on the next page for Jefferson's version with the Congress's editing.) Jefferson made several points in the paragraph: the colonists had freely submitted to the British king but not to the British parliament; they had tried repeatedly and unsuccessfully to gain the support of the British people for their cause; yet the British ("unfeeling brethren") had not only ignored the colonists' pleas but also worsened their difficulties by supporting the parliament. These actions, Jefferson concluded, gave the colonists no choice but to separate from England. The Congress cut Jeffer-

Weiss 3

Nor have we been wanting in attentions to our British brethren. we have warned them from time to time of attempts by their legislature to extend ^ [a] jurisdiction over ^ [these our states.] we have reminded them of the circumstances of our emigration & settlement here, [no one of which could warrant so strange a pretension: that these were effected at the expence of our own blood & treasure, unassisted by the wealth or the strength of Great Britain: that in constituting indeed our several forms of government, we had adopted one common king, thereby laying a foundation for perpetual league & amity with them: but that submission to their parliament was no part of our constitution, nor ever in idea, if history may be credited: and,] we ^ appealed to their native justice and magnanimity ^ [as well as to] the ties of our common kindred to disavow these usurpations which ^ [were likely to] interrupt our connection and correspondence. they too have been deaf to the voice of justice & of consanguinity, [and when occasions have been given them, by the regular course of their laws, of removing from their councils the disturbers of our harmony, they have, by their free election, re-established them in power. at this very time too they are permitting their chief magistrate to send over not only souldiers of our common blood, but Scotch & foreign mercenaries to invade & destroy us. these facts have given the last stab to agonizing affection, and manly spirit bids us to renounce for ever these unfeeling brethren. we must endeavor to forget our former love for them, and to hold them as we hold the rest of mankind enemies in war, in peace friends. we might have been a free and a great people together; but a communication of grandeur & of freedom it seems is below their dignity. be it so, since they will have it. the road to happiness & to glory is open to us too. we will tread it apart from them, and] ^ acquiesce in the necessity which denounces our [eternal] separation ^ !

^ an unwarrantable

^ us

^ have

^ and we have conjured them by

^ would inevitably

^ we must therefore

^ and hold them as we hold the rest of mankind, enemies in war, in peace friends.

Photocopy of the material to be analyzed (a primary source)

Fig. 1. Next-to-last paragraph of the Declaration of Independence, photocopied from Jefferson (318-19). The text is Jefferson's as submitted by the five-man committee to the Continental Congress. The Congress deleted the passages that are underlined and added the passages in the margin.

Figure caption and source

35j

Weiss 4

son's paragraph by almost two-thirds, leaving only the points about the colonists' appeals to the British, the refusal of the British to listen, and the necessity of separation.

Until recently, most historians accepted all the Congress's changes in the Declaration as clear improvements. Dumas Malone, author of the most respected biography of Jefferson, expresses "little doubt that the critics strengthened" the Declaration, "primarily by deletion" (222). Julian Boyd, a historian of the period and the editor of Jefferson's papers, observes that "it is difficult to point out a passage in the Declaration, great as it was, that was not improved by their [the delegates'] attention" (36). Carl Becker, considered an expert on the evolution of the Declaration, agrees that "Congress left the Declaration better than it found it" (209). These scholars make few specific comments about the next-to-last paragraph. Becker, however, does say that Jefferson's emphasis on the British parliament is an allusion to a theory of government that is assumed in the rest of the document, so that the paragraph "leaves one with the feeling that the author, not quite aware that he is done, is beginning over again" (211-12).

Quotation and paraphrase of three important scholars on one side of the disagreement

The agreement in favor of the Congress's changes was broken in 1978 when the journalist and humanities scholar Garry Wills published a detailed defense of Jefferson's original, particularly his next-to-last paragraph. According to Wills, "Jefferson's declara-

Quotation and paraphrase of the scholar on the other side of the disagreement

tion of independence is a renunciation of unfeeling brethren. His whole document was shaped to make that clear" (319). The British people had betrayed the colonists both politically (by supporting the intrusive parliament) and emotionally (by ignoring the colonists' appeals), and that dual betrayal was central to Jefferson's argument for secession (303). Wills contends that in drastically cutting the next-to-last paragraph, "Congress removed the heart of his argument, at its climax" (319).

Weiss's resolution of the disagreement

As an explanation of Jefferson's intentions, Wills's presentation is convincing. However, a close examination of the original and edited versions of the next-to-last paragraph supports the opinions of earlier historians rather than Wills's argument that the Declaration was damaged by the Congress. The paragraph may have expressed Jefferson's own intentions, but it was neither successful in its tone nor appropriate for the purposes of the Congress as a whole.

Thesis sentence

Supporting analysis of the Declaration, including quotations and comment (next three paragraphs)

Part of Jefferson's assignment "was to impart the proper tone and spirit" to the Declaration (Malone 221). He did this throughout most of the document by expressing strong feelings in a solemn and reasonable manner. But in the next-to-last paragraph Jefferson's tone is sometimes overheated, as in the phrases "invade & destroy us," "last stab to agonizing affection," and "road to happiness & to glory." At other times Jefferson sounds as if he is pouting, as in "we must endeavor to forget our former love for

Analysis of tone

Weiss 6

them" and "a communication of grandeur & of freedom it seems is below their dignity." Wills comments that critics have viewed this paragraph as resembling "the recollections of a jilted lover" (313). Wills himself does not agree with this interpretation of the tone, but it seems accurate. All the quoted passages were deleted by the Congress.

Analysis of appropriateness for purposes of Congress (next two paragraphs)

More important than the problem in tone is the paragraph's inappropriateness for the purposes of the Declaration as the Congress saw them. Specifically, the paragraph probably would not have convinced reluctant colonists and potential foreign allies of the justice and logical necessity of secession. The Congress needed the support of as many colonists as possible, but many colonists still felt strong ties to their friends and relatives in England (Becker 127-28; Boyd 31-32). They would probably have been unhappy with phrases such as "renounce forever" and "eternal separation" that threatened a permanent break in those ties. The Congress deleted those phrases, and it also gave greater stress to Jefferson's one hint of a possible reconciliation with the British: "We must . . . hold them as we hold the rest of mankind enemies in war, in peace friends." This thought was moved by the Congress from inside the paragraph to the very end, where it strikes a final note of hope.

First purpose of Congress

Second purpose of Congress

The Congress also strengthened the appeal of the Declaration to potential allies, who would have needed assurance that the colonists were acting reasonably

Weiss 7

and cautiously. Both Jefferson's and the Congress's versions note that the colonists often "warned" and "reminded" the British and "appealed to their native justice & magnanimity," but that the British were "deaf to the voice of justice & consanguinity" and left the colonists no choice besides "separation." However, Jefferson buried these statements in lengthy charges against the British, while the Congress stripped away the charges to emphasize the colonists' patience in exploring all avenues of redress and their reluctance in seceding. Instead of "beginning over again," as Becker says Jefferson's version seems to do, the revised paragraph clearly provides the final rational justification for the action of the colonists. At the same time, it keeps enough of Jefferson's original to remind the audience that the colonists are feeling people, motivated by their hearts as well as by their minds. They do not secede enthusiastically but "acquiesce in the necessity" of separation.

Summary, and restatement of thesis

Though the Declaration has come to be a statement of this nation's political philosophy, that was not its purpose in 1776. Jefferson's intentions had to bow to the goals of the Congress as a whole to forge unity among the colonies and to win the support of foreign nations. As Boyd observes, the Declaration of Independence "was the result not merely of a single author's lonely struggle for the right phrase and the telling point, but also of the focussing of many minds --among them the best that America ever produced" (38).

Weiss 8

Works Cited

Becker, Carl. The Declaration of Independence: A Study in the History of Political Ideas. New York: Knopf, 1956.

Boyd, Julian P. The Declaration of Independence: The Evolution of a Text. Princeton: Princeton UP, 1945.

Jefferson, Thomas. "Notes of the Proceedings in the Continental Congress." The Papers of Thomas Jefferson. Ed. Julian P. Boyd et al. 21 vols. Princeton: Princeton UP, 1950-74. 1: 309-27.

Malone, Dumas. Jefferson the Virginian. Vol. 1 of Jefferson and His Time. 6 vols. Boston: Little, 1948.

Wills, Garry. Inventing America: Jefferson's Declaration of Independence. Garden City: Doubleday, 1978.

36
Practical Writing

Writing an essay examination or a business letter or memorandum requires the same attention to unity, coherence, and development that writing an essay or research paper does (Chapters 1 and 35). The special problems of writing essay examinations, business letters, and memos are the subject of this chapter.

36a
Answering essay questions

In writing an essay for an examination, you summarize or analyze a topic, usually in several paragraphs or more and usually within a time limit. An essay question not only tests your knowledge of a subject (as short-answer and objective questions do) but also tests your control and synthesis of that knowledge and helps you see it in a new way (as other kinds of questions usually cannot do).

1
Preparing for an essay examination

Taking lecture notes, thoughtfully reading the assigned texts or articles, and reviewing regularly will help you prepare for any kind of examination. (See Appendix C on study skills.) In addition, for an essay examination you can practice synthesizing what you know by creating summaries or outlines that reorganize the course material. For instance, in a business course you could evaluate the advantages and disadvantages of several approaches to management. In a short-story course you could look for a theme running through all the stories you have read by a certain author or from a certain period. In a psychology course you could contrast various theorists' views of what causes a disorder like schizophrenia. Any one of these is a likely topic for an essay question. Thinking of such categories not only can help you anticipate the kinds of questions you may be asked but also can increase your mastery of the material.

2 Planning your time and your answer

When you first look at your examination, always read it all the way through at least once before you start answering any questions. As you scan the examination, determine which questions seem most important, which ones are going to be most difficult for you, and approximately how much time you'll need for each question. (Your instructor may help by assigning a point value to each question as a guide to its importance or by suggesting an amount of time for you to spend on each question.) You will want to provide your best answer for every question, so this initial planning is important.

To avoid straying from an essay question or answering only part of it, read it at least twice. Examine the words and consider their implications. Look especially for words like *describe, define, explain, summarize, analyze, evaluate,* and *interpret,* each of which requires a different kind of response. For instance, the instruction *Define dyslexia and compare and contrast it with two other learning disabilities* contains important clues for how an essay should be written. *Define dyslexia* tells you to specify the meaning of the term. A description of how children with dyslexia feel about their disability, however well done, would be irrelevant. Instead, you should say what dyslexia is—a perceptual impairment causing a reader to reverse or scramble letters—and extend the definition by providing distinctive characteristics, ways the impairment seems to work, examples of its effects, and so on. The words *compare and contrast it with two other learning disabilities* tell you to analyze not only its similarities to but also its differences from the other disabilities. Answering this part of the question thus involves thinking of categories for comparison, such as causes, treatments, frequency of occurrence, and severity of effect. An essay that described only similarities or only differences would not answer the question completely.

After you're sure you understand the question, make a brief outline of the main ideas you want to include in your essay. Use the back of the test sheet or exam booklet for scratch paper. Write a brief thesis sentence for your essay that responds directly to the question and represents your view of the topic. (If you are unsure of how to write a thesis sentence, see 1g.) Include key phrases that you can expand with supporting evidence for your view. This stage is much like the planning of an essay or a research paper. Though you don't have as much time to refine and rearrange your ideas, planning will help make your essay unified, coherent, well supported, and concise.

3
Starting the essay

A well-constructed thesis sentence will contribute much to an examination essay. Drawing on the brief thesis you devised during planning, you can begin an essay effectively by stating your thesis immediately and including in it an overview of the rest of your essay. Such a capsule version of your answer tells your reader (and grader) generally how much command you have and also how you plan to develop your answer.

The opening statement should address the question directly and exactly. The following thesis sentence, in response to the question below, does *not* meet these criteria.

Question

Given humans' natural and historical curiosity about themselves, why did a scientific discipline of anthropology not arise until the twentieth century? Explain, citing specific details.

Tentative thesis sentence

The discipline of anthropology, the study of humans, actually began in the early nineteenth century and was strengthened by the Darwinian revolution, but the discipline did not begin to take shape until people like Franz Boas and Alfred Kroeber began doing scientific research among nonindustrialized cultures.

This tentative thesis sentence says nothing about *why* anthropology did not arise as a scientific discipline until the twentieth century. Instead, it supplies an unspecific (and unrequested) definition of anthropology, vaguely reasserts the truth implied by the question, and adds irrelevant details about the history of anthropology. The following thesis—revised to address the question directly, to state the writer's view, and to preview the essay—begins the answer more effectively.

Revised thesis sentence

Anthropology did not emerge as a scientific discipline until the twentieth century because nineteenth-century Westerners' limited contact with remote peoples and the corresponding failure to see those other people as human combined to overcome natural curiosity and to prevent objective study of different cultures.

This thesis sentence specifies the writer's view of the two main causes of the slow emergence of anthropology—limited contact with remote peoples and, related to that, a narrow definition of humanity—that she will analyze in her essay.

4
Developing the essay

You develop your essay by supporting your thesis sentence with sound generalizations, which you support in turn with *specific* evidence. (See 4c.) Avoid filling out your essay by repetition. Avoid substituting purely subjective feelings about the topic for real analysis of it. (It may help to abolish the word *I* from your essay.)

The student answering the anthropology question must show that contact between Western and non-Western cultures was limited and must specify how the limitations dulled curiosity, prevented objective study, and hampered the development of anthropology. She also needs to demonstrate how a consequently narrow definition of humanity had the same results. And she *must* support her assertions with concrete evidence. For instance, she might cite nineteenth-century writings that illustrate feelings of superiority toward distant peoples.

The student would not be providing effective evidence if she introduced unsupported generalizations or substituted her subjective feelings for an objective analysis of the problem. For instance, a blanket statement that all nineteenth-century Westerners were narrow-minded or a paragraph condemning their narrow-mindedness would only pad the essay.

5
Rereading the essay

The time limit on an essay examination does not allow for the careful rethinking and revision you would give an essay or research paper. You need to write clearly and concisely the first time. If you do have a few minutes after you have finished the entire exam, reread the essay (or essays) to correct illegible passages, misspellings, grammatical mistakes, and accidental omissions. Verify that your thesis is accurate—that it does, in fact, introduce what you ended up writing about. Check to ensure that you have supported all your generalizations thoroughly. Cross out irrelevant ideas and details, and add any information that now seems important. (Write on another page if necessary, keying the addition to the page on which it belongs.)

36b

Writing business letters, job applications, and memos

When you write a letter to request information, to complain about a product or bill, or to apply for a job, or when you write a memo or report to someone you work with, you are addressing busy people who want to see quickly why you are writing and how they should respond to you. A wordy, incoherent letter or memo full of errors in grammar and spelling may prevent you from getting what you want, either because the reader cannot understand your wish or because you present yourself so poorly. In business writing, state your purpose at the very start. Be straightforward, clear, objective, and courteous, and don't hesitate to be insistent if the situation warrants it. Observe conventions of grammar and usage, for these not only make your writing clear but also impress a reader with your care.

1

Writing business letters and job applications

Using a standard form

Business correspondence customarily adheres to one of several acceptable forms. Use either unlined white paper measuring at least 5½″ × 8½″ or what is called letterhead stationery with your address printed at the top of the sheet. Type the letter if possible, single-spaced, on only one side of a sheet. Follow a standard form for each of the letter's parts. (The form described below and illustrated in the sample letter on the next page is one common model.)

The return-address heading of the letter gives your address (but not your name) and the date. (If you're using letterhead stationery, you need add only the date.) Align the lines of the heading on the left, and place the whole heading on the right of the page, allowing enough space above it to center the entire letter vertically on the page.

The inside address shows the name, title, and complete address of the person you are writing to, just as this information will appear on the envelope. Begin the address a few lines below the heading at the left side of the page.

The salutation greets the addressee. Place it two lines below the address and two lines above the body of the letter. Always follow it with a colon, not a comma or dash. If you are not addressing a particular person, use a general salutation such as *Dear Sir or Madam* or *Dear Symthe Shoes* (the company name). Use *Ms.* as the

17A Revere St.
Boston, MA 02106
January 1, 1986

Return address heading

Ms. Ann Herzog
Circulation Supervisor
Sporting Life
25 W. 43rd St.
New York, NY 10036

Inside address

Dear Ms. Herzog:

Salutation

Thank you for your letter of December 20, which notifies me that Sporting Life will resume my subscription after stopping it in error after I had received the July issue. Since I missed at least five months' issues because of the magazine's error, I expected my subscription to be extended for five months after it would have lapsed--that is, through June 1986. Instead, you tell me that the magazine will send me the back issues that it failed to send and that the January issue (which I haven't received) will complete my current subscription.

I have no interest in receiving the back issues of Sporting Life because the magazine is not useful or interesting unless it is current. Since Sporting Life erred in stopping my subscription prematurely, I still expect it to make up the difference on the other end of my subscription.

Unless I hear otherwise from you, I will count on your extending my subscription at least through June 1986. If Sporting Life cannot compensate for its error in this way, I will cancel my subscription and request a refund.

Body

Close — Sincerely,

Signature — *Janet M. Marley*
Janet M. Marley

Janet M. Marley
17A Revere St.
Boston, MA 02106

Ms. Ann Herzog
Circulation Supervisor
Sporting Life
25 W. 43rd St.
New York, NY 10036

Envelope

title for a woman when she has no other title, when you don't know how she prefers to be addressed, or when you know that she prefers to be addressed as *Ms.* If you know a woman prefers to be addressed as *Mrs.* or *Miss,* use the appropriate title.

The body of the letter, containing its contents, begins at the left margin. Instead of indenting paragraphs, you may place an extra line of space between them so that they are readily visible.

The letter's close begins two lines below the last line of the body and aligns at the left with the heading at the top of the page. Typical closes include *Yours truly* and *Sincerely.* Only the first word is capitalized, and the close is followed by a comma.

The signature of a business letter has two parts: a typed one, four lines below the close, and a handwritten one filling in the space. The signature should consist only of your name, as you sign checks and school documents.

Below the signature, at the left margin, you may want to include additional information such as *Enc.* (something is enclosed with the letter); *cc: Margaret Newton* (a carbon copy is being sent to the person named); or *CHC/enp* (the initials of the author/the initials of the typist).

The envelope for the letter (see p. 563) should show your name and address in the upper left corner and the addressee's name, title, and address in the center. Use an envelope that is the same width as your stationery and about a third the height. Fold the letter horizontally, in thirds.

Writing requests and complaints

Letters requesting something—for instance, a pamphlet, information about a product, a T-shirt advertised in a magazine—must be specific and accurate about the item you are requesting. The letter should describe the item completely and, if applicable, include a copy or description of the advertisement or other source that prompted your request.

Letters complaining about a product or a service (such as a wrong billing from the telephone company) should be written in a reasonable but firm tone. (See the sample letter on p. 563.) Assume that the addressee is willing to resolve the problem when he or she has the relevant information. In the first sentence of the letter, say what you are writing about. Then provide as much background as needed, including any relevant details from past correspondence (as in the sample letter). Describe exactly what you see as the problem, sticking to facts and avoiding discourses on the company's social responsibility or your low opinion of its management. In the clearest possible words and sentences, proceed directly from one point to the next without repeating yourself. Always include your opinion of how the problem can be solved. Many companies are required by law to establish a specific procedure for complaints about products and services. If you know of such a procedure, be sure to follow it.

Writing a job application and résumé

In writing to apply for a job or to request a job interview, you should announce at the outset what job you desire and how you heard about it. (See the sample letter below.) Then summarize your qualifications for the job, including facts about your education and employment history. Include only the relevant facts, mentioning that additional information appears in an accompanying résumé. Include any special reason you have for applying, such as a specific

3712 Swiss Ave.
Dallas, TX 75204
March 2, 1985

Personnel Manager
Dallas News
Communications Center
Dallas, TX 75222

Dear Sir or Madam:

In response to your announcement posted in the English department of Southern Methodist University, I am applying for the summer job of part-time editorial assistant for the Dallas News.

I am now enrolled at Southern Methodist University as a sophomore, with a dual major in English literature and journalism. As the enclosed résumé shows, I have worked on the university newspaper for nearly two years, I have published articles in my hometown newspaper, and I worked a summer there as a copy boy. My goal is a career in journalism. I believe my educational background and my work experience qualify me for the opening you have.

I am available for an interview at any time and would be happy to send you samples of my newspaper work. My telephone number is 744-3816.

Sincerely,

Ian M. Irvine

Enc.

RÉSUMÉ

Ian M. Irvine
3712 Swiss Ave.
Dallas, TX 75204
(214) 744-3816

<u>Position desired</u>	Part-time editorial assistant.
<u>Education</u>	
1983 to present	Southern Methodist University. Current standing: sophomore. Major: English literature and journalism.
1979–1983	Abilene (TX) Senior High School. Graduated with academic degree.
<u>Experience</u>	
1983 to present	Reporter on the <u>Daily Campus</u>, student newspaper of Southern Methodist University. Responsibilities include writing feature stories and sports coverage; proofreading; some editing.
Summer 1984	House painter and free-lance writer. Published two articles in the <u>Abilene</u> (TX) <u>Reporter-News</u>: "A Hundredth Birthday Party" (7/1/84) and "A New Way to Develop Photographs" (8/6/84).
Summer 1983	Copy boy at <u>Abilene Reporter-News</u>. Responsible for transmitting copy among writers, editors, and typesetters. Watched over teleprinter, ran errands, occasionally accompanied reporters and photographers on assignments.
<u>Special interests</u>	Fiction writing, photography, reading, squash.
<u>References</u>	Academic references available from the placement office at Southern Methodist University, Dallas, TX 75275.
	Employment reference: Ms. Millie Stevens <u>Abilene Reporter-News</u> Abilene, TX 79604
	Personal reference: Ms. Sheryl Gipstein 26 Overland Dr. Abilene, TX 79604

career goal. At the end of the letter, mention that you are available for an interview at the convenience of the addressee, or specify when you will be available (for instance, when your current job or classes leave you free).

The résumé that you enclose with your letter of application should contain, in table form, your education, your employment history, your other interests, and information about how to obtain your references. (See the sample résumé on the opposite page.) In preparing your résumé, you may wish to consult one of the many books devoted to application letters, résumés, and other elements of a job search. Two helpful guides are Richard N. Bolles, *What Color Is Your Parachute? A Practical Manual for Job-Hunters and Career Changers* (Berkeley: Ten Speed, 1985), and Tom Jackson, *The Perfect Résumé* (Garden City: Doubleday, 1981).

2 Writing business memos

Unlike business letters, which address people in other organizations, business memorandums (memos, for short) address people within the same organization. A memo can be quite long, but more often it reports briefly and directly on a very specific topic: an answer to a question, a progress report, an evaluation. Both the form and the structure of a memo are designed to get to the point and dispose of it quickly.

The memo has no return address, inside address, salutation, or close. Instead, as shown in the sample memo on the next page, the heading typically consists of the date, the addressee's name, the writer's name, and a subject description or title. (If you are sending copies of the memo to someone besides the addressee, give his or her name after *cc*, meaning "carbon copy." See the sample.) Type the body of the memo as you would the body of a business letter: single-spaced, double-spaced between paragraphs, and no paragraph indentions. Never sign a business memo, though you may initial your name in the heading.

Immerse your reader in your subject at the very beginning of the memo. State your reason for writing in the first sentence, but do not waste words with expressions like "The purpose of this memo is. . . ." Devote the first paragraph to a succinct presentation of your answer, conclusion, or evaluation. In the rest of the memo explain how you arrived at your answer, the facts on which you base your conclusion, and your method of evaluation. The paragraphs may be numbered so that the main divisions of your message are easy to see.

A business memo can be more informal in tone than a business letter, particularly if you know the addressee; but it should not be wordy. Use technical terms if your reader will understand them, but otherwise keep language simple and use short sentences. Provide only the information that your reader needs to know.

The sample memo below, from a sales representative to her district manager, illustrates these guidelines. Notice especially the form of the memo, the writer's immediate statement of her purpose, the clear structure provided by the three numbered paragraphs, and the direct tone of the whole.

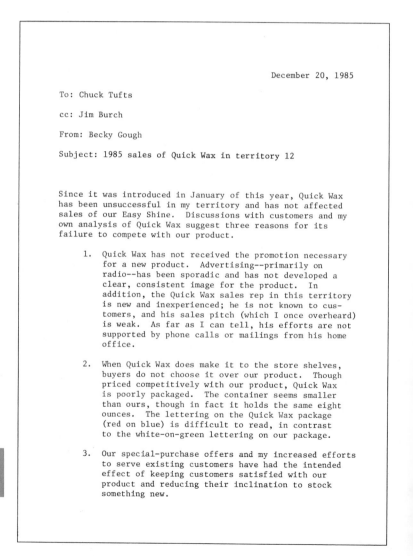

December 20, 1985

To: Chuck Tufts

cc: Jim Burch

From: Becky Gough

Subject: 1985 sales of Quick Wax in territory 12

Since it was introduced in January of this year, Quick Wax has been unsuccessful in my territory and has not affected sales of our Easy Shine. Discussions with customers and my own analysis of Quick Wax suggest three reasons for its failure to compete with our product.

1. Quick Wax has not received the promotion necessary for a new product. Advertising--primarily on radio--has been sporadic and has not developed a clear, consistent image for the product. In addition, the Quick Wax sales rep in this territory is new and inexperienced; he is not known to customers, and his sales pitch (which I once overheard) is weak. As far as I can tell, his efforts are not supported by phone calls or mailings from his home office.

2. When Quick Wax does make it to the store shelves, buyers do not choose it over our product. Though priced competitively with our product, Quick Wax is poorly packaged. The container seems smaller than ours, though in fact it holds the same eight ounces. The lettering on the Quick Wax package (red on blue) is difficult to read, in contrast to the white-on-green lettering on our package.

3. Our special-purchase offers and my increased efforts to serve existing customers have had the intended effect of keeping customers satisfied with our product and reducing their inclination to stock something new.

Appendixes

Appendix A
Avoiding Plagiarism

Plagiarism (from a Latin word for "kidnapper") is the presentation of someone else's ideas or words as your own. You plagiarize deliberately if you copy a sentence from a book and pass it off as your writing, if you summarize or paraphrase someone else's ideas without acknowledging your debt, or if you buy a term paper to hand in as your own. You plagiarize accidentally if you carelessly forget quotation marks around another writer's words or mistakenly omit a source citation for another's idea because you are unaware of the need to acknowledge the idea. Whether deliberate or accidental, plagiarism is a serious and often punishable offense.

You do not plagiarize, however, when you draw on other writers' material and acknowledge your sources. That procedure is a crucial part of honest research writing (see Chapter 35). Nevertheless, because a research paper requires by definition that you integrate other people's ideas with your own, you may not always be sure what constitutes plagiarism. This appendix shows you how to avoid plagiarism by acknowledging sources when necessary and by using them accurately and fairly.

A1
Knowing what to acknowledge

When you write a research paper, you coordinate information from three kinds of sources: (1) your independent thoughts and experiences; (2) common knowledge, the basic knowledge people share; and (3) other people's independent thoughts and experiences. Of the three, you *must* acknowledge the third, the work of others.

Your independent material

You need not acknowledge your own independent material—your thoughts, compilations of facts, or experimental results, expressed in your words or format—to avoid plagiarism. Such material includes observations from your experience (for example, a conclusion you draw about crowd behavior by watching crowds at concerts or shopping centers) as well as diagrams you construct from information you gather yourself. Though you generally should describe the basis for your independent conclusions so that readers can evaluate your thinking, you need not cite sources for them. However, someone else's ideas and facts are not yours; even when you express them entirely in your words and format, they require acknowledgment.

Common knowledge

Common knowledge consists of the standard information of a field of study as well as folk literature and commonsense observations. Standard information includes, for instance, the major facts of history. The dates of Charlemagne's rule as emperor of Rome (800–814) and the fact that his reign was accompanied by a revival of learning—both facts available in many reference books—do not need to be acknowledged, even if you have to look up the information. However, an interpretation of facts (for instance, a theory of how writing began) or a specialist's observation (for instance, an Asian historian's opinion of the effects of Chinese wall posters) is considered independent, not common, knowledge and must be documented.

Folk literature, which is popularly known and cannot be traced to particular writers, is considered common knowledge. Mother Goose nursery rhymes and fairy tales like "Snow White" are examples. However, all literature traceable to a particular writer should be acknowledged. Even a familiar phrase like "miles to go before I sleep" (from Robert Frost's poem "Stopping by Woods on a Snowy Evening") is literature, not folk literature, and requires acknowledgment.

Commonsense observations, such as the idea that weather affects people's spirits or that inflation is most troublesome for people with low and fixed incomes, are considered common knowledge and do not require acknowledgment, even when they also appear in someone else's writing. But a scientist's findings about the effects of high humidity on people with high blood pressure, or an economist's argument about the effects of inflation on immigrants from China, will require acknowledgment.

You may treat common knowledge as your own, even if you have to look it up in a reference book. You may not know, for example, the dates of the French Revolution or the standard definition of *photosynthesis*, although these are considered common knowledge. If you do not know a subject well enough to determine whether a piece of information is common knowledge, make a record of the source as you would for any other quotation, paraphrase, or summary. As you read more about the subject, the information may come up repeatedly without acknowledgment, in which case it is probably common knowledge. But if you are still in doubt when you finish your research, always acknowledge the source.

Someone else's independent material

You must always acknowledge other people's independent material—that is, any facts or ideas that are not common knowledge or your own. The source may be anything, including a book, an article, a movie, an interview, a microfilmed document, or a computer program. You must acknowledge not only ideas or facts themselves but also the language and format in which the ideas or facts appear, if you use them. That is, the wording, sentence structures, arrangement of thoughts, and special graphic format (such as a table or diagram) created by another writer belong to that writer just as his or her ideas do. The following example baldly plagiarizes the original quotation from Jessica Mitford's *Kind and Usual Punishment* (New York: Random, 1973), p. 9.

Original The character and mentality of the keepers may be of more importance in understanding prisons than the character and mentality of the kept.

Plagiarism But the character and mentality of prison officials (the keepers) is of more importance in understanding prisons than the character and mentality of prisoners (the kept).

Though the writer has made some changes in Mitford's original and even altered the meaning slightly (by changing *may be* to *is*), she has plagiarized on several counts. She has copied key words (*character, mentality, keepers, kept*), duplicated the entire sentence structure, and lifted the idea—all without acknowledging the source. As illustrated in the following section, the writer must either enclose the exact quotation in quotation marks or state the idea in her own words and in her own sentence. Whichever she does, she must acknowledge Mitford as the source.

You need to acknowledge another's material no matter how you use it, how much of it you use, or how often you use it. Whether you are quoting a single important word, paraphrasing a single sentence, or summarizing three paragraphs, and whether you are using the source only once or a dozen times, you must acknowledge the original author every time. See 35i for discussion and examples of how to acknowledge sources in your text.

If you read someone else's material during your research but do not include any of that material in your final draft, you need not acknowledge the source with a note because you have not actually used the material. However, your instructor may ask you to include such sources in your list of works cited (see 35h).

A2
Quoting, summarizing, and paraphrasing

When writing a research paper, you can present the ideas of others through direct quotation, through summary, or through paraphrase, depending on your purpose. (See 35e and 35g-2 for information on deciding when and how to employ these methods.) For **direct quotation,** copy the material from the source *carefully,* place it in quotation marks within your running text (see 24c for the style to use with poetry and long quotations), and acknowledge the source. Put quotation marks around even a single word if the original author used it in a special or central way. Do not change any wording, spelling, capitalization, or punctuation unless you indicate the change in brackets (see 25d and 26a). Be careful not to omit or add any words or punctuation marks accidentally. Use an ellipsis mark (three spaced periods) to indicate the exact point at which you have deliberately left out part of a direct quotation (see 25e).

To correct the plagiarism of Mitford's sentence above, the writer would place Mitford's exact words in quotation marks and cite the source properly.

QUOTATION According to one critic of the penal system, "The character and mentality of the keepers may be of more importance in understanding prisons than the character and mentality of the kept" (Mitford 9).

When you summarize or paraphrase, you state in your own words and sentence structures the meaning of someone else's writing. In a **summary** you extract the central idea from several sentences, paragraphs, or even pages, condensing it into one or more sentences of your own. In a **paraphrase** you follow the original more closely, often sentence by sentence, recording in your own words the author's line of reasoning. Since the words and the sentence structures are yours, you do not enclose either a summary or a paraphrase in quotation marks, although, of course, you must acknowledge the author of the idea. Here is a paraphrase of the Mitford quotation above.

PARAPHRASE One critic of the penal system maintains that we may be able to learn more about prisons from the psychology of the prison officials than from that of the prisoners (Mitford 9).

If you adopt the source's sentence pattern and simply substitute synonyms for key words, or if you use the original words and merely change the sentence pattern, you are not paraphrasing but plagiarizing, even if you acknowledge the source, because both methods use someone else's expression without quotation marks. The inadequate paraphrase below plagiarizes the original source, Frederick C. Crews's *The Tragedy of Manners: Moral Drama in the Later Novels of Henry James* (1957; Hamden: Shoe String, 1971), p. 8.

ORIGINAL In each case I have tried to show that all the action in a "Jamesian novel" may be taken as a result of philosophical differences of opinion among the principal characters, and that these differences in turn are explainable by reference to the characters' differing social backgrounds.

PLAGIARISM According to Crews, the action in a "Jamesian novel" comes from philosophical differences of

> opinion between characters, differences that can be explained by examining the characters' differing social backgrounds (8).

The plagarized passage lifts several expressions verbatim from the source, without change and without quotation marks: *action in a "Jamesian novel"; philosophical differences of opinion; the characters' differing social backgrounds.* Thus, even though the writer acknowledges the author's work (by giving Crews's name and the parenthetical page number, 8), he plagiarizes because he does not also acknowledge the author's words with quotation marks. The paraphrase below both conveys and acknowledges the author's meaning without stealing his manner of expression.

Paraphrase According to Crews, the characters in Henry James's novels live out philosophies acquired from their upbringing and their place in society (8).

In this paraphrase, although the writer retains Crews's essential meaning, he restates that meaning in a sentence that he himself has clearly constructed and designed to fit his larger purpose.

In paraphrasing or summarizing you must not only devise your own form of expression (or place quotation marks around the author's expressions) but also represent the author's meaning exactly without distorting it. In the following inaccurate summary the writer has avoided plagiarism but has stated a meaning exactly opposite that of the original. The original quotation, from the artist Henri Matisse, appears in Jack D. Flam, *Matisse on Art* (London: Phaidon, 1973), p. 148.

Original For the artist creation begins with vision. To see is itself a creative operation, requiring an effort. Everything that we see in our daily life is more or less distorted by acquired habits, and this is perhaps more evident in an age like ours when cinema posters and magazines present us every day with a flood of ready-made images which are to the eye what prejudices are to the mind.

Inaccurate summary Matisse said that the artist can learn how to see by looking at posters and magazines (qtd. in Flam 148).

The revision below combines summary and quotation to represent the author's meaning exactly.

Improved summary Matisse said that the artist must overcome visual "habits" and "prejudices," particularly those developed in response to popular cultural images (qtd. in Flam 148).

To be sure you acknowledge sources fairly and do not plagiarize, review this checklist both before beginning to write your paper and again after you have completed your first draft.

1. What type of source are you using: your own independent material, common knowledge, or someone else's independent material?
2. If you are quoting someone else's material, is the quotation exact? Have you inserted quotation marks around quotations run into the text? Have you shown omissions with ellipses and additions with brackets?
3. If you are paraphrasing or summarizing someone else's material, have you used your own words and sentence structures? Does your paraphrase or summary employ quotation marks when you resort to the author's exact language? Have you represented the author's meaning without distortion?
4. Is each use of someone else's material acknowledged in your text? Are all your source citations complete and accurate? (See 35i.)
5. Does your list of works cited include all the sources you have drawn from in writing your paper? (See 35h.)

See 35e and 35g-2 for additional discussion and examples of quoting, paraphrasing, and summarizing. Exercises on all three methods appear on pages 501–02 and 509.

Appendix B
Preparing a Manuscript

A legible, consistent, and attractive manuscript is a service to readers because it makes reading easier. This appendix discusses the materials necessary for manuscript preparation and some conventions of format. (Most of these guidelines are standard, but your instructor may request that you follow different conventions in some matters.)

B1
Choosing the appropriate materials

Handwritten papers

For handwritten papers, you can use regular white paper, 8½″ × 11″, with horizontal lines spaced between one-quarter and three-eighths of an inch apart. Don't use paper torn from a notebook, unlined paper, paper with narrow lines, colored paper, or paper other than 8½″ × 11″ (such as legal or stenographer's pads). Use the same type of paper throughout a project. Write on only one side of a sheet.

Use black or blue ink, not pencil. If possible, use an ink eraser or eradicator to correct mistakes. If you must cross out material, draw a single line through it. Don't scribble over or black out a mistake, and don't write corrections on top of mistakes.

Typewritten papers

For typewritten papers, use 8½″ × 11″ white bond paper of sixteen- or twenty-pound weight. Some instructors also accept the same size surface-coated bond paper (called "erasable" or "corrasable"), but ink smears easily on such paper. Onionskin sheets, paper torn from notebooks, colored paper, and paper smaller or larger than 8½″ × 11″ are unacceptable. Use the same type of paper throughout a project. Type on only one side of a sheet.

Use a black typewriter ribbon that is fresh enough to make a dark impression, and make sure the keys of the typewriter are clean. To avoid smudging the page when correcting mistakes, use a liquid correction fluid or a correction tape. Don't use hyphens or *x*'s to cross out mistakes, and don't type corrections (strikeovers) on top of mistakes.

Papers produced on a word processor

Two kinds of printers are used with most computerized word processors. Letter-quality printers work like regular typewriters to produce characters with solid lines. Dot-matrix printers form characters out of tiny dots, and the legibility of their type varies considerably. If you use a word processor with a dot-matrix printer, make sure the dots are close enough together to produce legible characters. In addition, make sure the tails on letters such as *j*, *p*, and *y* descend below the line of type, as they do in the typeface used here. Resist the temptation to use any of the unusual type sizes or styles that your printer may be capable of producing, for such embellishments can clutter your manuscript and distract readers from what you are saying. Before you submit a paper printed on a dot-matrix printer, show your instructor a sample of the type to be sure it is acceptable.

Be sure the printer ribbon is fresh so that it leaves a dark impression. Use standard-sized (8½″ × 11″) white bond paper of sixteen- or twenty-pound weight, not the lightweight green-striped paper associated with computer print-outs. If you use continuous paper folded like a fan at perforations, it will also come with a row of holes along each side for feeding the paper into the printer. Before submitting your paper, remove these strips of holes along the perforations and separate the pages at the folds.

B2
Following a standard format

A consistent physical format makes the script, margins, paging, title, and identification visually effective and avoids the illegibility and the confusion of inconsistencies. See the sample research papers in Chapter 35 (pp. 526–49 and 550–57) for examples of the items below. (For the special formats of source citations and list of works cited, which are not discussed here, see 35h and 35i.)

Script

Handwritten script should be reasonably uniform and clear. Be sure letters are easily distinguishable. Cross all *t*'s; dot all *i*'s with dots, not circles; form the loops of letters carefully. Make capital letters and small letters clearly different. Space consistently between words and between sentences. If your handwriting is difficult to read, submit a typed paper if possible. If you don't have access to a typewriter and your handwriting is illegible or unusual in size, decoration, or slant, make it more legible or conventional when writing the final manuscript. Indent the first line of every paragraph about an inch. Write on every line or every other line as specified by your instructor.

In script produced on a typewriter or word processor, indent the first line of every paragraph five spaces and double-space throughout. Leave one space between words and after commas, semicolons, and colons. Leave two spaces after sentence periods, question marks, and exclamation points. Use one space before and after as well as between the three periods of an ellipsis mark. To make a dash, use two consecutive hyphens with no space before or after. To make brackets when they are not on your typewriter or word-processor keyboard, leave an extra space on either side of the material you are bracketing and add them neatly in ink. Use handwriting as well to make other symbols that are not on your keyboard, leaving three or four spaces and then inserting the symbol in ink.

For both typed and handwritten script, try to avoid breaking words at the ends of lines. If you must break a word, follow the guidelines provided in Chapter 30. Don't start a line with any mark of punctuation other than a dash, an opening parenthesis, an opening quotation mark, or an ellipsis mark when one of these is called for.

Set off quotations of more than four lines of prose or three lines of poetry; two- or three-line poetry quotations may be set off or placed in the text (see 24c). In handwritten copy, indent all lines of a displayed quotation an inch from the left margin. In typewritten copy, indent all lines ten spaces. Double-space above and below each quotation, and double-space the quotation itself. (See 24c.)

Margins

Use one-inch margins on all sides of each page. The right margin will probably be uneven but should not be narrower than an inch. The top margin will contain the page number (see below). If you are using a word processor, be sure to instruct the computer to set appropriate margins. Don't let the lines of type run across the perforations on continuous fanfold paper.

Paging

Whether or not you provide a separate title page, begin numbering your paper on the first text page, and number consecutively through the end. Use Arabic numerals (1, 2, 3), and do not add periods, parentheses, hyphens, or the abbreviation "p." However, for every page after the first, place your last name before the page number in case the pages become separated after you submit your paper. (See p. 532 for an example.) Align the page number with the right margin, and position it about half an inch from the top of the page, at least two lines above the first line of text.

Title and identification

If you do not use a separate title page for an essay, provide your name and the date, plus any other information requested by your instructor, on the first text page. Place this identification an inch from the top of the page, aligned with the left margin and double-spaced. Double-space again, and center the title. Don't underline the title or place quotation marks around it, and capitalize the words in the title according to the guidelines in 26b. Quadruple-space between the title and the first line of text. (See p. 550 for an example of this format.)

For a research paper, your instructor may ask you to provide a separate title page. If so, follow the guidelines and example on pages 526–27. On page 1 of the paper repeat the title, centered an inch from the top of the page, and quadruple-space between the title and the first line of text. (See p. 530 for an example.)

B3

Proofreading, correcting, and submitting the final manuscript

Proofread each page of your paper carefully. Concentrate on spelling, punctuation, mechanics, grammar, and manuscript format. If a page has several errors, retype or rewrite the page. If it has one or two errors and you can't eradicate them, correct them in ink. Draw a single line through a word you want to delete. Don't try to correct a misspelled word without crossing out and rewriting the whole word. To replace a word or mark of punctuation, draw a line through the item, place a caret (^) underneath it, and write the new word or mark in the space above the old one. To add words or marks of punctuation, place a caret underneath the line at the point where you wish to insert the word or mark; then center the word or mark over the caret in the space above the line.

```
                                  organisms
An ecosystem is a community of ^argonisms interacting
                           the
with each other and with ^environment.
```

If you have to add more words than will fit between the lines of text, rewrite or retype the page.

When you submit your final paper, be sure the pages will stay together when the paper is shuffled in with others. Depending on the wishes of your instructor, you may fold the paper in half lengthwise, paperclip or staple the pages in the upper left corner, or place the paper in a special binder.

Appendix C
Improving Study Skills

Three basic qualities underlie effective study skills: organization, repetition, and motivation. This appendix will show briefly how to employ these qualities in reading, taking notes, and preparing for tests.

It is possible to study anywhere and at any time, but you will benefit from a place that is moderately comfortable, well lighted, and undistracting. Have handy the materials you'll need while studying, such as paper, pencils, pens, and a highlighter. Keep your expectations realistic. Don't plan to accomplish more in an hour or a day than you ever have before. Concentrate on specific goals, such as answering a question about a textbook chapter or even passing a test, rather than on more general, longer-term goals, such as getting a certain grade-point average or graduating from college. And plan to take a break after every hour or so of studying to refresh yourself.

C1
Remembering

In memorizing, you use short-term storage, where information may stay a few seconds or a few minutes, and long-term storage, where information may stay indefinitely—or at least through the final examination. Most academic learning requires a conscious effort to move material from short-term storage into long-term storage.

The more organized your learning is, the more it will penetrate your long-term memory. Read a book's introduction before you read the book; skim a whole chapter before you read the chapter. Organize information into small groups of ideas or facts that make sense to you. For instance, memorize French vocabulary words in related groups such as words for parts of the body or parts of a house. Keep the groups small: psychological research has shown that we can easily memorize about seven items at a time but have trouble with more.

As you accumulate new information, make associations between it and what you already know. For instance, to remember a sequence of four dates in twentieth-century English history, link the occurrences in England with simultaneous, and more familiar, events in the United States. Or use **mnemonic devices,** tricks for improving your memory. Say the history dates you want to remember are separated by five then four then nine years. By memorizing the first date and then 5 + 4 = 9, you'll have command of all four dates.

Reviewing the material you want to learn will improve not only how long but also how completely and accurately you remember it. Since you forget a great deal right after you read a chapter or listen to a lecture, try to spend five minutes going over the material immediately after you first encounter it. You will probably remember more from that brief review than you will from a much longer review several days later. In addition, try to spread subsequent study over half-hour sessions three or four days a week instead of concentrating all study time in a single, long session.

C2
Scheduling

To organize your time effectively for studying, examine how you spend your days. For a week, keep track of your activities and the time they absorb. How many of the 168 hours in a week do you spend eating, sleeping, watching television, attending classes, studying, working at a job, commuting, doing laundry, socializing, and so forth? If you think it will help you organize your time, make a chart like a calendar that divides the week into seven vertical columns (one for each day) and one horizontal row for each hour you are awake. Block out on the chart your activities that occur regularly and at specific times, such as commuting, attending classes, and working. Then fill in your other regular activities (such as exercise, eating, and studying) that do not necessarily occur at fixed times.

Set aside regular time for study each week. During any given week you will want to adjust how you spend the studying time to allow for different assignments in different courses. For courses requiring extensive reading or creative work such as writing, try to include several large blocks of time per week. If you have been given a long-term assignment (such as a research paper), include time for it in your planning.

When devising a weekly schedule, don't overorganize so that you have no time left for relaxing. An unrealistic schedule that assigns all available time to studying will quickly become so difficult to live by that you'll be forced to abandon it and start over.

C3
Reading

The assigned reading you do for college courses—in textbooks, journal articles, and works of literature—requires a greater focus on

C3

comprehension, analysis, and retention than does reading for entertainment or for practical information. For most course reading, especially textbook reading, you will benefit from at least three separate examinations of the material: once skimming; once reading carefully, word by word; and once reviewing. Though these processes may seem redundant and time-consuming, with practice you will be able to perform some steps simultaneously and follow all the steps almost habitually.

The purpose of **skimming** is to give you an overview of the material that will aid your understanding of any part of it. Your goal is not to comprehend all the details or even the structure of the author's argument. Rather, you want to achieve a general sense of how a piece of writing is organized and what its principal ideas are. The steps outlined below constitute a typical procedure for skimming a textbook chapter.

1. Examine the chapter title. What does it mean? What do you already know about this subject?
2. Read the first couple of paragraphs carefully to introduce yourself to the topic and to the author's writing style. An author often gives an overview of his or her ideas at the start.
3. Move through the chapter from heading to heading, reading each one as if it were a headline. Viewing the headings as the levels of an outline will give you a feeling for which ideas the author sees as central or as subordinate.
4. As you move from one heading to the next, scan the text and note any key words that are in color, **boldface,** or *italic* type.
5. Slow down for all pictures, diagrams, tables, graphs, and maps. These often contain concentrated information.
6. Read the last paragraph of the chapter or its summary carefully. These often give an overview of the main ideas of the chapter.
7. Take a moment to think over what you've skimmed. Try to recall the sequence of ideas. Ask yourself what the main idea or thesis is.

As soon as possible after you have skimmed a chapter, read it carefully for a thorough understanding of each idea or group of ideas. Here is a procedure you might follow for such word-by-word reading.

1. Distinguish the main ideas from the supporting ideas. Look for the chapter's thesis or central argument, for the central idea in each section or paragraph, and for terms the author takes pains to define and perhaps highlights with special type.
2. Read the chapter's structure as if it were a map of the author's ideas. Look for the introduction to the chapter, which outlines the ideas that follow; for the step-by-step explanations of main ideas found in the body of the chapter; for transitions between ideas that signal shifts in thought and highlight relationships; and for summaries or conclusions at the ends of sections or the end of the chapter that condense the text to its main concepts.
3. After reading a section or a group of ideas, test your comprehension by summarizing the material in your own words and then skimming it to check your understanding. Reread parts you have forgotten or misunderstood until you're sure of your comprehension.

4. Once you feel you understand the entire chapter, go back to underline important phrases or passages and to add marginal notes (or to make separate notes if you don't want to mark your book). Underline or take notes on only main ideas, key terms, and specific supporting evidence you've chosen to remember. In marginal notes, add your own ideas or summarize the author's.

When you review a chapter, reread headings, summaries, and key terms as well as the passages you have underlined or taken notes on. Concentrate on how the parts fit together. Stop to read carefully any passages that don't seem familiar or clear. Before a test, skim the material a section at a time, and then recite or write out the main ideas before going on to the next section. If you have trouble remembering, reread the section instead of skimming it.

C4
Taking notes in class

Your aim in taking notes from a class lecture or discussion is to record it as completely as possible while sorting out the main ideas from the secondary and supporting ones. By doing so, you not only provide yourself with complete material for study later but also learn about the instructor's integration of the course material.

As you take notes, use your own words as much as possible to help you comprehend and retain the material, but resort to the speaker's words if necessary to catch everything. If you miss some material while making notes, leave a space to be filled in later. Don't count on going back to copy over and expand your notes. You may not be able to recall the missing information, and copying is little more than a time-wasting, mechanical activity. If you have already read the textbook chapter related to the lecture, you may be tempted to omit from your notes any lecture material you could find in the text. But you would be missing an important opportunity to integrate all the components of the course—the text material, your instructor's views, and your own thoughts. And you would risk forgetting exactly how your instructor made use of the text.

If, when you review your notes, you discover holes in them or confusing shifts in thought, consult a fellow student for his or her version of that part of the lecture. When you feel you understand the material, underline key words and important ideas in the notes and add comments (or cross-references to the text) in the margins.

C5
Preparing for examinations

No matter how much time you have, what material you are studying, or what kind of test you will be taking, studying for an examination involves three main steps, each requiring about a third of the total preparation time: (1) reviewing the material; (2) organizing summaries of the material; and (3) testing yourself. Your main goals are to strengthen your understanding of the subject, making both its ideas and its details more memorable, and to increase the flexibility of your new knowledge so that you can recognize it and apply it in new contexts.

As you begin studying for a test, organize your class notes and reading assignments into manageable units. Reread the material, recite or write out the main ideas and selected supporting ideas and examples, and then skim for an overview. Proceed in this way through all the units, returning to earlier ones as necessary to refresh your memory or to relate ideas.

Allow time to reorganize the material in your own way, to create categories that will help you apply the information in various contexts. For instance, in studying for a biology examination, work to understand a process, such as how a plant develops or how photosynthesis occurs. Or in studying for an American government test, explain the structures of the local, state, and federal levels of government, or outline the differences among the levels. Other useful categories include advantages or disadvantages, causes or effects, and repeated ideas. Develop categories that bring together as much of the material as possible, and think through each one as completely as you can. Such analytical thinking will enhance your mastery of the course material and may even prepare you directly for specific essay questions (see 36a).

Spend the last portion of your preparation time testing yourself. Convert to a question each heading in your lecture notes or textbook and each general category you have devised. Recite to yourself or write out the answers to the questions, going back to the course material to fill in missing information. Be sure you can define and explain all key terms. For subjects that require solving problems (such as mathematics, statistics, chemistry, and physics), work out a difficult problem for every type on which you will be tested. For history, test yourself on events and their causes or consequences. For a subject like psychology, be certain you understand the principal theories of behavior and their implications. For a literature course, test your knowledge of each work by thinking of the author's style and meaning, the main characters, and the plot developments; and trace the development of movements, genres, or periods to be sure you comprehend the relations among works.

About cramming: Everything psychologists report about learning under stress suggests that cramming for an examination is about the least effective way of preparing for one. It takes longer to learn under stress, and the learning is shallower, more difficult to apply, and more rapidly forgotten. Information learned under stress is even harder to apply under conditions of stress, such as the stress of taking an examination. And the lack of sleep that usually accompanies cramming makes a good performance even more unlikely. If you must cram for a test, determine what is most important. Skim chapters and notes to select central ideas. Face the fact that you can't learn everything that will be on the test, and spend what time you have reviewing main concepts and facts.

Glossaries

Glossary of Usage
Glossary of Grammatical Terms

Glossary of Usage

This glossary provides notes on words or phrases that often cause problems for writers. The recommendations for standard written English are based on current dictionaries and usage guides like the ones listed in 32a. Items labeled **nonstandard** should be avoided in speech and especially in writing. Those labeled **colloquial** and **slang** occur in speech and in some informal writing but are best avoided in the more formal writing usually expected in college and business. (Words and phrases labeled *colloquial* include those labeled by many dictionaries with the equivalent term *informal*.) See Chapter 31 for further discussion of word choice and for exercises in usage. See 32b-2 for a description of dictionary labels. Also see 34a-1 for a list of commonly confused words that are pronounced the same or similarly. The words and definitions provided there supplement this glossary.

The glossary is necessarily brief. Keep a dictionary handy for all your writing, and make a habit of referring to it whenever you doubt the appropriateness of a word or phrase.

a, an Use *a* before words beginning with consonant sounds, including those spelled with an initial pronounced *h* and those spelled with vowels that are sounded as consonants: *a historian, a one-o'clock class, a university*. Use *an* before words that begin with vowel sounds, including those spelled with an initial silent *h: an orgy, an L, an honor.*

When you use an abbreviation or acronym in writing (see 28b), the article that precedes it depends on how the abbreviation is to be read: *She was once an HEW undersecretary.* (*HEW* is to be read as three separate letters, and *h* is pronounced "aitch.") *Many Americans opposed a SALT treaty.* (*SALT* is to be read as one word, *salt.*)

See also *article* in the Glossary of Grammatical Terms (p. 605).

accept, except *Accept* is a verb meaning "receive." *Except* is usually a preposition or conjunction meaning "but for" or "other than"; when it is used as a verb, it means "leave out." *I can accept all your suggestions except the last one. I'm sorry you excepted my last suggestion from your list.*

adverse, averse *Adverse* and *averse* are both adjectives, and both mean "opposed" or "hostile." But *averse* describes the subject's opposition to something, whereas *adverse* describes something opposed to the subject: *The president was averse to adverse criticism.*

advice, advise *Advice* is a noun, and *advise* is a verb: *Take my advice; do as I advise you.*

affect, effect Usually *affect* is a verb, meaning "to influence," and *effect* is a noun, meaning "result": *The drug did not affect his driving; in fact, it seemed to have no effect at all.* But *effect* occasionally is used as a verb meaning "to bring about": *Her efforts effected a change.* And *affect* is used in psychology as a noun meaning "feeling or emotion": *One can infer much about affect from behavior.*

aggravate *Aggravate* should not be used in its colloquial meaning of "irritate" or "exasperate" (for example, *We were aggravated by her constant arguing*). *Aggravate* means "make worse": *The President was irritated by the Senate's stubbornness because he feared any delay might aggravate the unrest in the Middle East.*

agree to, agree with *Agree to* means "consent to," and *agree with* means "be in accord with": *How can they agree to a treaty when they don't agree with each other about the terms?*

ain't Nonstandard for *am not, isn't,* or *aren't.*

all, all of Usually *all* is sufficient to modify a noun: *all my loving, all the things you are.* Before a pronoun or proper noun, *all of* is usually appropriate: *all of me, in all of France.*

all ready, already *All ready* means "completely prepared," and *already* means "by now" or "before now": *We were all ready to go to the movie, but it had already started.*

all right *All right* is always two words. *Alright* is a common misspelling.

all together, altogether *All together* means "in unison," or "gathered in one place." *Altogether* means "entirely." *It's not altogether true that our family never spends vacations all together.*

allusion, illusion An *allusion* is an indirect reference, and an *illusion* is a deceptive appearance: *Paul's constant allusions to Shakespeare created the illusion that he was an intellectual.*

almost, most *Almost* is an adverb meaning "nearly"; *most* is an adjective meaning "the greater number (or part) of." In formal writing, *most* should not be used as a substitute for *almost: We see each other almost* (not *most*) *every day.*

a lot *A lot* is always two words, used informally to mean "many." *Alot* is a common misspelling.

among, between In general, *among* is used for relationships involving more than two people or things. *Between* is used for relationships involving only two or for comparing one thing to a group to which it belongs. *The four of them agreed among themselves that the choice was between New York and Los Angeles.* Increasingly, though, *between* is used for relationships involving three or more comparable people or things: *Let's keep this just between the three of us, shall we?*

amongst Although common in British English, in American English *amongst* is an overrefined substitute for *among*.

amount, number *Amount* refers to a quantity of something (a singular noun) that cannot be counted. *Number* refers to countable items (a plural noun). *The amount of leftover ice we can save depends on the number of containers we have to put it in.*

an, and *An* is an article (see *a, an*). *And* is a coordinating conjunction. Do not carelessly omit the *d* from *and.*

and etc. *Et cetera* (*etc.*) means "and the rest"; *and etc.* therefore is redundant. See also *et al., etc.*

and/or *And/or* is awkward and often confusing. A sentence such as *The decision is made by the mayor and/or the council* implies that one or the other or both make the decision. If you mean both, use *and;* if you mean either, use *or*. Use *and/or* only when you mean three options.

and which, and who When *which* or *who* is used to introduce a relative clause, *and* is superfluous: *WCAS is my favorite AM radio station, which* (not *and which*) *I listen to every morning. And which* or *and who* is correct only when used to introduce a second clause beginning with the same relative pronoun: *Jill is my cousin who goes to school here and who always calls me at seven in the morning.*

ante-, anti- The prefix *ante-* means "before" (*antedate, antebellum*); *anti-* means "against" (*antiwar, antinuclear*). Before a capital letter or *i, anti-* takes a hyphen: *anti-Freudian, anti-isolationist.*

anxious, eager *Anxious* means "nervous" or "worried" and is usually followed by *about. Eager* means "looking forward" and is usually followed by *to. I've been anxious about getting blisters. I'm eager* (not *anxious*) *to get new running shoes.*

anybody, any body; anyone, any one *Anybody* and *anyone* are indefinite pronouns; *any body* is a noun modified by an adjective; *any one* is a pronoun or adjective modified by *any. How can anybody communicate with any body of government? Can anyone help Amy? She has more work than any one person can handle.*

any more, anymore *Any more* is used in negative constructions to mean "no more." *Anymore,* an adverb meaning "now," is also used in negative constructions. *He doesn't want any more. She doesn't live here anymore.*

anyplace Colloquial for *anywhere.*

anyways, anywheres Nonstandard for *anyway* and *anywhere.*

apt, liable, likely *Apt* and *likely* are interchangeable. Strictly speaking, though, *apt* means "having a tendency to": *Horace is apt to forget his lunch in the morning. Likely* means "probably going to": *Horace is leaving so early today that he's likely to catch the first bus.*

Liable is normally used to mean "in danger of" and should be confined to situations with undesirable consequences: *If Horace doesn't watch out, he is liable to trip over that lawn sprinkler.* In the strictest sense, *liable* means "responsible" or "exposed to": *If Horace trips over that lawn sprinkler, the owner will be liable for damages.*

as *As* is often used to mean *because, since, while, whether,* or *who.* It may be vague or ambiguous in these senses: *As we were stopping to rest, we decided to eat lunch.* (Does *as* mean "while" or "because"?) Usually a more precise word is preferable. See also 16c.

As never should be used as a substitute for *whether* or *who. I'm not sure whether* (not *as*) *we can make it. That's the man who* (not *as*) *gave me directions.*

as, like In formal speech and writing, *as* may be either a preposition or a conjunction; *like* functions as a preposition only. Thus, if the construction being introduced is a full clause rather than a word or phrase, the preferred choice is *as* or *as if* (see 16c): *The plan succeeded as* (not *like*) *we hoped. It seemed as if* (not *like*) *it might fail. Other plans like it have failed.*

When *as* serves as a preposition, the distinction between *as* and *like* depends on meaning. *As* suggests that the subject is equivalent or identical to the description: *She was hired as an engineer. Like* suggests resemblance but not identity: *People like her do well in such jobs.* See also *like, such as.*

as, than In comparisons, *as* and *than* may be followed by either subjective- or objective-case pronouns: *You are as tall as he* (subjective). *They treated you better than him* (objective). The case depends on whether the pronoun is the subject or object of a verb. To determine which case to use, supply the omitted verb: *I love you more than he* (*loves you*) (*he* is the subject of the missing verb *loves*). *I love you more than* (*I love*) *him* (*him* is the object of the missing verb *love*). See also 6e.

assure, ensure, insure *Assure* means "to promise": *He assured us that if we left early, we would miss the traffic. Ensure* and *insure* often are used interchangeably to mean "make certain," but some reserve *insure* for matters of legal and financial protection and use *ensure* for more general meanings: *We left early to ensure that we would miss the traffic. It's expensive to insure yourself against floods.*

as to A stuffy substitute for *about: The suspect was questioned about* (not *as to*) *her actions.*

at The use of *at* after *where* is wordy and should be avoided: *Where are you meeting him?* is preferable to *Where are you meeting him at?*

at this point in time Wordy for *now, at this point,* or *at this time.*

averse, adverse See *adverse, averse.*

awful, awfully Strictly speaking, *awful* means "awe-inspiring." As intensifiers meaning "very" or "extremely" (*He tried awfully hard*), *awful* and *awfully* are colloquial and should not be used in formal speech or writing.

a while, awhile *Awhile* is an adverb; *a while* is an article and a noun. Thus *awhile* can modify a verb but cannot serve as the object of a preposition, and *a while* is just the opposite: *I will be gone awhile* (not *a while*). *I will be gone for a while* (not *awhile*).

bad, badly In formal speech and writing, *bad* should be used only as an adjective; the adverb is *badly*. *He felt bad because his tooth ached badly*. In *He felt bad*, the verb *felt* is a linking verb and the adjective *bad* is a subject complement. See also 9b.

being as, being that Colloquial for *because*, the preferable word in formal speech or writing: *Because* (not *Being as*) *the world is round, Columbus never did fall off the edge.*

beside, besides *Beside* is a preposition meaning "next to." *Besides* is a preposition meaning "except" or "in addition to" as well as an adverb meaning "in addition." *Besides, several other people besides you want to sit beside Dr. Christensen.*

better, had better *Had better* (meaning "ought to") is a verb modified by an adverb. The verb is necessary and should not be omitted: *You had better* (not *better*) *go.*

between, among See *among, between.*

bring, take Use *bring* only for movement from a farther place to a nearer one and *take* for any other movement. *First, take these books to the library for renewal, then take them to Mr. Daniels. Bring them back to me when he's finished.*

bunch In formal speech and writing, *bunch* (as a noun) should be used only to refer to clusters of things growing or fastened together, such as bananas and grapes. Its use to mean a group of items or people is colloquial; *crowd* or *group* is preferable.

burst, bursted; bust, busted *Burst* is a standard verb form meaning "to fly apart suddenly" (principal parts *burst, burst, burst*). The past-tense form *bursted* is nonstandard. The verb *bust* (*busted*) is slang.

but, hardly, scarcely These words are negative in their own right; using *not* with any of them to indicate negation is redundant. *We have but an hour* (not *We haven't got but an hour*) *before our plane leaves. I could hardly* (not *I couldn't hardly*) *make out her face in the dark.*

but however, but yet These and similar expressions, in which *but* is combined with another conjunction, are redundant and should be avoided: *He said he had finished, yet* (not *but yet*) *he continued.*

but that, but what These wordy substitutes for *that* and *what* should be avoided: *I don't doubt that* (not *but that*) *you are right.*

calculate, figure, reckon As substitutes for *expect* or *imagine* (*I figure I'll go*), these words are colloquial.

can, may Strictly, *can* indicates capacity or ability, and *may* indicates permission: *If I may talk with you a moment, I believe I can solve your problem.*

can't help but This idiom is common but redundant. Either *I can't help wishing* or the more formal *I cannot but wish* is preferable to *I can't help but wish.*

case, instance, line Expressions such as *in the case of, in the instance of,* and *along the lines of* are usually unnecessary padding in a sentence and should be avoided.

censor, censure To *censor* is to edit or remove from public view on moral or some other grounds; to *censure* is to give a formal scolding. *The lieutenant was censured by Major Taylor for censoring the letters his men wrote home from boot camp.*

center around *Center on* is generally considered more logical than, and preferable to, *center around.*

climatic, climactic *Climatic* comes from *climate* and refers to weather: *Last winter's low temperatures may indicate a climatic change. Climactic* comes from *climax* and refers to a dramatic high point: *During the climactic duel between Hamlet and Laertes, Gertrude drinks poisoned wine.*

complement, compliment To *complement* something is to add to, complete, or reinforce it: *Her yellow blouse complemented her black hair.* To *compliment* something is to make a flattering remark about it: *He complimented her hair. Complimentary* also can mean "free": *a complimentary sample of our new product; complimentary tickets.*

conscience, conscious *Conscience* is a noun meaning "a sense of right and wrong"; *conscious* is an adjective meaning "aware" or "awake." *Though I was barely conscious, my conscience told me to confess.*

contact Often used imprecisely as a verb when a more exact word such as *consult, talk with, telephone,* or *write to* would be appropriate.

continual, continuous *Continual* means "constantly recurring": *Most movies on television are continually interrupted by commercials. Continuous* means "unceasing": *Cable television often presents movies continuously without commercials.*

convince, persuade In the strictest sense, to *convince* someone means to change his or her opinion; to *persuade* someone means to move him or her to action. *Convince* thus is properly followed by *of* or *that,* whereas *persuade* is followd by *to: Once he convinced Othello of Desdemona's infidelity, Iago easily persuaded him to kill her.*

could of See *have, of.*

couple of Used colloquially to mean "a few" or "several."

credible, creditable, credulous *Credible* means "believable": *It's a strange story, but it seems credible to me. Creditable* means "deserving of credit" or "worthy": *Asked to play "Red River Valley," Steve gave a creditable performance. Credulous* means "gullible": *The credulous Claire believed Tim's statement that he was quitting school.* See also *incredible, incredulous.*

criteria The plural of *criterion* (meaning "standard for judgment"): *Of all our criteria for picking a roommate, the most important criterion is a sense of humor.*

gl/us

data The plural of *datum* (meaning "fact"): *Out of all the data generated by these experiments, not one datum supports our hypothesis.* Usually, a more common term like *fact, result,* or *figure* is preferred to *datum.* Though *data* is very often used as a singular noun, it is still treated as plural in much formal speech and writing: *The data fail* (not *fails*) *to support the hypothesis.*

device, devise *Device* is the noun, and *devise* is the verb: *Can you devise some device for getting his attention?*

differ from, differ with To *differ from* is to be unlike: *The twins differ from each other only in their hairstyles.* To *differ with* is to disagree with: *I have to differ with you on that point.*

different from, different than *Different from* is preferred: *His purpose is different from mine.* But *different than* is widely accepted when a clause follows, particularly when a construction using *from* would be wordy: *I'm a different person now than I used to be* is preferable to *I'm a different person now from the person I used to be.*

discreet, discrete *Discreet* (noun form *discretion*) means "tactful": *What's a discreet way of telling Maud to be quiet? Discrete* (noun form *discreteness*) means "separate and distinct": *Within a computer's memory are millions of discrete bits of information.*

disinterested, uninterested *Distinterested* means "impartial": *We chose Pete, as a disinterested third party, to decide who was right. Uninterested* means "bored" or "lacking interest": *Unfortunately, Pete was completely uninterested in the question.*

don't *Don't* is the contraction for *do not,* not for *does not: I don't care, you don't care,* but *he doesn't* (not *don't*) *care.*

due to *Due to* is always acceptable as a subject complement: *His gray hairs were due to age.* Many object to *due to* as a preposition meaning "because of" (*Due to the holiday, there will be no class tomorrow*). A rule of thumb is that *due to* is always correct after a form of the verb *be* but questionable otherwise.

due to the fact that Wordy for *because.*

each and every Wordy for *each* or *every.* Write *each one of us* or *every one of us,* not *each and every one of us.*

eager, anxious See *anxious, eager.*

effect See *affect, effect.*

elicit, illicit *Elicit* is a verb meaning "bring out" or "call forth." *Illicit* is an adjective meaning "unlawful." *The crime elicited an outcry against illicit drugs.*

ensure See *assure, ensure, insure.*

enthused Used colloquially as an adjective meaning "showing enthusiasm." The preferred adjective is *enthusiastic: The coach was enthusiastic* (not *enthused*) *about the team's victory.*

especially, specially *Especially* means "particularly" or "more than other things"; *specially* means "for a specific reason." *I especially treasure my boots. They were made specially for me.*

et al., etc. *Et al.*, the Latin abbreviation for "and other people," is often used in source references for works with more than two or three authors: *Jones et al.* (see 35c, 35i). *Etc.*, the Latin abbreviation for "and other things," should not be used to refer to people. See also *and etc.*

everybody, every body; everyone, every one *Everybody* and *everyone* are indefinite pronouns: *Everybody* (*everyone*) *knows Tom steals. Every one* is a pronoun modified by *every, every body* a noun modified by *every*. Both refer to each thing or person of a specific group and are typically followed by *of: The game commissioner has stocked every body of fresh water in the state with fish, and now every one of our rivers is a potential trout stream.*

everyday, every day *Every day* is a noun modified by *every; everyday* is an adjective meaning "used daily" or "common": *Every day she had to cope with everyday problems.*

everywheres Nonstandard for *everywhere.*

except See *accept, except.*

except for the fact that Wordy for *except that.*

explicit, implicit *Explicit* means "stated outright": *I left explicit instructions. The movie contains explicit sex. Implicit* means "implied, unstated": *We had an implicit understanding. I trust Marcia implicitly.*

farther, further *Farther* refers to additional distance (*How much farther is it to the beach?*), and *further* refers to additional time, amount, or other abstract matters (*I don't want to discuss this any further*).

fewer, less *Fewer* refers to individual countable items (a plural noun), *less* to general amounts (a singular noun): *Skim milk has fewer calories than whole milk. We have less milk left than I thought.*

field The phrase *the field of* is wordy and generally unnecessary: *Margaret plans to specialize in* (not *in the field of*) *family medicine.*

figure See *calculate, figure, reckon.*

fixing to Avoid this colloquial substitute for "intend to": *The school intends* (not *is fixing*) *to build a new library.*

flaunt, flout *Flaunt* means "show off": *If you have style, flaunt it. Flout* means "scorn" or "defy": *Hester Prynne flouted convention and paid the price.*

flunk A colloquial substitute for *fail.*

former, latter *Former* refers to the first-named of two things, *latter* to the second-named: *I like both skiing and swimming, the former in the winter and the latter all year round.* To refer to the first- or last-named of three or more things, say *first* or *last: I like jogging, swimming, and hang gliding, but the last is inconvenient in the city.*

fun As an adjective, *fun* is colloquial and should be avoided in most writing: *It was a pleasurable* (not *fun*) *evening.*

further See *farther, further.*

get This common verb is used in many slang and colloquial expressions: *get lost, get with it, get your act together, that really gets me, getting on. Get* is easy to overuse; watch out for it in expressions like *it's getting better* (substitute *it's improving*) and *we got done* (substitute *we finished*).

good, well *Good* is an adjective, and *well* is nearly always an adverb: *Larry's a good dancer. He and Linda dance well together. Well* is properly used as an adjective only to refer to health: *You don't look well. Aren't you feeling well?* (*You look good,* in contrast, means "Your appearance is pleasing.")

good and Colloquial for "very": *I was very* (not *good and*) *tired.*

had better See *better, had better.*

had ought The *had* is unnecessary and should be omitted: *He ought* (not *had ought*) *to listen to his mother.*

half Either *half a* or *a half* is appropriate usage, but *a half a* is redundant: *Half a loaf* (not *A half a loaf*) *is better than none. We'd like a half bottle* (not *a half a bottle*) *of the house wine, please.*

hanged, hung Though both are past-tense forms of *hang, hanged* is used to refer to executions and *hung* is used for all other meanings: *Tom Dooley was hanged* (not *hung*) *from a white oak tree. I hung* (not *hanged*) *the picture you gave me.*

hardly See *but, hardly, scarcely.*

have, of Use *have,* not *of,* after helping verbs such as *could, should, would, may,* and *might: You should have* (not *should of*) *told me.*

he, she; he/she The pronouns *he* and *she* refer to male and female antecedents, respectively. When the antecedent could be either male or female, convention has allowed the use of *he* to mean "he or she": *After the infant learns to crawl, he progresses to creeping.* However, many people today object to this use of *he* because readers tend to think of *he* as male, whether or not that is the writer's intention. *He/she,* one substitute for *he,* is awkward and objectionable to most readers. The better choice is to use *he or she,* to make the pronoun plural, or to rephrase. For instance: *After the infant learns to crawl, he or she progresses to creeping. After infants learn to crawl, they progress to creeping. After learning to crawl, the infant progresses to creeping.* See also 8b-3.

herself, himself See *myself, herself, himself, yourself.*

hisself Nonstandard for *himself.*

hopefully *Hopefully* means "with hope": *Freddy waited hopefully for a glimpse of Eliza.* The use of *hopefully* to mean "it is to be hoped," "I hope," or "let's hope" is now very common; but since many readers continue to object strongly to the usage, you should avoid it. *I hope* (not *Hopefully*) *Eliza will be here soon.*

idea, ideal An *idea* is a thought or conception. An *ideal* (noun) is a model of perfection or a goal. *Ideal* should not be used in place of *idea: The idea* (not *ideal*) *of the play is that our ideals often sustain us.*

if, whether For clarity, begin a subordinate clause with *whether* rather than *if* when the clause expresses an alternative: *If I laugh hard, people can't tell whether I'm crying.*

illicit See *elicit, illicit.*

illusion See *allusion, illusion.*

impact Careful writers use both the noun and the verb *impact* to connote forceful or even violent collision. Avoid the increasingly common diluted meanings of *impact:* "an effect" (noun) or "to have an effect on" (verb). The diluted verb (*The budget cuts impacted social science research*) is bureaucratic jargon.

implicit See *explicit, implicit.*

imply, infer Writers or speakers *imply,* meaning "suggest": *Jim's letter implies he's having too good a time to miss us.* Readers or listeners *infer,* meaning "conclude": *From Jim's letter I infer he's having too good a time to miss us.*

in, into *In* indicates location or condition: *He was in the garage. She was in a coma. Into* indicates movement or a change in condition: *He went into the garage. She fell into a coma. Into* is also slang for "interested in" or "involved in": *I am into Zen.*

in ... A number of phrases beginning with *in* are unnecessarily wordy and should be avoided: *in the event that* (for *if*); *in the neighborhood of* (for *approximtely* or *about*); *in this day and age* (for *now* or *nowadays*); *in spite of the fact that* (for *although* or *even though*); and *in view of the fact that* (for *because* or *considering that*). Certain other *in* phrases are nothing but padding and can be omitted entirely: *in the case of, in nature, in number, in reality, in terms of,* and *in a very real sense.* See also 31c.

incredible, incredulous *Incredible* means "unbelievable"; *incredulous* means "unbelieving": *When Nancy heard Dennis's incredible story, she was frankly incredulous.* See also *credible, creditable, credulous.*

individual, person, party *Individual* should refer to a single human being in contrast to a group or should stress uniqueness: *The U.S. Constitution places strong emphasis on the rights of the individual.* For other meanings *person* is preferable: *What person* (not *individual*) *wouldn't want the security promised in that advertisement? Party* means "group" (*Can you seat a party of four for dinner?*) and should not be used to refer to an individual except in legal documents.

infer See *imply.*

in regards to Nonstandard for *in regard to* (or *as regards* or *regarding*). See also *regarding.*

inside of, outside of The *of* is unnecessary when *inside* and *outside* are used as prepositions: *Stay inside* (not *inside of*) *the house. The decision is outside* (not *outside of*) *my authority. Inside of* may refer colloquially to time, though in formal English *within* is preferred: *The law was passed within* (not *inside of*) *a year.*

instance See *case, instance, line.*

insure See *assure, ensure, insure.*

irregardless Nonstandard for *regardless.*

is because See *reason is because.*

is when, is where These are mixed constructions (faulty predication; see 15b) in sentences that define: *Adolescence is a stage* (not *is when a person is*) *between childhood and adulthood. Socialism is a system in which* (not *is where*) *government owns the means of production.*

its, it's *Its* is a possessive pronoun: *That plant is losing its leaves. It's* is a contraction for *it is: It's likely to die if you don't water it.* Many people confuse *it's* and *its* because possessives are most often formed with *-'s;* but the possessive *its,* like *his* and *hers,* never takes an apostrophe.

-ize, -wise The suffix *-ize* is frequently used to change a noun or adjective into a verb: *revolutionize, immunize.* The suffix *-wise* commonly changes a noun or adjective into an adverb: *clockwise, otherwise, likewise.* But the two suffixes are used excessively and often unnecessarily, especially in bureaucratic writing. Avoid their use except in established words: *The two nations are ready to settle on* (not *finalize*) *an agreement. I'm highly sensitive* (not *sensitized*) *to that kind of criticism. From a financial standpoint* (not *Moneywise*), *it's a good time to buy real estate.*

kind of, sort of, type of In formal speech and writing, avoid using *kind of* or *sort of* to mean "somewhat": *He was rather* (not *kind of*) *tall.*

Kind, sort, and *type* are singular and take singular modifiers and verbs: *This kind of dog is easily trained.* Agreement errors often occur when these singular nouns are combined with the plural demonstrative adjectives *these* and *those: These kinds* (not *kind*) *of dogs are easily trained. Kind, sort,* and *type* should be followed by *of* but not by *a: I don't know what type of* (not *type* or *type of a*) *dog that is.*

Use *kind of, sort of,* or *type of* only when the word *kind, sort,* or *type* is important: *That was a strange* (not *strange sort of*) *statement. He's a funny* (not *funny kind of*) *guy.*

later, latter *Later* refers to time; *latter* refers to the second-named of two items. See also *former, latter.*

lay, lie *Lay* is a transitive verb (principal parts *lay, laid, laid*) that means "put" or "place"; it is nearly always followed by a direct object. *If we lay this tablecloth in the sun next to the shirt Sandy laid out there this morning, it should dry quickly. Lie* is an intransitive verb (principal parts *lie, lay, lain*) that means "recline" or "be situated": *I lay awake all night last night, just as I had lain the night before. The town lies east of the river.* See also 7b.

leave, let *Leave* and *let* are interchangeable only when followed by *alone; leave me alone* is the same as *let me alone.* Otherwise, *leave* means "depart" and *let* means "allow": *Julia would not let Susan leave.*

less See *fewer, less.*

let See *leave, let.*

liable See *apt, liable, likely.*

lie, lay See *lay, lie.*

like, as See *as, like.*

like, such as When you are giving an example of something, use *such as* to indicate that the example is a representative of the thing mentioned, and use *like* to compare the example to the thing mentioned: *Steve has recordings of many great saxophonists such as Ben Webster, Coleman Hawkins, and Lee Konitz. Steve wants to be a great jazz saxophonist like Ben Webster, Coleman Hawkins, and Lee Konitz.*

Most writers prefer to keep *such* and *as* together: *Steve admires saxophonists such as* rather than *Steve admires such saxophonists as.*

likely See *apt, liable, likely.*

line See *case, instance, line.*

literally This adverb means "actually" or "just as the words say," and it should not be used to qualify or intensify expressions whose words are not to be taken at face value. The sentence *He was literally climbing the walls* describes a person behaving like an insect, not a person who is restless or anxious. For the latter meaning, *literally* should be omitted.

lose, loose *Lose* is a verb meaning "mislay": *Did you lose a brown glove? Loose* is an adjective meaning "unrestrained" or "not tight": *Don't open the door; Ann's canary got loose. Loose* also can function as a verb meaning "let loose": *They loose the dogs as soon as they spot the bear.*

lots, lots of Colloquial substitutes for *very many, a great many,* or *much.*

may, can See *can, may.*

may be, maybe *May be* is a verb, and *maybe* is an adverb meaning "perhaps": *Tuesday may be a legal holiday. Maybe we won't have classes.*

may of See *have, of.*

media *Media* is the plural of *medium: Of all the news media, television is the only medium with more visual than verbal content.*

might of See *have, of.*

moral, morale As a noun, *moral* means "ethical conclusion" or "lesson": *The moral of the story escapes me. Morale* means "spirit" or "state of mind": *Victory improved the team's morale.*

most, almost See *almost, most.*

must of See *have, of.*

myself, herself, himself, yourself The *-self* pronouns are reflexive or intensive, which means they refer to or intensify an antecedent (see 5a-2): *Paul and I did it ourselves; Jill herself said so.* Though the *-self* pronouns often are used colloquially in place of personal pronouns, especially as objects of prepositions, they should be avoided in formal speech and writing unless the noun or pronoun they refer to is also present: *No one except* me (not myself) *saw the accident. Our delegates will be Susan and* you (not yourself).

nohow Nonstandard for *in no way* or *in any way.*

nothing like, nowhere near As colloquial substitutes for *not nearly,* these idioms are best avoided in formal speech and writing: *The human bones found in Europe are not nearly* (not *nowhere near*) *as old as those found in Africa.*

nowheres Nonstandard for *nowhere.*

number See *amount, number.*

of, have See *have, of.*

off of *Of* is unnecessary. Use *off* or *from* rather than *off of: He jumped off* (or *from,* not *off of*) *the roof.*

OK, O.K., okay All three spellings are acceptable, but avoid this colloquial term in formal speech and writing.

on, upon In modern English, *upon* is usually just a stuffy way of saying *on.* Unless you need a formal effect, use *on: We decided on* (not *upon*) *a location for our next meeting.*

on account of Wordy for *because of.*

on the other hand This transitional expression of contrast should be preceded by its mate, *on the one hand: On the one hand, we hoped for snow. On the other hand, we feared that it would harm the animals.* However, the two combined can be unwieldy, and a simple *but, however, yet,* or *in contrast* often suffices: *We hoped for snow. Yet we feared that it would harm the animals.*

outside of See *inside of, outside of.*

owing to the fact that Wordy for *because.*

party See *individual, person, party.*

people, persons In formal usage, *people* refers to a general group: *We the people of the United States. . . . Persons* refers to a collection of individuals: *Will the person or persons who saw the accident please notify. . . .* Except when emphasizing individuals, prefer *people* to *persons.*

per Except in technical writing, an English equivalent is usually preferable to the Latin *per: $10 an* (not *per*) *hour; sent by* (not *per*) *parcel post; requested in* (not *per* or *as per*) *your letter.*

percent (per cent), percentage Both these terms refer to fractions of one hundred and should be avoided except when specifying actual statistics. Use an expression such as *part of, a number of,* or *a large* (or *small*) *proportion of* when you mean simply "part."

Percent always follows a numeral (*40 percent of the voters*), and the word should be used instead of the symbol (%) in formal writing. *Percentage* usually follows an adjective (*a high percentage*).

person See *individual, person, party.*

persons See *people, persons.*

persuade See *convince, persuade.*

phenomena The plural of *phenomenon* (meaning "perceivable fact" or "unusual occurrence"): *The Center for Short-Lived Phenomena judged that the phenomenon we had witnessed was not a flying saucer.*

gl/us

plenty A colloquial substitute for *very: He was going very* (not *plenty*) *fast when he hit that tree.*

plus *Plus* is standard as a preposition meaning *in addition to: His income plus mine is sufficient.* But *plus* is colloquial as a conjunctive adverb: *Our organization is larger than theirs; moreover* (not *plus*), *we have more money.*

practicable, practical *Practicable* means "capable of being put into practice"; *practical* means "useful" or "sensible": *We figured out a practical new design for our kitchen, but it was too expensive to be practicable.*

precede, proceed The verb *precede* means "come before": *My name precedes yours in the alphabet.* The verb *proceed* means "move on": *We were told to proceed to the waiting room.*

pretty Overworked as an adverb meaning "rather" or "somewhat": *He was somewhat* (not *pretty*) *irked at the suggestion.*

previous to, prior to Wordy for *before.*

principal, principle *Principal* is a noun meaning "chief official" or, in finance, "capital sum." As an adjective, *principal* means "foremost" or "major." *Principle* is a noun only, meaning "rule" or "axiom." *Her principal reasons for confessing were her principles of right and wrong.*

proceed, precede See *precede, proceed.*

question of whether, question as to whether Wordy for *whether.*

raise, rise *Raise* is a transitive verb that takes a direct object, and *rise* is an intransitive verb that does not take an object: *The Kirks have to rise at dawn because they raise cows.*

real, really In formal speech and writing, *real* should not be used as an adverb; *really* is the adverb and *real* an adjective. *Popular reaction to the announcement was really* (not *real*) *enthusiastic.*

reason is because Mixed construction (faulty predication; see 15b). Although the expression is colloquially common, formal speech and writing require a *that* clause after *reason is: The reason he is absent is that* (not *is because*) *he is sick.* Or: *He is absent because he is sick.*

reckon See *calculate, figure, reckon.*

regarding, in regard to, with regard to, relating to, relative to, with respect to, respecting Stuffy substitutes for *on, about,* or *concerning: Mr. McGee spoke about* (not *with regard to*) *the plans for the merger.*

gl/us

respectful, respective *Respectful* means "full of (or showing) respect": *If you want respect, be respectful of other people. Respective* means "separate": *After a joint Christmas celebration, the French and the Germans returned to their respective trenches.*

rise, raise See *raise, rise.*

scarcely See *but, hardly, scarcely.*

sensual, sensuous *Sensual* suggests sexuality; *sensuous* means "pleasing to the senses." *Stirred by the sensuous scent of meadow grass and flowers, Cheryl and Paul found their thoughts growing increasingly sensual.*

set, sit *Set* is a transitive verb (principal parts *set, set, set*) that describes something a person does to an object: *He set the pitcher down. Sit* is an intransitive verb (principal parts *sit, sat, sat*) that describes something done by a person who is tired of standing: *She sits on the sofa.* See also 7b.

shall, will *Will,* originally reserved for the second and third persons, is now generally accepted as the future-tense helping verb for all three persons: *I will go, you will go, they will go.* The main use of *shall* is for first-person questions requesting an opinion or consent: *Shall I order a pizza? Shall we dance?* (Questions that merely inquire about the future use *will: When will I see you again?*) *Shall* can also be used for the first person when a formal effect is desired (*I shall expect you around three*), and it is occasionally used with the second or third person to express the speaker's determination (*You shall do as I say*).

should, would *Should* expresses obligation for first, second, and third persons: *I should fix dinner. You should set the table. Jack should wash the dishes. Would* expresses a wish or hypothetical condition for all three persons: *I would do it. Wouldn't you? Wouldn't anybody?* When the context is formal, however, *should* is sometimes used instead of *would* in the first person: *We should be delighted to accept your kind invitation.*

should of See *have, of.*

since *Since* is often used to mean "because": *Since you ask, I'll tell you.* Its primary meaning, however, relates to time: *I've been waiting since noon.* To avoid confusion, some writers prefer to use *since* only in contexts involving time. If you do use *since* in both senses, watch out for ambiguous constructions, such as *Since you left, my life is empty,* where *since* could mean either "because" or "ever since."

sit, set See *set, sit.*

situation Often unnecessary, as in *The situation is that we have to get some help* (revise to *We have to get some help*) or *The team was faced with a punting situation* (revise to *The team was faced with punting* or *The team had to punt*).

so Avoid using *so* alone as a vague intensifier: *He was so late. So* needs to be followed by *that* and a clause that states a result: *He was so late that I left without him.*

some *Some* is colloquial as an adverb meaning "somewhat" or "to some extent" and as an adjective meaning "remarkable": *We'll have to hurry somewhat* (not *some*) *to get there in time. Those are remarkable* (not *some*) *photographs.*

somebody, some body; someone, some one *Somebody* and *someone* are indefinite pronouns; *some body* is a noun modified by an adjective; and *some one* is a pronoun or an adjective modified by *some. Somebody ought to invent a shampoo that will give hair some body. Someone told Janine she should choose some one plan and stick with it.*

someplace Informal for *somewhere.*

sometime, sometimes, some time *Sometime* means "at an indefinite time in the future": *Why don't you come up and see me sometime? Sometimes* means "now and then": *I still see my old friend Joe sometimes. Some time* means "span of time": *I need some time to make the payments.*

somewheres Nonstandard for *somewhere.*

sort of, sort of a See *kind of, sort of, type of.*

specially See *especially, specially.*

such Avoid using *such* as a vague intensifier: *It was such a cold winter. Such* should be followed by *that* and a clause that states a result: *It was such a cold winter that Napoleon's troops had to turn back.*

such as See *like, such as.*

supposed to, used to In both these expressions, the *-d* is essential: *I used to* (not *use to*) *think so. He's supposed to* (not *suppose to*) *meet us.*

sure Colloquial when used as an adverb meaning *surely: James Madison sure was right about the need for the Bill of Rights.* If you merely want to be emphatic, use *certainly: Madison certainly was right.* If your goal is to convince a possibly reluctant reader, use *surely: Madison surely was right. Surely Madison was right.*

sure and, sure to; try and, try to *Sure to* and *try to* are the preferred forms: *Be sure to* (not *sure and*) *buy milk. Try to* (not *Try and*) *find some decent tomatoes.*

take, bring See *bring, take.*

than, as See *as, than.*

than, then *Than* is a conjunction used in comparisons, *then* an adverb indicating time: *Holmes knew then that Moriarty was wilier than he had thought.*

that, which *That* always introduces restrictive clauses: *We should use the lettuce that Susan bought* (*that Susan bought* identifies the specific lettuce being referred to). *Which* can introduce both restrictive and nonrestrictive clauses, but many writers reserve *which* only for nonrestrictive clauses: *The leftover lettuce, which is in the refrigerator, would make a good salad* (*which is in the refrigerator* simply provides more information about the lettuce). See also 21c.

gl/us

their, there, they're *Their* is the possessive form of *they: Give them their money. There* indicates place (*I saw her standing there*) or functions as an expletive (*There is a hole behind you*). *They're* is a contraction for *they are: They're going fast.*

theirselves Nonstandard for *themselves.*

then, than See *than, then.*

these kind, these sort, these type, those kind See *kind of, sort of, type of.*

this here, these here, that there, them there Nonstandard for *this, these, that,* or *those.*

thusly A mistaken form of *thus.*

till, until, 'til *Till* and *until* have the same meaning; both are acceptable. *'Til,* a contraction of *until,* is an old form that has been replaced by *till.*

time period Since a *period* is an interval of time, this expression is redundant: *They did not see each other for a long time* (not *time period*). *Six accidents occurred in a three-week period* (not *time period*).

to, too, two *To* is a preposition; *too* is an adverb meaning "also" or "excessively"; and *two* is a number. *I too have been to Europe two times.*

too Avoid using *too* as an intensifier meaning "very": *Monkeys are too mean.* If you do use *too,* explain the consequences of the excessive quality: *Monkeys are too mean to make good pets.*

toward, towards Both are acceptable, though *toward* is preferred. Use one or the other consistently.

try and, try to See *sure and, sure to; try and, try to.*

type of See *kind of, sort of, type of.* Don't use *type* without *of: It was a family type of* (not *type*) *restaurant.* Or, better: *It was a family restaurant.*

uninterested See *disinterested, uninterested.*

unique As an absolute adjective (see 9e-5), *unique* cannot sensibly be modified with words such as *very* or *most: That was a unique* (not *a very* or *the most unique*) *movie.*

until See *till, until, 'til.*

upon, on See *on, upon.*

usage, use *Usage* refers to conventions, most often those of a language: *Is "hadn't ought" proper usage? Usage* is often misused in place of the noun *use: Wise use* (not *usage*) *of insulation can save fuel.*

use, utilize *Utilize* means "make use of": *We should utilize John's talent for mimicry in our play.* In most contexts, *use* is equally or more acceptable and much less stuffy.

used to See *supposed to, used to.*

wait for, wait on In formal speech and writing, *wait for* means "await"

(*I'm waiting for Paul*), and *wait on* means "serve" (*The owner of the store herself waited on us*).

ways Colloquial as a substitute for *way: We have only a little way* (not *ways*) *to go.*

well See *good, well.*

whether, if See *if, whether.*

which See *that, which.*

which, who *Which* never refers to people. Use *who* or sometimes *that* for a person or persons and *which* or *that* for a thing or things: *The baby, who was left behind, opened the door, which we had closed.* See also 12f.

who's, whose *Who's* is the contraction of *who is: Who's at the door? Whose* is the possessive form of *who: Whose book is that?*

will, shall See *shall, will.*

-wise See *-ize, -wise.*

with regard to, with respect to See *regarding.*

would See *should, would.*

would of See *have, of.*

your, you're *Your* is the possessive form of *you: Your dinner is ready. You're* is the contraction of *you are: You're bound to be late.*

yourself See *myself, herself, himself, yourself.*

gl/us

Glossary of Grammatical Terms

absolute phrase A phrase that consists of a noun or pronoun and a participle, modifies a whole clause or sentence (rather than a single word), and is not joined to the rest of the sentence by a connector: *Our accommodations arranged, we set out on our trip. They will hire a local person, other things being equal.* When the participle in an absolute phrase is a form of the verb *be* (*being, been*), the participle is often omitted: *They will hire a local person, other things equal.* See also 5c-3 and 21d.

abstract noun See *noun.*

acronym A pronounceable word formed from the initial letter or letters of each word in an organization's title: NATO (North Atlantic Treaty Organization). See also 20b and 28b.

active voice See *verb.*

adjectival A term sometimes used to describe any word or word group, other than an adjective, that is used to modify a noun. Common adjectivals include nouns (*wagon train, railroad ties*), phrases (*fool on the hill*), and clauses (*the man that I used to be*). See *clause* and *phrase.* See also 5c.

adjective A word used to modify a noun or a word or word group used as a noun.

> **Descriptive adjectives** name some quality of the noun: *beautiful morning; dark horse.*
>
> **Limiting adjectives** narrow the scope of a noun. They include **possessives** (*my, their*); words that show number (*eight, several*); **demonstrative adjectives** (*this train, these days*); and **interrogative adjectives** (*what time? whose body?*)
>
> **Proper adjectives** are derived from proper nouns: *French language, Machiavellian scheme.*

Adjectives also can be classified according to position.

> **Attributive adjectives** appear next to the nouns they modify: *full moon.*

Predicate adjectives are connected to their nouns by linking verbs: *The moon is full.* See also *complement.*

See also *comparison,* 5b-1, and Chapter 9.

adjective clause See *clause.*

adjective phrase See *phrase.*

adverb A word used to modify a verb, an adjective, another adverb, or a whole sentence. Any one-word modifier that is not an adjective, a word used as an adjective, or an article is an adverb: *If you go south you'll hit a more heavily traveled road.* (*South* modifies the verb *go; heavily* modifies the adjective *traveled;* and *more* modifies the adverb *heavily.*) See also *comparison,* 5b-1, and Chapter 9.

adverb clause See *clause.*

adverbial A term sometimes used to describe any word or word group, other than an adverb, that is used to modify a verb, an adjective, another adverb, or a whole sentence. Common adverbials include nouns (*This little piggy stayed home*), phrases (*This little piggy went to market*), and clauses (*This little piggy went wherever he wanted*). See *clause* and *phrase.* See also 5c.

adverbial conjunction See *conjunctive adverb.*

adverb phrase See *phrase.*

agreement The correspondence of one word to another in person, number, or gender. A verb must agree with its subject; a pronoun must agree with its antecedent; and a demonstrative adjective must agree with its noun. *Every week the commander orders these kinds of sandwiches for his troops.* (The verb *orders* and the pronoun *his* both agree with the noun *commander.* The demonstrative adjective *these* agrees with the noun *kinds.*) See Chapter 8.

Logical agreement requires consistency in number between other related words, usually nouns: *The students brought their books* (not *book*). See also 13a.

antecedent The noun, or word or word group acting as a noun, to which a pronoun refers: *Jonah, who is not yet ten, has already chosen the college he will attend.* (*Jonah* is the antecedent of the pronouns *who* and *he.*) See also 8b.

appositive A word or phrase appearing next to a noun or pronoun, or to a word or word group acting as a noun, which explains or identifies it and is equivalent to it: *My brother Michael, the best horn player in town, won the state competition.* (*Michael* is a restrictive appositive that identifies which brother is being referred to. *The best horn player in town* is a nonrestrictive appositive that adds information about *My brother Michael.*) See also 5c-5 and 21c-2.

article The word *a, an,* or *the.* Articles are usually classed as adjectives; they are sometimes called **determiners** because they always signal that a noun follows. See the Glossary of Usage (p. 586) for a discussion of choosing between *a* and *an* before a noun or abbreviation.

Articles often present problems for those whose native language is not English because many languages use articles differently or less frequently than English does. The main conventions for using articles in English can be summarized as follows:

gl/gr

1. *The* is a **definite article:** it precedes a noun when the thing named is already known to the reader (*Visitors may tour the house*). *A* and *an* are **indefinite articles:** they precede a noun when the thing named is not already known to the reader (*They share a house*).
2. Use *a, an,* or *the* with a singular count noun—that is, a singular noun that names something countable: *a glass, an apple, the mirror.* Count nouns can form plurals with the addition of *-s* or *-es* (*glass, glasses*) or in some irregular way (*child, children*).
3. Do not use *a* or *an* with a plural noun: *apples* (not *an apples*). And do not use *a* or *an* with a mass noun—that is, a singular noun that names something not normally countable: *mail* (not *a mail*), *supervision* (not *a supervision*). Unlike count nouns, mass nouns do not form plurals. Note, however, that many nouns are sometimes count nouns and sometimes mass nouns: in *We have room for you, room* is a mass noun meaning "space"; in *We have a room for you, room* is a count noun meaning "walled area."
4. Do not use *the* with a plural noun or a mass noun when the noun refers generally to all representatives of what it names: *Men* (not *The men*) *and women* (not *the women*) *are different. Democracy* (not *The democracy*) *fosters freedom* (not *the freedom*) *of expression* (not *the expression*). Use *the* when referring to one or more specific representatives of what the noun names: *The women came and went.*

This summary omits many special uses of articles. Fuller discussions can be found in many composition textbooks designed for students using English as a second language.

auxiliary verb See *helping verb.*

cardinal number The type of number that shows amount: *two, sixty, ninety-seven.* Contrast *ordinal number* (such as *second, ninety-seventh*).

case The form of a noun or pronoun that indicates its function in the sentence. Nouns have two cases: the **plain case** (*John, ambassador*), for all uses except to show possession; and the **possessive** (or **genitive**) **case** (*John's, ambassador's*). Pronouns have three cases: the **subjective** (or **nominative**) **case** (*I, she*), denoting the subject of a verb or a subject complement; the **possessive case,** for use as either an adjective (*my, her*) or a noun (*mine, hers*); and the **objective case** (*me, her*), denoting the object of a verb, verbal, or preposition. See *declension* for a complete list of the forms of personal and relative pronouns. See also Chapter 6.

clause A group of related words containing a subject and predicate. A **main (independent) clause** can stand by itself as a sentence; a **subordinate (dependent) clause** cannot.

MAIN CLAUSE	*We can go to the movies.*
SUBORDINATE CLAUSE	We can go *if Julie gets back on time.*

Subordinate clauses may function as adjectives, adverbs, or nouns.

> **Adjective clauses** modify nouns or pronouns: *The car that hit Fred was running a red light* (clause modifies *car*).
>
> **Adverb clauses** modify verbs, adjectives, other adverbs, or whole clauses or sentences: *The car hit Fred when it ran a red light* (clause modifies *The car hit Fred*).
>
> **Noun clauses,** like nouns, function as subjects, objects, or complements: *Whoever was driving should be arrested* (clause is sentence subject).

See also 5c-4.

collective noun See *noun.*

comma splice A sentence error in which two main clauses are separated by a comma with no coordinating conjunction.

COMMA SPLICE	The book was long, it contained useful information.
REVISED	The book was long; it contained useful information.
REVISED	The book was long, *but* it contained useful information.

See 11a and 11b.

common noun See *noun.*

comparative See *comparison.*

comparison The inflection of an adverb or adjective that shows its relative intensity. The **positive degree** is the simple, uncompared form: *gross, clumsily.* The **comparative degree** compares the thing modified to at least one other thing: *grosser, more clumsily.* The **superlative degree** indicates that the thing modified exceeds all other things to which it is being compared: *grossest, most clumsily.* The comparative and superlative degrees are formed either by adding the endings *-er* and *-est* or by preceding the modifier with the words *more* and *most, less* and *least.* See also 5b-1 and 9e.

complement A word or word group that completes the sense of a subject, an object, or a verb.

> **Subject complements** follow a linking verb and modify or refer to the subject. They may be adjectives, nouns or pronouns, or words or word groups acting as adjectives or nouns: *I am a lion tamer, but I am not yet experienced.* (The noun *lion tamer* and the adjective *experienced* complement the subject *I.*) Adjective complements are also called **predicate adjectives.** Noun complements are also called **predicate nouns** or **predicate nominatives.**

are also called **predicate adjectives.** Noun complements are also called **predicate nouns** or **predicate nominatives.**

Object complements follow and modify or refer to direct objects. The complement can be an adjective, a noun, or a word or word group acting as an adjective or noun: *If you elect me president, I'll keep the unions satisfied.* (The noun *president* complements the direct object *me,* and the adjective *satisfied* complements the direct object *unions.*)

Verb complements are direct and indirect objects of verbs. They may be nouns, pronouns, or words or word groups acting as nouns: *Don't give the chimp that peanut.* (*Chimp* is the indirect object and *peanut* is the direct object of the verb *give.* Both objects are verb complements.)

See also *object* and 5a-3.

complete predicate See *predicate.*

complete subject See *subject.*

complex sentence See *sentence.*

compound Consisting of two or more words that function as a unit. **Compound words** include **compound nouns** (*milestone, featherbrain*); **compound adjectives** (*two-year-old, downtrodden*); and **compound prepositions** (*in addition to, on account of*). **Compound constructions** include **compound subjects** (*Harriet and Peter poled their barge down the river*); **compound predicates** (*The scout watched and waited*) or parts of predicates (*He grew tired and hungry*); and **compound sentences** (*He smiled, and I laughed*). See also 5d.

compound-complex sentence See *sentence.*

compound predicate See *compound.*

compound sentence See *sentence.*

compound subject See *compound.*

concrete noun See *noun.*

conjugation A list of the forms of a verb showing tense, voice, mood, person, and number. The conjugation of the verb *know* in present tense, active voice, indicative mood is *I know, you know, he/she/it knows, we know, you know, they know.* See also Chapter 7.

conjunction A word that links and relates two parts of a sentence. **Coordinating conjunctions** (*and, but, or, nor, for, so, yet*) connect words or word groups of equal grammatical rank: *The lights went out, but the doctors and nurses cared for their patients as if nothing were wrong.* See also 5d-1. **Correlative conjunctions** or **correlatives** (such as *either . . . or, not only . . . but also*) are pairs of coordinating conjunctions that work together: *He was certain that either his parents or his brother would help him.* See also 5d-1. **Subordinating conjunctions** (*after, although, as if, because, if, when, while,* and so on) begin a subordinate clause and link it to a main clause: *The seven dwarfs whistle while they work.* See also 5c-4.

conjunctive adverb (adverbial conjunction) An adverb (such as *besides, consequently, however, indeed,* and *therefore*) that connects two main clauses in a sentence: *We had hoped to own a house by now; however, housing costs have risen too fast.* See also 5d-2.

connector (connective) Any word or phrase that links words, phrases, clauses, or sentences. Common connectors include coordinating, correlative, and subordinating conjunctions; conjunctive adverbs; and prepositions.

connotation An association called up by a word, beyond its dictionary definition. See 31b-1. Contrast *denotation.*

construction Any group of grammatically related words, such as a phrase, a clause, or a sentence.

contraction A condensation of an expression, with an apostrophe replacing the missing letters: for example, *doesn't* (for *does not*), *we'll* (for *we will*). See also 23c.

coordinating conjunction See *conjunction.*

coordination The linking of words, phrases, or clauses that are of equal importance, usually with a coordinating conjunction: *He and I laughed, but she was not amused.* See also 16a. Contrast *subordination.*

correlative conjunction (correlative) See *conjunction.*

count noun See *noun.*

dangling modifier A word or phrase modifying a term that has been omitted or to which it cannot easily be linked.

DANGLING	*Having arrived late,* the concert had already begun.
REVISED	Having arrived late, *we* found that the concert had already begun.
REVISED	*Because we arrived late,* we missed the beginning of the concert.

See also 14g.

declension A list of the forms of a noun or pronoun, showing inflections for person (for pronouns), number, and case. See Chapter 6. The following chart shows a complete declension of the personal and relative pronouns.

Personal pronouns	*Subjective*	*Objective*	*Possessive*
Singular			
First person	I	me	my, mine
Second person	you	you	your, yours
Third person			
Masculine	he	him	his
Feminine	she	her	her, hers
Neuter	it	it	its

Personal pronouns	*Subjective*	*Objective*	*Possessive*
Plural			
First person	we	us	our, ours
Second person	you	you	your, yours
Third person	they	them	their, theirs
Relative pronouns	who	whom	whose
	which	which	whose, of which
	that	that	—

gl/gr

degree See *comparison.*

demonstrative adjective See *adjective.*

demonstrative pronoun See *pronoun.*

denotation The main or dictionary definition of a word. See 31b-1. Contrast *connotation.*

dependent clause See *clause.*

derivational suffix See *suffix.*

descriptive adjective See *adjective.*

determiner A word such as *a, an, the, my,* and *your* which indicates that a noun follows. See also *article.*

diagramming A visual method of identifying and showing the relations among various parts of a sentence.

direct address A construction in which a word or phrase indicates the person or group spoken to: *Have you finished, John? Farmers, unite.*

direct object See *object.*

direct quotation (direct discourse) See *quotation.*

double negative A nonstandard form consisting of two negative words used in the same construction so that they effectively cancel each other: *I don't have no money.* Rephrase as *I have no money* or *I don't have any money.*

double possessive A possessive using both the ending *-'s* and the preposition *of: That is a favorite expression of Mark's.*

ellipsis The omission of a word or words from a quotation, indicated by the three spaced periods of an **ellipsis mark:** "*that all . . . are created equal.*" See also 25e.

elliptical clause A clause omitting a word or words whose meaning is understood from the rest of the clause: *David likes Minneapolis better than (he likes) Chicago.* See also 5c-4.

expletive A sentence construction that postpones the subject by beginning with *there* or *it* followed by a form of the verb *be: It is impossible to get a ticket; I don't know why there aren't more seats available.* (*To get a ticket* is the subject of *is; seats* is the subject of *aren't.*) See also 5e-4.

finite verb A term used to describe any verb that makes an assertion or expresses a state of being and can stand as the main verb of a sentence or clause: *The moose eats the leaves.* See also 5c-2. Contrast *gerund, participle,* and *infinitive*—all formed from finite verbs but unable to stand alone as the main verb of a sentence: *I saw the moose eating the leaves* (participle). Contrast also *verbal* (*nonfinite verb*).

fragment See *sentence fragment.*

function word A word, such as an article, conjunction, or preposition, that serves primarily to clarify the roles of and relations between other words in a sentence: *We chased the goat for an hour but finally caught it.* Contrast *lexical word.*

fused sentence (run-on sentence) A sentence error in which two main clauses are joined with no punctuation or connecting word between them.

FUSED	I heard his lecture it was dull.
REVISED	I heard his lecture; it was dull.

See 11c.

future perfect tense See *tense.*

future tense See *tense.*

gender The classification of nouns or pronouns as masculine (*he, boy, handyman*), feminine (*she, woman, actress*), or neuter (*it, typewriter, dog*).

genitive case Another term for possessive case. See *case.*

gerund A verbal that ends in *-ing* and functions as a noun. The form of the gerund is the same as that of the present participle. Gerunds may have subjects, objects, complements, and modifiers: *Working is all right for killing time.* (*Working* is the subject of the verb *is; killing* is the object of the preposition *for* and takes the object *time.*) See also 5c-2, *verbal,* and *participle.*

helping verb A verb (also called an **auxiliary verb**) used with a main verb in a verb phrase: *will give, has been seeing, could depend.* Helping verbs indicate tense and sometimes also indicate voice, person, number, or mood. **Modal auxiliaries** include *can, could, may, might, must, ought, shall, should, will,* and *would.* They indicate a necessity, possibility, capability, willingness, or the like: *He can lift 250 pounds. You should write to your grandmother.* See also 5a-2 and Chapter 7.

idiom An expression that is peculiar to a language and that may not make sense if taken literally: for example, *dark horse, bide your time,* and *by and large.* See 31b-3 for a list of idioms involving prepositions, such as *agree with them* and *agree to the contract.*

imperative See *mood.*

indefinite pronoun See *pronoun.*

independent clause See *clause.*

indicative See *mood.*

indirect object See *object.*

indirect quotation (indirect discourse) See *quotation.*

infinitive The plain form of a verb, the form listed in the dictionary: *buy, sharpen, rinse.* Usually in combination with the **infinitive marker** *to,* infinitives form verbals and verbal phrases that function as nouns, adjectives, or adverbs. They may have objects, complements, or modifiers: *Alex's goals are to make money and to live well.* (*To make* and *to live,* following a linking verb, are complements of the subject *goals. To make* takes the object *money* and *to live* is modified by the adverb *well.*) See also 5c-2 and *verbal.*

infinitive marker See *infinitive.*

infinitive phrase See *phrase.*

inflection The variation in the form of a word that indicates its function in a particular context. See *declension,* the inflection of nouns and pronouns; *conjugation,* the inflection of verbs; and *comparison,* the inflection of adjectives and adverbs.

inflectional suffix See *suffix.*

intensifier A modifier that adds emphasis to the word(s) it modifies: for example, *very slow, so angry.*

intensive pronoun See *pronoun.*

interjection A word standing by itself or inserted in a construction to exclaim or command attention: *Hey! Ouch! What the heck did you do that for?*

interrogative Functioning as or involving a question.

interrogative adjective See *adjective.*

interrogative pronoun See *pronoun.*

intransitive verb See *verb.*

inversion A reversal of usual word order in a sentence, as when a verb precedes its subject or an object precedes its verb: *Down swooped the hawk. Our aims we stated clearly.*

irregular verb A verb that forms its past tense and past participle in some other way than by the addition of *-d* or *-ed* to the plain form: for example, *go, went, gone; give, gave, given.* See also 5a; and see 7a for a list of irregular verbs. Contrast *regular verb.*

lexical word A word, such as a noun, verb, or modifier, that carries part of the meaning of language. Contrast *function word.*

linking verb A verb that relates a subject to its complement: *Julie is a Democrat. He looks harmless. Those flowers smell heavenly.* Common linking verbs are the forms of *be;* the verbs relating to the senses, such as *feel* and *smell;* and the verbs *become, appear,* and *seem.* See also 5a-3 and *verb.*

logical agreement See *agreement.*

main clause See *clause.*

mass noun See *noun.*

misplaced modifier A modifier so far from the term it modifies or so close to another term it could modify that its relation to the rest of the sentence is unclear.

MISPLACED	The boys played with firecrackers that they bought illegally *in the field.*
REVISED	The boys played *in the field* with firecrackers that they bought illegally.

A misplaced modifier that could modify the words on either side of it is called a **squinting modifier.**

SQUINTING	The plan we considered *seriously* worries me.
REVISED	The plan we *seriously* considered worries me.
REVISED	The plan we considered worries me *seriously.*

See also 14a to 14f.

mixed construction A sentence containing two or more parts that do not fit together in grammar or in meaning.

MIXED	Of those who show up will not all be able to get in.
REVISED	Not all those who show up will be able to get in.

See also 15a and 15b.

modal auxiliary See *helping verb.*

modifier Any word or word group that limits or qualifies the meaning of another word or word group. Modifiers include adjectives and adverbs as well as words, phrases, and clauses that act as adjectives and adverbs.

mood The form of a verb that shows how the speaker views the action. The **indicative mood,** the most common, is used to make statements or ask questions: *The play will be performed Saturday. Did you get us tickets?* The **imperative mood** gives a command: *Please get good seats. Don't let them put us in the top balcony.* The **subjunctive mood** expresses a wish, a condition contrary to fact, a recommendation, or a request: *I wish George were coming with us. Did you suggest that he join us?* See also 7g.

nominal A noun, a pronoun, or a word or group of words used as a noun: *Joan and I talked. The rich owe a debt to the poor* (adjectives acting as subject and object). *Baby sitting can be exhausting* (gerund acting as subject). *I like to play with children* (infinitive phrase acting as object).

nominative See *case.*

nonfinite verb See *verbal.*

nonrestrictive element A word, phrase, or clause that does not limit the term or construction it refers to and that is not essential to the meaning of the sentence's main clause. Nonrestrictive elements are usually set off by commas: *This electric mixer, on sale for one week only,* *can be plugged directly into your kitchen counter* (nonrestrictive adjective phrase). *Sleep, which we all need, occupies a third of our lives* (nonrestrictive adjective clause). *His wife, Patricia, is a chemist* (nonrestrictive appositive). See also 21c. Contrast *restrictive element.*

noun A word that names a person, place, thing, quality, or idea: *Maggie, Alabama, clarinet, satisfaction, socialism.* Nouns normally form the possessive case by adding *-'s* (*Maggie's*) and the plural by adding *-s* or *-es* (*clarinets, messes*), although there are exceptions (*men, women, children*).

> **Common nouns** refer to general classes: *book, government, music.*
>
> **Proper nouns** name specific people or places: *Susan, Athens, Candlestick Park.*
>
> **Collective nouns** name groups: *team, class, jury, family.*
>
> **Count nouns** name things that can be counted: *ounce, camera, pencil, person, cat.*
>
> **Mass nouns** name things that are not normally counted: *jewelry, milk, music, information.*
>
> **Concrete nouns** name tangible things: *ink, porch, bird.*
>
> **Abstract nouns** name ideas or qualities: *equality, greed, capitalism.*

See also 5a-2.

noun clause See *clause.*

number The form of a noun, pronoun, demonstrative adjective, or verb that indicates whether it is singular or plural: *woman, women; I, we; this, these; runs, run.* See also Chapter 8.

object A noun, a pronoun, or a word or word group acting as a noun that receives the action of or is influenced by a transitive verb, a verbal, or a preposition.

> **Direct objects** receive the action of verbs and verbals and frequently follow them in a sentence: *We sat watching the stars. Emily caught whatever it was you had.*
>
> **Indirect objects** tell for or to whom or what something is done: *I lent Stan my car. Reiner bought us all champagne.*
>
> **Objects of prepositions** usually follow prepositions and are linked by them to the rest of the sentence: *They are going to New Orleans for the jazz festival.*

See also 5a-3 and 5c-1.

object complement See *complement.*

objective See *case.*

ordinal number The type of number that shows order: *first, eleventh, twenty-fifth.* Contrast *cardinal number* (such as *one, twenty-five*).

parenthetical element A word or construction that interrupts a sentence and is not part of its main structure, called *parenthetical* because it could (or does) appear in parentheses: *Childe Hassam* (*1859–1935*) *was an American painter and etcher. The book, incidentally, is terrible.*

participial phrase See *phrase.*

participle A verbal showing continuing or completed action, used as an adjective or part of a verb phrase but never as the main verb of a sentence or clause.

> **Present participles** end in *-ing: My heart is breaking* (participle as part of verb phrase). *I like to watch the rolling waves* (participle as adjective).
>
> **Past participles** most commonly end in *-d, -ed, -n,* or *-en* (*wished, shown, given*) but often change the spelling of the verb (*sung, done, slept*): *Jeff has broken his own record* (participle as part of verb phrase). *The meeting occurred behind a closed door* (participle as adjective).

See also *gerund,* 5b-2, and 5c-2.

parts of speech The classes into which words are commonly grouped according to their form, function, and meaning: nouns, pronouns, verbs, adjectives, adverbs, conjunctions, prepositions, and interjections. See separate entries for each part of speech. See also 5a to 5d.

passive voice See *verb.*

past participle See *participle.*

past perfect tense See *tense.*

past tense See *tense.*

perfect tenses See *tense.*

person The form of a verb or pronoun that indicates whether the subject is speaking, spoken to, or spoken about. In English only personal pronouns and verbs change form to indicate difference in person. In the **first person,** the subject is speaking: *I am* (or *We are*) *planning to go to the party tonight.* In the **second person,** the subject is being spoken to: *Are you coming?* In the **third person,** the subject is being spoken about: *She was* (or *They were*) *going.*

personal pronoun See *pronoun.*

phrase A group of related words that lacks a subject or a predicate or both and that acts as a single part of speech. There are several common types of phrases:

> **Verb phrases** are verb forms of more than one word that serve as predicates of sentences or clauses: *He says the movie has started.*
>
> **Prepositional phrases** consist of a preposition and its object, plus any modifiers. They function as adjectives, as adverbs, and occasionally as nouns: *We could come back for the second show* (adverb). See also *preposition.*
>
> **Absolute phrases** consist of a noun or pronoun and usually a

participle. They modify whole clauses or sentences: *Our seats being reserved, we probably should stay.* See also *absolute phrase.*

Verbal phrases are formed from verbals (see 5c-2). **Infinitive phrases** consist of an infinitive and its object, plus any modifiers, and they sometimes also include a subject. They function as nouns, adjectives, and adverbs: *I'd hate to go all the way home* (noun). (See also *infinitive.*) **Participial phrases** consist of a participle and its object, plus any modifiers. They function as adjectives: *The man collecting tickets says we may not be too late.* (See also *participle.*) **Gerund phrases** consist of a gerund (the *-ing* form of a verb used as a noun) and its object, plus any modifiers, and they sometimes also include a subject. They function as nouns: *Missing the beginning is no good, though.* (See also *gerund.*)

plain case See *case.*

plain form The infinitive or dictionary form of a verb. See *infinitive.*

positive degree See *comparison.*

possessive See *case.*

predicate The part of a sentence other than the subject and its modifiers. A predicate must contain a finite verb and may contain modifiers and objects of the verb as well as object and subject complements. The **simple predicate** consists of the verb and its auxiliaries: *A wiser person would have made a different decision.* The **complete predicate** includes the simple predicate and any modifiers, objects, and complements: *A wiser person would have made a different decision.* See also 5a and 5b.

predicate adjective See *complement.*

predicate noun (predicate nominative) See *complement.*

prefix A letter or group of letters (such as *sub-, in-, dis-, pre-*) that can be added at the beginning of a root or word to create a new word: *sub- + marine = submarine; dis- + grace = disgrace.* See also 33b-2. Contrast *suffix.*

preposition A word that links a noun, a pronoun, or a word or word group acting as a noun (the object of the preposition) to the rest of a sentence: *If Tim doesn't hear from that plumber by four, he'll call someone else before dinner.* Common prepositions include those in the preceding example as well as *about, after, beside, between, for, in,* and *to.* See 5c-1 for a more complete list. See also *object* and *phrase.*

prepositional phrase See *phrase.*

present participle See *participle.*

present perfect tense See *tense.*

present tense See *tense.*

principal clause A main or independent clause. See *clause.*

principal parts The three forms of a verb from which its various tenses are formed: the **plain form** or **infinitive** (*stop, go*); the **past tense** (*stopped, went*); and the **past participle** (*stopped, gone*). See *infinitive, participle,* and *tense.* See also 5a-2 and Chapter 7.

progressive tense See *tense.*

pronoun A word used in place of a noun or noun phrase (its antecedent). There are eight types of pronouns, many of which differ only in function, not in form:

> **Personal pronouns** (*I, you, he, she, it, we, they*): *They want you to come with us.*
>
> **Reflexive pronouns** (*myself, themselves*): *Can't you help yourselves?*
>
> **Intensive pronouns** (*myself, themselves*): *I myself saw it. She herself said so.*
>
> **Interrogative pronouns** (*who, which, what*): *What was that? Which is mine?*
>
> **Relative pronouns** (*who, which, that*): *The noise that scared you was made by the boy who lives next door.*
>
> **Demonstrative pronouns** (*this, that, these, those*): *These are fresher than those.*
>
> **Indefinite pronouns** (*each, one, anybody, all*): *One would think somebody must have seen it.*
>
> **Reciprocal pronouns** (*each other, one another*): *I hope we'll see each other again.*

See also 5a-2, Chapter 6, 8b, Chapter 12.

proper adjective See *adjective.*

proper noun See *noun.*

quotation Repetition of what someone has written or spoken. In **direct quotation (direct discourse),** the person's words are duplicated exactly and enclosed in quotation marks: *Polonius told his son, Laertes, "Neither a borrower nor a lender be."* An **indirect quotation (indirect discourse)** reports what someone said or wrote but not in the exact words and not in quotation marks: *Polonius advised his son, Laertes, not to borrow or lend.* See also 13d and Chapter 24.

reciprocal pronoun See *pronoun.*

reflexive pronoun See *pronoun.*

regular verb A verb that forms its past tense and past participle by adding *-d* or *-ed* to the plain form: *dip, dipped, dipped; open, opened, opened.* See also 5a and Chapter 7. Contrast *irregular verb.*

relative pronoun See *pronoun.*

restrictive element A word, phrase, or clause that is essential to the meaning of a sentence because it limits the thing it refers to. Restrictive elements are not set off by commas: *The keys to the car are on the table.*

That man <u>*who called about the apartment*</u> *said he'd try to call you tonight.* See also 21c. Contrast *nonrestrictive element.*

rhetoric The principles for finding and arranging ideas and for using language in speech or writing so as to achieve the writer's purpose in addressing his or her audience.

rhetorical question A question asked for effect, with no answer expected. The person asking the question either intends to provide the answer or assumes it is obvious: *If we let one factory pollute the river, what does that say to other factories that want to dump wastes there?*

run-on sentence See *fused sentence.*

sentence A complete unit of thought, consisting of at least a subject and a predicate that are not introduced by a subordinating word. Sentences can be classed on the basis of their structure in one of four ways: *simple, compound, complex,* or *compound-complex.*

> **Simple sentences** contain one main clause: *I'm leaving.*
>
> **Compound sentences** contain at least two main clauses: *I'd like to stay, but I'm leaving.*
>
> **Complex sentences** contain one main clause and at least one subordinate clause: *If you let me go now, you'll be sorry.*
>
> **Compound-complex sentences** contain at least two main clauses and at least one subordinate clause: *I'm leaving because you want me to, but I'd rather stay.*

See also *clause* and Chapter 5.

sentence fragment A sentence error in which a group of words is set off as a sentence even though it begins with a subordinating word or lacks either a subject or a predicate or both. See also Chapter 10.

FRAGMENT	She wasn't in shape for the race. *Which she had hoped to win.* [*Which,* a relative pronoun, makes the italicized clause subordinate.]
REVISED	She wasn't in shape for the race, which she had hoped to win.
FRAGMENT	He could not light a fire. *And thus could not warm the room.* [The italicized word group lacks a subject.]
REVISED	He could not light a fire. Thus he could not warm the room.

sentence modifier An adverb or a word or word group acting as an adverb that modifies the idea of the whole sentence in which it appears rather than any specific word: <u>*In fact*</u>*, people will always complain.*

simple predicate See *predicate.*

simple sentence See *sentence.*

simple subject See *subject.*

simple tenses See *tense.*

split infinitive The often awkward interruption of an infinitive and its marker *to* by an adverb: *The mission is to boldly go where no one has gone before.* See also *infinitive,* and see 14f.

squinting modifier See *misplaced modifier.*

subject The noun, or word or word group acting as a noun, that is the agent or topic of the action or state expressed in the predicate of a sentence or clause. The **simple subject** consists of the noun alone: *The quick brown fox jumps over the lazy dog.* The **complete subject** includes the simple subject and its modifiers: *The quick brown fox jumps over the lazy dog.* See also 5a.

subject complement See *complement.*

subjective See *case.*

subjunctive See *mood.*

subordinate clause See *clause.*

subordinating conjunction (subordinator) See *conjunction.*

subordination The use of grammatical constructions to make one element in a sentence dependent on rather than equal to another and thus to convey the writer's sense that the dependent element is less important to the whole: *Although I left six messages for him, the doctor failed to call me back.* See also 16b. Contrast *coordination.*

substantive A word or word group used as a noun.

suffix A **derivational suffix** is a letter or group of letters that can be added to the end of a root word to make a new word, often a different part of speech: *child, childish; shrewd, shrewdly; visual, visualize.* See also 33b-3. **Inflectional suffixes** adapt words to different grammatical relations: *boy, boys; fast, faster; tack, tacked.* See also 5a and 5b.

superlative See *comparison.*

syntax The division of grammar that is concerned with the relations among words and the means by which those relations are indicated.

tag question A question attached to the end of a statement and consisting of a pronoun, a helping verb, and sometimes the word *not: It isn't raining, is it? It is sunny, isn't it?*

tense The form of a verb that expresses the time of its action, usually indicated by the verb's inflection and by helping verbs.

The **simple tenses** include the **present** (*I race, you go*); the **past** (*I raced, you went*); and the **future,** formed with the helping verb *will* (*I will race, you will go*).

The **perfect tenses,** formed with the helping verbs *have* and *had,* indicate completed action. They include the present perfect (*I have raced, you have gone*); the **past perfect** (*I had raced, you had gone*); and the **future perfect** (*I will have raced, you will have gone*).

The **progressive tense,** formed with the helping verb *be* plus the present participle, indicates continuing action (*I am racing, you are going*).

See also Chapter 7.

transitive verb See *verb.*

verb A word or group of words indicating the action or state of being of a subject. A **transitive verb** conveys action that has an object: *He shot the sheriff.* An **intransitive verb** does not have an object: *The sheriff died.* A **linking verb** connects the subject and a complement that describes or renames the subject: *The sheriff was brave.* Often the same verb may be transitive, intransitive, or linking, depending on its use in the sentence: *The dog smelled the bone* (transitive). *The dog smelled* (intransitive). *The dog smelled bad* (linking).

Transitive verbs also may be either in the **active voice,** when the subject is the agent of the action, or in the **passive voice,** when the subject is the recipient of the action. Active: *We all made the decision together.* Passive: *The decision was made by all of us.*

The inflection of a verb and the use of helping verbs with it indicate its tense, mood, number, and sometimes person: *shall go, were going, have gone.*

See 5a, 5e-3, and Chapter 7. See also *tense* and *mood.*

verbal (nonfinite verb) A verb form used as a noun (*Swimming is good exercise*), an adjective (*Blocked passes don't make touchdowns*), or an adverb (*We were prepared to run*). A verbal can never function as the main verb in a sentence. Verbals may have subjects, objects, complements, and modifiers. See *participle, gerund, infinitive,* and *phrase.* Contrast *finite verb.* See also 5c-2.

verbal phrase See *phrase.*

verb phrase See *phrase.*

voice The active or passive aspect of a transitive verb. See *verb.* See also 5e-3.

word order The arrangment of the words in a sentence, which plays a large part in determining the grammatical relation among words in English.

(Continued from page iv)

Bruce Catton, "Grant and Lee: A Study in Contrasts" from *The American Story*, Earl Schenck Miers, editor. © 1956 by Broadcast Music, Inc. Copyright renewed 1984. Reprinted by permission.

David L. Chandler, from "Air Bags — Life Saving and Unavailable," *The Boston Globe*, March 1985. Reprinted courtesy of The Boston Globe.

Arthur C. Clarke, from "The Star of the Magi," copyright © 1972 by Arthur C. Clarke. Reprinted by permission of the author and the author's agent, Scott Meredith Literary Agency, Inc., 845 Third Avenue, New York, N.Y. 10022.

Malcolm Cowley, from "Sociological Habit Patterns in Linguistic Transmogrification," *The Reporter*, vol. XV (20 September 1956). Copyright © 1956 by Malcolm Cowley. Reprinted by permission.

Definition of *conjecture* and synonym study for *real* © 1985 by Houghton Mifflin Company. Reprinted by permission from *The American Heritage College Dictionary, Second College Edition*.

Definition of *reckon*. By permission. From *Webster's Ninth New Collegiate Dictionary* © 1985 by Merriam-Webster, Inc., publisher of the Merriam-Webster® Dictionaries.

Emily Dickinson, poem #781 reprinted by permission of the publishers and the Trustees of Amherst College from *The Poems of Emily Dickinson*, edited by Thomas H. Johnson, Cambridge, Mass.: The Belknap Press of Harvard University Press, Copyright 1951, © 1955, 1979, 1983 by The President and Fellows of Harvard College.

Joan Didion, an excerpt from "Los Angeles Notebook" in *Slouching Towards Bethlehem* by Joan Didion. Copyright © 1967, 1968 by Joan Didion. Reprinted by permission of Farrar, Straus & Giroux, Inc.

Annie Dillard, from "Sojourner" in *Teaching a Stone to Talk: Expeditions and Encounters*. Copyright © 1982 by Annie Dillard. Reprinted by permission of Harper & Row, Publishers, Inc.

Peter F. Drucker, from "How Best to Protect the Environment," *Harper's* Magazine (January 1972). Copyright © 1971 by Minneapolis Star and Tribune Co., Inc. Reprinted by permission of the author.

Rene Dubos, from *Man, Medicine and Environment*. Copyright © 1968 by Encyclopaedia Britannica. Reprinted by permission.

Freeman Dyson, from *Disturbing the Universe*. Copyright © 1979 by Freeman Dyson. Reprinted by permission of Harper & Row, Publishers, Inc. Originally appeared in *The New Yorker*.

Barbara Ehrenreich, "Finding the 'Bright Side' to Nuclear War," *The New York Times*, 14 March 1985. Copyright © 1985 by The New York Times Company. Reprinted by permission.

Peter Eisinger et al., from *American Politics: The People and the Polity*. Copyright © 1978 by Little, Brown and Company (Inc.). Reprinted by permission.

Ralph Ellison, from "Harlem Is Nowhere" in *Shadow and Act*. Copyright 1953, © 1964 by Ralph Ellison. Reprinted by permission of Random House, Inc.

Nora Ephron, from "Bernice Gera, First Lady Umpire" in *Crazy Salad: Some Things About Women*. Copyright © 1973, 1975 by Nora Ephron. Reprinted by permission of Alfred A. Knopf, Inc., and International Creative Management.

Joseph Epstein, from *Ambition: The Secret Passion*, Copyright © 1980 by Joseph Epstein. Reprinted by permission of the publisher, E. P. Dutton, a division of New American Library; and Georges Borchardt, Inc.

Peter Farb, from *Word Play: What Happens When People Talk*. Copyright © 1973 by Peter Farb. Reprinted by permission of Alfred A. Knopf, Inc., and Brandt & Brandt Literary Agents, Inc.

Robert Frost, two lines from "The Death of the Hired Man" from *The Poetry of Robert Frost*, edited by Edward Connery Lathem. Copyright 1930, 1939, © 1969 by Holt, Rinehart and Winston. Copyright © 1958 by Robert Frost. Copyright © 1967 by Lesley Frost Ballentine. Reprinted by permission of Holt, Rinehart and Winston, Publishers, the Estate of Robert Frost, and Jonathan Cape Ltd., Publishers.

John Kenneth Galbraith, from *Economics and Public Purpose*. Copyright © 1973 by John Kenneth Galbraith. Reprinted by permission of Houghton Mifflin Company.

Barbara Garson, from *All the Livelong Day*. Copyright © 1972, 1973, 1974, 1975 by Barbara Garson. Reprinted by permission of Doubleday & Company, Inc., and International Creative Management.

William Gaylin, from *Feelings: Our Vital Signs*. Copyright © 1979 by Willard Gaylin. Reprinted by permission of Harper & Row, Publishers, Inc.

Stephen Jay Gould, reprinted from *The Panda's Thumb: More Reflections in Natural History* with the permission of W. W. Norton & Company, Inc. Copyright © 1980 by Stephen Jay Gould.

Donald Hall, from *String Too Short to Be Saved*. Copyright © 1979, 1961, 1960 by Donald Hall. Reprinted by permission of David R. Godine, Publisher, Boston.

Edward T. Hall, excerpt from *The Hidden Dimension*. Copyright © 1966 by Edward T. Hall. Reprinted by permission of Doubleday & Company, Inc., and Blassingame, McCauley & Wood.

Gilbert Highet, from *Poets in a Landscape*. Reprinted by permission of Curtis Brown, Ltd. Copyright © 1957 by Gilbert Highet.

Emmet John Hughes, from "The Presidency vs. Jimmy Carter," *Fortune* (4 December 1978). Reprinted by permission.

Ada Louise Huxtable, from "The Rayburn Building," *The New York Times*, 16 March 1965. Copyright © 1965 by The New York Times Company. Reprinted by permission.

Mac Jeffery, "Does Rx Spell Rip-off?" *The New York Times*, 7 August 1978. Copyright © 1978 by The New York Times Company. Reprinted by permission.

Suzanne Britt Jordan, from "That Lean and Hungry Look," *Newsweek*, 9 October 1978. Copyright 1978, by Newsweek, Inc. All Rights Reserved. Reprinted by permission.

Pauline Kael, from "Silliness." Reprinted by permission; © 1983 by Pauline Kael. Originally in *The New Yorker*, 27 June 1983.

Tracy Kidder, from *The Soul of a New Machine*. Copyright © 1981 by John Tracy Kidder. Reprinted by permission of Little, Brown and Company in association with the Atlantic Monthly Press, and Penguin Books Ltd.

Charles Kuralt, from *Dateline America*. Text copyright © 1979 by CBS Inc. Reprinted by permission of Harcourt Brace Jovanovich, Inc.

Lawrence A. Mayer, from "The Confounding Enemy of Sleep," *Fortune* (June 1974). Reprinted by permission.

Jan Morris, from *Destinations: Essays from Rolling Stone* by Jan Morris. Copyright © 1980 by Rolling Stone Press and Jan Morris. Reprinted by permission of Oxford University Press, Inc.

Iris Murdoch, from *The Nice and the Good*. Copyright © Iris Murdoch, 1968. Reprinted by permission of Viking Penguin Inc. and Chatto & Windus Ltd.

Newsweek, 7 July 1980, from "The New Immigrants." Copyright 1980, by Newsweek, Inc. All Rights Reserved. Reprinted by permission.

Robert Nisbet, from "Boredom" in *Prejudices* (Harvard University Press, 1982). Reprinted by permission.

Robert Ornstein, from "A Letter from the Director," *Human Nature* (August 1978). Copyright © 1978 by Human Nature, Inc. Reprinted by permission of the publisher.

William G. Ouchi, Ph.D., from *Theory Z: How American Business Can Meet the Japanese Challenge*, copyright © 1981. Reprinted by permission of Addison-Wesley Publishing Company.

Laurence Perrine, from "Fifteen Ways to Write Five Hundred Words," *The CEA Critic* (November 1962). Copyright by The College English Association, Inc., 1962. Reprinted by permission.

Readers' Guide to Periodical Literature, March 1977–February 1978, from entries under "Advertising." Copyright © 1977, 1978 by The H. W. Wilson Company. Material reproduced by permission of the publisher.

Roger Rosenblatt, from "Consistency as a Minor Virtue," *Time*, 7 February 1983. Copyright 1983 Time Inc. Reprinted by permission from *Time*.

Richard Rovere, reprinted with permission of Macmillan Publishing Company from *Arrivals and Departures*. Copyright 1959, © 1976 by Richard Rovere. Originally appeared in *The New Yorker*.

Max Shulman, from "Love Is a Fallacy." © 1951, © renewed 1979 by Max Shulman. Reprinted by permission of Harold Matson Company, Inc.

Lewis Thomas, from "The Art of Teaching Science," *The New York Times Magazine*. Copyright © 1982 by The New York Times Company. Reprinted by permission.

Barbara Tuchman, from "The Decline of Quality," *The New York Times Magazine*, 2 November 1980 Copyright © 1980 by The New York Times Company. Reprinted by permission.

Stewart L. Udall, from *The Quiet Crisis*. Copyright © 1963 by Stewart L. Udall. Reprinted by permission of Holt, Rinehart and Winston, Publishers.

Michael Walzer, from "The Community," *The New Republic*, 1 March 1982. Reprinted by permission of *The New Republic*. © 1982 The New Republic, Inc.

Judith Wax, from *Starting in the Middle* by Judith Wax. Copyright © 1979 by Judith Wax. Reprinted by permission of Holt, Rinehart and Winston, Publishers.

Bayard Webster, from "Should Vivisection Be Abolished?" *The New York Times*, 27 September 1983. Copyright © 1983 by The New York Times Company. Reprinted by permission.

Diane White, from "At Large," *The Boston Globe*, 27 January 1979. Reprinted courtesy of The Boston Globe.

E. B. White, from *One Man's Meat* by E. B. White. Copyright 1939 by E. B. White. Reprinted by permission of Harper & Row, Publishers, Inc.

E. B. White, from *The Wild Flag* (Houghton Mifflin). © 1943, 1971 by E. B. White. Originally in *The New Yorker*. Reprinted by permission.

George F. Will, from *Statecraft as Soulcraft: What Government Does* by George F. Will. Copyright © 1983 by G. F. W., Inc., A Maryland Corporation. Reprinted by permission of Simon & Schuster, Inc.

Kenneth L. Woodward, from "Life After Death?" *Newsweek*, 12 July 1976. Copyright 1976, by Newsweek, Inc. All Rights Reserved. Reprinted by permission.

Richard Wright, from pp. 217–218 in *Black Boy* by Richard Wright. Copyright 1937, 1942, 1944, 1945 by Richard Wright. Reprinted by permission of Harper & Row, Publishers, Inc., and Mrs. Ellen Wright.

William Zinsser, from *The Lunacy Boom* by William Zinsser. Copyright © 1966, 1968, 1969, 1970 by William Zinsser. Reprinted by permission.

Index

Index

Index

Index

Index

Index

Index

Index

Index

Index

Index

Plan of the book and guide to correction code and symbols

ORRECTION SYMBOLS IN ALPHABETICAL ORDER

oldface numbers and letters refer to chapters and sections of the handbook.

b	Faulty abbreviation, **28**
d	Misuse of adjective or adverb, **9**
gr	Error in agreement, **8**
ppr	Inappropriate diction, **31a**
wk	Awkward construction
ib	Error in bibliography form, **35c-2**
a	Error in case form, **6**
ap	Use capital letter, **26**
it	Missing source citation or error in form of citation, **35i**
oh	Coherence lacking, **1h-3, 3b**
on	Be more concise, **31c**
oord	Coordination needed or faulty, **16a**
s	Comma splice, **11a–b**
'	Error in diction, **31**
'ev	Inadequate development, **1, 3c**
'iv	Incorrect word division, **30**
'm	Dangling modifier, **14g**
mph	Emphasis lacking or faulty, **18**
xact	Inexact word, **31b**
n	Error in footnote form, **35i-3**
rag	Sentence fragment, **10**
s	Fused sentence, **11c**
l/gr	See Glossary of Grammatical Terms, *p. 604*
l/us	See Glossary of Usage, *p. 586*
r	Error in grammar, **5–9**
yph	Error in use of hyphen, **34d**
nc	Incomplete construction, **15c–e**
tal	Italicize (underline), **27**
:	Awkward construction
c	Use lowercase letter, **26f**
og	Faulty logic, **4**
nixed	Mixed construction, **15a–b**
nm	Misplaced modifier, **14a–f**
nng	Meaning unclear
ns	Error in manuscript form, **App. B**
o cap	Unnecessary capital letter, **26f**
o ^,	Comma not needed, **21j**
o ¶	No new paragraph needed, **3**

num	Error in use of numbers, **29**
p	Error in punctuation, **20–25**
. ? !	Period, question mark, exclamation point, **20**
^,	Comma, **21**
;	Semicolon, **22**
^'	Apostrophe, **23**
" "	Quotation marks, **24**
: — ( ) [ ] . . . /	Colon, dash, parentheses, brackets, ellipsis mark, slash, **25**
par, ¶	Start new paragraph, **3**
¶ *coh*	Paragraph not coherent, **3b**
¶ *dev*	Paragraph not developed, **3c**
¶ *un*	Paragraph not unified, **3a**
pass	Ineffective passive voice, **7h, 18d**
ref	Error in pronoun reference, **12**
rep	Unnecessary repetition, **31c-2**
rev	Revise or proofread, **2**
run-on	Run-on (fused) sentence, **11c**
shift	Inconsistency, **13**
sp	Misspelled word, **34**
spec	Be more specific, **3c, 4c**
sub	Subordination needed or faulty, **16b**
t	Error in verb tense, **7e–f**
t seq	Error in tense sequence, **7f**
trans	Transition needed, **3b-6, 3e**
var	Vary sentence structure, **19**
vb	Error in verb form, **7a–d**
w	Wordy, **31c**
ww	Wrong word, **31b-1**
//	Faulty parallelism, **17**
#	Separate with a space
⁀	Close up the space
℘	Delete
∾	Transpose letters or words
x	Obvious error
∧	Something missing, **15e**
??	Manuscript illegible or meaning unclear

THE LITTLE, BROWN HANDBOOK